# LANDSCAPES OF DEVELOPMENT

# Landscapes of Development

## An Anthology of Readings

**LAURA E. BERK**

Illinois State University

Wadsworth Publishing Company
I⊤P® An International Thomson Publishing Company

Belmont, CA • Albany, NY • Boston • Cincinnati • Johannesburg • London • Madrid • Melbourne
Mexico City • New York • Pacific Grove, CA • Scottsdale, AZ • Singapore • Tokyo • Toronto

**Education Editor:** Dianne Lindsay
**Assistant Editor:** Valerie Morrison
**Marketing Manager:** Becky Tollerson
**Project Editor:** Jennie Redwitz
**Print Buyer:** Barbara Britton
**Permissions Editor:** Bob Kauser
**Production:** Robin Gold, Forbes Mill Press
**Cover Design:** Bill Stanton
**Cover Images:** *Photos:* © 1998 PhotoDisc, Inc.; *Painting:* Bill Stanton
**Compositor:** Wolf Creek Press / Forbes Mill Press
**Printer:** Banta Book Group, Harrisonburg

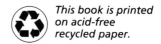 *This book is printed
on acid-free
recycled paper.*

Printed in the United States of America
    2  3  4  5  6  7  8  9  10

For more information, contact Wadsworth Publishing Company, 10 Davis Drive, Belmont,
CA 94002, or electronically at http://www.wadsworth.com

International Thomson Publishing Europe
Berkshire House
168-173 High Holborn
London, WC1V 7AA, United Kingdom

International Thomson Editores
Seneca, 53
Colonia Polanco
11560 México D.F. México

Nelson ITP, Australia
102 Dodds Street
South Melbourne
Victoria 3205 Australia

International Thomson Publishing Asia
60 Albert Street #15-01
Albert Complex
Singapore 189969

Nelson Canada
1120 Birchmount Road
Scarborough, Ontario
Canada M1K 5G4

International Thomson Publishing Japan
Hirakawa-cho Kyowa Building, 3F
2-2-1 Hirakawa-cho, Chiyoda-ku
Tokyo 102, Japan

International Thomson Publishing Southern Africa
Building 18, Constantia Square
138 Sixteenth Road, P.O. Box 2459
Halfway House, 1685 South Africa

**Library of Congress Cataloging-in-Publication Data**

Landscapes of development : an anthology of readings / [edited by]
    Laura E. Berk.
        p.   cm.
    Includes bibliographical references.
    ISBN 0-534-54378-2
    1. Child development.   2. Child development—cross-cultural
studies.   I. Berk, Laura E.
    HQ767.9.L355   1998                                                       98-28398
    305.231—dc21

# Contents

## PART V PATHWAYS TO MATURITY: MIDDLE CHILDHOOD TO ADOLESCENCE            339

# Preface

I n preparing this anthology of readings in child development, my goal is to expand students' knowledge of current, high-interest topics in a way not possible in a general textbook. As I planned the book's contents and invited authors to participate, its overall theme—increasingly prominent in contemporary theory and research—quickly took shape. Together, the contributions highlight the impact of diverse contexts on children's development. Each author places special emphasis on social and cultural influences. Children's relationships with parents, caregivers, teachers, peers, and (indirectly but no less important) government officials and advocates in the wider world are regarded as crucial for safeguarding their well-being. At the same time, the role of biological processes in development is given substantial attention, through such topics as prenatal and birth complications, genetic counseling, sleep, temperament, attention deficits, pubertal maturation, and adolescent depression.

In addition, all selections in this book explore the vital link between theory, research, and applications. Each contribution considers research-based practices aimed at supporting and furthering development. Many parts of the text discuss the current condition of children and families and show how theory and research have sparked successful interventions. In this way, the volume makes child development knowledge relevant for its readers.

Finally, all entries have been selected for both their depth of coverage and readability. Rather than focusing narrowly on single studies and the technicalities of research methodology, almost all the contributions present reviews of theory and research written in an appealing, accessible style. The few that do present single studies illustrate major contemporary methods (such as longitudinal and ethnographic research), provide unique insights into biological, social, and cultural contexts, and are prepared in a nontechnical style. The book is rich in everyday examples of children's experiences and behavior.

## Organization and Coverage

This anthology is organized chronologically, a strategy that permits students to get to know children of each age period especially well. The infancy, childhood, and adolescent sections contain selections on all domains of development—physical, cognitive, emotional, and social. Consequently, the articles can also be assigned in topical order, according to the instructor's preference.

The book opens with a section on Ethics of Research with Young Participants. In doing so, this collection of readings emphasizes that a caring, compassionate approach to children should permeate all aspects of their lives—including the settings and experiences in which child development knowledge is gathered. Five parts follow:

- Beginnings: Prenatal Development and Birth
- Joining a New World: Infancy to Early Childhood
- The Play and School Years: Early to Middle Childhood
- Pathways to Maturity: Middle Childhood to Adolescence
- Looking Back, Looking Forward: Lifespan Implications

Each of these sections addresses fascinating questions and pressing concerns in children's lives. For example: Do nighttime sleeping arrangements affect the baby's sense of security? How does children's memory for personally meaningful experiences form? What do children understand about their own and others' emotions? How and why do some countries forge child-care policies sensitive to children's needs, whereas others do not? What can adults do to ensure that children develop healthy, varied food preferences? How can parents and teachers best support children's aesthetic sensibilities in the visual arts and music? What disciplinary practices work best with young children? How can we help ethnic minority children successfully negotiate two cultural worlds? What can families and schools do to foster a healthy sense of autonomy in adolescence? What impact do stressful childhood experiences have on adult adjustment?

In answering these and other questions, each contribution draws on a rich, current research base. And almost all take up the impact of cultural values and societal conditions on development.

## Authors

A melting pot of experts from around the world contribute to contemporary child development research and the design of effective interventions and practices. The authors contributing to this book reflect this diversity. They come from North America, Australia, Europe, and Israel and represent a broad array of disciplines—developmental psychology, education, family studies, public health, sociology, anthropology, nutrition, and medicine. Many contributors are re-searchers nationally and internationally recognized for their work. Others are particularly knowledgeable in applied areas and have spent part of their careers working directly with children. They bring special expertise to the discussions of research-based applications that permeate this volume.

## Pedagogical Features

The pedagogical features of this book have been carefully designed to assist students in mastering its content and using what they have learned in their daily lives. The features are as follows:

- *Editor's Introductions*: "Advance organizers" for each chapter provide students with an overview of what they are about to read.

- *Chapter Quotes*: Quotes that reflect main points of each author's presentation are highlighted to strengthen students' comprehension and retention.

- *Bolded Terms and End-of-Book Glossary*: Key terms are bolded within each article and defined within the end-of-book glossary. The glossary contains over two hundred important terms and concepts in the field of human development. Its breadth reflects the extent to which the book's contents reinforce and extend the vocabulary to which students are introduced in a general textbook.

- *Evaluating Your Mastery, Critical Thinking, and Applying Your Knowledge*: Each article concludes with (1) multiple choice, true–false, and fill-in questions that permit students to evaluate their mastery; (2) short-answer essay questions that assist students in thinking critically about the implications of each chapter; and (3) learning activities that encourage students to become actively involved with the subject matter and apply what they have learned. The Critical Thinking questions and Applying Your Knowledge activities can serve as course assignments and springboards for class discussion.

## Acknowledgments

The many months I spent planning this book and working with contributing authors were generously supported by a Lillian de Lissa Fellowship, de Lissa Institute of Early Childhood and Family Studies, University of South Australia, and by the College of Arts and Sciences, Illinois State University. Special thanks to Glenn Cupit for arranging my three-month stay at the de Lissa Institute; to Ann Veale, Head of School, for handling many details that made my visit to Australia stimulating and productive; to Alexandra Diamond and Jessica Friedberg for working with me on the book's pedagogy; and to Gillian Harvey for assisting with manuscript preparation. The entire staff of the de Lissa Institute extended warm hospitality and friendship to me during my fellowship term. I am grateful to each one of them.

I have been privileged to work with a very talented editorial team at Wadsworth Publishing Company. My appreciation to Sabra Horne, with whom

I signed this project, for much enthusiasm as well as good humor in taking care of contractual arrangements while I was halfway around the globe. Peter Marshall, Publisher, was my editor during much of the time the book was in progress. I am grateful to him for several productive meetings in which he brought his wisdom and experience to bear on the book's contents and features. The end result has benefitted greatly from his involvement. Jennie Redwitz, Production Editor, and Robin Gold of Forbes Mill Press have done a masterful job of producing the text. Their meticulous, caring efforts are evident in the book's lovely cover, internal design, and photo program. Working with Jennie and Robin has been a pleasure every step of the way. A special thank you to Susan Badger, President, for encouraging me to bring this project to Wadsworth.

I would like to thank the following reviewers for their suggestions: Branca Babic, Midwestern University; Cheryl A. Camenzuli, Hofstra University; Jo Ann M. Farver, University of Southern California; Jesse Leinfelder, Nova Southeastern University; Angeline Lillard, University of Virginia; and Elsa K. Weber, Purdue University, Calvmet.

I am pleased to donate all royalties from this book to the de Lissa Institute of Early Childhood and Family Studies, University of South Australia, for the purpose of furthering the professional development of its staff and students.

*Laura E. Berk*

# PART I

# Ethics in Research
# with Young Participants

# 1

# Behavioral Research Involving Children

## A Developmental Perspective on Risk

### ROSS A. THOMPSON
### University of Nebraska

■

Research risks vary with the age of the child in complex ways: Some decrease with increasing age, while others increase as the child matures, and some remain essentially stable over development.

■

Young children are less likely to be stressed by a concern with the researcher's motives and intentions until they have developed an ability to derive psychological inferences about what other people are thinking or intending.

■

While younger children may be oblivious to the subtle cues, demands, and judgments of their performance that occur in a research context, older children and adolescents are not only likely to perceive these implicit messages accurately but may also be affected adversely by them....

■

With respect to research participation, these findings suggest that when children experience negative situations for which they are not responsible, younger children may nevertheless be vulnerable to a variety of negative self-conscious emotions, which reflect a negative self-assessment that may not be justified by the circumstances.

■

In research settings, therefore, young children are likely to respond to researchers with immediate respect and obedience, even when they encounter unreasonable or illegitimate demands, and are more susceptible to coercive research practices as a result.

■

This analysis of developmental changes in vulnerability to research risk suggestion, however, that along with the conventional risk-benefit analysis, ethical review must also be concerned with establishing and maintaining standards of *decent treatment* of the children who participate in social and behavioral research.

■

## EDITOR'S INTRODUCTION

Ross Thompson's developmental analysis of research risks is a fitting opening to a book that highlights the role of relationships and culture in child development. A caring and compassionate approach to children and adolescents must encompass the practices used to investigate their behavior. Compared with adults, children are less capable of benefiting psychologically from involvement in research investigating their behavior. Yet the risks to their physical and psychological well-being can, at times, be considerable.

How can we make sure that children and adolescents are subjected to the least research risk possible? As Thompson points out, one valuable resource is our expanding knowledge of age-related capacities and individual differences. Research risks vary with development in complex ways. Some risks increase with age, others decrease, and still others occur at many or all ages. And personal characteristics and life circumstances can make some children more vulnerable to harm than others.

Reconciling risks with a study's potential for advancing knowledge and improving children's life condition is crucial because an understanding of child development is of great value to society. Given the complexity of children's research risks, Thompson presents a powerful argument for adding standards of decent treatment to the risks-benefits equation. Among factors that require special consideration in research with young participants are reactions to stress, threats to self-concept, tendency to yield to authority figures, invasion of personal privacy, and debriefing following deceptive research procedures.

One of the most difficult components of the ethical review of social and behavioral research is assessing potential risks to research participants. While procedures for ensuring privacy, confidentiality of research materials, and informed consent can be relatively well-defined, assessing potential risks is inherently more ambiguous because it depends on characteristics of the particular research procedure in relation to the specific subject population. Moreover, members of **Institutional Review Boards (IRBs)** are often discouraged from conducting a fine-grained appraisal of research risk because of their limited expertise in the specific research field, a reluctance to question their colleagues' ethical competence, and a bias in favor of approval of research protocols (Williams, 1984).

Consequently, there is reason for concern that this component of the ethical review process is sometimes neglected, despite its importance for safeguarding subjects' rights as research participants. Concern is especially warranted in behavioral research involving children because of their unique vulnerability in research settings. Children are vulnerable because of their more limited cognitive competencies and experimental backgrounds, which constrain their capacities to understand and defend their rights as research participants and to make reasoned decisions concerning research participation. They are also vulnerable because of their limited social power, which impairs their ability to exercise independent decision making concerning research participation when parents (for example, school personnel) and researchers support their involvement in research. Finally, children are also vulnerable because of their ambiguous standing in the law (Baumrind, 1978; Melton, 1987), which undermines their control not only over participation in research (with parents exercising **proxy consent**), but also over the disposition of research materials, their withdrawal from research participation, and other decisions normally accompanying research involvement. For these reasons, social and behavioral research involving children mandates an even more sensitive appraisal of risk because children have limited capacities to resist intrusions into their rights as research participants.

The purpose of this article is to contribute to more sensitive risk-assessment by proposing the need for a complex portrayal of developmental changes in vulnerability to research risk. Children are heterogeneous population, varying in developmental competencies as well as in background characteristics. Research risks vary with the age of the child in complex ways: Some decrease with increasing age, while others increase as the child matures, and some remain essentially stable over development. Because vulnerability to research risk does not uniformly decline with age, risk-assessment must compass these developmental changes in vulnerability, as well as differences in the background characteristics of children.

I will outline some of these age-related changes in vulnerability to research risk, and I will also argue that judgments of risk with children must become increasingly focused on establishing and maintaining the standards of decent treatment of minors who are research participants. By supplementing the conventional risk-benefit assessment with more prescriptive treatment norms governing studies with children, researchers and IRB members can remedy some of the existing difficulties with risk-benefit assessment and underscore the special considerations mandated for children as research participants.

## DEVELOPMENTAL CHANGES IN VULNERABILITY TO RESEARCH RISK

The ethical review of research involving minors commonly begins with the reasonable assumptions

Thompson, R. A. (1990, March/April). Behavioral research involving children: A developmental perspective on risk. *IRB, 12*(2), 1–6. © The Hastings Center. Reprinted by permission.

that infants and young children are most vulnerable to research risks of various kinds and that vulnerability declines with increasing age. Within this linear model of developmental change, IRBs typically encourage stricter safeguards against research risk with younger subject populations because young children are most susceptible to violations of privacy and confidentiality, and coercive or distressing research practices due to their more limited cognitive skills, emotional competencies, and experimental backgrounds. With increasing age, and corollary developments in cognition, social understanding, and prior experience, children's vulnerability to many research risks decreases, and they become more capable of understanding and exercising their rights as research participants.

But it is also important to recognize that vulnerability to some research risks *increases,* rather than decreases, as the child matures. For example, until children have developed a capacity to think about themselves psychologically, which includes relatively coherent concepts of one's skills, personality attributes, and emotional tendencies, it is unlikely that threats to the **self-concept** will have the significance they do at older ages. Young children are less likely to be stressed by a concern with the researcher's motives and intentions until they have developed an ability to derive psychological inferences about what other people are thinking and intending. And, in general, the trust of infants and young children in their caregivers may protect them against the stresses inherent in research procedures when caregivers accompany them. Thus for some domains of research risk, younger children are buffered or protected from risk because of some of the same cognitive and experimental limitations which increase their vulnerability in other ways. From this alternative portrayal of linear developmental change, IRB members should be more concerned with the effects of certain research procedures in older children and adolescents, who are more vulnerable because of their capacities for self-reflection, psychological understanding of others, and critical thinking.

Taken together, this analysis suggests that any effort to portray developmental changes in vulnerability to research risk in comprehensive, linear models will underestimate this complexity of these changes. The common assumption that younger children are uniformly more vulnerable, for example, does not encompass certain aspects of research risk to which older children and adolescents are more susceptible. This suggests that a developmental analysis of research risk must necessarily be more complex, entailing multidimensional considerations that vary with the child's age. At some ages, certain domains of research risk will be paramount in assessing study proposals, while other domains of risk will be predominant when children at other ages are involved. Although this necessarily complicates the assessment of research risk, it also promises a more sensitive appraisal.

One alternative formulation that defines research risk in a multidimensional, developmentally graded manner is already encompassed within Department of Health and Human Services (DHHS) regulations.[1] In guidelines concerning research with children, definitions of "minimal risk" as well as "a minor increase" over minimal risk are comparably framed in terms of the typical life experiences of children at that age (for example, "minimal risk" involves risk of harm not greater than that "ordinarily encountered in daily life or during the performance of routine physical or psychological examinations or tests"). From a developmental perspective, therefore, these regulations imply that as a child's normative life experiences change with age in accord with the child's growing competencies, **norms** defining research risk must be comparably revised to encompass these changing experiences. Research procedures that would ordinarily not be permitted at an early age—because they exceed risk of harms the child normally encounters at that age—might be permissible at a later age as the child's normative experiences change. For example, extended periods apart from parents with unfamiliar adults might be questionable in research involving infants, but certainly not older children and adolescents.

But by providing a developmentally changing metric of research risk in this manner, DHHS regulations potentially permit research procedures that might otherwise be harmful in a research context, even though such procedures are part of the child's normative experience. Young children, for example, regularly encounter invasions of their bodily and personal privacy by parents, teachers, and other adults, but it is not clear whether this justifies similar privacy violations in research. Older children and adolescent commonly encounter experiences at school that threaten their self-image, including unfavorable academic performance evaluations by teachers, testing about personal or physical characteristics by peers, and spontaneous as well as elicited social comparison. But ethical principles of **nonmaleficence** and respect for persons would lead some to question whether these normative experiences justify considering comparable experiences in research context to be "minimal risk." In short, a new developmental portrayal of changes in changes in vulnerability to research risk is needed that is both sensitive to age-related changes in children's capabilities, experiences, and needs, and also helps to define standards of decent treatment of minors who are research participants.

## AN ALTERNATIVE DEVELOPMENTAL PORTRAYAL

Unfortunately, an alternative portrayal must necessarily be a more complex one because to describe adequately the kinds of risks to which children are susceptible as research participants at different ages, different risks must be considered independently as well as developmentally. As a catalyst to the generation of an alternative developmental portrayal of research risk, I offer in this section some general guidelines related to research vulnerability which appear to be well-supported by the research literature (Maccoby, 1983). These guidelines are framed as general propositions (or, at times, working hypotheses).

1. *In general, the younger the child, the greater the possibility of general behavioral and socioemotional disorganization accompanying stressful experiences; with increasing age, the child's growing repertoire of coping skills permits greater adaptive functioning in the face of stress.* The research literature on coping and **emotional self-regulation** indicates that young children rely on external support for coping with stressful circumstances (for example, caregivers and other adults, security objects, and so on), but that with increasing age children acquire a broadening repertoire of emotional self-regulatory strategies, which can be flexibly applied to diverse situations (Kopp, 1989; Thompson, 1990). As a consequence, infants and young children are at greater risk for becoming overwhelmed with stressful research procedures at the moment they occur, because their emotional self-regulatory skills are much more limited. However, the research also indicates that young children's coping skills are facilitated by the availability of trusted caregivers, and also by familiarity of the setting or procedures, or the availability of familiar objects. Thus research procedures that occur at home, school, or in a day-care center not only benefit from ecological validity, but also foster the young child's coping with the demands of research by permitting access to caregivers, security objects, or a structured environment with which the child is familiar.

2. *Threats to a child's self-concept become more stressful with increasing age as children develop a more comprehensive, coherent, and integrated self-image; become more invested in an enduring identity; and acquire more sophisticated understandings of components of the self by which the self-concept becomes progressively modified and reshaped.* The content, organization, and structure of self-understanding change markedly from infancy through adolescence: Whereas preschoolers are concrete, physicalistic, and material in how they describe themselves, older school-age children and adolescents exhibit

more abstract, psychological, and integrated systems of self-understanding. Moreover, these self-referent beliefs (for example, self-concept, self-image, self-esteem, and so forth) also become increasingly more differentiated and hierarchically integrated with increasing age (Damon & Hart, 1982; Harter, 1983). Whereas the preschooler tends to provide self-evaluative judgments in discrete situations without integrating these judgments into a comprehensive self-concept, the older grade-school child attempts to find consistency among diverse attributes of the self, and the adolescent begins to organize these self-perceptions into a broader, coherent self-referent system (that is, an **identity**). Finally, the evaluations of others assume an increasingly important role in shaping the child's self-perceptions.

These research conclusions have significant implications for vulnerability to research risk because they suggest that research experiences that threaten a child's self-concepts are likely to be more stressful for older children and adolescents because they are more likely to be internalized, provoke worried self-reflection, and threaten broader aspects of self-esteem. Moreover, because the self-concept becomes more refined with increasing age—that is, it reflects a more realistic appraisal of the child's genuine strengths and weaknesses, rather than the optimistic and unrealistic self-confidence of younger children (Dweck & Elliot, 1983)—threats to the self-concept are likely to have a greater impact on older children because they contribute to the child's own self-criticism.

3. *Social comparison information becomes a more significant mode of self-evaluation with increasing age.* As suggested above, it is not until the school-age years that children spontaneously tend to incorporate a comparative metric into their self-evaluations: They judge their performance partly by the standards of others' performances (Ruble, 1983). As a consequence, older children are more vulnerable to explicit or implied comparisons of their research performance with others and may incorporate this information into their own evaluations of their skills and abilities. By contrast,

preschoolers are likely to remain optimistic and self-confident even in the face of negative performance comparisons with others. Moreover, older children may also be more sensitive to the evaluations of others to whom their research performance is disseminated, such as parents and teachers. Thus the feedback children receive about their skills and abilities in research settings is likely to have a much different impact depending on the child's age and self-evaluative skills.

4. *The capacity to make sophisticated psychological inferences of others' motives, attitudes, and feelings increases with age. This domain of psychological inferences includes inferences about others' reactions to oneself.* Inferring what another person is thinking or feeling is a challenging cognitive task, and although young children exhibit a rudimentary awareness that others have psychological states that are different from their own, it is not until the grade-school years that the child is skillful at making basic psychological inferences of other's thoughts and feelings. However, it is not until middle to late childhood (between 8 to 12 years of age) that children begin to derive inferences about others' evaluations *of them* (Shantz, 1983). *As a consequence, while younger children may be oblivious to the subtle cues, demands, and judgments of their performance that occur in a research context, older children and adolescents are not only likely accurately to perceive these implicit messages but may also be affected adversely by them* (for example, reevaluate the legitimacy of their responses, feel pressured to divulge confidential information, and so on).

It is worth nothing, however, that this developing capacity to derive psychological inferences is a double-edged sword for researchers. While the older child may be more susceptible to implicit demands and judgments in the research setting, he or she is also likely to approach the setting with greater skepticism concerning the true purposes of the research activity, or the real intention of the researcher. In other words, a developing capacity to derive psychological inferences also fosters an ability to question the true motives and intentions of another. By contrast, younger children are more likely to accept the researcher's intentions at face-value and are thus more vulnerable to deceptive or manipulative research practices because of their more limited capacity critically to question the researcher's motives.

5. *Self-conscious emotional reactions*—like shame, guilt, embarrassment, and pride—emerge later in development than do the primary emotions. But once they are acquired, young children may be more vulnerable to their arousal because of their limited understanding of these emotions. In contrast to the appearance in early infancy of primary emotions like happiness, sadness, fear, and anger, self-conscious emotions emerge during the preschool years with the growth of rudimentary forms of self-understanding (Campos, Berrett, Lamb, Goldsmith, & Stenberg, 1983). But although preschool children can understand these emotions, there is evidence that they overextend their meaning to apply to a broader range of circumstances than those for which they are appropriate. For example, preschoolers and young school-age children report feeling guilty in situations for which they are not personally responsible, perhaps because of exaggerated perceptions of their own agency, or confusion concerning intentionality (Harter, 1983; Graham, Doubleday, & Guarino, 1984; Thompson, 1987). It is possible that this is also true of other self-conscious emotional reactions like shame and embarrassment. It is not until children are 7 to 8 years of age that they better understand the reasons for self-conscious emotions like guilt and restrict their use to more appropriate situations in which they are personally culpable for a negative situation.

These research findings suggest, therefore, that susceptibility to emotions like shame, guilt, and embarrassment show a curvilinear trend: Very young children are buffered against these experiences because of their very limited emotional understanding, but during the preschool and early grade-school years children may be especially susceptible to the arousal of the self-conscious emotions because of their overextended understanding of these concepts. With more refined understanding, vulnerability to these emotions may decline somewhat during the grade-school years to more adult-like levels (with perhaps another developmental resurgence of susceptibility during adolescence, accompanying the acute self-consciousness of this period). *With respect to research participation, these findings suggest that when children experience negative situations for which they are not responsible, younger children may nevertheless be vulnerable to a variety of negative self-conscious emotions, which reflect a negative self-assessment that may not be justified by the circumstances.*

6. *Young children's understanding of authority renders them more vulnerable to coercive manipulations than older children, for whom authority relations are better balanced by an understanding of individual rights. Furthermore, young children's trust of authorities makes them more vulnerable to being deceived in research.* While children in the preschool and early grade-school years regard authorities as legitimate and powerful individuals who mandate obedience because of their intrinsically superior qualities, older children legitimate authorities by virtue of their training or experience and obey because of respect for authority rather than unilateral reverence (Damon, 1977; Piaget, 1965; Shantz, 1983). Authority relations increasingly become viewed as a cooperative consensual compact adopted for the welfare of all. In research settings, therefore, young children are likely to respond to researchers with immediate respect and obedience, even when they encounter unreasonable or illegitimate demands, and are more susceptible to coercive research practices as a result. By contrast, older children are more likely to question a researcher's requests spontaneously, and to regard research participation as their cooperative contribution to the researcher's efforts. Their perceptions of the adult's legitimacy may be undermined by demands that they perceive as unreasonable. Furthermore, while younger children are likely unquestionably to believe researcher's instructions, the susceptibility of older children to deception is undermined both by their more mature understanding of authority relations, and also by their emerging capacity to speculate concerning another's intentions and motives.

Vulnerability to research risk varies with children's age. Compared with older children, these kindergartners are more susceptible to arousal of self-conscious emotions and to coercive manipulations. (Photo: Michael Newman/ PhotoEdit)

7. *Privacy interests and concerns increase and become more differentiated as children mature, and broaden from an initial focus on physical and professional privacy to include concerns with informational privacy.* With increasing age, personal privacy becomes an important maker of independence and self-esteem, but children's privacy concerns change with growth in self-understanding. Children initially exhibit greater concern with establishing a physical location of their own (that is, territorial privacy, such as a bedroom) and the integrity of personal possessions (that is, possessional privacy), but at later ages this concern extends to the control of another's knowledge of

one's associations, activities, and interests (that is, informational privacy) (Melton, 1983; Wolfe, 1978). This suggests that children become increasingly vulnerable to a broader variety of privacy intrusions in research settings as they grow older, with older children and adolescents more likely than younger children to experience certain inquires or requests as unduly intrusive and threatening. Moreover to the extent that researchers gain access to personal information about children without their consent (for example, data from school records via parental permission), older children are especially likely to view this as a breach of informational privacy.

8. *Owing to their more limited conceptual skills, younger children may benefit less from feedback during the research experience, including dehoaxing and* **debriefing procedures,** *than do older children and adolescents.* In particular, when children are provided with false feedback concerning their research performance, which is subsequently corrected during debriefing, younger children may benefit little from this effort for several reasons. First, understanding deception tactics requires **recursive reasoning** (for example, "I knew that you would think this way when I did that, so I did this ..."), which is conceptually very demanding for preschoolers and early grade-school children to understand. Second, deception tactics are also complex and may be especially difficult for young children to understand when explanations require dehoaxing a set of earlier, convincing instructions by the researcher, which children trusted to be true. Finally, because young children often have difficulty reevaluating past performance in light of a subsequent standard, they may not spontaneously reappraise their critical evaluations of earlier performance in light of what they are subsequently told about nature of the study.

As a result, negative emotional consequences from the earlier false feedback may not be ameliorated by a debriefing procedure. Insofar as debriefing is used to reduce the risks inherent in research deception, alternative approaches may be necessary when younger children are research participants. More generally, younger children are unlikely to gain significantly from debriefing procedures as a whole because of their limited conceptual apprehension of the research process, the nature of research goals and purposes, and the theoretical questions underlying the study. Thus younger children are, in general, less likely to experience debriefing as a benefit from research participation.

9. *With increasing age, children are likely to become more sensitive to cultural and socioeconomic biases in research, which reflect negatively on the child's background, family, or previous experiences.* With developmental changes in the breadth and coherence of the self-concept, children are likely increasingly to identify themselves as members of broader social groups, including racial, ethnic, and socioeconomic groups. As a consequence, their vulnerability (and sensitivity) to overt and subtle biases in the research process is likely to increase with age.

These propositions do not, of course, exhaust the range of developmental changes in capabilities and skills, which have important implications for children's changing vulnerability to domains of research risk. But taken together, they illustrate how vulnerability to risk changes in complex ways with development. For some domains of risk, children become more vulnerable as they mature; for other domains, vulnerability decreases with increasing age. As a consequence, a somewhat different set of considerations may be preeminent in the ethical review of research with children of one age compared with another. Importantly, in **longitudinal studies,** new research risks are likely to emerge for consideration as the cohort under study ages, even through earlier review found age-appropriate risk concerns to be satisfied with the younger cohort. Thus the ethical review of long-term longitudinal studies may require successive reviews to assure that the changing matrix of research risks are appropriately addressed as children mature.

In general, those considerations indicate that a more complex, but more sensitive, analysis of developmental vulnerability to research risk is needed to guide ethical decision making in research with minors. But while this developmental analysis introduces greater complexity to the ethical review process, research review is additionally complicated by the need to consider also individual differences in the backgrounds and characteristics of children at any period of development.

## INDIVIDUAL DIFFERENCES IN VULNERABILITY TO RESEARCH RISK

Just as the term "children" embraces a very heterogeneous developmental population, so also the term encompasses a diverse range of backgrounds, characteristics, and prior experiences for children of any age. In many instances, the special characteristics of the children who participate in research mandate special considerations in the ethical review of research. Consider, for example, the characteristics of maltreated children, who are frequently the focus of developmental research investigations. Many elements of risk-assessment must be calibrated somewhat differently for this subject population. For example, because maltreating parents may not be reliable advocates for their offspring's interests, and may also seek to avoid detection of their abusive behavior, issues of proxy consent must be reconsidered in studies using populations who have been maltreated or who are at risk for abuse. Furthermore, in the research setting, the young child's coping with the demands of research may be undermined rather than supported by the parent's presence because **maltreated children** are typically insecurely rather than securely attached to their parents and experience other difficulties in the parent-child relationship.

Maltreated children also share other characteristics that are likely to make them somewhat more vulnerable to certain domains of research risk: They exhibit an acute sensitivity to aggressive stimuli and may be more prone to perceive ambiguous situations as threatening, they have diminished self-esteem and impaired perceptions

of self-competence, and they respond atypically
to novel adults, sometimes showing aloof disin-
terest, at other times exhibiting clingy dependency.[2] As a consequence, maltreated infants,
children and adolescents may be at greater risk
in research procedures that are stressful, threaten
self-esteem, require focused interaction with a
stranger, or involve experiences that could
potentially be interpreted as aggressive or threatening. Moreover, just as the consequences of
maltreatment change with age, so also the research vulnerabilities of maltreated children vary
their developmental status (Aber & Cicchetti,
1984). Thus the domains of research risk to
which this special population are likely to be particularly sensitive will vary with the child's age.

Other kinds of research risk require special
consideration with particular populations of children. When at-risk samples are identified for
study (for example, adolescent substance abusers,
offspring of adults with emotional disturbances,
and so forth), researchers must be careful that the
perceptions of these children by custodians from
whom permission is sought (for example, school
personnel, day-care workers, and so on) are not
biased by the description of the selection criteria. Children can be victimized by research
process if they become labeled in disadvan-
tageous ways. When requesting parental consent
for the child's participation, researchers must ensure that parents do not embrace inappropriate
expectations concerning benefits to the child
from research participation, since parents of special children (for example, children who suffered
traumatic experiences; children with congenital
illnesses, and so forth) may regard *any* contact
with professionals as a means of assisting the
child.[3] Finally, when the children under study
have serious intellectual deficits (for example,
Down syndrome children), special care must be
taken to ensure that the child's assent is meaningfully obtained, the child's freedom to withdraw from participation is fully understood, and
that dehoaxing (when necessary) and debriefing
procedures are suited to the child's level of understanding.

Thus a developmental analysis of vulnerability to research risk is additionally complicated by
the necessity of considering seriously the special
vulnerabilities of children from populations
under study. Because of their backgrounds, congenital characteristics, unusual experience or
other attributes, children from these populations
may experience research procedures in a manner
that is substantially different from children from
typical middle-class backgrounds, and this means
that standard "minimal risk" or "decent treatment" must be calibrated differently depending
on these characteristics. And as the study of maltreatment indicates, these unique vulnerabilities
are themselves likely to vary with developmental
stage. Clearly, doing a careful ethical review of
research risk in studies with children is a difficult, demanding task.

## RISKS IN RELATION TO BENEFITS

In this discussion of developmental changes in research vulnerability, the focus had been on risks
to children's self-esteem, coping with stress,
threats of embarrassment, privacy intrusions, and
pressures to cooperate encountered in social and
behavioral research. To many, of course, these
risks are rather benign, especially by comparison
with the risks of physical harm, disability, or
infection that may be encountered in biomedical
studies. Many of these risks are encountered in
studies that satisfy "minimal risk" provisions of
IRB guidelines, and thus they do not receive special scrutiny. Furthermore, federal and professional ethics guidelines mandate that
risk-assessment must be considered in the context of the potential benefits of research findings,
and it is easy to justify limited risks to children in
behavioral research with great promise (for example, studies with potential social utilities,
which advance theoretical knowledge, and so
on). As a consequence, many researchers who
study children approach the ethical review process
as a threshold concern: Can the level of risk to

children be justified by the anticipated benefits of research results? Once a researcher (and an IRB) can answer affirmatively, institutional requirements of ethical review are satisfied.

This analysis of developmental changes in vulnerability to research risk suggests, however, that along with the conventional risk-benefit analysis, ethical review must also be concerned with establishing and maintaining standards of *decent treatment* of the children who participate in social and behavioral research. There are two reasons warranting a concern with an ethics of treatment norms where minors are concerned. First, as indicated earlier, children are vulnerable to certain domains of research risk because of their cognitive and experiential immaturity, limited social power, and ambiguous legal standing. Because of these characteristics, they are uniquely ill-equipped to defend their rights as research participants. In view of the fact that their status as developing persons makes them venerable to certain risks to which more mature individuals are not as susceptible, special provisions are warranted in the ethical review of research in which they participate.

Second, the **risk/benefit calculus** is a problematic basis for the ethical analysis of research, especially when children are involved. The reason is that this calculus requires the comparison of things that are comparable, and thus cannot be balanced against each other. Risks, for example, are borne largely by research participants, but in most social and behavioral research, participants seldom benefit directly from their involvement, especially if they are children. In other words, risks are proximal to children who participate, while benefits are distal. Furthermore, risks and benefits differ markedly in the accuracy of their estimation when ethical review is conducted. Risks to research participants can be estimated as soon as research procedures have been designed and subject populations selected, but benefits are contingent on the outcome of the study, and thus involve a prediction of unknowns at the time the research is proposed (indeed, this is what justifies the research activity). Estimating potential bene-

fits is also confounded by (a) the fact that the social utility of research findings is often applied years after research insights have been generated, and are usually contingent on corollary findings, trends in scholarly activity, and the timing of social needs and concerns; and (b) research studies often produce no identifiable social benefits because of unexpected methodological difficulties, resource constraints to continuing the research, and/or publication obstacles to the dissemination of findings. For these reasons, comparing risks and benefits in ethical review is often like comparing apples and oranges.

When adults are research participants, their appreciation of the contingency of research findings, their conditional applications to social problems, and the distal benefits they could potentially receive from research participation can be assumed. But with children, we can make no such assumptions, and proxy consent does not alleviate the problem that children experience research risks directly, but few of the benefits. Consequently, ethical review of research involving children should be guided not only by the risk/benefit calculus, but also by norms of decent treatment of minors who are research participants. Researchers should be encouraged, in other words, to assume special responsibility for minimizing stresses to children, however, minor they may be, even when the study as a whole passes the threshold of risk/benefits analysis. In short, a proscriptive ethics of decent treatment norms makes ethical analysis of research a graded rather than a threshold concern. Guided by a fully developmental analysis of vulnerability to research risk, researchers who study children can remain sensitive to various potential harms to children who participate, even when the proposed research is fully justified by the social benefits it promises.

## ENLISTING THE EXPERTISE OF DEVELOPMENTAL SCHOLARS

A developmental portrayal of changing vulnerability to research risks with age, coupled with serious consideration of the individual characteristics that may warrant special concern for the population under study, significantly complicates the ethical review of social and behavioral research involving children. The same is true of any ethical review process that supplements the conventional risk/benefit calculus with norms of decent treatment of children who are research participants. In the face of this, IRB members encounter considerable challenges in their efforts to appraise research risks to children in a sensitive, comprehensive fashion. As noted earlier, IRB members are sometimes discouraged from conducting a thorough analysis of research risk because of their limited expertise in the research field, together with a reluctance to question their colleagues' ethical judgments. In light of the increased complexity of ethical review foreshadowed in the present analysis, what is an IRB to do?

Clearly, the professionals who can claim expertise in this area are researchers themselves, so perhaps one recommendation from this analysis is the greater use of developmental researchers in the ethical review process. This could be accomplished through greater use of developmental experts as invited consultants in the research review process. This might also involve requesting greater, and more detailed, information from developmental scholars concerning the particular vulnerabilities of the children they propose to study. Finally, greater collegial interchange between developmentalists and IRB members concerning children's vulnerabilities and the creation of alternatives to research procedures that might unduly stress the children who participate would foster mutual awareness and understanding, while diminishing the adversarial stance commonly assumed by both parties. Researchers are skilled at methodological critique, but the enlistment of their methodological acumen in the ethical analysis of proposed research is a task in which developmental scholars should become involved. In the end, greater sensitivity to developmental changes in vulnerability to research risk is important not only for protecting children's interests, but also for affirming the humanistic values underlying research activity we all share.

## ACKNOWLEDGMENTS

This analysis was prepared as a contribution to a Work Group on Ethical Issues in Social and Behavioral Research with Minors convened and sponsored by the Office for Protection from Research Risk of the National Institutes of Health and was also part of a seminar on Ethics and the Professions at the University of Nebraska. The author is very grateful for the various contributions from colleagues on the OPRR Work Group: Barbara Stanley (chair), Charles MacKay, Judith Areen, Thomas Grisso, Ruth Macklin, Gary Melton, Mary Jane Rotheram-Borus, Joan Sieber, and Alexander Tymchuk. I am also grateful for the contributions of participants in the Ethics seminar and for specific comments provided by Robert Audi, Susan Crockenberg, and Robert LeVine. An extended version of this paper also appears in *Child Development 1990;61*:1–16.

## NOTES

1. 45 Code of Federal Regulations 46, Subparts A and D.

2. For a comprehensive review of this research literature, see Cicchetti, D. (1990). The organization and coherence of socioemotional, cognitive, and representational development: Illustrations through a developmental psychopathology perspective on Down syndrome and child maltreatment. In R. A. Thompson (Ed.), *Socioemotional Development. Nebraska Symposium on Motivation: vol. 36.* (pp. 275–382). Lincoln, NE: University of Nebraska Press.

3. For a discussion of these and related issues, see C. B. Fisher, & S. Rosendahl, (1990). Psychological risks and remedies of research participation. In C. B. Fisher & W. W. Tryon (Eds.), *Ethics in Applied Developmental Psychology.* Norwood, NJ: Ablex.

## EVALUATING YOUR MASTERY

1. Which of the following research risks increases with age?
   a. Threats to self-concept
   b. Vulnerability to socioemotional disorganization because of stress
   c. Susceptibility to self-conscious emotional reactions
   d. Vulnerability to coercive manipulations

2. Which of the following research risks shows a curvilinear age-related trend (increasing and then decreasing)?
   a. Threats to self-concept
   b. Vulnerability to socioemotional disorganization because of stress
   c. Susceptibility to self-conscious emotional reactions
   d. Vulnerability to coercive manipulations

3. Which group of children is likely to be more affected by judgments of their performance in research?
   a. Infants
   b. Preschoolers
   c. Adolescents
   d. Maltreated children

4. In research involving maltreated children,
   a. There is less concern about research risk.
   b. Proxy consent might have to be reconsidered.
   c. Threatening stimuli are unlikely to produce any reaction.
   d. Research risks show no change with age.

5. True or False: According to Thompson, a risk/benefit calculus is an acceptable basis for ethical analysis of research involving children.

6. True or False: Standards of "minimal risk" in research need to be adjusted for certain participants, such as adolescent substance abusers and children of parents with emotional disturbances.

7. In addition to risk/benefit analysis, ethical review of research involving children must be concerned with _____.

## Critical Thinking

Why are standards of decent treatment crucial in assessing the ethical integrity of research involving children?

## Applying Your Knowledge

1. Select a study recently published in a journal specializing in research on children. Describe the study's purpose and methodology, including the ages and characteristics of its sample. After considering this information, list potential risks to research participants. For each risk, suggest a way of

reducing children's vulnerability. Is any risk so threatening to children's well-being that the study should not have been carried out?

2. Interview a member of the Institutional Review Board (IRB) at your college or university about special precautions used in evaluating research involving children. Does the IRB take a developmental perspective on risk? Explain your answer.

# PART II

# Beginnings: Prenatal Development and Birth

# 2

## Genetic Counseling

## A Developing Area of Interest for Psychologists

SHOSHANA SHILOH

Tel Aviv University

A birth defect that was once perceived as an unfortunate stroke of fate is now seen as avoidable, with responsibility assigned to the parents and sometimes to health care professionals. The possibility to predict by genetic testing the risks for developing serious diseases, like breast cancer, has raised dilemmas that have grave psychological consequences.

Some genetic defects are life-threatening, others are benign, some are disfiguring, and some are unnoticeable. Some entail extremely difficult management, whereas others carry no daily burden. Some cause progressive degeneration, and others are static. Some start at birth, and some have late onset; some involve physical disabilities and some mental.

Genetic conditions have a bad reputation. Unlike other diseases that are experienced as ego-alien, genetic disorders are experienced as part of one's self, with no option to diminish the threat by projecting it onto an external cause.

It is estimated that every individual unknowingly carries three to five recessive mutated genes that do not affect his or her health status. It becomes important only if both partners are carriers of the same mutation, in which case each pregnancy has a 25 percent risk of being affected.

■

When parents first learn about their child's genetic problem, they experience loss of self-esteem, envy of other parents, and grief reactions, such as shock, denial, anxiety, guilt feelings, and anger.

■

Most studies show that genetic counseling does not produce dramatic changes in counselees' reproductive behavior and that the best predictor of postcounseling reproductive decisions are precounseling intentions.

■

One model for genetic counseling has the genetic and psychological counselors meeting the couple together as a team. The psychologist helps create an accepting atmosphere, regulates the pace of information flow, encourages counselees' expressions of reactions to the information, checks understanding, and repeats explanations.

■

## EDITOR'S INTRODUCTION

As the genetic origins of more chronic diseases and conditions are being discovered and diagnostic techniques for identifying genetic risk expand, genetic counseling is becoming an increasingly complex and challenging field. Shoshana Shiloh reviews research on diverse components of the genetic counseling process, underscoring the importance of the involvement of psychologists in helping counselees understand genetic information, clarify their values, make difficult choices, and adjust to future outcomes.

Genetic defects are experienced as highly personalized conditions, pose profound ethical and interpersonal dilemmas, and are infused with cultural meanings. Among the complex issues raised in Shiloh's review are the multiple personal and contextual influences on decision making in carrier testing and prenatal diagnosis; the stressful impact of these procedures, whether outcomes are positive or negative; factors that affect the comprehension of genetic information, with special emphasis on the way counselors communicate degree of risk; and a developmental perspective on parents' adjustment to the news that their child has a genetic abnormality.

Shiloh explains how psychologists can help counselees understand and use newly learned, often highly threatening genetic information. She suggests that genetic and psychological counselors can best promote individual and family decision making and coping by working together. Genetic counseling, she argues, needs to become an interdisciplinary field.

The entry of psychologists into the field of medicine, which has gained momentum in the last decade (Taylor, 1990), requires adapting to a variety of new settings. My intent with this article is to familiarize psychologists with an area especially suited to psychological applications: **genetic counseling**. Contrary to popular belief, many genetic conditions are far from rare. Although only some 3 percent of all pregnancies result in the birth of a child with a significant genetic defect, progress in the treatment and prevention of other diseases has meant that today genetic disorders account for about 40 percent of childhood mortality and 5 to 10 percent of all pediatric hospital admissions. Many chronic diseases—including diabetes, cancer, hypertension, and schizophrenia—are now known to have a genetic component, and advances in genetic diagnostic technologies are dramatically expanding the possibilities for genetic screening and prenatal diagnosis (Gelehrter & Collins, 1990). These advances gained impetus from the **Human Genome Project,** which was initiated in 1988 by the United States Department of Energy and the National Institutes of Health with the goal of obtaining the entire human DNA sequence (Watson, 1990).

These developments have spawned major issues for individuals and for society. Pregnancies once assumed normal until proven otherwise are now viewed as risky and fraught with abnormalities until potential defects are ruled out by genetic tests. A birth defect that was once perceived as an unfortunate stroke of fate is now seen as avoidable, with responsibility assigned to the parents (Lippman, 1992) and sometimes to health care professionals. The possibility to predict by genetic testing the risks for developing serious diseases, like breast cancer, has raised dilemmas that have grave psychological consequences (Struewing, Lerman, Kase, Giambarresi, & Tucker, 1995). Psychologists will be asked more

and more often to help both clients and professionals deal with the psychological implications of these dilemmas. Meeting this challenge requires an understanding of the issues involved.

Genetic counseling, the main clinical application of the new genetic knowledge, is defined as a communication process meant to help an individual or family (a) comprehend medical facts, including diagnosis, probable cause, and available management of a disorder; (b) understand how heredity contributes to the disorder and the risk of recurrence in relatives; (c) choose and follow the most appropriate course of action in view of risks and family goals; (d) make the best possible adjustment to a disorder in an affected family member; and (e) deal with the risk of recurrence of that disorder (Fraser, 1974). This definition is broad enough to apply to most genetic counselings: providing pre-**amniocentesis** counseling for pregnant women whose fetuses are at-risk for genetic defects because of the woman's age or other reasons; discussing genetic risks with blood-related couples considering marriage; contacting parents during the crisis following fetal or neonatal death; informing parents of their child's genetic condition and helping them decide about risky options for future pregnancies; meeting with family members or prospective spouses of clients to discuss family secrets; preparing a community for a genetic population screening program; explaining the meaning of genetic test results to individuals found to be carriers of a **mutated gene**; informing couples about genetically related causes of their infertility or about their abnormal chromosomal makeup that sometimes means an ambiguous sex genotype; and discussing with offspring of affected parents the possibility of developing the same genetic condition later in life. The interested reader can find valuable detailed descriptions of genetic counseling cases in two casebooks, one by Applebaum

I gratefully acknowledge Amiram Vinokur, Abby Lippman, Azy Barak, and Yona Teichman for their helpful comments on a draft of this article.

Shiloh, S. (1996). Genetic Counseling: A Developing Area of Interest for Psychologists. *Professional Psychology: Research and Practice, 27,* 475–486. © 1966 by the American Psychological Association. Reprinted with the permission of the author and publisher.

and Firestein (1983) and one by Marks, Heimler, Reich, Wexler, and Ince (1989). Although the diversity of problems makes generalizing difficult, there is sufficient common ground to identify general themes, especially with regard to the psychological dimension of genetic counseling. These general themes are the focus of the present review.

Some components of genetic counseling make it more psychological than other medical encounters. It is defined as a process of communication, and although this is an important element in most medical practices, it is the essence of genetic counseling and not a means to other ends. Genetic counseling deals with human problems associated with the occurrence or risk of occurrence of a genetic disorder in a family, not with the disorder itself (which may not even be present, as when the counselee is a carrier of the genetic disease and not a patient). Cure is not a stated objective in the definition of genetic counseling and neither are treatment or prevention, though they are often possible. The objectives listed earlier—learning, understanding, choosing, coping—although recognized in other medical settings in addition to the main goals of cure and treatment, are the ultimate goals of genetic counseling. Despite the stated objectives and the emphasis on psychological components, genetic counseling is handled by physicians (called medical geneticists ) who specialize in genetic disorders or by genetic counselors who have an academic background in genetics plus training in genetic counseling. Although there is growing consensus about the professional standards and practice guidelines for genetic counseling services that meet the psychological needs of clients (Thompson & Rothenberg, 1992), with special attention to predictive genetic testing of late-onset diseases (Went, 1994), it is inevitable that psychologists will become increasingly involved in the process.

The following review of selected studies highlights psychological knowledge about genetic counseling in four main issues: the meaning of genetic information, patients' and families'

coping with a genetic condition, recall and comprehension of information provided in genetic counseling, and decision making in the context of genetic risks. Pertinent psychological processes related to other current issues in health psychology are also discussed, including coping with stigmatic diseases, understanding and recall of medical information, and patients' making difficult medical decisions. The final section lays out four roles for psychologists in this field: providing direct services to counselees, consulting with counseling teams, training genetic counselors, and researching the psychological aspects of genetic counseling.

## PSYCHOLOGICAL MEANINGS OF GENETICS CONDITIONS

Addressing genetic diseases as a homogeneous entity is misleading. Defects in almost every physical and mental function are represented in the 5,710 diseases identified as genetic (McKusick, Francomano, & Antonarakis, 1992). Some genetic defects are life-threatening, others are benign, some are disfiguring, and some are unnoticeable. Some entail extremely difficult management, whereas others carry no daily burden. Some cause progressive degeneration, and others are static. Some start at birth, and some have late onset; some involve physical disabilities and some mental. The field today also deals with medical conditions other than genetic diseases that have a small, but important, genetic component, such as breast cancer. Coping with a specific genetic disorder depends on its unique characteristics. A review of the literature on specific genetic conditions, their associated difficulties, and the needs of afflicted individuals and families is beyond the scope of this article. Rather, themes common to many genetic conditions are addressed, with a word of caution: The specific nature of genetic conditions limits their generalizability, and the topics covered here are to be read as illustrations of themes and not as examples applicable to other conditions.

Genetic conditions have a bad reputation. Unlike other diseases that are experienced as ego-alien, genetic disorders are experienced as part of one's self, with no option to diminish the threat by projecting it onto an external cause. Genetic disorders are commonly perceived as permanent, irreversible, chronic, family-linked, stigmatizing, complex, and evocative of strong emotions, such as fear, pity, and guilt for passing the defect to off-spring (Kessler, 1979). Their universal meaning aside, the strong ties between cultural and health-related schemes (Landrine & Klonoff, 1992) load genetic conditions with cultural connotations. For example, some highly orthodox Jewish parents of children with genetic defects perceive their child's problem as God's punishment for their deeds, and others perceive it as God's test of their faith (Strauss, 1988). Psychologists working with genetic clients are expected to be particularly attentive to such connotations. There is an increasing recognition that sensitivity to the cultural context is necessary for effective genetic counseling with diverse cultural groups. Two cases in point are the introduction of genetic screening programs for Southeast Asian refugee populations in California (Nidorf & Ngo, 1993) and genetic counseling about **consanguineous marriages** in Arab or Israeli communities (Panter-Brick, 1991; Shiloh, Reznik, Bat-Miriam-Katznelson, & Goldman, 1995).

## Severity of Genetic Conditions

Not all genetic disorders are equally severe, and their severity evaluations depend on one's perspective. Psychological processes, like cognitive biases, can undermine the significance of threatening information in processing health-related facts (Jemmott, Croyle, & Ditto, 1988). Because evaluation of the severity of a threat is a major variable in coping with it (Folkman, 1984; Rosenstock, 1974), anyone who wishes to help

with such coping efforts must understand the evaluation processes involved. For example, hemophilia[1] was perceived as milder by patients than by carriers of the disease gene (Markova, et al., 1986), and parents of children affected with a cleft lip and/or palate[2] rated the condition of their own child as less severe than they viewed that same defect in general (Sagi, Shiloh, & Cohen, 1992). These results may indicate a tendency to compare one's condition to more severe cases; this tendency is referred to as the downward evaluation coping process, which can also be found among cancer patients striving to regain self-esteem (Taylor & Lobel, 1989). In another study, pregnant women rated the burden of various birth defects on scales that combined their perceptions of the defects with their ability to cope with them (Ekwo, Kim, & Gosselink' 1987). The less participants felt they could cope with the consequences of a genetic condition, the more likely they were to accept amniocentesis. These women were following the transactional model of stress and coping (Folkman & Lazarus, 1980; Lazarus & Folkman, 1984), which incorporates the evaluation of available coping resources into the definition of stress.

## Effects of Genetic Status on Health and Illness Perceptions

Perceptions of one's health status are central to one's self-concept. However, the clear distinction between healthy and sick is sometimes blurred in the context of genetic information. Such is the case when a healthy individual learns in genetic screening that he or she is a **carrier** of a mutated (pathological) gene. There are two broad categories of being a carrier of a mutated gene: one that does not have direct implications for the carrier's own future health and one that does. It is estimated that every individual unknowingly carries three to five recessive mutated

---

1. Hemophilia is a disorder of the blood clotting system that mainly affects males and results in excessive bleeding following trauma and spontaneous internal bleeding.

2. Cleft lip and/or palette is a polygenic congenital malformation in which the palate and sometimes the upper lip fail to close. It can be corrected by surgery.

genes that do not affect his or her health status. It becomes important only if both partners are carriers of the same mutation, in which case each pregnancy has a 25 percent risk of being affected. However, people in a screening program found to be carriers of the Tay-Sachs[3] gene expressed significantly more worries about their future health than did noncarriers and controls (Marteau, Van Duijn, & Ellis, 1992). These heightened perceptions of vulnerability can lead to better health practices with a more realistic view of the future, rather than a prevailing unrealistic optimism about susceptibility to health problems (Weinstein, 1984). However, they can also trigger psychological difficulties and alter marital and reproductive plans (Broide, Zeigler, Eckstein, & Bach, 1993).

The psychological impact of genetic screening programs received special attention following one carried out in the 1970s to detect carriers of the sickle-cell anemia[4] gene. It proved to be a devastating experience for many individuals, causing anxiety, confusion, loss of self-esteem, social stigmatization, and discrimination (Murray, 1984). These negative consequences were attributed to a failure to educate the community about the meaning of the test, insufficient counseling services for detected carriers, and insufficient safeguards of the confidentiality of results. The lesson was learned before the more sensitive Tay-Sachs screening program was introduced (Weatherall, 1991). The ethical dilemmas, personal consequences, and counseling needs associated with carrier screening were recently debated again, this time over population screening for cystic fibrosis[5] (Roberts, 1990).

An entirely different genetically related health status is being at risk for developing a genetic condition later in life. This status applies to offspring of patients diagnosed with a genetic disease determined by a dominant gene; for example, offspring of patients with Huntington's disease[6] have a 50 percent chance of inheriting the defective gene and developing the disease some time in the future. The psychological distress of this uncertainty is enormous. Considering the affect-illness-cognition and behavior interactions (Leventhal, Diefenbach, & Leventhal, 1992), it is not surprising that at-risk individuals were reported to engage in disturbing and dysfunctional behaviors, including actively looking for telltale symptoms in themselves and other family members, being extremely anxious at every benign sign, attempting to diminish their physical resemblance to the affected parent, and feeling guilty when a sibling was diagnosed with the disease. Disturbed family dynamic was also described, leading to patient preselection—the singling out in advance of an asymptomatic family member to eventually become the affected individual; denial of disease onset and even suicide were also reported (Kessler & Bloch, 1989). These psychological processes must be recognized before any effective counseling intervention can be applied. The recent advent of presymptomatic diagnostic tests, which can determine who among the at-risk persons has actually inherited the gene for the disease (without means to prevent or slow its occurrence), may solve the problems resulting from uncertainty; however, these tests bring other equally serious ethical and personal dilemmas, including difficulty in communicating about the disease, thoughts of suicide, depression, acute anxiety, and extensive use of personal defense mechanisms.

In view of these reactions, programs for predictive testing of Huntington's disease include the following preventative steps: evaluation of

---

3. Tay-Sachs is a neurodegenerative disease caused by a metabolic defect that results in accumulation of fat in the brain. It leads to death in infancy.

4. Sickle cell anemia is a genetic blood disease caused by a defect in the oxygen-carrying protein hemoglobin. It results in continuous destruction of red blood cells and severe anemia.

5. Cystic fibrosis is one of the most common genetic diseases. It is caused by a defect in ion transfer through cellular membranes that results in severe disease of the respiratory tract and exocrine glands.

6. Huntington's disease is a progressive, late-onset disorder expressed by severe dementia and involuntary movements.

counselees' reasons for seeking the test, readiness for the results, suicidal tendencies, and depression; enhancement of coping resources and social support; and psychological help to deal with negative reactions (Fox, Bloch, Faby, & Hayden, 1989). Follow-up studies showed that, after a short period of shock followed by relief attributable to reduced uncertainty, the distress levels of those with increased risk did not change significantly from the baseline: Their distress tended to decrease after 6 and 12 months by making extensive use of avoidance and denial coping mechanisms. The distress of the reduced risk group was significantly lower than their baseline in all follow-up contacts in one study (Wiggins, et al., 1992). However, in another study (Tibben, et al., 1992), a short period of relief was followed by deteriorating emotional states: Some participants returned to initial feelings of uncertainty by casting doubt on test results; they experienced survivor guilt and emotional numbness and found it difficult to cope with the effects of the test on the family. High degrees of distress were also found among spouses of carriers, a group that rarely seeks professional help. These initial studies underscore the need to connect presymptomatic testing programs with ongoing psychological support services to patients and their families.

Population-based clinical testing for illness predisposition enabled by recent discoveries of major disease genes, like the breast cancer gene, is also pertinent here. However, before generalizing from Huntington's disease to such conditions, one must remember that the implications of carrying the breast cancer gene are drastically different from carrying the Huntington's gene, with regard to both the risk of developing the disease and the effectiveness of preventative measures. Before such genetic testing becomes widely available, strategies to minimize the adverse psychological sequelae and maximize the benefits of testing should be put in place, aimed at enhancing informed decision making, minimizing adverse psychological consequences, and promoting adherence to recommended surveillance (Lerman & Croyle, 1994).

# COPING WITH GENETIC CONDITIONS

Coping with genetic threats is a process of several stages. With early detection of fetal genetic disorders becoming so widespread, coping often begins early in pregnancy at the time of prenatal diagnosis. Another stage of coping begins at the time a genetic condition is diagnosed and develops into an ongoing effort at adjustment to life with it.

## Prenatal Diagnosis

The most studied diagnostic procedure is amniocentesis, an invasive test in which a sample of amniotic fluid containing fetal cells is aspirated through the abdomen during the second trimester of pregnancy. Although many parents consider the option of prenatal diagnosis a blessing, some feel social pressure to use it. The test itself carries a small risk of miscarriage, jeopardizing a wanted pregnancy; in addition, it raises the possibility of having to make a decision about whether to terminate a wanted pregnancy should the result be positive (that is, the fetus is affected). Emotional reactions to prenatal diagnosis cannot be understood separately from the special emotional state of pregnant women and their spouses, which is characterized by stress, ambivalence, changes in self and body image, emotional instability, and changes in thinking processes (Reading, Cox, Sledmere, & Campbell, 1984). Studies on various populations have reported high levels of anxiety in women undergoing prenatal diagnosis around the time of the test, which tended to decrease after receiving negative results (Phipps & Zinn, 1986a; Tabor & Jonsson, 1987; Tunis, Golbus, Copeland, Fine, Rosinsky, & Seely, 1990). Especially marked decreases in anxiety and depression were observed in women with a monitoring coping style (being alert and sensitized to threat-relevant information; Phipps & Zinn, 1986b), probably because it provided them with environmental cues that reduced uncertainty and signaled safety. Other studies found

Although most babies are born healthy, about 3 percent of pregnancies result in the birth of a child with a serious genetic defect. For example, 1 in every 500 African-American babies is born with sickle cell anemia. Genetic counselors help at-risk couples choose among various courses of action and adjust to the consequences of their decisions. (Photo: Richard Hutchings/PhotoEdit)

that women undergoing amniocentesis experienced a greater increase in maternal-fetal attachment from before to after receiving test results than did pregnant control women at comparable times in their pregnancy who did not undergo the test; the tested women presumably suppressed their emotional ties with the fetus during the waiting period in preparation for an abnormal result (Phipps & Zinn, 1986a). There were also reports of heightened worries throughout pregnancy in women using prenatal diagno-

sis, even when the results were normal (Evers-Kiebooms, Swerts, & van den Berghe, 1988). This finding can be attributed to the simulation heuristic (Kahneman & Tversky, 1982): Learning what could go wrong without the possibility of ruling out all possible defects raised the ease with which women imagined birth defects and increased their sense of vulnerability.

When test results show an abnormal fetus, the question of abortion becomes central. Although in general most women regain their psychological well-being shortly after abortion (see review by Dagg, 1991), women who have an abortion because of abnormal findings in prenatal diagnostic tests were found to experience it as especially stressful and hard to cope with (Jorgensen, Uddenberg, & Ursing, 1985). Such reactions may arise because of the following: pregnancies in these cases are usually wanted, genetic disorders evoke guilt feelings, amniocentesis falls in the second trimester when fetal movements are already felt and bonding with the fetus has been established, and abortion at that stage of pregnancy is performed by induced childbirth. The negative reactions in these cases increase if abortion is advocated because of the need for a fast decision, and the reactions become even sharper when the woman feels external pressures to abort (Blumberg, 1984). Genetic counselors recommended that counseling aimed at relieving some of the burden associated with this situation be started as soon as possible, preferably even before the decision to diagnose. It should include the following: reassuring women about the normality of their anxieties; providing information about the procedures (the test or the abortion); organizing support groups of other women and of spouses; discussing the possible reactions and decisions of any test results in advance; helping the couple reach a decision and supporting them afterward with their decision; and helping them understand and deal with reactions of other children in the family, especially those who are affected with the same condition diagnosed in the fetus (Beck-Black, 1990; Blumberg, 1984).

## After Diagnosing a Genetic Condition

When parents first learn about their child's genetic problem, they experience loss of self-esteem, envy of other parents, and grief reactions, such as shock, denial, anxiety, guilt feelings, and anger (Antley, Bringle, & Kinney, 1984). Counselors have the difficult job of supporting families at such critical moments. A number of counseling approaches have been suggested, drawing on a variety of theoretical backgrounds. Tadmor (1986) described a model for the behavior of medical staff in cases of neonatal death, aimed at recovering the couple's perceived personal control. Beck-Black and Weiss (1989) advocated social support groups for parents of children with genetic conditions.

A developmental perspective for conceptualizing family adjustment to cystic fibrosis (CF) can illustrate some of the issues involved in coping with genetic diseases (Carter, Urey, & Eid, 1992), bearing in mind the warning about generalizing from one condition to another. The first stage, the patient's infancy and early childhood, involves a search for an accurate assessment, anticipation of the severity of the child's condition, and adjustment to the somewhat unpleasant and time-consuming home treatments essential for routine prophylactic care of the child with CF (inhalation therapy, chest percussions, and many oral medications). The school-age stage involves adjustment to the child's increased needs for autonomy, parental loss of total control over the child's physical well-being, and risk of behavior or adjustment problems. Adolescent and young adult CF patients demand emancipation in the face of disease-induced dependency. The patients have to deal with negative changes in self-image caused by physical appearance, diminished stamina, demanding treatment regimen, and delayed sexual development. To minimize their differentness from their peers, many adolescents with CF deny the severity of their illness by violating life style restrictions and not complying with treatment regimens. At the same time, they develop an increasing awareness of their prognosis and proximity to terminal stages. Despite increased longevity, individuals with CF seldom survive beyond young adulthood. The terminal stage is the most painful and stress-producing stage of the illness. Parental feelings of helplessness and guilt grow as the child's health deteriorates and sometimes persist well beyond the death of the child. Understanding family and patient adjustment to such heavy demands necessitates **multifactorial** models that include the following: child, parent, and family characteristics; family premorbid functioning and coping efforts after diagnosis; disease status; formal and informal family support networks; and characteristics of the health care system.

Coping efforts of individuals afflicted with genetic problems were grouped by Kessler (1984) around four topics: pursuing hope, learning information, constructing meaning, and acquiring new coping methods. These are similar to the topics identified in the theory of cognitive adaptation to threatening events (Taylor, 1983). Both formulations revolve around issues of control, which seem to offer a potentially powerful integrating concept for understanding and predicting coping with genetic problems. Genetic counseling can offer various ways to regain different dimensions of personal control: cognitive—a better understanding of the condition; decisional—an opportunity to choose among various courses of action; and behavioral—availability of an instrumental response that may directly influence or modify the threat (like using prenatal diagnosis or an effective treatment for the disease). Recent findings in a follow-up study on genetic counselees support the notion that (a) counselees' perceived personal control is increased after genetic counseling in comparison to prior perceptions, and (b) perceived personal control mediates the effects of genetic counseling on counselees' use of more **problem-focused** and less **emotion-focused coping styles** (Shiloh, Berkenstadt, Miran, Bat-Miriam-Katznelson, & Goldman, 1995).

Many of the parents' coping efforts relate to their previous lifestyles, experiences with health problems, and particular coping styles, beliefs, and cultural backgrounds. Families accepting the positive meaning of their child's genetic condition (God's will) displayed better adaptation than families accepting the negative (punishment) meaning (Strauss, 1988). In a study on mothers of children with spine bifida, those with more supportive families and marriages and less conflicted and controlling families reported lower levels of psychological symptoms (Kronenberger & Thompson, 1992). With regard to the controversy about the role of self-blame in coping with health problems (Sholomskas, Steil, & Plummer, 1990), there is evidence that personal attributions to genetic problems can coexist with appropriate understanding of the medical facts (Weil, 1991) and that it can be adaptive: Over 40 percent of mothers interviewed about the causes of their child's genetic problems attributed it to their own past behaviors. Behavioral self-blame, as compared with external attributions (usually to doctors' behaviors) was found to be associated with more optimal parental perceptions, mood states, and interactions with their children (Affleck, McGrade, Allen, & McQueeney, 1985).

## COMMUNICATING AND LEARNING GENETIC INFORMATION

The information genetic counselors convey to clients is extremely complex and replete with uncertainties. It is associated not only with hereditary recurrence, but also with the effectiveness of prophylactic measures in some conditions or the variability of expression in others. Because educating counselees about their genetic condition is the essence of genetic counseling, the counselor has to have knowledge of what and how clients understand and recall genetic information in general and risk information in particular.

### Learning Genetic Information

Most studies that focus on educational aspects of genetic counseling show that counseling effectively increases counselees' knowledge of their problems, but that learning is still less than optimal (literature reviewed by Kessler, 1989). Failure of counselees to learn genetic information is attributed to their personal characteristics, like low education and emotional defense mechanisms, or to counseling attributes, like counselors' communication skills and non-use of educational aids. Several studies showed a relationship between learning of genetic information and its relevance for the counselee, with high relevance facilitating counselees' learning. For example, recurrence risk was remembered better by families considering having more children than those who were not (Lippman-Hand & Fraser, 1979c), and women choosing amniocentesis had a better recall of the risks of the procedure than those who decided against the test (Ekwo, Seals, Kim, Williamson, & Hanson, 1985). Some authors draw a distinction between recall and understanding of the information conveyed in genetic counseling (Bringle & Antley, 1980), further emphasizing the importance of the personal over the general meaning of that information.

### Risk Information

Counselees' processing of risk information (that is, the chances that a genetic defect will occur in the future) closely follows the literature on risk perceptions (Shiloh, 1994; Slovic, 1987). A study of audiotaped counseling sessions and follow-up interviews characterized reactions to risk information as a "binary perception" process, in which numeric risk information is translated into two broad binary categories: The event will or will not happen (Lippman-Hand & Fraser, 1979b). Counselees thus emphasized the uncertainty of the information, which they tried to resolve by a set of personally relevant evaluations, like whether they were themselves infected with the genetic defect. In contradiction to basic assumptions of normative models* of judgment and decision making (Edwards, 1961), an interaction was observed in many of the interviews between evaluation of the severity of the genetic problem (outcome utility) and the perception of its risk (subjective probability). The recurrence risk became, in the eyes of many counselees, part of the overall severity of the condition, rather than a separate piece of information.

There are large differences between counselees' interpretations of objective recurrence risks, and the same risk figures are perceived as high or low by different counselees. These differences have been attributed to demographic variables, like **parity**, a family history of a child with Down's syndrome, and age (Ekwo, et al., 1985). Other studies have found that motivation influences risk information processing in a way that facilitates preferred decisions: A negative correlation was found between the counselees' motivation to have more children (measured before counseling) and postcounseling subjective risk perceptions (Shiloh & Saxe, 1989). This finding supports the view that, although motivated reasoning is generally confined to what can be defended as rational (Kunda, 1990), in health issues there is a constant tension between accuracy motives and the desire to arrive at a favorable conclusion (Croyle, 1992). Other judgmental heuristics can be demonstrated in genetic risk perceptions. Postcounseling subjective perceptions of recurrence risks were better predicted by expectations of risk before counseling than by the objective risk provided in counseling (Shiloh & Saxe, 1989), an expression of the anchoring heuristic whereby people's judgments under uncertainty are determined by the point from which they began their deliberations (Tversky & Kahneman, 1974).

## Communication Styles

Some studies have investigated how the information is communicated by genetic counselors in terms of "framing effects" (Tversky & Kahneman, 1981), asserting (a) that people might change their decisions according to how the problem is presented, (b) that they are usually unaware of these influences, and (c) that they would prefer not to be influenced by presentation variables. Lippman-Hand and Fraser (1979b) described the tendency of genetic counselors to use evaluation words like *low chance* in communicating recurrence risks below 10 percent. One study asked participants to compare mathematically equal statements (or frames) of genetic risks presented as percentages or proportions: Participants who used numerical reasoning tended to perceive percentages as having a greater risk magnitude than equivalent odds. When person reasoning was used, proportions with denominators of 10 or less tended to be perceived as having greater risk magnitude than equivalent percentages, presumably because these participants tended to imagine actual individuals rather than evaluate abstract figures (Kessler & Levine, 1987). In another study, risk perceptions were affected by whether they were presented as single risks or in comparison with other risk figures: The former resulted in overweighing low probabilities and underweighing high probabilities (Shiloh & Sagi, 1989). Presenting genetic risks as negative chances versus positive chances of having a healthy child was found to affect participants' decisions to use prenatal diagnosis (Marteau, 1989), similar to previous findings about the effects of positive versus negative presentations on choice among therapeutic options (McNeil, Rauker, Sox, & Tversky, 1982).

In practice, this line of research is especially important with regard to findings that counselors intentionally or unintentionally presented genetic risks to women in ways that could influence their decisions to use prenatal diagnosis (Marteau, Plenicar, & Kidd, 1993). A better understanding of the ways in which presentation styles affect counselees' perceptions and decisions

---

* Editor's Note: *Normative* means standard, or typical. In a normative model of decision-making, people are assumed to decide on the basis of typical degree of risk, irrespective of other personally relevant information.

may help with the development of guidelines for communication in genetic counseling that protect against biases.

## DECISION MAKING IN GENETIC COUNSELING

One of the main objectives of genetic counseling is to help counselees decide among available options. New genetic technologies constantly add new options (such as presymptomatic tests for late-onset genetic conditions) and new genetic therapies and interventions. Although the available choices would appear to increase counselees' control over their destiny, they are actually experienced by many as an additional burden. Decisional difficulties and dilemmas are therefore expected to be major reasons for seeking psychological help. Most of what is known about genetic-related decisions revolves around matters of reproduction, whereas studies on decisions about predictive genetic testing are still sparse. This scarcity explains why the former studies far outweigh the latter in the following discussion of issues related to decision making in genetic counseling (for a more extensive review on decision making in genetic counseling, see Shiloh, 1995).

### Descriptions of Decisions and Decisional Process

Decisions in genetic counseling can often be described as a chain of consecutive choices (that is, a decision tree), for example, whether or not to use prenatal diagnosis and, then, whether or not to continue a pregnancy with an affected fetus (Beeson & Golbus, 1985). Both counselees and health professionals may confuse these two decisions and assume that a decision to use prenatal diagnosis implies a choice—to terminate the pregnancy of an affected fetus. Evidence is accumulating that these are separate decisions. Some 50 percent of parents of children with a cleft lip and/or palate indicated their intention to use

prenatal diagnosis for this defect, but only 25 percent would terminate an affected fetus (Sagi, Shiloh, & Cohen, 1992). Disentangling decisions is sometimes the key to helping counselees weigh and choose among options. Perceived benefits of prenatal testing, such as the ability to prepare oneself emotionally, were found to predict both the intentions to use the test and to abort an affected fetus. In contrast, perceived severity and risk of the identified defect were found to predict only the intention to diagnose, whereas attitude toward abortion was a significant predictor only of the intention to abort an affected fetus (Sagi, Shiloh, & Cohen, 1992).

That a particular decision can result from different considerations was recently noted with regard to predictive testing for Huntington's disease. The two main reasons for testing were reduction of uncertainty (emotional) and planning for the future (instrumental) (Meissen, Mastromauro, Kiely, McNamara, & Myers, 1991), both of which can be interpreted as expressions of need for control. Differences were found between testing motivations of at-risk individuals and their partners: The former focused on their own future health, and the latter focused on implications for their children (Evers-Kiebooms, Swerts, Cassiman, & van den Berghe, 1989). It is therefore important for psychologists who are involved in genetic counseling to be sensitive to differing agendas and to different views of options, even within the same family.

Attempts have been made to apply general decision-making models, such as the Subjective Expected Utility (Edwards, 1961) and the theory of reasoned action (Fishbein & Ajzen, 1975), to describe the right decision-making process in genetic counseling (Bringle & Antley, 1980; Pauker & Pauker, 1987). However, like in the literature on behavioral decision making, researchers have concluded that rational decision models are inappropriate for describing genetic counselees' decision processes (Beeson & Golbus, 1985). Recent attempts to apply a health-specific decision model, the health belief model (Rosenstock, 1974), to explain decisions made by genetic counselees proved more successful. Beliefs about the health threat, the effectiveness of the available action in reducing that threat, and barriers for performing that action were found to be predictive of genetic counselees' intentions to do carrier testing and prenatal diagnosis for genetic defects (Rowley, Loader, Sutera, Walden, & Kozyra, 1991; Sagi, Shiloh, & Cohen, 1992).

One descriptive model specific to the process of decision making in genetic counseling focused on counselees' desire to reduce uncertainty (Lippman-Hand & Fraser, 1979a). In this model, subjective perceptions of personal and medical facts are combined into a cognitive scenario of trying out the worst, leading to a decision the decider feels he or she can cope with should the worst happen. Another model presented a flow-chart describing counselees' decision process (Frets, Duivenvoorden, Verhage, Ketzer, & Niermeijer, 1990), in which variables explaining the decisions include reproductive outcome before genetic counseling, desire to have children, and interpretation of the information gained from genetic counseling.

## Decision Difficulties

A follow-up study on couples 2 to 3 years after genetic counseling (Frets, Duivenvoorden, Verhage, Peters-Romeyn, & Niermeijer, 1991) showed that 43 percent had problems making reproductive decisions. The following variables were associated with problems in the decision-making process: no postcounseling relief, anticipation of a high risk level, presence of an affected child in the family, a decision against having children, and lack of support from family members for the decision. The authors suggested a structured follow-up 3 to 6 months after genetic counseling to identify couples that would benefit from additional supportive counseling.

Most of the decisions associated with genetic counseling revolve around matters with which people have no experience, and many feel are not for them to decide. These are major life decisions: having a child (or another child) consid-

ered at-risk for a genetic defect; marrying if there is a special risk factor involved, like in consanguinity; using donor insemination to avoid increased genetic risks when both spouses carry the same gene for a genetic disease; undergoing genetic prenatal tests that carry a certain risk for miscarriage; and deciding whether or not to continue a pregnancy after learning that the fetus is affected with a genetic disease or, worse, when the test results are inconclusive. The newer applications of genetic technology raise new decisional dilemmas, such as deciding whether to undergo genetic testing for risk of developing future diseases or, worse, whether to test one's children for such risks. The grave consequences of these decisions that are embedded in profound moral and interpersonal dilemmas are frequently uncertain, because information is largely probabilistic. An indication of such difficulties in deciding to undergo predictive genetic testing is seen in the recent finding that, although most people at risk for genetic diseases say they would get tested in the future (Hietala, Hakonen, Aro, Niemela, Peltonen, & Aula, 1995; Markel, Young, & Penney, 1987; Sujansky, et al., 1990), many do not (Evers-Kiebooms, 1990; Hoffman, 1994; Meissen et al., 1991).

## Nondirective Genetic Counseling

An additional difficulty for genetic counselees stems from the fact that, unlike in most medical counseling, the genetic counselor refrains from recommending a course of action, leaving the decision and responsibility for the outcome to the counselee (Wertz & Fletcher, 1988). This attitude represents the historical development of genetic counseling, shifting away from **eugenics** toward a client-oriented paradigm (Kessler, 1979). In view of the general trends toward more patient participation in medical decision making and more partnership in doctor-patient relationships (Quill, 1983; Speedling & Rose, 1985), the accumulated experience with genetic counseling offers a setting for examining such medical encounters. Forty-two percent of genetic counselees wanted to hear the counselor's opinion of the right decision, but most counselors tried to remain neutral (Somer, Mustonen, & Norio, 1988). It is doubtful, though, whether communication of information about genetic disorders, however balanced, can ever be neutral or value free (Lippman & Wilfond, 1992). Furthermore, there is evidence that counselors' neutrality is itself interpreted by counselees in ways that influence their perceptions of the information provided: Genetic risk perceptions were positively correlated with perceptions of the counselor as neutral, probably because of the reasoning that neutrality conceals bad news (Shiloh & Saxe, 1989).

## Influences of Genetic Counseling on Decisions

Some 26 to 57 percent of counselees reported having been influenced by the counseling (literature reviewed by Kessler, 1989). Those who reported having been influenced by genetic counseling came to counseling with the expectation of getting information relevant to a reproductive decision; they discussed their decision extensively with their counselor and were more educated than clients who said they were not influenced (Wertz & Sorenson, 1986). A consistent observation is the lack of correlation between counselees' reports of influence and actual changes in their plans after counseling (Abramovsky, Godmilow, Hirschhorn, & Smith, 1980). Most studies show that genetic counseling does not produce dramatic changes in counselees' reproductive behavior and that the best predictor of postcounseling reproductive decisions are precounseling intentions (Sorenson, Scotch, Swazey, Wertz, & Heeren, 1987). Moreover, contrary to some expectations, there was an increase in the number of clients initiating or intending pregnancies at 6-month follow-up, compared with those who intended pregnancies before counseling (Sorenson et al., 1987). This increase may relate to findings that precounseling expectations of risk tend to be higher than the actual risk learned in genetic counseling (Sagi, Shiloh, & Cohen,

1992; Shiloh & Saxe, 1989). Information about options of prenatal diagnosis not known before counseling may also influence planning in families with genetically affected children (Evers-Kiebooms, Denayer, & Van den Berghe, 1990). Other effects of genetic counseling on counselees' decisions include changes in confidence in the decision made (Wertz, Sorenson, & Heeren, 1984) and in agreement on the decision between husband and wife (Sorenson & Wertz, 1986).

Reproductive decisions made by couples after they receive genetic counseling correlate with the same social, familial, personal, and financial considerations as those used by the general population, and the information discussed in genetic counseling has only limited influence on their plans (Sorenson, et al., 1987). According to Welshimer and Earp (1989), genetic information interpreted in a personalized way, which is sometimes biased to support previous intentions, is integrated into a previously held cognitive set of beliefs and attitudes regarding childbearing. These intriguing findings do not necessarily imply that genetic information has no impact on counselees' decisions. There is evidence that genetic information affects counselees' decisions only indirectly through cognitive transformations. Postcounseling reproductive intentions, although unrelated to the objective recurrence risks, were significantly correlated with the subjective perceptions of these same risks (Shiloh & Saxe, 1989).

## Decisional Aids

Counseling techniques were designed to guide genetic counselors in their efforts to help counselees reach decisions more effectively according to various theoretical criteria for an effective decision-making process, without directly advising them on what to decide. One of the most ambitious techniques used principles of prescriptive decision analysis to deal with the decision to use amniocentesis for prenatal diagnosis (Pauker & Pauker, 1987). The model explicitly presented the possible outcomes of performing the test, and the counselees were asked to choose between abortion and carrying a pregnancy to term without the benefit of amniocentesis, where the likelihood of an affected child was varied in a structured sequence. Their attitudes were measured on a utility scale, which the counselor used in a normative model to recommend the decision that would give the couple the highest expected utility [chance of favorable outcome]. A qualitative summary of the experience using this technique with 849 genetic counselees over a decade (Pauker & Pauker, 1987) reported that it enhanced communication between the counselor and couple and encouraged couples to confront their attitudes, clarify their values regarding specific reproductive outcomes, and incorporate them together with their current risks into a logical decision about prenatal diagnosis. Some counselees, however, found quantification of their feelings and gambling on such issues hard and disturbing. Other potentially useful counseling techniques were the balance sheet (Janis & Mann, 1977), used by Leonard and Beck-Black (1984) to raise and clarify counselees' considerations for and against specific options, and the structured imagination of alternative outcome scenarios, which was found helpful in reaching a decision, especially by women who had trouble discussing their emotions (Arnold & Winsor, 1984).

## IMPLICATIONS FOR PSYCHOLOGISTS

The psychosocial aspects of genetic counseling and genetic technology have been of concern in genetic centers throughout the world. Multidisciplinary teams engaged in research and practice include physicians, genetic counselors, psychologists, social workers, and genetic nurses whose work together has proved challenging and enriching (Evers-Kiebooms, Fryns, Cassiman, & Van den Berghe, 1992). In the United States, the National Society of Genetic Counselors celebrated its tenth anniversary in 1989 with a membership of over 600 counselors, nurses, and social workers. As genetic knowledge increases, the need for trained genetic counselors expands, strengthening the status of this new profession (Marks, 1989). To the best of my knowledge, there are no statistics on the number of psychologists working in genetic clinics. Despite general agreement about the importance of psychological issues in genetic counseling, the entry of psychologists into this highly professional, competitive, and rapidly developing field will not be easy. The pace will depend in part on their efforts to adapt psychological knowledge to the highly complex subject matter of medical genetics. Nevertheless, considering the rising needs, it is reasonable to assume that more and more psychologists will be engaged in the future in genetic centers and will have to address the implications of genetic counseling in their general practice.

I delineate four roles in genetic counseling for psychologists: providing direct services to clients, training health care providers, consulting with genetic counselors, and researching genetic counseling. Among these, research and training are straightforward and readily accomplished, whereas direct services to clients and consultations within genetic clinics, although greatly needed, may be problematic and require more time.

## Providing Direct Services to Genetic Counselees

Although genetic counseling will remain mainly the task of medical professionals, who have the expertise to diagnose and analyze hereditary and health consequences of genetic disorders and risks, a psychologist on the genetic counseling team seems essential. Early in the counseling process, psychologists can assess individual differences among counselees in psychological and familial status, traits, needs, expectations, and conceptions of what is wrong, which may lead to more personalized counseling. When predictive testing for late-onset conditions is contemplated, persons at psychosocial risk who will need special counseling and support can be identified. Later in the process, psychologists can intervene in crisis situations, provide family and supportive counseling, and help resolve personal and interpersonal problems raised by the genetic counseling. After the educational phase of genetic counseling, psychologists can help counselees (a) understand and personalize the newly learned, often threatening, genetic information; (b) clarify their values; (c) make difficult decisions; and (d) develop and strengthen coping resources to adjust to future outcomes.

One model for genetic counseling has the genetic and psychological counselors meeting the couple together as a team (Antley, Bringle, & Kinney, 1984). The psychologist helps create an accepting atmosphere, regulates the pace of information flow, encourages counselees' expressions of reactions to the information, checks understanding, and repeats explanations. Not all professionals agree these roles should be taken up by psychologists. Kessler (1979) argued that the genetic counselor, not a psychologist, should undertake the role of psychotherapist, help reorganize personal strengths and resources, enhance coping, and provide emotional support. Such a genetic counselor is uncommon, however, because most see themselves as mainly information givers, a role they explicate as nondirective counseling (Wertz & Fletcher, 1988).

Counselees' desire for psychological intervention as part of genetic counseling has not been studied, but many of the researchers cited earlier indicated that most counselees interviewed in their studies were eager to discuss their difficulties with a professional. Thus, having an option for psychological help should be appreciated by many genetic counselees. However, any new psychological intervention in this field must be accompanied by evaluation studies to determine its impact on both counselees and professionals.

## Consulting with Genetic Counseling Teams

Genetic counselors work under great pressure. In a cynical article, Partington (1986) described genetic counselors as counseling when they themselves are uncertain about the genetic outcomes, are required by the counselees to answer existential questions for which they are not prepared, and are frequently misunderstood by the counselees. Ultimately, despite best intentions, they make unavoidable mistakes.

In addition to the serious psychological problems addressed in this article, genetic counselors often have to discuss sensitive issues with their counselees, like parenthood through donor insemination, nonpaternity, and the obligation to inform other family members about a genetic risk and disclose information the counselee might want to hide even from close relatives. Counselors may experience serious moral dilemmas when they have to support counselees' decisions that run counter to their personal values, like terminating a pregnancy for a reason the counselor feels is inappropriate; offering available options, such as a risky prenatal diagnosis, even when the problem seems insignificant; or relaying information on an insignificant finding discovered in genetic tests that may be misinterpreted by the counselee and cause unnecessary alarm. One way to minimize these burdens is to lay down professional guidelines and regulations for specific dilemmas, practically an unachievable task (Foss, 1989). In the final analysis, genetic counselors must face these dilemmas and solve each specific case in accordance with moral and professional standards.

Psychologists in a consulting role can alleviate some of the genetic counselors' burden. They can help the counselor decide how to handle a particular case. They can provide theoretical justifications, empirical evidence, and practical advice on how to handle crises, couple disagreement, communication difficulties, emotional states, and counselees' demands and accusations. They can provide support, help clarify counselor's values, and encourage open discussion of feelings and stresses by the genetic team.

## Training Genetic Counselors

In 1988, there were only 12 master's degree programs for training genetic counselors in the

United States and Canada. Most included theoretical and practical courses on interviewing and counseling and on psychosocial and ethical aspects of genetic counseling (Scott, Walker, Eunpu, & Djurdjinovic, 1988). The rapid growth of genetic services is increasing the need for qualified psychologists to teach courses for genetic counselors, either in formal programs for new genetic counselors or in on-the-job courses for active genetic counselors. A theoretical course on the psychological aspects of genetic counseling should include, in addition to basic psychological information, a review of the issues related to genetic counseling, like those covered in this article.

## Researching Psychological Aspects of Genetic Counseling

Out of some 9,000 articles that appeared in the major genetic and obstetric journals from 1985 to 1989, only 45 presented empirical data from distinct studies dealing with psychological, social, and ethical issues of genetic counseling (Lippman, 1991). Most were descriptive studies of attitudes and reactions of counselees to genetic counseling and prenatal diagnosis. Prospective, interdisciplinary studies are required to close the many gaps in knowledge about the impact of the new genetic technologies. The Human Genome Project has devoted approximately $3 million a year for the past 5 years to exploring the legal, ethical, and social policy issues raised by the project. This declared goal of the Human Genome Project may accelerate developments already occurring at a rapid pace. An increasing number of social scientists are working in close contact with medical genetics units and developing ties that are producing highly qualitative research. This trend justifies the current call for psychosocial genetics as a distinct emerging scientific field (Harper, 1993). This is a challenge for psychologists, who are eminently qualified to conduct studies on human reactions and behavior related to genetic counseling. Psychological theory and methodology and a balance between qualitative and quantitative approaches are essential. The few studies reviewed in this article that applied psychological theories and methods—anchored in general, cognitive, clinical, social, and health psychology—may prove stimulating and helpful to clinicians as well as to those interested in the theoretical aspects of genetic counseling.

Psychological researchers may find that genetic counseling is not only an interesting research area per se, but also can provide a real-life laboratory to test some of the issues examined by psychologists, including risk perception, decision making, interpersonal communication, stress and coping, and family dynamics. When one considers the wealth of possibilities for practical study of theoretical concepts, surprisingly little attention has been given to genetic counseling in the psychological literature, even in health psychology, perhaps because most psychologists are not familiar with genetic counseling. It is hoped that this review will help familiarize psychologists with this potentially fruitful area.

## EVALUATING YOUR MASTERY

1. Research on the psychological consequences of prenatal diagnosis reveals which of the following?
   a.   Decreased anxiety around the time of testing
   b.   Heightened attachment to the fetus before receiving test results
   c.   A rise in worries throughout pregnancy, even after test results rule out certain defects
   d.   Considerable stress for those who decide to abort after learning of abnormal findings

2. Shiloh's example of family adjustment after learning that a child has cystic fibrosis shows that
   a.   Parent and child adaptation is limited to just after the genetic disease is disclosed.
   b.   Parent and child adaptation continues throughout childhood and adolescence.
   c.   Parent adaptation is limited to an initial period of shock; children must continually adjust throughout childhood and adolescence
   d.   Because cystic fibrosis victims live a normal life span, parents and children need not adapt to a terminal illness.

3. Which of the following factors was NOT reported to affect the degree to which genetic information is accurately understood during genetic counseling?
   a.   Presenting risk as percentages (for example, 10 percent) versus proportions, or odds (1 in 10)
   b.   The counselee's age and sex, which often influences their understanding of probabilistic information
   c.   Presenting risks alone versus in comparison to other risks
   d.   Presenting risks as negative chances versus positive chances of a healthy child

4. Which of the following is true about decision making on the basis of genetic information?
   a.   The availability of many new tests relieves anxiety.
   b.   The chain of consecutive choices is rational, based on risk and an objective appraisal of information.
   c.   Personal perceptions of health threat and available actions for reducing threat predict decisions about genetic testing
   d.   Non-health-related decision models generalize to decision making about genetic issues

5. True or False: A genetic counselor can unintentionally influence the way a person makes decisions about genetic risks by remaining neutral throughout the counseling session.

6. True or False: Follow-up counseling is needed because many people have problems making reproductive decisions for several years after obtaining genetic counseling.

7. True or False: Most studies show that genetic counseling produces dramatic changes in counselees' reproductive behaviors.

8. Match each of the following genetic diseases with their description:
   a. A metabolic defect the results in accumulation of fat in the brain
   b. A defect in ion transfer through cellular membranes that results in severe respiratory disease
   c. A late-onset disease that results in severe dementia and involuntary movements
   d. A defect in the oxygen-carrying protein hemoglobin that results in continuous destruction of red blood cells
   e. Malformation of the spinal cord, leading to paralysis

   _____ sickle cell anemia

   _____ cystic fibrosis

   _____ Tay-Sachs disease

   _____ spina bifida

   _____ Huntington's disease

## Critical Thinking

A pregnant woman with a history of Tay-Sachs disease in her own and her husband's families has come to a genetic counselor for help in deciding whether to seek prenatal diagnosis. List factors identified by research that might affect the woman's decision making. Which factors are most important for the counselor to keep in mind while providing the woman with genetic information? Why are those factors especially important?

## Applying Your Knowledge

Your best friend has just completed her master's degree in genetic counseling and is beginning to establish her practice. She seeks your opinion about whether she should work closely with a psychological counselor. Explain the value of establishing interdisciplinary genetic counseling teams. Who else would you include on the team, and why?

# 3

# Interventions to Ease
# the Transition to Parenthood

## Why They Are Needed
## and What They Can Do

### CAROLYN PAPE COWAN & PHILIP A. COWAN
### University of California, Berkeley

■

If a life transition experienced by approximately 90 percent of contemporary married couples can be expected to be accompanied by stress and distress for many parents, it is likely that this strain will permeate some of all of the relationships in the family, which, in turn, can be expected to compromise children's optimal development.

■

New mothers and fathers describe shifts in their friendship networks and their connection to work outside the home that make it increasingly difficult to juggle the competing demands of work and family life or to preserve time for friendships or leisure.

■

The most noteworthy effects of the intervention were on parents' marital satisfaction and stability 18 months into parenthood. In contrast to the drop in marital satisfaction found in most longitudinal studies, marital satisfaction between 6 and 18 months postpartum remained stable in couples who had been in a couples group.

■

A number of ambitious programs for new families considered to be at high risk for distress or compromised development use interdisciplinary teams, some of which incorporate hospital and home visits that begin in pregnancy and continue into the early months or years of parenthood.

■

These examples of intensive interventions designed to help high-risk families get off to a healthier start show that many expectant or new parents will respond to highly trained health and mental health paraprofessionals and professionals who offer a nurturant relationship over an extended period of time.

■

Parents' adjustment to parenthood as individuals and couples forecasts the quality of the relationship they develop with their children in the preschool period, which, in turn, is a central predictor of their children's subsequent cognitive, social, and emotional adaptation to elementary school.

■

## EDITOR'S INTRODUCTION

Carolyn and Philip Cowan review evidence indicating that the birth of a baby profoundly alters the family system, leading to both individual and marital distress for the large majority of new parents that can last from months to years. Even parents who are in low-risk circumstances—economically well off, happily married before childbirth, and functioning well psychologically—experience these changes. Disrupted sleep schedules, less time for husband and wife to devote to each other, and new financial responsibilities prompt an increase in conflict and a decline in marital satisfaction. In addition, entry of the baby into the family usually causes the roles of husband and wife to become more traditional.

As the Cowans note, both men and women are at increased risk for mental health problems during the transition to parenthood—an outcome that can profoundly affect the parent–infant relationship. These findings offer powerful support for interventions targeting expectant and new parents that focus on resolving personal distress and enhancing the marital and parent–child relationships. Reviewing existing programs, the authors point out that many end just as the baby is born, leaving parents on their own to manage this challenging transition. Yet, interventions that extend beyond the baby's birth and focus on preventive mental health services are highly successful.

Effective intervention efforts must adapt to families' life situations. The Cowans consider strategies that work well with low-risk parents, such as couples groups, and more intensive programs for high-risk parents, including troubled adults, teenage parents, parents living in poverty, and parents struggling to adjust to the birth of a child with disabilities.

Men and women have been having babies since human life began. Not until the last half of the twentieth century, however, did the transition to parenthood become the subject of intensive analysis by sociologists, psychologists, and health and mental health professionals. Academicians' and health providers' interest appears to have been stimulated by a study by LeMasters (1957), a sociologist, who made the apparently shocking claim that 83 percent of new parents had experienced "moderate or severe crisis" in their marital and family life in the first years following the birth of their first child. Using various methods and outcome measures, investigators over the next three decades challenged LeMasters' assertion that the transition to parenthood constitutes a crisis for a marriage (Hobbs, 1965; White & Booth, 1985). These investigators concluded that (a) new parenthood was a stressful but essentially manageable, normative transition (Hobbs & Cole, 1977), or (b) the decline in adjustment and marital satisfaction new parents experienced was not appreciably different from the waning of marital intimacy experienced over time by childless couples (McHale & Huston, 1985; White & Booth, 1985).

Neither of these responses to LeMasters seemed to settle the controversy about crisis. After early retrospective studies, investigators in the 1980s began to *follow* couples from pregnancy into the early childrearing years. These longitudinal studies revealed negative changes in many aspects of men's and women's adaptation as individuals and as couples (see reviews by Belsky & Pensky, 1988; Cowan & Cowan, 1988; Worthington & Buston, 1987). Along with shifts in partners' stress levels, division of family labor, and leisure time, almost every study noted a decline in men's and women's marital satisfaction.

Is the transition to parenthood likely to create long-term strain in men, women, and marriage? The answer to this question has important

theoretical and practical implications. Theories of life course and family development (see Cowan, 1991; Hinde & Stevenson-Hinde, 1988) imply that major life changes and transitions create conditions of risk. New challenges can outstrip existing resources, trigger new problems, or amplify preexisting vulnerabilities and inadequacies. Explicit in some of these theories is the idea that the challenges of transitions can also stimulate the development of new coping skills and higher levels of adaptation. The transition to parenthood is an interesting test case for lifespan developmental theories because, unlike most expected and unexpected traumatic transitions that have been studied extensively, becoming a parent is widely regarded as a positive change in the life of a couple. If the transition to parenthood does increase the probability of problematic outcomes in parents and children, then the hypothesis that life transitions constitute conditions of risk would be supported.

Increased marital and family risk associated with the transition to parenthood has implications for the provision of health and mental health services. If a life transition experienced by approximately 90 percent of contemporary married couples can be expected to be accompanied by stress and distress for many parents, it is likely that this strain will permeate some or all of the relationships in the family, which, in turn, can be expected to compromise children's optimal development. In that case, it would seem reasonable to create targeted or even universal preventive intervention programs designed to enhance parents' coping skills and reduce their stress or to provide remedial help for couples already in difficulty when the transition begins. If there is no significant increase in risk or negative outcomes attributable to this transition, then intervention programs on a wide societal scale would be unnecessary.

The first section of this article argues that, despite some remaining areas of controversy in

Cowan, C. P., & Cowan, P. A. (1995). Interventions to ease the transition to parenthood: Why they are needed and what they can do. *Family Relations, 44,* 412–423. © 1995 by the National Council on Family Relations, 39389 Central Ave. NE, Suite 550, Minneapolis, MN 55421. Reprinted by permission.

The preparation of this article was supported in part by National Institute of Mental Health grant no. MH-31109.

comparing and interpreting studies, we can conclude with some confidence that the transition to parenthood constitutes a period of stressful and sometimes maladaptive change for a significant proportion of new parents. This conclusion is based on findings that individual and marital distress in parents of young children can be predicted from risk indicators obtained before partners enter parenthood. Furthermore, longitudinal studies of low risk couples make it clear that stress and distress in parents during the early years of family formation are associated with negative developmental outcomes for their children in the preschool and elementary school periods (Cowan & Cowan, 1992). These data provide solid justification of the need for preventive intervention programs designed to ease the transition to parenthood for parents and their babies.

Curiously, systematic longitudinal research on the transition to parenthood has focused primarily on two-parent families in relatively favorable socioeconomic and relationship circumstances. We summarize the findings from this research in the second section of this article. Although it can be demonstrated that a meaningful proportion of nominally low-risk couples experience significant problems during the transition-to-parenthood period, there are virtually no services to provide help until the problems escalate to the point where one or both parents or their children require the assistance of the mental health system. In contrast with the dearth of interventions for so-called low-risk partners becoming parents, interventions for *mothers* considered to be at high risk by virtue of their low socioeconomic status or single parenthood have been launched in many geographic locales. These programs have been justified by evidence that mothers who are young, unmarried, and poor tend to suffer health or emotional problems themselves, are more likely to require health and mental health services, and have children who are at risk for developmental and academic problems (McLoyd, 1990). Yet, most interventions for high-risk mothers have been designed in the absence of systematic data documenting links between specific risks and outcomes.

In sum, on one hand we have extensive research on the risks and distress experienced by a substantial proportion of relatively advantaged men and women becoming parents, but no services to help ease the transition. On the other hand, we have a variety of intervention programs for high-risk mothers and sometimes their babies, but almost no systematic longitudinal before-to-after parenthood studies to identify the key risk and protective factors that need to be targeted in interventions. In the middle sections of this article, we describe evaluations of interventions for expectant and new parents in low-risk and high-risk populations. In the final section, we attempt to integrate ideas from these two virtually nonoverlapping bodies of work.

## ELEVATED RISK IN THE TRANSITION TO PARENTHOOD: JUSTIFYING THE NEED FOR INTERVENTION

We begin with a brief description of documented changes in family life as partners become parents. Our summary is derived from results of longitudinal studies of couples having a first child; the mean age of the parents is the late twenties, and the socioeconomic status ranges from working or lower-middle class to upper-middle class. For primary reports and extensive reviews of this research, the reader is referred to two special issues of journals (Cox, 1985; Palkovitz & Sussman, 1988) and a number of books (Belsky & Kelly, 1994; Berman & Pedersen, 1987, Boukydis, 1987; Clulow, 1982; Cowan & Cowan, 1992; Grossman, Eichler, & Winickoff, 1980; Michaels & Goldberg, 1988).

### What Changes During the Transition to Parenthood?

When designing longitudinal studies of men and women becoming parents in the 1980s, researchers wisely shifted their focus away from the vague question of whether the transition to parenthood constitutes a crisis for couples and pursued a more differentiated set of descriptive questions about the nature of change in individual and family life from midpregnancy into the first or second postpartum year. Studies such as the ones by Belsky and his colleagues in Pennsylvania (for example, Belsky & Rovine, 1990; Belsky, Spanier, & Rovine, 1983) and by us and our colleagues in California (Cowan & Cowan, 1992; Cowan et al., 1985) were guided by multidomain theoretical models that hypothesize that the transition to parenthood represents a transformation not simply of the parents as individuals but of the developing **family system**. We proposed that changes in each of five family domains must be examined in order to understand which families are doing well and which are at risk for compromised development. These domains are (a) the quality of relationships in the new parents' families of origin, (b) the quality of the new parents' relationship as a couple, (c) the quality of relationship that each parent develops with the baby, (d) the balance between life stress and social support in the new family, and (e) the well-being or distress of each parent and child as individuals.

Taken as a group, studies of the transition to parenthood show that new parents experience shifts in all five domains. Anecdotal, qualitative accounts reveal inner psychological and interpersonal changes in both partners' relationships with their parents, sometimes resulting in closer relationships, sometimes in more distance (Cowan & Cowan, 1992; Leifer, 1980). The family becomes organized around each parent's relationship with the child, and the quality of this relationship changes quickly, especially in the early months of the child's life (Brazelton & Cramer, 1990). Measures of overall perceived life stress and social support in parents' lives do not seem to show much systematic change in the early childrearing years (Cowan & Cowan, 1992), but new mothers and fathers describe shifts in their friendship networks and their connection to work outside the home that make it increasingly difficult to juggle the competing demands of work and family life or to preserve time for friendships or leisure (Crawford & Huston, 1993). Some theoretical analyses of the transition to parenthood assert that personality change accompanies the parenthood transition (Antonucci & Mikus, 1988), but few studies examine that claim. What is more certain is that having a baby brings with it not only a new identity as parent, but a rearrangement of parents' investment in their other roles—son/daughter, partner, lover, worker, friend (Cowan et al., 1985). This reorganization involves psychological energy and may or may not reflect actual time spent in each of these roles.

Finally, on a descriptive level, it is clear that the transition to parenthood is accompanied by marked shifts in the marital relationship. The division of labor in the family becomes more traditional (Cowan & Cowan, 1988; Entwisle & Doering, 1981; Macdermid, Huston, & McHale, 1990), less time is available for the couple (LaRossa & LaRossa, 1981), and the meaning and frequency of sex shifts, sometimes differently for men and women (Osofsky & Osofsky, 1984). What makes this a systemic rather than a personal issue for couples is that changes in each domain of family life combine or interact to affect how men and women adapt to becoming parents (Belsky, Rovine, & Fish, 1989; Cowan & Cowan, 1992).

## Does the Transition to Parenthood Elevate Risk for Individual or Marital Distress?

The question of central relevance to this article is whether the shifts that couples experience in their transition to parenthood are accompanied by increased levels of individual and marital distress. Evidence supports an affirmative answer.

*Individual adaptation.* Both men and women are at increased risk for depression during the transition to parenthood (for example, Cutrona, 1982). Estimates of the incidence of **postpartum depression** in women range from .01 percent to 50 percent (Hamilton, 1962). Campbell and her colleagues (Campbell, Cohn, Flanagan, Popper, & Myers, 1992) report that approximately 10 percent of postpartum women develop clinical depression serious enough to interfere with their daily functioning. There are no epidemiological data documenting the incidence of postpartum depression or other psychological distress for new fathers. In our study of 100 relatively well-functioning couples, one mother *and one father* experienced postpartum clinical depressions that required hospitalization and treatment in the first months of parenthood.

Few investigators document symptoms of depression and negative mood in nonclinical samples of parents of young children (for exceptions, see Cutrona, 1982; Feldman, 1987; Fleming, Ruble, Flett, & Shaul, 1988). Even when they do, they rarely report what proportion of the sample scores in the clinically distressed range. In our own sample, 30 percent of both mothers and fathers scored above the cutoff on the Center for Epidemiological Studies Depression Scale (CES-D; Radloff, 1977) at 18 months postpartum, and 20 percent of the mothers and 30 percent of the fathers were still above the cutoff when their children were 3 1/2 years old. Given recent evidence that adults' high scores on the CES-D are predictive of future psychiatric risk, even when more rigorous interview data do not result in a **DSM** classification of mood disorder (Gotlib, Lewinsohn, & Seeley, 1995), it is clear that a substantial proportion of new mothers and an unknown number of new fathers are in acute emotional distress during the family formation period. Furthermore, we know that in a significant percentage of cases, this postpartum distress continues over a period of years (Kumar & Robson, 1984), and that parents' depression poses risks for the quality of both marital and parent-child relationships (see, for example, Field, Healy, Goldstein, & Guthertz, 1990).

*Marital adjustment*. Both LeMasters' conclusion, which first raised the issue of potential risks for partners becoming parents, and the conclusion that the transition to parenthood is not stressful can be questioned on methodological grounds. The initial studies were all retrospective, asking participants to compare their present postpartum state with recollections of their prebaby experiences. In addition, Hobbs' work (1965; Hobbs & Cole 1977) that focused on the first few months of parenthood used simple checklists of "bothersome events," with no empirical validation of cutoff scores to assess parents' levels of distress. Even with these weak criteria of distress, Hobbs' studies found 20 percent of the sample in the distressed range, yet concluded that the impact of the transition was minimal.

In the past two decades, longitudinal studies of the transition to parenthood became the norm. In a prospective longitudinal survey of couples in 1980 and again in 1983, White and Booth (1985) included what they believed to be a key comparison between couples who did and did not become parents over the 3-year period. Although they found greater increases in problems and disagreements in the couples who became parents, the authors concluded that there were no basic differences between the two samples in overall marital happiness or frequency of marital interaction. Because marital quality declined in both the parent and nonparent samples, White and Booth argued that decreased marital quality in single sample studies of couples who are parents is an artifact of a decay found generally in marital relationships over time. Despite the improved longitudinal method, there were two limitations of the White and Booth study. First, their telephone interview survey method may have restricted the reports of personal and marital distress (Laslett & Rapoport, 1975). Second, although longitudinal, the study did not focus on the transition itself because the age of the children in the parent sample varied by as much as 3 years.

In another study begun as an investigation of young married couples, Huston and his colleagues also found little difference between those who had and had not become new parents (McHale & Huston, 1985; Macdermid, Huston, & McHale, 1990). In our own longitudinal study of first-time parents (Cowan & Cowan, 1992), with participants ranging in age from 21 to 47 years and in relationships ranging in length from

4 months to 12 years, we also followed a childless comparison group of couples who had not yet decided about whether to become parents but who were recruited from the same sources as the expectant parents (obstetrician–gynecologists and public service media announcements). We found significantly more negative changes in the marital relationship of the new parents than in the childless couples. The decline in marital quality for parents was greater in older, longer-married new parent couples, and the decline for men was not evident until midway through the second postpartum year. Because older couples were not included in the White and Booth (1985), McHale and Huston (1985),·or Macdermid, Huston, and McHale (1990) studies, and because their assessments were made at an earlier point in the transition, their results may have minimized the impact reported by many other investigators who followed more heterogeneous samples over a longer period.

Thirteen of 15 prospective longitudinal transition to parenthood studies we reviewed in 1988 (including White and Booth's and our own), all using pre- and postbaby marital measures, support the conclusion that marital satisfaction declines after the birth of a first child. Studies conducted in Germany (Engfer, 1988; Schneewind, 1983) and England (Clulow, 1982) arrive at the same conclusion. Although simply adding up studies with findings supporting one side or another has its own difficulties, we feel relatively assured in concluding that, especially in heterogeneous samples of couples, there is a statistically significant risk that many marriages will suffer increases in conflict and declines in satisfaction in the years after couples have children. In addition, the relative congruence of findings from studies using different methods and samples from different geographical locations helps to resolve the potential criticism that the convenience samples of new parents studied so far are not representative of the population of couples having first babies. We believe that the strength of the present findings lies in the fact that the basic results have now been replicated in more than 20 studies in different locales within the United States and overseas.

The conclusion that the transition to parenthood is associated with elevated risk of a decline in marital quality itself does not resolve four important questions: (a) Does the transition to parenthood *cause* the decline in marital quality? (b) How many couples experience serious negative changes in individual and marital adaptation after the baby arrives? (c) Who are the individuals and couples at risk for distress during this period? and (d) Do these negative shifts in parents have consequences for subsequent family relationship quality and the children's development?

## Do We Need Childless Couples as Controls?

Because most studies of the transition to parenthood fail to compare couples having babies with childless couples, it is necessary to consider White and Booth's central argument (1985): A decline in satisfaction is not caused by parenthood *per se,* but occurs as a function of disenchantment in relationships over time. In response, Belsky and Pensky (1988) observe that "Families not expecting or rearing a baby differ from those that are in a variety of important ways above and beyond the mere status of parenthood" (p 137). They have also suggested that the relationship of nonparent couples may have been less stable to begin with. In other words, even when differences between parents and childless couples are found, it is not possible to determine whether they are caused by the difference in parenthood status or by preexisting differences in personality, motivation, or relationship quality.

A further complication of the White and Booth argument is that studies have not examined the longer-term marital shifts in either parents or nonparents. In our study, a 6-year follow-up revealed that 20 percent of couples who had become parents had divorced, but 50 percent of the couples who remained childless had also dissolved their marriages. This finding accords with national demographic data suggesting that, despite increasing marital dissatisfaction in new parents, the presence of a child tends to keep the marital relationship intact (Bumpass & Rindfuss, 1979).

It seems that a childless comparison group, an intuitively obvious research strategy choice, may raise more questions than it resolves. But without a comparison group, can we evaluate the hypothesis that the transition to parenthood *causes* an increase in risk status or actual distress? Although it flies in the face of conventional wisdom, the question of causality may be relatively unimportant from the point of view of intervention and public policy. If we demonstrate that a substantial number of couples show *increasing* individual and marital distress after becoming parents, and if their distress has negative implications for their own or their children's development (see below), then preventive and remedial services may be necessary to ease the transition for men and women who are creating new families.

## How Frequent and Severe Are Negative Changes in Marital Quality?

Belsky and Rovine (1990) attempted to advance the study of marital change across the transition to parenthood by moving beyond the study of central tendencies to examine variations in patterns of marital change from late pregnancy to 3 years postpartum. Using four self-report indices of husbands' and wives' marital quality, they found that from 30 percent to 59 percent of the participants showed a decline in marital quality, whereas 10 percent to 30 percent (depending on the gender of the spouse and the measure) showed a modest positive increase. Our own study showed decreasing marital satisfaction in 45 percent of the men and 58 percent of the women, with increasing marital satisfaction in 18 percent of the couples not participating in one of our intervention groups. Of course, the exact proportion of couples showing declining or improved marital quality depends in part on the sample and in part on the statistical criteria for delineating decline, no change, and improvement. The point we emphasize here is that from one-third to one-half of the men and women in

two large longitudinal studies experienced some decline in marital quality after having a baby.

Belsky and his colleagues have noted, and our findings correspond, that the mean decline in marital satisfaction on the Short Marital Adjustment Test (Locke & Wallace, 1959) or the Dyadic Adjustment Scale (Spanier, 1976) is a small to moderate 10 to 15 points, from scores of about 125 (relatively happy) falling to around 110 (10 points above the clinical cutoff of 100, indicating some level of marital distress). We cannot be totally reassured by this description of modest mean change. In fact, some couples decline much more than 10 points. In our study, 18 percent of the participants declined more than 20 points in marital satisfaction scores between late pregnancy and 18 months postpartum, with about 6 percent showing a decline greater than 40 points and one couple declining from their combined (his and her) mean score of 128 to 28. About 15 percent of the men and women moved from above to below the clinical cutoff in marital satisfaction, whereas only 4 percent shifted from below to above the cutoff. Twenty-eight percent of the men and women were below the clinical cutoff in marital satisfaction at one or more points during their transition to parenthood. There is little doubt, then, that a significant proportion of partners becoming parents experience a reduction in the quality of their marriage and that some are in relationships that the partners and marital therapists would judge to be distressed.

## Who Are the Couples Most At Risk?

Despite significant shifts from before to after the birth of a first child in the five domains of family life assessed in the studies we have cited, there is also remarkable consistency of well-being or distress over time—within and between family domains. This means that it possible to identify individuals and couples who are at heightened risk for later distress and dysfunctional behavior patterns on the basis of assessments made before their babies are born. Parents' individual symptoms, life stress, social support, and marital adjustment *measured before the birth of the child* account for a substantial portion of the variance in both men's and women's adaptation to parenthood (Belsky & Rovine, 1990; Cowan & Cowan, 1992; Cox, Owen, Lewis, & Henderson, 1989; Fleming et al., 1988; Grossman, Eichler, & Winickoff, 1980; Heinicke, Beckwith, & Thompson, 1988). A baby's arrival is unlikely to destroy very well-functioning marriages *or* generate closer, more satisfying relationships between already troubled partners.

## Parents' Adaptation and Children's Development

Results from five research teams reveal that mothers' and fathers' psychological adaptation and marital quality before their babies are born predicts their parenting effectiveness during the first year or two of their child's life (Belsky & Rovine, 1990; Cowan & Cowan, 1992; Cox et al., 1989; Grossman, Eichler, & Winickoff, 1980; Heinicke, Diskin, Ramsay-Klee, & Oates, 1986). Belsky and his colleagues found similar results in families followed at 3 years postpartum, and our research team has traced links between parents' individual and marital distress before the child was born and parent-child relationship quality 4 and 6 years later (Cowan, Cowan, Schulz, & Heming, 1994). Pre- and postbirth data contribute both independently and additively to the prediction of both parenting quality and children's adaptation. The quality of the parent-child relationship emerges in part from the history of parents' adjustment—as individuals and as couples—to the process of becoming a family. Along with the family's current life circumstances and characteristics of the child, this history helps to explain a substantial amount of the variance in the effectiveness as parents.

Data from studies that follow couples beyond the immediate transition to parenthood highlight the necessity of taking a family systems view of what happens to development when partners become parents. When stress is experienced by a parent, a couple, or a child, it has a tendency to spill over or get amplified in relationships with other family members, regardless of where the stress begins (Belsky & Kelly, 1994; Clulow, 1982; Cohn, Cowan, Cowan, & Pearson, 1992; Crockenberg, 1981; Fidele, Golding, Grossman, & Pollack, 1988). Children's social and academic adaptation to elementary school is predicted best by combining information about parents' adaptation to parenthood and the tone of their relationship as a couple in the preschool years (Cowan et al., 1994). Children's emotional adjustment, using externalizing and internalizing behavior problems as an index, is predicted more fully when information is added about parents' memories of being parented (Belsky & Isabella, 1985; Cowan, Cohn, Cowan, & Pearson, 1996).

What conclusions can be drawn from the data we have summarized so far? Because of ambiguities in the meaning of control groups, we cannot really determine whether couples who are making the transition to parenthood are at greater risk of personal or marital distress than childless couples. We know that results from longitudinal studies of relatively low-risk families show that before their babies are born, a substantial proportion of expectant parents are at risk for amplification of their difficulties as individuals and as couples once they become parents. During the transition period, between one third and one half are experiencing as much marital distress as couples who are already in therapy for marital difficulties. We reemphasize the point that this evidence of distress has been obtained in studies of relatively advantaged families, suggesting that the designation of these families as "low risk" does a disservice to their actual experiences. We have the tools now to predict who the individuals and couples in most distress will be, based on what we can learn from self-report instruments obtained in middle to late pregnancy. Finally, parents' well-being or distress during the family-making period is a precursor of their children's academic achievement, success with peers, and behavior problems in early elementary school.

In our view, the pattern of findings we have reported provides strong justification for considering the provision of intervention programs for expectant and new parents. The data suggest that it would be wise to focus on the resolution of both personal and marital distress, on parents' distressing experiences with their parents, and on the enhancement of marital and parent-child relationship skills. If this justification is strong for the low-risk families who have been the objects of so many studies, it seems even stronger when we consider parents at high-risk or already in distress as they start their families. Even so, further study is needed to show precisely how high-risk status affects both men's and women's transitions to parenthood and how the changes of the transition ultimately affect their relationship quality and the children's development.

## INTERVENTIONS FOR LOW-RISK FAMILIES

Just as the early transition to parenthood studies focused on women, the few early interventions developed by professionals and paraprofessionals in the medical and mental health community were addressed to mothers during pregnancy, childbirth, and the first year or so of parenthood. Despite research findings emphasizing the vulnerability of the couple relationship during this transition, and the centrality of marital quality to subsequent family relationships, systematically evaluated interventions to help *couples* function more optimally during the transition to parenthood are virtually nonexistent.

Programs addressed directly or indirectly to easing the transition to parenthood for individual parents span a range from those focused on pregnancy and childbirth, to parent support groups, to several more comprehensive programs combining information about child development, parent-child relationships, and parents' social support. There is scant attention in the published literature to details of the goals or content of these programs and virtually no focus on the level of

skill, training, or supervision of intervention staff. Often because funding is limited, few studies involve follow-ups to evaluate the longer term effectiveness of the program on family functioning beyond the end of the intervention.

### Pregnancy and Birth

Although prepared childbirth classes now commonly include men, they focus on preparation for the labor and delivery of the baby and rarely address men's or women's adjustment to pregnancy or parenthood. Few evaluate the impact of the intervention on men, women, or their relationships as couples. As May and Perrin (1982) point out, "most expectant fathers do not discuss their own emotional reactions with others (not even their spouses) and thus feel somewhat isolated as they make these adjustments" (p. 74). "An expectant father who is having difficulty in adjustment to the pregnancy must himself be considered at risk for emotional disruption" (p. 83). Heming's (1985) analysis of risk in the families in our project shows that men who did not feel ready for or accepting of the birth of their first baby had lower self-esteem, reported more symptoms of depression, and had greater marital dissatisfaction when their babies were 18 months old. Further analyses revealed that when men have very strong feelings about not being ready to become fathers, but go along with the pregnancy for the sake of preserving the couple relationship, it is very likely that the relationship will end in divorce before the child enters elementary school (Cowan & Cowan, 1992). Of the seven men in our study who fit this description, all had dissolved their marriages by the time their first child was 5 years old. This suggests that one target of preventive intervention might be couples who are in the process of considering starting a family.

Data on the effectiveness of prepared childbirth classes are sparse. Duncan and Markman (1988) used information gathered from expectant parents before and after they attended classes to compare couples with and without prepared childbirth. They report stable levels of marital satisfaction, state anxiety, and birth-related problems from 3 months before to 9–10 weeks after birth in parents who attended classes, and sharp decreases in marital satisfaction and increases in anxiety and postbirth problems in parents with no classes. Given the stability of anxiety and problems from before to after birth in parents with this intervention, it is unfortunate that the classes end just as the baby is due to be born, leaving mothers and fathers virtually on their own to manage any concern or distress during the rest of the transition to parenthood.

## Parent's Well-Being

A few systematically evaluated programs have attempted to help new parents adapt to becoming a family. They range from self-help and support groups with and without leaders to more intensive ongoing counseling with mental health professionals.

*Counseling for mothers.* In one of the earliest interventions to ease the transition to parenthood for women, Shereshefsky and Yarrow (1973) trained mental health professionals to work regularly with individual expectant mothers during pregnancy and to offer several appointments to their husbands. In weekly sessions with a therapist from one of several different counseling orientations, each expectant mother was helped with "psychological preparation for the stresses of pregnancy, delivery, and parenthood" during the third trimester of pregnancy (p. 156). Perhaps the investigators' primary emphasis on women was evident, given that almost all the men declined the offer of counseling. When all the mothers in the study were interviewed 6 months after birth, women who had participated in a type of counseling described as *anticipatory guidance* had maintained their prebaby levels of marital satisfaction, whereas the marital satisfaction of mothers with no counseling or other counseling methods had declined. The authors noted that *the quality of the marital relationships of both counseled and comparison mothers*

*was the most significant predictor of women's adaptation to parenthood.*

*Programs for fathers.* Levant's (1988) review of programs designed to help men in their role as fathers described a high level of program development activity. This resulted in the emergence of pilot programs to address changes in the role of contemporary fathers. Levant found no studies of *pre*-parenthood programs for men; there were several of a limited nature for new fathers, but almost none had evaluation components. He described the fatherhood course at Boston University for fathers—half of whom were married, half divorced, a few remarried—whose children ranged from infancy to young adulthood. Levant and a graduate student in counseling psychology with training in leading groups and parent-child interaction offered an 8-week course using a skills training format. Fathers were encouraged to role play incidents particular to their own family situation and were provided videotaped instant feedback. Although not advertised as counseling, the second half of the course encouraged fathers to speak about their thoughts and feelings when they interacted with their children; to recognize their own sensitivities in order to become more accepting of their children's feelings and behavior; and to express their feelings in a nondefensive, open manner. The men's before and after intervention responses were compared to those of control group families. Fathers who had participated in the course showed improved sensitivity and a reduction in undesirable responses to their children. The men appeared to shift their views of ideal family life, and their children's perceptions suggested that they saw improvement in their relationships with their fathers.

*For parents and babies.* For some years, the Minnesota Early Learning Design program (MELD; Junge & Elwood, 1986) has provided long-term parent support groups from pregnancy to 2 years postpartum. Implemented in four stages according to the age of the child, the discussions in the groups cover information about pregnancy, nutrition and health needs, child development, parent-child relationships, and parents' needs. The group leaders are parents who are trained to work in pairs. They meet biweekly for 2 to 3 hours in various settings, including homes, churches, and community agencies. The program's philosophy centers on support, mutual learning and cooperation, and appreciation of differences between parents within each group and has been modified for use with young mothers, bicultural groups, and parents of preschoolers. It is unfortunate that this ambitious program has had minimal evaluation, for it could teach a good deal about what works best for whom. A systematic study is apparently underway.

## The Marital Relationship

To our knowledge, there are still no preventive mental health services available in the United States, Canada, Germany, or Great Britain in which trained mental health professionals encourage expectant couples to focus on marital issues before they experience enough distress to seek counseling or therapy. Outside of our own longitudinal study evaluating professionally led couples groups for expectant and new parents, we know of only one preventive intervention study that addressed the marriages of expectant couples who were not already in difficulty.

*The First Baby Project*. This program was developed at the Tavistock Institute of Marital Studies in London, England (Clulow, 1982). It offered expectant couples at birth clinics a series of six groups, held monthly throughout the last trimester of pregnancy and the first 3 months of parenthood. One male-female team from the Institute of Marital Studies and female co-leaders from the British Home Visitors Service co-led groups in which they focused on the marriages of couples during their transition to parenthood. Like our Becoming a Family Project in California, The First Baby Project was based on the idea of enhancing parents' well-being as individuals and as couples to prepare the way for smoother adaptation to parenthood and the development of more nurturant parent-child relationships.

Clulow described mixed results of the intervention. Although some participants completed the series of six meetings and reported that the discussions had helped their adjustment to parenthood, a number of couples did not return to the groups after they gave birth. What Clulow found most disconcerting was that couples did not often use the groups to work on marital difficulties. In fact, he observed that when spouses in a couple felt different from others in their group, they were likely not to return to the group. Yet, when the Health Visitors came to parents' homes after birth to check on the babies' health, they often heard hints or direct reports about marital tension. Because the groups were not consistently well attended and did not seem to stimulate talk of marital strain, Clulow seemed discouraged about the potential for a group intervention to assist partners with marital issues. The leaders could not discern any positive effects of the group discussions on the couples' relationships; this assessment was made all the more difficult by the absence of any pre-intervention, base-line assessments of the marriages.

*The Becoming A Family Project*. Our intervention study was designed to (a) examine the effects of the transition to parenthood on men, women, and marriage; (b) identify the risk factors and buffers associated with adaptation in parents, children, and couples; (c) target the intervention to modify the risk factors and strengthen the buffers; and (d) assess the impact of the intervention of the five domains of life in our conceptual model by following couples into the early years of parenthood (Cowan & Cowan, 1992). We randomly assigned 24 expectant couples to the intervention, 24 couples to a pre-post assessment but no group, and 24 additional couples to a post-baby assessment. The couples group intervention offered expectant couples a safe setting in which we could monitor the unexpected shifts and distress in each of the aspects of life in our conceptual model over a 6-month period. By meeting with couples weekly during the last 3 months of pregnancy and the first 3 months of parenthood, we hoped to help men

Fostering a positive transition to parenthood through couples' intervention can have long-term consequences for parent-child relationships. Men, for example, describe themselves as more involved in their roles as fathers. (Photo: Victoria Whitington)

and women capitalize on their strengths and get reassurance and help when they felt vulnerable, so that the stress of the transition would not precipitate a marital crisis.

Four expectant couples met with their staff couple each week for 24 weeks and their babies joined the groups once they were born. Over the 6 months of meetings, we worked with each participant to explore the pleasures, the strains, and the unexpected dilemmas they experienced as individuals, as couples, and as parents. We took time to anticipate and flesh out partners' dreams for their families before the babies were born. This process was followed by months of experimenting with small shifts in each of the family domains in order to make the early months of parenthood less stressful and more satisfying. During the 6 months of work in the groups, partners described many feelings about their relationships with *their* parents. With our encouragement, many spouses brought old or new

marital issues to the group for help, while others listened intently and talked more privately at home. The groups ended when the babies were 3 months old.

Two years into the study, we compared shifts in the new parent couples and the couples who had not had babies. The childless couples described almost no systematic shifts in the five domains of life, but the new parent couples reported change in all of them, as we described earlier. When we compared new parents with and without the group intervention, we found positive intervention effects for husbands, for wives, and for the relationship between them. For example, men who had participated in a couples group described themselves as more psychologically involved in their roles as fathers than men with no intervention. Women who had participated in a couples group maintained their prior level of role satisfaction, but women with no group were more unhappy with their role arrangements. Men and women from the groups also reported fewer negative changes in their sexual relationships after giving birth than parents without intervention.

The most noteworthy effects of the intervention were on parents' marital satisfaction and stability 18 months into parenthood. In contrast to the drop in marital satisfaction found in most longitudinal studies, marital satisfaction between 6 and 18 months postpartum remained stable in couples who had been in a couples group. In contrast to the 12.5 percent separation and divorce rate of the no-treatment couples when their babies were 18 months old, the marriages of *all* of the couples who had participated in the groups were still intact.

Analyses of the measures at a 3½ year follow-up showed that the intervention effects on parents' individual and marital adaptation began to wane during the preschool period. Satisfaction with marriage, which had declined steadily in the no-treatment couples from pregnancy to 3½ years after birth, now began dropping in the treatment couples, and the first couple from the intervention subsample had separated, making a 4 percent to 16 percent contrast in the separation rates of intervention and no-treatment couples. Although these samples are too small to test for statistical significance, our figures for the couples with no intervention are comparable to Eiduson's (1981), in which 15 percent of her new-parent sample were divorced by 3 years after the birth of a first child; they also correspond with figures in a national study of divorce by Bumpass and Rindfuss (1979). These figures make our intervention sample's low rate of divorce (4 percent) almost 4 years after becoming parents noteworthy.

What are the mechanisms that account for these positive intervention effects? It is important to note that parents in our intervention groups experienced many of the shifts described by the comparison parents, but they tended to feel less disappointed or distressed about them after the intervention groups ended. They reported that having a setting in which both part-

ners were encouraged to work together on their dilemmas and disappointments in an ongoing way as they faced the challenges of new parenthood helped highlight the concerns men were having and kept the women from feeling that the entire burden of making a family and caring for the baby was theirs. Studies of couples in marital therapy (Gurman & Kniskern, 1978) reveal that when both spouses are working on the marriage, they have lower rates of marital dissolution. The impact of our intervention suggests that when both partners take advantage of marital help from mental health professionals during the transition from couple to family, they, too, experience less marital dissatisfaction and lower rates of marital dissolution—at least for the first few years after the intervention.

We think that tolerance toward the alteration of so many aspects of their lives is encouraged when intervention parents discover that most new parents in their group are experiencing similar shifts and feeling vulnerable. They appear to attribute their unexpected shifts—toward less egalitarian role arrangements, for example—less to low motivation on the part of their partners and more to the transition to parenthood. The normalizing process that occurs in a group of parents at the same stage of family life may provide a substitute for the naturally occurring support and commiseration available in times past when most couples stayed among family and friends in the cities and towns where they grew up. We have found that professional group leaders can create a safe environment in which both men and women can explore the kinds of intimate and troubling family matters that partners say they do not discuss on their own.

Our emphasis so far has been on intervening with couples and focusing on the couple relationship, in part because of the strong relations among marital, child, and family adaptation. This approach can be validated only when interventions with couples produce positive changes in their marital relationships that are followed by positive changes in other aspects of their family lives.

# INTERVENTIONS FOR HIGH-RISK FAMILIES

We have seen that even in families with more op-timal resources, the transition to parenthood brings a kind of disequilibrium that amplifies the parents' existing vulnerabilities and leads a signif-icant proportion to experience increased strain and distress. It makes sense that there will be heightened risks when these shifts are experi-enced by troubled adults, by teenagers becoming parents, and by families struggling with the added stressors of living in poverty or having children with medical or psychiatric disabilities. In aggre-gate, studies of these high-risk groups (see, for example, McLoyd's review, 1990) find an elevated incidence of physical, cognitive, and social prob-lems in the children, and of what is judged to be ineffective parenting by the mothers (overcontrol, undercontrol, low warmth, disengagement).

What is not clear is the extent to which these risks and levels of distress are attributable to the transition to parenthood. Studies of high-risk populations in the family-making years focus neither on the systematic and expected changes from pregnancy to the postpartum period nor on the level of continuity or predictability over time of parents' functioning. What is missing, from our perspective, is identification of the specific risk factors, assessed before and after the birth of a child, that are associated with maladaptive changes. As Coie and his colleagues (1993) point out, research-based factors are needed as guide-lines in order to target specific preventive and therapeutic interventions. As we have seen, the quality of the parents' marriage has been identi-fied as a key factor in both parents' and children's adaptation in low or moderate risk samples, which suggests that the couple relationship is an obvious target for intervention during the transi-tion to parenthood. What do we know about the key factors in parents' and children's later com-promised adaptation in high-risk families? Is it the family background and intergenerational transmission of problems? Is it the quality of single mothers' intimate relationships or social support? What mediates or moderates the links between risks and positive or negative outcomes? It is not that we lack justification for early inter-ventions with these families, but more systematic pre-to-post birth information (for example, Osofsky & Osofsky, 1984) would help identify targets of intervention most likely to produce clinically meaningful results.

A number of ambitious programs for new families considered to be at high risk for distress or compromised development use interdiscipli-nary teams, some of which incorporate hospital and home visits that begin in pregnancy and continue into the early months or years of par-enthood. Several programs provide groups for the mothers and day care for the children as well. Most of the published studies of interventions for new, high-risk families report some success, and many address one or more of the aspects of fam-ily life outlined in our model: a mother's psycho-logical distress, her relationship with her baby, life stress, and social support. Because few of these mothers are expected to live with their ba-bies' fathers, the interventions do not address those relationships explicitly, at least not in pub-lished accounts.

Olds and Kitzman (1993) reviewed studies of 31 home visiting programs explicitly designed for pregnant women and parents of young chil-dren. All 31 studies employed randomized trials, which is a methodologically rigorous design by which families are randomly assigned to two groups, typically to receive home visiting services or care as usual. The authors found variations in the theoretical base, specific goals, intensity of service, level of skill or training of intervention staff, and outcomes chosen as criteria to evaluate intervention effectiveness. In a similar review of home visiting programs without randomized designs, Powell (1993) makes the helpful distinc-tion between two general frameworks under-lying most visiting programs: a parent education model, which assumes that parenting compe-tence stems from access to expert information about child development, and a psychodynamic view in which the agent of change is assumed to be the relationship between the parent and intervention staff. A number of programs that contain systematic evaluations tend to focus on relationships—between intervener and mother, between mother and child, or between mother and other sources of support. To illustrate the range of approaches and effects reported by different investigators working with high-risk mothers, we describe several programs briefly.

## Parent Education Programs

Olds' program, now replicated in three geographic locations (Olds, Kitzman, & Cole, 1995), is an excellent example of a parent education program. He carefully constructed a home visiting program in which nurses provide information about health and child development to low-income mothers. In addition to finding positive pre to post effects for intervention mothers compared to controls, Olds' recent work shows that the programs are differentially effective for mothers who enter the programs with different levels of resources; whether mothers with higher or lower levels of resources benefit more depends on the specific resources and the specific outcomes investigated.

## Parent-Child Relationship Programs

Meisels, Dichtelmiller, and Liaw (1993) reviewed studies of programs for mothers whose babies are disabled, premature, or low birth weight. The authors contrasted interventions of high and low intensity, with a focus on the child, the parent-child relationship, or both, a few following families beyond infancy. None of the child-focused or low-intensity programs found positive treatment effects for both the child and the parent-child interactions, whereas almost one third of the parent-focused and two thirds of the jointly focused programs did. Most programs reported some positive results soon after the intervention ended, and studies with longer term follow-ups suggest that there may be sleeper effects that emerge as long as 5 years after the intervention in the children's cognitive development, inde-

pendent play, and social skills (Meisels, Dichtelmiller, & Liaw, 1993).

After finding that an intervention with a 3-month nurse home visiting program was not effective with pregnant women with low social support and many stressors in their lives (Barnard, Booth, Mitchell, & Telzrow, 1988), Barnard and her colleagues (Barnard, Morisset, & Spieker, 1993) designed a more comprehensive intervention to help high-risk women focus on their social skills and relationships with other individuals in their lives. Based on the notion that an individual's capacity to parent a child follows in part form the person's capacity to have satisfying relationships with other adults, nurses with master's level training in parent-child nursing provided ongoing help to mothers in both home and clinic settings, beginning in the second trimester of pregnancy and continuing until the child's first birthday. The comparison group included similar mothers in a shorter information and resources model. At the end of this 18-month intervention, the mothers in the more intensive intervention made more contact with their nurse visitors, and the nurses did more direct, problem-related intervention than the monitoring and referral done by staff in the shorter program. The mothers rated the comprehensive intervention more positively and showed enhanced social competence and interaction with their children when compared to mothers in the shorter intervention.

Heinicke (1995) has also developed a relationship-focused intervention for high-risk mothers and babies that includes psychodynamic, cognitive-behavioral, and advocacy components and a no-intervention comparison. Intervention parents are offered weekly home visits once their babies are born until 12 months later. The intervention staff on this study have at least master's level training in clinical psychology, counseling, or social work (Heinicke, personal communication, March 31, 1995). Preliminary results show intervention effects changes in the mother's perceptions of support from her partner, responsiveness to her infant's needs, and encouragement of the baby's autonomy and mastery of cognitive experiences. There were no significant differences between intervention and nonintervention babies' cognitive performance at the end of the intervention, although longer term evaluation is continuing.

## Programs Focused on Parents' Family of Origin Experiences

Two intensive interventions with an explicit theoretical and developmental base attempt to break the cycle in which problematic relationships are transmitted across generations. These researchers are explicitly attempting to optimize a new mother's chances of creating a more nurturant and responsive relationship with her baby than she had with her own mother. Egeland and his colleagues in Minnesota (Egeland & Erickson, 1993; Erickson, Korfmacher, & Egeland, 1994) conducted a comprehensive and intensive program of home visits along with a group intervention for 154 high-risk mothers and their infants, who were randomly assigned to their STEEP program (Steps Toward Effective Enjoyable Parenting) or a comparison group. The 12-month intervention was designed to improve the interaction and relationship between mother and infant, particularly the quality of mother-infant attachment as assessed by the Ainsworth Strange Situation. The home visits began in the second month of pregnancy and continued until the babies were 12 months old. Guided by attachment theory, the group intervention invited mothers to talk about their early relationships with their mothers. Group facilitators—mothers who were caring; accepting of individual differences in values, beliefs, and styles; and experienced at working with low-income individuals—were trained to use educational, therapeutic, and supportive strategies. The paraprofessional intervention staff attempted to modify the mothers' inner working models based on the theory that the women's new insights about their upbringing would allow them to empathize with their own early needs and become more able to respond to the needs of their babies.

Preliminary results indicate that, in the months after the intervention, mothers had lower depression and anxiety scores, were more competent in managing their daily lives, and showed a greater ability to provide a stimulating and organized home environment for their babies than mothers without the intervention. Despite these benefits for the mothers, there were no significant changes in the mothers' adult attachment categories or differences in the babies' security of attachment when the babies were 13 and 19 months old (immediately and approximately 6 months after the intervention).

These investigators took on a most ambitious task with very needy women, one that would be a challenge for mental health professionals with many years of supervised training. Because the mothers' adult attachment categories did not change as they had hoped, Egeland and Erickson (1993) speculated that the ability to understand how past history influences current feelings and behavior may not be realistic with parents with limited cognitive abilities or severe abuse in their histories. We share their concern that their facilitators may have been inadequately prepared to work with mothers with such troubled histories and that the intervention may not have been long enough or intense enough to have the hoped-for impact.

Lieberman and Pawl (1993) described a northern California program with an orientation and conceptual base similar to that of the Minnesota group. This project, which focused on mothers and babies with already troubled relationships, used therapists with more specialized professional training in clinical work than those on the Minnesota staff had. Mother-baby dyads were referred to the program by pediatricians or other health professionals because the attachment relationship was observed to be in difficulty. The authors describe that the goal of the therapy is "to create a space between parent and child where the relationship becomes a vehicle rather than an obstacle to the fulfillment of individual needs." The hope is that "both parent and child will be able to manage autonomy in the context of emotional closeness and intimacy" (p. 573). The therapists work weekly with mothers and babies throughout the second year of life, fostering both parent-therapist and parent-child relationships through ongoing empathetic feedback and discussion and separate visits with the mother and baby when warranted.

When contrasted with a comparison group of mother-baby pairs with secure attachment relationships, mothers and babies in Lieberman and Pawl's (1993) intervention showed benefits of the therapy: The mothers were rated as having more empathy for their toddlers and as initiating interactions with them more frequently than comparison mothers. In contrast to the results of the Minnesota program, the children in the California intervention showed improved relationship adaptation with their mothers in terms of less anger, avoidance, and resistance. In fact, scores of intervention toddlers were equivalent on these measures to those of securely attached dyads in the control group.

One unusual and welcome aspect of Lieberman and Pawl's (1993) studies is an assessment of the process of the intervention in order to determine which components are contributing to the effects. They found that improvement was most marked in dyads in which the mother was able to use the therapeutic sessions to explore and work through her feelings of anger, sadness, and ambivalence toward the important people in her life, including her parents and her child. These promising results with families already in dysfunctional relationships underscore the importance of the intensity of the intervention, the level of training and supervision of the staff, and the need for more adequate measures of the intervention *process* to test which components of interventions lead to the benefits.

These examples of intensive interventions designed to help high risk families get off to a healthier start show that many expectant or new parents will respond to highly trained health and mental health paraprofessionals and professionals who offer a nurturant relationship over an extended period of time. We have seen that when

parents develop trusting relationships with program staff in programs that enable them to examine and understand their own early and current experiences in key relationships, they show benefits that include increased confidence, better recognition of their babies' needs, more developed social and parenting skills, and the ability to provide a more nurturing family environment. In a few of these studies, particularly those in which the work addresses the mother-baby relationships explicitly and gives ongoing feedback to the mother, the children themselves ultimately show enhanced cognitive and emotional development when follow-ups continue some years beyond the intervention.

## DISCUSSION AND CONCLUSIONS

Let us begin by summarizing the findings we have presented:

1. The incidence and severity of *risk for distress and dysfunction* is elevated in many domains of family life during the transition to parenthood. The incidence of *actual distress* during this period is surprising, even in couples who are in relatively well-functioning relationships and who are economically comfortable.

2. In addition to new parents' reports indicating significant change, there is also *a high degree of consistency or predictability of both risks and actual distress* from mothers and fathers' level of adaptation during pregnancy to their after-birth status.

3. Parents' adjustment to parenthood as individuals and couples forecasts the quality of the relationships they develop with their children in the preschool period, which, in turn, is a central predictor of their children's subsequent cognitive, social, and emotional adaptation to elementary school. Although few transition-to-parenthood studies were conceived in a risk framework, the results demonstrate that we can identify expectant

*parents* at risk for distress and *children* at risk for difficulty in adapting to their first years of formal schooling. We have, then, the prime prerequisites for considering and planning preventive interventions to promote healthier adaptation in parents and young children.

4. For parents at low or moderate risk, a couples group intervention with mental health professionals as leaders revealed benefits for fathers, for mothers, and for their marital satisfaction and stability. For high-risk mothers, a number of comprehensive interventions led to greater support, increased self-esteem, and greater responsiveness to their babies. A few programs, usually those with staff who had clinical training, found enhanced development in the children as well.

5. Interventions have been targeted at one or more of the five domains of family life that combine to affect individual parents' adaptation: feelings about the self, relationships with the family of origin, social support networks, parent-child relationships, and relationships with intimate partners.

Although not all parents will accept the offer of intervention, programs to ease the transition to parenthood in high risk populations have clearly attracted thousands of women over the past decades. We have seen that it is possible to design interventions that help new mothers and fathers in both low- and high-risk populations become more sensitive and nurturant as partners and parents. When interventions are specifically focused on the parent-child relationship, when the staff bring clinical skills adequate to address parents' family-of-origin issues, and when the program intensity matches the needs of the participants, children may reap the benefits of their parents' gains with their own enhanced cognitive, social, and emotional development.

Despite these promising results with the more comprehensive interventions, it is not realistic to expect the benefits of any intervention during the transition to parenthood to serve as a

lifetime inoculation against all future problems; follow-up booster programs to monitor and bolster the strengths will be needed to ensure that parents and children maintain the earlier gains. Although we have much to learn and test in the field of preventive intervention, we are encouraged by the stories these systematic studies tell.

## Low-Risk and High-Risk Transitions to Parenthood

Our organization of this article into sections describing low- and high-risk studies and interventions was dictated by the fact that the literatures were virtually nonoverlapping. Having surveyed both bodies of research on the transition to parenthood period, we believe it is time to reconsider this dichotomy. First, the loose and vague use of risk metaphors and concepts makes it difficult to compare and replicate study results. More attention must be paid to the distinction between risk (a potential for negative outcomes) and actual distress or disorder. Many apparently advantaged men and women are at risk during the transition to parenthood, and some show signs of serious distress as individuals (depression), as couples (marital distress and dissolution), and as parents (parenting stress, difficulties in managing their children). That is, low risk does not mean problem free. Conversely, although research rarely tells this side of the story, many high-risk women and couples adapt well to the transition to parenthood. We need to pay more attention to the protective factors and to define risks in relation to specific outcomes. We have seen that spouses who appear to possess many resources seem to enter a zone of risk to their relationships as they make major life transitions. Researchers have yet to discover whether and how the transition to parenthood constitutes an additive risk for expectant mothers who are already defined as at high risk in other ways.

Analogous to what Sameroff and Chandler (1975) termed a "continuum of caretaking casualty," we believe that there is a continuum of preexisting risk and distress that tends to get magnified by the disequilibration of the transition to parenthood. Not all new parents need or want assistance in managing this challenge, but some men and women all along this continuum clearly welcome services designed to enhance their coping skills and reduce their level of stress. Evidence from many studies suggests that helping new parents can ultimately provide important developmental and mental health benefits to the adults and, in the longer run, to some of their children.

The continuum of risk and distress is especially important in defining the parameters of prevention (Coie, et al., 1993). At the low end of the continuum of preexisting risk and distress, we have opportunities for primary prevention. Primary prevention focuses on individuals prior to the manifestation of a problem or disorder, with the goal of enhancing competence and reducing inadequate coping patterns so that the incidence of problematic outcomes in a population will be reduced. As we move up the risk-distress continuum, we move into the territory of secondary prevention, targeted toward individuals and families who are already showing precursors of dysfunction or signs of health or mental health problems. The goal here is to avoid more serious disorders and reduce current levels of distress. Like the low-risk/high-risk dichotomy, the distinction between primary and secondary prevention is not absolute. Participants in primary and secondary prevention programs vary in their initial levels of adaptation, but the distinction helps to define the target population, the aims of the intervention program, and the criteria for success.

## What Are the Characteristics of Successful Interventions?

In reviews of intervention studies addressed to the family formation period, Heinicke and his colleagues (Heinicke, 1993; Heinicke, Beckwith, & Thompson, 1988) concluded that a carefully integrated multicomponent approach to new families appears to be most effective. Using the intervention studies available at the time, they showed that the most effective programs pro-

vided 11 or more contacts with parents over at least a 3-month period and ongoing, nurturant, and supportive relationships with the staff. Reviewers of the studies we have summarized here draw similar conclusions. It seems clear that the intensity of the intervention and the ability of sensitive staff to develop ongoing, meaningful relationships with participants makes a difference in parents' receptivity and to the ultimate effectiveness of the program. Many of the programs we have described, which are only a fraction of the published studies, have offered many more sessions than 11, but all of the programs with successful results have offered participants an empathetic and clinically skilled staff trained to work directly with complex relationship issues.

Possibly due to space constraints, there is rarely adequate attention in the literature to the rationale, content, and process of preventive interventions, or to the skills, training, and supervision of intervention staff. We need more systematic examination of the process that occurs during the intervention in order to understand which components of which interventions, with which staff, will be most effective with which families. As program goals shift from primary to secondary prevention, effective results will necessitate increasing levels of qualifications, skills, and training of intervention staff and greater length, frequency, or intensity of contact with participants.

Timing of intervention evaluations appears to be crucial. We find that it takes time for parents to experiment with the new ideas and strategies from our ongoing couples groups. Although there were no statistically significant effects 3 months after our groups ended, we found substantial intervention effects 1 year later. Similarly, Meisels, Dichtelmiller, & Liaw, (1993) reported stronger intervention effects 5 years after the intervention ended.

## Directions for Future Research

Although we have cited a number of studies of interventions designed to ease the transition to parenthood, especially in high-risk samples, comprehensive and systematic research on the topic is in its infancy. Even though changes during the transition to parenthood have been well documented with interview and self-report measures, there has been very little observational study of changes in couple and family relationships *beginning in pregnancy*.

Like the early stages of psychotherapy research, the field has been preoccupied with demonstrating *whether* interventions work. With the exception of Olds and his colleagues (1993, 1995), there has been little attention to determining optimal matches between intervention strategies and participant characteristics and to which treatment components are responsible for the effects. The question of who benefits most (and least) from intervention must be central in future research on the transition to parenthood. Answers to this question will allow more precise targeting and recruitment of participants and opportunities to tailor interventions to specific problems using specified strategies. We see intervention research not only as a tool to evaluate effectiveness but also as a potential contributor to theories about family transition. If it can be shown that specific interventions produce specific changes that affect specific outcomes, theories of the mechanisms that link risks and outcomes will become more differentiated and useful.

## Implications for Family Policy

We recognize that this may not be an ideal time to recommend additional services for new families, given current economic concerns surrounding the provision of health care and other social programs. Nevertheless, the results of longitudinal studies of low to moderate risk families, along with data from interventions with parents all along the continuum of risk, suggest that without intervention, the problems and vulnerabilities of new parents will spill over into other relationships in the family, leaving the children at risk for compromised development.

With little support from business and government, men and women who are parents of young children are virtually on their own to address the competing needs of their children, their marriage, and their families. We believe that as long as it is up to each man and woman to work out a satisfying balance of gender role and work-family issues during the transition to parenthood period, the relationships between them—and between them and their children—will be vulnerable to strain. Gershenson (1993) summarized the situation vividly: "Repeatedly, successful demonstration programs terminate when grant funds are no longer available" (p. 8). He calls this situation "a conundrum: a decline in the quality of human services in the face of ostensibly proven ability to improve them.... We observe successful demonstrations like meteors: momentarily illuminating our hopes and expectations only to disappear" (p. 9). In our view, a serious concern about the preservation of strong family relationships argues for the allocation of increased resources for programs to strengthen families all along the risk continuum. Programs to ease the transition to parenthood seem an obvious place to begin.

## EVALUATING YOUR MASTERY

1. The Cowans identify five domains that distinguish families doing well and those at risk for adjustment difficulties: (1) relationships with family of origin; (2) couples' relationship; (3) each parent's relationship with the baby; (4) the balance of life stress and social support, and (5) the well-being of each parent. Research indicates that new parents experience shifts in which of the following domains?
   a.   1 and 2
   b.   1, 2, and 4
   c.   1, 2, 4, and 5
   d.   1, 2, 3, 4, and 5

2. During the transition to parenthood, both men and women are at increased risk for
   a.   Eating disorders
   b.   Job loss
   c.   Depression
   d.   Hospitalization

3. Decline in marital quality following the birth of a baby is greater for
   a.   Men
   b.   Younger couples married for a brief time
   c.   Older, longer-married couples
   d.   Noncareer-oriented mothers

4. In the Cowans' intervention study in which expectant couples attended a group intervention,
   a.   Only participating wives experienced positive effects.
   b.   Participating husbands had difficulty becoming psychologically involved in their roles as fathers.
   c.   Marital satisfaction of participating couples declined despite the intervention.
   d.   The marriages of all participating couples remained intact, whereas a considerable number of comparison couples divorced.

5. Considering intervention programs for new parents, which of the following have been successful?
   a.   Programs focusing on the parent–child relationship
   b.   Programs focusing on the parents' family-of-origin experiences
   c.   Home visiting programs providing information about health and child development to low-income mothers
   d.   All of the above
   e.   None of the above

6. True or False: A baby's arrival is unlikely to destroy a very well-functioning marriage.

7. True or False: A baby's arrival can bring unhappy, poorly functioning couples closer together.

8. True or False: Distress experienced by couples during pregnancy is a good predictor of risks and actual distress in the family after the baby is born.

9. True or False: Successful interventions provide meaningful relationships with program staff and contacts with parents over at least a three-month period.

## Critical Thinking

1. The impact of the transition to parenthood is a challenging topic of study, requiring careful selection of childless comparison groups. In designing a study on the transition to parenthood, what type of comparison group would you use? What characteristics would these individuals have, and what factors would you try to control?

2. The Cowans take a family systems view of the impact of parents' relationship on children. Describe this view, and explain how individual and marital distress can affect the baby's well-being and subsequent development.

## Applying Your Knowledge

On the basis of evidence reviewed by the Cowans, describe the ingredients of two successful interventions to ease the transition to parenthood: one for low-risk couples (economically well off and happily married before childbirth) and one for high risk parents (for example, affected by poverty or teenage parenthood).

# PART III

# Joining a New World:
# Infancy to Early Childhood

# 4

## Cultural Variation in Infants' Sleeping Arrangements

### Questions of Independence

GILDA A. MORELLI,
Boston College

BARBARA ROGOFF
University of California, Santa Cruz

DAVID OPPENHEIM
University of Haifa

DENISE GOLDSMITH
Salt Lake City

■

Folk wisdom in the United States considers the early night-time separation of infants from their parents as essential for the infants' healthy psychological development.

■

In many non-U.S. communities it is customary for infants to sleep with their mothers for the first few years of life, at least in the same room and usually in the same bed.

■

Although middle-class U.S. parents and child-care specialists regard sleeping problems as among the most common disturbances of infancy, our goal is not to prescribe any changes but rather to come to a broader understanding of cultural practices in which middle-class U.S. and Mayan families, like all other families, participate.

■

All 14 Mayan mothers slept in the same bed with their infants through the first year
of life and into the second year. In none of the 18 U.S. families did parents sleep
with their newborns on a regular basis.

■

The idea that sleeping arrangements were not an issue for the Mayan families is
supported by the lack of bedtime routines carried out in the nightly transition to
sleep. Events surrounding bedtime for the U.S. families played a significant role in
the organization of family evening activities.

■

In Mayan families, sleeping arrangements are not an issue until the child is displaced
from the mother's side by a new baby.

■

The findings suggest that encouraging independence during infancy is an important
goal for many U.S. families and that parents believe that sleeping apart helps train
children to be independent.

■

It is interesting from a cultural perspective that some parents would prefer that their
children become attached to and dependent on an inanimate object (for example,
a blanket) rather than a person.

■

## EDITOR'S INTRODUCTION

The research of Gilda Morelli and her collaborators indicates that child-rearing
practices associated with the most basic physical behaviors—in this case, infant
sleeping—vary greatly around the world. The authors' interviews with middle-
class American and Guatemalan mothers, and their accompanying literature review, reveal that only a minority of human parents follow the practice, common
in middle-class American homes, of putting babies to bed in a room by themselves. Instead, many U.S. ethnic minorities and non-U.S. communities practice
*cosleeping:* Babies sleep with their mothers for the first few years of life.

The authors show how cultural values and beliefs underlie infant sleeping
practices. Their work also reveals that infant sleeping arrangements affect other
aspects of family life. Whereas sleep problems are not an issue for Mayan parents,
bedtime struggles occur often in the U.S. where young children are required to
fall asleep each night without assistance.

It was time to give him his own room . . . his own territory. That's the American way.

REFLECTIONS OF A MIDDLE-CLASS U.S. MOTHER

Among middle-class families and child-care experts in the United States, it is assumed that the proper sleeping arrangement for infants and parents is separate. The purpose of this article is to examine this assumption as a cultural practice. A **sociocultural approach** involves understanding how practices within a community relate to other aspects of the community's functioning, such as adult work roles, physical space arrangements, climate, and values and goals regarding desired characteristics of citizens. One of the most valuable aspects of comparisons across cultural communities is that they make us aware of the cultural basis for and the assumptions underlying our own practices, whoever we are (Cole, 1985; Munroe, Munroe, & Whiting, 1981; Rogoff, 1990; Rogoff & Morelli, 1989; Whiting & Edwards, 1988).

In this study, we review work demonstrating that the middle-class U.S. practice of separating infants from their mothers is unusual compared with the practice in most communities around the world, and we examine speculations regarding values and other practices that may be associated. Then we make an explicit comparison of practices and rationales described by parents of infants in two communities: a small Guatemalan Mayan town and a middle-class sample from a U.S. city.

Folk wisdom in the United States considers the early night-time separation of infants from their parents as essential for the infants' healthy psychological development. This widespread belief is reflected in the advice parents have received since the early 1900s from child-rearing experts regarding **cosleeping**. Spock (1945) wrote, "I think it's a sensible rule not to take a child into the parents' bed for any reason" (p. 101). Brazelton (1978, 1979) and Ferber (1986), pediatricians and writers nationally known as specialists on parenting, also warned parents of the dangers of sleeping with their infants. The concerns of such authors included possible smothering by a restless parent (Bundesen, 1944), the increased likelihood of catching a contagious illness (Holt, 1957), the difficulty of breaking the habit when the child grows older (Spock, 1945), and sexual overstimulation for the oedipal child (Spock, 1984). Although several accounts now acknowledge the value placed on cosleeping by some families (Brazelton, 1990), or advocate the practice (Thevinin, 1976), pediatricians generally advise parents to avoid cosleeping (Lozoff, Wolf, & Davis, 1984).

Research indicates that cosleeping is not commonly practiced by middle- to upper-class U.S. families. Lozoff, Wolf, & Davis (1984) found that only 35 percent of urban Caucasian 6- to 48-month-olds slept with their parents for all or part of the night on a regular basis. Crowell, Keener, Ginsburg, and Anders (1987) reported even lower figures: A mere 11 percent of the 18- to 36-month-olds they studied shared a bed with their parents 3 or more nights a week, and only 15 percent shared a room with them. Valsiner and Hall (1983) found that 18 out of 19 infants from well-educated U.S. families slept in a room separate from their parents from before 3 months of age. Over half of the infants studied by Hong and Townes (1976) slept in their own rooms by 2 months of age, 75 percent by 3 months, and 98 percent by 6 months. Other researchers have noted that by 6 months, middle-class U.S. infants' designated sleeping place is in a room separated from their parents (Keener, Zeanah, & Anders, 1988; Richman, Miller, & Solomon, 1988; Whiting & Edwards, 1988). From these and other studies it appears that in the U.S. middle class, cosleeping is not a frequently occurring event in

Morelli, G., Rogoff, B. Oppenheim, D., & Goldsmith, D. (1992). Cultural variation in infants' sleeping arrangements: Questions of independence. *Developmental Psychology, 28,* 604–613. © The American Psychological Association. Reprinted by permission of the publisher and author.

infancy and early childhood (Mandansky & Edel-brock, 1990; Rosenfeld, Wenegrat, Haavik, Wenegrat, & Smith, 1982).

In many non-U.S. communities it is customary for infants to sleep with their mothers for the first few years of life, at least in the same room and usually in the same bed. J. W. M. Whiting (1964) reported that infants sleep in bed with their mothers in approximately two thirds of the 136 societies he sampled around the world, and in the remainder the babies were generally in the same room with their mothers. Infants regularly slept with a parent until weaning in all but 1 (the United States) of the 12 communities studied by B. B. Whiting and Edwards (1988); in the U.S. community no cosleeping was observed. In a survey of 100 societies, American parents were the only ones to maintain separate quarters for their babies (Burton & Whiting, 1961; see also Barry & Paxson, 1971; McKenna, 1986). These findings are consistent with other work on sleeping arrangements in urban Korea (Hong & Townes, 1976) and urban and rural Italy (Gaddini & Gaddini, 1971; Gandini, 1990; New, 1984).

Communities that practice cosleeping include both highly technological and less technological communities. Japanese urban children usually sleep adjacent to their mothers in early childhood and generally continue to sleep with a parent or an extended family member until the age of 15 (Caudill & Plath, 1966; Takahashi, 1990). Parents often separate in order to provide all children with a parental sleeping partner when family size makes it difficult for parents and children to share a single room. Space considerations appear to play a minor role in cosleeping practices for Japanese families (Caudill & Plath, 1966).

Within the United States, demographic, ethnic, and economic correlates of cosleeping have been identified. There is less cosleeping by mothers with some college education than by mothers with a high school education (Wolf & Lozoff, 1989). Black U.S. children are more likely than White U.S. children to fall asleep with a caregiver present, to have their beds in their parents' room, and to spend all or part of the night cosleeping with their parents (Lozoff, Wolf, & Davis, 1984; Ward, 1971). Thirty-six percent of infants growing up in eastern Kentucky shared their parents' beds as newborns, and 48 percent shared their parents' room. Over 65 percent of infants from this community slept with or near their parents through the first 2 years of life (Abbott, 1992); again, space did not seem to be the issue.

Previous literature has identified a stress on independence training as being connected with middle-class parents' avoidance of cosleeping (Munroe, Munroe, & Whiting, 1981). Kugelmass (1959) advocated separate rooms for children on grounds that it would enable them to develop a spirit of independence. The rare middle-class U.S. families who do practice cosleeping often recognize that they are violating cultural norms (Hanks & Rebelsky, 1977). In contrast, Brazelton (1990) noted that "the Japanese think the U.S. culture rather merciless in pushing small children toward such independence at night" (p. 7). Parents in communities where cosleeping is common may regard cosleeping as important for the development of interpersonal relationships (Caudill & Plath, 1966).

In the present study, we examine differences between a U.S. middle-class community and a non-Western community in the sleeping arrangements of infants, including where the babies sleep and nighttime feeding and waking practices, as well as parents' rationales for and comfort with their infants' sleeping arrangements. We are particularly interested in the values expressed by parents regarding the consequences for children of cosleeping or sleeping apart. We also investigate practices that may be associated with sleeping arrangements, such as special activities occurring around bedtime. The transition to sleep may be a difficult process for young children that is eased by the presence of their caregivers or by substitute attachment objects or special bedtime activities (Albert, 1977; Wolf & Lozoff, 1989).

Although middle-class U.S. parents and child-care specialists regard sleeping problems as among the most common disturbances of infancy, our goal is not to prescribe any changes but rather to come to a broader understanding of cultural practices in which middle-class U.S. and Mayan families, like all other families, participate.

## METHOD

### Participants

Eighteen Caucasian, middle-class mothers living in a U.S. city (with 7 girls and 11 boys aged 2 to 28 months, median age = 16 months) and 14 Mayan mothers living in a rural Guatemalan community (with 7 girls and 7 boys aged 12 to 22 months, median age = 19 months) were interviewed on topics related to the sleeping arrangements of their youngest child.

U.S. families were randomly selected from birth information supplied by the Bureau of Vital Records and were invited to take part in the study. Mayan families were selected from a small town in highland Guatemala. The families from the two communities were similar in number of children (*Mdn* = 2, range = 2–7 for the U.S. sample; *Mdn* = 3, range = 1–9 for the Mayan sample). Approximately one-third of the children were firstborn in both communities. The U.S. mothers averaged 30 years of age (range = 22–39, based on 13 respondents) and the Mayan mothers averaged 26 years (range = 19–42). The U.S. mothers had completed more years of schooling, with a median of 14 grades (range = 12–18, based on 14 respondents), compared with a median of 3 grades for the Mayan mothers (range = 0–9). All of the Mayan mothers were the primary daytime caregivers for their toddlers; two-thirds of the U.S. mothers were. Most families included a father; all of the 18 U.S. fathers and 11 of the 14 Mayan fathers were living with the child and mother. The religious affiliations of the families were Mormon (58 percent, based on 12 respondents), and the remainder were Catholic, Protestant, or Jewish; over half of the Mayan families were Catholic (64 percent), and the remainder were Protestant.

### Procedure

Parents were interviewed in their homes, with family and community members often included in the session. A North American researcher familiar with the language, community, and families interviewed the Mayan sample, with a community member assisting in translation when parents preferred speaking Mayan. A second North American researcher interviewed the U.S. sample.

Family sleeping arrangements at the time of the interview were determined by asking parents to draw a map of their home indicating relative positions of rooms as well as beds and identifying each person's present sleeping location. Parents were asked about their infant's sleeping locations from the time of birth, about other practices associated with sleeping arrangements (for example, night feedings), and why they made the choices they did. Questions were grouped topically, but the interviewer used her judgment to decide the order in which they were asked. Information on family background was also gathered. The interview was tailored in ways appropriate to each community. It took approximately 60 minutes to interview an American family. Mayan interviews took longer (approximately 120 minutes) because the questions were embedded in a larger study.

### Sleeping Arrangement Variables

Questions on infants' sleeping locations, night feedings, and bedtime routines were parallel in the two communities. Questions exploring rationale for and comfort with decisions were tailored to each community because the practices and issues were different for each.

*Infant's sleeping location* is categorized as being in the mother's bed (which we term *cosleeping*, after Lozoff, Wolf, & Davis's, 1984, definition), in the mother's room, or in another room. We also report any changes in location since the infant's birth and information on who else besides the mother shared the infant's bed or room.

*Night feedings* includes information on whether the baby is breast or bottle fed, where night feedings occur (in mother's bed, mother's room, or another room), and where the baby is put to sleep following night feedings.

*Bedtime routines* are reported in terms of whether the infant fell asleep alone or in someone's company, whether the infant fell asleep at the same time as the mother or separately, whether the infant received special bedtime activities (for example, bedtime story, lullaby, bathing, or toothbrushing routines), and whether the infant used a security object for falling asleep.

*Sleeping arrangement issues and reflections* differ in format in the two communities because of their very different practices. For the Mayan families, we report on the issues that appear when toddlers are shifted away from cosleeping with the mother, usually at age 2 or 3, and on some of the Mayan parents' reflections on U.S. middle-class infants' sleeping arrangements.

For the U.S. families, we report the parents' rationales for the infant's sleeping location (and changes in location), their comfort with the infant's sleeping location, their perceptions of the relation between the baby's sleeping location and development, and their attitudes toward cosleeping. Table 4-1 lists coded categories and representative statements by U.S. parents.

## Reliability

**Reliability estimates** were unnecessary for data that did not involve judgments by the researchers (for example, sleeping location, night feedings, bedtime routines). The reflections of the U.S. parents on sleeping arrangements were grouped into coding categories requiring judgments; 50 percent of them were selected for reliability assessment using percentage of agreement scores. The values ranged from 75 percent to 100 percent, with a median of 88 percent.

## RESULTS

The practices of the Mayan and U.S. middle-class families with regard to sleeping locations, night feedings, and bedtime routines are reported first. We then follow up the differences in practices by examining parents' reflections on the different issues with questions tailored to the community's practices.

## Sleeping Location

*Mayan families*. All 14 Mayan mothers slept in the same bed with their infants through the first year of life and into the second year (see Table 4-2); 1 child had spent some time sleeping apart from her mother, on a cot in the same room, but was now sleeping with her mother again. In this case, the sleeping arrangement reflected changes in the presence of the father, from whom the mother was now separated.

Most of the Mayan toddlers (8 of them) also slept in the same bed with their fathers. Of the 6 who did not share a bed with their fathers, 3 had fathers sleeping in another bed in the same room (in 2 cases, father was sleeping with other young children), and the other 3 involved absent fathers. Four of the toddlers had a sibling (newborn to 4 years of age) in the same bed with them and their mothers, and of these, 2 also had the father in the same bed. Ten of the 14 toddlers had siblings sleeping in the same room with them, either in the same bed or another bed. Of the 4 toddlers who had no siblings sleeping in the same room, all were only children; one of these had paternal uncles sleeping in the same room.

*U.S. families.* In none of the 18 U.S. families did parents sleep with their newborns on a regular basis (see Table 4-2). Rather, most mothers and fathers (15 families) chose to share a room with their newborn infants, often placing them in a bassinet or crib near the parents' bed. This was a temporary arrangement; by 3 months of age 58 percent of the babies were already sleeping in separate rooms. This figure climbed to 80 percent by the 6th month of life. When the babies were moved to a room apart from their parents, first-borns were placed in a room of their own, but most second- and laterborns (89 percent) were moved into rooms with siblings. However, none of them shared a bed with a sibling.

**Table 4.1  Issues Related to Sleeping Arrangements, Coding Categories, and Associated Representative Statements: United States**

| Topic | Coding category | Representative statement by parents |
|---|---|---|
| Reasons for sleeping near baby | Pragmatic (e.g., reference to temporary phenomenon such as illness, room renovations, or convenience) | "My husband's mother … decided to come to visit, so he (baby) stayed (in parent's room) until she left." |
| | Developmental (e.g., reference to vulnerability or infant features associated with physical or psychological attributes) | "I could look over and see, yes he is still alive. He's still there, he's still breathing." |
| | Affectionate/emotional (security, closeness, comfort) | "I think he was able to look over and feel comfortable. It was a good experience for him, and for me, for the closeness." |
| Sleeping near mother and baby's development | Develop security or closeness | "I think that being in our room was probably healthy for him … he could see our bed … and feel more comfortable." |
| Reasons for moving baby out of mother's room | Pragmatic (e.g., reference to temporary phenomenon such as illness, room renovations, or convenience) | "It is kind of a strain for a couple to tiptoe in (the bedroom) and be quiet." |
| | Developmental (e.g., reference to infant features associated with physical or psychological attributes) | "My baby was sleeping through the night, he didn't need me anymore. |
| | Foster independent or autonomous behavior | "It was time to give him his own space, his own territory." |
| | Fear of establishing a difficult-to-break habit | "She just might as well get used to it (sleeping by self)." |
| Sleeping apart from mother and baby's development | Develop independent or autonomous behavior | "I think it would have made any separation harder if he wasn't even separated from us at night." |
| Comfort with sleeping apart from mother | Comfortable | "It was not bad because we put him right across the hall. I wouldn't say a big adjustment." |
| | Ambivalent | "There is good and bad both ways." |
| | Uncomfortable | "But I don't know how they are doing. I can't check up on them. No it is not comfortable having (him) in the other room." |
| Reasons for not sleeping with the baby | Fear of establishing a difficult-to-break habit | "Once you start it (cosleeping) it will continue. They (friends who cosleep) are sorry now that they have started it because now he is older and they can't get him out." |
| | Safety issues | "We might roll over him, hurt him … he could get smothered." |
| | Uncomfortable with idea | "I … don't think that I ever want him right in the same bed as me. I don't really know why." |
| | Concerns about encouraging dependency | "I think that he would be more dependent … if he was constantly with us like that" (i.e., asleep near them). |

**Table 4.2  Sleeping Locations in the Two Communities**

| Location | U.S. (n = 18) | | Mayan (n = 14) | |
|---|---|---|---|---|
| | 0–3 months | After 6 months | 0–3 months | After 6 months |
| In mother's bed with father and/or sibling(s) | 0 | 2 | 10 | 10 |
| In mother's bed, with no other bedmates | 0 | 0 | 4 | 4 |
| In separate bed, in mother's room | 15 | 2 | 0 | 0 |
| In another room, with a bedmate | 0 | 0 | 0 | 0 |
| In own bed in another room, with a roommate | 0 | 6 | 0 | 0 |
| In another room, alone | 3 | 8 | 0 | 0 |

In 3 of the 18 U.S. families, parents chose not to share a room with their babies from the time the babies were brought home from the hospital. These 3 newborn infants slept in their own rooms, despite the fact that 2 of them had siblings with whom they could have shared a room. For 1 family this meant keeping the infant in the living room.

Of the 15 families in which parents had slept near their newborn infants and then moved their babies to a separate room, 3 moved the infants back in the second half year of their baby's lives. Two babies were moved to cribs located in their parents' rooms; 1 baby was moved to her parents' bed. In addition, 1 family moved their child from a separate bed in the parents' room to the parents' bed when the child was 1 year old.

## Night Feedings

*Mayan families.* The pattern of night feeding arrangements in the Mayan families was for the baby or toddler to sleep with the mother until shortly before the birth of another child (about age 2 or 3) and to nurse on demand. The mothers reported that they generally did not notice having to feed their babies in the night. Mothers said that they did not have to waken, just to turn and make the breast accessible. Hence night feedings were not an issue for the Mayan mothers or for their infants and toddlers.

*U.S. families.* All but 1 of the 18 U.S. mothers reported having to stay awake during night feedings (which, for most mothers, lasted 6 months or so). Ten mothers chose not to feed their babies in their rooms, even though 7 of them had infants sleeping there and 8 of them were breastfeeding. Two mothers (both breastfeeding) fed infants in the parental room, but not in the parental bed; and 6 mothers (all breastfeeding) elected to feed their babies in the parental bed, but 5 of them regularly returned babies to their own beds when finished. The 1 mother whose infant regularly remained in bed with her following feedings was the only mother who said that nightly feedings did not bother her.

## Bedtime Routines

*Mayan families.* The idea that sleeping arrangements were not an issue for the Mayan families is supported by the lack of bedtime routines carried out in the nightly transition to sleep. There was not a separate routine to coax the baby to sleep. Most of the babies simply fell asleep when sleepy, along with the rest of the family or before if they got tired. Seven of the babies fell asleep at the same time as their parents, and most of the rest fell asleep in someone's arms. Ten of them were nursed to sleep (as they are nursed on demand during the daytime as well). Of the 4 who were no longer nursing, 1 fell asleep alone with a bottle, 1 fell asleep with a bottle and his mother going to bed with him, and 2 who had been nursed to sleep until recently (and were being weaned) usually fell asleep on their own but were cuddled by their father or older brother on the occasions when they needed company at bedtime.

None of the babies received a bedtime story; there were no reports of bathtime or toothbrushing in preparation for bed; none of the babies sucked their thumbs; only 1 was reported to use a security object for falling asleep (a little doll—this belonged to the 1 child who had for a time had a bed by herself!). There was thus no focus on objects as comfort items for falling asleep.

None of the Mayan families sang special children's lullabies to the babies at bedtime; some laughed at the idea. However, 4 of the mothers admitted with embarrassment that they sometimes sang their babies church songs at bedtime. (One added that she does this when she feels badly about not having taken the baby out during the day.) The babies were not changed into pajamas in preparation for bed. (They do not have specialized nightclothes; nor do the parents.) However, 11 of them were changed into their oldest clothes for sleeping. The other 3 just slept in the clothes they had worn during the day. Thus it appears that no special preparations or coaxing are needed for these babies, whose sleeping occurs in the company of the same people with whom they spend the day.

*U.S. families*. Events surrounding bedtime for the U.S. families played a significant role in the organization of family evening activities. Besides the daily evening activity of putting on nightclothes and brushing teeth, 10 of the 18 parents engaged in additional routines such as storytelling. Routines varied in their degree of elaborateness, with some parents spending just a few minutes reading a story to their babies and other parents investing a fair amount of time getting their child ready for sleep. One mother jokingly said, "When my friends hear that it is time for my son to go to bed, they teasingly say 'See you in an hour'."

Once infants were in bed, 11 were expected to fall asleep by themselves. It is interesting that 5 of the 8 infants who fell asleep alone took a favorite object such as a blanket to bed with them (data are missing for 3 children). By comparison, only 2 of the 6 infants who fell asleep in the company of another person (data are missing for 1 child) needed to do the same.

## Reflections of Parents on Sleeping Arrangements

*Mayan families.* Most of the families regarded their sleeping arrangements as the only reasonable way for a baby and parents to sleep. In addition, in five interviews the subject of how U.S. families handle sleeping arrangements came up. Invariably, the idea that toddlers are put to sleep in a separate room was received with shock, disapproval, and pity. One mother responded, "But there's someone else with them there, isn't there?" When told that they are sometimes alone in the room the mother gasped and went on to express pity for the U.S. babies. Another mother responded with shock and disbelief, asked whether the babies do not mind, and added with feeling that it would be very painful for her to have to do that. The responses of the Mayan parents gave the impression that they regarded the practice of having infants and toddlers sleep in separate rooms as tantamount to child neglect. Their reactions and their accounts of their own sleeping arrangements seemed to indicate that their arrangements were a matter of commitment to a certain kind of relationship with their young children and not a result of practical limitations (such as number of rooms in the house).

In Mayan families, sleeping arrangements are not an issue until the child is displaced from the mother's side by a new baby. At the time or before the new baby is born, the toddler is weaned and may be moved to sleep beside the father in the same bed or in another bed in the same room. One mother and father told us that their little boy got very angry at his mother (when the next child arrived) and even cried when he was moved to his father's bed; he wanted to be the last born—he did not want someone else to take his place beside his mother. For most families, though, this transition is usually made without difficulty. Parents sometimes try to prevent any difficulties by getting the child accustomed to sleeping with another family member before the new baby is born. The transition is sometimes difficult for Mayan mothers and fathers. Mothers may regret letting the child move from their care to that of another family member, and fathers may lose sleep as they often become responsible for the displaced child. One father of a toddler told us that his older son, whose wife was expecting a second child in 4 months, needed to move their 2-year-old firstborn to another bed soon, even though she did not want to move. The older man told us that the firstborn needed to become accustomed to sleeping apart from the mother or the father would have trouble later. "I know," said the older man, "because I went through this … If the first child doesn't sleep through the night, apart from the parents, when the new child comes, the father suffers. He has to get up in the night to give the child something."

If there are older siblings, they often take care of the displaced child if needed during the night, allowing the father to sleep. Of the 10 Mayan families with older siblings, in 5 of them the older siblings had moved to sleep with the father when our subjects were born (3 in the same bed with mother and the new baby, 2 with father in another bed in the same room), in 2 they had moved to sleep with a sibling in the same room, in 2 they had moved to a separate bed in the same room, and in 1 they slept with the mother and the new baby as father slept in a separate bed in the same room. It is noteworthy that even when the children are displaced from their mother's side, they still sleep in the same room with her, usually at someone else's side.

***U.S. families.***[1] U.S. parents chose to sleep near their newborn infants for pragmatic reasons (mentioned by 78 percent, for example, "Because I nurse them … it is sort of convenient to have them here") as well as for developmental and affectionate reasons (57 percent and 64 percent mentioned these). Of the parents who slept near their babies starting at birth, an overwhelming majority (92 percent) felt that sleeping near infants helped foster the development of an affectionate tie between them and their babies. (Table 4-1 contains a description of coding categories and representative statements by parents.)

Although these parents acknowledged that sleeping near their infants was a meaningful experience for both them and their babies, all but 1 family decided to move their infants to separate quarters within the 1st year of life (most moves occurred during the first 3 to 6 months).[2] When asked about the reasons for shifting sleeping quarters, parents often talked about the infant's developmental readiness for separation (69 percent): "She didn't need to be watched as close"; "He was old enough to be by himself." This suggests that a perceived decrease in the vulnerability of the infant and readiness for separation played an important role in the parents' decision to move the infant out of the parents' room. Pragmatic factors (for example, "It was time for me to go back to work") were cited as important in the decision-making process by 54 percent of the families. Fostering independence and preventing conflict over separation were given as reasons for moving the baby out of the parents' room by 38 percent and 15 percent of the families, respectively. Most U.S. families did not consider the transition from sleeping near parents to sleeping apart from them in these early months to be stressful for the infants. One family speculated that a baby might find the move stressful if the baby was a firstborn.

Twelve of the 14 families who moved their babies out of their rooms expressed satisfaction with their decision.[3] Many emphasized that the move allowed continued proximity to their babies. Half of the parents told us that the baby's room was close to their room, making it easy for them to monitor their infant's movements. Some families also made a regular habit of keeping doors slightly ajar so that they could better hear their babies' cries. Just 2 mothers who moved their babies out of their room were unhappy with their decision. For 1 mother, the baby's move to the living room severely hampered her daytime activities.

Three parents participating in the study never had their infants sleep in the same room with them. Two of the 3 families made this choice because of concerns related to independence training. All 3 families were comfortable with their decision to maintain separate sleeping quarters; 2 families commented that the rooms were sufficiently close to allow them to hear their infants in case of an emergency.

Most of the 17 families who slept in different rooms from their infants (from birth, or within months following the baby's birth) focused on issues related to independence training when discussing what their practices meant for their baby. Sixty-nine percent of these families believed that it was important for their infants' developing independence and self-reliance to sleep apart from them, with some reporting that separations at night made daytime separations easier and would help reduce their babies' dependence on them.

The findings suggest that encouraging independence during infancy is an important goal for many U.S. families and that parents believe that sleeping apart helps train children to be independent. But the age at which parents think it is appropriate for infants to sleep apart is somewhat variable, ranging from 0 to usually 3 to 6 months. This range of variability is narrow compared with worldwide sleeping practices.

Sixteen of the 18 U.S. mothers reported that they would not want to sleep with their baby on a regular basis. The explanations for avoiding cosleeping included the fear of establishing a habit that would be difficult to break (50 percent; for example, "She would like it and not want to leave"), concern about encouraging dependency in their baby (19 percent), safety reasons (44 percent; for example, "I was so afraid that I would crush him"), or simply being uncomfortable with the idea (44 percent). However, the majority of parents (77 percent) did report allowing occasional night visits, often as a way to comfort their infants. But some families felt that it was just not acceptable to bring a baby into the parental bed for any reason.

Sleeping within listening distance (but not within touch) of babies during the first months of life is a practice preferred by most of the U.S. middle-class mothers participating in the study. As parental perceptions of the developing infant shifted, it seemed increasingly inappropriate to the U.S. mothers for their babies to be within their beds or bedrooms. Cosleeping was often seen as a bad habit that is difficult to break or as a practice that impedes the development of independence.

## DISCUSSION

Mayan and U.S. middle-class families differed in the way they managed their infants' and young children's sleeping arrangements. Cosleeping, a practice found in many communities worldwide, was common in the Mayan community (Burton & Whiting, 1961; Whiting & Edwards, 1988; Whiting, 1964; see also Barry & Paxson, 1971; McKenna, 1986). Mayan infants slept with their mothers, and often their fathers and siblings, from birth onward, with changes in sleep location not expected until around the time of the birth of a sibling.

None of the middle-class U.S. parents, by comparison, coslept with their newborn infants on a regular basis. Rather, many parents chose to sleep near their babies in the same room but moved them to separate rooms by 3 to 6 months of age. Some parents, however, chose not to share a room even with their newborn infants. The pattern observed in our U.S. sample is similar to what has been described for other Caucasian middle- and upper-class families living in the United States (Hong & Townes, 1976; Keener, Zeanah, & Anders, 1988; Richman, Miller, & Solomon, 1988; Valsiner & Hall, 1983; Whiting & Edwards, 1988). U.S. middle-class parents may differ somewhat in their sleeping arrangements for their newborn infants, but they are working toward a common goal, which is to have infants sleep in rooms of their own as early as possible. In fact, it seems as though U.S. parents are more comfortable with the idea of newborn infants sleeping in a room alone than with the idea of 1-year-olds sharing a room with their parents.

The few U.S. parents who had difficulty achieving the goal of sleeping apart from their babies and had moved them back to the parents' room after they had already been sleeping in separate quarters felt their decision was necessary but were unhappy about it. Discussion of their infants' present sleeping locations suggested that these parents knew that they were going against conventional practices and were reminded of it by family and community members alike, who expressed surprise and concern about the consequences of the parents' decision for both the infants' and the parents' well-being.

The practice of sleeping with babies may relate to concerns with infant survival. According to LeVine (1980), concerns about survival take precedence during infants' first years of life and shape infants' early caregiving environment. In our middle-class U.S. sample, many parents' decisions regarding newborns were based on their perceptions of infant vulnerability. U.S. parents were comforted by the fact that they could check up on their babies during the night to make sure that they were still breathing. (But note that U.S. parents chose not to sleep with their babies.) Once parents felt that their babies' health was not in jeopardy (around the 3rd to 6th month of life), they expected them to sleep apart. The Mayan practice of cosleeping may help minimize threats to infant survival, which are considerably greater than in the U.S. middle class because of malnutrition and illness.

McKenna (1986) argued that cosleeping was a **panhuman** practice with survival value for infants during much of our evolutionary past (see also Konner & Super, 1987). His view is based on the claim that infants rely on cues from parents when sleeping to help them regulate their breathing, allowing them to survive "breathing control errors" (p. 53) that might play a role in sudden infant death syndrome. Evidence that infants in some communities wake and feed about every 4 hours at night (as they do in the daytime) for at least the first 8 months of life adds to the argument that forcing babies to be alone through the night may go beyond the limits of some infants' physiological systems (McKenna, 1986; Super & Harkness, 1982).

Decisions about infants' sleeping arrangements, like other parenting decisions, also relate to the community's values and goals regarding desired characteristics of citizens. Some Mayan parents who reflected on the possibility of sleeping apart from their infants and toddlers emphasized qualities related to **interdependence**. It seems that their arrangements reflect commitment to this type of relationship with their young children. Speculations at one interview lend support to this idea:

> Upon being asked how she teaches her 13-month old that there are some things not to handle, the mother said she tells her, "Don't touch it, it's no good, it could hurt you," and the baby nods seriously at mother and obeys, and knows not to touch it. (This was a common statement by the Mayan mothers.)

> The interviewer commented that U.S. babies don't understand so young, and instead of understanding and obeying when they are told not to touch something, they might get more interested in it. With much feeling, another mother who was present at the interview (in which we reported on U.S. sleeping arrangements) speculated that perhaps U.S. children do that because of the custom of separating children from parents at night. "In our community the babies are always with the mother, but with North Americans, you keep the babies apart. Maybe that's why the children here understand their mothers more; they feel close. Maybe U.S. children feel the distance more." She went on to speculate that if children do not feel close, it will be harder for them to learn and understand the ways of the people around them.

In many respects, Mayan infants and toddlers were regarded as not yet accountable (they were not punished for misdeeds, being considered unable to understand) and not yet ready to be treated as individuals who could be separated from their families, especially their mothers. On the other hand, the mothers generally reported that their infants and toddlers understood social rules and prohibitions from an early age. Almost all of the Mayan mothers reported that they could trust their young children not to put objects in their mouths and not to touch prohibited objects. Contrast this with the vigilance with which U.S. parents watch over their children around small objects until age 2 or 3. The mothers in our U.S. sample reported that they did not trust their young children with small objects. This difference is consistent with the Mayan mothers' speculation that the relationships fostered in sleeping close with babies may relate to the Mayan babies' learning from those around them (see also Rogoff, Mosier, Mistry, & Göncü, 1993, on Mayan babies' keenness of observation and alertness to their social surroundings).

The relation between cosleeping and interdependence was noted by Caudill and Plath (1966) in their work on Japanese families. Japanese parents believe that their infants are born as separate beings who must develop interdependent relationships with community members to survive; cosleeping is thought to facilitate this process (Caudill & Weinstein, 1969). In contrast, U.S. parents believe that infants are born dependent and need to be socialized to become independent. Abbott (1992) argues that the Eastern Kentucky practice of parents sleeping with or near their children through the first 2 years of life is a strategy used by parents to foster the development of interdependence. Our U.S. middle-class mothers indicated that having newborns sleep in the parents' room fostered their feelings of closeness and the newborn's sense of security and emotional attachment. However, for the U.S. middle-class families, the fostering of closeness in this fashion seemed to be limited to the newborn period and involved parents sleeping in sight or hearing of but not in contact with their newborns.

In criticizing cosleeping, many U.S. mothers talked about the need to train babies to be inde-

pendent and self-reliant from the first few months of life, and they reported concern with establishing a habit that would be difficult to break. A number of authors share this view (Edelman, 1983; Hoover, 1978; Spock, 1945). This reveals an assumption that from birth children should become accustomed to the requirements of later life, an assumption that child-rearing practices in infancy should be continuous with those of childhood (Benedict, 1955). This is an assumption that is not shared by many communities where infants are treated differently than young children; in such communities infants are assumed not to have sense or to understand and to have needs different than those of children. Rather than making the break in closeness with mother at or shortly after birth, infants are treated as part of a mother-infant unit until about the end of the 2nd year (when the appearance of a new baby and the need for weaning often occur). This latter view of infancy is consistent with Mayan beliefs and practices surrounding sleeping arrangements and with Kawakami's (1987) statement regarding Japanese child rearing: "An American mother-infant relationship consists of two individuals ... On the other hand a Japanese mother-infant relationship consists of only one individual, that is, mother and infant are not divided" (p. 5).

Loss of privacy and associated concerns about sexual intimacy were also mentioned by some of the U.S. mothers when discussing their decision not to sleep with their babies on a regular basis. One U.S. mother said, "My husband did not like that idea (cosleeping). He was afraid that it would be unnatural, too much intimacy." It appears that unlike the Mayan community, who view sleeping as a social activity, some U.S. families see sleeping as a time for conjugal intimacy.

It is possible that spending extended periods of time alone may provide training in self-comforting and self-regulation (LeVine, 1980, 1990; Munroe, Munroe, & Whiting, 1981). Although many U.S. parents believe that their infants are asleep during the night, this is not always true. Anders (1979) found that 78 percent of nine-month-olds were not removed from their cribs from midnight to 5 A.M., satisfying conventional criteria for sleeping through the night. Yet 57 percent of these infants woke up during these hours. When babies wake in the absence of a caregiver, they are responsible for dealing with their own emotional or physiological distress (for example, fear, hunger, cold). The fear of sleeping alone was well put by one U.S. middle-class 3-year-old who developed nightmares and trouble sleeping. He went into his parents' room and complained, "If there was a human in the same room, I wouldn't be 'fraid.'" When he was moved into his baby brothers' room, his sleeping troubles disappeared (V. K. Magarian, personal communication, July 1991).

However, Wolf and Lozoff (1989) questioned the relation between sleeping alone and independence training. They noted that "if leaving children to fall asleep alone truly fosters independence, it is perhaps surprising that during historical periods in the U.S. in which 'independence' was most vividly demonstrated, such as the colonial period or the westward movement, children were not likely to fall asleep alone" (p. 292). It might be that infants and young toddlers who sleep alone during the night find it more difficult (rather than easier, as assumed by middle-class parents) to separate from their parents during the day (E. Z. Tronick, personal communication, September 1991).

The struggle seen around bedtime between many U.S. middle-class parents and their children may be related to the stress infants experience when required to make the transition to sleep without assistance (Albert, 1977; see also LeVine, 1990). It may also reflect a conflict of goals, with parents wanting their child to go to sleep as soon as possible because of fears engendered by having to sleep on his or her own (Gandini, 1986). For the U.S. toddlers, bedtime was associated with separation from family social life: All toddlers went to bed earlier than their parents, and most were expected to fall asleep alone, in their own rooms. Anders (1979) and LeVine (1990) reported similar findings. In contrast, most Mayan babies went to sleep when their parents did or fell asleep in the midst of ongoing social activity.

This is consistent with a general pattern, observed in communities around the world, in which there is little distinction between daytime and nighttime events for infants and toddlers (LeVine, 1990).

Bedtime routines, common in many U.S. families, including those we observed, are thought to help ease the child's nightly transition from being with others to being alone (Albert, 1977; Crowell et al., 1987; Lozoff, Wolf, & Davis, 1984). Many of the U.S. children who were expected to fall asleep alone took objects to bed with them that were seen by their parents as offering solace to their children. This finding replicates that of Wolf and Lozoff (1989), who found that middle-class children who did not have an adult present as they fell asleep were more likely to use **transitional objects** or to suck their thumbs at night. The nightly passage to sleep appears to be difficult for young children who have to do it alone; security objects and bedtime routines may be used to help infants in the transition to sleep. This view is consistent with findings showing that infants who sleep near or with their parents tend not to use transitional objects (Gaddini & Gaddini, 1971; Hong & Townes, 1976) and with our finding that Mayan toddlers did not use security objects for falling asleep.

It is interesting from a cultural perspective that some parents would prefer that their children become attached to and dependent on an inanimate object (for example, a blanket) rather than a person. U.S. parents feel obliged, in many cases, to avoid giving their children comfort during the night or while getting to sleep. One mother reported putting a pillow over her head to drown out the sounds of her crying baby as she fell asleep—consistent with the advice of some child-rearing specialists (such as Ferber, 1986).

The Mayan infants, who generally go to sleep with the rest of the family or in the company of a family member, appear not to experience bedtime as an issue for negotiation with parents or as a time of stress. However, Mayan families face a transition at age 2 or 3 when a new sibling is expected and toddlers are weaned from the breast and their mother's bed. Parents report attempts to prevent difficulties at this transition by moving the child from the mother's side to sleep with another person before the new baby is born. Most children are reported to make the transition without difficulty.

The Mayan children generally continue to sleep with others throughout their childhoods. In a study of 60 9-year-olds in this Mayan community, only 8 percent were in a bed by themselves, and none were in a separate bedroom (Rogoff, 1977). Most (63 percent) shared a bed with siblings, 20 percent shared a bed with one or both parents, and 8 percent shared a bed with a grandmother or aunt. The idea of sleeping alone was disagreeable to the Mayan 9-year-olds, who expressed pity for U.S. 9-year-olds when told that they sleep in rooms of their own. And Mayan adults often find a sleeping companion if for some reason their family is away. Sleeping alone is seen as a hardship.

In both the middle-class U.S. and the Mayan communities, sleeping arrangements reflect child-rearing goals and values for interpersonal relations. It is not our aim to determine causality in the patterns we observed or to make recommendations for change in either community. It is instructive simply to note the patterns and to come to a broader understanding of cultural practices in which all families participate. In the Mayan community, infants and toddlers sleep with their mothers, and when a new baby appears they make a transition to sleeping with another family member or to a separate bed in the same room. Bedtime has social continuity with the relationships in which the Mayan children participate throughout the day and is not specially marked with transition routines or aided by attachment objects. In the U.S. middle-class community, infants generally sleep in a room separate from their parents by the second half of the first year of life. Infants seem to adjust to the changes made in their sleeping arrangements and may develop sleep patterns and rhythms similar to those of family members as they make adjustments associated with sleeping separate from

their parents. The transition to sleep and to spending long hours alone is eased by attachments to objects and by special transition routines at bedtime. The transition is often stressful for parents and children alike, with parents at times acting in an adversarial role with their children in order to force adherence to what is seen by many as a cultural imperative—children sleeping alone—that aids in developing self-reliance and independence, personal characteristics valued by the community.

## NOTES

1. Some of the findings reported in this section involve a few cases of missing data. The percentages do not include these cases.

2. One family made cosleeping a regular family practice when their son was 1 year of age, after having had the infant in a separate bed in the parents' room. The mother already had a history of falling asleep with the infant while nursing; the decision was one of convenience, prompted by the baby's increasing resistance to sleeping alone. Nonetheless, the parents were ambivalent about their decision to cosleep. They felt that cosleeping provided their son with emotional security but, at the same time, they wanted their privacy.

3. The 3 families who made additional changes in their babies' sleeping arrangements after their infants had been moved to separate rooms were unhappy about their decisions, although they reported that their decisions were necessary (because of medical concerns or space issues). One mother exclaimed, "I am a human being, and I deserve some time and privacy to myself."

## EVALUATING YOUR MASTERY

1. Cosleeping promotes
   a. Infants' use of transitional objects
   b. The development of interdependence
   c. Elaborate bedtime routines
   d. The development of self-reliance

2. Most American families move their babies to a separate room within
   a. 6 months
   b. 6 months to 1 year
   c. 1 to 1.5 years
   d. 1.5 to 2.0 years

3. All of the following are explanations American parents give for not sleeping in the same room as their child *except*
   a. Concern about encouraging dependence in the baby
   b. Physical safety
   c. Belief that infants are born independent
   d. Fear of establishing a habit that would be difficult to break

4. The arrival of a new baby in the Mayan family results in the next youngest child
   a. Sleeping with the father and/or older siblings
   b. Sleeping alone in a separate room
   c. Sleeping with a grandparent
   d. Continuing to sleep with the mother

5. True or False: Cosleeping is rare and only occurs in a few non-Western communities.

6. True or False: Night feeding is an issue for both Mayan and American mothers because they both must wake for it.

7. One of the primary reasons given for American infants sleeping in a separate room from their parents is that child-rearing practices in infancy should be [consistent with/different from] those of childhood.

### Critical Thinking

1. Why are security objects and bedtime routines so important for children who sleep in a separate room from their parents?

2. Some cultures believe that parent-infant cosleeping helps build interdependent relationships. How might this practice promote the development of infant-caregiver attachment?

### Applying Your Knowledge

Interview several parents of infants and preschoolers, asking about sleeping arrangements and the reasons for them, use of transitional objects, and bedtime routines. Is the patterning of these factors within each family consistent with the findings of Morelli and her colleagues? Explain.

# 5

# Symbolic Functioning in Preschool Children

JUDY S. DeLOACHE & NANCY M. BURNS
University of Illinois

■

Young children's comprehension of scale models is interesting, not because models play an important role in children's everyday lives, but because of what they can reveal about early symbolization and cognition in general.

■

Being very familiar with the layout of the room and the furniture in it did nothing at all to help [2.5-year-olds] appreciate the correspondence between the room and the model of it.

■

This research demonstrates that achieving representational insight can be very difficult, even when the symbol actually looks like what it stands for and even when children are explicitly told about the existence of the relation.

■

Our research leads us to believe that representational specificity may be important developmentally. Generic representation is easier to understand and appears earlier; specific representation is more difficult and develops later.

■

One implication is that a good approach to teaching young children about a new symbolic relation would be to make as much contact as possible between it and a symbol system they already understand.

■

The clear message about materials is that, contrary to a common adult intuition, symbolic functioning may not be facilitated and may even be harmed by the use of concrete symbolic objects.

■

## EDITOR'S INTRODUCTION

The most obvious aspect of children's psychological development during toddlerhood and the preschool years is an extraordinary increase in representational activity. Judy DeLoache and Nancy Burns focus on the years from 2 to 3, when children are first introduced to the diverse symbol systems of their culture. They describe a series of investigations addressing the understanding of two kinds of symbols: scale models and pictures.

Their findings reveal that even when symbolic materials are very concrete and strongly resemble the things for which they stand, young children often do not grasp their representational nature. For example, 2.5-year-olds do not realize a scale model's dual function—as both an interesting play object and as a representation of another object. Symbolic appreciation of pictures is advanced over models, emerging between 2.0 and 2.5 years of age. Because pictures are not very attractive as play objects, young children find it easier to focus on their symbolic purpose. Furthermore, research on both types of symbols reveals that specific representation—the realization that a photo or model can stand for a particular object or place rather than for objects or places in general—is challenging for young preschoolers.

DeLoache and Burns conclude with suggestions for helping preschoolers become aware of symbol-referent relations. Contrary to what most adults assume, concrete symbolic objects that invite children to treat them as playful materials are not the best way to foster symbolic understanding in very young children.

Our capacity for the flexible and creative use of symbols is what most sets humans apart from other species. In modern, industrial societies, there are many symbol systems that must be mastered for full participation in society. We must speak fluently and use gestures comprehensible to others. We must be able to count and do math, to read and to write. We need to understand the media of our culture, including pictures, TV, and movies. In addition, it is becoming increasingly important to have computer and other technological skills.

The start toward mastering these various symbolic media is made in the first few years of life. Most infants produce their first words and gestures around the end of their first year. Most American preschoolers can count and understand something about numbers; many can identify letters and some can even read. They look at picture books, watch TV, and accompany their families to movies.

Preschool curricula are designed to foster symbolic skills. To facilitate symbolic play, a variety of materials are made available, including dolls and other replica objects. Teachers lead children in letter and counting games and songs. Children are read to during the ubiquitous story time and encouraged to interact with books on their own.

In addition, most preschools provide materials of an explicitly educational nature. For example, sets of blocks of graduated sizes are used to represent different numerical quantities. Addition is demonstrated by showing that when three individual yellow blocks, each 1 inch long, are placed end to end, they are equal in length to a single blue block that is 3 inches long. Alphabet letters constructed of wood, plastic, sandpaper, and so forth constitute another example of concrete symbolic tokens that are very common.

The assumption made about these materials is that their concrete, tangible nature will help young children acquire the abstract concepts they represent. Is this assumption warranted? Our research on very young children's understanding of symbols suggests that it is not. One implication of this research is that symbolic materials for very young children must be selected with great care. Young children often do not understand the relation between a symbol and its referent, even when that relation seems to be totally transparent to an adult or older child.

The basis for these cautionary statements is research we have been doing for several years on very young children's understanding of scale models, pictures, and maps. In this work, we and our colleagues examined children's appreciation of the representational nature of symbols, that is, our subjects' realization that a symbol—a model, picture, or map—stands for something other than itself. We discovered several factors that make it more or less likely that young children will achieve this basic representational insight.

## YOUNG CHILDREN'S UNDERSTANDING OF SCALE MODELS

Young children's comprehension of scale models is interesting, not because models play an important role in children's everyday lives, but because of what they can reveal about early symbolization and cognition in general. In our research, we examined 2.5- and 3.0-year-old children's appreciation of the symbolic relation between a scale model and the full-sized room it represented. The model contained miniature versions of all the items of standard living room furniture that were in the room, and the corresponding objects were in the same spatial arrangement within the two spaces. Each child received an extensive orientation in which we explicitly described and demonstrated the overall correspondence between the two spaces, the individual

DeLoache, J., & Burns, N. M. (1994). Symbolic functioning in preschool children. *Journal of Applied Developmental Psychology, 15,* 513–527. Reprinted by permission.

correspondences between the items of furniture within them, and the correspondence between two toys—a stuffed dog ("Big Snoopy") and a miniature plastic dog ("Little Snoopy").

Our young subjects watched as the miniature toy was hidden somewhere in the model, and they were then asked to find the larger, analogous toy concealed in the corresponding place in the room itself. For example, a child would observe Little Snoopy being placed behind the miniature armchair in the model and would search for Big Snoopy in the room. The child was instructed that "Big Snoopy is hiding in the same place in his room." After retrieving the analogous toy in the room (Retrieval 1) the child was brought back to the model and asked to find the toy he or she had actually observed being hidden (Retrieval 2). To succeed in this task, children must (a) recognize the correspondence between the model and the room, (b) map the elements of one space onto those of the other, and (c) use their knowledge of where the miniature toy was hidden to figure out where the larger toy must be.

In the original study using this task, a large difference appeared in the performance of young children only a few months apart in age (De-Loache, 1987). As Figure 5.1 shows, a group of 3-year-olds succeeded in retrieving the toy on 77 percent of their Retrieval 1 trials, whereas a group of 2.5-year-olds succeeded only 15 percent of the time. The large difference in the performance of the two groups was not due to differences in memory for the location of the original toy. Both age groups were highly successful at retrieving the toy they had actually observed being hidden (88 percent and 83 percent on Retrieval 2 for the older and younger children, respectively).

Note that the high Retrieval 2 performance indicates that the children's failure on Retrieval 1 was not due to the lack of motivation or to a total lack of comprehension. The 2.5-year-olds understood everything about the task except the crucial feature. They knew there was a toy hidden in the room and they knew they were sup-posed to find it. What they did not realize was that they had any way of knowing where it was. They thought they were playing a guessing game and they were happy to do so.

This basic pattern of results has been replicated many times (DeLoache, 1989a, 1989b, 1990, 1991; DeLoache, Kolstad, & Anderson, 1991; Dow & Pick, 1990). Because both group and individual performance tends to be very good or very poor, we have concluded that the key variable is **representational insight**—awareness that the model stands for or represents the room. Given this insight, the task is trivially easy for a child of this age. Without this insight, the child has no basis for knowing where to find the analogous toy.

We tried a variety of stratagems to improve the performance of 2.5-year-olds in this task, that is, to help them become aware of the correspondence between the room and model. In one study (DeLoache, 1989b), we verbally labeled the hiding place ("I'm hiding Little Snoopy behind his *couch*"). There was absolutely no effect on performance. In another, we gave the children extensive experience with the room prior to the testing. Young children came to the room in small groups and played there three times a week for 3 weeks. Being very familiar with the layout of the room and the furniture in it did nothing at all to help them appreciate the correspondence between the room and the model of it. Several other efforts to help 2.5-year-olds similarly failed, indicating that achieving representational insight in this task is very difficult for them.

It is not, however, impossible. We succeeded in a few instances in getting 2.5-year-olds to appreciate a model-room relation. In one successful effort, we dramatically decreased the degree of size difference between the model and the larger space it represented. The model was the same size as that used in the previous research, but the larger space was only twice as large as the model. Because they were so similar in scale, the two spaces were extremely similar perceptually (although the subject was never allowed to see them at the same time). In addition, they were

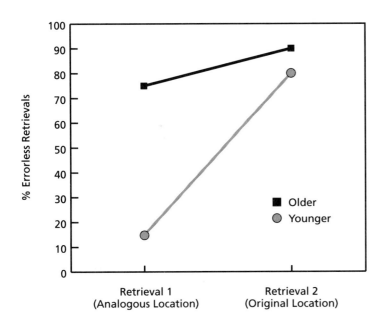

**FIGURE 5.1** Percentage errorless retrievals achieved by the two age groups.

both surveyable spaces, whereas in the other studies, the model was a surveyable space but the room was a surrounding space. Everything else about the space was the same as before. As Figure 5.2 shows, the performance of a group of 2.5-year-olds in this similar-scale task was much better than that of a group of the same age in the standard, dissimilar-scale model task.

This result is important because it demonstrates that it is possible for 2.5-year-old children to appreciate a symbolic relation involving a scale model. Thus, their failure in numerous other model studies is not due to a total inability to appreciate such a relation.

Why, then, is it so difficult for 2.5-year-olds to detect the correspondence between a scale model and a larger space? An important part of the answer to that question has to do with the inherently dual nature of models. A scale model is both a symbol and a real object, and success in our model task requires thinking about it in two ways at the same time, both as the object that it is and as a symbol for something it is not. Watching little Snoopy being hidden in the model, the child must also think about Big Snoopy in the

room. In other words, appreciation of the symbolic nature of a scale model requires a dual representation.

## Dual Representation

We have evidence that one reason for the poor performance of 2.5-year-olds in the model task is that they failed to achieve a dual representation of the model. They certainly represented it as an object; they watched the experimenter hide things in it and they successfully retrieved them. But, because the model was so salient and attractive to them as a concrete object, as an appealing toy, they represented only that aspect of it; they failed to appreciate its relation to the room. Watching Little Snoopy being hidden in the model, the child thought only about Little Snoopy.

The evidence in support of this dual representation hypothesis comes primarily from a series of studies comparing 2.5-year-olds' understanding of models versus pictures. The dual representation hypothesis led to a counterintuitive prediction—that 2.5-year-old children should do

**FIGURE 5.2** Percentage errorless retrievals by 2.5-year-olds as a function of the extent of size differences between two spaces.

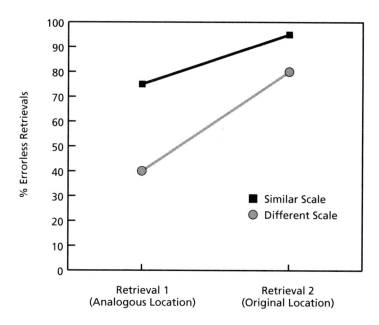

better when given information about the location of a hidden object by pictures than when the same information is conveyed using a scale model. A picture is, of course, a concrete object. However, although pictures have a certain "double reality" (Sigel, 1978), they are not very salient or interesting as objects, and their primary function is to represent something else. When we look at a picture, we normally think only of what it depicts, not of the picture as an object itself. Thus, a picture should not require a dual representation in the way a model does and should, therefore, be easier for very young children to interpret.

This prediction that performance should be better with pictures than a model is counterintuitive on other grounds, however. We generally consider real objects to be more salient, more informative, and more memorable than pictures. Furthermore, there is a large body of studies showing better performance with objects than pictures in a wide variety of tasks (for example, Daehler, Lonardo, & Bukatko, 1979; DeLoache, 1986; Hartley, 1976; Sigel, 1953; Sigel, Anderson, & Shapiro, 1966; Sigel & Cocking, 1977; Sigel & Olmsted, 1970; Sorce, 1980; Steinberg, 1974).

The predicted picture-superiority effect has been found in a series of studies, using varying materials and procedures. In the first test (DeLoache, 1987), a group of 2.5-year-olds participated in two tasks—the *standard-model task* and a *picture task* using four color photographs. Each photograph depicted one of the four items of furniture used as hiding places in the room. On each trial, the experimenter pointed to one of the photographs to indicate where the toy was hidden in the room. ("This is where Snoopy is hiding; he's hiding back [under] here.") In another study (DeLoache, 1991), only one picture was used. In one condition, there was a wide-angle color photograph that depicted a large portion of the room, including all the furniture to be used as hiding places. In another condition, a lightly colored line drawing of the same scene was used. In both studies, all children participated in the two tasks (model and picture) on different days, with task order counterbalanced across children.

As predicted, 2.5-year-old children successfully used the information in the pictures to find the hidden toy. They found the toy on 70 percent

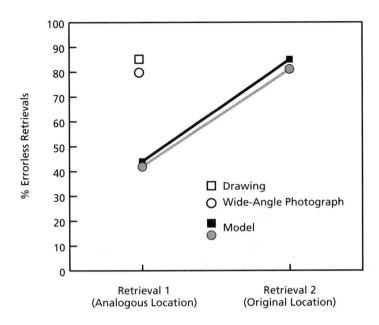

**FIGURE 5.3** Percentage errorless retrievals by 2.5-year-olds for pictures versus model. The squares represent picture and model performance for those subjects who received the line drawing in the picture task, and the circles represent subjects who received the wide-angle photograph.

of the trials in the earlier study and, as Figure 5.3 shows, they were even more successful with the wide-angle photograph and line drawing (81 percent and 86 percent). Thus, having seen the experimenter point at the picture of the couch, for example, they usually went to the couch in the room and searched behind it for the toy. The same children were much less successful in the model task.

Although these results supported the dual representation hypothesis, there was one aspect of the study that could be cause for concern—the method by which the correct location was communicated to the child. In the model task the location of the toy in the room is conveyed by a hiding event, whereas in the picture task the experimenter simply points to the correct picture. It could be that it is easier to represent a simple point to a single object than it is to represent a hiding event that involves the relation between two objects. Such a difference could then lead to the superiority of pictures over the model, but have nothing to do with the need for dual representation.

To evaluate this possibility, we did a study crossing medium (model or pictures) with method (hiding or pointing). Two of the resulting four conditions were simply replications. In the first condition, the miniature toy was hidden in the model, and in the second condition, the experimenter pointed to one of four pictures. In the third condition, the experimenter simply pointed to the correct object in the model to indicate where the toy was hidden in the room. In the final condition, the miniature toy was hidden behind one of the four pictures. To illustrate, consider the case in which the larger toy was hidden behind the dresser in the room: (a) in the *hide-model condition,* the child watched as the miniature toy was hidden behind the miniature dresser in the model; (b) in the *point-picture condition,* the experimenter pointed to the photograph of the dresser; (c) in the *point-model condition,* the experimenter pointed to the miniature dresser in the model; and (d) in the *hide-picture condition,* the experimenter hid the miniature dog behind the picture of the dresser. Appropriate instructions were given in each condition. Four groups of 2.5-year-old children participated in the four conditions.

The results provided strong support for the dual representation hypothesis. As Figure 5.4

**FIGURE 5.4** Percentage errorless retrievals (Retrieval 1 only) by 2.5-year-olds as a function of medium (scale model versus picture) and method (hiding versus pointing).

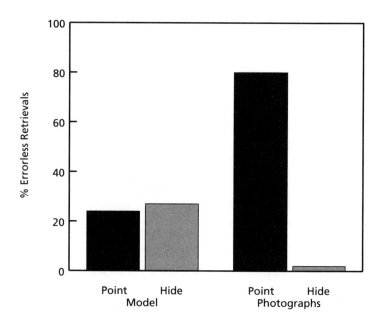

shows, the performance of the two replication groups was indeed the same as that found in previous studies; the 2.5-year-old subjects were very successful in the point-picture condition (78 percent) and quite unsuccessful in the hide-model condition (25 percent). The crucial condition was the point-model condition, and the data were unequivocal. Performance was exactly the same (25 percent) as in the hide-model condition. Thus, the picture-superiority effect cannot be attributed to a difference in the method of communicating the location of the toy in the room. Children failed with the model, regardless of how the correct location was indicated.

Support for the dual representation hypothesis also came from the hide-picture condition, in which performance was zero. Not a single child ever succeeded on a single trial. Why should this condition have been so incomprehensible to the children? One reason is that this condition also requires a dual representation. In this case, the child must treat a symbol (a photograph) both as a symbol for something else and as an object (a hiding place). We apparently induced our subjects to treat the pictures as objects; their high

Retrieval 2 scores indicated that they represented them as hiding places. However, responding to the pictures as objects seems to have blocked responding to what they depicted, that is, interpreting them as symbols as something else.

A second reason why performance in this condition was so terrible is that, in addition to requiring a dual representation, it violated the normal symbolic function of pictures. By 2.5 years of age, children have had extensive experience with pictures and have learned a great deal about them. They know that pictures are normally responded to in terms of their depicted referents, not in terms of themselves as objects. In other words, the hide-picture condition confronted our young subjects with an anomalous use of symbols. Their retrieval score of zero suggests that they did indeed find the situation anomalous.

This research demonstrated that achieving representational insight can be very difficult, even when the symbol actually looks like what it stands for and even when children are explicitly told about the existence of the relation. As we have seen, an important part of the difficulty in understanding the relation between a scale model

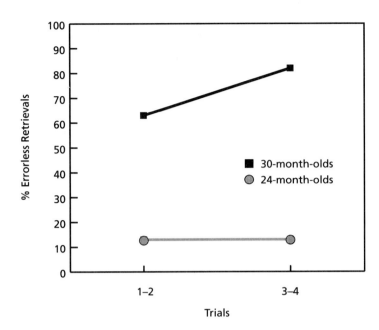

**FIGURE 5.5** Percentage errorless retrievals by the two age groups in the two trial blocks.

and what it stands for arises from the three-dimensional nature of the model—from the fact that the model is both a concrete object and a symbol and hence requires a dual representation.

One might be tempted to conclude that our discovery that young children have great difficulty achieving representational insight with scale models is an interesting but isolated phenomenon, and that the same difference would not arise with other, more familiar kinds of symbols. One would be wrong in drawing such a conclusion. The same basic pattern occurs for a different symbol system; one that is very common and familiar, even to very young children.

## YOUNG CHILDREN'S UNDERSTANDING OF PICTURES

We studied very young children's understanding of pictures in exactly the same way we studied their understanding of models (Burns, 1990; DeLoache & Burns, 1994). We started by simply asking whether children even younger than the 2.5-year-olds we had already studied could understand the relation between a picture and what it represented. We know, of course, that children of this age and younger can identify pictures; they can point to named objects and can label depicted objects and people. What we wanted to know was whether they would understand that a picture can give them information about the world—that it can tell them something they do not know.

In our first study (DeLoache & Burns, 1994), we compared the performance of a group of 2.0-year-olds in the picture task described earlier (using the wide-angle photograph and line drawing) to that of a group of 2.5-year-olds. Somewhat to our surprise, the results were remarkably like those in the original model study. As Figure 5.5 shows, the 2.5-year-olds understood the relation between the picture and what it represented (72 percent correct retrievals overall). In contrast, the 2.0-year-olds seemed to have no idea that the picture told them anything about the location of the hidden toy. Their score of 13 percent was solely attributable to one of the eight subjects who found the toy on every trial. The other seven 2.0-year-olds *never* had an errorless retrieval.

**FIGURE 5.6** Percentage errorless retrievals by the three age groups in the
two trial blocks.

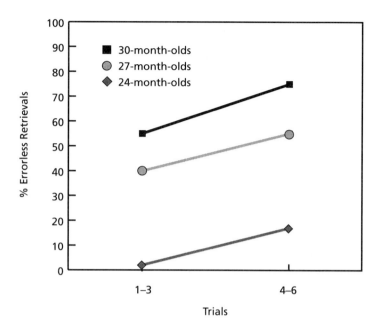

Intrigued by this result, we conducted a series
of studies further probing 2.0-year-olds' understanding of pictures. We reasoned that perhaps a
source of difficulty was the necessity to generate
an image of the hidden toy in its hiding place.
Recall that the pictures depicted the room and its
furnishings, and the experimenter pointed to the
appropriate location, telling the child that was
where the toy was hidden. If 2.0-year-olds have
difficulty constructing an image to guide their
search, their failure in our study might have had
more to do with limited imaginative capabilities
than with limited understanding of pictures.

To test this idea, we used pictures that actually depicted the toy in its hiding place. For example, one picture showed a Big Bird toy on the
floor behind an armchair. Another depicted Big
Bird hidden inside a basket. Thus, the child did
not have to imagine the toy in the designated
location. We again tested 2.0- and 2.5-year-old
children, and we also tested a group of children
intermediate in age between the other two
groups (M = 27 months).

The results were quite clear. As Figure 5.6
shows, the 2.5-year-olds were again successful,

especially on the second block of trials, whereas
the 2.0-year-olds were again remarkably unsuccessful. Performance on the first block of trials
was zero; on the second block, the scores for all
but one subject were again zero. One child
caught on and was correct on all of the last three
trials. Thus, the poor performance of 2.0-year-
olds in the previous picture study was not due
to problems constructing an image to guide
their search.

We conducted two further studies to try to
increase the performance of 2.0-year-olds in our
picture task. In one, we gave each subject an
extensive orientation that incorporated several
features we thought might help the children realize the correspondence between the pictures
and what they represented: The experimenter
showed the child all of the hiding locations that
would be used and labeled each one. With the
child watching, the experimenter placed the toy
in each of these locations. The test photographs,
each of which depicted the toy hidden in one of
the locations, were also shown to the child in relation to the actual scenes they depicted. The experimenter explicitly pointed out the relation

between the picture of the hidden toy and the toy actually in that location. Thus, before the experimental trials began, the child had seen all of the experimental materials, had seen the toy in each of the hiding places, and had had the correspondence between each picture and its referent explicitly described. This extended orientation had very little impact; performance was 16 percent, not significantly better than the 6 percent achieved with the standard orientation.

The final study in this series was designed to see if 2.0-year-olds' performance might be improved by demonstrating how a picture comes to depict its referent. During the orientation, the experimenter used a Polaroid camera to take pictures of the toy in appropriate locations in the room and pointed out the relation between each of the newly developed pictures and the corresponding object it depicted. During the test trials, the experimenter went into the room, hid the toy, activated the camera, and returned with a Polaroid picture that showed where the toy was hidden. Again, we had a small effect on the children's performance. The errorless retrieval rate was 27 percent (which was not significantly better than the 6 percent in the first study).

Earlier we asked why 2.5-year-olds have so much difficulty understanding that a scale model represents a room. Now we must ask why 2.0-year-olds have so much difficulty understanding pictures. We propose that the answer has to do with the *type* of representational relation that is involved in our picture and model tasks.

The symbols—picture or model—in our research are all specific representations. They all stand for something particular that actually exists: the room and the objects within it. These symbols have representational specificity.

## Representational Specificity

Many symbols are generic representations; they stand for a general idea or for a class of objects. The Statue of Liberty stands for various abstract principles and ideals, but no specific real entity. A commercial dollhouse represents houses in general, but no particular house, past or present.

Our research leads us to believe that representational specificity may be important developmentally. Generic representation is easier to understand and appears earlier; specific representation is more difficult and develops later. The 2.0-year-old children who did so poorly in our picture studies could identify Big Bird and all the other objects in the pictures we showed them. Nevertheless, they did not realize, even thought we told them, that the picture represented the present location of that particular Big Bird toy in that particular place in the room. The 2.5-year-olds who failed our model task saw the model as a toy room. They understood that the miniature chair in the model represented a chair, and that the little table corresponded to tables in general. These children still found it extremely difficult to realize that the miniature room represented the larger room that was next door, and that the little chair and table stood for the particular chair and table in that room.

Why is representational specificity so elusive for young children? We suggest that it may in large part have to do with infants' and toddlers' earliest experience with symbols—with the type of symbolic objects infants and young children typically encounter and the context in which they encounter them. A major source of early symbolic experience for children in our culture is picturebook reading. Virtually all of the pictures in young children's books are generic representations—the apples, dogs, and zebras in their baby books stand for those classes of objects in general, and not for any specific entities. In addition, young children's experience with books is highly decontextualized: It takes place in particular settings with particular people and has little or nothing to do with other experience. Children learn in these interactions how to treat pictures; they learn that you name and talk about depicted objects, but otherwise you respond to them very differently from how you respond to the real things they represent.

These young children are probably aware that the toy zoo they are constructing represents zoos in general. Understanding representational specificity—that the model can stand for a particular zoo—is a more difficult achievement. (Photo: Laura Berk)

## IMPLICATIONS FOR PRESCHOOL PRACTICE

Symbols are important in the life and education of young children. One crystal-clear finding from the research we discussed here is that we can never take for granted that young children will understand the basic relation between a symbol and its referent, no matter how obvious it seems to us or how familiar the materials are to the young child. Our scale model looks a lot like what is represents, but 2.5-year-olds remain oblivious to the correspondence. Pictures, such as the color photographs we used, not only look like what they represent, but they are a very familiar medium to infants and toddlers. Nevertheless, 2.0-year-olds showed surprising difficulty understanding pictures as a source of information.

Preschool teachers and parents are, of course, well acquainted with examples of a similar phenomenon. Young children who can faultlessly sing the alphabet song, and maybe even identify letters, are often unaware of what the letters stand for. Similarly, children recite numbers long before they understand anything about enumeration.

As our work and these examples reveal, representational insight is the crucial first step in understanding and using any symbol system. It is not an easy step.

How can one help a young child become aware of a symbol-referent relation? Our research shows it can be surprisingly difficult to help children achieve representational insight. One way we induced 2.5-year-olds to succeed with our standard-model task was to capitalize on their understanding of pictures. We found that children who first succeeded in our picture task were subsequently successful in the model task as well. Apparently, experience with one symbol system they understand can help young children understand a different one that they would not otherwise appreciate.

One implication is that a good approach to teaching young children about a new symbolic relation would be to make as much contact as possible between it and a symbol system they already understand. For example, one might employ pictures such as those used in our studies to introduce maps.

The concept of dual representation that emerged from our model research has many implications for preschool practice, especially with regard to materials. As our research reveals, one cannot necessarily rely on intuition about what materials will facilitate or impede symbolic functioning. The picture-superiority effect we found is counterintuitive in any context other than our model studies.

The clear message about materials is that, contrary to a common adult intuition, symbolic functioning may not be facilitated and may even be harmed by the use of concrete symbolic objects. Such objects are abundant in the homes and preschools in which toddlers spend their time. Plastic magnetic letters and numbers can be found on the refrigerators of thousands of homes across the United States. Letters and numbers of sandpaper and other materials are common in our preschools, as are appealing books shaped like their subject matter (for example, a book about tools in the shape of a hammer). The stores are full of "educational" toys of this ilk, one example being a set of plastic alphabet letters that join together (not in the proper order) to form a track for a Sesame Street train. These materials are designed or purchased with the explicit goal of helping young children learn about the alphabet and number system.

According to the dual representation hypothesis, these materials are probably counterproductive with respect to the very thing they are supposed to foster. They all invite children to treat them as objects. As we learned from the model studies, responding to something as an object—the natural inclination of very young children—makes it more difficult to appreciate it as a symbol.

There is some evidence, other than from the research discussed here, for the applicability of the dual representation concept to educational materials. In his research on the development of math skills, Stigler (personal communication, May 16, 1992) had occasion to use blocks (like those mentioned in the beginning of this article) that are designed for teaching arithmetic skills. He also designed computer analogs in which the same concepts are conveyed by combining bars of different lengths on a computer screen. Stigler observed that children often seem to do better when using the computer than when using the real objects. Our interpretation is that the concrete real objects, the blocks, distract the children somewhat from the abstract principles they represent. The two-dimensional images on the computer screen present no such challenge.

The use of other sorts of models in preschool teaching would be similarly suspect. For example, a teacher who uses a model of the human body to communicate to children about their own bodies might not be very effective if the children fail to make the connection between their own bodies and the doll.

Along these lines, we are currently investigating the use of dolls in children's eyewitness testimony. According to the dual representation hypothesis, very young children should find it difficult or impossible to understand an instruction to "pretend this doll is you; show me where he touched you." Our preliminary results are as expected; many young children do not seem to know how to interpret such suggestions, and performance is actually somewhat poorer using the dolls than not using them. Please note that the use of dolls in questioning young children who are capable of interpreting a doll as a representation of themselves may, as intended, facilitate their recall.

Finally, our discovery of the difficulty that young children have with representational specificity has implications for working with this age group. Children who understand a symbol in a generic sense (interpreting the model as a miniature room) may not understand its potential for specific reference (knowing it stand for the real room next door). It should help children come to appreciate the representational specificity of symbols if their attention is explicitly directed to the relation between symbols and their real-world referents. For example, when reading standard picture books to toddlers, one could discuss how the book content relates to their own direct experience. Presumably, it would be especially useful to make photo albums with pictures of events a child had personally experienced and to discuss them with the child.

In summary, research on young children's understanding and use of symbols makes us appreciate what challenges children face in sorting out the myriad symbols with which they are confronted daily. We know enough to be certain that there are numerous factors that help children gain insight into symbol-referent relations and numerous other factors that impede such insight. Our research to date has identified some of these factors, and future research will help us learn about others. Such knowledge should assist in the planning of curriculum and materials to facilitate the symbolic functioning of preschool children.

## EVALUATING YOUR MASTERY

1. Children's comprehension that a model of a room represents a real room develops between:
   a.   1.5 and 2.0 years of age
   b.   2.0 and 2.5 years of age
   c.   2.5 and 3.0 years of age
   d.   3.0 and 3.5 years of age

2. Which of the following helped young children achieve the representational insight that a model of a room stands for a real room?
   a.   Verbally labeling Little Snoopy's hiding place
   b.   Giving children extensive experience in the real room
   c.   Permitting children to play with Little Snoopy and Big Snoopy
   d.   Dramatically decreasing the size difference between the model and the room it represented

3. One reason for the poor performance of very young preschoolers in the model task is that they
   a.   Have difficulty remembering Little Snoopy's hiding place
   b.   Cannot pay attention long enough to find Big Snoopy
   c.   Have difficulty with generic representation of the model
   d.   Fail to achieve a dual representation of the model

4. Among preschoolers, understanding of pictures emerges _____ understanding of models.
   a.   Earlier than
   b.   Later than
   c.   At the same time as

5. True or False: DeLoache and Burns believe that young children's mastery of the picture and model tasks depends on the development of representational specificity.

6. True or False: The representational experiences young children typically have in picture-book reading are very similar to the representational demands of the model task.

## Critical Thinking

1. Why is specific representation more difficult for young preschoolers than generic representation?

2. Describe how make-believe play encourages children to look for new correspondences between the play scene and real world. How does this facilitate symbolic representation?

## Applying Your Knowledge

1. DeLoache and Burns suggest that a good approach to teaching young children about a new symbolic medium is to relate it to a symbol system they

already understand. Using this idea, create a plan for helping 3-year-olds grasp the meaning of a simple map of their classroom or play yard.

2. Visit a toy store, select five toys designed to teach preschoolers the representational meaning of letters or numbers, and evaluate the appropriateness of each based on DeLoache and Burns's conclusions about the early development of symbol–referent relations.

# 6

## The Psychological and Social Origins of Autobiographical Memory

KATHERINE NELSON

CUNY Graduate School

■

All that seems to truly distinguish episodic recall from generic event memory is the sense that "something happened one time" in contrast to the generic "things happen this way."

■

Remembering, then, involves reconstructing past events using presently existing schemas....

■

Recent research on episodic memory in early childhood indicates that children have at least some well-organized specific and general event memories, similar to those of adults....

■

A possible function of memory talk distinct from rehearsal is that of reinstatement.

■

Memories become valued in their own right—not because they predict the future and guide present action, but because they are shareable with others and thus serve a social solidarity function.

■

■

Deaf children of hearing parents might be expected to be delayed in establishing
early memories because of their lack of opportunities to engage in talk about
past experience.

■

## EDITOR'S INTRODUCTION

Katherine Nelson addresses *autobiographical memory,* long-lasting recollections of
personally meaningful events that each of us weaves into a life story. Her analysis
of research sheds new light on the origins of autobiographical memory and the
related, mysterious phenomenon of *childhood,* or *infantile, amnesia,* the inability of
older children and adults to recall events that happened to them before age 3 or 4.

An understanding of autobiographical memory, Nelson points out, requires
an appreciation of several everyday memory forms. *Episodic memory* is our memory for personally experienced events. *Autobiographical memory* is a type of episodic
memory—events that are unique and personally significant in our lives. A second
type of episodic memory is *generic event memory,* or memory for repeated events,
such as getting ready in the morning, going to class, or running errands on Saturday morning. We sketch the broad outlines of these familiar events, leaving out
details, thereby forming *scripts,* or general representations of what occurs and
when it occurs in a particular situation. For example, you probably have difficulty recalling exactly what you wore three or four days ago because you scripted
it—fused many instances of getting ready in the morning into an inclusive structure of main acts, such as taking a shower, getting dressed, and eating breakfast.
Autobiographical memory is quite different from general event memory. Because
it focuses on unique events that are invested with personal significance, it is very
detailed. Notice how well you recall what you wore on a special day, such as a
birthday or graduation.

What explains infantile amnesia and its opposite—the development of autobiographic memory after age 3? Examining developmental research, Nelson
builds a convincing case that autobiographical memory requires language and the
ability to converse with others. As parents, teachers, and caregivers talk with
young children about the past, these adults guide children in constructing a personal life story. As a result, cultural values about what is important to remember
and the narrative form of personal memory are transmitted to children, who
"enter into the social and cultural history of their family and community."

Remembering past events is a universally familiar experience. It is also a uniquely human one. As far as we know, members of no other species possess quite the same ability to experience again now, in a different situation and perhaps in a different form, happenings from the past, and know that the experience refers to an event that occurred in another time and in another place. Other members of the animal kingdom . . . cannot travel back into the past in their own minds. (Tulving, 1983, p. 1)

This passage introducing Tulving's book on **episodic memory** makes a strong claim, similar to the more familiar claim of the uniqueness of human language. If remembering past events is uniquely human, as Tulving claims, the point calls out for further investigation. What is the significance of this ability for human social and psychological functioning? How and why does it arise **phylogenetically** and **ontogenetically**? Is it related to other uniquely human functions such as language, symbolic cognitive processing, and the establishment of complex cultures?

Tulving's claim is controversial and has been argued extensively (see commentators on Tulving, 1984). For the purposes of this article, I take it as an assumption to be examined, but I confine the assumption only to the late-developing type of episodic memory that humans possess, namely **autobiographical memory**. And I examine the assumption in the course of addressing the question of why a specific kind of episodic memory—autobiographical memory—may develop in human childhood.

For the developmental account outlined here, it is important to distinguish not only between semantic and episodic memory, as Tulving has, but also between generic event memory, episodic memory, and autobiographical memory, taking autobiographical memory as a subtype of episodic. **Generic event memory** (not specifically con-sidered by Tulving) provides a schema derived from experience that sketches the general outline of a familiar event without providing details of the specific time or place when such an event happened, whether once or many times. A basic type of this kind of general schema is the **script** (Schank & Abelson, 1977) that specifies the sequence of actions and empty slots for roles and props that may be filled in with default values, in the absence of specifications. Generic event memory may also be considered for some purposes a type of semantic memory in that it crosscuts the distinctions that Tulving set forth.

Both of Tulving's memory types (and those considered in this article) fall under the **declarative memory** system distinguished by Squire (1992) or the **explicit memory** system described by Schacter (1992), which involve conscious recollection of previous experiences. The present distinctions among memory types are adopted primarily for the purpose of interpreting the developmental research and providing an explanation for the establishment of a "life history" memory.

In contrast to generic event memory, an episodic memory has the phenomenal characteristic of referring to something that happened once at a specific time and place. But the specific identification of time and place does not seem to be necessarily part of episodic recall, although adults can often reconstruct an episodic memory from different types of cues and find a way of identifying a specific time and place at which a specific event was experienced, even if the location is not available in declarative form. All that seems to truly distinguish episodic recall from generic event memory is the sense that "something happened *one* time" in contrast to the generic "things happen this way." Yet it is not at all clear that this somewhat vague impression (of "one time") will bear the weight of Tulving's claim of human uniqueness. We simply do not know whether other animals, or even human

Nelson, K. (1993). The psychological and social origins of autobiographical memory. *Psychological Science,*
*1,* 1–8. © 1993 The American Psychological Society. Reprinted by permission of Cambridge University
Press and the author.

infants, experience a phenomenal difference between remembering and knowing, differentiating between one-time happenings and usual happenings. They very well might.

Equally important, not all episodic memory is *autobiographical memory*. This point is critical to the theoretical and empirical explication of the development of autobiographical memory. To take a simple example, what I ate for lunch yesterday is today part of my episodic memory, but being unremarkable in any way, it will not, I am quite sure, become part of my autobiographical memory. It has no significance to my life story beyond the general schema of lunch. In contrast, the first time I presented a paper at a conference is part of my autobiographical memory: I remember the time, place, and details of the program and participants, and I have a sense of how that experience fits into the rest of my personal life story. It is important to make this distinction at the outset because, as recent research has established, very young children do have episodic memories, but do not yet have autobiographical memory of this kind.

Autobiographical memory as used here is specific, personal, long-lasting, and (usually) of significance to the self-system. Phenomenally, it forms one's personal life history. Prior to the development of this system, memories do not become part of a personally known life history, although of course they may be important in other ways to one's life, and one may derive a strong sense of one's early history from hearing about it from other people.

Autobiographical memory has its onset during the early childhood years. Surprisingly, it is only recently that this onset has been thought of in developmental terms. In the past, it has usually been conceived of in terms of **childhood** (or **infantile**) **amnesia,** the phenomenon, first identified by Freud (1963) and familiar to all who reflect on it, that memories for events from the early years of our lives—before about 3 to 4 years—are not available to adult consciousness, although many memories from later childhood usually are easily called up.

The onset of autobiographical memory is simply the inverse of infantile amnesia. In the present framework, the critical questions are when and why an autobiographical system— in which some memories are retained for a lifetime—becomes differentiated from a general episodic system.

Most of the research on childhood amnesia— the period of life before the onset of autobiographical memory—has come from studies of adults' recall of childhood memories, beginning with a questionnaire study by Henri and Henri in 1897 (see review by Dudycha & Dudycha, 1941). As in many studies that followed, they asked adults ($N = 120$) to recall their earliest memories from childhood and reported the data in terms of the number of childhood memories from a given age range. No memories were reported from before 2 years, but 71 percent of the subjects had some memories from the period between 2 and 4 years of age. Summarizing over large number of such studies, Pillemer and White (1989) found that the earliest memory is reported on average at about 3½ years. They noted that there are actually two phases of childhood amnesia, the first a total blocking of memories, usually prior to about 3 years, and the second, between 3 and 6 years, a significant drop-off of accessible memories relative to later memories. Such a pattern has been verified by the analysis of the **forgetting curve** for adult recall of childhood memories (Wetzler & Sweeney, 1986). However, it is important to note also that there is considerable variability both in age of earliest memory—from 2 years to 8 years or even later—and in number of memories reported from early childhood. In the early empirical literature on the topic, the age of earliest memory has been negatively correlated with IQ, language ability, and social class, and females tend to have earlier memories than males.

It is commonly objected that the data on early childhood memories are unreliable and unverifiable, but for the following reasons these objections do not invalidate the conclusions drawn. First, those who can reliably date their memories—

because they experienced moves or other disruptions during early childhood—or whose parents can verify events (Usher & Neisser, 1991) exhibit the same general age relations as those suggested by the overall research. For example, it is rare to find anyone who claims to remember a specific incident from before the age of 2 years. Moreover, a study of memory for the birth of a sibling, which could be definitively dated, showed the same age relation as the questionnaire data: Children could remember the event if it occurred when they were 3 years or older, but not before that age (Sheingold & Tenney, 1982).

The validity of any given memory is not relevant within the present theoretical framework. Although the validity of a memory may be of concern if one is interested in such issues as whether children are reliable witnesses, it is of less concern if one is interested in when they begin to retain memories in the autobiographical memory system. Memories do not need to be true or correct to be part of that system.

The term childhood amnesia implies that something was there and is lost. This in turn implies that we need to find an explanation either in terms of loss or in terms of some force that interferes with retrieval of memories that still exist, as Freud proposed. The alternative possibility explored here is that something develops that leads to a new organization of memory or the establishment of a new memory system or function. These possibilities can be evaluated only in terms of the study of memory during the period prior to and subsequent to the emergence of autobiographical memory. The adult research, on the basis of which so much of the discussion has been based, can tell us only that the phenomenon is real; it cannot reveal anything about its development.

## EVIDENCE FROM DEVELOPMENTAL RESEARCH

Research on memory in very early childhood is very recent, coming mostly from the past 15 years. My colleagues and I began investigations of children's event memory in the mid-1970s, and our early studies revealed that 3-year-olds are quite good at telling what happens in general in a familiar event such as having lunch at the preschool or going to McDonald's, but they are relatively poor at telling what happened on one particular occasion (Nelson, 1978; Nelson & Gruendel, 1981). These early findings suggested to us an explanation for infantile amnesia, namely, that children do not preserve episodic memories, although they may remember bits of information from specific events in their schematic event memory. In early childhood, we believed, all information retained from experience is absorbed by the generic memory system. Recently, Gopnik and Graf (1988) and Perner (1991) have suggested similar "overwrite" mechanisms.

However, this hypothesis—that young children have generic memory only—has not stood up to empirical test. Subsequent research indicated that very young children do remember novel events, within limits, and sometimes quite readily report episodes that they find interesting (Hudson, 1986; Ratner, 1980). When asked about routine events, they simply give routine answers, but when asked about novel events, they are sometimes able to respond with details even when as young as 2½ years. More recent research has verified that children do have specific episodic memories and can remember them for extensive periods—sometimes as long as 2 years—prior to the age of the earliest autobiographical memories reported by adults (see Fivush & Hudson, 1990, for reviews). Why do these memories not persist into later childhood and adulthood?

Not only does this research invalidate the proposal that memory is at first completely generic, but it calls into question some other theoretical proposals as well. For example, there is nothing in this recent evidence to support the idea that young children's memories are especially threatening, either positively or negatively affect laden, as Freud's theory would suggest.

Schachtel (1947) and Neisser (1962) suggested that autobiographical memories are the outcome of a reconstructive process based on schemas or

What determines whether this opportunity to view these parrots closely will become part of these preschoolers' autobiographical memories? According to recent research, as this teacher converses with the children about the event, it becomes personally significant and more memorable for the children. (Photo: Frederick Ebbeck)

frames of reference, along the lines suggested by Bartlett (1932). Remembering, then, involves *reconstructing* past events using presently existing schemas, and the claim is that adult schemas are not "suitable receptacles" for early childhood experience; "adults cannot think like children" and thus cannot make use of whatever fragments of memories they may retain. In this view, **socialization** and the impact of language force a drastic change in the child's schemas at age 6.

The recent developmental data cast doubt on this proposal as well. Although very young children often need extensive probing to elicit their memories, suggesting that they may retain only random and unschematized fragments, there is also evidence of specific episodic memories that have the same form as we might find in older children. A fragment from a 2½-year-old girl talking to herself when alone in her room is illustrative:

> We *bought* a baby, cause, well because, when she, well, we *thought* it was for Christmas, but *when* we went to the s-s-store we didn't have our jacket on, but I saw some

dolly, and I *yelled* at my mother and said I want one of those dolly. So after we were finished with the store, we went over to the dolly and she *bought* me one. So I have one.

In this example, Emily was recounting to herself what apparently was a significant episode in her life (she had not rehearsed this recent episode with her parents or others; see Nelson, 1989, for further details). This recount is well organized, with clear and concise temporal and causal sequencing. It—and others like it—does not suggest that the preschool child's schemas are dramatically different from those of the older child and adult.

Indeed, recent reports of young children's free recall of salient episodic memories (Engel, 1986; Hudson, 1990; Tessler, 1991) support the conclusion that the basic ways of structuring, representing, and interpreting reality are consistent from early childhood into adulthood. These studies indicate that young children, in both their script recounts and their specific memory recounts, typically tell their stories in a sequence that accurately reflects the sequence of the experience itself and that has the same boundaries that seem natural to adult listeners (Nelson, 1986).

Of course, there may be other differences between adult and child memories, including what is noticed and remembered of an event. The extensive cueing and probing often required to elicit details from a young child suggest that adult and child may have different memories of the same event. An analysis of the content of crib talk (talk to self alone before sleep) by the child Emily, recorded from 21 to 36 months, supports the suggestion that adult and child may focus on different events and different aspects of events. Emily's memories were concerned mostly with the quotidian, unremarkable, routines of her life. They were not concerned with the truly novel events of her life (from the adult's point of view), such as the birth of her baby brother or her airplane trips to visit relatives (Nelson, 1989). Thus, interest in—and therefore memory for—aspects of experience that seem unremarkable to adults, and indifference to what adults find interesting, as well as lack of facility with language and differences in the knowledge base, may account for why children sometimes seem to have organized their knowledge in a different form or have remembered only fragments from an episode that adults consider memorable.

In summary, recent research on episodic memory in early childhood indicates that children have at least some well-organized specific and general event memories, similar to those of adults; thus, the suggestion that a schematic reorganization may account for infantile amnesia is not supported. However, recent research that has shown that children learn to talk about their past experiences in specific ways does provide some clues as to what may be developing and how.

## NARRATIVE CONSTRUCTION OF MEMORY

Over the past decade, a number of researchers have studied the ways in which parents engage in talking about the past with their very young children. These studies, some focused on the specific language forms used, others on the content of talk, and still others on narrative forms and differences in communicative styles, have revealed the active role that parents play in framing and guiding their children's formulation of "what happened."

Hudson (1990) concluded from a study of her own daughter's memory talk between 21 and 27 months that eventually Rachel began to "interpret the conversations not as a series of questions to be answered but as an *activity of remembering*" (p. 183). Hudson endorses a *social interaction model* of the development of autobiographical memory, a model that Pillemer and White (1989) and Fivush and Reese (1991) have also invoked. In this view, children gradually learn the forms of how to talk about memories with others, and thereby also how to formulate their own memories as narratives. The social interaction model differs from the schematic change model in that it claims that children learn *how* to formulate their memories and thus retain them in recoverable form.

Several studies at the City University of New York (and elsewhere) have found that parents not only engage in memory talk but also differ among themselves in the number of memory-relevant questions they ask, the kind of memory they attempt to elicit, and the ways in which they frame the talk. Engel (1986) studied mother-child conversations about past episodes with children from 18 months to 2 years and identified two styles of mother talk, one described as *elaborative,* the other more *pragmatic.* The elaborative mothers tended to talk about episodes in narrative terms of what happened when, where, and with whom. Pragmatic mothers referred to memory primarily in instrumental terms, such as "where did you put your mittens?" For pragmatic mothers, memory is useful for retrieving information relevant to ongoing activities. For elaborative mothers, memory provides the basis for storytelling, constructing narratives about what mother and child did together in the there and then. Engel found that children of elaborative mothers contributed more information to the memory talk at 2 years than children of pragmatic mothers.

Tessler (1986, 1991) studied the effect of adult talk during an experience on children's subsequent memory for the experience in two naturalistically designed experiments. She observed differences in mothers' style of interaction similar to those identified by Engel and found that children of narrative (or elaborative) mothers remembered more from a trip to a natural history museum a week later, when probed with a standard set of questions, than did children of pragmatic-type mothers. Most strikingly, none of the children remembered any of the objects that they viewed in the museum if they had not talked about them together with their mothers. In a second study, Tessler found that there was no difference between children experiencing different types of interaction with mothers during an event in recognizing elements of the experience, but there were differences in the amount of information recalled from the experience, with the children of narrative mothers recalling significantly more. Again, things that were not talked about were not recalled. These findings indicate not only that talk about the past is effective in aiding the child to establish a narrative memory about the past, but that talk during a present activity serves a similar purpose. In both cases, adults who present the activity in a narrative format, in contrast to a focus on identification and categorization, appear to be more effective in establishing and eliciting memories with their young children. Could this be important in establishing an autobiographical memory system? The social interaction hypothesis would certainly suggest so.

## EFFECTS OF LANGUAGE ON MEMORY

What is it that talking about events—past and present—contributes to memory? The social interaction hypothesis emphasizes learning to structure memories in narrative form. Another suggestion might be the effects of **rehearsal**. However, there

are two indications that rehearsal is not the major contributor. First, children are frequently unresponsive to maternal probing (Fivush & Fromhoff, 1988), suggesting that often the event being talked about was not what the child remembered but what the adult remembered. Second, available evidence suggests that events that do seem rehearsed are not subsequently remembered. For example, Emily sometimes recounted an event many times during an evening's session of crib talk but did not apparently remember the event months later (Nelson, 1989) or when probed years later (Nelson, unpublished data). Emily seemed to be attempting to understand the events she took part in, and to use them in her representation of her world, but not for holding on to memories of specific episodes. Long-term follow-up studies of memories rehearsed in early childhood are obviously important but are very rare. In one instance, similar to the findings from Emily, J. A. Hudson (personal communication, April 1992) has indicated that her daughter at 8 years remembers nothing of the events they rehearsed together when she was 2.

In a unique follow-up study, Hudson and Fivush (1991) reported on the long-term memories of sixth graders for a class trip they took as kindergartners. Some memories of the trip could be retrieved when the children were probed and viewed pictures taken at the time, but none of the children spontaneously recalled the event. These children would have been on the edge of the amnesia barrier at age 5 or 6 when they experienced the event; however, the trip may not have seemed personally significant, or may have been absorbed into the generic memory of class trips as years went by.

A possible function of memory talk distinct from rehearsal is that of **reinstatement**. Reinstatement is a concept that has been invoked in infant memory studies by Royce-Collier and Hayne (1987). The idea is that a learned response (for example, kicking to make a mobile move) that would otherwise be lost over time may be reinstated and thus preserved if a part of the context is represented within a given time period. A study by Fivush and Hamond (1989) with 2-year-old children found a similar effect; specific memories that tended to be lost over a period of weeks could be retained if they were reinstated by providing an experience similar to the original event at least once within a specific period of time—in this case, 2 weeks. In a memory test 3 months later, children whose memory had been reinstated remembered significantly more than children who had not had this experience. Equally important, the reinstated group remembered as much at 3 months as they had at 2 weeks; that is, there was no subsequent loss.

## FUNCTIONS OF EARLY MEMORY

At this point, it may be possible to construct an integrated picture of the development of memory in early childhood and the establishment of an autobiographical memory system. The proposal rests on the assumption that the basic episodic memory system is part of a general mammalian learning-memory adaptive function for guiding present action and predicting future outcomes. The most useful memory for this function is generic memory for routines that fit recurrent situations, that is, a general event schema (or script) memory system. Memory for a specific episode presumably becomes part of that system when a new situation is encountered, and thus it becomes apparent that a new schema must be established. A new experience alerts the organism (person, animal) to set up a new schema, which at first may be equivalent to an episodic memory, but with further experience with events of the same kind comes to be more and more scriptlike. Indeed, research on novel and repeated events with preschool children found that this was precisely what happened (Hudson & Nelson, 1986). The more frequently an event (such as going to the beach or the zoo) had been experienced, the more scriptlike the child's account became. Events experienced five or more times tended to be formulated in general present-tense terms and to confuse slot-fillers (for example, animals seen) for different episodes of the event.

This general scheme leaves us with a problem, however: How is the basic memory system to know whether a novel event is the first of a recurrent series of events that should therefore be remembered (that is, schematized for future reference) or is an aberration that is of no functional significance? (Of course, if the aberration is life-threatening, it is likely to be entered into the general memory and knowledge system as important information for that reason alone.) The point is, the system cannot know on the basis of one encounter what significance the event might have with respect to future encounters.

The solution for a limited memory system is either to integrate the new information as part of the generic system or to keep the novel memory in a separate, temporary, episodic memory for a given amount of time to determine if it is the first of a series of recurrent events and thus should become part of the generic system. Then, if the event reoccurs, the memory may be transferred to the more permanent generic memory system. If a similar event does not recur during that test period, the episode is dropped from memory as of no adaptive significance.

Reinstatement would play an important part in this proposal. Reinstatement signals that the episode is not a one-time occurrence and thus the memory should be retained for future reference. Reinstatement would extend the amount of time that a memory is held in the episodic system, as found by Royce-Collier and Hayne (1987) and by Fivush and Hamond (1989). In the basic functionally based system being described here, all memory is either generic knowledge—scriptlike—or temporarily episodic. The basic episodic system is claimed to be a *holding pattern,* not a permanent memory system. I suggest that this basic system characterizes human infants and young children and probably our close primate relatives as well, and perhaps other mammals.

Thus far then, the proposed system can account for the good generic event memory found in early childhood, as well as the availability of episodic memories that may persist for 6 months, or longer if there are conditions of reinstatement.

But this proposal does not account for the establishment of an autobiographical memory system in which some specific memories may persist for a lifetime. This raises the question as to what function the autobiographical system serves beyond that of the long-lasting generic plus temporary episodic system just described.

The claim here is that the initial functional significance of autobiographical memory is that of sharing memory with other people, a function that language makes possible. Memories become valued in their own right—not because they predict the future and guide present action, but because they are shareable with others and thus serve a social solidarity function. I suggest that this is a universal human function, although one with variable, culturally specific rules. In this respect, it is analogous to human language itself, uniquely and universally human but culturally—and individually—variable. I suggest further that this social function of memory underlies all of our storytelling, history-making narrative activities, and ultimately all of our accumulated knowledge systems.

The research briefly reviewed here supports these speculations. Children learn to engage in talk about the past, guided at first by parents who construct a narrative around the bits and pieces contributed by the child (Eisenberg, 1985; Engel, 1986; Hudson, 1990). The timing of this learning (beginning at about 2½ years and continuing through the preschool years) is consistent with the age at which autobiographical memory begins to emerge. The fact that the adult data suggest a two-phase process, as noted earlier, including the absence of memories in the first 2 to 3 years, followed by a sparse but increasing number of memories in the later preschool years, supports the supposition that the establishment of these memories is related to the experience of talking to other people about them. Also, the variability in age of onset of autobiographical memory (from 2 to 8 years or later) and its relation to language facility is consistent with the idea that children's experiences in sharing memories of the right kind

and in the right form contribute to the establishment of autobiographical memory.

The social interaction hypothesis outlined earlier clearly fits these data well. This proposal is not simply one of cultural transmission or socialization, but rather a **dialectical** or Vygotskian **model** in which the child takes over the forms of adult thought through transactions with adults in activity contexts where those forms are employed in this case, in the activities where memories are formed and shared. The problem that the child faces in taking on new forms and functions is to coordinate earlier memory functions with those that the adult displays, incorporating adult values about what is important to remember, and the narrative formats for remembering, into his or her own existing functional system.

This, then, is the functional part of the proposal, suggesting that sharing memories with other people performs a significant sociocultural function, the acquisition of which means that the child can enter into the social and cultural history of the family and community. However, identifying this function, and some of the social-linguistic experiences that support it, does not in itself explain why personal autobiographical memories continue to persist. For that explanation we must call on an additional function of language.

Recall that reinstatement through action was shown to be effective in establishing the persistence of a memory of an event. I hypothesize that an important development takes place when the process of sharing memories with others through language becomes available as a means of reinstating memory. (See also Hudson, 1990.) Further, I suggest that language as a medium of reinstatement is not immediately available when mothers and their young children first begin to exchange talk about a remembered experience.

Rather, reinstatement through language requires a certain level of facility with language, and especially the ability to use the verbal representation of another person to set up a representation in one's own mental representation system, thus recognizing the verbal account as a reinstatement of one's prior experience. Using another person's verbal representation of an event as a partial reinstatement of one's own representation (memory) depends on the achievement of language as a representational system in its own right, and not only as either an organizing tool or a communication tool. This achievement is, I believe, a development of the late preschool years (Nelson, 1990).

In summary, the theoretical claim here is that language opens up possibilities for sharing and retaining memories in a culturally shared format for both personal and social functions. Sharing memory narratives is important to establish the new social function of autobiographical memory, as well as to make reinstatement through language possible. Following Vygotsky's (1978) model of **internalization,** after overt recounting becomes established, covert recounting or re-experiencing to oneself may take place, and take on the function of reinstatement.

If memory is not talked about, to oneself or to others, should it persist? Once an autobiographical memory system is established, it takes on a personal as well as a social value in defining the self, as other scholars (for example, Fivush, 1988) have recently argued. Thus, replaying a memory, even without talking about it specifically, overtly or covertly, might well reinstate it and cause it to persist, once the autobiographical system is set in motion.

A number of lines of research are suggested by this proposal. For example, a shift in linguistic communities should disrupt autobiographical memory, because of its dependence on linguistic representations, and there is some evidence from D. Pillemer's (personal communication, March 1990) work that such is the case. Also, the number of recounting opportunities should be important, and this might be variable across families

and communities. Deaf children of hearing parents might be expected to be delayed in establishing early memories because of their lack of opportunities to engage in talk about past experiences. Cultural differences in discourse practices might be expected to lead to differences in autobiographical memory. Most of our present evidence is from middle-class Western children. In other cultures, for example, cultures that discourage children's participation in adult talk, such as the Mayan (Rogoff & Mistry, 1990), autobiographical memory might be a very late development, or take on different cultural forms such as shared myths.

To conclude, autobiographical memory may be thought of as a function that comes into play at a certain point in human childhood when the social conditions foster it and the child's representational system is accessible to the linguistic formulations presented by other people.

Finally, to return to Tulving's claim, memory, that is, autobiographical memory, "is a universally familiar experience. It is also a uniquely human one." It is uniquely human because of its dependence on linguistic representations of events, and because human language itself is uniquely human. As Miller (1990) has recently stressed, human language is unique in serving the dual function of mental representation and communication. These dual functions make possible its use in establishing the autobiographical memory system. And because such memory is at once both personal and social, it enables us not only to cherish our private memories, but also to share them with others, and to construct shared histories as well as imagined stories, in analogy with reconstructed true episodes. Once the child has begun to share memories with others, he or she is well on the way to sharing all of the accumulated cultural knowledge offered at home, in school or in the larger world.

## EVALUATING YOUR MASTERY

1. Which of the following is most likely to become part of 5-year-old Susan's autobiographical memory?
   a. The peanut butter sandwich she had for lunch yesterday
   b. The time she usually goes to bed
   c. Great grandmother Tillie's ninetieth birthday celebration
   d. Her monthly haircut at Sandy's Salon

2. Which of the following represents Nelson's view of autobiographical memory?
   a. Memories were once there but lost.
   b. Memories emerge spontaneously.
   c. Memories are reorganized through social experience.
   d. Memories develop through exploration of the physical world.

3. Which of the following is true about early childhood memory?
   a. Basic ways of representing reality are the same in early childhood as in adulthood.
   b. Children represent reality in very different ways than adults do.
   c. Children do not represent reality until 3 to 4 years of age.
   d. Both children and adults have difficulty forming specific episodic memories.

4. Which child is likely to remember more about a trip to a natural history museum one week after the experience?
   a. David, whose mother is highly intelligent
   b. Eric, whose mother takes him on lots of outings
   c. Sean, whose mother likes to talk about what happened, when, and with whom
   d. John, whose mother likes to ask, "How many animals did you see? What are their names?"

5. Children of [elaborative/pragmatic] mothers contribute more to memory discussions at 2 years of age.

6. According to Nelson, [rehearsal/reinstatement] is a possible function of memory talk with others.

7. True or False: The functional significance of autobiographical memory is that of sharing memory with other people.

## Critical Thinking

1. When adults talk about the past with their young children, what other aspects of development are they supporting in addition to autobiographical memory? Explain.

2. Why might deaf children of hearing parents be expected to be delayed in establishing early autobiographical memories?

## Applying Your Knowledge

Ask a parent to discuss a significant one-time experience with his or her preschool child, such as a special excursion or a birthday party. Did the parent use an elaborative or pragmatic style to talk about the past? Explain how that style might affect the child's autobiographical memory. Do the child's recollections reflect the parent's style?

# 7

🪶

# Intersubjectivity in Caregiver-Child Communication

## VICTORIA WHITINGTON & CHRISTY WARD
### University of South Australia

■

Followers of Vygotsky have used the term intersubjectivity to capture the complex, multidimensional nature of children's relationships with significant adults, regarded as essential for optimal development.

■

Clearly, emotion is an essential component of intersubjectivity, and infants and children are very sensitive to emotional indicators in their communication with close adults.

■

In Vygotsky's sociocultural theory, development takes place within the zone of proximal development, or, a range of tasks that are too challenging for children to accomplish by themselves, but that they are able to master with the assistance of a more skilled partner.

■

Children brought up in societies where they participate in the daily work of adults at an early age are in a prime position to observe and learn how to be a successful member of the community.

■

The level of education of caregivers has been shown to be important in the responsivity of their interactions.

■

Intersubjectivity achieved with toddlers has some qualities in common with that of infants, but the greatest attainment of this period is spoken language.

■

It is important to note that the ability to share meanings with adults, be they parents or caregivers, prepares the child to share meanings with peers.

■

Because caregivers are responsible for groups of children, it is important to capitalize on moments when routines create conditions for one-to-one communication.

■

## EDITOR'S INTRODUCTION

Given the large number of mothers of infants and preschoolers in the labor force, Victoria Whitington and Christy Ward argue that relationships between substitute caregivers and young children are central to children's development. To capture the essential ingredients of the caregiver-child tie, Whitington and Ward draw on the concept of intersubjectivity, inspired by Vygotsky's sociocultural theory. Development-enhancing communication, they point out, involves more than a transfer of information from one partner to another; it requires joint, mutual understanding, realized through subtle verbal and nonverbal cues.

Whitington and Ward discuss age-related changes in the roles of caregivers and children in establishing intersubjectivity. Over time, children who have experienced sensitive interaction become increasingly capable of contributing to its future realization. The authors explain the relevance of intersubjectivity to other well-known Vygotskian concepts—namely, the zone of proximal development and scaffolding. Furthermore, they point out that intersubjectivity is achieved in different ways, depending on the style of interaction valued by the child's culture. But in all societies, intersubjectivity is crucial for two key social processes that foster development: (1) creating bridges between what children currently know and what they are about to experience, and (2) providing opportunities and support for involvement in meaningful activities.

The authors consider special obstacles to achieving intersubjectivity in child care settings and suggest ways to increase its occurrence. Their discussion is rich in illustrations of adult–child communication in which intersubjective, shared understandings are realized.

A nine-month-old baby is in her mother's arms as the mother talks with the child's caregiver. The baby looks at a colorful mobile hanging from the ceiling.

Caregiver (following the baby's gaze): That's a lovely color, isn't it? (The baby smiles and holds out her hand to touch one of the birds, but she cannot reach it.)

Caregiver: Would you like to touch it? Here it is. (She pulls the bird over so the child can touch it. The baby's face lights up with joy.)

In Australia, 48.6 percent of mothers with children between birth and 5 years of age are employed, 14.3 percent of them full time (Australian Bureau of Statistics, 1993). In the United States, these figures are even higher: 65 percent of American children under age 6 have mothers in the labor force (U.S. Bureau of the Census, 1996). As rearing young children is increasingly shared with nonparental caregivers, the quality of care offered outside the home is of great interest to parents and professionals alike. Indeed, parents in Australia, the United States, and elsewhere in the Western world expect that this care will foster the development of their children in much the same way as their own care does (Hoffman & Lilja, 1988; see also F. Ebbeck, Chapter 11 of this volume).

Evaluations of child care have typically been structured along the lines of the academic disciplines. Researchers have examined children's emotional, cognitive, and social progress separately, paying particular attention to cognitive and language development. Vygotsky's sociocultural theory of development proposes that, instead, we view children in a more holistic way and emphasize the child's development in social context (Ratner & Stettner, 1991). From this vantage point, relationships between children and their substitute caregivers are at the heart of high-quality child care (Smith, 1993; Stremmel & Fu, 1993).

Followers of Vygotsky have used the term **intersubjectivity** to capture the complex, multidimensional nature of children's relationships with significant adults, regarded as essential for optimal development. Generally speaking, intersubjectivity refers to the process whereby two individuals who begin with different understandings arrive at a joint understanding (Berk & Winsler, 1995). In child-care centers and family day-care homes, even widely endorsed standards for adult–child ratios—1:4 for babies, 1:7 for toddlers, and 1:10 for preschoolers—can lead organizational matters to take precedence over the quality of adult–child interaction. Therefore, in such settings, we cannot assume that intersubjectivity will take place; it might have to be a conscious focus for caregivers.

The purpose of this article is to describe the concept of intersubjectivity in detail, using examples from infants, toddlers, and preschoolers in child care contexts. Strategies for early childhood programs will be suggested that increase the likelihood that intersubjectivity will be attained.

## WHAT IS INTERSUBJECTIVITY?

Since its introduction by Newson and Newson (1975), the concept of intersubjectivity has generated much research and discussion in the fields of early childhood development, care, and education. An extensive body of research on mothers and young children provides the starting point for investigating the young child's experiences with professional caregivers. (Despite the fact that most research on intersubjectivity has been carried out on mothers and children, both males and females can be effective principal nurturers of very young children, either as parents or professional caregivers.)

Rogoff (1990) defines intersubjectivity as "the mutual understanding that is achieved between people in communication" (p. 67). She

The authors would like to thank the staff and children of Goodwood, MacKinnon Parade, and St Morris Community Childcare Centres for their assistance.

emphasizes that communication that fosters development is not simply a transfer of information from one person to another; both parties desire communication and work toward that goal. For example, Trevarthen's (1979) investigation of communication between infants and mothers illustrates how the building of **attachment** takes place through intense interaction, often with the baby in control, or taking the lead, once the pair is mutually focused. As Trevarthen comments, "Our findings with infants 2 to 3 months of age lead us to conclude that a complex form of mutual understanding develops even at this age. It is both naturally accepted and strongly regulated by the infant" (p. 343).

Moreover, regardless of whether intersubjectivity is established within face-to-face communication or as individuals work on a task together, it combines both verbal and nonverbal cues. Beginning in infancy, children communicate in many ways—through vocalization, gesture, facial expression, and body movements, and caregivers often respond in kind, not just with verbal comments but with hugs, pats, rocking, and gentle tone of voice. Even in adult–adult interaction, researchers speculate, as much as 65 percent of communicative messages are nonverbal (Birdwhistlell, 1970).

Clearly, emotion is an essential component of intersubjectivity, and infants and children are very sensitive to emotional indicators in their communication with close adults. Affective cues provide information about the meaning of situations and words and about what is important in their surroundings and what is not (Ratner & Stettner, 1991). Children, of course, also send affective messages to adults, as research by Mundy, Kasari, and Sigman (1992) illustrates. They found that 20-month-old toddlers displayed greater positive emotion when gesturing to gain **joint attention** with an adult than when gesturing to request an object.

The vital contribution to development of the diverse communicative ingredients just described is starkly evident when they are absent. Research on infants of depressed mothers reveals that by 18 months, they are less securely attached, exhibit more behavior problems, and perform less well on cognitive tasks than do babies of nondepressed mothers (Murray, 1991). Likewise, studies of hearing mothers and their deaf children, who do not share the same modes of communication, indicate that intersubjectivity is hard to establish under these conditions. Hearing mothers have great difficulty in discarding their habitual auditory mode of communication, which is useless with their deaf child (Jamieson, 1994) Hearing mothers of deaf toddlers score lower on maternal sensitivity, positive affect, shared understanding, and turn-taking than do mothers of toddlers who share the same mode of communication, a difference that increases between 12 and 18 months of age (Meadow-Orlans, 1993). Hearing mothers of deaf children need to adopt the more appropriate visual mode, so that mutually responsive two-way interaction is possible.

In relationships unaffected by these barriers, mothers' responses to young babies are generally "stimulating, attentive, confirmatory, interpretive, and highly supportive" (Trevarthen, 1979, p. 340). Intersubjectivity in parent–infant relationships has been shown to contribute significantly to secure attachment and to subsequent development (Main, Kaplan, & Cassidy, 1985; Murray, 1991). Furthermore, Leadbeater (1989) believes that the interchanges between infants and mothers to provide a vital foundation for intimate relationships in adult life.

Although intersubjectivity demands that partners reach out to each other, it is not a symmetrical relationship, that is, partners are not necessarily equal (Rommetveit, 1985). The child has an innate drive to communicate with others and learn about the world, but the adult, who already knows about that world, creates meaning for the child, taking on the role of "interpreter" of experience. In the early years of development, the adult is in an especially powerful position with respect to communication. If she does not engage the child, or engages only minimally, then emergence of the child's sense of self, a crucial precursor to the development of self-esteem, can be affected adversely (Gallimore, Tharp, & John-Steiner, 1992; Murray, 1991; Trevarthen & Hubley, 1978). Furthermore, adults often need to go more than halfway to establish intersubjectivity with young children, for whom many tasks and aspects of the surrounding world are new. Older children's greater knowledge, experience, and communicative skill means that they can more easily contribute to the achievement of mutual understanding. The active role that adults take in establishing intersubjectivity with infants begins with following the child's gaze and then responding, rather than initiating and creating focuses for the infant to follow. Indeed, early language has been shown to be facilitated where the caregiver, follows and then responds to the infant's focus of attention, rather than directing it (Dunham, Dunham, & Curwin, 1993).

Of course, intersubjectivity is not achieved in every interaction between parent and child. In this sense it is not an all-or-nothing concept. Rather, it can be conceptualized on a continuum. Some interactions will contain a closer "meeting of minds and hearts" than others. Skilled partners, those who generally achieve a high level of intersubjectivity in their communication, will expect and work toward that end. They will also be better at correcting "misses" when they do occur.

## INTERSUBJECTIVITY, SCAFFOLDING, AND THE ZONE OF PROXIMAL DEVELOPMENT

In Vygotsky's sociocultural theory, development takes place within the **zone of proximal development,** a range of tasks that is too challenging for the child to accomplish alone but that the child can master with the assistance of a more skilled partner. According to Vygotsky (1984), interactions between the child and the adult create this zone of proximal development. Although Vygotsky said little about exactly how the zone is established, contemporary researchers have used the

metaphor of **scaffolding** to describe this process. It refers to "a changing quality of support over the course of a teaching session in which the adult adjusts the assistance provided to fit the child's current level of performance. As competence increases, the adult permits the child to take over her guiding role and apply it to his own activity" (Berk & Winsler, 1995, p. 172). Gradually, these interactions are internalized; the child turns them inward, using them to communicate with the self and to guide and manage his or her own thought and behavior. As adult–child communication becomes part of children's thinking, adults transfer values, beliefs, essential knowledge, problem-solving strategies, and skills to the next generation.

Intersubjectivity is a key part of this movement of ideas from the social, interactive plane to the internal, thinking plane because adult and child must achieve shared meaning for transfer to take place. Consider this example of a caregiver and 30-month-old child exploring characteristics of a giraffe together:

Child: (pointing to a low table with toy African animals) Can I play with the animals?

Caregiver: Of course you can.

Child: What do giraffes do?

Caregiver: Well, they've got very long legs and very tall necks, and they can run very fast, and they can make their necks stretch right up to the trees to eat the leaves. And they can make their necks go right down to eat the grass. (She demonstrates these actions with a giraffe from the table.)

Child: And that giraffe's got a tail. (The child plays with the giraffe, making it eat high up and low down, then tries unsuccessfully to make it stand.)

Child: The big giraffe can stand?

Caregiver: Yes, you just need to put the legs like this. (The caregiver demonstrates. The child proceeds to stand the giraffe up, then play with the giraffe using the ideas than had been discussed. Then the caregiver moves away.)

In this example, the caregiver responds to the child's initiatives, follows the child's cues, and adjusts the information and stimulation she provides to the child's capacity to take it in.

## INTERSUBJECTIVITY ACROSS CULTURES

Intersubjectivity is achieved in different ways, depending on the style of interaction valued by the child's culture. Among Westerners, talking is the principal mode of communication between children and adults, perhaps because infants and their caregivers are often physically separated. In many non-Western village and tribal cultures young children experience close bodily contact with their mothers who carry them in slings throughout the day, and cosleep with them at night. Therefore mothers are more likely to use other types of communication such as posture, smell, touch, and even silence (Rogoff, Mosier, Mistry, & Göncü, 1993). In certain cultures such as the Kaluli of Papua New Guinea and the people of Western Samoa, children are not considered appropriate communicative partners for adults (Schieffelin & Ochs, 1987). Typically, other children fulfill this crucial function by caring for younger children, taking on the role of the expert, scaffolding their learning, and interacting so that shared meaning is created. Children brought up in societies where they participate in the daily work of adults at an early age are in a prime position to observe and learn how to be a successful member of the community. In these cultures, children do not need the extensive explanation necessary in a culture where such participation is not possible.

Despite diversity in the partners and patterns of interaction through which intersubjectivity is established, Rogoff and her colleagues (1993) propose that two key processes in parent-child communication are common to many cultures. First, adults *create bridges* between what children already know and what they are about to experience. For example, when taking a toddler to an agricultural show or state fair for the first time, an adult might say, "It's a bit like a zoo in that there are lots of animals there, but they are mostly farm animals. And there are also rides for children, like a carousel." Second, adults structure children's participation in the culture by *providing opportunities and support* for involvement in meaningful activities. For example, regardless of culture, children are guided in participating in tasks appropriate to their age. They might be given smaller scale eating implements and congratulated enthusiastically when they begin to use them appropriately. They might be given modified tools, then guided in the use of them while helping an adult accomplish a task. These objects vary depending on the culture, so while one child is learning to use a small spoon or a hammer, another child might be acquiring skills in the use of chopsticks or a machete.

Successful implementation of these two processes, creating bridges and providing opportunities and support, presumes intersubjectivity between adult and child. The child wants to take part, and the adult wants the child to acquire culturally valued ways of thinking and behaving; consequently, both share a goal. Furthermore, when the adult has a good sense of what the child knows, he or she can build an effective bridge to new knowledge and skills and provide a context that maximizes the child's opportunity to learn.

## CONTEXTS IN WHICH INTERSUBJECTIVITY IS LIKELY TO OCCUR

Intersubjectivity is most likely to be experienced in close relationships. For young children, these include associations with parents, other family members, caregivers, and peers.

The earliest context for development of intersubjectivity is thought to be the subtle, communicative interactions between infants and parents (Trevarthen, 1977). Some researchers consider the capacity to achieve intersubjectivity to be innate—that is, they regard infants as social beings born equipped to share meaning with those around them (Brazelton, 1983; Newson, 1977; Trevarthen, Hubley, & Sheeran, 1975, cited in Rogoff, 1990). Others believe the capacity for intersubjectivity is learned—that parents interact with their infants as though the infant's behavior had meaning. Infants' cries, body movements and facial expressions are responded to as meaningful communications, and, over time, infants pick up this two-way rhythm and mutual interaction develops (Kaye, 1982, cited in Rogoff, 1990).

All researchers agree, however, that both partners contribute to intersubjectivity. When the parent is attentive, patient, and warm, the child feels sufficient trust and security to focus on and participate in social interaction. When the parent expresses joy and enthusiasm and shows interest in the child's activities, she sustains the child's attention, a prerequisite for shared communication (Wood, Bruner, & Ross, 1976; Azmitia & Perlmutter, 1986, cited in Berk & Winsler, 1995). The child, the other partner in the interaction, also plays a strong role. Murray (1991) reported that by at least six weeks infants show evidence of wanting interpersonal engagement that is appropriately tuned to their needs. When interaction with their mothers was interrupted, infants tried hard to re-engage her by a variety of strategies depending on the type of interruption. These included quiet observation, frowning and thrashing, and puzzlement or confusion, all of which caused increased solicitness by their mothers. When these strategies failed, the infants withdrew from engagement with the surroundings and became self-absorbed.

Compared with parent–child interaction, the caregiver–child relationship as a context for the development of intersubjectivity has been less thoroughly studied (File, 1995; Smith, 1993). Whereas adults at home rarely are responsible for more than two children who are close in age, adults in child-care settings have several to many children in their charge, a situation that demands special skills. These care-givers must create a nurturing, stimulating environment for each child in their care. Infants and toddlers, particularly, require individual responses: It is appropriate to group them for activities only occasionally, unlike preschool children who can often be effectively grouped. Caregivers in these settings need to work hard to become effective partners in communication with their young charges, and the younger the children are, the more the caregiver needs to build bridges and offer support. In addition, many routines necessary for children who cannot manage themselves, such as toileting, feeding, and keeping clean, must be conducted in such as way that they enhance children's development. Clearly, this role requires great skill to be done well. In the following example the caregiver manages to achieve intersubjectivity simultaneously with six babies while she and another caregiver are feeding them.

Six infants, five in low baby chairs and one seated at a small table, are having a snack with their two caregivers. Four of the children choose their own fruit as the plate is passed around by one caregiver, Robert. The second caregiver, Sally, is spoonfeeding the other two infants, Emily and Claire. As Sally does so, she skillfully interacts with the other four children.

One child, Stephen, sees the fruit tray and begins banging his hands on the tray. The caregiver looks over at him.

> Sally: Yeah, it's coming, Stephen … it's coming … it's coming. Hang in there. We'll be as quick as we can.
>
> (Sally turns to feed Emily.)
>
> Sally: There you go, Emily. That's apple and banana. How's that? Is that good?
>
> (Claire begins to make complaining noises.)
>
> Sally: Yes, yours is here too. Are you hungry?
>
> (Sally looks toward Stephen who is excitedly banging his tray again and making babbling sounds.)
>
> Sally: Are you hungry? Are you hungry, Stephen?
>
> (She begins to feed Claire.)

Sally: Let's get that really nice and smooth for you.

(She stirs the pureed apple and banana to be offered to Claire.)

Sally: How's that? That's very well done! (Claire eats the spoonful offered.)

(Matthew, another child, says 'Daw-gy' and points to a picture on the wall. Sally follows his gaze and puts her finger on the picture.)

Sally: What is it? What's that? A koala bear.....Is it?

(Stephen bangs on his tray again and babbles excitedly as the other caregiver, Robert, passes the fruit plate to the child sitting next to Stephen.)

Sally: (Looking at Stephen) Say, "Hurry up, Robert."

The caregiver follows the children's focuses of attention and interprets these in the light of her considerable knowledge of each child. She also hears and responds to the emotional content of their communications to her. It is a skilled demonstration of the achievement of intersubjectivity in a group setting.

Intersubjectivity is an important contributing ingredient of adult–child interactions that foster **secure attachment,** so factors found to affect the development of attachment are also likely to influence the development of intersubjectivity. Howes and Matheson (1992) suggest that attachments grow out of the combination of emotional care (comforting, holding, touching, warmth), and physical care (feeding, cleaning, changing). It is most likely to form between a professional caregiver and child when care is provided by the same adult for a substantial period of each day, or almost daily, and the child enters day-care in the first year (Ainslie & Anderson, 1984). Discussing attachment as an organizing principle in day-care, Raikes (1996) states that caregivers will have difficulty developing attachment relations with young children unless there are generous adult-child ratios, small group sizes, and responsive care. The level of education of caregivers has

been shown to be important in the responsivity of their interactions. Berk's investigation (1985) of caregivers with varying levels and types of education showed that college-educated caregivers had more 'child-oriented attitudes and behaviors' than did those with only high school certificates. College-educated caregivers were more likely than their counterparts to support and extend children's interactions and to develop children's verbal skills.

## DEVELOPMENT OF INTERSUBJECTIVITY

Intersubjectivity is a developmental process. As infants grow into toddlers, and then into preschoolers, gains in cognition, language, and emotional expressiveness and understanding result in changes in the contribution they can make to establishing intersubjectivity. In response, the adult's role changes as well. This process can be compared with scaffolding in that, over time, children take increasing responsibility for creating intersubjectivity, until eventually both parties make similar contributions.

### Intersubjectivity in Infancy: Birth to 14 Months

From birth, both child and adult are active in attaining intersubjectivity. During this period, intersubjectivity depends on the baby's developing ability to attend to and interact with people and objects, and on the adult's capacity to sensitively tailor her messages to the child's level of attention and understanding (Rogoff, 1990).

According to Göncü (1993a), intersubjectivity involves the capacity to recognize and coordinate intentions, which improves with age. Trevarthen and Hubley (1978) describe two types of intersubjectivity in infancy: primary and secondary. Primary intersubjectivity is the earliest form, observed in babies younger than 9 months, who perceive and use objects and communicate with people, but express these two sets of intentions separately. Young babies can build a shared focus around emotional states, but they cannot yet share their knowledge or intentions about things. For example, when mother and baby smile at one another, each experiences the other's joy in the interaction (Trevarthen, 1988). Yet before 9 months, infants cannot formulate a shared reference to objects or to other people who are not participating in the interaction.

Before the development of language, intersubjectivity is achieved in two main ways. First, interchange of information occurs through cues, or signals, between the adult and infant. These include body movements, especially of the head, hands, and feet; body tension; postural cues; sounds such as variations in vocalizations and cries; and facial expressions (Garton, 1992; Rogoff, 1990). Second, intersubjectivity requires mechanisms of joint attention—for example, joint eye gaze (Jamieson, 1994). All this information is transmitted during mundane, ordinary day-to-day interactions of adult and infant, but the parent or caregiver "must be able to respond to even the subtlest of signals sent by the child, just as the child intuitively does to the [caregiver]" (Halverson, 1994, p. 171).

Around nine to ten months, a change occurs in the infant's ability to express intentions using language, and secondary intersubjectivity appears. Now the infant deliberately seeks to share a focus, or experience, about events and things external to the interaction itself (Trevarthen & Hubley, 1978). This is reflected in such behaviors as getting the adult to help perform a task with an object, showing another person an object through pointing, accompanied by an exclamatory vocalization, returning affection in the form of a hug or kiss, waving bye-bye, playing peek-a-boo, and holding a cup to the adult's or a doll's mouth. The most important feature of these new behaviors is that they combine the infant's interests in objects or events with acts of communication. They involve the baby's intention to share with another person some form of recognized system of meaning about an event or object (Trevarthen & Hubley, 1978).

## Intersubjectivity in Toddlerhood: 14 to 36 Months

Intersubjectivity achieved with toddlers has some qualities in common with that of infants, but the greatest attainment of this period is spoken language. As a result, toddlers bring a newfound power to their interactions. They also combine language with communicative techniques mastered in infancy. For example, a toddler might call out "Mummy, come here!" and wail at the same time. As Rogoff (1990) points out, with language comes "engagement that is less closely supported by (children's) partners and more tuned to the skills and understandings of society" (p. 79). Nevertheless, caregivers must continue to carefully adjust their messages to toddlers' emerging capacities. Consider this example:

The play area is somewhat wet after a rainy night. A caregiver pushes two toddlers on the swings, when a third child who had been playing in the sand pit runs over. He clearly wants to tell her something.

> Child: I got wet pants.
>
> Caregiver: Are your pants wet?
>
> Child: No.
>
> Caregiver: (Thinks, then speaks to the child.) Your pants were wet but now you've changed them.
>
> Child: Yes, my mummy washed these pants. (The child smoothes his pants with both hands and smiles.)
>
> Caregiver: Those ones are dry.
>
> Child: Yes. (He smiles happily and runs off.)

In this interactive sequence, knowledge of context was crucial for the caregiver to help the child verbalize his intended message and not be misunderstood. Often toddlers assume that adults know more than they do about the child's experiences; they simply expect listeners to respond in an appropriate fashion (Göncü, 1993a).

At times, toddlers in child care can be responded to as a group, should an event capture the interest and attention of many children. In the following example, a sudden, loud rainstorm stopped everyone in the room. One child began speaking quietly to himself:

> Child: I want to watch the rain, then I'll come back.
>
> Caregiver: (Sees the child run to the window) Jack, do you want to see the rain?
>
> Child: OK (nods).
>
> (Other children gather at the window and door, which the caregiver has opened.)
>
> Caregiver: I'll grab a cushion, and we can watch the rain.
>
> Other children: We need a pillow!
>
> Caregiver: Yes, sure, here you go. Sit on the cushion and watch the rain. Jack, did you want to sit on the pillow and watch the rain, or are you just looking through the window?
>
> Child: (nods)
>
> Caregiver: You do? Sit on the pillow. I love watching the rain. (sings) The rain is falling down, pitter, patter, pitter patter....
>
> (The children join in.)

In these examples, children take an active role in creating shared meaning. At the same time, caregivers must meet them more than half way. They need to know the children and their contexts well, to take into account affect, to listen to their words and know what they are likely to mean, to fill in the gaps that the children cannot yet express.

## Intersubjectivity During the Preschool Years: 30 to 60 Months

With older children, "a shared focus of attention serves as a starting point for joint activity and enables the participants to expand their existing knowledge and understanding to new situations" (Göncü, 1993b, p. 186). Children of this age are much more equal partners in conversing with adults than they were previously. Their interactions with peers also become richer, and play

possibilities increase greatly. Although the focus of this article is intersubjectivity in adult–child relationships, it is important to note that the ability to share meanings with adults, be they parents or caregivers, prepares the child to share meanings with peers. Consequently, early intersubjective adult–child communication provides the foundation for satisfying play experiences and close, rewarding friendships (Budwig, Strage & Bamberg, 1986, and Trevarthen, 1989, cited in Göncü, 1993b).

Between 2 and 6 years of age, children gradually become capable of making a greater effort to understand another person and to establish shared knowledge—with adults and peers. The following example illustrates the development of this skill:

> Caregiver: Cindy, you didn't tell me about your holiday yet. Where did you go?
>
> Child: After Jingo?
>
> Caregiver: Pardon?
>
> Child: After the clown's show. (The child clarifies; she is referring to Jingo the clown.)
>
> Caregiver: Yes, where did you go after Jingo had been here?
>
> Child: We went to Bright.
>
> Caregiver: It was white? (Again, the caregiver doesn't understand the child.)
>
> Child: It was Bright. (The child repeats and clarifies.)
>
> Caregiver: Bright ... Oh, you went for a holiday at Bright, didn't you?
>
> (The child continues, telling the caregiver that she caught a fish on her holiday, when a second child enters the conversation.)
>
> Caregiver: Did you have to scale the fish as well?
>
> Child 1: No, we eated them. (The child misunderstands the meaning of the word scale.)
>
> Child 2: You need to peel them ... peel them. (The second child tries to clarify.)
>
> Caregiver: (confirming Child 2's meaning) Mmmmmm ... you need to take the scales off, don't you?

Child 2: You can't do it with your hands; you need a peeler.

Caregiver: Or a knife … a really sharp fishing knife.

Child 1: They peeled the fishes with a fork. (The child now shares meaning with the other two.)

As is evident in this conversation, the two main partners struggle equally to create shared meaning, and a second child assists in attaining joint understanding. Preschool children are clearly much more sophisticated communicators than their younger counterparts; they do not need their partners to take as much responsibility as they used to for the interaction, except in instances when the context or topic under discussion is unfamiliar. Nevertheless, commitment to the relationship is still very important. Preschoolers need an understanding social context in which to develop.

Entrance to the preschool years brings children to a more equal role in intersubjective relations, one in which they can take an active role in helping their partners to understand and in correcting "misses" when they do occur.

## CREATING AND FACILITATING INTERSUBJECTIVITY WITH CHILDREN

A sociocultural approach to development regards the child not as a solitary meaning maker, but, rather, as a member of a two-person team that creates meaning together. File (1995) suggests a number of questions caregivers might ask as they evaluate the quality of their communication with infants, toddlers, and preschoolers:

- What understandings of this concept did the children and I create and share?

- How effective was our dialogue in achieving a shared sense of meaning?

- How can I lead this child's development? (pp. 311–312)

These questions contrast with the often-stated query: What can this child do on her own?

To effectively plan experiences that make the caregiver-child relationship central during the early childhood years, child-care staff members must continually support one another and carefully review the quality of their interactions with children. During planning and evaluation meetings, they can ask these questions:

- Are we attending to what children are in fact, noticing?

- How do we react when children talk to us, and what does our body language suggest?

- Are we willing to accept the nonstandard answer and follow along with a child's thinking, in an effort to build on and enhance that child's understanding? (Maxwell, 1996, p 32).

As several examples in this article reveal, to attain intersubjectivity readily with young children, caregivers must strive to understand the child's life outside the caregiving situation. There are many ways to do so. For example, caregivers can provide a photograph album for each child, to which parents contribute and which contains pictures of significant people and events in the child's life. Home visits and informal daily chats with parents as they deliver and collect their children are additional strategies, as are daybooks in which caregivers and parents can note significant experiences in the child's daily life.

Because caregivers are responsible for groups of children, it is important to capitalize on moments when routines create conditions for one-to-one communication. Nappy (diaper) changing and meal preparation provide valuable opportunities for interacting on an individual basis with children. Where possible, contextual factors mentioned earlier, including adult-child ratios, group size, staffing stability, and caregiver awareness of the role of intersubjectivity in development, should be improved.

This child wants to learn to saw wood at the woodworking table. Her teacher responds to the child's goal by establishing a shared focus of attention, discussing the activity with her, and supporting her skill development by guiding her movements while protecting her safety. As a result, intersubjectivity is attained, and the child moves forward in development. (Photo: Frederick Ebbeck)

Finally, it is worth looking at the relationship between caregivers and parents through the lens of intersubjectivity. Although each has a more intense relationship with the child than with the other, this, too, is a partnership. When a supportive relationship between caregivers and parents develops, they are likely to find themselves teaching and learning from one another as they join forces in their common goal of providing an optimum environment for the child.

## CONCLUSION

The concept of intersubjectivity is a useful one for caregivers as they attempt to do their difficult job well. It describes how, from birth, adults and young children work as a team to create shared meaning and understanding. Intersubjectivity is related to other well-known constructs in early childhood development and education: attachment, scaffolding, and the zone of proximal development. Each sheds light on how intersubjectivity can be achieved and its consequences for development. A major challenge for the early childhood profession is to find ways to create environments where intersubjectivity can occur often in the context of group care. The joint meaning-making that grows out of intersubjectivity is not only important for development, but crucial for community life and the transmission of culture from one generation to the next. The meeting of minds and hearts between people is the root of our identity, individually and as a group; that is, we bring each other into being. As Gallimore, Tharp, and John-Steiner (1992) sum up, "Through the processes of intersubjectivity community and individuals create each other; culture and cognition create each other" (Gallimore, Tharp, & John-Steiner, 1992, p. 23).

## EVALUATING YOUR MASTERY

1. Which of the following is an essential component of intersubjectivity?
   a. Working on a task together
   b. Exchange of emotional cues
   c. Engaging in conversation
   d. Looking at the same object

2. Research on hearing mothers of deaf children indicates that _____ facilitates intersubjectivity.
   a. Sharing the same mode of communication
   b. Secure attachment
   c. Performing cognitive tasks
   d. Maternal sensitivity during feeding

3. Which of the following is true?
   a. Intersubjectivity is achieved in the same way in all cultures.
   b. Infants take a more active role in establishing intersubjectivity than do preschoolers.
   c. When parent and child communicate effectively, intersubjectivity is achieved in every interaction.
   d. Intersubjectivity is most likely to be experienced in close relationships.

4. Which of the following is likely to support the attainment of intersubjectivity in child-care centers?
   a. Care of the child by several adults, who take frequent turns
   b. Large group sizes, permitting frequent peer interaction
   c. Well-educated professional caregivers
   d. Enrolling a baby after the first year

5. _____ and _____ are two key processes in establishing intersubjectivity that are common to many cultures.

6. Professional caregivers [can/cannot] achieve intersubjectivity simultaneously with several babies.

7. To attain intersubjectivity readily with young children, caregivers [need to/ do not need to] understand the child's life outside the caregiving situation.

## Critical Thinking

1. Explain how intersubjectivity is necessary for successful scaffolding and creation of the zone of proximal development.

2. What developments between the years of 2 and 6 gradually permit children to make "a greater effort to understand another person and to establish shared knowledge"?

## Applying Your Knowledge

Arrange to observe an infant and a preschool child, each interacting with a familiar adult—either a parent or professional caregiver. To what extent does each pair achieve intersubjectivity? What behaviors did you rely on to decide? Cite similarities and differences in the way the infant and the preschooler contribute to intersubjectivity.

# 8

✑

# Young Children's Understanding of Everyday Emotions

JANET KUEBLI

St. Louis University

■

By helping children to understand emotions, we hope to help them channel their feelings in self-enhancing ways and also prepare them to deal with similar experiences in the future.

■

Researchers hypothesize that a fundamental prerequisite underlying emotional experience is having a self-concept; that is, children need a sense of an "I" who owns and knows her or his own emotions states and expressions in order to experience them.

■

Children's early knowledge of some emotional situations may considerably outpace their ability to talk about those emotions.

■

The goal of emotion socialization is usually to redirect or change the way children spontaneously express their emotions to conform more closely with social rules or conventions.

■

There is evidence that emotions downplayed or left undefined in some cultures are central to how other cultures make sense of experience.

■

Becoming conscious of the roles we play in children's emotion socialization empowers us to provide children with better opportunities in their daily lives for understanding themselves and others.

■

## EDITOR'S INTRODUCTION

Parents and early childhood educators must grasp children's developing capacity to understand emotion so they can build on and enhance that capacity, help children respond in compassionate ways to others, and encourage children to express emotion in socially acceptable ways. Janet Kuebli explains how emotion understanding changes from infancy to early childhood.

Children's developing cognitive capacities—self-awareness, language for talking about emotion, and insights into the causes and consequences of feelings—support their increasing ability to interpret and evaluate emotional states. In addition, emotion understanding is socially influenced. Adults teach children about emotion—both directly, by telling them which feelings are all right to display in various situations and reinforcing their behavior, and indirectly, by modeling acceptable emotional expressions, discussing how they themselves reacted to emotionally arousing experiences, and attributing meaning to the child's emotional displays.

Kuebli emphasizes that talking with children about emotion is especially important because language helps children organize and transform their emotional lives. Emotion talk varies from society to society and differs for boys and girls, so emotional understanding is strongly influenced by culture and gender.

What young children understand about emotion states and behaviors is of importance to early childhood educators who deal with children's feelings every day. Children, like adults, experience many emotions in the course of each day. Strong emotions arising from their own experiences may be very confusing for children. Children also have to make sense of other people's emotional reactions or feelings; therefore, we often try to help children talk about their own and others' feelings. We think of this especially when children encounter traumatic life events, such as when a child's parents divorce or someone in the family is very sick or dies.

Children may also need help in understanding everyday emotions. Teachers and parents may, for example, suggest ways that children can cope with feelings of distress, fear, or shyness on the first day of school or explain how it is possible to feel sad and happy at the same time about moving to a new school. Sometimes we urge children to talk about their anger or sadness as a way of handling minor daily conflicts and disappointments. By helping children to understand emotions, we hope to help them channel their feelings in self-enhancing ways and also prepare them to deal with similar experiences in the future.

As children mature, we also expect them to master their emotions to some extent. Learning to express some feelings and how to mask others are common everyday lessons in children's lives. Hochschild (1983) calls this learning how to do "emotion work." Getting along with others often means handling feelings in a socially acceptable fashion. Children who get mad because they have to wait their turn or who laugh at a crying child who has taken a fall and skinned a knee sometimes are encouraged to think about how others feel. A child who overexuberantly boasts about being a winner may be urged to remember how it also feels to be the loser. In some cases the ability to regulate and manage emotions tells us that a child is ready for new challenges.

Over the last decade, researchers have shown keen interest in the nature of children's understanding of emotion, especially as it relates to social-cognitive development. Much of this work has concerned school-age children. Results from these studies suggest, not surprisingly, that emotion understanding becomes more complex and sophisticated during elementary school. At these ages, for example, children begin to appreciate the fact that they can experience more than one emotion at a time (Carroll & Steward, 1984; Donaldson & Westerman, 1986; Harter & Buddin, 1987; Wintre, Polivy, & Murray, 1990). They also begin to take into greater account the situations that cause emotional reactions (Barden, Zelko, Duncan, & Masters, 1980; Brody & Harrison, 1987; Camras & Allison, 1989; Strayer, 1986). At this time children's skill in hiding their feelings also shows considerable improvement (Davis, 1992; Saarni, 1984, 1985), as does their understanding of emotions that involve self-evaluations, such as pride, guilt, and shame (Graham, 1988; Graham, Doubleday, & Guarino, 1984; Harter & Whitesell, 1989).

Emotion-understanding studies with younger children are by comparison less common. New research, however, has begun to yield information both about what younger children know about emotions and how this understanding may develop. At the heart of the studies with younger children are two related issues. The first concerns identifying links between early developments in emotion understanding and language. The second issue centers on how children's emotion understanding is socialized in the course of children's interactions with others. One major conclusion derived from these studies is that conversations about feelings are an important context for learning about emotions and how to manage them.

This article considers the general nature of emotional experience first. The focus turns next to several studies on children's early emotion

Kuebli, J. (1994, March). Young children's understanding of everyday emotions. *Young Children, 49*(3), 36–47. © National Association for the Education of Young Children. Reprinted by permission.

vocabulary and concepts, followed by research on how emotions are discussed by young children with others. The studies described here, while not exhaustive of the work in this area, provide a selective overview of what is known about emotion understanding in young children. Finally, I suggest ways that teachers can use these findings to facilitate children's understanding of their own and others' feelings.

## EMOTIONAL EXPERIENCE

According to Lewis (Lewis, 1992; Lewis & Michalson, 1983), it's useful to think of emotional behavior as consisting of a variety of components. One of these components, **emotional experience,** refers to how individuals interpret and evaluate their emotions. Other components include (a) emotion states and (b) their expressions, which may be conveyed either verbally or through nonverbal changes in facial expressions, physical posture, or movement. The componential model of emotion proposes that our emotional experiences, states, and expressions do not always correspond to each other. On some occasions we may be unaware of our emotions or simply unable to name the particular feelings we are having. At other times we might intentionally express one emotion while experiencing a different feeling, or we might recognize our feelings but lack insight into the reasons for having them.

Among these various emotion components, emotional experience is considered the most cognitive (Lewis & Saarni, 1985) because it relies upon basic mental processes of attention, perception, and memory. We cannot begin, thus, to understand our feelings until we pay attention to them. Emotional experience further entails arriving at cognitive judgments and insights about our own emotion states and expressions. Emotional experience, in effect, depends upon being able to introspect or reflect upon ourselves (Lewis, 1992). Cognitive processes that underlie emotional experience essentially bring our emo-

tions into consciousness and provide the basis for our having emotional experiences.

The developmental timetable for the emergence of various emotion states and expressions has already been well documented (for example, Campos, Barrett, Lamb, Goldsmith, & Stenberg, 1983). Newborns, for example, display joy, interest, disgust, and distress; around eight months most babies show surprise, anger, fear, and sadness (Stenberg, Campos, & Emde, 1983; Izard & Malatesta, 1987). Embarrassment, empathy, pride, shame, and guilt only begin to appear at the end of infancy, usually after the age of 18 months. Much less is known about the developmental course of emotional experience and understanding. The components model of emotion, however, suggests that it is not necessary for emotional states, expressions, and experience to develop in lock-step fashion all together. This model may explain why children have emotions and express them before they are able to reflect upon and understand their feelings (Lewis, 1992; Michalson & Lewis, 1985).

Researchers hypothesize that a fundamental prerequisite underlying emotional experience is having a **self-concept**; that is, children need a sense of an "I" who owns and knows her or his own emotion states and expressions in order to experience them. Even prior to forming a self-concept, however, children acquire several important cognitive skills related to self-understanding, which may also underlie their capacity for emotional experience. Collectively these skills are known as **self-referential behaviors**. They are first evident at ages between 15 and 24 months and include acquiring (a) an awareness of oneself as separate from others, (b) knowledge that objects independent of oneself have a permanent existence, (c) a sense of oneself as a causal agent, and (d) the ability to visually recognize oneself (Bertenthal & Fisher, 1978; Harter, 1983; Kagan, 1981; Lewis & Brooks-Gunn, 1979; Lewis, Sullivan, Stanger, & Weiss, 1989; Sroufe, 1979). Harter (1983) refers to these developments as contributing to the formation of an "**existential self.**" Existential awareness of self forms the foundation for the child's initial self-concept. Together, these cognitive abilities enable children to make themselves objects of thought. Thereafter, emotional experience probably develops gradually, most likely in concert with changes in children's self-concepts. Emotions are, thus, integral to children's sense of who they are, helping them to form their own personal views of the world around them.

## LEARNING WORDS AND CONCEPTS FOR EMOTIONS

Emotion theorists suspect that learning to talk is another critical factor in the development of emotional experience; acquiring word labels for emotions is regarded as particularly important for developments in children's understandings of emotions. Certainly, parents refer to emotions in conversations with their children, almost from birth. Emotion communication enables others to draw attention to children's expressions of emotion. No doubt, this communication accelerates the development of emotional experience and understanding (Izard & Malatesta, 1987). Children's emotional self-understanding may start with being able to name emotion states and behaviors. From maternal reports, diary studies, and direct observations, we know that children begin to use emotion terms around the ages of 20 to 24 months (see Bretherton, Fritz, Zahn-Waxler, & Ridgeway, 1986, for a review of research on how children learn to talk about emotions.) By 36 months children use emotion words to talk about both themselves and others, and in reference to events in the present, past, and future (Bretherton & Beeghly, 1982).

To learn about children's first emotion words, Bretherton and Beeghly (1982) gave mothers of 28-month-olds a list of terms for emotions as well as for mental states (for example, knowing, remembering, dreaming), physiological states (for example, hunger, fatigue), and perceptual states (for example, seeing, hearing, tasting). Mothers indicated which words on the list their children used. At this age about 75 percent of the children had acquired the emotion words *mad* and *scared*, and well over half used *happy* and *sad*. Nearly all of the children used the emotion-behavior term *cry;* however, *surprise,* apparently a late acquisition, was reported for only 13 percent of the children. Additionally, children used emotion words to refer to both self and others, rather than only to self or only to others. This suggests that children's early emotional understanding of themselves and others may be closely related rather than developing separately. Finally, emotion terms were more common than mental-state words but less frequent than words for perceptual or physiological states. Notably, however, children talked about causes for emotions more often than causes for other kinds of states of being. This finding underscores the importance of emotional understanding as central to how children make sense of what happens to them.

In several experimental studies, researchers have looked at preschoolers' ability to label facial expressions. Michalson and Lewis (1985), for example, asked two- to five-year-olds "What kind of face" another child was making in a series of snapshots. They found that children knew the labels for *happiness* and *sadness* at earlier ages than they knew the terms for *anger, surprise, disgust,* or *fear.* In fact, children did not produce many verbal labels at all until after age three, and even by five years of age children had difficulty naming the surprise, disgust, and fear expressions. When asked to point to the face that matched the emotion label given by the experimenter, however, children as young as two demonstrated they knew something about the situations in which certain facial expressions were likely. Seventy percent of two-year-olds matched the happy face with a birthday-party drawing. These results tell us that children's early knowledge of some emotional situations may considerably outpace their ability to talk about those emotions. Less than

**Table 8.1 Some Characteristics of Young Children's Emotion Language and Understanding**

| Approximate age of child | Description |
|---|---|
| Birth to 18 months | Display emotions and respond to emotions in others at preverbal stage |
| | Use emotion cues of others to guide own responses to new or ambiguous situations |
| | Do not produce or comprehend emotion terms with a few exceptions |
| 18 to 20 months | Use first emotion words in vocabulary (e.g., cry, happy) |
| | Begin to discuss emotions spontaneously in conversations with others |
| 2 to 3 years | Increase emotion vocabulary most rapidly |
| | Correctly label simple emotions in self and others, and talk about past, present, and future emotions |
| | Talk about the causes and consequences of some emotions and identify emotions associated with certain situations |
| | Use emotion language in pretend play |
| 4 to 5 years | Show increased capacity to verbally reflect on emotions and to consider more complex relations between emotions and situations |
| | Understand that the same event may call forth different feelings in different people and that feelings sometimes persist long after the events that caused them |
| | Demonstrate growing awareness about controlling and managing emotions in accord with social standards |
| 6 to 11 years | Exhibit conceptual advances in their understanding of complex emotions (e.g., pride and shame) and of mixed or multiple emotions |
| | Show marked improvements in the ability to suppress or conceal negative emotional reactions and in the use of self-initiated strategies for redirecting feelings |
| | Take into fuller account the events leading to emotional reactions |

half of the two- and three-year-olds, however, matched the sad and disgust faces with the correct pictures; whereas, the majority of the four- and five-year-olds made the correct match. This more gradual development trend in understanding negative emotions has also been observed in several other studies (for example, Borke, 1971; Glasberg & Aboud, 1982; Reichenbach & Masters, 1983).

Clearly, preschoolers become more adept at talking about their own and others' emotions. The largest and most rapid increase in the number of terms children have for emotions occurs between the ages of two and three (Ridgeway, Waters, & Kuczaj, 1985), but children continue to acquire new emotion words after this time. During the preschool period, caregivers also increasingly urge children to "use words" rather than act out their feelings. Research shows that young children are learning more than just an emotion vocabulary. Specifically, children learn more about the nature of emotional processes, including new insights about the causes and consequences of feelings.

Denham and Zoller (1991) were particularly interested in what preschoolers think causes various emotions. The two researchers showed children puppets with happy, sad, fearful, or angry faces and then asked them to think of what would make the puppets "feel that way." Results showed that the children more often associated happiness with nonsocial causes (for example, playing or going somewhere without reference to being with others) than with social ones. By contrast, the reasons children gave for sadness and anger were mostly social in nature. Children said that being hurt or left by others caused sadness, for example; their reasons for anger included being punished, fighting, or not liking someone else. Interestingly, neither social nor nonsocial reasons were given for feeling fearful; instead, children said fear was caused by make-believe creatures, such as monsters or ghosts. One notable gender difference in the responses was that girls gave more reasons for sadness than did boys. This outcome is intriguing in light of research with adults and adolescents in which females report thinking about sadness in relation to themselves and experiencing depression more often than do males (Brody, 1984; Conway, Giannopoulos, & Stiefonhofer, 1990).

Some preschoolers also have begun to recognize that a single event sometimes causes different feelings in different people. In one study (Gove & Keating, 1979) three- and five-year-olds heard a short story in which only one of two characters won a game. All of the older children, but only two thirds of the younger ones, judged that the victor would feel happy, while the loser would be sad in this social situation. This result is somewhat at odds with what Denham and Zoller found, but the differences may be products of the methods used in the two studies. In addition, although preschoolers demonstrate an increasing ability to reason about the causes and consequences of single emotions, few children prior to the age of five grasp the concept of mixed or conflicting feelings. That is, while preschoolers may say that one feeling can follow another one sequentially, they tend to deny that two different emotions can be experienced simultaneously (Harter & Buddin, 1987). Even after short training about mixed emotions, four- and five-year-olds have shown little improvement in their understanding of mixed emotions (Peng, Johnson, Pollock, Glasspool, & Harris, 1992). Younger children's greater difficulty with multiple feelings may be tied to their limitations in the cognitive skills necessary for integrating opposing emotions.

## SOCIALIZATION OF EMOTION UNDERSTANDING

Studies on children's emotion concepts have sought to document at what ages children demonstrate higher levels of understanding about emotions. Other research has focused on identifying experiences in children's lives that influence the particular forms emotion understandings can take. A key assumption is that children's insights into their own emotions are socially shaped in important ways (for example, Lutz, 1985; Gordon, 1989). Whereas research on the content of emotion concepts has concentrated on older children, studies examining how emotions are socialized have usually been conducted with younger children.

The goal of **emotion socialization** is usually to redirect or change the way children spontaneously express their emotions to conform more closely with social rules or conventions. Sometimes this means substituting one feeling for a different one, as when we smile after receiving a disappointing gift (Saarni, 1984) or look on the bright side of things that worry or sadden us. Saarni (1985; Saarni & Crowley, 1990) outlines three general classes of processes by which emotions may be socialized. First, *direct* socialization refers to occasions when others chide or praise children's immediately prior emotional behaviors. In this case an adult's behavior reinforces the child's expression of emotions. Reinforcement, either reward or punishment, gives children explicit information about the way certain emotions are valued by others. Didactic teaching is another direct form of socialization often used with children to convey social conventions for expressing emotions. A child may be told, for example, that "girls don't brag" about their successes or that "boys don't cry" about their failures.

Emotions are also socialized *indirectly*. A classic example is when a child imitates someone else's emotional reactions, such as one child's fearful reluctance to try something new being copied by another child who only moments before was a willing and eager participant. We can view this situation, in part, as a case in which one person's emotional reactions are "catching." There are times when uncontrolled laughter seizes a group of children in this way or sadness sweeps through a classroom. Adults also provide ready models, of course, for children's emotional reactions. Research shows that children faced with a situation in which they do not know how to react will scan a caregiver's face in search of cues for the appropriate emotional response. This behavior, known as **social referencing,** has been studied extensively with infants. One study, for example, showed that eight-month-olds' reactions to a stranger were influenced by their mothers' immediately prior emotional reactions toward that person (Feinman & Lewis, 1983). Although fewer studies have considered this phenomena among preschoolers, the notion in all cases is that children learn about emotion states, expressions, and events by watching others and imitating their emotional behaviors.

A third channel for emotion socialization involves *expectancy communication.* For Saarni and Crowley (1990) **emotion expectancies** are beliefs about how emotions should be felt and expressed that are conveyed to children, verbally or nonverbally, in advance of particular events in which children's own emotional reactions are called forth. Saarni and Crowley liken the process to hypnosis, in which adults, first, plant "suggestions" in children's minds about how to respond in certain situations. If children subsequently encounter the same or similar situations, they may use this information to guide their own emotional responses. In this way children remember and act upon at later points in time the information previously acquired about emotions. So, when we tell young children, for example, about how we felt afraid (or excited) at their age, going on a Ferris wheel ride or sleeping away from home the first time, these verbal suggestions may be internalized as expectancies upon which children subsequently rely. By such means, Saarni and Crowley (1990) contend, strategies for managing emotions initiated "out-

side" the child are imported into children's own private, emotional lives.

A general, theoretical framework for studies on emotion socialization is found in the works of Cooley (1902), Mead (1956), and Vygotsky (1978), who each discussed links between emotion, self, and cognition. These writers proposed that (a) we become conscious of ourselves through how others know us and (b) consciousness is forged, in large part, through social activity and discourse. Mead, for example argued that self-consciousness only arises when we take on the attitudes of others toward ourselves. He wrote

> The child can think about his conduct as good or bad only as he reacts to his own acts in the remembered words of his parents. (1913, p. 146).

The imagined judgments of others "drawn from the communicative life" (1902, p. 179) were also essential to Cooley's **looking-glass self**:

> In imagination we perceive in another's mind some thought of our appearance, manners, aims, deeds, character ... and are variously affected by it. (1902, p. 184).

Although Vygotsky did not explicitly write about emotion development, he believed that children became self-conscious by using

> The same forms of behavior in relation to themselves that others initially used in relation to them. (1981, p. 157).

In particular, Vygotsky stressed the role that everyday social speech plays in children's development.

Contemporary researchers speculate that asking about emotions provides children with "reflective distance" from feeling states themselves (Stern, 1985; Bretherton et al., 1986; Dunn, Brown, & Beardsall, 1991). Discussing emotions is thought to distance children from the rush and immediacy of affective responses. Distancing gives children space in which to interpret and evaluate their feelings and to reflect upon causes and consequences. Emotion discourse may further allow adults and

Children observe, experience, and talk about a rich variety of emotions during play with agemates, as this sandbox scene reveals. Through everyday interactions, preschoolers come to better understand the causes and consequences of emotions and the feelings typically associated with certain situations. These emotion concepts help children reflect on and manage their own emotions, thereby transforming their emotional lives. (Photo: Laura Berk)

children to work out socially acceptable meanings of feeling states. Especially significant may be the way adults attribute meaning to children's own emotional behavior and development (Lutz, 1983). The way we talk about emotions with children, thus, has the potential to uniquely organize and transform their emotional lives.

Researchers also assume that preschoolers begin to formulate emotion concepts specific to their own culture or subculture (Lutz, 1983; Lutz & White, 1986; Miller & Sperry, 1987). From this perspective emotion concepts are viewed as embedded in broader cultural knowledge about situations and social relationships. How children come to understand emotions will presumably depend on the particular cultural vocabulary and meaning systems available to children for talking about emotions (Levy, 1984; Lutz & White, 1986; Gordon, 1989) and on existing social norms about ways emotions should be felt and expressed.

Both psychologists and anthropologists have studied how emotions are variously viewed and talked about in different cultures. There is evidence that emotions downplayed or left undefined in some cultures are central to how other cultures make sense of experiences. Cross-cultural comparisons indicate that Americans and Chinese, for example, identify different types of causes for pride (Stipek, Weiner, & Li, 1989), and Japanese culture emphasizes shame more than other groups do (Lewis, 1992). Americans also report experiencing emotions longer and more intensely than do Japanese subjects (Matsumoto, Kudoh, Scherer, & Wallbott, 1988). In contrast to the Western culture's sense of sadness as an emotion, Tahitians classify sadness as a physical illness or body state (Levy, 1984). How adults approach childrearing, moreover, is thought to be related to their knowledge and beliefs about emotions (Lutz & White, 1986; Miller & Sperry, 1987; Markus & Kitayama, 1991). Yet, until recently, few researchers have directly observed adult-child conversations about emotions. The few studies so far have, not surprisingly, focused mostly on how mothers talk with young children.

Miller and Sperry (1987), for example, interviewed three working-class mothers of two-and-one-half-year-old daughters and observed how they socialized anger and aggression. Notably, the mothers led lives in which violence and aggression were all too commonplace; they typically discussed these events in their daughters' presence but usually while talking to other family members or friends. It is striking that at least one child's own stories about anger and aggression were closely patterned after her mother's recollections. In this way what children overhear others relating about emotional events may be one context for learning about emotions. Miller and Sperry observed a second important context—episodes of anger between mothers and daughters. Mothers sometimes intentionally provoked their daughters' anger by teasing or trading insults with them as a way of teaching the girls how to stand up for themselves. Miller and Sperry also found that, rather than talking explicitly about the emotional state of anger itself, families referred to those emotion behaviors that only indirectly expressed anger (for example, *fight, hit, punch).*

Children's interactions with their mothers and a sibling have been examined by Dunn and her associates. Their analyses of these three-way interactions included tracking how the amount and kind of emotion talk that occurs in the home changes as young children grow older. One study's home observations conducted when younger siblings were 18 and 24 months old revealed that family members' references to emotion states and to their causes and consequences increased over time (Dunn, Bretherton, & Munn, 1987). Mothers' comments during these interactions usually served to guide or explain children's feelings rather than simply to bring attention to children's emotions. This suggests that mothers, consciously or not, actively worked at shaping their children's emotional experiences, much like the mothers in the Miller and Sperry study.

Moreover, the more frequently mothers and older siblings referred to feeling states at the 18-month visit, the more often the younger child talked about emotions at the 24-month visit. In other research Dunn and Kendrick (1982) found that two- and three-year-olds whose mothers commented more often about a new baby's feelings were more likely to have friendly interactions with that sibling one year later.

Dunn has also examined sibling conflicts as contexts for emotion socialization. Between the ages of 14 and 36 months, younger siblings' ability to tease and upset their older siblings appears to increase significantly (Dunn, Brown, & Beardsall, 1991; Dunn & Munn, 1985). This finding demonstrates how young children are learning to anticipate and influence others' feelings. Dunn and colleagues (1991) further found that mothers and children who engaged in more frequent emotion talk were more apt to also discuss the causes and consequences of siblings' disputes. Finally, three-year-olds from families with more emotion talk showed a better understanding of others' emotions three years later at age six. These results provide additional support for the contention that emotion talk provides an important context for learning about feelings.

Together, these studies indicate that exposure to different types and amounts of emotion talk may be related to individual differences in children's emotion understanding (Gordon, 1989). Especially intriguing in this regard are reports of differences in how mothers talk about emotions with daughters and sons. In the study by Dunn and colleagues (1987), for example, references to emotions were more frequent in mother-daughter, than mother-son, conversations at both 18 and 24 months; and by 24 months girls also talked about feeling states more often than boys did. Gender differences have also been reported by Fivush (1989; 1991). Reasoning that conversations about past emotions might provide even more reflective distance, Fivush asked mothers to talk with children about specific events in their child's past. In one study with 30-to 35-month-olds, Fivush (1989) found that mothers attributed more talk about sadness to daughters and more talk about anger to sons. Mother-daughter conversations also focused more on feelings, whereas mother-son pairs were more apt to discuss causes and consequences for emotions.

When fathers talk about the past with young children, they, too, seem to talk differently about emotions with daughters than with sons. Kuebli and Fivush (1992) found that both mothers and fathers of 40-month-olds talked about a greater number and variety of emotions with daughters than they did with sons; again, sadness was more often a topic in conversations with girls. At the age of 40 months, differences were not yet apparent in how boys and girls talked about emotions. Mother-child interviews conducted just before the children started kindergarten, however, revealed that the number of girls' references to emotions nearly quadrupled over this time, whereas boys' references had remained about the same (Kuebli & Fivush, 1993). These results suggest that girls' and boys' emotional lives may be socialized in somewhat different ways. In related research, moreover, adult women were found to be more likely than men to say they are emotional, to value the expression of emotions, and to report experiencing a variety of emotions (Allen & Haccoun, 1976; Allen & Hamsher, 1974; Balswick & Avertt, 1977; Fitzpatrick & Indvik, 1982).

## APPLICATIONS FOR EARLY CHILDHOOD EDUCATORS

For educators and parents, it is certainly not earthshaking to find that children learn about emotions from us; but, emotions are sometimes so "close to the skin" and fleeting that it is easy for feelings to slip out of one's conscious awareness. Becoming conscious of the roles we play in children's emotion socialization empowers us to provide children with better opportunities in their daily lives for understanding themselves and

others. Teachers have some unique occasions for structuring children's activities in ways that can encourage children to talk about their own and others' emotions. Consider the following recommendations for meeting this objective.

1. Evaluate whether the emotional climate of the classroom itself is conducive to expressing emotions. In other words, caregivers need to legitimate children's feelings in order for children to feel it is acceptable to talk about and reflect upon their emotions. Leavitt and Power (1989) contend that we give meaning to children's emotions when we recognize and respond to their feelings. Essentially this means entering into authentic emotional relationships with children and regarding them as "emotional associates" (Leavitt & Power, 1989, p. 37) who are capable of interpreting and understanding their own and others' emotions.

2. Consider the physical environments in which children may learn about feelings. Play centers no doubt vary in the opportunities they afford for emotional engagement and reflection. Family-living or dramatic-play sections, for example, may encourage children to act out social interactions into which emotions figure. Well-stocked play centers can also provide sources of suggestions to children's imaginations for reworking earlier emotional altercations or experiences. Either from the sidelines or as players ourselves, adults can observe the way individual children play out emotion scripts dramatically. Introduce themes and ask questions that prompt children to vicariously explore the causes and consequences of emotions. Similarly, puppets and dolls are excellent vehicles for emotion play.

3. The arts center provides another valuable context for emotion conversation. Encourage children to make pictures that tell about personal events in their lives. This idea, borrowed from therapists who work with disturbed children, adapts well for children whose "troubles" are within the typical range of life experiences. Children might be encouraged to "draw about the time when ..." they were upset with another

child, afraid of something new, and so forth. Engaging children in conversations about their pictures, either as they are being created or afterwards, can give children chances to reflect upon their emotions. Children can also dictate the stories and feelings that go with their pictures. Older children may want to construct longer picture stories, several pages in length. Sometimes, children will enjoy "reading" back their picture stories to someone else, either during group times or on their own to other children and teachers.

4. Stories written for children are yet another readily available resource for talking about emotions. Books can be selected that show other children being emotional and dealing with their feelings. Children and teachers can discuss the causes and consequences of story characters' emotions and then link them with children's own experiences. Certainly, other media (for example, TV, movies, plays, children's magazines) provide similar options.

5. Tape recorders and video equipment can be used advantageously as well. Children might audiotape or videotape each other telling stories in which they recreate emotions. Subsequent viewing of these mini-productions can serve as a springboard for later discussion about choices children have in responding to their own or others' emotions. Audiovisual projects can also be sources of collaborative production and pride. We show children that we value their emotions if we put the emotion work they do in projects of this sort on display for others to see and share. Invite parents or other classes for a film showing, or put on loan children's story tapes for other children's listening.

6. Dealing with children's quarrels and disputes offers a final classroom context in which children can develop their understanding of emotions. Fighting children learn more about anger and aggression if we do more than simply separate them. Ask each child to "tell what happened" from his or her perspective without interruption by the other participant(s). Teachers can convey back what the child says, asking for any corrections or clarifications before calling on the other child to tell her or his part in the altercation. All children should be urged to examine their personal contributions to the conflict. Teachers can also ask children to talk about how the events made them feel and how they think the other child feels, along with what they each could do differently next time. In this way teachers can help children to manage their feelings rather than simply to suppress or deny them; by doing so, Leavitt and Power (1989) claim that we enhance children's ability to develop authentic emotional understandings and relationships.

## CONCLUSION

Research on young children's emotion understanding and socialization is still very new. Based on what we know so far, however, we can expect that children will show individual differences in the kinds of emotion understandings they possess. Differences will be apparent among children of different ages and even in the rate at which age-mates gain new insights into emotions; moreover, children's family backgrounds and histories are likely to translate into different ways of conceptualizing and using emotions. Cross-cultural evidence on emotion understanding should make teachers particularly sensitive to multicultural variation in the ways emotions figure in children's lives. Despite the differences, however, research also suggests that the basic processes by which children learn about emotions are similar, although much more needs to be learned about the nature of these mechanisms. What is, perhaps, fundamentally important is realizing that a great deal of what young children understand about feelings is apparently learned in the informal curriculum provided by their social interactions with others. Emotions frequently are at the heart of these interactions, and children may greatly benefit when we direct their attention to talking about these experiences.

## EVALUATING YOUR MASTERY

1. Which of the following is a fundamental prerequisite for emotional experience?
   a. Knowledge that objects have a permanent existence
   b. Self-concept
   c. Ability to display joy, interest, disgust, and distress
   d. First meaningful gestures

2. Which of the following is true?
   a. Surprise is among the first emotion words acquired.
   b. Young children use emotion words to refer only to the self, not to others.
   c. Children label happy and sad emotions before angry and surprised.
   d. Understanding of negative emotion is attained before understanding of positive emotion.

3. Research by Denham and Zoller (1993) shows that preschoolers more often associate happiness with _____ causes and sadness with _____ causes.
   a. Nonsocial; social
   b. Social; nonsocial
   c. Social; social
   d. Nonsocial; nonsocial

4. Which of the following is an example of emotion socialization in infancy?
   a. Looking-glass self
   b. Social referencing
   c. Playing social games, such as peek-a-boo
   d. Labeling babies' emotional states

5. Tom tells his son Chad that when he went to the dentist as a child, he felt scared but simply tried to think about something pleasant. Tom is engaging in which of the following:
   a. Social referencing
   b. Indirect emotion socialization
   c. Self-referential behaviors
   d. Emotion expectancy communication

6. Discussing emotions with children helps them [distance from/experience more intensely] the rush and immediacy of affective responses.

7. True or False: Japanese individuals report experiencing emotion more intensely than do Americans.

8. True or False: Physical as well as social environments in early childhood programs can assist children in learning about feelings.

## Critical Thinking

1. Kuebli points out that adults socialize children's expression of emotion in both direct and indirect ways. Provide an example of each. Why is emotion socialization important for children's development?

2. How do parents talk differently about emotions with daughters and sons? How might this difference affect the development of girls' and boys' emotional lives?

## Applying Your Knowledge

1. Plan a series of play activities for young children aimed at helping them understand their own and others' emotions. Explain how each activity supports the development of emotion understanding.

2. Visit your local library and explore the shelves of books for young children. Select several books that help children learn about emotion. Describe how each does so.

# 9

*

# "Children of the Dream" Revisited

## 70 Years of Collective Early Child Care in Israeli Kibbutzim

ORA AVIEZER
Oranim Israel

MARINUS H. VAN IJZENDOORN
Leiden University, Netherlands

ABRAHAM SAGI
University of Haifa

CARLO SCHUENGEL

■

Kibbutzim had created a psychological ideology that was used to justify collective sleeping arrangements as contributing to the children's well-being as well as mental health.

■

The family has become the principal authority and has assumed additional caregiving functions, whereas the caregivers' influence has declined and become secondary. Thus, a process is taking place in which responsibilities are being redefined, although the sense of the community's commitment to its children has been preserved.

■

■

Although it is generally agreed that kibbutz children grow up to become well-functioning adults, the findings indicate that they experience less emotional intensity in interpersonal relations, possibly as a result of their experiences in infancy.

■

The increase in infants' insecurity probably reflects a child-care environment in which infants experience inconsistent care as a result of parental absence during the night without an adequate replacement.

■

## EDITOR'S INTRODUCTION

How do children reared collectively in Israeli kibbutzim (cooperative settlements) fare in psychological development? In answering this question, Ora Aviezer and her colleagues highlight the contributions of a variety of relationships—mother, father, professional caregiver, and peers—to young children's social competence and emotional well-being.

In traditional kibbutz collective child-rearing, starting shortly after birth children slept away from their home and parents in a children's house, watched over by women who took turns checking on sleeping infants and toddlers. Today, only a few kibbutzim maintain this practice. But where communal sleeping occurred in the past and still occurs today, kibbutz infants are exposed to multiple caregivers with frequent caregiver turnover during the night. The authors trace the high incidence of insecure mother-infant attachment among kibbutz babies, especially of the insecure-resistant type, to this sleeping practice. Yet long-term negative consequences are tempered by the infant's social network as a whole. In contrast with the mother–infant relationship, the father-infant relationship is unaffected by communal sleeping. And daytime child care by professional caregivers is both stable and of high quality. As Aviezer and her collaborators demonstrate, this extended network is a better predictor of future development than is the mother-child relationship by itself. Furthermore, kibbutz children develop very close ties with peers. By age 2, social interaction with agemates is especially mature, and children form a strong identity with the group. Consequently, peers provide an added source of social support.

Research on the early development of kibbutz children bears on the question of whether child care common in Western nations (daily daytime separations because of maternal employment) interferes with emotional and social development. The studies reviewed in this article answer no, as long as that care is stable and of high quality. Indeed, as long as nighttime separations, which led to attachment insecurity, are no longer practiced in Israeli kibbutzim, children fare well.

An Israeli **kibbutz** (plural, **kibbutzim**) is a cooperative, democratically governed, multigenerational community with an average population of 400 to 900 people. Each kibbutz is economically and socially autonomous but is also affiliated with one of three kibbutz organizations called "kibbutz movements" that offer support and guidance to individual kibbutzim. In the past, the kibbutz movements were deeply divided by political and ideological differences that were expressed even on the level of child-care practices. With the passage of time, however, most of these differences have lost their significance, and many kibbutz members today favor the idea of establishing a single united kibbutz movement. Every kibbutz member works for the kibbutz economy and is in turn provided by the community with housing, food, clothing, health and educational services, recreation, and other living needs. In the past, kibbutzim had been fairly isolated agricultural communities in which living conditions were exceedingly hard. Today kibbutz economies are based on a diversity of industries and agricultural activities and are able to provide members with a satisfying standard of living.

The kibbutz is known as being one of the very few utopian experiments that have succeeded in establishing a radically different way of living and of raising children. As many as four generations have been brought up in kibbutzim since the first such communities were founded at the turn of the century. The kibbutz child-rearing system, also called collective education, has been treated in the literature as furnishing a "natural laboratory" for testing the consequences of child-rearing methods that derived from a unique philosophy and from practices markedly different from those used in the West (Beit-Hallahmi & Rabin, 1977; Bettelheim, 1969; Rapaport, 1958; Spiro, 1958).

Our goal in this article is to evaluate the positive and negative aspects of collective child rearing, particularly in regard to the socioemotional consequences for young children. We begin with a short review of the historical roots of the kibbutz movement and the guiding principles of collective education. This is followed with a description of educational practices in the past and of the changes that brought kibbutz child care to its present form. Then in the second part of the article, the results of studies on kibbutz children are reviewed within the context of dynamic changes in kibbutz life both recently and in the past and with reference to developmental research. Particular emphasis is given to attachment relationships and their consequences. Finally, the development of social competence and relationships with peers is reviewed and discussed.

## HISTORICAL BACKGROUND

The early pioneers of the kibbutz movement were idealistic young people who rejected the culture of the **shtetl** that had dominated the life of Eastern European Jews for centuries and sought to create instead a new society founded on socialist and Zionist principles (Melzer, 1988; Selier, 1977). The task they set for themselves was in no way minor. They proposed to create a collective society that emphasized production and physical labor, striving at the same time to achieve both national and personal independence under conditions of perfect equality. The Marxian precept "from each according to his ability, to each according to his needs" was established as the primary and essential principle of kibbutz life. The political aspirations of kibbutzniks dictated their settlement in remote locations, where they were constrained to cultivate barren land in a harsh climate and a hostile environment. In these circumstances, the decision to raise children collectively contributed to the protection and well-being of the young. Children were thus

Aviezer, O., Van IJzendoorn, M. H., Sagi, A., & Schuengel, C. (1994). "Children of the Dream" revisited: 70 years of collective early child care in Israeli kibbutzim. *Psychological Bulletin, 116,* 99–116.

housed in the only brick building on kibbutz grounds and never went hungry, whereas the adults of the community lived in tents and their food was rationed. Early in kibbutz history, this reality interacted with an awareness of the role of child rearing in furthering the goals of the collective by discouraging individualism, abolishing inequalities between the sexes, and bringing up a person who was better socialized to communal life (Gerson, 1978).

One of the principal goals of early kibbutzim was to alter the patriarchal organization of the family that was typical of Eastern European Jewish culture; in this culture, women were economically dependent on men and parental authority over children was absolute. Collective education was assigned an important place in achieving this goal. It was instituted so as to free women from the burdens of child care, thereby allowing them to participate in the socioeconomic life of the community on an equal footing with men. Men, on the other hand, would share in the duties of child care and become nurturing rather than authoritarian figures in the lives of their children. Moreover, bringing children up collectively was regarded as essential in fostering the solidarity of the group and restraining individualistic tendencies in both children and adults. Educational practices in kibbutzim were accordingly established so as to reflect the egalitarian and democratic philosophy of the kibbutz community (Gerson, 1978).

The kibbutz community therefore assumed total responsibility for all of the material needs of its children in the way of food, clothing, and medical care and for seeing to their spiritual well-being, the latter including mental health, developmental progress, and parental counseling (Gerson, 1978). This responsibility extended to each child individually, who was in a sense regarded as being a "kibbutz' child"; and it also created an informal communal **socialization** network (Rabin & Beit-Hallahmi, 1982). Thus, child care and education were, first and foremost, conceived of as being social mechanisms. It was only later that the needs of children became a central concern in the consciousness of the community (Alon, 1976) and that kibbutzim tended to assume the character of a "child-centered community" (Lewin, 1990; Rabin & Beit-Hallahmi, 1982) in which psychological theory came to influence educational conceptualizations and practices (Kaffman, Elizur, & Rabinowitz, 1990).

## THE GUIDING PRINCIPLES OF COLLECTIVE EDUCATION

During the formative years of collective education, **psychoanalytic theory** was eagerly adopted as an educational guide. A token of this influence is already apparent in the work of Bernfeld, a reforming pedagogue whose utopian visions were widely accepted among young German Jews who immigrated to Palestine and joined the kibbutz movement (Melzer, 1988). Given that one of the principal goals of the kibbutz founders was to change family relations, it is not surprising that psychoanalytic views about the pathological consequences of conflicts in parent-child relations should have had a special appeal for them (Lavi, 1984, 1990a). Kibbutz educators interpreted these views as furnishing support for the ideas of dividing the task of socialization between parents and educators (caregivers and teachers) and of nonreliance on parents alone in educating infants and young children. Maintenance of two emotional centers for kibbutz children—the parental home and the children's house—was thought to protect children against their parents' shortcomings while preserving the benefits of parental love (Golan, 1959). The practice of having children sleep away from the parental home was justified on the grounds that it spared them from the trauma of exposure to the so-called "primal scene" and from the conflicts with parents that are imminent in the **Oedipus complex** (Golan, 1959).

Observers of the kibbutz have characterized parental involvement as emotional and directed toward need gratification, whereas caregivers have been described as being goal directed and instrumental (Bar-Yosef, 1959; Rabin & Beit-Hallahmi, 1982). This role division was considered to be beneficial for children because the objective attitudes and professional approach of caregivers were conducive to the children's mastery of autonomous behavior and social learning without in any way compromising their parents' love (Gerson, 1978; Golan, 1958). In addition, living among peers from an early age was regarded as being an inseparable part of bringing up future kibbutz members because it presented children with a supportive environment for dealing with the kind of human values perceived to be at the core of kibbutz life, such as sharing and consideration for others (Hazan, 1973).

## COLLECTIVE EDUCATION IN PRACTICE: PAST AND PRESENT

There has never been a simple one-to-one correspondence between child-rearing practices on kibbutzim and the beliefs of adult members. Socioeconomic and physical conditions, as well as new psychoeducational theories, have always had an impact on how kibbutz children are brought up, and ideological differences have existed between the different kibbutz organizations since their foundation. Individual kibbutzim, moreover, adopted day-to-day practices that accommodated their particular needs and the prevailing emotional atmosphere of the community (Lavi, 1990a). It is nevertheless possible to describe the practices that are typical of a collective kibbutz upbringing and to present these practices from a dynamic perspective of historical changes.

### Past Trends

Before the 1940s, the medical model dominated approaches to child care both inside and outside the kibbutz (Gerson, 1978; Lewin, 1986). Cleanliness was maintained in infant houses to the point of sterility, infant feeding was rigorously scheduled, parental visits were restricted, and

caregivers (Hebrew: singular, **metapelet**; plural, **metaplot**) were trained in hospitals (Lewin, 1986). Caregivers were regarded as the experts and the ultimate authority in kibbutz children's care (Gerson, 1978). Characteristically, a very small staff of two or three caregivers took care of a large group of between 12 and 18 children. Some of these early practices can be better understood when one takes into account the ecological context of kibbutzim at the time; these were isolated communities far from medical facilities. Moreover, because of the prevalence of serious diseases in this pioneering period, the major concern was to keep babies alive, which was indeed managed quite successfully by the kibbutzim (Gerson, 1978). These years were naturally difficult for many families, some of whom left the kibbutz.

After World War II and Israel's War of Independence, the emphasis shifted from physical health to the emotional needs of children and mothers. This change was supported by a gradual improvement in economic conditions and the increasing influence of the conceptualizations of Bowlby (1951) and Spitz (1946) in regard to "maternal deprivation," which replaced both the medical model and classical psychoanalysis (Lavi, 1984). Parental participation in child care through the infants' first year, particularly on the part of mothers, was also allowed to increase. Mothers were granted maternity leave, which over the years was expanded from 6 weeks to a period of 3 or 4 months. In addition, demand feeding replaced schedule feeding, and breast-feeding was encouraged. As a result of changes that evolved in the 1970s, infants no longer live in the infant house on arrival from the hospital but remain at home with their mothers for the duration of maternity leave (Kaffman, Elizur, & Rabinowitz, 1990). Daily visits of mothers were instituted in the early 1960s for the purpose of allowing mothers to spend time with their children (this period was humorously referred to as the "love hour"). The growing awareness in kibbutzim that children need intimacy for their emotional growth, as well as space and stimulation for activity, has been translated into improvements of the physical environment in the children's houses, a reduction of the size of groups to 4–7 children, and an improvement in the caregiver to children ratio. Training of caregivers has shifted its emphasis to developmental knowledge, educational practices, and the caregivers' role in supporting children's emotional development as it is expressed in tasks such as weaning, toilet training, and nocturnal fears (Lewin, 1985).

In the late 1960s, under the influence of Piaget's theory, children's cognitive development was emphasized (Lewin, 1985). Piaget's views of development as a product of interactions between children and their environment were easily accommodated by the egalitarian philosophy of collective education. The nature of children's activity, creativity, and play became the center of attention, as well as age-related curricula (for example, Haas, 1986; Lewin, 1983).

## Collective Sleeping Arrangements

Collective sleeping arrangements for children away from their parents constitute probably the most distinctive characteristic of kibbutz practices in collective child raising. Many cultures practice multiple caregiving (for example, Barry & Paxton, 1971; Konner, 1977; Morelli & Tronick, 1991; Tronick, Winn, & Morelli, 1985), and the pattern is in many ways similar to the practice in kibbutzim (Rabin & Beit-Hallahmi, 1982). However, a worldwide sample of 183 societies showed that none of them maintained a system of having infants sleep away from their parents (Barry & Paxton, 1971). The major reasons for instituting collective sleeping for children in the early years of kibbutzim were (a) the concern for children's safety, and (b) women's equality and training children for communal life (Fölling-Albers, 1988b; Lavi, 1984). These aims were later interpreted by kibbutz educators as concordant with fundamental psychoanalytic ideas. Thus, kibbutzim had created a psychological ideology that was used to justify collective

sleeping arrangements as contributing to the children's well-being as well as mental health.

The children's house on a kibbutz in fact functions as the children's home in almost every respect. Only a few kibbutzim still maintain communal sleeping arrangements for children; in those where the custom continues, however, this facility serves as the place in which children spend most of their time, eat their meals, are bathed, and sleep at night, in much the same way as they might do at home—hence the term "children's house." The children's house is designed to fulfill all such functions. It consists of a number of bedrooms that are each shared by three or four children, a dining area, showers, and a large space for play activities and learning. Children have private corners in their bedrooms where they keep their personal things, and these corners are decorated according to the child's preference. Family time is in the afternoon and evening, when both parents try to be available. Children are returned to the children's house for the night by their parents, who put them to bed; a caregiver or a parent then remains with them until the night watchwomen take over.

Two night watchwomen are responsible for all children in the kibbutz under 12 years of age. The women are assigned on a weekly rotation basis, and they monitor the children's houses from a central location, usually the infant house, by making rounds and through the use of intercoms. In most cases, night watchwomen are not complete strangers to the children (Ben-Yaakov, 1972). However, the weekly rotation system makes sensitive response to the infants' needs nearly impossible. Moreover, intervention by an unfamiliar adult when infants experience distress may elicit a response of **stranger anxiety** (Bronson, 1968; Spitz, 1965). Thus, although collective sleeping may allow for sufficient monitoring of children's safety, it leaves children with only a precarious and limited sense of security. Independent support for this view was recently offered in a study that found that the longest period of uninterrupted sleep (defined as the longest continuous period scored as sleep without any identified awakening) was more extended for children sleeping at home than for children in communal dormitories (Ophir-Cohen, Epstein, Tzischinsky, Tirosh, & Lavie, 1993). It should be noted that this measure of sleep was derived from the recently developed Automatic Scoring Analysis Program conducted on actigraphic data* (Sadeh, Lavie, Scher, Tirosh, & Epstein, 1991). On the basis of the same actigraphic technique of data collection and analysis, Epstein (1992) recently compared sleeping patterns in 1–6-year old kibbutz children when they slept collectively with their sleeping patterns at home 1 year later. The findings showed that sleep efficiency (defined as the ratio of sleep to total sleep time) in collective sleeping was low and that it improved when children were moved to sleep at home to a level of efficiency similar to that of family-reared children. This improvement occurred despite overcrowding in kibbutz family homes that had not yet been adapted to accommodate the children on a permanent basis. A more detailed discussion of this topic follows in a later section.

Most kibbutzim had abandoned collective sleeping by the beginning of the 1990s (this practice is currently in effect in only 3 of the country's 260 kibbutzim). Doubts about children's collective sleeping had been voiced as early as in the 1950s, and a small number of kibbutzim have always maintained home-based sleeping arrangements (Lavi, 1984). The movement to change children's sleeping arrangements gained momentum in the 1960s and 1970s, along with an upsurge in familistic tendencies (Fölling-Albers, 1988b; Tiger & Shepher, 1975). This trend was reinforced by the growing prosperity of kibbutz economies, which resulted in the building of better family homes for members on the one hand and the weakening of ideological identifications of young kibbutz members on the other (Lavi, 1990b). Familistic trends accelerated significantly in the 1980s, as had been predicted by some researchers (for example, Beit-Hallahmi, 1981; Rabin & Beit-Hallahmi, 1982). Moreover, these trends have continued, notwithstanding serious economic problems that required many kibbutzim to commit themselves to heavy financial obligations to be able to make the necessary modifications for family housing (Melzer & Neubauer, 1988).

The success of familism in kibbutzim reduced women's participation in community life (Gerson, 1978; Lavi, 1984), pushing their struggle for equality into the background. Collective education failed to free kibbutz women from child care as their primary responsibility or from leading a dual-career life combining motherhood and work. Frustrated by their work options, many kibbutz women invested in motherhood (Keller, 1983), and women were the leading proponents for changing the practice of collective sleeping for children. Thus, along with the men, they helped to preserve the sex-typed occupational structure of kibbutzim (for example, the absence of men in the caregiver's role), rather than attempting to change it (Fölling-Albers, 1988a).

## Present Practices

Kibbutz infants are exposed to multiple caregiving very early in their lives (Lavi, 1990a). In their first 3 months, kibbutz infants receive exclusive maternal care in the family's residence. They are brought to the infant house as soon as their mothers return to work part time. During the initial period of their stay in the infant house, they are cared for jointly by the mother and the metapelet. Mothers are almost exclusively in charge of feeding, and they arrange their work schedule accordingly; caregivers are responsible for the infants between maternal visits. During the second half of the infants' first year, caregivers gradually assume responsibility for the children's various needs as the mothers increase

---

* Editor's note: An *actigraph* is a small, computerized movement detector that can be attached to someone's arm or leg. Data obtained are automatically scored to reveal the duration of sleep and wakefulness during the monitoring period.

**Table 9.1  Overview of the Distribution of Caregiving Responsibilities During Early Childhood**

| Caregiving responsibility | Age period | | | | | |
| --- | --- | --- | --- | --- | --- | --- |
| | 0–6 weeks | 6 weeks–6 months | 6–9 months | 9–4 months | 14 months-kindergarten | Postkindergarten |
| Feeding | Parent(s): on demand | Parent(s): if possible, every 3–4 hours | Parent(s): weaning, caregiver begins to take over | Caregiver (3 meals per day) | Caregiver | Caregiver |
| Washing/ diapering | Parent(s): between feedings | Parent(s), caregiver | Parent(s), caregiver | Caregiver | Caregiver | Caregiver |
| Play | Parent(s) | Parent(s), caregiver, love hour | Parent(s), caregiver, love hour | Parent(s), caregiver, love hour | Parent(s), caregiver, love hour | Parent(s), caregiver, love hour |
| Socialization | Not available | Parent(s) | Parent(s), caregiver | Parent(s), caregiver | Parent(s), caregiver | Parent(s), caregiver, peers |
| Education | Not available | Not available | Not available | Caregiver | Caregiver | Caregiver |
| Night care* | Caregiver, watchwomen | Caregiver, watchwomen | Caregiver, watchwomen | Caregiver, watchwomen | Caregiver, watchwomen | Caregiver, watchwomen |

Note: The information included here is based on data from Ben-Yaakov (1972) and Rabin and Beit-Hallahmi (1982). The picture of the kibbutz child-rearing system is continuously changing. For this reason, the information provided here may not be adequate in light of recent developments. However, it represents the system in its most characteristic form.

* In home-based sleeping, provided by parents. In collective sleeping, parents wake up children in the morning up until 9–14 months of age.

their work load. Thus, by the infants' second year, they come under the full care of the caregivers, who play an increasingly larger role in their socialization with respect to issues such as table manners, sharing, play habits, and knowledge of the environment.

Table 9.1 contains an overview of the caregiving responsibilities during early childhood in the kibbutz. This description represents a summary of various periods; the delegation of responsibilities may change further.

Children join the toddler group, which is larger than the infant group (10–12 children), at about the middle of their second year, but the 1:3 ratio of adults to children is maintained. At this stage, caregivers are responsible for a wide range of the children's needs (for example, administering of medication, toilet training, appropriate nutrition, and growth and age-appropriate activities of individual children). When children approach 3 years of age, they move to the nursery class, which is somewhat larger and where the ratio of adults to children is reduced to 1:4. Parents are welcome to spend time in the children's house; they visit whenever they can, and caregivers try to accommodate them.

Home-based sleeping has changed the proportion of time spent by kibbutz children in the children's house to a pattern similar to that of nonkibbutz day-care settings. Children come to the children's house in the morning and go home during late afternoon. Maternal responsibilities for infants' care throughout the first year have remained the same, but the love hour practice is no longer officially observed. Most parents, even among those originally opposed to home-based sleeping, are now satisfied with the change in sleeping arrangements (Lavi, 1984). Children's sleeping at home has clearly changed the balance between the two emotional centers of the family and the community. The family has become the principal authority and has assumed additional caregiving functions, whereas the caregivers' influence has declined and become secondary. Thus, a process is taking place in which responsibilities are being redefined, although the sense of

the community's commitment to its children has been preserved.

Collective education in the 1990s is therefore faced with the need of negotiating new ways of expressing the influence of the collective without infringing on the autonomy and privacy of families. This is not an easy task, considering the heterogeneous nature of multigenerational kibbutz populations. Also, recent economic difficulties and difficulties in providing adequate professional manpower have resulted in demands to reduce the costs, of early care by restructuring it to resemble nonkibbutz day care in Israel (Sagi & Koren-Karie, 1993). Clearly, early child care in kibbutzim is changing. As in the past, the changes are taking place within the context of general processes in which collective responsibility is being reduced and new ideas for the accountability of the community for the actions of individual members and the resultant consequences are being negotiated. This topic is, however, beyond the scope of the present article.

## SUMMARY OF THE HISTORICAL REVIEW

The kibbutz approach to child rearing established a radically different method of raising children that was legitimized by both socialist and psychoanalytic ideas. Its original conceptualization as a social mechanism for promoting the goals of a new society led to the institution of unique childcare practices. More specifically, the practices of nonmaternal care for infants and toddlers, children dwelling with their peers in children's houses instead of with their families, and the division of the tasks of socialization between parents and caregivers (teacher) differed markedly from the educational practices common in Western societies (see Lamb, Sternberg, Hwang, & Broberg, 1992; Melhuish & Moss, 1991).

The course of the evolution of early care in kibbutzim reflects the changes occurring in the physical and socioeconomic conditions of these communities, as well as changes in ideology, educational conceptualizations, and knowledge. During the early period of kibbutzim, collective education was, in part, determined by the difficult conditions of existence; thus, children's health and physical development were regarded as the primary criteria for child care. The rigors of the environment, adherence to the medical model, inexperience and lack of knowledge, and ideological zeal all contributed to the strict practices involving kibbutz children and their parents. Growing knowledge about young children's emotional and cognitive development and improved economic conditions later led to a shift in emphasis to emotional needs and to a restructuring of early care in kibbutz education. The definition of children's well-being thus came to include more than mere physical health and resulted in an emphasis on caregiving practices and furnishing children with a stimulating environment.

A historical overview of early child care in the kibbutz reveals an important shift in the relative weights assigned to the two major agents of socialization: the family and the community. In the beginning, the influence of the community was preeminent. Thus, its representatives—the caregivers—were granted ultimate authority over educational practices. In later years, there has been a gradual ascendancy of familism, expressed by more intense parental involvement. The institution of home-based sleeping has finalized the process by transferring most caregiving functions to the family. The practice of collective sleeping arrangements for children, which is rapidly disappearing, has become a historically unique phenomenon that deserves an evaluation in terms of its socioemotional consequences.

## THE KIBBUTZ SYSTEM OF EARLY CARE: A RESEARCH REVIEW

As noted earlier, child rearing in kibbutzim has attracted a fair amount of attention motivated by interest in the developmental outcomes of its unique practices. Any comprehensive system such as kibbutz child care can be evaluated from

a variety of points of view. In what follows, we briefly consider studies of parental attitudes, caregivers' roles, and the quality of care offered by collective education. We then evaluate in depth the developmental consequences of kibbutz child rearing, with an emphasis on socioemotional development.

## Parental Attitudes

A hypothesis frequently proposed about kibbutz mothers is that their lower than usual participation in the care of their children may result in guilt feelings that lead to insecure mother-child relationships (for example, Fölling-Albers, 1988b; Liegle, 1974). According to Bettelheim (1969), however, kibbutz women suffer from maternal guilt feelings because of their subconscious rejection of their own mothers. No empirical evidence corroborates either of these claims. Lewin (1990) found that most kibbutz mothers regard the infant house and metapelet as assisting them in their motherhood. However, women's prominent support of familistic trends suggests that recent generations of mothers lay claim to a larger share in the caregiving role than did mothers in the founding generations of the kibbutzim (Kaffman, Elizur, & Rabinowitz, 1990; Lavi, 1984; Spiro, 1979; Tiger & Shepher, 1975). Kibbutz mothers entertain specific notions about themselves in the role of educators. They perceive themselves as being more nurturant and influential in the development of interpersonal behavior in their children. They attribute to the metapelet a more demanding role and regard themselves as less influential than her in regard to such age-related behaviors as dressing and toilet training. In comparison, day-care mothers perceive themselves as being more nurturant and influential than caregivers in every domain of child development (Feldman & Yirmiya, 1986).

## The Role of Caregivers

Caregivers are assigned a central role in kibbutz education. Their influence on children's development of autonomy and socialization to kibbutz life is considered paramount, and their constant and stable presence is thought to potentially compensate for poor maternal functioning (Gerson, 1978). Indeed, metaplot have been reported to perceive themselves as the most important influence in children's social development and physical care (Kaffman, Elizur, & Rabinowitz, 1990); however, they have also been reported to be uncertain about their professional role when mother–infant relations require intervention (Harel, 1986). The trust kibbutz mothers have expressed in their infants' caregivers has been attributed to the sharing of responsibilities and the openness of kibbutz child-care services to parental and community supervision (Feldman & Yirmiya, 1986; Lewin, 1990) and to the professional expertise of caregivers (Harel, 1986). Like kibbutz mothers, most metaplot (who are often mothers themselves) have been supportive of home-based sleeping and of infants remaining with their mothers for more extensive periods after their birth (Kaffman, Elizur, & Rabinowitz, 1990).

Systematic observations of caregivers' interactions with toddlers have shown that the approach of metaplot toward children is positive but is adversely affected by poor physical conditions and caregivers' fatigue (Gerson & Schnabel-Brandes, 1990). Gerson and Schnabel-Brandes suggested that the metaplot's strong commitment to the ideological and pedagogical values of the kibbutz and their strong involvement with the children contribute to their positive approach. However, Rosenthal (1991) found that superior training and experience rather than ideological commitment distinguished kibbutz metaplot from caregivers in other Israeli day-care settings.

## Quality of Early Care in the Kibbutz

In a recent overview of Israeli day-care centers by Sagi and Koren-Karie (1993), the quality of kibbutz child care was rated as being the best in the country. The specific advantages indicated by these authors were the high quality of physical and educational environments in the kibbutz system, the small group size (8–12 children), a good caregiver to child ratio (1:3–1:4), and the level of caregivers' commitment. Note that these standards of care had developed in the kibbutz long before the quality of nonmaternal care had become an issue of professional concern, and their advantage had already become evident. For instance, Gewirtz (1965) attributed the decline of smiling he found among infants from institutions and day nurseries, as compared with infants reared in families and kibbutzim, to less stimulation and availability of caregivers in those child-care settings in which custodial care and poor children to adult ratios prevailed.

Rosenthal (1991) examined three Israeli child-care settings in regard to the educational quality of the physical environment, the content and emotional tone of each program, and the characteristics of the daily interactions of the children with their caregivers. Her findings corroborated Sagi and Koren-Karie's (1993) assessment. The kibbutz environment was significantly better than the environment of both center care and family day care. Emotional atmosphere and children's daily interactions in the kibbutz resembled those in family day care, in which group size and adult-child ratio are similar. However, kibbutzim scored significantly better in these respects than did center care. In addition, children's social orientation and active learning are determined by developmentally appropriate activities, which are another aspect of quality care (Howes, Phillips, & Whitebook, 1992; Rosenthal, 1991). Rosenthal (1991) also measured the extent to which toddlers in the various settings engaged in active learning and social interaction as an indication of the quality of their experience. She found that kibbutz children were more active in both learning and social exchanges and attributed this finding to their experience in an environment that combined structural aspects and processes of better quality care as delineated by Phillips and Howes (1987).

Yet, caregivers' stability, which is another important aspect of quality care, seems to be a relative weakness in the kibbutz child-care system. Gerson and Nathan (1969) surveyed the entire caregiver population of the kibbutz movement and found a 25 to 33 percent annual turnover rate. Caregiver turnover rates were highest for toddler groups and lowest for infant groups. Although no current data are available on the topic, Lewin (1982) reported that caregiver turnover has always been a problem and has not decreased over the years. Turnover rates are related to the quality of a caregiver's work environment, the position often being characterized by low salaries and low prestige (Whitebook, Howes, & Phillips, 1989). It is interesting to note that caregiving does not have much prestige in kibbutzim either, despite proclaimed convictions concerning its importance (Gerson & Nathan, 1969). A possible reason is that early care is often regarded as a task that women can perform instinctively without formal training (Gerson, 1976). Although turnover rates reported for kibbutzim are somewhat lower than those in the United States (Whitebook, Howes, & Phillips, 1989), they are nevertheless high enough to suggest substantial instability. In a comprehensive system of care—such as that found in kibbutzim—that delegates many parental tasks to caregivers, the consequences of such instability may be even more severe. Yet, the cohesive, intimate nature of the kibbutz community, with its high degree of familiarity and involvement among people, may contribute to a sense of consistency and predictability for both children and parents. The sharing of caregiving responsibilities may be viewed as a source of instability in the children's house. However, unlike other child-care environments, kibbutz caregiving takes place within the context of enduring relationships. These relationships, in turn, can sustain adults' mutual trust (Feldman & Yirmiya, 1986) and support children's sense of living in a stable, secure environment (see Rabin, 1965). One can conclude that the quality of kibbutz care has been excellent in regard to its structural dimensions and basic caregiving characteristics; at the same time, however, caregiver stability has been relatively weak and may therefore have had adverse effects on children's socioemotional development (Howes, Phillips, & Whitebook, 1992).

## THE DEVELOPMENTAL CONSEQUENCES OF KIBBUTZ CHILD REARING

In this section, we consider the research on the developmental consequences of kibbutz child rearing, which has been in force for more than 4 decades. Classical evaluations of kibbutz child rearing were based on **participant observation techniques** and **clinical impressions** that focused on nonmaternal care for small children. Succeeding research efforts concentrated on comparing kibbutz children with their counterparts outside the kibbutz on measures that have often furnished global assessments of development, with implications for future personality characteristics. Exposure to multiple relationships in early childhood, which is inherent in group care, became the main issue in this regard. The current wave of research has been concerned with the socioemotional development of kibbutz children and has focused on attachment theory. Within the context of a growing worldwide prevalence of nonmaternal and group care in early childhood, studies have concentrated on the effects of the unique characteristics of collective upbringing on interpersonal relations and personality formation.

### Classical Evaluations of Kibbutz Child Rearing

The general impression of most early observers of kibbutz children was that their relations with their parents were warm and affectionate; however, the delegation of child-care functions to caregivers was judged to be a potential obstacle to the formation of exclusive relationships between mothers and infants and a potential impediment for future personality development (Bettelheim, 1969; Irvine, 1952; Spiro, 1958; Winograd, 1958). However, both Spiro (1958) and Bettelheim (1969) concluded that kibbutz children appeared to grow into well-functioning and adapted adults, despite early indications of emotional insecurity (Spiro, 1958) and some interference with the development of personal identity, emotional intimacy, and individual achievement (Bettelheim, 1969).

Spiro (1958) observed, in an anthropological study, that kibbutz children often felt rejected by their caregivers and had to face aggression from their peers. Their emotional pain resulted in introversion and resistance in their interpersonal contacts with kibbutz members and outsiders. However, Spiro did not perceive the reality of kibbutz children as similar to institutions in which emotional deprivation prevails (Bowlby, 1951). Bettelheim (1969) believed that the "children of the dream," as he called kibbutz children, would experience early in their childhood a balanced mixture of trust and mistrust of the environment. The relatively large number of caregivers would be a source of mistrust, but the availability of caregivers in all situations and the continuous presence of the peer group would prevent the development of **separation anxiety**. According to Bettelheim, the absence of extremely positive or negative emotions in the experience of kibbutz children underlies an "emotional flatness" that he observed in their personalities. Unfortunately, many of the early observations were unsystematic (some were even based on secondhand reports) and often relied on small unrepresentative samples without control groups. Hence, they have been criticized as anecdotal and speculative (Lavi, 1990a; Rabin & Beit-Hallahmi, 1982).

## The Early Studies

The first systematic empirical investigation of the effects of collective child rearing was conducted by Rabin (1958, 1965). Rabin compared the performance of kibbutz children of various ages with that of children from a rural semicommunal setting (moshav) on a battery of tests of mental and social development to assess the hypothesis that kibbutz children suffer from partial psychological deprivation because of their repeated transitions between the parental home and the children's house. His results indicated a significant developmental lag in the socioemotional and verbal learning of kibbutz infants, although it was not considered to be pathogenic. This lag was found to have disappeared by 10 years of age, when there was evidence of early independence and less problematic puberty (Rabin, 1965). These results highlighted the differential effects of group environment in regard to multiple interpersonal relations at different ages. Although the presence of multiple "significant others" in infancy may be overwhelming to the tender personality, it may be supportive of **ego** development later in middle childhood and adolescence.

Rabin's work, however, faced various criticisms. Golan (1958) argued that the developmental delay found in kibbutz infants did not result from maternal deprivation. He attributed it to the caregiver's focus on satisfying infants' physical needs at the expense of providing them with personal contact and arranging an adequate environment for play. Furthermore, Kohen-Raz (1968) criticized Rabin's sample as small and unrepresentative. He studied a larger sample of infants and found that the developmental level of kibbutz infants was equal to that of family-raised Israeli infants and to that of an American normative sample. In addition, contradictory findings of new studies challenged Rabin's conclusions about kibbutz infants. Gewirtz (1965) found that the smiling response of kibbutz infants through the first 18 months was similar to that of family-raised infants. Greenbaum and Landau (1977) found that kibbutz infants possessed advanced linguistic skills comparable to those of family-reared infants in spite of less time spent with their mothers; Holdstein and Borus (1976) found the same for kibbutz preschoolers. It was therefore concluded that collective education had no adverse effects on infant development (Kohen-Raz, 1968), and the nurturing, stimulating character of the kibbutz environment was underscored (Holdstein & Borus, 1976).

Rabin's (1965) findings represented the development of kibbutz infants as observed during the 1950s, when his study had been conducted.

Because Rabin did not assess the quality of child care as a variable separate from interpersonal relationships, it would be difficult to argue that one or the other was an exclusive cause. Moreover, it is important to note that most of the early studies used developmental measures that evaluated social-verbal learning rather than socioemotional experience. Thus, given the wide consensus that the quality of day care is an important factor in children's development (Clarke-Stewart, 1989; Fein & Fox, 1988; Howes, 1988b), it is not surprising that improvements in the quality of early child care in the kibbutz were associated with improved performance on developmental measures; these measures do not, however, allow for direct assessment of emotional development.

## Long-Term Effects of Collective Early Care

Long-term effects are an important aspect of the consequences of early care. Kibbutz children, adolescents, and young adults have been judged to be emotionally healthy, constructive, and successful. Rabin (1965) based these conclusions on **projective psychological tests** (for example, Rorschach, Draw a Person, Sentence Completion, and Thematic Apperception Test) in which he found indications of intellectual achievements, greater personality maturity, and ego strength. Also, Zellermayer and Marcus (1971) noted the scarcity of delinquency and drug abuse. In one of the few longitudinal studies of kibbutz-raised individuals, Rabin and Beit-Hallahmi (1982) interviewed Rabin's (1965) subjects 20 years after they had originally been studied. They found that collective-raised and moshav-raised adults were very similar in terms of their level of education and achievements. Furthermore, they were found to be similar in their functioning as spouses and in their identification with their parents. However, Rabin and Beit-Hallahmi also found some empirical support for a lower capability among kibbutz-reared adults to establish intimate friendships. This was attributed to the differential effect of the early experiences of the two groups. Similarly, a reduced

need for affective involvement and emotional intimacy, as assessed by the Family Relations Test (Anthony & Bene, 1957), was found by Regev, Beit-Hallahmi, and Sharabany (1980) among school-aged children and by Weinbaum (1990) among kindergartners who lived in kibbutzim with communal sleeping arrangements. Berman (1988) summarized a number of studies that investigated the effects of traditional collective upbringing (including communal sleeping) and concluded that such an upbringing had an impact on personality development by causing "a consistent interference with emotional experience, creativity, and the quality of object relations as expressed especially in intimate relationships" (p. 327). Thus, although it is generally agreed that kibbutz children grow up to become well-functioning adults, the findings indicate that they experience less emotional intensity in interpersonal relations, possibly as a result of their experiences in infancy. However, a direct assessment of the emotional experience of infants in collective child care and its consequences had to await new theoretical formulations and research procedures of the kind offered by attachment theory.

## ATTACHMENT RESEARCH: INFANT'S RELATIONSHIPS AND THEIR CONSEQUENCES

Bowlby's (1951) publication on maternal deprivation, as well as the work of researchers such as Spiro, Rabin, and Bettelheim, inspired changes in kibbutz child-care practices (Lavi, 1984). Still, the primary research orientation was that of classical psychoanalytic theory, and it was not until the 1970s and 1980s that **attachment theory** became one of the leading paradigms. The conceptual framework and research procedures of attachment theory, particularly, the **strange situation paradigm** (Ainsworth, Blehar, Waters, & Wall, 1978), opened new avenues for investigating issues that have concerned kibbutz research since the 1950s, including the effects on infant development of early exposure to multiple caregivers in the context of group care.

According to attachment theory, the security of infants' attachment to their caregivers is determined by the quality of the care they receive (Bowlby, 1969/1982). Sensitive responses to infants' signals and needs are associated with **secure attachments,** whereas rejection of infants' communications and inconsistent care are related to **insecure attachments** (Ainsworth, et al., 1978). A multiple caregiving arrangement exposes infants to repeated separations from their primary caregivers as well as to new relationships. When nonmaternal care involves group care, the feasibility of providing sensitive care to individual children within a group and the nature of relationships with additional caregivers become important issues for examination. The increasing numbers of children who are exposed to various multiple caregiving arrangements lend additional importance to the study of these issues. Therefore, our review of attachment research in kibbutzim examines the relationships of kibbutz infants and the consequences of these relationships in terms of socioemotional development.

## Infants' Relations with Parents

The first studies focused on children's relations to their mothers and concluded that collective upbringing does not interfere with the intensity of attachment relations. In a stressful situation very similar to the strange situation paradigm, 2- to 4-year-old kibbutz children (Maccoby & Feldman, 1972) and 8- to 24-month-old kibbutz infants (Fox, 1977) used their mothers as a **secure base**. However, neither Maccoby and Feldman nor Fox were able to apply the extensive classification system of attachment behavior in the strange situation (Ainsworth et al., 1978). This is probably the reason why they chose to measure the intensity of attachment as if it were a personality trait. In current conceptualizations, attachment is viewed as a strategy of dealing with the emotions elicited by stressful events and with the status of the attachment figure in this process.

Three fundamental strategies have been identified: (1) denial of negative emotions and avoidance of the attachment figure, who is not expected to provide relief (A); (2) open communication with the attachment figure about negative emotions (B); and (3) preoccupation with negative emotions and ambivalence toward the attachment figure, who for the child is both a source of stress and a potential "haven of security" (C; Main, 1990). The classification of attachment behavior in the strange situation paradigm is based on several strategies. A child's attachment to the primary caregiver can be classified as **insecure-avoidant** (A), **secure** (B), or **insecure-resistant** (C). The view of attachment as a relationship organization underlies much of the later research.

Sagi, Lamb, Lewkowicz, and colleagues (1985) used the strange situation paradigm (Ainsworth, et al., 1978) and its classification system to study the relationships of 85 communally sleeping kibbutz infants with their parents and caregivers. They also examined the relationships with their mothers of 36 Israeli infants attending city day-care facilities. They found that only 59 percent of kibbutz infants were securely attached to their mothers, as compared with 75 percent of Israeli day-care infants and the 65 percent–70 percent levels found in most studies. Among children with insecure attachments in both Israeli samples, anxious-ambivalent relationships were overrepresented. Skewed distributions of attachment relationships, including that found by Sagi and his colleagues, have raised concern that the strange situation may not be cross-culturally valid (Grossmann, Grossmann, Spangler, Suess, & Unzner, 1985; Sagi, Lamb, Lewkowicz, et al., 1985). However, recent secondary analyses and meta-analyses (Sagi, Van IJzendoorn, & Koren-Karie, 1991; Van IJzendoorn & Kroonenberg, 1988), as well as analyses of cross-national data (Lamb, Thompson, & Gardner, 1985; Sagi, 1990; Van IJzendoorn, 1990), have indicated that this procedure is valid for assessing universal communicative patterns between adults and infants that may be affected by stress (Van IJzendoorn & Kroonenberg, 1988) or by cultural preferences (Sagi, 1990). Clearly, more research was needed to find precursors of attachment relationships in kibbutz children so as to understand that unusual rates of insecure relationships.

Communal sleeping in children's houses—the unique characteristic of a collective upbringing—was postulated by Sagi and his colleagues to be a possible antecedent for the development of insecure attachments, and a new study was designed to investigate this assumption. Before we describe this study, it should be noted that, until the mid-1980s, decisions about sleeping arrangements were closely related to ideological differences among the major kibbutz movements. The traditional, more politically socialist movement advocated communal sleeping and emphasized conservative interpretations of kibbutz ideology. Moreover, the transition to home-based sleeping brought further changes. The relative weight of the children's house and the influence of the metapelet were reduced in home-based sleeping, whereas the educational practices of both caregivers and parents were characterized as more permissive than in communal sleeping (Lavi, 1990b). Thus, it can be argued that sleeping arrangements were associated with a host of other important variations. However, the influence of these variations on developmental outcomes was not assessed separately from sleeping arrangements. Nathan (1984), in his summary of the relevant research, concluded that children who were raised in different sleeping arrangements were very similar on outcome variables including behavior disorders, social adjustment, self-image, and adolescents' autonomy from parents.

In a new **quasi-experimental study,** 23 mother-infant dyads from traditional kibbutzim (with communal sleeping arrangements) and 25 dyads from nontraditional kibbutzim (where family-based sleeping was instituted) were observed in the strange situation paradigm (Sagi, Van IJzendoorn, Aviezer, Donnell, & Mayseless, 1994). The distribution of attachment relationships for communally sleeping infants was confirmed and was even more extreme than in the earlier study: Only 48 percent of the infants were securely attached to their mothers. However, the distribution for infants in family-based sleeping arrangements was completely different. Eighty percent of these infants were securely attached to their mothers, a rate similar to that found among urban Israeli infants (Sagi, Lamb, Lewkowicz, et al., 1985).

To rule out alternative explanations for the effect of communal sleeping arrangements, assessments were also made of the ecology of the children's house during the day, maternal separation anxiety, infants' temperament, and mother-infant play interactions. The two groups (that is, family-based and communal sleepers) were found comparable on all of these variables. Thus, it was concluded that collective sleeping, experienced by infants as a time during which mothers were largely unavailable and inaccessible, was responsible for the greater insecurity found in this group. Inconsistent responsiveness was inherent in the reality of these infants, because sensitive responding by mother or caregiver during the day sharply contrasted with the presence of an unfamiliar person at night. Inconsistent responsiveness has previously been considered to be an important antecedent condition of insecure, ambivalent attachment (Ainsworth, et al., 1978).

Figure 9-1 represents the distribution of attachment classifications with mothers and illustrates how the collective kibbutz samples differ from other groups in Israel and elsewhere in the world. The plot is based on an earlier correspondence analysis of the then-known studies of attachment (see Van IJzendoorn & Kroonenberg, 1988). In addition, we calculated the relative positions of the subgroups of kibbutzim both with and without collective sleeping from Sagi and colleagues (1994). The first dimension in Figure 9.1 shows a progression of an overrepresentation of the A classification on the left to an overrepresentation of the C classification on the right, the second dimension indicates a B versus A plus C overrepresentation. The plot clearly shows that the collective kibbutz samples are very much at variance with other Israeli samples and samples

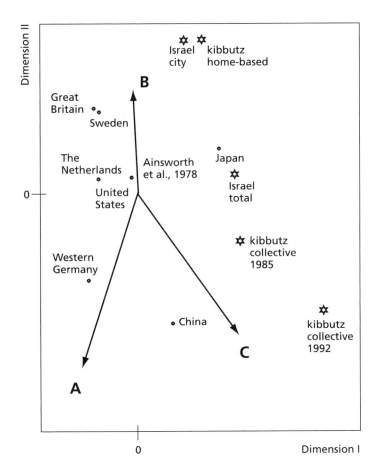

**FIGURE 9.1** Distributions of attachment classifications in various countries and in various Israeli samples (based on Van IJzendoorn & Kroonenberg, 1988). This plot is based on the meta-analysis by Van IJzendoorn and Kroonenberg of almost 2,000 worldwide attachment classifications. The distribution of attachment classifications is plotted for each country. The origin of the plot represents global distributions. The distance between points represents discrepancy; the direction of the discrepancy is indicated by the three vectors. Van IJzendoorn and Kroonenberg provided locations of the data points. Only Ainsworth, Blehar, Waters, and Wall's (1978) [American] sample and the Israeli samples have individual data points. Added to Van IJzendoorn and Kroonenberg's plot is the sample of Sagi, Van IJzendoorn, Aviezer, Donnell, and Mayseless (1994). This sample is indicated by kibbutz home-based and kibbutz collective 1992. This information is also accounted for in the Israel total.

from other countries. The anomalous position of the collective kibbutz samples is accounted for by the overrepresentation of insecure and, particularly, ambivalent attachments. Thus, Sagi, et al.'s (1994) recent findings underscore the sensitivity of the strange situation paradigm to the nature of infants' emotional communications with their caregivers, even though they are derived from experiences in variable rearing conditions embedded in various cultural contexts.

More evidence about problematic aspects of communal sleeping can be derived from the **Adult Attachment Interview** (AAI; Main & Goldwyn, 1991), which assesses adults' current mental representations with regard to their early childhood attachment relationships. Sagi and colleagues (1992) presented the AAI to 20 mothers

from kibbutzim maintaining collective sleeping arrangements and to 25 mothers from home-sleeping kibbutzim. Parent-child concordance in attachment classifications was relatively low for the communally sleeping group (40 percent) and relatively high for the home-sleeping group (76 percent). Possibly, caring for infants within the ecology of collective sleeping may have disrupted the transmission of parents' internal model of relationships into their parenting style.

Sagi, Lamb, Lewkowicz, et al. (1985) also observed communally sleeping kibbutz infants with their fathers in the strange situation paradigm; they found that independent of the infants' attachment to mothers, the rates of secure attachments to fathers (67 percent) were no lower than those commonly found in other populations.

This suggests that communal sleeping has presented no particular problem for infants' relationships with their fathers. Moreover, an examination of the behavior patterns of mothers and fathers at home with communally sleeping infants aged 8–16 months revealed that kibbutz mothers and fathers behave differently toward their infants during natural interactions, in a manner similar to mothers and fathers in other cultures. However, unlike other cultures, kibbutz infants showed no preference for one parent over the other (Sagi, Lamb, Shoham, Dvir, & Lewkowicz, 1985). The infants' lack of preference was interpreted as an indication that neither parent was functioning as the primary caregiver because kibbutz infants were being cared for in the children's house. It is possible, however, that the infants' behavior reflects their experience with parents who do not regard any part of child care as being the exclusive responsibility of only one parent (Shamai, 1992). In addition, kibbutz fathers tend to spend more time with their infants than do their urban counterparts (Sagi, Koren, & Weinberg, 1987); thus, it is possible that the time infants spend together with their parents may in itself be an important contribution to the relationships between parents and children (Clarke-Stewart, 1988).

Research on children in day care (Farran & Ramey, 1977; Goossens & Van IJzendoorn, 1990; Howes, Phillips, & Whitebook, 1992; Howes, Rodning, Galluzzo, & Meyers, 1988), and on kibbutz children (Fox, 1977; Sagi, Lamb, Lewkowicz, et al., 1985) has suggested that caregivers and teachers function as attachment figures in addition to the parents. Sagi, Lamb, Lewkowicz, , et al. (1985) observed 84 kibbutz infants with their caregivers (metaplot) in the strange situation. They classified 53 percent of the infant-metaplot relationships as secure, independently of the classifications of these infants' relationships with their mothers and fathers. Goossens and Van IJzendoorn (1990), in a Dutch sample, and Howes, Phillips, and Whitebook (1992), in an American sample, found similar rates of secure relationships between children and

their caregivers (57 percent and 51 percent, respectively). Although these rates of security were somewhat lower than those commonly found between infants and parents, Sagi and Van IJzendoorn (in press) and Van IJzendoorn, Sagi, and Lambermon (1992) concluded, from an evaluation of two data sets (Goossens & Van IJzendoorn, 1990; Oppenheim, Sagi, & Lamb, 1988), that it is justified to argue that infants indeed develop attachment relationships to their professional caregivers and that these relationships reflect the interactive history of the caregiver-infant dyad. Note that the rates of secure relationships with mothers found in kibbutzim where communal sleeping is in force (59 percent) actually resemble rates found for secure relationships with caregivers (51 percent–57 percent). One can conclude that in an environment of multiple caregivers, children form multiple attachment relationships that are independent of each other.

Note that the traditional argument favored by attachment theory (Main & Weston, 1981; Sroufe, 1985) about the lack of concordance in the attachment relationships of a single infant to its mother and father has been recently challenged by Fox, Kimmerly, and Schafer (1991). Their meta-analytic study on the concordance of infant-mother and infant-father attachment showed a significant—albeit small—degree of similarity between these two relationships. One might speculate that the concordance of attachment between parental and nonparental caregivers is weak or absent because **assortative mating** is much less likely to play a role. Steele, Steele, and Fonagy (1993) proposed that the concordance between infant-mother and infant-father attachment quality exists because of the concordance between maternal and paternal **attachment representations**. In a combination of studies on the concordance of attachment representations in husbands and wives, Van IJzendoorn and Bakermans-Kranenburg (1996) found a modest association: Secure wives are more often married to secure husbands than might be expected by chance. If attachment is transmitted across generations, this association would lead to a correspondence between infant attachment to father and infant attachment to mother. Although pertinent data are lacking, the same association seems unlikely between parental and nonparental attachment representations. In the same vein, maternal modeling of caregiving behaviors that might determine the quality of infant attachment is more likely between a child's mother and father than between the child's parents and nonparental caregivers. In an environment of multiple caregivers, therefore, attachment relationships might be independent, at least for parental and nonparental caregivers. More data on attachment networks and attachment representations in the kibbutz are needed to confirm these speculations.

## Consequences of Attachment Relationships

These recent findings of attachment research in a sense support Rabin's (1965) argument that kibbutz infants suffer from a partial psychological deprivation; they also suggest that collective sleeping is an important contributing factor to this effect. Such a conclusion would be in accord with the findings of earlier research that collective sleeping has a long-lasting moderating impact on socioemotional needs and styles (Berman, 1988; Regev, Beit-Hallahmi, & Sharabany, 1980). Rabin conjectured that partial deprivation of this kind in infancy has a very limited long-term effect on development. Additional data must be examined to assess whether the quality of early relationships, as assessed in the strange situation paradigm, has a long-term developmental effect.

Oppenheim, Sagi, and Lamb (1988) assessed a broad spectrum of socioemotional competencies of most of the subjects in the sample of Sagi, Lamb, Lewkowicz, et al. (1985) when they were 5 years old in an attempt to understand the consequences of early relationships. They found that secure attachment to the caregiver during infancy was the strongest predictor of children being empathic, dominant, independent,

achievement oriented, and behaviorally purposive in kindergarten; on the other hand, no significant relationships were found between these socioemotional developments and the quality of children's attachment to their parents. These results suggest that the influence of attachment relationships may be viewed as domain specific. Because infants' relations with caregivers had been formed in the context of the infant house, they are the best predictor of children's socioemotional behavior in similar contexts.

However, one can expect attachment relationships in a multiple caregiver environment to interact in such a way that the predictive power of individual relationships is weaker than that of their combination (Howes, et al., 1988; Tavecchio & Van IJzendoorn, 1987). Van IJzendoorn, Sagi, and Lambermon (1992) examined a sample of kibbutz children and a sample of Dutch children for the predictive power of the extended network of infants' relationships (mother, father, and professional caregiver) in comparison with the family network (mother and father) and the mother-infant relationships. They found that secure extended-network relationships were the best predictor of later advanced socioemotional functioning, although this finding was much stronger for kibbutz children. In the Dutch sample, the security of the extended network was related to children's higher developmental quotient and autonomous behavior in preschool. However, in the kibbutz sample, security of the extended network was related to a higher IQ and more independent behavior in kindergarten, as well as to higher ego resilience, ego control, **field independence,** dominance, goal-directed behavior, and empathy. Security of the family network in the kibbutz was also related to some of these variables, whereas infant-mother relationships were, by themselves, unrelated to any of the children's outcome variables. Thus, one can conclude that the quality of early relationships does predict future development. However the ecology of infant care in regard to the extent of the child's exposure to multiple relationships determines the relative contribution of individual relationships to developmental outcome.

Moreover, there is evidence here, as well as in Howes, et al. (1988), that within a matrix of multiple relationships, secure relationships with professional caregivers are not only feasible but also contribute to the child's well-being by either adding to a network of secure attachments or, possibly, compensating for their absence. Relationships between professional caregivers and children thus have the potential of adding a significant dimension to children's socioemotional development without interfering with the parent-child relationship, as was strongly believed by kibbutz educators (Gerson, 1978).

## Summary and Discussion

The study of kibbutz child rearing from the perspective of attachment theory has allowed a direct assessment of the impact of multiple caregiving in infancy both on children's experience as infants and on their future development. Investigations of collective child rearing, with its unique philosophy and practices, highlight issues that may be pertinent to other multiple-care arrangements but tend to be overlooked or underrated. On the basis of data available from studies of kibbutz children, one can conclude that early extensive day care and the repeated separation from parents inherent in such care do not necessarily interfere with the formation of close relationships between parents and children. The similarly high rates of secure attachments found in kibbutzim practicing family-based sleeping and in Israeli day care centers, and their difference from both samples of communal sleeping (see Figure 1), suggest that neither day care nor kibbutz care can in itself explain the unusual rates of insecure attachments found in kibbutzim with collective sleeping arrangements. Rather, the increase in infants' insecurity probably reflects a child-care environment in which infants experience inconsistent care as a result of parental absence during the night without an adequate replacement.

Nevertheless, understanding the effects of collective sleeping, which is an extreme practice, may highlight the effects of the repeated separations from mothers that are inherent in any multiple caregiving arrangements. Two variables have been proposed to attenuate the effects of separations on the quality of infant attachment: high-quality alternative caregiving (Goossens, 1987; Howes et al., 1988), which may alleviate the stress that infants experience in situations of maternal absence, and maternal compensating efforts, which may moderate the effects of temporary traumatic separations (for example, those occurring as a result of hospitalizations) so as not to result in long-term insecurity (Van IJzendoorn, Goldberg, Kroonenberg, & Frenkel, 1992). Collective sleeping arrangements have been problematic in both respects. Although kibbutzim have provided high-quality child care during the day, the quality of night care in the infant house has been poor because it has most often been provided by strangers who can offer only a precarious sense of security to the infants. On the other hand, maternal compensation is not very likely, because even sensitive parents may not feel an urgency to compensate for their absence during the night in a situation in which routinely implemented separations are the norm for all of the children in the community. This circumstance points to the dangers inherent in maintaining multiple care arrangements for infants without also guaranteeing alternative caregiving of adequate quality.

A number of studies have shown that quality of caregiving (Droege & Howes, 1991; Howes, et al., 1992; Rosenthal, 1991) is relevant to children's socioemotional development in that it determines the quality of children's experience in day care and affects parent-child relations (Goossens, 1987; Howes, et al., 1988). In this regard, therefore, one should consider the discrepancy between the quality of collective child care during the day and during the night. More specifically, the low-quality aspect of kibbutz child care, which is associated with collective sleeping, must be controlled for when dealing with the broader controversy about the impact of extensive day-care experience in infancy on socioemotional development (Belsky, 1988; Clarke-Stewart, 1988, 1989; Gamble & Zigler, 1986). Indeed, the finding of normal rates of secure attachment among kibbutz infants, who experience early and extensive care of high quality during the day and who sleep at home at night, is consistent with studies that suggest that high quality of care is an important determinant of children's socioemotional experience (for example, Howes, 1990; Howes, Phillips, & Whitebook, 1992).

We have until now emphasized the increased rates of insecure attachment in situations of collective sleeping. However, one should not overlook the fact that almost 50 percent of the mothers of communally sleeping infants have been able to provide their infants with a sense of a consistent, secure relationship. This group underscores the need to understand **resiliency** in the face of adverse conditions (Belsky, 1990).

The finding that both the extended network and the family network in kibbutzim have more predictive power than does the mother-child relationship may be explained by the greater involvement of kibbutz fathers and caregivers in child care. Recall that the increased involvement of others in child care was regarded as beneficial to both women and children and had an important ideological value. In Israel, kibbutz fathers tend to spend more time with their infants than do nonkibbutz fathers (Sagi, Koren, & Weinberg, 1987), possibly because the organization of kibbutz life allows both parents equal time to spend with their children. More time for leisure and availability of Israeli fathers have been found to determine the extent of their play and affiliative behaviors, whereas their attitudes and perceptions regarding fatherhood have predicted caregiving and play (Levy-Shiff & Israelashvili, 1988).

As a result of the high value placed by kibbutz culture on parental involvement (Shamai, 1992), no aspects of child care have been viewed by parents of either sex as being the exclusive responsibility of one parent or the other. Yet, the duties of professional caregiving have never been assumed by kibbutz men. Thus, it would seem that kibbutz fathers are relatively privileged because they have more leisure time with their children within a culture that values paternal involvement in child care but does not regard the father as having primary responsibility. However, in the name of women's equality, which uses masculine criteria for achievement (Palgi, Blasi, Rosner, & Safir, 1983), maternal involvement in child care has been reduced. It would appear, then, that in comparison with other child-rearing environments, collective education has supported father-child relationships while being ambiguous toward mother-child relationships. This may explain the differential influence exerted by collective education combined with communal sleeping on infants' relationships with their mothers and fathers and the similarity in rates of security between mothers and caregivers (Sagi, Lamb, Lewkowicz, et al., 1985). Recently published autobiographical recollections of kibbutz-raised women support this conclusion (Leshem, 1991).

The kibbutz data suggest that as women increase their involvement in out-of-home employment and increasingly share the duties of caring for their children with other caregivers (professionals or family members), the relative influence of the mother-child relationship may also change. Role changes within families, as they translate into daily functioning, may affect parental relationships with infants, and different childrearing conditions may increase or decrease the influence of these relationships on children's development (Belsky, 1990). Given the processes of change experienced by many families, there is a need for more information about the attitudes of parents toward child care and parenting roles; such information will provide a better understanding of the interrelationships among child-care ecology, parental functioning, and children's relations with parents. The consequences of these changes for children's development in different ecologies and cultures remain an empirically open question. We have thus far focused on children's relations with various adults, but the collective orientation of the kibbutz has also been manifested in the role assigned to the peer group in the socialization of children. Therefore, our review would be incomplete without a discussion of the relations of kibbutz children with their peers.

## RELATIONS WITH PEERS

In the educational conceptualization of collective education, the peer group was viewed as offering a natural environment for children's activity because it both directs their behavior and protects their independence (Golan, 1961). Group activities and sharing, as well as respect for the rights of others, were emphasized by adults from an early age (Rabin & Beit-Hallahmi, 1982). At the time, this view was at odds with the prevailing belief that young children were unable to benefit from group life because of their competition for the attention and love of adults (Freud, 1973; Isaacs, 1948) and their egocentric and noncommunicative thinking (Piaget, 1959). Group living among children from the time of infancy, as practiced in kibbutzim, has intrigued some observers who have been impressed by the unexpected presence of emotional ties between infants and toddlers. Bettelheim (1969) and Kaffman (1965) described close relations between such infants and detected distress when one of the infants was absent. Zaslow (1980) found that individual group members were sought out as early as the end of the first year, and such closeness was influenced by sharing a room in the infant's house, mutual responsiveness, and close relations between parents. Spiro (1958) observed 10-month-old infants playing together so often that they seemed to be a subgroup within the large group and described the peer group as a constant source of stimulation as well as security. Winograd (1958) observed mutuality and empathy in the behavior of children much younger than the age at which such behaviors were assumed to be meaningful.

Recent research on infants and toddlers together (Eckerman & Didow, 1988) suggests that the observations just reported have captured a natural social capacity readily displayed by kibbutz children because of the intensive social character of their environment. Although infant sociability is viewed as a natural capacity, it must be distinguished from social competence, which refers to effectiveness with peers through coordinated interactions and reciprocal actions within a relevant affective context. Early peer encounters have been thought to provide children with the social experience necessary to support the development of social competence (Eckerman & Didow, 1988; Howes, 1988a). Moreover, it has been suggested that peer familiarity facilitates social interaction and the development of specific relationships based on the continued presence of the partner (Doyle, Connolly, & Rivest, 1980; Howes, 1988a). Kibbutz infants and toddlers are exposed to peers very early, the peer group is stable, and peer familiarity is very high. In addition, adults value the role of peers in children's lives. These features of peer experience have been found to facilitate social competence in young children (Howes, 1988a); thus, one can expect social competence to be well developed among kibbutz children.

Two kinds of studies have assessed social competence in kibbutz infants, toddlers, and preschoolers: investigations of group processes and peer relationship formation and assessments of play quality as a demonstration of social skills. The data indicate that kibbutz children are competent in both respects. Faigin (1958) found that 2-year-old toddlers had already developed a strong identity with the group, expressed in concepts such as "we" and "ours" and by mutual defense of group members in between-groups competitions and rivalries. Although leadership belongs to the metapelet, the group functions as a socializing agent in terms of controlling the behavior of its members. Laikin, Laikin, and Costanzo (1979), as well as Y. Harel (1979), explored group processes in toddler groups and identified group behaviors at very young ages, however, role taking, following group "rules," and negotiations in regard to objects and toys were found to be behaviors that develop with age. Play in groups formed according to children's choice, which increased in frequency between the ages of 24 and 30 months, involved more mature and intensive social interactions than parallel play or whole-group activities not involving choice (Harel, 1979).

Ross, Conant, Cheyne, and Alevizos (1992) recently published a study that investigated toddlers' relationships and conflict interventions in two kibbutz groups whose members' average age was 20 months. They found that unique adjustments were made by children in their interactions with specific partners and observed conflicts as well as positive interactions. These adjustments tended to be mutual and spanned broad periods of time, thus taking the form of reciprocal relationships in which conflicts and positive interactions were integrated. Considerations of rights and fairness seemed to guide third-party conflict interventions, which sometimes involved attempts to mediate, compensate, or reprimand; however, alliances more than fairness determined the outcome of a conflict. These behaviors were taken as an indication that very young children are able to sort out the nature of social exchanges in which they were not initially involved. The nature of peer relations in these groups, with their siblinglike familiarity that afforded members a comfortable context for acquiring social experience, may have made such sophisticated behaviors possible.

Studies that have evaluated play quality and social behavior among kibbutz and urban Israeli children reveal that kibbutz children are very skilled social players. Toddlers from kibbutzim were found to be more likely to engage in positive social interaction with peers than family day-care and center day-care children (Rosenthal, 1991). Kibbutz toddlers were more involved in associative-dramatic play and showed less unoccupied behavior and parallel play. Functional play appeared earlier in kibbutz nursery school children, but it was more frequently observed among urban kindergarten children (Meerovitch, 1990). Finally, kibbutz children displayed coordinated play more frequently and were less competitive in group encounters and less involved in object exchange and struggle over toys; however, they were also less affectively involved with their peers and more verbally aggressive than were urban nursery school children. When kibbutz children were not interacting with peers, they spent more time in solitary play and interaction with caregivers and less time watching their peers (Levy-Shiff & Hoffman, 1985). However, communally sleeping preschoolers exhibited lower levels of effective problem solving but higher autonomy in daily routine tasks, despite parents' reports that did not indicate that kibbutz children were less attached to them (Levy-Shiff, 1983).

The data suggest that although social competence is developmental, the social environment that provides the context for its acquisition has a strong impact. The attitudes of adults toward early peer interaction influence the social environment of children and thus may play an important role in children's social experience (Howes, 1988a). Indeed, kibbutz caregivers emphasize group behaviors at a very early stage (Faigin, 1958; Rabin & Beit-Hallahmi, 1982). In interviews, caregivers have reported that they encourage children to help one another and to share (Laikin, Laikin, & Costanzo, 1979), as well as to engage in social rather than individualistic achievements (Meerovitch, 1990). In addition, adult actions and attitudes have been observed to have an impact on children's behaviors. Y. Harel (1979) reported that children used initiations and rule-setting behaviors to which they had previously been introduced by their caregivers, and Zaslow (1980) identified close relationships between parents as a variable related to closeness between infants. Richman's (1990) findings supported the hypothesis that kibbutz children will behave more prosocially than nonkibbutz children because prosocial behavior reflects children's experience with expectations in their environment. Moreover, he found that kibbutz kindergarten children whose parents and caregivers were themselves kibbutz born helped more and that kibbutz children whose metaplot were kibbutz born shared more. Richman thus concluded that the expectations of kibbutz-born adults concerning prosocial behavior have had an impact on the children they bring up.

The research reported thus far suggests that peers are emotionally important to kibbutz infants and toddlers and that prosocial behaviors are found at a very early age among kibbutz children. However, social behaviors are developmental, and adults play an important part in the learning of such behaviors. It seems reasonable to assume that the influence of the peer group derives from its stable presence and from the continuity of interpersonal relationships that it allows, as well as from adult emphasis on the importance of the group and of group rules and values. The pervasiveness of the early peer group may also be illustrated with studies that have shown that early peers do not tend to marry each other in adulthood because they seem to consider themselves more like siblings (Shepher, 1971).

However, a complex picture regarding the development of social competence emerges from this review. It seems that young kibbutz children display advanced group-oriented skills and sophisticated behaviors in peer interactions together with indications of greater affective distancing and lower levels of affective problem-solving skills. Affective behavior and problem-solving skills—neither of which are group-oriented skills—are involved in social competence and have been predicted on the basis of the quality of attachment relationships (Sroufe & Fleeson, 1986), which also determine children's social competence in interactions with peers (Easterbrooks & Lamb, 1979; Sroufe & Fleeson, 1986). Within this framework of attachment theory, both lower problem skills and lower capacity for intimacy can be related to the higher rates of insecurity found among communally sleeping infants (Sagi, Lamb, Lewkowicz, et al., 1985; Sagi et al., 1994), thereby explaining the coexistence of high sociability and low intimacy.

Thus, the intensive social nature of the environment of kibbutz children could support their acquisition of advanced social skills, whereas the complicated socioemotional nature of their experience in communal sleeping underlies their affective behaviors and style. This theoretical basis allows one to predict that home-based kibbutz toddlers will be more competent than their collectively sleeping counterparts. Indeed, Laikin, Laikin, and Costanzo (1979) found more mature social interaction in groups of home-based sleeping toddlers than in communally sleeping groups, which they explained in terms of different interactive needs. Alternatively, the higher competence of home-based toddlers may be attributed to the more extensive nature of their interpersonal experience in their families. Unfortunately, these conclusions are only tentative because no research, to the best of our knowledge, has directly explored the association between family interactions and social competence among kibbutz children from the two ecologies. Moreover, because the studies of social competence in kibbutz children represent a variety of theoretical formulations, operational definitions, and measurements, it is difficult to derive a single conclusive interpretation. The various facets of social development in very young children who experience an intensive social environment, as increasing numbers of children do, and the specific conditions that shape social development are topics for further research, which may be especially interesting to pursue with kibbutz children.

## SUMMARY AND CONCLUSIONS

Collective child-rearing represents a special case of group care because children's exposure to multiple significant others and to peer-group living, although serving adults' goals, was put into practice as a result of the belief of adults that it was beneficial to children. The present review shows that collective kibbutz education has undergone tremendous changes in the course of the 70 years of its existence. Initially, an extreme form of collectivism, motivated by economic needs and ideological convictions, was instituted. Its intended goal was to nourish a "new type" of human being that would be untainted by the shortcomings that those who instituted the practice had observed in their own upbringing.

Judged strictly in terms of this ambition alone, collective education can be regarded as a failure. The family as the basic social unit has not been abolished in kibbutzim. On the contrary, familistic trends have become stronger than ever, and kibbutz parents have reclaimed their rights to care for their own children. Collective education has not produced a new type of human being, and any differences found between adults raised on and off the kibbutz have been minimal. Moreover, research results indicate that collective sleeping arrangements for children negatively affect socioemotional development in the direction of a more anxious and restrained personality. Collective sleeping, which may have been justified in early periods in the history of kibbutzim, was abolished as it became clear that it did not serve the emotional needs of most kibbutz members. Its disappearance demonstrates the limits of adaptability of parents and children to inappropriate child-care arrangements.

However, setting aside communal sleeping as too radical a practice, collective child rearing seen from a broader perspective has to its credit remarkable achievements unprecedented in other cultures. It has furnished high-quality care for all of the children in the community without exception and long before multiple caregiving was contemplated for the population at large. Only in Eastern Europe have such attempts been made, at the cost of providing mediocre care (Weigl & Weber, 1991). Collective education has developed a long-term practice of normal multiple caregiving that is supported by caregivers and parents, as well as the community. Thus, with the discontinuance of collective sleeping,

secure relationships have come to prevail to an extent similar to that found among nonkibbutz children. Collective education affords children the benefit of a network of relationships in a supportive environment.

The kibbutz practice of raising children in peer groups from infancy highlights the role of peers in children's social experiences and the contribution of these experiences to the development of social competence. However, social competence is a multifaceted construct that includes group-oriented skills as well as intimacy, affective behavior, and emotional style. Group-oriented skills can be facilitated by a social environment of familiar peers in which group behaviors are supported by adults' guidance. The affective dimension seems to require secure relationships with sensitive and responsive adults; these relationships may provide the foundation for the capacity to enter intimate relations with others. Further research is needed to understand the complexities of children's social competence.

The kibbutz, as a unique experiment in nature (Beit-Hallahmi & Rabin, 1977), has contributed to theories of early socioemotional development while reiterating the detrimental effects of poor-quality care in institutional settings (Bowlby, 1951; Spitz, 1946). Nevertheless, leaving aside the practice of communal sleeping arrangements, the kibbutz child-care system demonstrates the potentials of sharing tasks and responsibilities of child rearing with nonparental caregivers—without detrimental effects for either the children or the parents involved—and underscores some of the conditions that have to be taken into account in the current day-care debate regarding the influence of extensive day-care experiences during infancy on later socioemotional development.

## EVALUATING YOUR MASTERY

1. Which of the following theories of the pathological outcomes of parent–child conflicts influenced kibbutz founders to rear children collectively?
   a. Behaviorist
   b. Psychoanalytic
   c. Social learning
   d. Sociocultural

2. Which of the following might have been evoked by the practice in kibbutzim of having night watchwomen rotate on a weekly basis to monitor sleeping infants?
   a. Secure attachment
   b. Friendliness with strangers
   c. Cognitive impairments
   d. Disturbed sleep

3. Which of the following characterizes modern kibbutz child rearing?
   a. The family as the principal authority
   b. The caregiver as the principal authority
   c. The family and caregiver with equal authority
   d. Both family and caregiver with little authority; older siblings take primary responsibility

4. In a comparison of mother-infant dyads from traditional and nontraditional kibbutzim, Sagi and his colleagues (1985) found that communally sleeping infants were more likely to be:
   a. Securely attached
   b. Insecurely attached
   c. Overly dependent
   d. Emotionally responsive

5. True or False: The practice of having infants sleep away from their parents is widespread in nonindustrialized societies around the world.

6. True or False: Parent–child concordance, or similarity, in attachment classification is low for communally sleeping infants, high for home-sleeping infants.

7. True or False: Communal sleeping in Israeli kibbutzim leads to infant insecure attachment to both mothers and fathers.

8. True or False: The security of kibbutz infants' attachment to their caregivers (but not to their parents) is a strong predictor of their emotional and social functioning at age 5 in kindergarten.

9. True or False: In a multiple caregiver environment, individual relationships in infancy are a better predictor of later socioemotional functioning than are extended-network relationships.

## Critical Thinking

1.  Explain how collective sleeping arrangements in Israeli kibbutzim lead to inconsistent care.

2.  Summarize the positive and negative aspects of collective child rearing in Israeli kibbutzim, and discuss their implications for modern day care arrangements for infants and young children of employed mothers. List ingredients of day care that are essential for ensuring healthy emotional and social development.

## Applying Your Knowledge

A mother and father about to place their 5-month-old infant in day care ask you about the single most important factor in selecting a placement. How would you respond? Justify your recommendation using research findings in Aviezer and her colleagues' review of research on collective child care in kibbutzim.

# 10

## Quality of Child Care as an Aspect of Family and Child-Care Policy in the United States

SANDRA SCARR & DEBORAH PHILLIP,
University of Virginia

KATHLEEN McCARTNEY
University of New Hampshire

MARTHA ABBOTT-SHIM
Georgia State University

■

By comparison with other industrialized countries in the world, the United States neglects essential provisions that make it possible for parents in other countries to afford to rear children and to find and afford quality child care for their children.

■

In the United States, parents pay more than 90 percent of child-care costs because we do not have a national policy that supports child care for working parents.

■

The quality of care provided infants and young children is currently a topic of much debate in the United States and elsewhere.

■

The most shocking finding from our observations of ratios in classrooms in the three states is the degree to which ordinary practice violates the states' own regulations.

■

More staff training and more enforcement of existing regulations seem to be
essential to improve the quality of child care in the centers we observed.

■

Additional resources are needed for training, for better salaries and benefits to retain
caregivers, for Head Start expansion into a child-care system, for direct subsidies to
centers and family providers of care for the poor, for enforcement of regulations,
and much, much more.

■

## EDITOR'S INTRODUCTION

This article is the first of several in this book to address the relevance of a nation's
social and political context for children's development and well-being. As increasing numbers of infants and young children in Western nations have parents who
are employed, the quality of the settings in which they spend their days becomes an
issue of vital significance. Sandra Scarr and her collaborators provide an overview
of American child-care policy, which reveals the United States lags far behind other
industrialized nations in provision of paid, job-protected maternal leaves following
childbirth and of high quality, affordable child care. The authors' study of child-
care center quality, conducted in four states, underscores the consequences of lack
of national standards. Scarr and her colleagues link the alarmingly inadequate state
of American child-care services to a history of government policy toward women
in the labor force that differs greatly from Europe, where national child-care policies that protect and promote children's development are widespread.

The quality of child-care services in the United States should be understood within a context of child-care policy at the federal and state levels. Similarly, **child-care policy** needs to be examined within the larger context of family-support policies that do or do not include parental leaves to care for infants (and other dependent family members) and family allowances that spread the financial burdens of parenthood.

Maynard and McGinnis (1993) presented a comprehensive look at the current and predictable policies that, at federal and state levels, affect working families and their children. They note the many problems in our "patchwork" system of child care—problems of insufficient attention to quality and insufficient supply for low-income families. Recent legislation is a step toward improving the ability of low-income families to pay for child care (by subsidizing that part of the cost of such care that exceeds 15 percent rather than 20 percent of the family income) and some steps toward training caregivers and improving regulations. Maynard and McGinnis note the seeming political impasse over parental leaves, even unpaid leaves, and the impact of this lack of policy on the unmet need for early infant care.

We should step back from the current morass of family and child-care policies in the United States and look at what other nations have done and continue to do for their working families. By comparison with other industrialized countries in the world, the United States neglects essential provisions that make it possible for parents in other countries to afford to rear children and to find and afford quality child care for their children.

## PAID PARENTAL LEAVE

In the summer of 1990, President Bush vetoed a plan for *unpaid* parental leaves at the birth of or adoption of an infant. The legislation was bitterly opposed by the business community, especially small businesses represented by the U.S. Chamber of Commerce. The United States is the only industrialized country in the world that does not have mandated, paid, job-protected, maternal leaves following the birth of a child. By contrast, let us look at the *paid* parental leave policies of representative European countries, as shown in Table 10.1.

Most industrialized countries compensate mothers in the form of an untaxed cash supplement for the time away from employment in the child's first 4 to 9 months of life. The level of compensation varies from 50 percent to 100 percent of wages, but most pay mothers (and often fathers) 75 percent or more of their usual wage to stay home with the new infant. Many countries have additional leave time, up to a year or more, that is compensated at lower levels. Parents are also paid to stay home with children who are ill.

The history of paid maternal leaves (mothers take more than 90 percent of the time afforded by these leaves) is that following World War II, with its economies in shambles, Europe realized that women were needed in the labor force to rebuild. If women were to be attracted to and retained in the labor force, some provision would have to be made for childbearing and early child-rearing. In addition, most European countries had declining populations before the War and adopted a consciously pronatalist policy following the War. If women were expected to work and bear children, clearly governments were going to have to compensate them and make the combined roles attractive. Thus, paid, job-protected, maternal leaves became an instrument of government policy to rebuild economies and to increase birth rates (they hoped, but failed).

In the United States, after World War II, women who had worked at all manner of jobs during the War were told to go home to make places in the work force for some 2 million returning veterans (Hewlett, 1986). Economists

Scarr, S., Phillips, D., McCartney, K., & Abbott-Shim, M. (1993). Quality of child care as an aspect of family and child care policy in the United States. *Pediatrics, 91,* 182–188. Reprinted by permission.

**Table 10.1  Paid Parental Leaves in Western Countries[1]**

| Country | Date | Duration of Paid Leave | Available to Fathers | Supplementary Unpaid or Paid Parental Leave |
|---|---|---|---|---|
| **Benefit Level at 100% Earnings[2]** | | | | |
| Norway | 1984 | 4 months | Y | Y |
| Austria | 1987 | 16 weeks | | 10 more months, at lower level[3] |
| FR Germany | 1987 | 14 weeks[4] | Y | 1 year at flat rate[5] |
| Portugal | 1984 | 3 months | | Y |
| Netherlands | 1984 | 12 weeks[4] | | |
| **Benefit Level at 90% Earnings** | | | | |
| Sweden | 1987 | 9 months plus 3 months at flat rate | Y | Up to 18 months; 6 hour work day, up to 8 years |
| Denmark | 1987 | 24 weeks | Y | Y |
| France | 1987 | 16 weeks[4] | | Up to 2 years |
| UK | 1987 | 6 weeks + 12 weeks at flat rate | Y | Maternity leave |
| **Benefit Level at 80% Earnings** | | | | |
| Finland | 1987 | 11 months | Y | Y |
| Italy | 1984 | 5 months[6] | | Y |
| Belgium | 1984 | 14 weeks | | |
| Ireland | 1982 | 14 weeks | | |
| **Benefit Level at 75% Earnings** | | | | |
| Spain | 1982 | 14 weeks | | |
| Israel | 1984 | 12 weeks | | |
| Canada | 1984 | 17 weeks, 15 paid | | |
| **Benefit Level at 50% Earnings** | | | | |
| Greece | 1982 | 12 weeks | | |

[1] From Kamerman (1989). Y = yes.

[2] Up to maximum covered under Social Security.

[3] Plus 2 years for low-income single mothers if they cannot find child care.

[4] Six weeks must be taken before expected birth; in other countries this time is voluntary.

[5] Last 6 months available only on an income-tested basis.

[6] One hundred percent paid for first 4 weeks; 2 months' leave before birth mandated.

expected a massive recession and unemployment after the War; they failed to anticipate the pent-up consumer demand for housing, automobiles, and refrigerators that fueled a massive boom in the US economy in the late 1940s and early 1950s.

Although most women did not leave the labor force, they were excluded from well-paying industrial jobs and returned to lower paid, pink-collar occupations. Government withdrew any provisions that would "encourage" women to enter and stay in the labor force, especially after childbirth. The extensive child-care system that the federal government had established during the war was dismantled. Thus, the history of government policy toward women in the labor force is vastly different in Europe and the United

Because of weak family-support policies, far too few children in the United States receive the high-quality child care they need to develop at their best. (Photo: Laura Berk)

States. From a 1990s perspective, it certainly seems that they were right and we were wrong.

## FAMILY ROLES

Another deterrent to mothers' participation in the labor force is the lack of full participation by husbands in home and child-care responsibilities. Garry Trudeau, in the comic strip *Doonesbury,* often captures family dilemmas by reversing usual male and female roles. In one cartoon, he pictures a driving woman boss making demands on an overworked employee father, who seems to have to cope also with all the planning and child-care responsibilities for his family. In it Trudeau captures the essence of women's problems in juggling work and home. The father says, "J.J. tries to help, of course, but just the fact that she calls it 'helping' tells you the whole story. The fact is, if I don't do things—the vacuuming, shopping, laundry, making play dates—they won't get done." Amen.

Data on time use by full-time employed husbands and wives—childless couples and parents—

confirm Trudeau's view (Bernardo, Shehan, & Leslie, 1987). In families without children, wives work at combined job and home responsibilities about 52 hours a week, about 5 hours more than their husbands. When there is an infant or preschool child in the home, mothers work 16 to 24 hours more per week than fathers; mothers work a combined total of 80 to 90 hours a week. Figure 10.1 shows these results. The old saying about a woman's work is never done could not be more true, if she is a mother.

## TAX POLICY

Policy on family allowances and tax relief for child care are among a large set of family supports that may reduce the economic disadvantage of parents as compared with childless couples.

In all European countries and in Canada, families with children are given an allowance of some sort to help them with the expenses of parenthood. Sometimes, the allowance is only the equivalent of $50 to $100 per month; in other countries, the allowance is several hundreds of dollars per child per month.

In the United States, tax policy is a primary consideration affecting day care for most working, nonpoor families, but the tax exemption for dependents has declined in real value from 1950 to 1990 by about two thirds. This means that rearing children in the 1990s costs parents significantly more than was true in earlier decades. The phasing down of the dependent-care credit for middle- and high-income families has lessened that benefit for millions of American families, but the 1987 tax reform legislation increased the dependent-care credit for the working poor.

Congress recently increased the earned-income tax credit for the working poor, especially for parents of small children, thus expanding this mechanism. The earned-income tax credit has become one of the major antipoverty initiatives, providing support to more and more parents; the number of eligible families increased from about

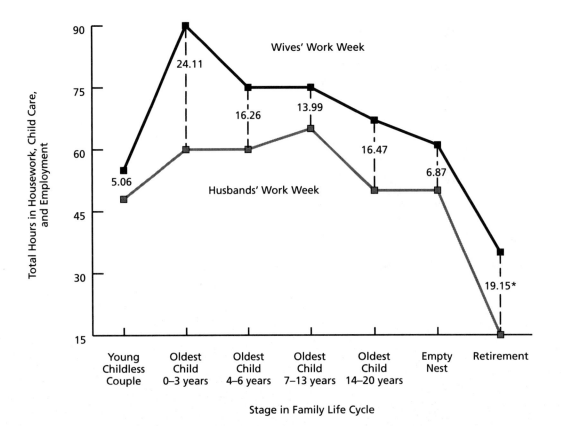

**FIGURE 10.1** Mean total hours in work weeks of husbands and wives who are employed full-time, by stage in their family-life cycle.

6.5 million in the Reagan era to about 12 million in 1989. The average amount of credit also increased from less than $300 per family from 1981 to 1986 to almost $600 in 1990. "In all, the IRS expects 13.8 million families to be eligible for the credit this year—more than one in every 10 households in the country. Treasury and congressional analysts estimate that the working poor will get an average of $700 a family, assuming they can figure out the new form" (Wessel, 1991).

As of 1991, parents of infants are eligible for an extra "wee tots" benefit, designed to help mothers of babies younger than 1 year of age stay at home or to help parents buy expensive infant care when they return to work. A second new provision is a special credit for parents who purchase health insurance for their children.

All in all, the earned-income tax credit has become a major mechanism for partially offsetting the extra costs of parenthood for the working poor. It encourages participation in the labor force both for single mother and for married mothers whose husbands are in low-wage jobs, and it helps such parents buy better quality child care.

## CHILD-CARE PROVISIONS

It may surprise U.S. parents to learn that in Europe, parents pay no more than 5 percent to

15 percent of the true costs of their children's out-of-home care. In the United States, parents pay more than 90 percent of child-care costs because we do not have a national policy that supports child care for working parents. Again, the European policy of publicly supported day care is part of a comprehensive family support system designed to foster child development and to attract mothers back to the labor force after the child's first year. In addition to maternal leaves, publicly supported child care is another provision needed to help mothers return to the work force when their children are younger than school age.

Most countries support child-care centers, although many also support family day care by paying the providers directly, providing training for them, and inspecting their homes for health and safety. Child care for preschoolers and after-school care for primary school children is simply an expected public expense, as is all of education. In this country, parents must support all of the costs of child care unless they are poor, with a small tax credit for middle-income families.

What is most surprising to Europeans who visit child-care settings in the United States is the lack of national standards. The fact that each state sets, and allegedly enforces, different regulations strikes them as very odd. How can it be that Georgia can have seven infants for each caregiver and Massachusetts can have half that ratio? Are the needs of infants in Georgia so different from the needs of infants in Massachusetts?

The fact that parents must pay nearly all of the costs of child care in the United States has serious ramifications for our whole system, or nonsystem, of care. As Maynard and McGinnis (1993) estimate, the actual expenditure on child care in the country averages about $2,600 per child per year. To provide good care would require about $5,000 per year, which many parents cannot afford. In European countries the real cost of infant and preschool care is $7,000 to $10,000 per child per year because caregivers and teachers are paid wages on the primary school scale. Also, the trained European caregivers have health and so-

cial welfare benefits just as any other citizen does. In this country, salaries of most full-time child-care personnel are below the poverty level, and they have few if any benefits. The real costs of child care in the United States would triple, if the women who care for children in centers and in their own homes were to make a decent wage and have health, unemployment, disability, retirement, and other desirable benefits.

## A STUDY OF CHILD-CARE CENTER QUALITY

Child-care centers are the fastest growing segment of the child-care market. The quality of care provided infants and young children is currently a topic of much debate in the United States and elsewhere. We conducted research on quality of child-care centers in 120 centers in three states: Massachusetts, Virginia, and Georgia. These states have regulations on child-to-caregiver ratios, group size, and staff qualifications and training, which vary considerably. Four types of centers were sampled: nonprofit, local for-profit, for-profit national chains, and church-sponsored (which are unregulated in Virginia and in 10 other states).

Six children (2 infants, 2 toddlers, and 2 preschoolers) were randomly sampled from three classrooms in each center, for a total of 720 children. Three caregivers in each center were observed across a day by three trained observers, who noted adult-child ratios, scored children's social behaviors, and completed quality measures of the classrooms and the overall center. Quality of care was scored in several ways using infant, toddler, and preschool scales (Infant and Toddler Environmental Rating Scale [ITERS], Early Childhood Environmental Rating Scale [ECERS]), the Assessment Profile of Early Childhood Programs (Abbott-Shim & Sibley, 1987), and global ratings of caregiver behaviors with children. Children's social/emotional behaviors with teachers and peers were observed across the day by two observers. Children's temperament and social/

### Table 10.2  Measures Used in the Study

| Measure | Source | Informant/Rater |
|---|---|---|
| Child assessment | | |
| Child Behavior Survey | Waters, 1989 | Mother, caregiver |
| EAS Temperament Survey | Buss and Plomin, 1984 | Mother, father, caregiver |
| Manageability Index | Scarr et al, 1987 | Mother, father, caregiver |
| Perceived Social Competence | Harter and Pike, 1984 | Child |
| Observation of Social Behavior in the Classroom | Adapted from Ruopp et al., 1979 | Research team |
| Observation of Day Care Drop-off and Pick-up | Newly constructed | Caregiver |
| Family interview | | |
| Emotional and Instrumental Social Support | Marshall, 1989 | Mother, father |
| Family Demographics | Newly constructed | Mother |
| Parental Stress Index | Abidin, 1983 | Mother, father |
| History of Child Care | National Longitudinal Survey of Youth (NORC, 1984) | Mother |
| Life Role Salience Scales | Amatea et al., 1986 | Mother, father |
| Maternal Separation Anxiety | Hock et al., 1983 | Mother, father, caregiver |
| Parental Modernity Scale | Schaefer and Edgerton, 1981 | Mother, father |
| Parental Discipline Interview | Scarr, Pinkerton, and Eisenberg, unpublished | Mother, father |
| Revised Ways of Coping Scale | Vitaliano et al., 1985 | Mother, father |
| Wechsler Adult Intelligence Scale-Revised Vocabulary Subscale | Wechsler, 1981 | Mother |
| Child-care environment | | |
| Center Day Care Profile | National Child Care Staffing Study, 1987 | Director |
| Early Childhood Environmental Rating Scale | Harms & Clifford, 1980 | Research team |
| Infant and Toddler Environmental Rating Scale | Harms, Cryer, & Clifford, 1987 | Research team |
| Assessment Profile for Childhood Programs | Abbott-Shim & Sibley, 1987 | Research team |
| Caregiver Global Rating Scale | Arnett, 1987 | Research team |
| Caregiver Interactions With Children | Howes, 1987 | Research team |

emotional development were rated by teachers, parents, and observers. Attachment, measured by the **Q-Sort** items developed by Waters, to mother, father, and caregiver are of particular interest. Table 10.2 shows the measures used in the study.

Parents were interviewed for 2.5 hours in their homes about family background and the child's history of care. Mothers were given the Wechsler Adult Intelligence Scale-Revised, Vocabulary subtest. Parents also did extensive ratings of their child's social/emotional development.

Analyses tested the following hypotheses: (1) Quality of care is related to state regulations about staff ratios, director and staff training, and staff wages. Stability of child-care staff was also hypothesized to be important. (2) Sponsorship of centers will partially determine quality of care, with unregulated, church-sponsored care proving the lowest quality overall. (3) Quality of care is predicted to be related to children's developmental and adjustment status, so that children in higher quality, stable care will have better developmental status than those in lower quality care. (4) Family background factors will have profound effects on children's developmental status. (5) There will be interactions between family

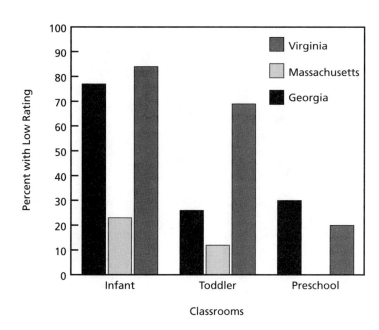

**FIGURE10.2** Percent of low-rated classrooms, by professional standards.

background and quality of child care that favor children from disadvantaged backgrounds in high-quality care. High-quality centers can serve as a positive intervention for children from high-risk backgrounds. Public-policy makers will be informed of the results of this study, which asks the fundamental questions, "Does quality of child care matter?" and "Is typical center-based child care in the United States of sufficient quality to promote our children's sound development?"

Because the analyses of this study are still in progress, we summarize the preliminary outcomes.

## Descriptions of Quality

Analyses of quality, conducted by Phillips and Mekos, examined the percentage of classrooms for infants, toddlers, and preschoolers that fall below professionally acceptable standards of quality; the compliance of programs with two sets of national quality guidelines; and the compliance of programs with their own states' regulations.

*Professional Standards.* ITERS (Abbott-Shim & Sibley, 1987) and ECERS (Harms & Clifford, 1980; Harms, Cryer, & Clifford, 1987) assess

developmental appropriateness of care, including teacher-child interactions, health and safety provisions, qualities of physical environment, appropriateness of play materials, and daily activities. Figure 10.2 shows the percentage of classrooms rated below 3.00 ("minimally acceptable" or "inadequate") on the Harms-Clifford 7-point environmental rating scale (Harms & Clifford, 1980).

It is shocking to see that the vast majority of infant classrooms in both Georgia and Virginia were rated by trained observers as being of low quality. The majority of toddler classrooms in Virginia were also of poor quality. Because three observers spent an entire day in each center and established good reliabilities across sites, these results are credible, if distressing. Massachusetts has the most demanding standards, and their programs are most often of high quality by professional standards.

*Health, Education, and Welfare Day-Care Regulations (HEWDCR): Recommended Ratios.* In the early 1970s, an interagency task force on child-care quality proposed that the federal government accept standards of care that incorporate the caregiver ratios shown in Figure 10.3: 1:3 for

**FIGURE 10.3** Percent of classroom out of compliance with recommended ratios (Health, Education, and Welfare Day-Care Regulations)

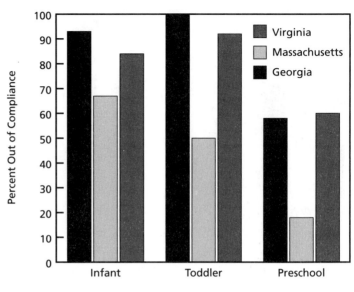

infants, 1:4 for toddlers, and 1:8 for preschool children. These proposed regulations were never accepted, but they remain as a benchmark of what we ought to demand of child care that is federally funded. Figure 10.3 also shows the percentage of programs in the three states that do not comply with the recommended ratios.

More than 90 percent of the infant and toddler classrooms in Georgia do not meet the ratios recommended by HEWDCR. More than 80 percent of the infant and toddler rooms in Virginia exceed the recommended ratios. Again, Massachusetts has more demanding ratio requirements, and a greater percentage of those classrooms meet these standards.

*National Association for the Education of Young Children (NAEYC) Recommended Ratios.* When the NAEYC began its accreditation programs some 7 years ago, it defined ratios for children of different ages, as shown in Figure 10.4. Note that the ratios are not as demanding as those of the HEWDCR, but note also that the standard of 1:4 for infants is above that of Massachusetts and at the state-mandated level for Virginia. By

NAEYC guidelines, close to 80 percent of the infant and toddler classrooms in Georgia are out of compliance. In Virginia about 40 percent of the infant classrooms are out of compliance, and almost 80 percent of the toddler rooms violate these standards. Again, Massachusetts centers are much more likely than the other states to meet these standards, as shown in Figure 10.4.

*State Regulations.* The most shocking finding from our observations of ratios in classrooms in the three states is the degree to which ordinary practice violates the states' own regulations. The actual state-mandated ratios for infants, toddlers, and preschoolers is shown in Table 10.3.

Massachusetts requires twice as many adults to children in both infant and toddler classrooms as Georgia. Virginia is far more demanding than Georgia, but not as stringent as Massachusetts. Training requirements, not surprisingly, are also more stringent in Massachusetts than in Virginia or in Georgia.

When we observed in classrooms, we noted ratios of adults to children every 10 minutes and averaged them across the day. Figure 10.5 shows

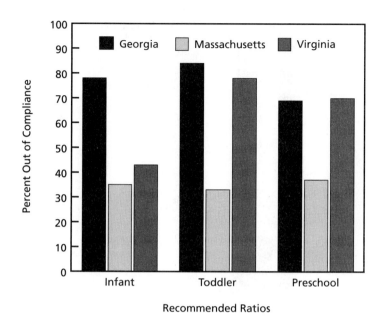

**FIGURE 10.4** Percent of classrooms out of compliance with recommended ratios (National Association for the Education of Young Children).

**Table 10.3  State Regulations**

|      | Ratio | | | Training |
|------|--------|---------|-----------|----------|
|      | **Infant** | **Toddler** | **Preschool** | |
| GA   | 1:7    | 1:10/12 | 1:15      | Some every 3 y |
| MA   | 2:7    | 2:9     | 1:10      | 20 h/y |
| VA   | 1:4    | 1:5     | 1:10/12   | 8 h/y |

the percentage of classrooms in each state at each age level that were out of compliance *on average* with their own state regulations. If we had reported those centers that were *ever* out of compliance, practically all would be on the list.

In Virginia, half the toddler classrooms are not meeting the state-mandated requirement of 1:5 for young toddlers, and 37 percent of the infant classrooms fail to meet the state's requirement for 1:4. In Massachusetts, almost half of the infant classrooms are not meeting that state's mandated ratio of 2:7. Preschool classrooms, where the state regulations permit a larger ratio of children to adults, were less frequently violated.

## Enforcement of State Regulations

Jeffrey Arnett, a consultant to the Child Care Quality Study of the University of Virginia Child Care and Family Project, interviewed 10 child-care center directors in each state and several officials in the states' regulatory agency for child care. The issue of enforcement looms large when one sees the extent of violations of existing state regulations. In these interviews, he found that attitudes of directors toward regulatory agencies varied considerably by state. In Georgia, the regulators are more likely than in Virginia to be seen as helping centers to meet state regulations, whereas in Virginia they seem

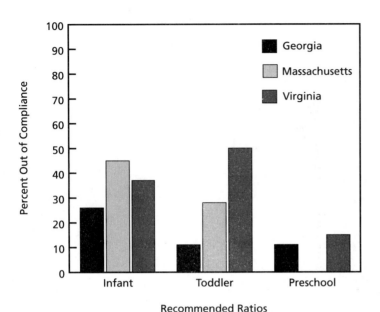

**FIGURE10-5** Percent of classrooms out of compliance with state-managed regulations.

to be seen as adversaries—albeit rather ineffectual adversaries who visit only once a year on an announced occasion. Funds for regulation are so short in Virginia that the state is now proposing to go to only one announced visit every 2 years! In Georgia, on the other hand, state regulators make one announced and one unannounced visit every year and consult with those centers that need help in meeting state regulations. In Massachusetts, state regulators visit annually and seem to be seen in rather neutral terms by the center directors.

The importance of enforcement of state regulations cannot be exaggerated, given these data on actual ratios that occur in the ordinary practices of centers. We also observed violations of health and safety regulations, developmentally inappropriate programming, and punitive interactions between caregivers and children, but those are beyond the scope of this paper. More staff training and more enforcement of existing regulations seem to be essential to improve the quality of child care in the centers we observed.

## Effects of Good and Poor Quality Care on Children

Although we have not completed all of the data reduction, we (Scarr, McCartney, and Eisenberg) have analyzed some of the effects of family and center care quality on children's social and emotional development. Briefly, family stress, parental intellectual status, and economic characteristics, of course, have impact on how well the children are faring. Children in families that report high levels of stress are performing less well on ratings of social and emotional development, both by teachers and by parents, than children who are in families less stressed. But child–care quality also contributes to children's well-being, as rated both by parents and by teachers. The amount of variance explained by differences in quality of child care is small but reliable across all ages of children and across the three states. Various measures of quality, including group size, ratios, and professional measures of quality of program (ITERS, ECERS, Profile), all contributed to ratings of emotionality, activity, sociability, shyness, attachment, dependency, and manageability. Children in high-quality programs are rated as less emotional, less shy, less dependent, more manageable, and more sociable. Thus, controlling for family effects, there is still evidence that the quality of care that infants and young children experience every weekday has influence on their social and emotional development.

## IMPLICATIONS FOR QUALITY

To provide a high-quality system of child care in the United States will require massive infusions of public money. Parents, especially in low-income, working families, cannot pay much more than they already do. Additional resources are needed for training, for better salaries and benefits to retain caregivers, for **Head Start** expansion into a child-care system, for direct subsidies to centers and family providers of care for the poor, for enforcement of regulations, and much, much more.

We also need minimum standards for care that receives public support. Since all child care should receive public support, we argue for national minimum standards, above which the states could improve their standards of care.

Again, Doonesbury gets it right—high-quality care is expensive. In one of Trudeau's cartoons, Joannie Caucus is interviewing the *male* director of a child-care center, who tells her of all the wonderful facilities and personnel he has at the center. She is so impressed that she says "Dr. Tenney, you are the answer to a parent's prayers." She then asks what the rates are, and he replies, "$400 a day." It might not cost that much to provide acceptably high-quality care, but the real cost is much more than our system currently invests in the care of children.

We cannot afford to wait much longer before public monies are demanded for child care, as they were in the early century for free public education for every child. The demographics of maternal employment, inadequate wages for single breadwinners, and projections for the labor force all point toward the need for more and better child care. We can finance an improved system in a variety of ways—by increased subsidies to families, by direct payments to caregivers, by using public school mechanisms, and so forth. But we cannot afford to let the current inadequate hodgepodge continue. The future of the nation rests on the adequate development of all our children, and early care in quality settings is essential to that development.

## EVALUATING YOUR MASTERY

1. The United States is the only industrialized country in the world that does not have
   a. Federally subsidized child care for low-income families.
   b. Mandated, paid, job-protected maternal leaves.
   c. Tax relief to subsidize the cost of parenthood.
   d. Standards for caregiver-child ratios in child-care centers.

2. Estimates indicate that an employed mother with an infant or preschool child works a combined total of ____ hours a week to meet both job and home responsibilities.
   a. 50 to 60
   b. 60 to 70
   c. 70 to 80
   d. 80 to 90

3. In the United States, standards for day care are set _____; in Europe they are set _____.
   a. Nationally; locally
   b. Locally; locally
   c. By the states; nationally
   d. Nationally; by the states

4. In the United States, most full-time child-care personnel
   a. Are well paid and have good benefits.
   b. Are poorly paid but have good benefits.
   c. Are poorly paid and have few if any benefits.
   d. Are well paid but have few if any benefits.

5. In Scarr, Phillips, and Abbott-Shinn's study of quality of child-care centers in three states:
   a. The majority of infant classrooms in Georgia and Virginia were rated as low quality.
   b. Programs almost always met their own state standards for caregiver-child ratios.
   c. Programs in Virginia were higher quality than those in Massachusetts.
   d. Programs in Georgia were higher quality than in both Massachusetts and Virginia.

6. True or False: The extensive child-care system that the U.S. federal government established during World War II continues today.

7. In Europe, parents pay no more than _____ percent of the true costs of their children's out-of home care, whereas in the United States, parents pay more than ____ percent.

8. True or False: In Scarr, Phillips, McCartney, and Abbott-Shim's study, child-care quality contributed to children's well-being in all three states.

## Critical Thinking

Explain how the history of U.S. government policy toward women in the labor force has affected the availability of parental leave for child birth and child illness and the quality of child care.

## Applying Your Knowledge

Find out what the child-care center standards for caregiver-child ratios and caregiver training are in your state. Compare them to acceptable standards described by Scarr, Phillips, McCartney, and Abbott-Shim. How are those standards likely to translate into quality of child-care experiences for young children?

# 11

# Child-Care Policy in Australia

MARJORY EBBECK

University of South Australia

FREDERICK EBBECK

Royal Melbourne Institute of Technology

■

Through its policies and regulations and its present and past practices in subsidizing child-care center construction, the Australian government has made child care possible and affordable for most families who need it.

■

One major program initiative was the funding and construction of community-based and other nonprofit child-care centers.

■

A recent initiative, implemented in 1996 and 1997 and accepted by all states, will impose a national standard for staffing on child-care centers, family day-care homes, and out-of-school-hours care programs.

■

The NCAC [National Childcare Accreditation Council] aims to assist centers in becoming more openly accountable to their users and to encourage parents to become more involved in the work and management of the center.

■

Today, Australia recognizes high-quality child care as vital for families with employed parents and, therefore, as crucial for the well-being of its own economy.

■

## EDITOR'S INTRODUCTION

Marjory and Fred Ebbeck describe child care policy in Australia, where the very recommendations suggested by Scarr, Phillips, McCartney, and Abbott-Shim for upgrading American child care have been implemented. As the first country in the world to develop a national child-care quality improvement system, Australia serves as an inspiring example for the United States and other nations seeking to upgrade child-care services. Widespread government funding of child-care centers is available in Australia, but it is linked to accreditation. Adapting the standards and procedures of the National Academy of Early Childhood Programs in the United States (a nonprofit organization that accredits U.S. centers on a voluntary basis), Australia makes government funding contingent on quality. The accreditation system involves first-hand observation of caregiving practices, ratings of the extent to which they offer children development-enhancing experiences, and checks and balances that make it unusually fair and objective. Ebbeck notes that the national accreditation system has sensitized Australian parents to issues of quality. As informed consumers who demand good care for their children, parents have begun to select centers on the basis of accreditation rating. As a result, parents are yet another force that upgrades the quality of child care services.

Child-care policy in Australia has made tremendous strides during the past ten years, to
the point where today it leads the world in standards of quality and coverage. For example, Australia is the first country in the world to develop
a national child-care quality improvement system, funded and supported by the Australian
government (National Childcare Accreditation
Council, 1993). Although accreditation through
this system is not mandatory, unless centers are
accredited, they are not eligible for the considerable government monies available to subsidize
children's care. Through its policies and regulations and its present and past practices in
subsidizing child-care center construction, the
Australian government has made child care possible and affordable for most families who need
it. Child care is readily available in both urban
and rural areas. How has this come about, and
why has the government taken such an interest
in the development of this very important
human service?

This essay reviews Australian child-care policies and practices, placing special emphasis on
the government initiative known as the **Quality
Improvement and Accreditation System
(QIAS),** introduced in 1993 and managed by
the Australian National Childcare Accreditation
Council (NCAC). The goal of the NCAC initiative was to address concerns about the quality
of existing child care, given rapid growth in
numbers of preschool-aged children with employed mothers and government-funded child-
care places.

## SOME FACTS AND FIGURES

Table 11.1 describes the various kinds of government-funded child care in Australia.[1] In 1996,
there were more than 7,800 centers in the funded
child-care sector, serving 558,700 children (Economic Planning and Advisory Commission,
1996). This represents an increase of 231,600 gov-
ernment-supported child-care places, or 140 percent, over the previous three years. If we consider

the last twelve years, the rise has been greater than
500 percent. Moreover, this rapid rate of growth
is likely to continue. The 1993 Bureau of Statistics Survey estimated that 490,000 additional child
care places were needed. In 1995, the government
asked its Economic Planning and Advisory Commission (EPAC) for recommendations about the
future demand for child care. The EPAC (1995)
Interim Report calculated that by the year 2011,
formal child care for children age 4 and under will
expand even further, by about 600,000 places.

Given these statistics, it is not surprising that
paid child care in Australia has become a
$2.4 billion a year industry with 70,000 employ-
ees. More than 60 percent of costs are met by the
Australian government (see Table 11.2). Consequently, child care is "big business"—one major
reason that quality is a serious issue. Even more
important, the average amount of time children
spend in child care has risen dramatically, to a
point where it is possible to accumulate 12,500
child-care hours before starting primary school.
This is only 500 hours less than children spend
in classrooms during their entire thirteen years
of compulsory schooling (NCAC, 1993). Therefore, in addition to being big business, child care
is too important a factor in the lives of young
children to be left to chance.

## THE HISTORY OF
## AUSTRALIAN CHILD CARE

Formal child care services entered the political
arena in the mid-1970s, when rising numbers of
mothers in the paid workforce created a social
dilemma. The Child Care Act of 1972 was the
Australian government's first specific provision to
fund existing child-care centers and provide financial assistance to nonprofit organizations for
establishing and operating new centers for children of employed mothers. The advent of the
Labor government at the end of 1972 assisted the
cause of child care, as it was sympathetic to the
needs of mothers who elected full-time employment instead of full-time motherhood.

### Table 11.1  Various Kinds of Child Care in Australia

| Type | Description |
|---|---|
| Long Day Care (LDC) (Center-based) | Care for children in licensed day-care centers for as much as 8 hours or more per day, 5 days per week, 48 weeks per year. Such centers can be community based or private. |
| Family Day Care (FDC) | Long day care provided for children in the caregiver's own home. It is usually geared for children younger than 5 years old, but older children can be accommodated before and after school hours. FDC has a national focus for support. |
| Multifunctional Aboriginal Children's Services (MACS) | An integrated child-care services center incorporating long day care, part-time and occasional care, play groups, emergency care and out of school hours care. MACS is a model designed to meet Aboriginal needs. Special funding arrangements are made to meet the particular needs of the Aboriginal community. |
| Multifunctional Centers | Centers that operate in rural areas, meet the needs of both working and nonworking parents and provide a range of care at one location, e.g., services extended by adding care facilities to existing preschool centers. |
| Occasional Care (OC) | Child care provided at a center on an hourly basis or sessional basis for parents who need care to attend an appointment, to take care of personal matters, to undertake casual or part-time work, to provide temporary respite from full-time parenting, or to provide developmental opportunities for children. |
| Outside School Hours Care (OSHC) | Care provided for school-age children (5–12 years) during outside school hours in the term time and vacation time. Related terms are "before and After School Hours Care," which refers to care during term time only and "Year Round Outside School Hours Care." |
| Work-Related Child Care | Child care provided while the parent is involved in paid work, is looking for a job, or is studying or training for work. It is usually long day care or occasional care, either center-based or family day care. It can be located at the parent's workplace or elsewhere. It is distinguished from other types in that employed parents can claim extra child-care government subsidies. |

Source: Economic Planning and Advisory Commission, 1996, pp. 183–188.

### Table 11.2  The Child-Care Sector as an Industry

**Importance of child care:**

Accounts for 0.5% of GDP . . . . . . . . . . . . . . . . . . . . . . . . . . . . . . . . . . . . . . . . . . . . . . . . . $2.4 billion

Majority of costs (60%) are met by government   . . . . . . . . . . . . . . . . . . . . . . . . . . . . . . . . . . $1.5 billion

Number of children aged 0–11 in formal care including preschool (1993) . . . . . . . . . . . . . . . . . . . . 596,000

Percentage of children aged 3–4 in formal care, including preschool (1993) . . . . . . . . . . . . . . . . . . . . 60%

**Commonwealth-funded services:**

Total employees (1995) . . . . . . . . . . . . . . . . . . . . . . . . . . . . . . . . . . . . . . . . . . . . . . . . . . . 71,000

Increase in employment 1992–1995 . . . . . . . . . . . . . . . . . . . . . . . . . . . . . . . . . . . . . . . . . . . . . 70%

Number of child-care services . . . . . . . . . . . . . . . . . . . . . . . . . . . . . . . . . . . . . . . . . . . . . . . . 7,800

Number of child-care places . . . . . . . . . . . . . . . . . . . . . . . . . . . . . . . . . . . . . . . . . . . . . . . . 301,400

Increase in child-care places since 1983 . . . . . . . . . . . . . . . . . . . . . . . . . . . . . . . . . . . . . . . . . 555%

Number of children . . . . . . . . . . . . . . . . . . . . . . . . . . . . . . . . . . . . . . . . . . . . . . . . . . . . . 558,700

Source: Economic Planning and Advisory Commission, 1995, p. 23.

In 1973, the annual conference of the Australian Labor Party emphasized the need for a national child-care service that would be government sponsored and community based and include a variety of child care services. The party announced that it would accept major financial responsibility for the establishment and operation of approved preschool and child-care centers from January 1974, with priority being given to services for families in greatest economic need and for mothers in the labor force. In this way, the government's receptiveness to the needs of employed mothers and their children was a major impetus for early federal financial support for child care in Australia. In the spirit of this heightened awareness of the needs of many families for child care as well as preschooling, the government launched its Children's Services Program, which established priorities for expanding services and allocated funding to effect its program.

One major program initiative was the funding and construction of community-based and other nonprofit child-care centers. Women's political lobby groups regarded this as a major advance in both provision of affordable services and in upgrading the standard of care. Not only were the costs of constructing buildings met by the federal government, but some cost-sharing arrangements with state governments were negotiated, especially for continuing operating expenses, thereby reducing the financial burden on families. In addition, a floor of quality was established through state licensing bodies, which devised minimum program standards to be reached.

An increase in the number of community-based centers was accompanied by the beginnings of the professionalization of child care. Developments in staff training brought the educational preparation of child-care staff at least up to the level of preschools. Government-sponsored Technical and Further Education (TAFE) colleges (two-year institutions of higher education) began to offer child-care courses, and Colleges of Advanced Education responsible for preparing preschool teachers extended this

entry-level preparation to diploma and degree levels. Today, education and training for child care is achieved at two levels: (1) at the fully professional level, through a two-year Diploma in Social Science (Child Care) offered by the TAFE colleges or by Registered Training Providers (private trainers); in universities, through the four-year degree of B.Ed. (early childhood education) or B.Soc.Sc. (human services); (2) at the subprofessional level, through a one-year Certificate in Child Care (sometimes called an Associate Diploma), granted by TAFE colleges or private providers.

These developments exacerbated existing divisions in funding and quality between government-sponsored community (nonprofit) and private (profit-making) child-care centers. This dichotomy lessened somewhat only recently, when in 1991 the Australian government extended subsidies to private centers. In 1993–1994, private centers received $235 million under the Child Care Assistance Program.

Table 11.3 shows the Australian government's child-care contribution to families, which increased more than four-fold between 1985 and 1996, from nearly $3 million to $13.2 million. Significant in these figures is the percentage of total family payments allocated to child care: 4.9 percent in 1985 and 9.3 percent in 1996. As these figures reveal, child care became an even greater government priority over this period.

As is common in most countries, a change in government leads to policy changes, which affect priorities and services. The present government, although skeptical of the prior federal commitment to child care, does not plan major changes, with the exception of placing community-based and private child-care centers on an equal footing as far as financial subsidies are concerned. Inevitably, this means that funding for community-based centers will decrease, and they will have to charge parents fees comparable with those in the private sector. No changes are anticipated in the two major family financial assistance schemes—namely, Childcare Assistance,

**Table 11.3 Australian Government's Contribution to Families for Child Care ($M)**

|                                                  | 1985–1986 | 1990–1991 | 1994–1995 | 1995–1996 | 1996–1997 |
|--------------------------------------------------|-----------|-----------|-----------|-----------|-----------|
| Child-Care Services                              | 147       | 246       | 906       | 1108      | 1239      |
| Child Care as a Percentage of Total Family Payments | 4.9   | 4.5       | 8.8       | 8.8       | 9.3       |

Source: Economic Planning and Advisory Commission, 1996, p. 37.

which subsidizes low-income families so they can access child care easily, and the Childcare Cash Rebate, which subsidizes child-care costs associated with employment.

## THE ROLE OF STATE GOVERNMENTS

In Australia, the eight state and territory governments have licensing control over child care. Therefore, standards and requirements for operation have varied from state to state, a situation that has not always been to the advantage of the child-care industry. However, a recent initiative, implemented in 1996 and 1997 and accepted by all states, imposed a national standard for staffing on child-care centers, family day-care homes, and out-of-school-hours care programs.

State standards for operating child-care centers ensure a baseline of quality for buildings, equipment, child–staff ratios, health and safety, programs for the care and education of children, and (to a certain extent) qualifications of staff. For example, in South Australia, the Children's Services Act of 1985 has specific sections mandating a children's services consultative committee[2]; regional advisory committees; licensed child-care centers; licensed baby-sitting agencies; approved family day care and licensed family day care agencies; registered children's services centers (such as the Aboriginal and rural centers mentioned earlier); and appeals (for services that fail to meet baseline standards). In effect, such Acts place the responsibility for licensing and enforcing standards in the hands of a particular

government agency, and the degree to which standards are met depends considerably on the political persuasion of state governments and their willingness to devote resources to this process. Generally speaking, the state acts do not necessarily ensure that high-quality services are delivered, although most state authorities do check on centers from time to time. The matter of enhancing and controlling quality has largely been assumed by the Australian government, through its national Quality Improvement and Accreditation System.

## THE QUALITY IMPROVEMENT AND ACCREDITATION SYSTEM (QIAS)

No system of accreditation that seriously addresses the quality and developmental appropriateness of child-care programs for young children can be implemented on a shoestring budget. Any worthwhile system is time-consuming and costly. In addition, no system is likely to please all people involved in the process. Nevertheless, the single greatest factor in raising Australian child-care standards in recent years has been the introduction of the government-sponsored QIAS.

The model for the QIAS was inspired by the work of the U.S. National Association for the Education of Young Children (NAEYC). Its accrediting body, the National Academy of Early Childhood Programs, devised a voluntary accreditation system for center-based care, in hopes of upgrading the generally dismal quality of child-care services in the United States (Helburn, 1995; Phillips, Howes, & Whitebook, 1992). It was also hoped that the accreditation system would eventually be adopted as a national standard for American child care programs (NAEYC, 1991), although this has not yet occurred (see Scarr, Phillips, McCartney, & Abbott-Shim, Chapter 10 in this volume). Australia, in contrast, has moved far beyond the voluntary status of accreditation in the United States to develop a truly national program that has become, more or less, mandatory for child-care centers. Government subsides can be allocated only to child-care programs that are accredited or in the process of being accredited. Funding, therefore, has become an important stimulus for compliance and action.

Introduced in 1993, the QIAS is supported by the Australian government to the extent of $2.2 million a year, which covers most of the costs of monitoring and evaluating. In addition, each center seeking accreditation is expected to pay a registration fee (currently, $100). The QIAS is managed by the NCAC, which is supported by and answerable to the Australian government through the Minister for Family Services. At present, the QIAS and the NCAC relate only to center-based "long day" care, but there is considerable support from within the industry and government to extend the accreditation scheme to out-of-school-hours care (for 6- to 12-year-olds) and family day care. It is quite likely that extension into these other two important services will be accomplished within the year following the preparation of this article.

The EPAC Report, advising the government on the future demand for child care, noted that whereas parents have the opportunity to exercise their preferences for the kind of care they want for their children, the criteria they use in decision making can be very unreliable. (A similar, research-based conclusion has been reached in the United States; see Helburn, 1995.) Parents often draw on a wide range of information from many sources, including the relationship established with their child's caregiver and their own personal beliefs about the needs of young children. The QIAS, however, has led many parents to become more discerning; they are beginning to ask about accreditation ratings and scrutinize centers for quality on the basis of more sophisticated information. This change in parental behavior is largely the result of years of hard work by child advocates within the industry and associated consciousness-raising about the importance of the early years in development, which culminated in the national accreditation system. Private (for-profit) child care providers are recognizing the power of parental expectations as market forces and, on the whole, are raising their standards. Indeed, today they must do so to survive.

## Five Stages of Accreditation

The QIAS involves a self-study by the center and direct observations by a peer reviewer. It also has a number of checks and balances that introduce fairness and objectivity. The process has five stages:

1. *Registration* (payment of a $100 fee).

2. *Self-Study:* The center reviews its policies and practices in relation to benchmarks of quality (represented by 52 principles of child care practice) established by the NCAC. At the conclusion of the Self-Study, the center rates itself by whether it believes it qualifies for a one-, two-, or three-year accreditation status. (The longer the time interval between assessments, the higher the quality of a center's program. More frequent reviews of centers not judged excellent are designed to upgrade quality.)

3. *Peer Review:* The peer review is crucial for ensuring uniformity of standards across Australia. The NCAC appoints a Reviewer, an experienced professional currently working in child care and trained in reviewing practices, who visits the center and notes what he or she sees happening in relation to the 52 principles mentioned earlier. On the basis of these observations, the reviewer recommends the center for a one-, two-,

or three-year accreditation status. The reviewer is given the center's own ratings and justifications, which emanated from the self-study. Similarly, the center is informed of the reviewer's ratings and comments. When there is a difference of opinion, the center can exercise a "right of reply" to the NCAC immediately following the review.

4. *Moderation:* A panel of three nationally appointed moderators, after considering the written evidence, mediates any difference of opinion between the center staff and the reviewer and makes a recommendation to the NCAC. Moderators are chosen for their broad experience in the field of early childhood education and for their impartiality. Therefore, they add an additional dimension to the accreditation process—namely, a national perspective.

5. *NCAC Final Decision:* The NCAC receives all advice and materials generated in stages 2 to 4 and renders the final accreditation rating. In determining this rating, neither the moderators nor the Council know the identity of the center or the peer reviewer. In addition, the Council does not know the identity of the moderators. The intent is to make the process as fair and objective as possible.

## Key Elements of the Accreditation Process

A crucial ingredient of the accreditation system is the establishment of an accreditation committee within each center to conduct the self-study, made up of management, staff and parents. The committee meets regularly, keeps minutes of its deliberations, and shares its findings with the center community. By mandating this committee, the NCAC aims to assist centers in becoming more openly accountable to their users and to encourage parents to become more involved in the work and management of the center. Parent involvement tends to be higher in community-based (nonprofit) than in private (for-profit)

centers. Nevertheless, the view of the NCAC is that regardless of the program's financial base, parents can enhance the quality of their children's experiences by participating in some aspect of the work of the center.

The NCAC's 52 principles of child care practice are the key to effective self-study and accreditation. The principles cover four key areas:

1. *Interactions:* Between caregiver and child; child and child; caregiver and parent; and caregiver and caregiver.

2. *Program:* Daily activities that meet the total education and developmental needs of young children, including infants, toddlers, preschoolers, and children with special needs.

3. *Nutrition, Health and Safety Practices:* Health and welfare practices; food preparation; nutrition, hygiene, emergency procedures; building maintenance; and other practices that protect the physical well-being of children.

4. *Center Management and Staff Development:* Staff and parent involvement in center evaluation; dissemination of information to staff about the beliefs and cultures of families and the local community and the philosophy of the center; and opportunities for staff to increase their knowledge and skills.

Accompanying each principle are descriptions of attitudes and activities that define four grades of care: unsatisfactory, basic, good quality, and high quality (see Table 11.3). The NCAC's accreditation decision is based on an overall assessment of quality, which combines ratings across the various principles. Seventeen of the principles are deemed core, or essential for any good quality service; examples are listed in Table 11.4. If a center receives an unsatisfactory rating on any core principle, it is denied accreditation.

How successful have Australian child care centers been in achieving accreditation? During the first year of the QIAS, of 2,392 centers assessed, 854 (35.7 percent) were granted accreditation for three years; 246 (10.3 percent) for two years; 993

## Table 11.4  Examples of Core and Noncore Principles in the Four Areas Covered in the QIAS Total of 52 Principles

**Part A: Interactions**

*Ai (Interactions between staff and children)*

Principle 2:   Staff treat all children equally and try to accommodate their individual needs: They respect diversity of background.

Principle 3:   Staff treat all children equally and try to accommodate their individual needs: They treat both sexes without bias.

*Aii (Interactions between staff and parents)*

Principle 10: There is verbal and written communication with all families about the center.

**Part B: Program**

Principle 17: The program incorporates learning experiences appropriate for each child, as indicated by development records maintained by the center.

Principle 18: The program gives children the opportunity to make choices and take on new challenges.

Principle 22: Toileting and nappy (diaper) changing procedures meet individual needs and are positive experiences.

Principle 23: (not core) The program is regularly evaluated in the light of stated goals.

**Part C: Nutrition, Health, and Safety Practices**

Principle 35: Staff try to ensure that children are clothed appropriately for indoor and outdoor play and for sleep.

Principle 41: (not core) Potentially dangerous products are inaccessible to children.

**Part D: Center Management and Staff Development**

Principle 48: Staff and parents consult on the program and evaluate it together.

Principle 49: New staff are informed about the philosophy and goals of the center.

Principle 50: (not core) The center provides regular learning and training opportunities for staff.

**Examples of standards set for quality of care:**

**Principle 2:**

Unsatisfactory:  • Staff communication and interaction shows no recognition that children come from a diversity of backgrounds.
                 • Staff ignore differences in family values and practices.
                 • Staff make no attempt to communicate with children from non-English-speaking backgrounds.

Basic:           • Staff show some awareness of differences, but it is occasional rather than consistent.
                 • Staff use nonverbal communication to include non-English-speaking children in groups.

Good Quality:    • Staff communicate and interact positively with all children, regardless of background, and incorporate some experiences that show that such differences are valued.
                 • Staff attempt to include individual experiences for non-English-speaking children.

High Quality:    • In their interactions, staff consistently demonstrate sensitivity to a wide variety of backgrounds and family structures.
                 • Staff consult with families about the care of each child.
                 • Staff encourage parents to participate in the center and share some aspects of their lifestyle with the children and staff.
                 • Staff encourage positive attitudes in all children to the different backgrounds of others.

Source: National Childcare Accreditation Council, 1993, pp. 5–7.

A national commitment to high-quality child care has led to a world-class quality improvement system in Australia. These busy, contented children, their parents, and the nation as a whole benefit. (Photo: Laura Berk)

(41.5 percent) for one year; and 299 (12.5 percent) were not accredited and asked to improve quality in areas deemed unsatisfactory. These latter centers were required to complete a plan of action detailing how they would raise their standards. After a plan of action is accepted by NCAC, a substandard center is labeled "Working Toward Accreditation," and government subsidies are temporarily extended. Clearly, accreditation standards are rigorous. At the same time, poor-quality centers are encouraged to upgrade their services and attain accreditation through the incentive of financial gain.

*Implementation Issues.* The NCAC, as it encourages child-care centers to scrutinize their own practices for quality, has also been taking a close look at the efficiency and effectiveness of the QIAS procedures. No system works perfectly when first implemented.

The accreditation process is expected to take about six months. When the scheme was in its initial phase of operation, however, some centers waited as much as a year from time of registration to notification of accreditation status. Efforts are being made to reduce the length of the process, but some lapse of time between self-study and peer review can be advantageous, permitting centers to begin engaging in self-improvement before external evaluation. Nevertheless, additional resources are needed to streamline the accreditation system. As part of this streamlining effort, there is general consensus that the 52 principles could be reduced in number to about 30, while still retaining all essential aspects of quality.

Finally, because the current Australian government favors decentralization, the possibility of transferring responsibility for accreditation to the individual states and territories has been raised. This option is being soundly resisted by the centers themselves as well as by many politicians sensitive to the needs of all Australia's children. The great strength of the QIAS is that it is national. If accreditation were to revert to the states, quality care for young children would inevitably lose ground, as it would have to compete with each state and territory's other priorities and for a fair share of its economic resources. As the NCAC (1993) *Handbook* notes,

> State and local government licensing laws and regulations (licensing requirements) generally provide an industry-wide "floor" below which no centre is permitted to operate.... For a long time it was widely believed that specifying minimum acceptable levels ... would guarantee that the child care provided was of good quality.
>
> However, such factors only *contribute* to quality—that is, they create an environment in which good quality care *can* be provided.... By emphasizing actual outcomes for children [the QIAS] shifts the focus from meeting minimum standards to striving toward the highest levels of care. (p. iii)

## LOOKING TOWARD THE FUTURE

Involvement of the Australian government in child care has led to remarkable outcomes. Tying considerable financial subsidies to demonstrated standards in meeting children's developmental needs has forced the child-care industry to lift itself by its own bootstraps, producing a world-class service in terms of quality. The initial impetus for the QIAS came from Australia's political commitment to social justice and, in particular, to the needs of women. Today, Australia recognizes high-quality child care as vital for families with employed parents and, therefore, as crucial for the well-being of its own economy. In this respect, Australia differs strikingly from the United States, which has neglected essential government provisions that enable parents to find and afford quality child care for their children (Scarr, et al., Chapter 10 in this volume).

The extension of the QIAS model to other areas of organized child care in Australia, such as family day care and out-of-school-hours programs serving older children, is on the horizon. Nevertheless, child advocates and policy makers must guard against complacency, remaining ever watchful that high-quality services remain affordable to families in current times of economic stringency. But historically, Australian values have acknowledged the need to "put children first" by helping parents with child rearing during the early years. This makes the future a bright one for Australian children in child care.

## NOTES

1. Preschool education is not included, even though it can be considered a type of child care. This article does not dwell on Australian preschool services, which predate expansion of child care to meet the needs of employed mothers. It is important to note, however, that the Australian government funds a half-day of universal preschool education during the year before formal schooling. It is estimated that 90 percent of all children attend (Senate Employment Education and Training References Committee, 1996).

2. This committee is composed of representatives of a variety of early childhood services (for example, long-day care, out-of-school-hours care) and of parents. It canvases the views of these constituencies on significant issues and can influence policy. The chair of the Children's Services Consultative Committee and several of its members are appointed by the state Minister of Education and confirmed by Parliament.

## EVALUATING YOUR MASTERY

1. Provision of nationally funded child care in Australia dates back to
   a.  The 1970s
   b.  The 1980s
   c.  The turn of the century
   d.  1993

2. A major impetus for federal financial support for child care in Australia was
   a.  The need to intervene with children from low-income families.
   b.  The government's receptiveness to the needs of employed women.
   c.  To substitute for lack of preschool education.
   d.  The desire of researchers to study the impact of group care on development.

3. The Australian government's child care contribution to families _____ between 1985 and 1996.
   a.  Decreased more than four-fold
   b.  Decreased slightly
   c.  Increased more than four-fold
   d.  Increased slightly

4. The QAIS
   a.  Has had only a minor impact on the quality of Australian center-based child care
   b.  Is unlikely to be extended to family day care
   c.  Has led parents to become more discerning about the quality of child care
   d.  Has yet to build in procedures for protecting against biased evaluations

5. True or False: Australia is moving toward national standards for staffing child-care centers, family day-care homes, and out-of-school hours care programs.

6. True or False: Accreditation committees within centers ensure parent involvement in the accreditation process.

7. True or False: Few Australian child-care centers have been successful in achieving accreditation.

### Critical Thinking

1. Why are state licensing standards for child care (as opposed to licensing standards set and enforced by the federal government) not always in the best interests of children?

2. What aspects of the QAIS make it uniquely suited to encouraging unsatisfactory child-care centers to upgrade the quality of services they provide?

### Applying Your Knowledge

Ask several parents of infants or preschool children what qualities they would look for in selecting a child-care center and why they regard those features as important. To what is extent are the parents knowledgeable about child-care quality?

# PART IV

# The Play and School Years:
# Early to Middle Childhood

# 12

*ॐ*

# Children's Eating

## The Development of Food-Acceptance Patterns

LEANN L. BIRCH
Pennsylvania State University

SUSAN L. JOHNSON
University of Colorado

JENNIFER A. FISHER,
Pennsylvania State University

■

The positive response to sweetness and the rejection of bitter and sour tastes are "built-in," but from very early in life, even responses to these basic tastes change with the child's repeated experience with food and eating.

■

Our recommendation to parents and caregivers is to set a clear and consistent expectation that the child will taste new foods when they are offered. This policy works best if initiated when the child first begins to try new foods, during late infancy prior to the increased autonomy and independence of the toddler period.

■

We suggest that caregivers can increase the chances that children will come to accept a wide variety of foods by providing children with repeated opportunities to try new foods in positive or relatively neutral social contexts and by avoiding coercive feeding practices.

■

The ready availability of high-fat foods, their association with positive social contexts, and children's predisposition to learn to like high-fat and other high-energy foods contributes, as every parent and teacher knows, to the increased incidence of childhood obesity.

■

It appears that as we age, an increasing number of environmental and psychological factors can influence and even override sensitivity to internal cues that tell us how much to eat.

■

Parental control exerted to regulate the quantity of food that children consume results in a decrease in development of the children's self-control of energy intake and ultimately, perhaps, in increases in children's amount of body fat.

■

## EDITOR'S INTRODUCTION

This article focuses on an essential aspect of child health: food acceptance patterns, or which foods children select and how much they eat. As Leann Birch, Susan Johnson, and Jennifer Fisher explain, children's natural preference for the sweet taste and for high-energy foods that satisfy hunger affect their food acceptance. Furthermore, young children readily reject unfamiliar foods, an adaptive response that shields them from ingesting toxic substances. They also have an innate capacity to adjust how much they eat to the energy density (caloric content) of available foods. At the same time, food preferences vary widely from culture to culture, in-dicating that they are profoundly influenced by experience. Birch, Johnson, and Fisher's program of research reveals that repeated opportunities to taste new foods gradually increase children's acceptance of them. Offering a variety of foods in an emotionally positive eating atmosphere in which coercive feeding practices are avoided fosters healthy eating behaviors. Under these conditions, children's natural ability to self-regulate their energy intake is sustained, thereby protecting them from the widespread modern health risk of overweight and obesity.

For caregivers and parents, young children's health and well-being are of primary concern. Because we have been made aware of the important links between nutrition and children's health and growth, young children's eating (or not eating) can generate a high degree of anxiety in caregivers. The purpose of this article is to review what is known about the factors that influence the developing child's food-acceptance patterns, including children's sensory responsiveness, their innate preferences and ability to learn about food and the consequences of eating, and the effect of child-feeding practices on children's **food-acceptance patterns**. The term food-acceptance patterns encompasses which foods are selected and how much is consumed. Our focus will be primarily on the evidence showing how early experience contributes to the development of food-acceptance patterns and the control of food intake. This information should be useful in designing strategies to foster the development of healthy patterns of food intake and in reducing caregivers' anxieties about child feeding. Because an extended discussion of the practical implications of these findings is beyond the scope of this article, we refer the interested reader to Ellyn Satter's two excellent books on child feeding for additional practical information (Satter, 1986, 1987).

## EARLY SENSORY RESPONSIVENESS AND FOOD ACCEPTANCE

In the absence of adult coercion, young children eat what they like and leave the rest. In making their food choices, they are blissfully ignorant of the caloric content and nutrient value and do not hesitate to express their likes and dislikes. These food-acceptance patterns begin in infancy with the reflexive facial expressions elicited by the basic tastes. The taste system is functional at birth; newborns respond with a positive expression to sweet and a negative expression to sour and bitter, and by about four months, they begin to show a preference for salt (Cowart & Beauchamp, 1986). The infant's reflexive facial expressions in response to sweet, sour, and bitter are unambiguous. Adults viewing infants tasting sweet substances interpret the expression as "she likes it" and the responses to bitter and sour as "he doesn't like it." In fact, one theory on emotional development posits that emotional expressiveness has its roots in these initially reflexive facial expressions (Chiva, 1983). Caregivers interpret the infant's facial and gestural responses to foods and make decisions about whether to continue feeding a food, to stop the feeding, or to try a different food. The fact that these early responses to the basic tastes are reflexive ones suggests that food acceptance patterns may be "hardwired"—fixed and difficult to change, but research on the development of children's food-acceptance patterns reveals that this is not the case. The positive response to sweetness and the rejection of bitter and sour tastes are "built-in," but from very early in life, even responses to these basic tastes change with the child's repeated experience with food and eating.

Foods are complex stimuli, and they provide input to several sensory systems in addition to taste. Foods have textural components (such as crunchiness, creaminess, or greasiness), and the smell of food contributes greatly to much of what we commonly refer to as the taste or flavor of food. A food's appearance also can influence its attractiveness. Thus, our food preferences result from our response to a complex combination of stimulation, involving the food's taste, smell, appearance, and tactile characteristics. Children's responses to these characteristics are strongly influenced by prior experience with the food.

If we look at diets across cultures, dramatic differences exist in what substances are considered food, in what items tend to be valued and preferred, as well as in which substances are seen as unappealing or disgusting (Fallon, Rozin, & Pliner, 1984). Humans are omnivores. This means that we need a variety of foods to obtain adequate nutrition, unlike specialized species who can survive on one or a few foods. Along with this need for variety comes the ability to adapt readily to consuming whatever edible substances happen to be available in our environment. This adaptability implies that learning and experience must play central roles in shaping our food-acceptance patterns.

Although there is striking cross-cultural diversity in adult diets, as mammals we all begin life consuming an exclusively milk diet. By the time children are 5 or 6 years old, they are consuming many of the foods that make up the adult diet of their culture, and within that cultural group they will have developed individual patterns of food likes and dislikes; for example, many American 6-year olds love hamburgers, but in India a Hindu child would probably find the idea of eating a hamburger disgusting. From a developmental perspective this implies that learning occurs relatively rapidly in the first few years of life.

In some of our initial research on children's food preferences, we investigated the question of which of the many dimensions of foods are central in forming children's food preferences (Birch, 1979); for example, how central are textural characteristics relative to the food's flavor in determining whether a food will be accepted or rejected? Our initial work revealed that sweetness was a primary determinant of children's preferences for foods, and this came as no surprise; however, a second factor, familiarity, was also important in determining preference. This is not a characteristic of the food but a function of the child's experience: Children tended to prefer foods that were familiar over those that were not, relatively independent of the foods' sensory characteristics. Based on that observation we have conducted a program of research designed to investigate how children's early experience with food and eating shapes the development of their

preferences and food-acceptance patterns. Much of that work will be reviewed in this article. This work has practical implications for constructing social and physical settings for child feeding, and these points will also be developed.

## LEARNED FOOD PREFERENCES: REPEATED EXPOSURE AND ASSOCIATIVE LEARNING

Infancy and early childhood involve a dramatic dietary transition from consuming an exclusively milk diet to eating a variety of foods; at one point, all foods were new to the child. To obtain adequate nutrition, children must come to accept some of the new foods that parents offer. However, in general, infants and young children do not readily accept new foods (unless they happen to be sweet!). We have investigated this rejection of the new, or **neophobia,** and how children's initial rejection of new foods can be altered. Fortunately, many of children's initial rejections of new foods can be changed to acceptance. How? By simply providing the child with a number of opportunities to sample the new food.

In several experiments we have shown that as exposure to a food increases, so does the child's preference for the food (Birch & Marlin, 1982). We offered samples of new foods to children repeatedly during the course of their ongoing preschool program. We encouraged the children to take a small taste of the food, and we compared the changes in preference that resulted from this procedure to changes obtained when the child did not taste but only looked at and smelled the food (Birch, McPhee, Shoba, Pirok, & Steinberg, 1987). Repeated exposure enhanced acceptance only when children actually tasted the foods; looking at and smelling the food did not increase children's acceptance. These changes in acceptance of new foods occur relatively slowly, often requiring 10 exposures before clear changes in acceptance are achieved (Sullivan & Birch, 1990).

Unfortunately, in many cases children don't have repeated opportunities to eat new foods because caregivers often interpret the child's initial rejection as reflecting a fixed and persistent dislike of the food. If the caregiver views the child's initial rejection as reflecting a dislike that cannot be altered, then she may not serve this food to the child again. As a result, caregivers may become frustrated and anxious about feeding the child, possibly resorting to coercive feeding techniques, which can have a negative impact on food selection and the regulation of energy intake (see "How parents influence their children's eating behaviors" later in this chapter). In addition, the child may learn to accept few foods and may be labeled as "finicky" or as a "picky eater." Results of several experiments indicate that if caregivers are willing to persist in offering a new food, repeated exposure can be a slow but effective means of expanding the variety of foods that children will accept. The effect of repeated exposure on food acceptance is not restricted to young children; it is also effective with infants (Sullivan & Birch, 1994) and adults (Pliner, Pelchat, & Grobinski, 1993).

Research with animals reveals that changes in food acceptance resulting from repeated exposure are probably a result of "learned safety" (Kalat & Rozin, 1973). This means that when the child learns (via repeated consumption) that eating the new food is not followed by illness, the food is gradually accepted. Putting edible substances into the body is a risky business; they can be toxic. Viewed in this light, the child's initial rejection of new foods takes on an adaptive character. Rather than reflecting a lack of cooperation or negativism, the child's rejection of new foods can be viewed as a normal, adaptive, protective response. Over time, when the consumption of a new food is not followed by nausea and vomiting, the child ultimately accepts the food. Conversely, when eating is followed by such negative consequences, a conditioned aversion results, and the child rejects and avoids the food.

Based on these findings, we encourage caregivers to be persistent and to continue to offer new foods that are initially rejected. A schedule that includes two opportunities to try the food each week seems to work well. The child should not be coerced but should have the chance to taste the food in an unpressured setting. Our recommendation to parents and caregivers is to set a clear and consistent expectation that the child will taste new foods when they are offered. This policy works best if initiated when the child first begins to try new foods, during late infancy prior to the increased autonomy and independence of the toddler period. By the time the child reaches the "terrible twos," a time when many of the child's experiences with new foods occur, eating can easily become a focal point for power struggles, and having a well-established routine for tasting new foods can minimize negative interactions surrounding feeding.

## CONTRIBUTIONS OF ASSOCIATIVE LEARNING TO FOOD-ACCEPTANCE PATTERNS

### Social Context

We have indicated that our food likes and dislikes are influenced by learning, most of which occurs in the absence of explicit teaching, during children's routine experiences at mealtimes. Young children eat frequently during the day and thus have many opportunities for experiences that can shape their food-acceptance patterns. For young children, eating is a social occasion because they need help; they cannot yet prepare and serve their own food, and they may also need help in feeding themselves. Siblings, peers, and adults are often present at meals and snacks, when they can serve as models. In fact, we have seen that one way to increase children's acceptance of disliked vegetables is to expose children to peers who happen to like the disliked food (Birch, 1980).

Caregivers may attempt to control the child's eating via a variety of child-feeding strategies. The emotional tone of the social interactions surrounding feeding can shape children's food-acceptance patterns when associations are formed between food and the child's emotional response to the feeding interaction. Meals are an important context for family or child care staff-child interaction, and meals also have a temporal structure that has meaning. Children learn very early that certain foods are served in particular order at meals and that particular social occasions require special foods. Even 2-year-olds can tell you what foods should be served at birthday parties and that dessert comes after the vegetables. In Western cultures, sweet desserts come at the end of the meal, probably because we still find them palatable even when we are relatively satiated, after consuming other courses. This sequencing of courses in Western cuisines fosters the use of sweet, palatable foods as effective rewards for finishing the previous course ("Finish your vegetables and you may have dessert"). We have investigated the impact of the use of foods in these social contexts on the formation of children's preferences for foods, and these findings reveal that some common feeding practices may have unintended and untoward effects on children's food-acceptance patterns. When foods are given to children in positive social contexts (as rewards, or paired with positive social interaction with an adult), children's preferences for those foods are enhanced (Birch, Zimmerman, & Hind, 1980). The opposite effect on food acceptance can occur when caregivers force children to eat "nutritious" foods to obtain rewards. ("Eat your vegetables and you can watch TV"). The strategy of having a child eat a food in order to obtain a reward tends to reduce the child's liking for the food she is rewarded for eating (Birch, Marlin, & Rotter, 1984). In summary, via associative learning, social contexts of feeding that are perceived by the child as positive enhance liking; those that are negative reduce liking.

It may not be immediately obvious how this associative learning can contribute to the formation of food-acceptance patterns inconsistent with good nutrition. This occurs because there tends to be a consistent association between

A relaxed, positive mealtime atmosphere in which children are given repeated opportunities to try new foods fosters healthy food acceptance patterns. (Photo: Laura Berk)

foods and the social contexts in which they are given: Foods presented in positive social contexts and as rewards tend to be palatable foods high in fat, sugar, and salt. These foods, preferred by children even without much prior experience, are the same foods that current dietary guidelines tell us to consume in moderation. While our findings reveal that these child-feeding practices can enhance children's preferences for these foods, parents who use coercive feeding practices are often unaware of the effects these practices have on children's food-acceptance patterns. The same parents are concerned that their children are consuming too many "unhealthy" foods that are high in fat, salt, and sugar and not enough healthy, nutritious foods.

Based upon the research presented above, we suggest that caregivers can increase the chances that children will come to accept a wide variety of foods by providing children with repeated opportunities to try new foods in positive or relatively neutral social contexts and by avoiding coercive feeding practices. Parents should be aware that while coercive feeding tactics (such as rewarding children for eating foods they do not spontaneously consume) may have the immediate effect of increasing intake, they can also have negative long-term effects on children's food-acceptance patterns.

## Learned Preferences for High-Energy Foods

We have seen that children's preferences for foods are shaped by their innate reactions to the basic tastes in foods, and that via associative learning, the quantity and quality of their early experience with foods have a major impact on their developing food-acceptance patterns. Recent research has revealed that the physiological consequences of ingesting food can also modify children's preferences and can influence how much of those foods is consumed. Children can learn to associate the flavor cues in foods with the physiological consequences of eating those foods. The clearest example of this sort of learning was mentioned earlier: The case of the **conditioned aversion,** which results when consumption of a food is associated with subsequent nausea and vomiting. This learning is very powerful, and even previously preferred foods may be consistently avoided after such an association.

Recent research has revealed that children also form associations between foods' sensory cues and the positive physiological consequences (feeling pleasantly full, for example) that normally follow eating an energy-dense food. In this research, children were given repeated opportunities to consume fixed amounts of high- and low-energy-density versions of the same distinctively flavored food. The foods used included yogurt and puddings, which can be made either high or low in energy density by varying either the fat or carbohydrate content. When adults were asked to taste the different preparations, they could not tell with reliability whether the preparations were high or low energy, nor did they consistently prefer one preparation over the other. After repeated opportunities to eat these foods as snacks, children showed clear preferences for the high-energy versions, and this result was obtained whether the high-energy version was made with added fat or with carbohydrate (Birch, McPhee, Steinberg, & Sullivan, 1990; Johnson, McPhee, & Birch, 1991). The children's preferences for the high-energy foods were particularly clear when they were hungry, providing additional support for the fact that preferences were mediated by the physiological consequences of the food's energy density (Kern, McPhee, Fisher, Johnson, & Birch, 1993). These findings indicate that, in addition to the child's natural preference for the sweet taste, the child is biased to learn to prefer foods that are high in energy. This ability to learn to associate a food's flavor cues with the physiological consequences of eating that food can be viewed as serving an adaptive function, especially in contexts of food scarcity. Forming associations between the food's sensory cues and the food's energy content would lead to learning to prefer foods with high-energy contents. In the United States today, where for many of us foods are readily available and overconsumption is our most prevalent nutritional problem, rates of obesity among children have increased more than 50 percent in the last 20 years (Dietz, 1991). The ready availability of high-fat foods, their association with positive social contexts, and children's predisposition to learn to like high-fat and other high-energy foods contributes, as every parent and teacher knows, to the increased incidence of childhood obesity. Reduced energy expenditure must be considered also as one cause of increased childhood obesity.

## CHILDREN'S ABILITY TO REGULATE ENERGY INTAKE

Do young children "know" how much to eat? In the late 1930s Clara Davis observed that when presented with a variety of nutritious foods, children self-selected a diet sufficient to maintain adequate health. This path-breaking research suggested that young children possessed an innate ability to regulate food intake, independent of adult supervision. Davis, however, pointed out that part of the "trick" of her experiment was providing children with a set of simply prepared, healthful foods from which they could choose (Davis, 1928). In a recent series of experiments, we have been investigating how children's responsiveness to the caloric content of foods serves as a control of food intake. In the initial studies we looked at whether children adjusted their food intake in response to differences in the caloric content of foods (Birch & Deysher, 1985, 1986). This research was prompted by the earlier research of Davis, as well as that of Fomon (1974), which examined infants' ability to adjust their milk intake in response to changes in the formula's energy density. Fomon's work revealed that infants older than six weeks adjusted the amount of formula intake according to the energy density of the given formula, consuming more of the energy-dilute formula and less of the energy-dense version.

To determine whether the responsiveness to energy density seen in infants persisted into childhood, we first looked at the effect that varying the caloric density of a meal's first course had on children's food intake in subsequent meals. In these experiments children were observed during a pair of meals, eaten on different days. The meals, which consisted of a first and second course, differed only in the caloric content of the first course. The children first consumed a fixed amount of a first course (half a cup of yogurt, for example) that was either low or high in calories. A few minutes later the children were offered a variety of foods from which they could self-select a meal, consuming as much of the foods as they wished. We reasoned that if children were responsive to the caloric density of foods in controlling their food intake, they would eat less in the self-selected portion of the meal following the high-calorie first course. In fact, this is what children did; they adjusted their intake in the second course almost calorie for calorie with the energy in the first course, so that their total

caloric intake for the first and second meals were the same whether or not they consumed the high-calorie first course or the low-calorie first course. Our findings are consistent with the idea that children may possess the ability to regulate how much to eat based on the caloric content of the foods they eat. In fact, our experience has been that children may rely on this sensitivity to caloric density to a greater extent than do adults. When children and adults were presented with the same low- and high-energy courses, the children showed the most precise regulation of caloric intake (Birch & Deysher, 1985). It appears that as we age, an increasing number of environmental and psychological factors can influence and even override sensitivity to internal cues that tell us how much to eat.

Our research indicates that children have some innate capacity to adequately "know" how much to eat based on foods' differing energy density. This "knowledge" is manifest in a sensitivity to the caloric content of foods not only within a given meal but also over a number of meals. This may seem quite contrary to what parents and practitioners believe about children's meal-to-meal eating behavior. For instance, children are often inconsistent in what and how much they eat, consuming large portions of food at lunch one day and very little of the food offered at lunch on other days. It is therefore not surprising that caregivers and practitioners often approach child feeding with concern and frustration, as children may seem incapable of meeting their energy needs without adult supervision or intervention. However, we have found that although children's meal-to-meal energy intake is somewhat erratic, children are consistent in the total amount of calories they consume during 24-hour periods. In examining children's caloric intake over the course of a 24-hour period, we found that total daily intake varied, on the average, by only about 10 percent (Birch, Johnson, Andresen, Peters, & Schulte, 1991; Birch, Johnson, Jones, & Peters, 1993). Although our measurements were made in a relatively controlled laboratory school setting, similar patterns of children's food intake have been observed in other less-controlled contexts (Shea, Stein, Basch, Contento, & Zybert, 1992).

## INDIVIDUAL DIFFERENCES IN THE REGULATION OF ENERGY INTAKE

The percentage of young American children being classified as obese has continued to increase over the last several decades, with current estimates indicating that 25 percent of young children are obese and nearly one third of young children are overweight (Dietz, 1991). Casual observation reveals large individual differences among children in degree of body fatness, suggesting that all children may not be equally adept at adjusting what they eat in relation to how much their body needs.

We have begun to characterize individual differences in children's ability to regulate energy intake and identify the influences that result in these differences. Recent experiments at our laboratory have begun to focus on the individual child to determine the kinds of relationships that exist between an individual's eating behaviors and his body fatness. Building on our previous work, we investigated differences among children in their ability to respond to energy-density cues. Using our standard experimental procedure, on two separate occasions we gave children a drink that was high or low in calories; if a child received the high-calorie version the first time, the second time she drank the low-calorie version. A short time after the children finished the drink, they were invited to eat a self-selected lunch, that is, *they* chose what they wished to eat from a variety of foods that included a main dish, fruit, vegetables, and milk, as well as a dessert. We measured their energy intake at lunch on both occasions and from this information determined whether or not each child adjusted lunch intake in response to the calorie content of the first-course drink. In addition to collecting this consumption data, we also obtained information on the children's body-fat stores by measuring height, weight, and skinfolds. Our findings indicated that children varied in their ability to regulate energy intake and that this variation was related to their body-fat stores: The children who showed less evidence of regulating their energy intake also had the greatest body-fat stores. This indicates that a systematic relationship exists between children's ability to regulate energy intake, their eating style, and their weight outcome.

Individual differences in the accuracy of energy-intake regulation are probably due, at least to some extent, to genetic variability, that is, some genetic predisposition or familial similarity exists in patterns of body fatness and food-intake regulation, and these biological characteristics account for some portion of individual differences in body type. These predispositions can be shaped or altered by various environmental factors, however. These factors include food availability, the type and variety of foods consumed, and the more social aspects of feeding, such as parents'/caretakers' attitudes and behaviors related to food and eating. Parents' child-feeding strategies and parents' eating styles will be the focus of the last portion of this article.

## HOW PARENTS INFLUENCE THEIR CHILDREN'S EATING BEHAVIORS

Research on parenting style and child development outcomes reveals that **authoritarian** or rigid control over children's behavior is associated with unfavorable developmental outcomes; for example, parents who use an overly restrictive style have children who are less self-reliant than are children of democratic parents. In contrast, **democratic parenting** fosters the development of a child's self-esteem and self-control (Baumrind, 1973). Costanzo and Woody (1985) have developed a model whereby they associate problematic outcomes in children with overrestrictiveness of the parent. They suggest that parents, motivated by concern for their children, are likely to impose more control over their children in areas of development (1) that they value highly or (2) in which they believe that their child may be especially at risk. The researchers further suggest that parents' attempts to impose control inhibit the child's likelihood of developing *self*-control in that particular area of development.

Costanzo and Woody's model can be applied to the eating domain by considering the relationship between parents' child-feeding strategies and children's regulation of energy intake. Many parents impose rules and regulations regarding eating that are both implicit and explicit. These rules include such practices as using foods as bribes and rewards or making access to highly desirable foods contingent upon the consumption of less desirable ones ("If you finish your Brussels sprouts, I will give you a cookie"). We have already presented evidence that these practices can systematically alter children's food preferences in directions incompatible with healthy diets. These control strategies can negatively affect children's food-acceptance patterns in a second way: decreasing children's ability to self-regulate energy intake (Birch, McPhee, Shoba, Steinberg, & Krehbiel, 1987). When we instructed one group of children to focus on "cleaning their plates," or the amount of food remaining on the plate, these children were much less responsive to energy-density cues than children who had been taught to focus on internal cues, such as feelings of hunger or fullness. More recent work has revealed that parents who use controlling child-feeding strategies have children who are less likely to exhibit self-control in regulating their energy intake (Johnson & Birch, 1993). We asked parents to complete the Child Feeding Questionnaire, an instrument designed to assess the degree of control parents use within the child-feeding domain. This questionnaire asks parents whether they believe that they need to regulate when and how much their children eat in addition to what they eat. The completed questionnaire also reveals information regarding the rules and regulations that parents establish with respect to eating. The children from these families participated in a pair of consumption trials to assess their responsiveness to energy-density cues of their diet. We found that parents who reported using more control over their children's food intake had children who showed less evidence of self-regulation of energy intake (Johnson & Birch, 1993). Furthermore, children who were less responsive to energy-density cues had larger body-fat stores. Together these findings suggest that parental control exerted to regulate the quantity of food that children consume results in a decrease in development of the children's self-control of energy intake and ultimately, perhaps, in increases in children's amount of body fat.

## CONCLUSIONS FOR CHILD CARE PROVIDERS

A primary responsibility of parents and caregivers is to try to ensure that children are healthy. Part of providing an optimal environment for growth and health is to make sure that children get enough to eat and also that they consume a wide variety of foods. Parents and caregivers establish standards or rules about food and eating in part because they are concerned for children's welfare. These rules provide children with the tools and information necessary to gain an understanding of the importance of healthy eating. Cuisine rules and rules of etiquette are necessary and positive when they provide the opportunity for children's learning and allow for the development of proper eating behaviors (Birch, 1993). But when these strategies are overpowering, when they control but do not empower the child, they become problematic.

Our research supports what parents and caregivers informed about good child-development practice have been doing for the past 50 years: assume responsibility for providing children with a variety of healthful foods in a positive social environment and then allowing children the freedom to eat what they wish.

## EVALUATING YOUR MASTERY

1. Food acceptance patterns begin in
   a. Infancy with reflexive facial expressions to basic tastes
   b. Early childhood with exposure to a wide variety of foods
   c. Middle childhood, when taste buds mature
   d. Adolescence, when exposure to fast foods restricts preferences

2. Which of the following factors is central in determining young children's food preferences?
   a. Texture
   b. Tartness
   c. Familiarity
   d. Salt content

3. Repeated exposure to new foods enhances children's acceptance when children _____ the food.
   a. Taste
   b. Smell
   c. Touch
   d. Assist in preparing

4. To promote food acceptance in young children, new foods should be offered _____ beginning in _____.
   a. One a week; infancy
   b. Twice a week; infancy
   c. Once a week: toddlerhood
   d. Twice a week; toddlerhood

5. What factor is likely to lead to a strong preference for foods high in fat, sugar, and salt?
   a. Forcing a child to eat them
   b. Using them as rewards
   c. Rarely serving them
   d. Serving them with bitter and sour foods

6. In the United States, rates of obesity among children have increased more than ___ percent in the last 20 years; ___ percent of young children are obese and nearly ____ percent are overweight.

7. True or False: Infants and preschoolers have a built-in capacity to adjust their food intake to the energy density of foods—and rely on it to a greater extent than do adults.

8. True or False: Children who show less evidence of regulating their energy intake have the greatest body-fat stores.

9. _____ parenting results in a decrease in children's self-control of energy intake.

## Critical Thinking

1. Two-year-old Steven has a four-year-old brother Murray, who loves Chinese and Mexican food. How can Murray's food preferences influence Steven's?

2. Why is children's natural preference for the sweet taste and for high-energy foods adaptive?

3. Why has childhood obesity increased dramatically in the United States?

## Applying Your Knowledge

Roberta dislikes peas and carrots, but her mother wants her to learn to like these vegetables. Prepare a list of research-based suggestions for how Roberta's mother can increase her daughter's food acceptance. Also prepare a list of behaviors that Roberta's mother should *not* use if she wishes to achieve her goal.

# 13

## Young Children's Understanding of the Mind

### Imagery, Introspection, and Some Implications

DAVID ESTES
University of Wyoming

■

The distinction between the mind and external reality is woven into the very fabric of our lives.

■

Their use of mental terms suggests that young children may have more conceptual understanding of mental phenomena than was previously recognized.

■

These preschool children thus seemed to recognize the existence of the mind and to understand something of how thoughts differ from things they represent.

■

Children consistently claimed that they could transform mental images of an object "just by thinking about it," but not the object itself or a photograph of the object.

■

Preschoolers not only have considerable conceptual understanding about the characteristics of mental images, but they also seem to have direct introspective access to the products of the imagination.

■

This research constitutes yet another demonstration of developmental psychology's tendency to underestimate the knowledge and abilities of preschool children.

■

Metacognition is a multifaceted construct encompassing awareness, evaluation, and control of thinking.

■

Rather than merely providing opportunities for imaginative play, adults might more actively employ young children's ability to construct and discuss "pictures in the head" as a way to promote metacognitive development.

■

Early childhood practices that use the imagination to promote the development of metacognition have the potential to help children become more vigorous, reflective, and creative thinkers.

■

## EDITOR'S INTRODUCTION

David Estes addresses a burgeoning area of research into children's theories of mind—in particular, their developing awareness of their own thoughts and ability to distinguish mental states from external reality. These understandings are of interest to researchers because they are powerful tools in predicting and explaining our own and others' everyday behavior. Just as children cannot make sense of the physical world without a grasp of time, space, and the permanence of objects, so they cannot understand themselves and their social world without a theory of mind.

According to Piaget's theory, young children are profoundly deficient in their understanding of the mind. Yet Estes shows that Piaget used methods that required preschoolers to explain abstractions and therefore vastly underestimated their knowledge of mental activity. When given age-appropriate experimental tasks, 3- to 5-year-olds have no difficulty accurately indicating how mental and physical entities differ. For example, they say that they can transform a mental image of an object "just by thinking about it," but not a real object or a photograph, and they offer sophisticated explanations as to why. And children as young as 4 are introspective beings who are well aware of their capacity to manipulate mental images.

Estes's findings are part of a growing body of evidence indicating that preschoolers' knowledge and abilities—although not yet complete—are considerably more advanced than they were recently assumed to be. Young children's capacity to reflect on mental life is evidence of the beginnings of metacognition, or awareness, evaluation, and control of thinking. Because metacognition is essential for competent cognitive performance of many kinds, Estes argues that more emphasis should be placed on enhancing it in early childhood education.

This article addresses two fundamental and closely related questions about early understanding of the mind: (a) Do young children grasp the conceptual distinction between the mind and the external world, and (b) are they conscious of their own thoughts? I argue that by 4 years of age children already have both a basic grasp of the distinction between the mind and external reality, and at least some capacity for introspection. These claims sharply contrast with more negative views of young children's understanding of the mind, which can be found both in Piaget's early work and in more recent research.

This article is not a general review of the flourishing area of research on children's **theories of mind**. Readers familiar with that literature will note that I touch only briefly on children's understanding of **false belief,** an issue that has come to dominate current research on early understanding of the mind. I focus instead on children's *awareness* of their own thoughts and their understanding of the **ontological** distinction between internal mental states and the external world. Special emphasis is given to research by my colleagues and me on early understanding of mental images, about which I try to show that young children are especially knowledgeable. After describing this research program and the view of the young child it supports, I suggest some general implications for early childhood education, the gist of which is that early childhood programs can and should use young children's precocious understanding of the imagination to focus more explicitly on the development of metacognition.

## THE MIND-WORLD DISTINCTION, FOLK PSYCHOLOGY, AND INTROSPECTION

The distinction between the mind and external reality is taken for granted by most adults. We believe that our thoughts are fundamentally different from the objects and events in the external world. Some philosophers might argue that to divide up the world in this way is to create what is ultimately a false dichotomy. Some psychologists with behaviorist tendencies might argue that our conscious mental states do not have the causal status we attribute to them. But regardless of our philosophical allegiances or our formal psychological theories, we all constantly use this basic distinction between the mind and the external world, the subjective and the objective realms, to make sense of our own experience and the behavior of others. This distinction might be considered the foundation of what has been called the adult's commonsense folk psychology (Churchland, 1979) or theory of mind (Wellman, 1990).

The distinction between the mind and external reality is woven into the very fabric of our lives. We know, for example, that we can think about doing something, can plan some course of action, but that even an elaborate plan can remain solely in the mind and never be carried out. We also know that our fantasies, no matter how vivid, are not real in the way that external objects or events are real. When we think longingly about something, for example, a cold glass of water when we are thirsty, we know that we cannot really see it, or touch it, or share it with someone else.

The distinction between "mere" thoughts and objective reality may be obvious to normal adults, but do young children understand this distinction? It is clear that even very young children must recognize this distinction on some level. It is implicit in their behavior. Try to get a thirsty preschooler to be satisfied with an imaginary glass of water. But to what extent do young children have explicit conceptual understanding of this distinction?

Intimately related to the question of young children's conceptual understanding of the mind-world distinction is another question, one that

Estes, D. (1994). Young children's understanding of the mind: Imagery, introspection, and some implications. *Journal of Applied Developmental Psychology, 15,* 529–548. Reprinted by permission.

more directly concerns the nature of early subjective experience: How conscious are young children of their own thoughts? As adults, we are sometimes spontaneously aware of our thoughts. Moreover, we can actively engage in introspection. Recognizing the distinction between the mind and the external world, we can turn our attention inward and report on the contents of our minds.[1] When can children do this? When do they become capable of some legitimate if rudimentary form of introspection? Without some conscious awareness of their thoughts, some minimal introspective access to an ongoing mental life, it is hard to see how children could ever come to conceive of a distinction between mind and world, for how would it be possible to selectively attend to the contents of the mind? Conceptual understanding of the mind-world distinction and a capacity for introspection thus seem to be intimately related.

## PIAGETIAN REALISM

Piaget (1928, 1929) addressed both these issues in his early work. He concluded that young children lack both a conceptual understanding of mental phenomena and introspective access to their own thoughts.[2] According to Piaget, failure on the part of young children to grasp the mind-world distinction accounts for many of the ways that they differ from older children and adults. It accounts for **egocentrism**: Because young children do not make a sharp distinction between themselves and the external world, they are not aware of their own thought as being subjective and internal. Consequently, they fail to realize that other people also have thoughts that may differ from their own.

Failure to sharply distinguish between the mind and the external world also causes the subjective and objective realms to become confused in the young child's experience. One side of this confusion leads the child to "psychologize" all of external reality, so that even inanimate objects are endowed with consciousness and intention,

resulting in childhood **animism**. The other side of this confusion leads the child to "physicalize" or externalize immaterial mental states and processes, to elevate "the products of one's own psyche (thoughts, dreams) to the status of real, material events visible to others" (Kuhn, 1992, p. 223). Piaget (1929) called this tendency childhood realism. He concluded that

> On the average the essential discoveries that thought is not matter and that it is distinct from the phenomena it deals with is not made before the age of 11 ... The child cannot distinguish a real house, for example, from the concept of mental image or name of the house. (p. 55).

So, according to this view, it is not until late childhood that children understand the immaterial, subjective, symbolic nature of mental phenomena.

Childhood realism as described by Piaget is more than just a conceptual deficiency. It also involves a corresponding experiential deficiency—young children have little awareness of their own thoughts. For Piaget, young children's minimal conceptual understanding of mind and their minimal awareness of "the thinking self within" were intimately intertwined (1929, p. 37). He concluded that before 7 or 8 years of age children are completely incapable of introspection. As children mature, an increasing conceptual grasp of mental phenomena develops in tandem with a "consistent effort on the part of thought to become more and more conscious of itself" (1928, p. 143; see also Flavell, 1963, p. 156).

The view that young children are profoundly deficient both in their conceptual understanding of the mind and in their awareness of mental phenomena has been and continues to be an influential doctrine in developmental psychology and related disciplines (for example, Keil, 1979). Despite its continuing influence, there are reasons to question the accuracy of this view. First, naturalistic research has shown that by around 3 years of age children are spontaneously using mental terms such as *think* and *know* to refer to mental states, much as adults do (Bartsch & Wellman,

1995). Their use of mental terms suggests that young children may have more conceptual understanding of mental phenomena than was previously recognized. Second, there is reason to question the appropriateness of some of the methods used by Piaget and other proponents of childhood realism. Asking young children "What does it mean, to think?" (1929, p. 329) or "What is a dream?" (1929, p. 107), as Piaget did, forces them to try to define notoriously difficult abstractions. Questions such as these might well obscure any knowledge that children actually possess about the nature of mental phenomena.

## EXPERIMENTAL STUDIES OF CHILDREN'S UNDERSTANDING OF MENTAL ENTITIES

Motivated by these reservations about the validity of Piagetian realism, Henry Wellman and I devised some experimental tasks we thought would be more age appropriate for very young children, yet sensitive enough to detect whatever conceptual understanding they might have about mental entities such as thoughts and dreams (Wellman & Estes, 1986). We were guided by an intuitive analysis intended to make explicit some of the central components of commonsense adult thinking about the differences between mental and physical entities. According to this analysis, mental and physical entities differ on at least three criteria. First, real physical things provide behavioral and sensory evidence. They can be seen and touched and used. Mental entities, mere thoughts about things in contrast to the things themselves, do not afford this kind of behavioral and sensory evidence. Second, real physical things are public. They have an objective existence. Mental entities such as thoughts and dreams are private and subjective. Third, physical things also have consistency in the sense that they are relatively permanent over time. Mental entities are not. Thoughts are fleeting. They do not have an independent existence over time the way

that physical objects do. These criteria, although they do not constitute an exhaustive philosophical analysis, do seem to capture some of the main elements of everyday thinking about this distinction. (For a more detailed discussion of these criteria, see Wellman, 1985).

In an initial series of studies (Wellman & Estes, 1986), we wanted to see whether young children understand these criteria and can use them to distinguish between mental and physical entities. In the first study, 3-, 4-, and 5-year-olds heard descriptions of several pairs of contrasting characters. In each pair, one character had a subjective experience and the other character had a corresponding objective experience. Subjective experiences were described as either thinking, pretending, remembering, or dreaming. After hearing each pair of characters described, children were asked a series of questions based on the reality criteria of behavioral and sensory evidence, publicness, and consistency. They answered by pointing to drawings of one or both of the characters. For example, after hearing about one boy who was only thinking about a cookie and another boy who actually had a cookie, children were asked to "Show me the boy who can see the cookie? ... not touch the cookie? ... eat the cookie? ... let his friend eat the cookie? ... save the cookie and eat it tomorrow?"

Children did quite well on these questions. Performance greatly exceeded chance at all ages, ranging from 72 percent correct for the 3- year olds to 92 percent correct for the 5-year-olds. Although younger preschoolers were somewhat less consistent than older ones, their errors appeared to be random rather than due to any systematic conceptual confusion. We tried to think of plausible alternative explanations for this high level of performance. One possibility might be that children at this age do not understand that mental terms such as *think* refer to internal mental states, so they interpret statements containing mental terms to mean that the object in question is simply absent or not currently possessed by the person in question. According to this interpretation, "He was thinking about a cookie" might have been taken to mean merely that "He doesn't have a cookie." If they interpreted our descriptions this way, they could have answered the questions in this study correctly, but from our point of view for the wrong reason: A real but absent object cannot be seen or touched because it is somewhere else; a thought about an object is just not the kind of thing that can be seen or touched. Notice that this interpretation of their performance would be consistent with childhood realism: Mental terms are given an objective meaning. In this case they just refer to the absence of some real object.

We tested this possibility in a second study. Preschoolers heard brief vignettes as in the previous study, but this time involving only one character at a time. The character either possessed some object (for example, a cupcake), did not possess the object, or was just thinking about or pretending to have the object. Half of the vignettes about characters who were only thinking or pretending included an explicit statement emphasizing that the character did not really possess the object; half of these vignettes contained no such statement. We reasoned that if young children tend to give mental terms a *realist* or *objectivist* interpretation by taking them to refer simply to the absence or nonpossession of some real object, then they should be most prone to this construal when the object's absence is explicitly emphasized. Questions similar to the ones in the previous study followed each vignette, and this time children were asked to explain their answers.

The results are easy to summarize. Performance was even better than in the previous study, possibly because children had to keep up with only one character rather than two. Three-, 4-, and 5-year-olds answered correctly on 87 percent, 96 percent, and 94 percent of the questions, respectively. Correct performance did not vary across the different types of vignettes, suggesting that preschoolers do not tend to interpret mental terms to mean merely that some real object is absent.

Children's explanations for their answers in this study provided additional evidence for their understanding of how mental and physical entities

During the preschool years, children develop a remarkable understanding of the mind and its activities. This four-year-old is aware that thinking about playing with the playdough and actually playing with it are very different experiences. (Photo: Laura Berk)

differ. When asked to explain why someone who does not currently possess an object cannot see it or touch it, a large proportion of their explanations (79 percent) referred appropriately to the absence of the object or to its location (for example, "It's not there," "He doesn't have it," "It's too far away"). In contrast, when explaining why someone just thinking about or pretending to have something cannot see it or touch it, they tended to use other kinds of appropriate explanations. In about one third of these explanations, they mentioned the mental status of the item, often spontaneously substituting another mental term (for example, "He was just *imagining* it") for the one used in the vignette (that is, *think* or *pretend*). They also sometimes referred to the reality status of the item, saying that a mental entity—a thought about something—is "not real," even though the adult interviewer purposely avoided using the terms *real* or *not real*. In their explanations for why a thought about something cannot be seen or touched, they sometimes did refer to its location, but in such cases the location was given as "in the head," "in the brain," or "in the mind."

These preschool children thus seemed to recognize the existence of the mind and to understand something of how thoughts differ from the things they represent. But there are different kinds and degrees of understanding, especially when the object of understanding is the mind itself. In these studies, children were only required to distinguish between descriptions of common subjective and objective situations involving other people. They might be able to make such distinctions with only a very vague and low-level conceptual knowledge about the mind, while possessing little or no awareness of their own thoughts or capacity for introspection. That is, preschoolers may have the rudimentary conceptual and linguistic tools necessary to answer simple questions about hypothetical everyday situations like those included in our two initial studies, yet still be unable to apply the mind-world distinction to themselves and distinguish between their own actual mental states and external reality. This issue was addressed in the next series of experiments. (For a more detailed account of these experiments, see Estes, Wellman, & Woolley, 1989).

## PRESCHOOLER'S UNDERSTANDING OF MENTAL IMAGES

An obvious methodological problem presents itself immediately, however. How is it possible to question someone, especially a small child, about an actual, currently existing mental state? How can a single specific thought be isolated from the stream of consciousness so that it can be referred to and questions can be asked about it? The technique devised for this purpose capitalizes on certain characteristics of mental imagery, which turns out to be an exceptionally useful tool for assessing young children's conceptions and awareness of mental phenomena. For many adults, the mental image of a simple physical object, when actively maintained in the imagination, has a distinctiveness that contrasts with the often fleeting and evanescent quality of the stream of consciousness, in which one thought flows into another without sharp boundaries. The relative stability and distinctiveness of actively maintained mental images make it possible to refer to them as separate entities, in much the same way we refer to physical objects. We can thus ask questions about a particular mental image, which in turn makes it possible to design experiments that contrast mental images with other kinds of things.

The transformability of mental images provides additional methodological leverage. Most people say they can transform mental images in ways that simulate the kinds of transformations that physical objects undergo in the external world, such as rotation. Most adults, for example, would say that they can look at a cup, close their eyes, and imagine it tilting upside down. Although in their work on mental imagery Piaget and Inhelder (1971) claimed that transformational or kinetic imagery is not acquired until the period of concrete operations in middle childhood, other evidence suggests that younger children may possess some capacity for transformational imagery (for example, Marmor, 1975). If preschool children do have at least a rudimentary capacity to transform images, then they should be able to report that they can do this, but only if they have introspective access to this mental process. In other words, in order for children to provide convincing reports under controlled conditions that they are transforming mental images, this process not only must actually be occurring in the mind but also must be accessible to consciousness as well. This logic motivated the next series of experiments.

In these experiments, children were questioned about three kinds of things: (a) simple physical objects (for example, a cup, a balloon, a pair of scissors), (b) photographs, and (c) mental images of these objects. All children were questioned about multiple instances of objects, photographs, and images. In the *mental-image condition* of a typical experiment, children heard the following instructions and questions:

> See this cup. I want you to close your eyes and try to make a picture of this cup in your head. Did you do it? Okay. Now what about that picture of the cup in your head? Can you see it with your eyes? … Can you touch it with your hands? … Can you use it to get a drink of water? … Can I see it with my eyes?

And finally, a mental transformation question: "Just by thinking about it, can you make that picture of the cup in your head turn upside down?"[3] In the other conditions, the same children were asked the same questions about the actual object, referred to as "the cup on the table," and about a photograph of the object. Before being questioned about a photograph, they were allowed to examine it and then watched as the adult placed it in a small plastic box (designed for 4 x 6 in. index cards) and closed the lid. In this example, children would then be questioned about "the picture of the cup in the box."

The graph at the top left of Figure 13-1 shows an ideal pattern of correct responses for images, photographs, and objects. A mental image cannot be seen, touched, used in the same way as the object it represents, or seen by someone else, but it can be mentally transformed. For a photograph in a closed box, negative responses are correct for all questions, and for the object itself a positive response is correct on all but the mental transformation question.

The real visible object served as a kind of baseline to ensure that the task and questions were understood. The contrast of primary interest was between the mental image and the hidden photograph. If young children are realists in the Piagetian sense, then they should tend to conceive of mental images as being physically real, like real pictures in the head. If this were the case, then referring to mental images as "pictures in the head" should tend to reinforce their realist

tendencies and lead them to respond similarly to questions about mental images and hidden photographs. So the basic idea was to set up a contrast between a mental representation and an inaccessible physical representation, refer to them in similar terms as "the picture in your head" and "the picture in the box," and then see whether children talked about them differently.

They did. Typical patterns of performance by 3-, 4-, and 5-year-olds are shown in the other graphs in Figure 13.1. At all ages the pattern of responses was very different for mental images than for hidden photographs and real objects. The biggest deviation from the ideal pattern was on the "Can you see it with your eyes?" question for mental images. A substantial number of the 4-, and 5-year-olds said they could see mental images with their eyes. This anomalous performance on the *see* question for images is notable because in a phenomenological sense we do see mental images. That there were considerably more errors on this question than on the other questions about images suggests that these children were in fact forming and experiencing mental images in response to instructions.

Also notable is the unequivocal crossover on the transformation question at each age. Children consistently claimed that they could transform mental images of an object "just by thinking about it," but not the object itself or a photograph of the object. So, with some allowance for inattention and contrariness, the overall pattern of responses by the preschoolers in these studies conforms quite well to the ideal pattern of correct responses.

This quantitative summary fails to do justice to the sophistication of many of the explanations these preschoolers were able to provide for their answers. Here are some examples:

- A 5-year-old on why she cannot touch a mental image: "How could you reach inside your head? Besides, it's not even there."
- A 4-year-old on why he cannot see a mental image: "You can't see it with your eyes, but you can see it in your brain with your eyes closed."

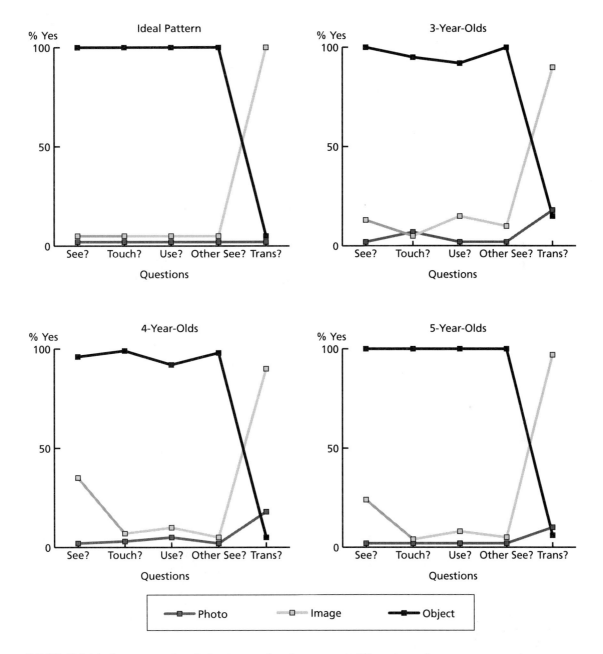

**FIGURE 13.1** Ideal pattern and typical patterns of performance at different ages in mental imagery experiments. ("Other See?" = Can I [the interviewer] see it with my eyes?" "Trans?" = the mental transformation question.)

- A 3-year-old on whether the interviewer could see the picture in her head: "No, people can't see my 'magination' [sic]."

The following descriptions of how they transform mental images are from a 3-, 4-, and 5-year-old, respectively:

- "I can't really do it, but I can pretend to do it."

- "Because I just imagine my hands in there too, and then I turn the cup upside down with my dream hands."

- "I thunk [sic] a special way. I can make things come true in my head."

Finally, here is a comment from a 4-year-old that does not bode well for the future of civilization:

- "Your mind is for moving things and looking at things when there's not a movie or a TV around."

Explanations such as these, coming as they do in the context of generally correct response patterns, suggest that preschoolers not only have considerable conceptual understanding about the characteristics of mental images, but they also seem to have direct introspective access to the products of the imagination. These children sounded as if they were matter-of-factly forming, transforming, and answering questions about mental images. It is also worth noting that they looked like they were engaging in mental effort in these experiments. When asked to form and transform mental images, they displayed such typical concomitants of hard visual thinking as squinting, grimacing, and head tilting.

Nevertheless, despite these converging findings one could still argue that this research does not conclusively demonstrate that young children have some consciousness of their mental states, because the evidence is based solely on their verbal reports. Perhaps children acquire the mentalistic language of everyday life (Stich, 1983) so rapidly that by 3 or 4 years of age their proficiency with this "mentalese" (fully activated by the demand characteristics of our experi-

ments) is sufficient to give the false impression of a sophisticated conceptual and experiential understanding of the mind. Another way to say this would be that the understanding I want to place in the child might really be more in the language the child is learning to use. To answer this objection, we need some method for obtaining objective evidence, independent of their verbal reports, that young children are really engaging in mental imagery when they say they are.

## CHILDREN'S AWARENESS OF MENTAL ROTATION

We have this kind of evidence for adults. It comes from Shepard's **mental-rotation paradigm** (Shepard & Cooper, 1982). In tasks requiring adults to judge whether two similar-looking geometric figures are identical, reaction times (RTs) display a very strong linear relation to the angular discrepancy between the two figures. The standard interpretation of this robust finding is that adults mentally rotate one figure into correspondence with the other to judge whether they match. The more one figure is rotated away from the other the longer this process takes. And most adults explain their performance on this task in just this way—by explicitly referring to the process of mental rotation (Shepard & Cooper, 1982). For adults, then, the mental-rotation paradigm provides complementary and converging evidence for the existence of a specific mental process: Verbal reports of the subjective experience of mental rotation are corroborated by objective RT data.

This combination of subjective and objective evidence is the key to demonstrating conclusively that young children have some conscious access to their mental processes. But RT tasks typically require sustained attention across repeated trials, and such concentration is virtually impossible for young children unless they find a task intrinsically rewarding. It is not surprising that attempts to use mental-rotation tasks with very young children have produced conflicting findings (for example, Marmor, 1975; Platt & Cohen, 1981).

To overcome this obstacle, a mental-rotation task was incorporated into a computer game designed to be intrinsically rewarding for young children. This procedure was tested in an initial study that included 41 preschoolers ranging in age from 4 to 5½ years. Children were asked to judge as quickly as possible (by pressing one of two buttons protruding through holes in a plastic keyboard cover) whether two monkeys flashed on the screen were holding up the same arm or different arms. On each trial one monkey was always upright, and the other was either upright or rotated clockwise in 30-degree increments up to 180 degrees. On half the trials the monkeys had the same arms raised; on the other trials they had different arms raised. The computer automatically recorded responses and RTs. After a correct response, the computer randomly played one of several brief tunes. Incorrect responses were followed by silence. The experimenter controlled the presentation of trials by clicking the mouse when the child was ready to proceed. Sessions consisted of 56 trials (8 trials at each of the 7 angles) and lasted about 20 minutes. Each session began with a brief orientation and warm-up, but there were no instructions to use mental rotation or any other strategy. During and following the session, children were asked to explain how they made their judgments (for example, "When you were looking at the two monkeys on the screen, how could you tell when they had the same arm up?").

In preliminary analyses of this ongoing study, children were classified as *rotaters* or *nonrotaters* depending on whether their RTs displayed a significant linear trend. Nineteen of these preschoolers (46 percent of the current sample: range = 4 years; 4 months to 5 years; 6 months, mean = 5 years; 0 months) had RT patterns that met this criterion, indicating that a substantial proportion of children in this age range spontaneously used mental rotation. Rotaters made significantly fewer errors than nonrotaters (14 versus 24 mean errors on 56 trials), $t(39) = 3.90$, $p < .001$.

Having established that some preschoolers spontaneously use mental rotation, the question of primary interest could be addressed: Are they conscious of this mental process? About one third of the rotaters (6 of 19) did not refer to mental rotation or any other mental process in their explanations (for example, "I look at them very closely and then I see what's right"). However, about two thirds of the mental rotaters (13 of 19) provided mentalistic explanations for their performance. Seven of these children offered nonspecific mentalistic explanations that referred to the mind, the brain, or a general mental process such as thinking or imagining (for example, "Because I just think of it in my brain"). More strikingly, about one third (6 of 19) of the children whose RT patterns indicated they were engaging in mental rotation were able to provide explicit descriptions of this process (for example, "Because you can imagine that it's standing up … By just thinking").

The preliminary findings from this study provide additional support for the conclusions reached in the previous studies. Convincing descriptions of mental rotation, coming from children whose RT patterns confirm they are using mental rotation, demonstrate that by 5 years of age some children spontaneously form and manipulate mental images on a task for which this is a productive strategy, and they are aware of doing so. It is worth emphasizing the untutored spontaneity of both their use of mental rotation (shown by their RT patterns), and their descriptions of mental rotation (in their explanations of their performance). There were no instructions to use mental rotation, and the question requesting them to explain how they made their judgments was open-ended and nonleading. Thus, not only did a substantial proportion of these preschoolers use mental rotation in the absence of instructions to do so; two-thirds of the rotaters accounted for their performance by referring to the action of the mind or brain or to a mental process, and half of these children described mental rotation explicitly. This combination of subjective reports and objective RT data provides conclusive evidence for conscious awareness of a mental process in preschoolers. A comprehensive series of studies is in progress to replicate and extend these preliminary findings and try this methodology with younger children.

## IMPLICATIONS FOR OUR VIEW OF THE YOUNG CHILD

Although there is certainly much more to be learned about young children's understanding of the mind, the research reviewed here provided initial answers to the two questions posed at the beginning of this article. First, before 4 years of age, children recognize the distinction between the mind and the external world. They know that mental entities such as visual images are subjective and immaterial and are therefore fundamentally different from the physical objects that occupy the external world. Second, around 4 years of age, children also have at least a rudimentary capacity for introspection. In response to adult instructions and questioning, they can take their own thoughts (in the form of mental images) as objects of reflection and discussion. And by 5 years of age, some children spontaneously use mental rotation and have conscious access to this mental process. These studies clearly demonstrate that relatively early in the preschool years children have considerable understanding of mental phenomena on both a conceptual and an experiential level. This is decisive evidence against any strong version of childhood realism. Young children already have a solid foundation for a commonsense understanding of the mind.

This research constitutes yet another demonstration of developmental psychology's tendency to underestimate the knowledge and abilities of preschool children. As in a number of other conceptual domains investigated over the past several years (Cox, 1991; Gelman & Baillargeon, 1983), when we examine young children's understanding of the mind with age-appropriate tasks and without preconceptions, we find previously undetected signs of competence. Childhood realism banished young children to a kind of weird dreamland where the subjective and objective realms were always in danger of being confused. The performance of the children in these studies makes such a view untenable.

Though it is clear from this research that young children do not typically confuse their own thoughts with external reality, they are certainly still busy trying to sort out what exists from what does not. So are scientists. Young children may not know whether monsters really exist, for example, just as astronomers do not yet know whether extraterrestrial life exists. But although preschool children may be uncertain about the existence of monsters, they do know that a "real" monster (should monsters exist) and an imaginary monster would be fundamentally different kinds of things. Failing to give them credit for understanding the basic distinction between imagination and reality is not only patronizing to children but probably confusing to them as well. They obviously still have a lot to learn about the intricacies of the mind and the subtleties of human psychology, but then we all do. This is a lifetime enterprise. Yet, without minimizing the awesome tasks of development that lie before them, we should view young children not as qualitatively different creatures, but as more like us than we had recognized. They already share with us the distinction between the mind and the external world, one of the foundational assumptions of our basic worldview.

## QUALIFICATIONS, CAVEATS, AND OTHER VIEWS

Some qualifications and caveats to this glowing view of the young child's understanding of mind are in order here. Although this research demonstrates that by 4 years of age children already recognize the distinction between the mind and the world, other research suggests that their understanding of how mind and world are related may not be so advanced. Specifically, a large body of research indicates that before 4 or 4½ years, children have difficulty with experimental tasks requiring them to demonstrate an understanding of false beliefs (for example, that an object is some place other than where it is believed to be), and, by inference, the notion of belief in general (Perner, 1991). This general finding is robust, but its meaning and significance remain a matter of some dispute. Space does not permit a detailed treatment of this debate, but it is important to note that some researchers regard success on false-belief tasks, which typically occurs sometime during the fifth year, as a behavioral index of a radical shift in the young child's developing understanding of the mind. According to this view, only with successful performance on false-belief tasks can the young child be said to have understood the representational nature of mind (Perner, 1991). Others dispute this discontinuity view and argue that 3- and even 2-year-olds can demonstrate some understanding of the concept of false belief under appropriate circumstances (for example, Chandler, Fritz, & Hala, 1989). As Flavell (1992) recently concluded, we are still unsure just what the average 3-year-old knows about belief.

The false-belief debate primarily concerns children's conceptual understanding of the mind. Recent work by Flavell and his colleagues (Flavell, Green, & Flavell, 1993) on children's understanding of the stream of consciousness has more bearing on the other issue addressed in this article—preschoolers' experience of the mind. Although the research of Flavell and his colleagues deals less directly with the issue of children's capacity for introspection, their conclusion that 4-year-olds have little understanding of the stream of consciousness does suggest a more negative view of young children's awareness of mental phenomena than the research presented here.

Perhaps the central issue in this field is whether there are sharp discontinuities in children's developing understanding of the mind. Do young children have what is by adult standards a severely deficient conceptual and experiential understanding of the mind? Or, is their understanding of the mind adult-like in its essentials as far back as our methods allow us to see? It may turn out that young children do have some starkly anomalous misunderstandings about the nature of mental phenomena (for example, regarding the possibility of false beliefs or the existence of a stream of consciousness) that exist side by side with the remarkable degree of understanding of other aspects of the mind they exhibited in the studies reported here. My own view is that continued research will tend to smooth out the apparent discontinuities and remove the apparent deficiencies in children's developing understanding of the mind.

## IMPLICATIONS FOR EARLY CHILDHOOD EDUCATION

In addition to its implications for how we view the young child—our conception of the child's conception of the world—the research reported here has potential implications for early childhood education. Specifically, I believe this research provides empirical justification for moving toward a more explicitly metacognitive approach to the education of young children.

Metacognition is a multifaceted construct encompassing awareness, evaluation, and control of thinking. Although some disagreement exists over how best to define this construct (Brown, Bransford, Ferrara, & Campione, 1983; Cavanaugh & Perlmutter, 1982), the understanding that children exhibited in the preceding studies should fit any reasonable definition of metacognition: If mental images are cognitions, then explicit conceptual knowledge about mental images, combined with the ability to intentionally form, transform, and monitor the occurrence of mental images, should certainly qualify as metacognition.

Metacognition is increasingly recognized as an essential component of competent performance in a variety of domains (Flavell, Miller, & Miller, 1993; Jacobs & Paris, 1987; Weinert & Kluwe, 1987). Flavell (1979) suggested that metacognitive training be incorporated into mainstream education, and a number of experimental programs have been devised to instruct both normal and learning-disabled school-aged children in metacognitive skills, often with promising results (Campione, 1987). The research reported in the present article provides additional evidence that preschool children also have the capacity to benefit from metacognitive training.

Placing special emphasis on metacognition in the education of young children is not a revolutionary proposal. In fact, emphasizing and elaborating some already well-established themes in early childhood education would naturally make it more metacognitive. For instance, an accepted goal of **developmentally appropriate practice** (Bredekamp, 1987) is to help children express in language what they think and feel, an objective that necessarily involves helping them become more aware of their thoughts and feelings. This is already an implicit form of metacognitive training.

Enhancing metacognition can also be seen as an implicit goal of **constructivist approaches to early childhood education,** Sigel's distancing curriculum being a notable example (Sigel, 1990). Constructivist preschool programs are based in part on the assumption that discrepancy resolution is the engine driving cognitive development. To stimulate the natural process of discrepancy resolution, **Socratic techniques** such as provocative questions and probing dialogue are used in conjunction with carefully chosen activities to guide children toward noticing and resolving conflicts in their beliefs and reasoning. Children must become aware of their discrepant beliefs in order to resolve them, making the process of discrepancy resolution necessarily metacognitive. Thus, although it is rarely stated in this way, enhancing metacognition is already an implicit goal of established early childhood educational practices. Making this goal more explicit and pursuing it more systematically would only extend accepted practices.

A more overt emphasis on metacognition in the preschool classroom might be achieved in a variety of ways, but I believe an especially promising approach would be to provide children with more direct guidance in the active use of the imagination. Again, using the imagination to promote metacognitive development would not be a radical departure from existing practices. Nurturing the imagination has been a recurring theme in the history of early childhood educational philosophy (Speidel & Troy, 1985), but direct and systematic guidance to help children learn to use the imagination is not a central focus of current mainstream early childhood education.[4] Attempts to stimulate the imagination in most preschool programs typically involve only indirect means such as arranging situations and providing props to encourage imaginative or dramatic play.

Rather than merely providing opportunities for imaginative play, adults might more actively employ young children's ability to construct and discuss "pictures in the head" as a way to promote metacognitive development. In good preschools, children are not left completely to their own devices when they are acquiring other kinds of skills. For example, most preschool teachers naturally talk with children about the construction of physical representations and provide noncoercive assistance and plenty of opportunities for practice to help children develop external representational skills, such as drawing. But even preschool teachers who are actively trying to promote children's thinking skills probably rarely talk directly with children about the construction and manipulation of internal representations. Just as children benefit from instruction and guided practice as they are learning to work with external representations, so might they benefit from sensitive, noncoercive guidance and practice as they learn to create and use internal representations. Talking explicitly about mental images and designing activities that exercise the imagination would be one natural way to give early childhood education a more metacognitive flavor.

A **meta-imagination** component in the early childhood curriculum has much to recommend it. First, as we have seen, metacognition is increasingly recognized as an essential ingredient of academic success, and enhancing metacognition is already an implicit goal of accepted early childhood practices. Indirectly stimulating children's playful use of the imagination is also widely accepted in the early childhood profession as a way to promote cognitive growth, creativity, and flexible thinking (Bruner, 1983; Fein, 1982), so more direct use of the imagination to promote metacognitive development should not be a radical departure from the current philosophy of most early childhood educators. Besides making sense to educators, this approach also should be natural for young children. Because preschoolers already have a solid understanding of mental imagery, they should be especially responsive to techniques and activities that employ imagery. Helping children to become proficient in using mental imagery should naturally promote metacognitive development by encouraging them to consciously reflect on, evaluate, and manipulate their thoughts.

Finally, it is worth noting that cognitive scientists and intellectual historians increasingly recognize the power of the visual imagination as an instrument for promoting creativity and insight in science and art (Barlow, Blakemore, & Weston-Smith, 1990; Bronowski, 1978; Miller, 1984; Shepard, 1988). Numerous scientists, artists, and writers, from Albert Einstein (Hadamard, 1945) to Tony Hillerman (Hillerman & Bulow, 1991), have emphasized the importance of visual imagery in their creative work. Given the imagination's potential power as a tool for discovery and insight, nurturing young children's precocious understanding of the imagination more directly and systematically may prove to be an especially fertile way to introduce a greater emphasis on metacognitive development into early education.

These initial speculations about the potential role of imagery and metacognition in early education are offered with the humble recognition that basic developmental research in both these domains is still in its childhood. Developing the specific techniques and practices to implement the kind of preschool program envisioned here would obviously require a long process of testing and refinement and the close collaboration of researchers and practitioners, but I believe we know enough now to justify and guide such a program of applied research.

Early childhood practices that use the imagination to promote the development of metacognition have the potential to help children become more vigorous, reflective, and creative thinkers. The ultimate aim of such practices would be to instill in young children a beginning appreciation for the pleasures and adventurers of the life of the mind. A less grandiose but still worthwhile result would be to help children recognize early in life that the mind is something more than just a backup device to be used only "when there's not a movie or TV around."

## NOTES

1. It is essential to distinguish between this basic meaning of introspection—the simple capacity to attend to and report on one's thoughts—and other more elaborate and controversial meanings of this term. In the way it is used here, introspection is not necessarily intended to imply either conscious access to functionally significant cognitive processes or a capacity for complex self-examination.

2. Two points need to be made about Piaget's early work. First, in some passages in his early writings, he sounds more positive about children's understanding of the mind (for example, 1929, p. 125) than in others. Nevertheless, a close reading of his early work will show that the summary provided here captures the general thrust of his ideas and is consistent with current interpretations of Piagetian realism (for example, Kuhn, 1992). Second, Piaget seems to have considered this early work only preliminary research and was surprised when the world seized upon it as the definitive description of the mind of the young child (Boring, 1952). Although he worked prodigiously for several more decades, he never focused directly on these issues again. We thus have Piaget at a disadvantage. He is unavailable to defend his conclusions or revise them in the light of more

recent research. It is unfortunate that some developmentalists appear to have lost sight of the incalculable magnitude of Piaget's contribution. It should be obvious that his pioneering work has provided the foundation and impetus for the later research that calls into question some of his initial tentative conclusions.

3. Of the 138 preschoolers who participated in this series of studies, 6 said they were unable to form a mental image and were not questioned further.

4. Some current preschool curricula do include a few suggested activities in which children are asked to follow explicit instructions to use their imaginations (for example, Copple, Sigel, & Saunders, 1984, p. 235). Others have advocated making some form of imagery training a primary goal of early childhood education (for example, Greeson & Zigarmi, 1985). And no doubt many parents and teachers informally coach children in using the imagination. For example, see the description by Richard Feynman (1988)—a Nobel prize-winning physicist noted for his revealing pictorial depictions of the quantum domain—of how his father taught him to use his imagination to understand the physical world. Despite such exceptions, systematic training of the imagination is not part of most adults' conception of early childhood education.

## EVALUATING YOUR MASTERY

1. Piaget incorrectly assumed that
   a.   Babies are aware of their own mental life.
   b.   Preschoolers can distinguish mental states from external reality.
   c.   School-age children believe inanimate objects have lifelike qualities.
   d.   Discovery of the distinction between thought and reality occurs after age 11.

2. By age ___, children spontaneously use mental terms, such as *think* and *know.*
   a.   3
   b.   6
   c.   9
   d.   12

3. In Wellman and Estes' research, 3- to 5-year-olds
   a.   Distinguished between mental states and objective reality.
   b.   Could not distinguish between mental states and external reality.
   c.   Were confused by the experimenter's questions about mental states and external reality.
   d.   Were disinterested and therefore did not pay attention to questions about mental states and external reality.

4. Using the mental rotation paradigm, Estes found that 5-year-olds
   a.   Do not use mental rotation but realize it can be used to solve some problems.
   b.   Do not use mental rotation and are not aware of it as a possible strategy.
   c.   Can use mental rotation and are sometimes consciously aware of it.
   d.   Can use mental rotation but are never aware of it as a possible strategy.

5. True or False: When questioned about a "picture in the head" and a "picture in a box," 3- to 5-year-olds talk about them differently.

6. True or False: Young children consistently claim that they cannot transform a mental image of an object "just by thinking about it."

7. True or False: Around age 4, children have some capacity for introspection.

## Critical Thinking

What does Estes mean by "a metacognitive approach to early childhood education?" How would this approach be evident in an early childhood program?

## Applying Your Knowledge

1. List the wide range of behaviors reported by Estes that indicate preschool children recognize the existence of the mind. Then observe several 3- to 5-year-olds at play and (if possible) ask them some questions aimed at revealing their understanding of mental activity. To what extent are your findings similar to those reported by Estes?

2. According to Estes, young children's understanding of the mind indicates that they might benefit from direct guidance in active use of the imagination. Design several activities for preschoolers that would encourage imaginative thinking—and awareness of such thinking.

# 14

## Vygotsky's Theory: The Importance of Make-Believe Play

### Illinois State University

■

A basic premise of Vygotsky's theory is that all uniquely human, higher forms of mental activity are jointly constructed and transferred to children through dialogues with other people.

■

Vygotsky pointed out that fantasy play first appears at a time when children must learn to postpone gratification of impulses and accept the fact that certain desires will remain unsatisfied.

■

Play constantly demands that children act against their impulses because they must subject themselves to the rules of the make-believe context or the game they have chosen to play.

■

Make-believe also fosters young children's ability to reason about impossible or absurd situations—a finding highly consistent with Vygotsky's emphasis that fantasy play assists children in separating meanings from the objects for which they stand.

■

■

In Western industrialized societies, play first appears between caregivers and children; children initially learn pretense and games under the supportive guidance of experts. From these interactions, children acquire the communicative conventions, social skills, and representational capacities that permit them to carry out make-believe on their own.

■

Teachers' effective playful involvement with children requires early childhood environments that are developmentally appropriate. Especially important are generous adult-child ratios, a stable staff that relates to children sensitively and responsively, and settings that are richly equipped to offer varied opportunities for make-believe.

■

These findings suggest that multi-age groupings in early childhood programs offer additional opportunities to promote make-believe and that older siblings from ethnic-minority families may be particularly adept at such scaffolding—indeed, they may be as capable as adults!

■

## EDITOR'S INTRODUCTION

The years of early childhood can be termed the high season of imaginative play. We all know young children "who spend hours in conversation with their dolls; who invest the smallest cast-off objects with secret significance; who on being interrupted at play react with blurred shock, flashing at the intruder the wary, glazed look of a suddenly awakened cat" (Rafferty, 1988). If we take children seriously, then anything so compelling and engrossing in the life of the young child must be profoundly significant.

In this article, Laura Berk introduces Vygotsky's perspective on the origins and developmental significance of make-believe play. In Vygotsky's theory, make-believe, like other higher mental functions, has social origins. Adults *scaffold* young children's fantasy play, facilitating its early emergence and elaboration. Once in place, make-believe serves as a vital zone of proximal development in which children's cognitive and social skills advance ahead of their development in other contexts. While pretending, children enact the rules of social life, subordinate their behavior to those rules, and generate for themselves critical lessons in how to renounce impulsive action in favor of deliberate, self-regulatory activity. According to Vygotsky's theory, make-believe is the preeminent educational activity of the preschool years.

In most theories of cognition and cognitive development, the social and the cognitive make contact only minimally. Rather than being truly joined and interactive, they are viewed as separate domains of functioning. At best, the social world is a surrounding context for cognitive activity, not an integral part of it. Early childhood educators have a long tradition of regarding what the young child knows as personally rather than socially constructed—a tradition that follows from the massive contributions of Piaget's cognitive-developmental theory to our field.

The ideas of the Russian developmental psychologist Lev Vygotsky, who early in this century forged an innovative theory granting great importance to social and cultural experience in development, have gained increasing visibility over the past decade. In Vygotsky's (1933/1978) **sociocultural theory,** the "mind extends beyond the skin" and is inseparably joined with other minds (Wertsch, 1991, p. 90). Social experience shapes the ways of thinking and interpreting the world available to individuals. And language plays a crucial role in a socially formed mind because it is our primary avenue of communication and mental contact with others, it serves as the major means by which social experience is represented psychologically, and it is an indispensable tool for thought (Vygotsky, 1934/1987). A basic premise of Vygotsky's theory is that all uniquely human, higher forms of mental activity are jointly constructed and transferred to children through dialogues with other people.

Vygotsky's ideas are stimulating a host of new ways to educate young children that emphasize opportunities for discussion and joint problem solving. A central Vygotskian concept that has played a formative role in these efforts is the **zone of proximal development,** which refers to a range of tasks that the child cannot yet handle alone but can accomplish with the help of adults and more skilled peers. As children engage in cooperative dialogues with more mature partners, they internalize the language of these interactions and use it to organize their independent efforts in the same way (Berk, 1992). According to sociocultural theory, supportive guidance from adults that creates a **scaffold** for children's learning is essential for their cognitive development. Such communication sensitively adjusts to children's momentary progress, offering the necessary assistance for mastery while prompting children to take over more responsibility for the task as their skill increases (Wood & Middleton, 1975; Wood, 1989). Furthermore, **cooperative learning**—in which small groups of peers at varying levels of competence share responsibility and resolve differences of opinion as they work toward a common goal—also fosters cognitive maturity (Forman, 1987; Tudge, 1992).

These Vygotskian ideas about teaching and learning have largely been implemented in academically relevant early childhood contexts, such as literacy, mathematics, and science (Forman, Minick, & Stone, 1993; Moll, 1990), but a close look at Vygotsky's writings reveals that they recur as major themes in his view of play. Although Vygotsky's works contain only a brief 12-page statement about play, his discussion is provocative, innovative, and ahead of his time. In accord with his emphasis on social experience and language as vital forces in cognitive development, Vygotsky (1933/1978) emphasized representational play—the make-believe that blossoms during the preschool years and evolves into the games with rules that dominate middle childhood. Vygotsky accorded fantasy play a prominent place in his theory, granting it the status of a "leading factor in development" (p. 101), as the following frequently quoted remarks reveal:

> Play creates a zone of proximal development in the child. In play, the child always behaves beyond his average age, above his daily behavior; in play it is as though he were a head taller than himself. As in the

Berk, L. (1994, November). Vygotsky's theory: The importance of make-believe play. *Young Children, 50*(1), *30–39.* © National Association for the Education of Young Children. Reprinted by permission.

focus of a magnifying glass, play contains all developmental tendencies in a condensed form and is itself a major source of development. (p. 102)

As we discuss Vygotsky's theory and the research stimulated by it, we will see that he situated play squarely within a sociocultural context. Adults and peers scaffold young children's play, nurturing the transition to make-believe and its elaboration throughout the preschool years. Representational play serves as a unique, broadly influential zone of proximal development within which *children advance themselves* to ever-higher levels of psychological functioning. Consequently, Vygotsky's theory has much to say to teachers about the importance of promoting make-believe in preschool and child-care programs.

## DEVELOPMENT AND SIGNIFICANCE OF MAKE-BELIEVE PLAY

Vygotsky began his consideration of the importance of play by suggesting that if we can identify its defining features, we can gain insight into its functions in development. To isolate the distinctiveness of play, Vygotsky explored characteristics regarded by other theorists as central to playful activity and found them wanting. For example, the common assumption that play is pleasurable activity is not specific to play. Many other experiences, such as eating a favorite treat, being granted the undivided attention of a parent, or listening to an exciting story, are at least as gratifying and sometimes more so than is play. Furthermore, certain playful experiences—games that can be won or lost—are not pure fun for the child when they result in disappointing outcomes.

A second way of understanding play is to highlight its symbolic features, as Piaget (1945/1951) did in his characterization of make-believe as a means through which children practice representational schemes. Yet symbolism is another

feature that is not exclusive to play. Both Piaget and Vygotsky noted that it also characterizes language, artistic, and literacy activities during the preschool years.

Vygotsky concluded that play has two critical features that, when combined, describe its uniqueness and shed light on its role in development. First, all representational play *creates an imaginary situation* that permits the child to grapple with unrealizable desires. Vygotsky pointed out that fantasy play first appears at a time when children must learn to postpone gratification of impulses and accept the fact that certain desires will remain unsatisfied. During the second year, caregivers begin to insist that toddlers delay gratification (for example, wait for a turn) and acquire socially approved behaviors involving safety, respect for property, self-care (for example, washing hands), and everyday routines (for example, putting toys away) (Gralinski & Kopp, 1993).

The creation of an imaginary situation in play, however, has often been assumed to be a way in which children attain immediate fulfillment of desires not satisfied in real life. Vygotsky pointed out that this commonly held belief is not correct. A second feature of all representational play is that it *contains rules for behavior* that children must follow to successfully act out the play scene. Games that appear in the late preschool period and flourish during the school years are clearly rule based. Even the simplest imaginative situations created by very young children proceed in accord with social rules, although the rules are not laid down in advance. For example, a child pretending to go to sleep follows the rules of bedtime behavior. Another child, imagining himself to be a father and a doll to be a child, conforms to the rules of parental behavior. Yet a third child playing astronaut observes the rules of shuttle launch and space walk. Vygotsky (1933/1978) concluded, "Whenever there is an imaginary situation, there are rules" (p. 95). A child cannot behave in an imaginary situation without rules.

These attributes of play—an imaginary situation governed by rules—provide the key to its role in development. According to Vygotsky, play supports the emergence of two complementary capacities: (a) the ability to separate thought from actions and objects, and (b) the capacity to renounce impulsive action in favor of deliberate, self-regulatory activity.

## Separating Thought from Actions and Objects

In creating an imaginary situation, children learn to act not just in response to external stimuli but also in accord with internal ideas. Infants and very young children, Vygotsky (1933/1978) explained, are reactive beings; momentary perceptions trigger their behavior. A baby who sees an attractive toy grabs for it without delay. A toddler runs after a ball that has rolled into the street without considering consequences "[I]n play, things lose their determining force. *The child sees one thing but acts differently in relation to what he sees. Thus, a condition is reached in which the child begins to act independently of what he sees*" (p. 97).

Just how does imaginative play help children separate thought from the surrounding world and rely on ideas to guide behavior? According to Vygotsky, the **object substitutions** that characterize make-believe are crucial in this process. When children use a stick to represent a horse or a folded blanket to represent a sleeping baby, their relation to reality is dramatically changed. The stick becomes a pivot for separating the meaning "horse" from a real horse; similarly, the blanket becomes a pivot for distinguishing the meaning "baby" from a real baby. This adjustment in thinking occurs because children change the substitute object's real meaning when they behave toward it in a pretend fashion.

Vygotsky emphasized that young children have difficulty severing thinking—or the meaning of words—from objects; they do so only gradually. Indeed, such research reveals that object substitutions become more flexible as children get older. In early pretense, toddlers use only realistic objects—for example, a toy telephone to talk into or a cup to drink from. Around age 2, children use less realistic toys, such as a block for a telephone receiver. Sometime during the third year, children can imagine objects and events without any direct support from the real world, as when they say to a play partner, "I'm calling Susie on the phone!" while pretending to dial with their hands or without acting out the event at all. By this time, a play symbol no longer has to resemble the object or behavior for which it stands (Bretherton, O'Connell, Shore, & Bates, 1984; Corrigan, 1987).

According to Vygotsky (1930/1990), in helping children separate meaning from objects, the pretending of early childhood serves as vital preparation for the much later development of abstract thought, in which symbols are manipulated and propositions evaluated without referring to the real world. And in detaching meaning from behavior, make-believe also helps teach children to choose deliberately from among alternative courses of action. This capacity to think in a planful, self-regulatory fashion is also strengthened by the rule-based nature of play, as we will see in the following section.

## Renouncing Impulsive Action

Vygotsky pointed out that the imaginative play of children contains an interesting paradox. In play, children do what they most feel like doing, and to an outside observer, the play of preschoolers appears free and spontaneous. Nevertheless, play constantly demands that children act against their immediate impulses because they must subject themselves to the rules of the make-believe context or the game they have chosen to play. According to Vygotsky (1933/1978), free play is not really "free"; instead, it requires self-restraint—willingly following social rules. As a result, in play the young child displays many capacities that "will become her basic level of real action and morality" in the future (p. 100). By enacting rules in make-believe, children come to better understand social norms and expectations and strive to behave in ways that uphold them. For example, a child occupying the role of parent in a household scene starts to become dimly aware of parental responsibilities in real situations and gains insight into the rule-governed nature of the parent-child relationship (Haight & Miller, 1993).

When we look at the development of play from early to middle childhood, the most obvious way in which it changes is that it increasingly emphasizes rules. The greater stress on the rule-oriented aspect of play over time means that children gradually become more conscious of the goals of their play activities. Vygotsky (1933/1978) summarized, "The development from games with an overt imaginary situation and covert rules to games with overt rules and a covert imaginary situation outlines the evolution of children's play" (p. 96). From this perspective, the fantasy play of the preschool years is essential for further development of play in middle childhood—specifically, for movement toward game play, which provides additional instruction in setting goals, regulating one's behavior in pursuit of those goals, and subordinating action to rules rather than to impulse—in short, for becoming a cooperative and productive member of society. Play, in Vygotsky's theory, is the preeminent educational activity of early childhood.

## IMPACT OF IMAGINATIVE PLAY ON DEVELOPMENT

Was Vygotsky correct in stating that make-believe serves as a zone of proximal development, supporting the emergence and refinement of a wide variety of competencies? A careful examination of his theory reveals that the benefits of play are complex and indirect; they may take years to be realized (Nicolopoulou, 1991). Still, considerable support exists for Vygotsky's view that play contributes to the development of a diverse array of capacities in the young child.

Sociodramatic play, the coordinated and reciprocal make-believe with peers that emerges around age 2½ and increases rapidly until age 4 to 5, has been studied thoroughly. Compared with social nonpretend activities (such as drawing or putting together puzzles), during social pretend

activities, preschoolers' interactions last longer, show more involvement, draw larger numbers of children into the activity, and are more cooperative (Connolly, Doyle, & Reznick, 1988). When we consider these findings from the standpoint of Vygotsky's emphasis on the social origins of cognition, it is not surprising that preschoolers who spend more time at sociodramatic play are advanced in general intellectual development and show an enhanced ability to understand the feelings of others. They are also seen as more socially competent by their teachers (Burns & Brainerd, 1979; Connolly & Doyle, 1984).

A growing body of research reveals that make-believe play strengthens a variety of specific mental abilities. For example, it promotes memory. In a study in which 4- and 5-year olds were asked either to remember a set of toys or to play with them, the play condition produced far better recall. Rather than just naming or touching the objects (strategies applied in the "remember" condition), children who played with the toys engaged in many spontaneous organizations and uses of the materials that enabled them to memorize effortlessly (Newman, 1990). In this way, play may provide a vital foundation for more sophisticated memory strategies mastered during middle childhood that depend on establishing meaningful relationships among to-be-remembered information. Other research confirms that opportunities to engage in fantasy play promote children's storytelling and story memory (Pellegrini & Galda, 1982; Saltz, Dixon, & Johnson, 1977).

Language is also greatly enriched by play experiences. As children engage in play talk, they often correct one another's errors, either directly or by demonstrating acceptable ways to speak. For example, in enacting a telephone conversation, one kindergartener said, "Hello, come to my house please." Her play partner quickly countered with appropriate telephone greeting behavior: "No, first you've got to say 'what are you doing?'" (Ervin-Tripp, 1991, p. 90). Vocabulary expands during make-believe as children introduce new words they have heard during recent experiences. One 4-year-old playing

As this child eats lunch with her make-believe companion, she creates an imaginary situation in which she follows socially approved rules and masters her own behavior. According to Vygotsky, make-believe play supports the emergence and refinement of a wide variety of competencies. (Photo: Laura Berk)

nurse remarked to an agemate, "I'm going to give you a temperature" (p. 90). Although her first use of the term was not correct, active experimentation increases the chances that she will notice more about the context in which "temperature" is applied and move toward correct usage. Furthermore, the linguistic skills required to express different points of view, resolve disputes, and persuade peers to collaborate in play are numerous. Play offers an arena in which all facets of conversational dialogue can be extended.

Make-believe also fosters young children's ability to reason about impossible or absurd situations—a finding highly consistent with Vygotsky's emphasis that fantasy play assists children in separating meanings from the objects for which they stand. A repeated finding in the cognitive development literature is that through much of early and middle childhood, thinking is tied to the here and now—to concrete reality, but under certain conditions, young children attain a "theoretical" mode of reasoning.

Consider the following syllogism: All cats bark. Rex is a cat. Does Rex bark? Researchers had a group of 4- to 6-year-olds act out problems like this with toys. A second group of children were told that the events were taking place on a pretend planet rather than on Earth. A control group merely listened and answered the question. Children in the two "play" conditions gave more theoretical than factual responses and were also able to justify their answers with theoretical ideas—for example, "In the story, cats bark, so we can pretend they bark" (Dias & Harris, 1988, 1990). Entering the pretend mode seems to enable children to reason with contrary facts as if they were true—findings that provide striking verification of Vygotsky's (1933/1978) assumption that in play, the child is well "beyond his average age, above his daily behavior" (p. 102).

Finally, young children who especially enjoy pretending or who are given encouragement to engage in fantasy play score higher on tests of imagination and creativity. When children use play objects in novel ways, the objects seem to stimulate the discovery of new relationships and enhance children's ability to think flexibly and inventively (Dansky, 1980; Pepler & Ross, 1981).

In sum, fantasy play contributes to social maturity and the construction of diverse aspects of cognition. For people who have questioned whether play activities, so indigenous and absorbing to children, must be curbed in favor of more "productive" activities or whether play constitutes a powerful zone of proximal development, the findings just reviewed clearly grant play a legitimate and fruitful place in children's lives.

## SCAFFOLDING CHILDREN'S MAKE-BELIEVE PLAY

The Piagetian view, dominant for the past three decades, claims that make-believe emerges spontaneously when children become capable of representational thought. Piaget and his followers assumed that children lack the cognitive competencies to share play symbols with others—both adults and peers—until well into the preschool period (for example, Fein, 1981). Not until recently have researchers seriously addressed the social context of children's play experiences. Their findings challenge the notion that fantasy play is an unprompted phenomenon arising solely from tendencies within the child. Instead, new evidence suggests that make-believe, like other higher mental functions, is the product of social collaboration.

### Adult-Child Play

Twenty-four-month-old Elizabeth is being carried upstairs for a diaper change by her mother.

> *Elizabeth:* My going Sherman Dairy. (Sherman Dairy is the family's favorite dessert restaurant.)
> *Mother:* You're going to Sherman Dairy?
> *Elizabeth:* Yeah.
> *Mother:* Is Andrew the cook? (Andrew is a 4-year-old friend who is playing with Elizabeth's sister.

> *Elizabeth:* Yep. (Pause) *My* cook.
> *Mother:* (Putting Elizabeth on the changing table and beginning to change her) You're the cook? You can cook with your dishes, right? Do you have some pots and pans?
> *Elizabeth:* Yep. (Adapted from Haight & Miller, 1993, p. 46)

In the play sequence above, 2-year-old Elizabeth initiates a make-believe scenario in which a trip upstairs for a diaper change is transformed into a journey to buy ice cream. Her mother encourages her to expand the imaginative theme and act it out with toys. The play episode is elaborated and sustained as her mother asks questions that help Elizabeth clarify her intentions and think of new ideas.

Vygotskian-based research on play emphasizes that make-believe is, from its beginnings, a social activity (El'konin, 1966; Garvey, 1990). In Western industrialized societies, play first appears between caregivers and children; children initially learn pretense and games under the supportive guidance of experts. From these interactions, children acquire the communicative conventions, social skills, and representational capacities that permit them to carry out make-believe on their own.

In the most extensive study of caregiver scaffolding of make-believe, Haight and Miller (1993) followed the development of pretend play at home of nine middle-class children between 1 and 4 years of age. Social make-believe was common across the entire age span, consuming from 68 to 75 percent of children's total pretend time. Furthermore, mothers were the children's principal play partners until 3 years of age. By age 4, children played approximately the same amount with their mothers as they did with other children (siblings and peers). Children's pretending with mothers, however, was not caused by a lack of child playmates at the youngest ages. Several investigations reveal that 1- and 2-year-olds who have fairly continuous access to other children prefer to play with their mothers (Dunn & Dale, 1984; Miller & Garvey, 1984). These findings confirm the Vygotskian view that play with care-givers gradually gives way to play with peers as children's competence increases.

Further evidence that caregivers teach tod-dlers to pretend stems from Haight and Miller's observation that at 12 months, make-believe was fairly one sided; almost all play episodes were ini-tiated by mothers. From age 2 on, when pre-tending was better established, mothers and children displayed mutual interest in getting make-believe started; half of pretend episodes were initiated by each. At all ages, mothers typi-cally followed the child's lead and elaborated on the child's contribution. Thus, although pretense was first introduced to 12-month-olds by their mothers, it quickly became a joint activity in which both partners participated actively in an imaginative dialogue and in which the adult gradually released responsibility to the child for creating and guiding the fantasy theme.

Children's object substitutions during make-believe are also largely traceable to episodes in which their mothers showed them how to engage in object renaming or suggested a pretend action to the child (Smolucha, 1992). By the time their children are 2 years old, mothers talk more about nonexistent fantasy objects, a change that may prompt children to widen the range of object substitutions in their play (Kavanaugh, Whitting-ton, & Cerbone, 1983). Furthermore, many par-ents and early childhood teachers surround children with toys designed to stimulate pretend themes. By offering an array of objects special-ized for make-believe, caregivers communicate to children that pretense is a valued activity and maximize opportunities to collaborate with them in integrating props into fantasy scenes.

## Consequences of Supportive Caregiver-Child Play

In their longitudinal study, Haight and Miller (1993) carefully examined the play themes of mother-child pretense and found that it appeared to serve a variety of functions, including com-municating feelings, expressing and working

through conflicts, enlivening daily routines and teaching lessons. These diverse social uses of caregiver-child play suggest that adult support and expansion of preschoolers' make-believe should facilitate all the developmental outcomes of play already discussed, although as yet, no sys-tematic research on the topic exists.

Accumulating evidence does show that chil-dren's make-believe play with their mothers is more sustained and complex than is their solitary make-believe play. One- to–3-year-olds engage in more than twice as much make-believe while playing with mothers than while playing alone. In addition, caregiver support leads early make-believe to include more elaborate themes (Dunn & Wooding, 1977; Fiese, 1990; Haight & Miller, 1993; O'Connell & Bretherton, 1984; O'Reilly & Bornstein, 1993; Slade, 1987; Tamis-LeMonda & Bornstein, 1991; Zukow, 1986). In line with Vygotsky's zone of proximal development, very young children, for whom make-believe is just emerging, act more competently when playing with a mature partner than they otherwise would. In Haight and Miller's study, suggestive evidence emerged that mother-child play promotes effec-tive child-child play. Children whose mothers ranked high in pretending when their children were 1 year old ranked high in peer play at 4 years. And children of the most enthusiastic and imaginative parents were among the most highly skilled preschool pretenders.

## Critical Features of Adult-Child Play

Although mother-child play has been granted considerable research attention, a search of the literature revealed no studies of teachers' partici-pation in young children's play. Yet evidence on the effect of adult-child play suggests that it is vital for teachers in preschool and child-care pro-grams to engage in joint play with children.

Teachers' effective playful involvement with children requires early childhood environments that are developmentally appropriate. Especially important are generous adult-child ratios, a stable staff that relates to children sensitively and

responsively, and settings that are richly equipped to offer varied opportunities for make-
believe. These factors are critical because they
ensure that teachers have the necessary time,
rapport, and play props to encourage children's
imaginative contributions and to scaffold them
toward social pretend play with peers.

At the same time, adults walk a fine line in
making effective contributions to children's pretense. The power of adult–child play to foster development is undermined by communication
that is too overpowering or one sided. Fiese
(1990) found that maternal questioning, instructing, and intrusiveness (initiating a new activity
unrelated to the child's current pattern of play)
led to immature, simple exploratory play in
young children. In contrast, turn taking and joint
involvement in a shared activity resulted in high
levels of pretense. Furthermore, adult intervention that recognizes children's current level of
cognitive competence and builds on it is most
successful in involving children. Lucariello
(1987) reported that when 24- to 29-month-olds
were familiar with a play theme suggested by
their mother, both partners displayed advanced
levels of imaginative activity and constructed the
scenario together. When the theme was unfamiliar, the mother took nearly total responsibility
for pretense.

## Promoting Social Pretend Play
## with Peers

At preschool, Jason joins a group of children in
the block area for a space shuttle launch. "That
can be our control tower," he suggests to Vance,
pointing to a corner by a bookshelf.

"Wait, I gotta get it all ready," states Lynette,
who is still arranging the astronauts (two dolls
and a teddy bear) inside a circle of large blocks,
which represent the rocket.

"Countdown!" Jason announces, speaking into
a small wooden block, his pretend walkie-talkie.

"Five, six, two, four, one, blastoff!" responds
Vance, commander of the control tower.

Lynette makes one of the dolls push a pretend button and reports, "Brrm, brrm, they're
going up!" (Berk, 1993, p. 311)

When pretending with peers, children make
use of the many competencies they acquire
through their play with adults. Yet pretend play
with peers must also be responsive and cooperative to result in satisfying play experiences and to
serve as a zone of proximal development in
which children advance their skills and understanding. According to Göncü (1993), social play
with peers requires intersubjectivity—a process
whereby individuals involved in the same activity who begin with different perspectives arrive
at a shared understanding. In the play episode
just described, the children achieve a high level
of **intersubjectivity** as they coordinate several
roles in an elaborate plot and respond in a
smooth, complementary fashion to each other's
contributions.

The importance of intersubjectivity for peer
social play is suggested by the work of several
major theorists. Piaget (1945/1951) notes that
for children to play together, they must collectively construct play symbols. Likewise, Vygotsky (1933/1978) claimed that in pretense with
peers, children jointly develop rules that guide
social activity. And Parten (1932) labeled the
most advanced form of peer social participation
**cooperative play,** in which children orient toward a common goal by negotiating plans, roles,
and divisions of labor.

Recent evidence indicates that intersubjectivity among peer partners increases substantially
during the preschool years, as the amount of
time children devote to sociodramatic play rises.
Between 3 and 4½ years, children engage in
more extensions and affirmations of their partners' messages and fewer disagreements, asser-
tions of their own opinions, and irrelevant
statements during play (Göncü, 1993). Interestingly, preschoolers have much more difficulty establishing a cooperative, shared framework in
"closed-end" problem solving, in which they
must orient toward a single correct solution to a

task (Tudge & Rogoff, 1987). Here again is an example of how children's competence during play is advanced compared with other contexts. By middle childhood, the social skills mastered during sociodramatic activities generalize to nonplay activities.

When we look at the features of harmonious child-child play, the relevance of warm, responsive adult communication for encouraging such play becomes even clearer. Even after sociodramatic play is well underway and adults have reduced their play involvement, teachers need to guide children toward effective relations with agemates. Observational evidence indicates that teachers rarely mediate peer interaction except when intense disagreements arise that threaten classroom order or children's safety. When teachers do step in, they almost always use directive strategies, in which they tell children what to do or say (for example, "Ask Daniel if you can have the fire truck next") or solve the problem for them (for example, "Jessica was playing with that toy first, so you can have a turn after her") (File, 1993, p. 352).

A Vygotskian-based approach to facilitating peer interaction requires that teachers tailor their intervention to children's current capacities and use techniques that help children regulate their own behavior. To implement intervention in this way, teachers must acquire detailed knowledge of individual children's social skills—the type of information teachers typically gather only for the cognitive domain. When intervening, they need to use a range of teaching strategies because (like cognitive development) the support that is appropriate for scaffolding social development varies from child to child and changes with age. At times the adult might model a skill or give the child examples of strategies (for example, "You could tell Paul, 'I want a turn'"). At other times, she might ask the child to engage in problem solving ("What could you do if you want a turn?") (File, 1993, p. 356). In each instance, the teacher selects a level of support that best matches the child's abilities and momentary

needs and then pulls back as the child acquires new social skills.

Children can be socialized into sociodramatic play by a variety of expert partners. In a recent comparison of the make-believe play of American and Mexican siblings, Farver (1993) found that American 3½- to 7-year-olds tended to rely on intrusive tactics; they more often instructed, directed, and rejected their younger siblings' contributions. In contrast, Mexican children used more behaviors that gently facilitated—invitations to join, comments on the younger child's actions, suggestions, and positive affect. In this respect, Mexican older siblings were similar to American mothers in their scaffolding of play, a skill that appeared to be fostered by the Mexican culture's assignment of caregiving responsibilities to older brothers and sisters.

These findings suggest that multi-age groupings in early childhood programs offer additional opportunities to promote make-believe and that older siblings from ethnic-minority families may be particularly adept at such scaffolding—indeed, they may be as capable as adults! Because of their limited experience with the caregiving role and their more conflictual relationships with siblings, children from ethnic-majority families may need more assistance in learning how to play effectively with younger peers. In classrooms with a multicultural mix of children, children of ethnic minorities who are skilled at scaffolding can serve as models and scaffolders for agemates, showing them how to engage young children in pretense.

## CONCLUSION

The vast literature on children's play reveals that its contributions to child development can be looked at from diverse vantage points. Psychoanalytic theorists have highlighted the emotionally integrative function of pretense, pointing out that anxiety-provoking events—such as a visit to the doctor's office or discipline by a parent—are likely to be revisited in the young child's play but with roles reversed so that the child is in command and compensates for unpleasant experiences in real life. Piaget underscored the opportunities that make-believe affords for exercising symbolic schemes. And all theorists recognize that pretense permits children to become familiar with social role possibilities in their culture, providing important insights into the link between self and wider society.

Vygotsky's special emphasis on the imaginative and rule-based nature of play adds an additional perspective to the viewpoints just mentioned—one that highlights the critical role of make-believe in developing reflective thought as well as self-regulatory and socially cooperative behavior. For teachers who have always made sure that play is a central feature of the early childhood curriculum, Vygotsky's theory offers yet another justification for play's prominent place in programs for young children. For other teachers whose concern with academic progress has led them to neglect play, Vygotsky's theory provides a convincing argument for change—a powerful account of why pretense is the ultimate activity for nurturing early childhood capacities that are crucial for academic as well as later-life success.

# EVALUATING YOUR MASTERY

1. According to Vygotsky, which of the following is a unique feature of make-believe play?
   a.  Pleasurable activity
   b.  Symbolism
   c.  Rules for behavior
   d.  Wish fulfillment

2. Which of the following aspects of make-believe play help the child separate actions from objects?
   a.  Object substitutions
   b.  Play partners
   c.  Parent involvement
   d.  Realistic toys

3. From early to middle childhood, play:
   a.  Becomes more imaginative
   b.  Becomes more solitary and introspective
   c.  Increasingly emphasizes rules
   d.  Increasingly emphasizes object substitutions

4. Preschoolers who spend more time in sociodramatic play:
   a.  Have trouble adjusting to school
   b.  Are better able to understand the feelings of others
   c.  Cannot understand the difference between appearance and reality
   d.  Are more artistically inclined

5. True or False: According to recent research, caregivers in Western industrialized nations teach young children how to pretend.

6. True or False: Questioning and instructing is the best way for adults to support the development of young children's make-believe play.

7. _____ is necessary for children to engage in satisfying play experiences with peers.

8. True or False: Teachers need to mediate peer interaction, guiding children toward effective sociodramatic play.

## Critical Thinking

1. Explain how make-believe play "creates a zone of proximal development in the child."

2. Why is it vital for teachers in preschool and child-care programs to engage in joint make-believe with children? What features of early childhood environments are necessary to support teachers' involvement in children's play?

**Applying Your Knowledge**

Observe 2- and 3-year-olds during a free-play period at a child-care center, and record the episodes in which caregivers play with them. How effectively are adults stimulating the development of make-believe? Explain.

# 15

# Art as Development

ANN VEALE

University of South Australia

■

Art is a means of expression through symbol making, a means of understanding one's own culture and cultural heritage, and a way of developing cultural understanding of different cultures.

■

The philosophy of the Reggio curriculum is based on the belief that art is a natural form of symbolic expression, central to the educational process, and integral to the rest of the curriculum.

■

As well as learning visual skills, children also need to develop the verbal language to talk about the dimensions of art.

■

Children enhance their perception and symbol-making skills through experiences with art materials and through their developing awareness of the visual environment around them.

■

Adults need to consciously scaffold the child's development in each of these areas, as they would in any other cognitive domain.

■

## EDITOR'S INTRODUCTION

This is the first of two articles to address nurturing children's aesthetic sense as crucial for optimal development. Ann Veale builds a case for education in the visual arts as a basic right of the child. She points out that appreciation of beauty and design in visual images is relevant to many aspects of everyday life and can be fostered in all children, not just the artistically gifted. As young children spend more time outside their homes, early childhood programs and schools must take more responsibility for artistic development. Experience with varied media, time to build expressive skills and explore visual qualities of the environment, and opportunities to acquire language for talking about the dimensions of art are essential aspects of art education. Veale draws on case histories of adult artists to show that early experience has long-term consequences for artistic development. She concludes by suggesting a variety of ways in which educators can enrich children's visual sensitivity during the preschool and school years.

## WHY ART?

Art is expressed as a right of the child in the *International Convention on the Rights of the Child*, adopted by the General Assembly of the United Nations on November, 1989. Several articles in the Convention relate to education, play, culture, and creative activities (Articles 28, 29, 30, and 31). The Convention states, "[Governments] shall respect and promote the right of the child to participate freely in cultural life and artistic life and shall encourage the provision of appropriate and equal opportunities for cultural, artistic, recreational and leisure activity" (Article 31, 2 United Nations General Assembly, 1989). One of the most moving testaments to artistic activity as vital to children's well-being relates to the Jewish ghetto of Treason, Czechoslovakia, in the 1940s. Deprived of their most basic human rights, the child-residents found the need and the means for artistic expression through drawing and poetry writing. They had few drawing tools, shared what they had, and used everything they could find on which to paint and draw. Their drive to engage in art seemed as important as life itself. Friedl Dicker-Brandejs, an artist, lived there and became a drawing teacher to the children. Many examples of their art work can still be seen in the Jewish Museum in Prague (1993) and in its publication, *I Have Not Seen a Butterfly Around Here.*

Art is also a means of enhancing our everyday life. It influences our appreciation of design and aesthetic dimensions in non-art applications, such as the cover design of a compact disc, the arrangement of collections of objects in a display, or the scene in a photograph. Art education can enhance the development of every child through experience and participation; its benefits are not restricted to the realm of the artistically gifted.

Seeing is a significant sensory means of learning. Visual art, although based on the visual medium, is suffused with other sensory experiences, such as touch, smell, and texture. Art is also a means of expression through symbol making, a means of understanding one's own culture and cultural heritage, and a way of developing understanding of different cultures. Every child is surrounded with visual images in life. Some of these lie beneath their conscious awareness. For full awareness, children need to be able to discriminate and talk about visual images. Visual impressions come through many daily experiences—watching television, going to the local shopping center, attending church, playing on the beach, or participating in a family barbecue.

The visual arts are seen by some as the realm of the "gifted" and as representing the expression of emotion rather than serious thought. Therefore, making art is viewed as less worthy than the serious study of subjects of more obvious utility, such as literacy, science, and mathematics. In this article, I demonstrate that art education shapes our artistic understanding and influences our lives in significant ways that are not always recognized as art. Aesthetic dimensions are qualities apparent in everyday life, such as in the design and layout of a letter, the format of a page of word processing, the way food is served on a plate, and the choice of functional and well-designed tools for our homes and offices. Although many of these aesthetic choices are a part of our everyday decisions, we are not consciously aware of their relation to the visual arts.

Artists and designers are disciplined creative thinkers who communicate their vision in ways that can be "read" and recognized by other people. The ability to respond to a work of art is not just something that we have or do not have, but something that can be developed and **scaffolded** by teaching and exposure to artifacts in art museums. Our early visual experience as children shapes our aesthetic preferences. This varies from culture to culture, depending whether that early exposure is to sand painting, religious art, basket making, or calligraphy. Familiarity with art media and immersion in artistic activities enable children to understand how artists use symbols to communicate ideas.

## ART IN CHILDREN'S PROGRAMS

In developed countries, employed parents have less time for the traditional cooking and craft activities in which children learn first-hand about rolling dough, decorating a cake, or planting a garden. Young children get this experience in programs outside their home. Therefore, early childhood educators have a greater responsibility to provide a range of sensory experiences to augment what modern families can provide.

Before children are ready to use art media in expressive ways, they need time and opportunity to explore and develop skills with a range of media. This is not a simple matter of "any medium will do." Children need to try a range of materials because it is impossible to predict which art media a child will find salient. Exposure to line drawing, applying paint, using fingers for modeling, and constructing with three dimensional materials are fundamental personal learning experiences with the building blocks of art.

Choice of the means of art making have been governed by theories about the suitability of art materials for different age groups. Recent advances have led us to realize that in selecting art experiences for children, we should not be too constrained by notions of **developmentally appropriate practice** (Bredekamp, 1987). Whereas earlier theories of art education focused on developmental stages (Lowenfeld & Britain, 1964), more recent perspectives indicate that these ideas reduce our expectations of what is suitable for children and what their capabilities are. The idea that children are capable of going beyond their present level of abilities has been strongly influenced by a major early developmental theorist, Vygotsky, and his concept of the **zone of proximal development,** which has paved the way for a new understanding of adult's role in providing the scaffolding for children's artistic development.

## CONTEMPORARY MODELS OF CHILDREN'S ART PROGRAMS

An early childhood education program in the city of Reggio Emilia in northern Italy has attracted international interest (Edwards et al, 1994). Artwork of children in the Reggio Emilia preschools invited educational attention because it exceeded expectations based on "developmental appropriateness." The philosophy of the Reggio curriculum is based on the belief that art is a natural form of symbolic expression, central to the educational process, and integral to the rest of the curriculum. Children are encouraged to take a problem-solving approach to learning and to develop projects over long periods of time that allow expansion of ideas and the achievement of ambitious goals.

The Reggio teachers act as facilitators of children's artistic development. Their role is not passive; they challenge children's preconceived ideas and provoke new competencies as children begin to interact with the materials. Later, children are reminded of the sequence they followed in the creative process—for example, through visual images recorded by photography or through written transcripts of children's verbal descriptions. In this way, teachers act as a group memory, preserving the progress of children's ideas. Finally, adults and children are collaborators; they work as partners by alternating leadership and negotiating activities and next steps. The outward sign of this unique relationship in art is that each of the Reggio centers has an **atelier,** or art studio, and an **atelierista,** or specialized art teacher. Thus, the art program is scaffolded by the structure of the art environment, by the collaborative roles of the adults and the art teacher with children, and by active stimulation of children's thinking and recalling of events.

The project approach to curriculum at Reggio taps into content from three broadly defined sources. First, extended projects can result from children's natural interaction with their environment. Second, they can originate in children's and staff's mutual interests. Third, they can arise directly from teacher concerns about children's learning of specific cognitive or social concepts (New, 1990). Whichever way projects are initiated, the distinguishing feature of the Reggio Emilia pedagogy is its focus on scaffolding children's development by means of developmental processes rather than a preoccupation with short-term objectives. Dr. Loris Malaguzzi, former director and spokesperson for the Reggio Emilia preschools, states " … schools either through content poverty or through excess of planning … fail to promote children's resources and potentials …" (Rabitti, 1991, p.1). Collaborative curriculum planning between adults and children in Reggio Emilia programs demonstrates confidence in children's artistic potential rather than a narrow focus on novelty and change to keep children interested.

Among contemporary programs in Australia, the Mia Mia model at Macquarie University in Sydney has shown how a successful art program can be mounted in a campus child-care center. The center aims to provide a model of excellence in Australian center-based day care for children from 6 weeks to 5 years of age. The visual arts program is the outcome of a unique collaboration between the staff of the center and Ursula Kolbe of the Institute of Early Childhood, an art educator who has participated as an artist-in-residence (Kolbe, 1996b). There are many parallels between the philosophies of Reggio Emilia and Mia Mia, although they evolved independently in distant parts of the world.

## ARE ALL ART MEDIA NECESSARY?

There are differences in the way that children and adults respond to each art medium. One medium might "open up" a person's avenue of expression, whereas other media do not arouse the same potential. Failure to offer the full range of experiences, including "messy activities," might close the door to children whose personal responsiveness might not be awakened in another way. Therefore, there is a need to offer children a range of visual means of expression. This can include work with fabrics and fibers, metal and clay sculpture, mobiles, kite making, portraits, botanical illustrations, and landscape paintings.

The basic media are the same for children as they are for adult artists. We need not "sugar coat" art experiences to make them palatable for children. Adults sometimes take the view that changing art experiences every day keeps children's interest. This constantly changing artistic menu does not necessarily further the aims of a visual art curriculum. It might fulfill the adult's need for variety and change in daily work, yet deny children the time to build artistic skills to the point where they are a satisfying means of expression. Consider, for example, a four-year-old child who struggled to draw a turtle that lived in a shallow aquarium. His problem seemed solved when the last of many such drawings showed the mosaic effect of the segmented shell, from the vantage point of looking down on the turtle. If this child had been directed to draw something else, he may never have solved the visual dilemma, nor have realized that he could solve it. Knowing a turtle through daily, close observation created the circumstances where the child set himself the goal of rendering what he saw by means of line drawing and was granted the opportunity to realize his goal without interruption. The Reggio Emilia philosophy also encourages a broad timeline within which children can continue to explore artistic themes over weeks—editing, changing, polishing, and improving techniques.

Television viewing adds diversity to the range of visual images to which children are exposed. For example, the Ninja Turtles theme seemed to strike a chord with children of a wide age range, yielding drawings by two-and-one-half to eight-year-olds. Contemporary films and cartoons evoke potent visual responses from children through color, movement, and sound.

## COMMUNICATING ABOUT ART

As well as learning visual skills, children also need to develop the verbal language to talk about the dimensions of art. Talk can be about color, texture, lines, patterns, mass, shape or space (Hardiman & Zernich, 1981). Because many adults have not had the opportunity to develop their own artistic vocabulary, they do not feel comfortable in this domain. To "read" an artist's message requires attention and effort at understanding. Desiring to show interest in children's progress with a drawing, adults often ask, "What's in your picture?" thereby suggesting that a drawing must have a recognizable form. Faced with pressure to name their drawing, many children invent an explanation to please the adult.

Through talking about art with children and actively encouraging them to advance in their observation of visual qualities, adults help children become more perceptive as artists. Exploration of items of environmental appeal, such as shells, plants, and rocks, while talking about their sensory characteristics leads to first-hand knowledge through close acquaintance combined with verbal reflection.

## DOES EARLY EXPERIENCE CONNECT WITH LIFE AS AN ARTIST?

Anecdotal evidence from adults who recall their early experience of art or music points to the potency of timely exposure to expressive media. However, the connection between early experiences and later vocations does not necessarily follow a straight line. For example, taking children to art galleries does not necessarily result in artistic leanings. Nevertheless, providing a rich sensory basis of experience may emerge in unforeseen ways later, as the following vignettes illustrate:

*The story of Lucy*: Lucy is a potter who is a popular and a commercial success; she cannot keep up with the demand for her work. Lucy's mother recalls the beginnings of Lucy's vocation as a potter. When the children were young, the family lived in a regional town in Australia. She played outdoors; liked using available natural materials; and modeled objects out of mud, sand, and water, which dried and hardened in the hot sun. Lucy was given a potter's wheel for her twenty-first birthday and has now given up her profession of nursing in favor of becoming a full-time potter. Many themes in Lucy's pottery are linked to personally meaningful events, including events in which she did not participate directly. For example, Lucy made a large pottery urn that features the white rocking horse of her mother's childhood, after reading about it in her mother's memoirs.

In this instance, Lucy used her mother's words, but in the Victoria and Albert story, she celebrates two cats who live in her brother's family home in England. She has not met the real cats yet. However this has not stopped her from portraying them as decoration on her pottery. Although the two cats are only drawn in caricature, there is reality in the writing. The words grace a circular platter that represent a somewhat spherical cat; "Yes he may be well endowed with abdominal fur ... which may give the misleading appearance of stockiness ... but underneath this sleek pelt lies a superb lithe and muscular body. He is Albert." Through personal and deeply felt family links, Lucy's artistic outcome is sophisticated and caring.

*The story of Ingrid*: When asked about the earliest recollections of her interest in art, Ingrid responded that her mother had some facility with drawing. She remembers pestering her mother to "draw for me." Ingrid was given drawing materials and enjoyed ordering them by color. As a baby, color was very salient in her developing awareness. The first real word she spoke was "blue," the name of her favorite color. Ingrid's early color experiences included using glossy colored squares of paper for her art work. She also remembers pouring over illustrated children's books, studying the drawings in Enid Blyton's books and as a 6-year-old, appreciating the illustrations by Eileen A. Soper, whose name she still remembers, including the detail of the middle initial.[1]

Ingrid was very interested in techniques of drawing that enabled hair to look shiny and fabrics to look like satin. At times, she relied on copying to learn how to draw, although her efforts were not always appreciated. For example, she recalls a mortifying moment when she showed a figure drawing to her father, and he noticed that it had no neck (Personal Communication, 1996). Ingrid has found satisfaction in her career as an art teacher and has rediscovered her capacity for artistic expression in new directions as a mature adult.

*The story of Josie*: Josie is a successful director of an early childhood program where visual art flourishes. Her childhood was suffused with art and artists. Her great grandfather was a sculptor, her father was a noted landscape painter, and she has moved among significant artistic figures since childhood. Her early experiences in art were based on access to plenty of art materials, including real artists' brushes and watercolor paper, and the experience of drawing with pastels on gray paper. Using art materials no different from those of serious artists, she drew prolifically.

Despite the fact that she was surrounded by professional artists, Josie remembers being surprised the first time she heard art described as "work." The artistic vision she projects into her program for young children is a reflection of the childhood circumstances that nurtured her own development.

These vignettes have common threads. All three artists clearly identify the beginnings of their lifetime interest in art during early childhood. Each had access to the tools of art, which came to be a significant factor in their discovering meaning through art. It is also notable that all three are also successful in fostering the artistic expression of children—an ability that might have been catalyzed by insight into their own symbolic expression.

## THE DEVELOPMENT OF SYMBOL SYSTEMS

Children enhance their perception and symbol-making skills through experiences with art materials and through their developing awareness of the visual environment. Educators can enrich children's experiences by providing an aesthetic context for teasing out their visual interest. A teacher of four-year-olds places a Chinese vase containing white lilies on a low table adjacent to the painting easels. The selection of paints matches the colors on the vase, and having small fine brushes, as well as the usual sizes, permits children to create similar designs. This structuring of painting materials is an indirect way of scaffolding the visual environment to make discovery possible.

Adults can "stretch" children's visual understanding in other ways—for example, through photographs or arrays of natural materials, such as shells, rocks, plants, flowers, and leaves. Such materials are also suitable for showing children a wide range of authentic visual forms from cultures other than one's own—not just token symbols, such as windmills for the Netherlands or teepees for Native-American groups. Authentic symbols might be batik fabrics from Bali, wooden drums from Africa, weaving from the Navaho Indians, wood carving from the Maori of New Zealand, and patterned silks from Asia.

As Ingrid's story reveals, picture books can be a source of visual experience. Using their visual qualities in combination with language can greatly expand children's exposure to artistic means. Stories by Ezra Jack Keats[2] can serve as a

Providing children with an aesthetic environment, rich opportunities to experiment with artistic media, and the verbal language to talk about art stretches their visual sensitivity and understanding. (Photo: Laura Berk)

basis for discussing collage pictures, as can picture stories without words by Jeannie Baker.[3] Baker, especially, uses collage to create images of the changing environment and passage of time in a way that children can understand. Illustrators such as John Burningham[4] in *Mr. Gumpy's Outing* use line drawings to complement a story that has wit and challenges thinking.

In recent years, international children's art exchanges have been common, particularly between Asian countries, such as Vietnam and the United States and Australia. The Reggio Emilia touring art exhibit is another example. These displays reflect the growing interest in comparative studies of children's art. Imaginative art programs for children and parents have been developed at the Museum of Modern Art in New York (Silberstein-Storfer & Jones, 1981) and by Barbara Piscitelli (1991) at the Queensland Art Gallery in Australia. In both, young children and parents share opportunities to view art in a gallery and then participate in collaborative art experiences in a studio.

## KEEPING CHILDREN'S VISUAL OPTIONS OPEN: THE SCHOOL-AGE CHILD

Many parents report that children who apparently showed spontaneity and originality in their art work as very young children seem to lose their visual adventurousness once they attend school. Further inquiry reveals that in the overcrowded school curriculum, there is often little time for art. Seen as less important, it can be restricted to Friday afternoons when children are tired.

A distinctive feature of the Reggio Emilia program is that preschoolers sustain their interest in projects for long periods. This unlimited time and scope for extending knowledge in a social situation where children and adults work together is a key factor that lifts the ceiling on what children can achieve. Similarly, where elementary-age children continue to experience artistic guidance and stimulation, their art production continues to flourish. With the establishment of new programs for after-school and vacation care for school-age children, an unparalleled opportunity exists for children to be offered expanded options and large chunks of time to be able to develop beyond the extent that schools offer. The limited budgets of these care programs might, however, restrict such possibilities.

Older children can also engage available technologies to document their work—through photographic, video, and color copying. In some after-school programs, children fax their artistic productions to parents while they are at work or traveling.

## HOW TO PLAN FOR CHILDREN'S DEVELOPMENT IN ART

Theoretical perspectives on children's development in art have been subject to changing dynamics in this century. Victor Lowenfeld viewed children as passing through a succession of stages that paralleled Piaget's theory of intellectual development. According to Lowenfeld, fostering of children's development was largely achieved by providing the appropriate art tools for the child's stage (Lowenfeld & Britain, 1964). Subsequent directions reflect interest in the development of symbol systems, influenced by the theories of Nelson Goodman (1976) and his symbolic domains, by Arnheim (1974) and his aesthetic dimensions (which derive from **Gestalt psychology**), and by the Project Zero approach, which applies Howard Gardner's **intellectual-domain view of artistic development** (Davis & Gardner, 1993). In all these contemporary perspectives, the child is viewed as constructing meaning by means of symbol exploration.

At the same time, theorists were interested in the child's perception of works of art. This added a new thrust to art education, transforming it from an exclusive focus on the child as art maker to one of the child as having the right to an art heritage. This approach is evident in current curriculum guidelines that structure content in three

areas: (1) creating, making, and presenting; (2) art criticism and aesthetics; and (3) past and present artistic contexts (Australian Education Council, 1994). Adults need to consciously scaffold the child's development in each of these areas, as they would in any other cognitive domain.

Current practices in art education are firmly grounded in art knowledge as a discipline. They also highlight the responsibility of the educator to guide and extend the developmental process in a way that steers children into the zone of proximal development through planned intervention and the provision of sustained experiences. Those who provide art instruction may not necessarily be artists themselves, but they can be "co-artists" with children, with some guidance as to how to support the child's symbolic development (Kolbe, 1996a). In the Reggio Emilia program, a special place where materials are kept (the atelier) separates visual productivity from other areas of the environment. This has the practical advantage of providing a sequestered space where unfinished work can be cared for and finished products referred to and reflected on by adults and children alike. It also raises the status of art as a valued activity.

## DEVELOPING CHILDREN IN ART

The vignettes of artists' recollections of their art development, presented earlier in this article, attest to the influence of early experiences in making art. The presence of a knowledgeable sympathetic adult with whom to talk about color, drawing, and the dimensions of art scaffolds children's developing skills. Access to high-quality children's books can be a way of opening up a dialogue for art talk. Early experience can also have symbolic significance in the metaphorical sense, as it might linger in the "mind's eye" to be recollected later. Philosopher Maxine Greene (1978) talks about "wide awakeness" and "attentiveness to one's own history." She suggests that "one's own self-formation may open up to critical awareness, much that is taken for granted...." For children, pictures in the family photograph album and family heirlooms with emotional significance and cultural and historical associations can help make these connections.

All three artists described in this article emphasize the importance of their early exposure to drawing, modeling, or colors. It provided the ground work for developing expertise in their preferred medium and creating personal meaning from the materials. What they have chosen to express in their art is an amalgam of their life experiences and their personalities. The artists' means of expression embodies skill and form, through which personal meaning is created and communicated.

## NOTES

1. Blyton, Enid (1950). *Five Fall into Adventure*. Illustrated by Eileen A. Soper. London: Hodder-Stoughton.

2. Keats, Ezra Jack (1964). *Whistle for Willie*. London: The Bodley Head.

3. Baker, Jeannie (1991) *Window*. London: MacRae Books.

4. Burningham, John (1970) *Mr. Gumpy's Outing*. London: Jonathon Cape.

## EVALUATING YOUR MASTERY

1. Veale recommends that children work on long-term rather than short-term art projects because
   a.   It is more economical; teachers need only buy one set of materials.
   b.   Extra time permits children to discover symbol-making possibilities.
   c.   Most young children cannot cope with changes.
   d.   Planning is easier for teachers.

2. An atelier enables children to
   a.   Use a range of materials
   b.   Work on art projects at home
   c.   Collaborate with one another
   d.   Have a place where work can be catalogued and cared for

3. Children should experiment with a wide range of art media
   a.   Because their attention span is limited
   b.   To find the medium in which they can best express themselves
   c.   To find a basis for collaborating with other children
   d.   To understand other people's artwork

4. Why is it important for children to talk about visual images?
   a.   So they can answer when adults ask, "What's in your picture?"
   b.   To advance their observation of visual qualities
   c.   To build their vocabularies
   d.   So they can understand adult descriptions of visual media

5. Visual experiences in early childhood have a [profound/limited] impact on artistic development.

6. The Reggio Emilia program stresses developing projects over a [short/long] period of time, focusing on the child's [process/product].

7. Adults [should/should not] become involved in children's art experiences; they should be [passive observers/co-artists].

### Critical Thinking

1. Veale describes an example of a 4-year-old boy drawing a turtle. What does that example imply about effective curriculum planning in art for young children?

2. How have theoretical perspectives on children's artistic development changed in recent years? Why is a stage approach no longer emphasized?

### Applying Your Knowledge

1. Veale indicates that we are surrounded by art, without even realizing it. Cite examples of subtle aesthetic choices you encounter on a daily basis. Suggest ways of using each of those choices to enhance children's artistic sensitivity.

2. List ingredients of a visual arts program that enhance children's aesthetic development. Then visit a child care center, kindergarten, or elementary

school and find out about its visual arts curriculum. Evaluate children's experiences using Veale's recommendations.

3. Interview a friend or an acquaintance who has an intense interest in the visual arts, and ask about early childhood experiences. Was attraction to visual media present early in life? Explain.

# 16

## Young Children's Responsiveness to Music

JANET McDOWALL

University of South Australia

■

In summary, research shows that children's music perceptual skills develop from an early age. However, certain limitations, such as an inability to focus on two simultaneous musical features, influence musical responsiveness into the early years of school.

■

Children's playful responses to music sometimes involve other areas of the early childhood curriculum, as seen in the delightful examples of a 4-year-old's spontaneous drawings of nursery rhymes....

■

Research locates the rudimentary beginnings of musical cognition in toddlerhood, followed by extensive development in early childhood, when children demonstrate increased understanding of such musical concepts as sound/silence, pitch, rhythm, and style.

■

Overall, research in the area of young children's affective responses to music shows that children in preschool and the early school years do associate music and emotion. Like adults, they are limited in their ability to explain their responses.

■

Young children are reasonably open to various styles of music, but preference for classical music declines toward the end of the early childhood years.

■

While broadening children's musical experience, adults often find they are discovering music *with* children. That is, they open up new worlds of interest for themselves.

■

## EDITOR'S INTRODUCTION

Although only a few will become accomplished musical performers, virtually all children will become avid listeners of music. Janet McDowall reviews research on young children's responsiveness to music and their ability to profit from training.

By the end of the first year, infants have a remarkable ability to perceive subtle variations in melodies. During the preschool years, children can recognize musical elements, such as tempo and articulation. In the first few years of elementary school, these discriminations improve, and children can detect more than one at a time—an attainment that greatly enhances their ability to respond to music. Children's movement, musical play, and "think-aloud" comments while listening grant researchers access to their musical cognitions. Increased understanding of such concepts as sound/silence, pitch, rhythm, and style takes place during early childhood. Although people of all ages find it difficult to explain their affective reactions to music, children's verbal descriptions of feeling states become more specific with age. As McDowall explains, preference for particular types of music is a complex product of musical exposure, social influence, listener characteristics, and characteristics of the music itself. Young children are particularly receptive to diverse forms of music, and exposure to a range of musical styles sustains their open-mindedness.

McDowall's analysis shows that training can enhance all aspects of musical responsiveness—perception, cognition, affective reactions, and preferences. If we begin early, all children can become more sensitive, knowledgeable, and evaluative musical listeners.

This article focuses on young children as listeners to music, in most cases their main form of musical activity. Easy access to recorded music in contemporary Western societies through television, radio, tapes, and CDs ensures that music is a pervasive aspect of life. Hence most children have extensive musical experience as listeners.

An overview of current research is presented, based on recent music psychology and music education literature. Several aspects of children's experience are addressed including perception of musical sound, musical cognition, affective responses to music, and musical preferences. These research findings have important practical implications for education during the early childhood years.

## CHILDREN'S MUSICAL PERCEPTION

According to Campbell (1991), "Perception lies at the heart of the musical experience. How and what we perceive, organize and derive from our interaction with the environment differentiate and integrate our understanding of the musical experience" (p. 35).

Research shows that musical perception begins early in life. In the first few days, infants can already discriminate simple melodic patterns, such as a series of tones arranged in ascending and descending order (Morrongiello, 1986). Over the first year, they organize sounds into increasingly elaborate patterns. Four- to 6-month-olds even have a sense of musical phrasing. They prefer Mozart minuets with pauses between natural phrases to minuets with awkward breaks (Krumhansl & Jusczyk, 1990).

Two experiments by Trehub, Bull, and Thorpe (1984) reveal remarkable attainments in perception of melodies by the end of the first year. Experiment 1 revealed that 8- to 11-month-olds can discriminate a 6-tone melody from the following five variations or transformations: an overall change in pitch (transposition to a new key), a change in dis-

tance between tones (intervals) with overall contour remaining the same; a change in octave of some tones but melodic contour retained; and a change in both octave of some tones and melodic contour. Experiment 2 was similar to Experiment 1, but included an additional variation in which the order of tones was rearranged. Eight- to 10-month-olds discriminated all transformations apart from the transposition and contour-preserving variations. According to the authors, "In general, infants treat new melodies or tone sequences as *familiar* if these sequences have the same melodic contour and frequency range as a previously heard sequence and as *novel* if either the contour or range differs" (p. 829).

In reviewing research on the effects of training on children's perceptions of music, Morrongiello (1992) concluded that "research with young listeners illustrates that formal training is not necessary for the development of sensitivity to the structure of one's native music" (p. 29). However, she also noted "the direct impact on development of music perception skills that can result from formal training in music during childhood" (p. 29).

The effects of both maturation and training can be seen in an investigation of 4- and 5-year-old American and Argentinean children's recognition of chord changes, as indicated by their verbal responses (Costa-Giomi, 1994). Following a short period of training, 5-year-olds were better than 4-year-olds at discerning harmonic changes when listening to only the accompaniment of a song. However, both 4- and 5-year-olds were unable to indicate chord changes when the stimuli included both accompaniment and melody. Poor scores on the melody plus harmony stimuli might have been caused by children's attention being drawn to more than one musical element, thus preventing them from focusing on the harmony. There were no significant differences between scores of Argentinean and American children.

How easily can young children divide their attention among various aspects of music, and to what extent is their capacity to do so affected by training? As Sims (1991) notes, "Since music is characterized by the simultaneous interaction of a number of elements … determining how children respond to more than one element at a time seems important to a more complete understanding of children's responses to music" (p. 299). Addressing this issue, Sims had preschoolers identify single and combined musical elements in listening, movement, and verbal labeling activities. An experimental group was given instruction in detecting the following musical characteristics: tempo (fast/slow), articulation (smooth/choppy), and their four possible combinations. A control group participated in posttesting only. Both the experimental and control children responded to a listening test in which they labeled examples as fast/slow, as smooth/choppy, and as combinations of these elements. A second test was a movement-to-music activity using the piece, "Kangaroo," from *Carnival of the Animals* by Saint-Saëns. In this music, short detached sound clusters suggest a hopping kangaroo, which contrast with smooth sections that suggest stopping. In the final phrase, "hopping" music is played at a slower tempo; to match movement to music at this point, children must make a double discrimination (slow tempo and choppy articulation). Following the movement activity, children were asked to identify the final phrase as smooth or choppy (stopping or hopping).

Results showed that the experimental group made 23 percent more correct responses than did the control group on single-characteristic discriminations. However, neither group did particularly well with double discriminations. An incidental finding is of particular interest: Although the control group did not express musical ideas well verbally, the experimental group *did* learn to do this, indicating that "[young] children are receptive to learning and using language to describe music" (p. 304).

In a second study, Sims (1991) replicated and extended the first, to determine whether children could combine musical elements using singing as a nonverbal response mode. Children ranging from 2 years 9 months to 5 years 11

These children have been highly sensitive to musical patterns, including melody and phrasing, since their first year of life. To foster musical development, adults can encourage young children to listen and move to music, explore musical instruments, and talk about their experiences. (Photo: Laura Berk)

months participated. Testing included replication of the listening task from the first study plus asking children to sing "Rain Rain," a song well known to them, four times, using the pairs of musical characteristics. In a second singing task, the instructor asked each child to "sing 'Rain Rain' with me, just the way that I sing it," a technique called simultaneous imitation. After singing each version, the child was asked whether the song had been fast or slow and smooth or choppy. On the listening task, older children did better than younger children on single and, especially, double discriminations. Furthermore, children singing with the experimenter "approximated the tempo and style of articulation of the model when singing with her" (p. 307). However, when children were asked to sing alone, "No child's performance reflected the correct relationships for all four versions" (p. 307). In sum, preschoolers could recognize and simultaneously imitate specified musical characteristics, although they were not yet capable of producing them independently.

Carrying this line of research further, Sims (1995) attempted to determine whether it might be possible to identify the grade levels at which it becomes relatively easy for elementary schoolchildren to "(a) make musical discriminations during listening when elements are presented simultaneously and (b) produce sung responses demonstrating combinations of musical elements in response to verbal instructions" (p. 208). Students in Grades 1 through 5 participated in a listening test using examples of classical music. Once again, the test was designed to assess participants' ability to discriminate and label music fast or slow, smooth or choppy, or combinations (fast or slow *and* smooth or choppy). A random subset of these children also participated individually in a singing test involving the song 'Rain Rain' using the fast/slow and smooth/choppy elements one at a time then in combination. Children's ability to discriminate and produce combined musical characteristics improved greatly around second and third grades.

Researchers face formidable difficulties in studying children's musical perception. For instance, the role of language requires careful attention to avoid confusion. Perhaps the most common example involves the terms 'high' and 'low,' denoting pitch but also having spatial and loudness meanings. These labels were the focus of a study by Flowers and Costa-Giomi (1991), who investigated English- and Spanish-speaking preschool children's use of verbal and nonverbal means (clapping) to indicate pitch changes. On the verbal task, Spanish speaking children used the terms "agudo" and "grave" as the counterparts of "high" and "low." Children participated in two lessons on "high/low" or "agudo/grave" and then were tested on their ability to indicate octave pitch changes in the tune "Twinkle Twinkle Little Star." Results showed that "Spanish-speaking children were more correct in their application of agudo/grave than were English speaking children in their application of high/low to two-octave pitch changes in the context of a familiar song" (p. 10). Clearly, educators need to be alert to the potentially confusing effects of language associated with musical perception.

Heller and Campbell (1981) emphasized music as a means of expression for all children, not just for the particularly talented. They likened perceptual learning and development in music to speech development. However, they claimed, "Early sensory stimulation in music is probably critical to the refinement of those implicit rules necessary for successful musical perception" (p. 22). The difficulty of testing this claim is immediately obvious. It would require longitudinal investigation of musical exposure in everyday life, an approach that contrasts starkly with the mainly laboratory based, experimental research that has dominated this field of study. Whether or not there is a **sensitive period** for mastery of musical perception is a worthy area of inquiry, in that it deals with a view that is probably intuitively held by many early childhood educators with particular interest in young children's musical development.

In summary, research shows that children's music perceptual skills develop from an early age. However, certain limitations, such as an inability to focus on two simultaneous musical features, influence musical responsiveness into the early years of school. For example, young children's movement to music is likely to reflect only one musical characteristic, such as tempo, at a time, rather than multiple features, such as tempo/volume/articulation. Language can also operate as a limiting factor, as in children's use of the terms high and low. To some extent, training can enhance children's perceptual skills, but maturation operates as a ceiling on this process.

## CHILDREN'S MUSICAL COGNITION

Zimmerman (1993), in an overview of developmental research in music, states, "It has been determined that the child is born with highly efficient neural arrangements that predispose him to make sense of his perceptual experiences and to engage in thinking" (p. 1). In attempting to discern and describe such cognitive processes in relation to music, researchers have studied a range of children's responses. These include movement, musical play, and musical "think alouds."

## Movement Responses

Conducting a naturalistic study over a period of 8 weeks, Metz (1989) used movement to investigate 2-, 3-, and 4-year-olds' musical cognition. Music learning centers were set up twice weekly in each of three classrooms, and children were "free to come and go as they wished to any center, such as the play table, painting easel, or craft table" (p. 49). The music centers were bounded by portable Plexiglas panels suspended from the ceiling, creating an area of approximately 12 × 12 feet. A tape recorder was provided, with excerpts from a range of compositions, chosen for variety in style and media. During the first three weeks of the study, the researcher was an observer. In the following five weeks, she assumed the dual roles of observer and teacher. In the first phase, when children were responding without teacher intervention, "Awareness of musical elements was observed in all age groups in the following rank order of visibility: sound and silence, overall style, and fast and slow. Children did not seem to distinguish loud music from fast music or quiet music from slow music, nor did they seem to respond specifically to high or low pitch" (p. 54). In the second phase, when the researcher was both teacher and observer, increases in music-related responses were observed. Child-teacher interaction was a key factor during this period. First, the researcher *modeled* body technique. Some peer modeling was also evident, but the researcher's modeling appeared to be more effective in producing music-related outcomes. Second, she *described* children's body movements in relation to musical elements or body technique, which sometimes led children to add further descriptions. Third, she made *suggestions* to prompt particular movement responses. Findings revealed that the three types of teacher encouragement were interrelated. For instance, for modeling to be effective, it had to be combined with describing and suggesting. Metz concluded, "Because musical elements have a natural link to movement concepts, the marriage of music and movement may be an ideal medium for teaching and learning in the preschool" (pp. 58–59).

## Musical Play

Musical play can be the means by which a conceptual understanding of music is more fully developed in the classroom (Shehan-Campbell & Scott-Kassner, 1995). For the early childhood educator, *observation* of children's play can provide information about children's musical cognition.

For example, working with 13- to 23-month-old toddlers in a day-care center over a 5-month period, Suthers (1995) examined children's playful responses to a range of musical experiences. Three types of musical activities were presented: play mats, sound lines, and cassette tapes. On the play mats were various sound makers, including percussion instruments, junk materials, sound-making toys, and kitchen utensils. The sound lines also offered opportunities for play with objects. A variety of soundmakers were suspended on a rope between two fixed posts. Careful attention was paid to safety issues. For instance, items on the sound lines had to be light enough not to cause harm if they bumped a child. Recorded music was chosen with care: "The cassette tapes used covered a range of musical genres and a variety of cultural traditions. All the music selected was strongly rhythmic and encouraged the toddlers to respond by moving and dancing" (p. 144). The researcher took the role of a participant observer in that she responded to the children's initiatives but did not direct their play. Children participated in various ways, mainly in solitary and parallel play situations or in interaction with an adult. Types of play included exploration, practice play, and imaginative play. Suthers suggested that these experiences provided children with opportunities to make discoveries about musical characteristics, such as tone color,

**FIGURE 16.1** A four-year-old's drawings of two nursery rhymes: "Jack and Jill" and "Humpty Dumpty."

dynamics, durational aspects of music, pitch differences, and even structural devices such as musical question and answer when children interacted with the researcher.

Children's playful responses to music sometimes involve other areas of the early childhood curriculum, as seen in the delightful examples of a 4-year-old's spontaneous drawings of nursery rhymes in Figure 16-1. These are part of a series by the same child, each representing a familiar song. They include a carefully drawn line of music (reversed quarter notes), which are not linked to any particular aspect of the song and simply seem to say, "This is music." However, perhaps these music notes also express the child's intuitive knowledge of certain characteristics of music, such as separate but connected sounds and its linear aspect—that it moves through time.

The little research that has been conducted on children's musical play has focused on beginning behaviors. Interesting as this is, more advanced experiences await research attention. For instance, what of the playful behaviors of children who have sufficient skill to respond to music in ways that are well beyond exploratory levels? This often involves "making up" music, "working out" previously

heard pieces, and creating variations on these. For some children, this is a natural process, as in the case of 14-year-old Louise, a keen violin player whose weekly musical schedule includes playing traditional Scottish fiddle and second violin in a community orchestra as well as beginning to contribute to a folk/rock group. Her parents report that starting in the preschool years, she *played with,* rather than just played, music. Formal tuition on several instruments has been paralleled by rich, informal experiences. Her musical life has included such spontaneous activities as working out television theme songs and commercial jingles on an electronic keyboard to (more recently) copying parts from rock recordings and working on/playing with arrangements of these on her violin, with her 16-year-old sister playing guitar. Instruments have always been close at hand. It is often simply a case of walking through the kitchen, picking up an instrument, playing for a few moments, then moving on in the same way that she might stop to get a glass of water, and equally as unselfconscious. On the basis of this kind of anecdotal evidence, it seems likely that interesting discoveries await researchers who investigate children's musical play beyond the very early years.

## Musical Think Alouds

Using a "think aloud" process, information can be collected on children's cognitions *while* they listen to music. Richardson (1996) explored the music listening processes of children in grades 1 through 8. All were musically trained in that they had general music instruction as part of their normal schooling and were studying an instrument outside of school. Their thinking aloud was tape recorded while they listened through head phones to ten short musical examples chosen to include variety of style, genres, and performing media. The researcher's instructions included, "What I mean by think aloud is that I want you to tell me everything you are thinking about the music from the time the music starts until it stops" (Richardson and Whitaker, 1996, p. 43). Analysis of transcripts revealed that children mainly talked within identifiable categories: musical characteristics; what they were reminded of; how they felt; and how they liked or disliked the music. The main developmental difference was comparing and predicting, which was more frequent in the higher grades.

The power of the "think-aloud" process is very clear in the following example from a transcript of a 7-year-old boy listening to Varese's *Hyperprism,* a work from 1923 for percussion, woodwind, and brass instruments:

> Interesting, very funny. Not the kind of music I would listen to ... Strange instruments that I don't know of. There might be an orchestra, I'm not sure. This is ... doesn't sound like regular music to me. This feels like good music I would listen to when I was sad or mad and this music when the drummers come on I feel like I am booming up and down and when I am getting boomed up and down by my dad ... and this kind of sound feels like I am being used as a salt-shaker ... this trumpet makes me feel like I am being stretched out as long as I can go like a piece of elastic ... This instrument makes me feel hot. This drum makes me feel

like I am being used as a door that is getting slammed. This ... makes me feel like I am a track. This ... this makes me feel like I am a bird. I have a strange feeling right now. It sounds like water when the sound comes up and down.... This trumpet makes me feel like I am going to explode. (Richardson & Whitaker, 1996, p. 44)

Typical cognitive processes, such as evaluation and comparison, as well as use of musical knowledge from past experience can be seen in this child's verbalizations. The kinesthetic nature of this child's responses are particularly apparent.

Research locates the rudimentary beginnings of musical cognition in toddlerhood, followed by extensive development in early childhood, when children demonstrate increased understanding of such musical concepts as sound/silence, pitch, rhythm, and style. To learn about musical cognition, we need to recognize and observe various aspects of children's musical experience, including movement, musical play, and verbal responses.

## CHILDREN'S AFFECTIVE MUSICAL RESPONSES

Affective, or feeling, responses to music are common experiences for most adults. But is this also the case with children?

Giomo (1993) investigated 5- and 9-year-olds' sensitivity to mood in music. Using a nonverbal (pictorial) response format, he focused on the following mood dimensions: softness/intensity; pleasantness/unpleasantness; solemnity/triviality. Both age groups performed at better-than-chance levels when responding to twelve brief but complete classical pieces, and no age differences emerged. This study suggests that preschool children are sensitive to the affective dimensions of music and that this sensitivity continues into the primary years.

A study by Meerum Terwogt and van Grinsven (1991) included children in three age groups: younger children aged 5 to 6 years; older

children; and adults. They were asked to link selected excerpts of classical music to one of four
mood states: happiness, sadness, fear, and anger.
Responses were recorded using a series of facial
expressions, and participants were asked to justify
their mood choice. All, even the 5- and 6-year-
olds, made what the authors described as "a fairly
systematic distinction between music that is emotionally positive or negatively weighted" (p. 106).
Within the negative area, "sad" music was easily
discerned but "angry" and "fearful" excerpts
were less easily distinguished. The authors noted
that all participants had difficulty expressing
choice of mood states in words and suggested that
verbal analysis is difficult for everyone. Unlike
older participants, young children appeared to be
satisfied with general descriptions, such as "it is
beautiful," and circular justifications, such as "the
piece gives a happy impression because it is so
happy/merry/cheerful" (p. 106). They also
tended to resort to singing, whistling, or moving
in trying to describe the music.

Kratus (1993) extended this line of research,
addressing gender differences and the impact of
particular musical elements on interpretations of
emotion. Six- to 12-year-olds were asked to
identify the emotions happy, sad, excited, and
calm in music, in response to excerpts from
J. S. Bach's *Goldberg Variations,* a set of pieces for
harpsichord. The percentages of participants at
each age level and in each gender agreeing with
the majority interpretation were well above the
chance figure of 50 percent, with no significant
differences between age groups or genders.
Agreement on happy-sad was significantly higher
than on excited-calm. Results underscored the
importance of rhythm and articulation in children's interpretations of emotion in music. Kratus
suggests, "There is no need for elementary music
educators to teach their students to associate the
emotions of happy, sad, excited or calm with
music because elementary students can already
interpret emotion consistently" (pp. 17–18). He
also notes that "relationships between the element of rhythmic activity and children's emotional responses help to explain why children

tend to prefer music with faster tempos....
[Teachers and] music therapists who use music
with little rhythmic activity and legato [smooth]
articulation should be aware that children may interpret such music as being sad" (p. 18).

Adults often associate music with other aspects of their lives. For example, a particular piece
of music may trigger a recollection of a place, a
person, or an event. Children also make such associations, as shown in a study by McDowall
(1991) in which 8-year-olds listened to musical
excerpts in a range of styles, including popular
and classical. Children were asked to write a description of each example. Most mentioned musical characteristics, such as tempo or volume, but
some showed sensitivity to other facets, particularly to the mood of the music, as in "nice soft
calm," "flowy," and "soft lovely gentle." Children
were also asked if the music reminded them of
anything. Responses were very mixed. In many
instances, children associated music with particular people, such as family members or friends.
Some responses were emotional, as "my friend
who died" and "sad days" in response to the slow,
dramatic tenor aria "Nessun Dorma" from the
opera *Turandot* by Puccini.

Overall, research in the area of young children's affective responses to music shows that children in preschool and the early school years do
associate music and emotion. Like adults, they are
limited in their ability to explain their responses.

## CHILDREN'S MUSICAL PREFERENCES

Musical preferences are "affective reactions to a
piece of music or to a certain style of music that
reflect the degree of liking or disliking for that
music" (Finnas, 1989, p. 2). Peery and Peery
(1987) identify three major influences on musical preferences. First, musical training or repeated
exposure to either a particular piece or style increases preference for that music: "What you
hear is what you like." Second, social factors
make a difference: "You like what significant

others like." Third, characteristics of the music affect preferences. The literature on adult musical preferences is extensive; only a few studies provide information on young children.

Peery and Peery (1986) investigated the effects of exposure to classical music on the musical preferences of 4 year-olds. During a 10-month period, children in an experimental group participated in a wide range of classroom experiences with classical music in weekly 45-minute sessions. These included listening to classical music and active involvement, such as singing classical themes and playing musical games. A control group had no special music program. At the outset, there were no significant group differences in musical preferences for popular and classical music. However, a posttest revealed a decrease in liking for classical music by the control group, whereas the experimental group maintained their pretest preference. The authors suggest that a "'what you don't hear, you come to like less' factor may be at work" (p. 30). They claim their findings "clearly suggest that musical preferences may begin to shift, sometime in the fifth year, away from music that is infrequently heard and socially avoided" (p. 31).

According to LeBlanc (1987), musical preference decisions result from the interaction of the listener's characteristics with input from the cultural environment and the nature of the music itself. Several studies have addressed aspects of LeBlanc's theory. For example, LeBlanc, Sims, Siivola, and Obert (1996) investigated musical preferences for classical, traditional jazz, and rock among listeners of a wide age range: grade 1 through college and other adults, including senior citizens. Ratings for the three styles were reasonably close across age levels, with a general tendency for preference to assume a gentle U-shaped curve corresponding to grade or age. Higher ratings in the lowest grades and at college level and beyond show that the younger and older participants expressed greater preference overall than did those in secondary school—a period in which there may be less tolerance for musical diversity.

Montgomery (1996) also examined the effect of musical characteristics on preferences. Using excerpts of orchestral music from early Romantic opera, she focused on the role of tempo among elementary and middle-school pupils. Children in the lower grades rated this style of music more favorably than did children in higher grades, a preference that declined steadily with age. Higher mean preference ratings were given to musical examples with faster tempos at every grade level. In keeping with research on children's responses to mood in music (Kratus, 1993), Montgomery's study highlights the salience of tempo in children's musical experience.

The complex nature of the variables involved in preference formation means that research tends to focus only on a small portion of the whole picture. Despite this limitation, a few generalizations can be made. First, young children are reasonably open to various styles of music, but preference for classical music declines toward the end of the early childhood years. Second, children clearly prefer faster rather than slower tempos. This is consistent with how they respond to music emotionally.

## APPLICATIONS FOR PARENTS AND EARLY CHILDHOOD EDUCATORS

Young children perceive musical sounds and respond to music in richly diverse ways, both in formal situations and as part of informal play experiences. Music evokes feelings and memories in children. At an early age, they begin to form clear musical likes and dislikes. For those who help shape children's life experiences, including educators and parents, research provides an informed basis for decisions influencing children's musical development.

### Exposing Children to Music

Compared with older children and adolescents, children in the early childhood years are more accepting of music that differs from the narrow range of popular styles pervading the media. As Shehan-Campbell and Scott-Kassner (1995, p. 160) state, "Young children from preschool through age eight are usually remarkably open to all kinds of music. This period of children's lives seems to be a good time to introduce them to a wide range of excellent music of many styles, genres, and cultures." A similar view is expressed by Wright (1991):

> Young children should be introduced to an eclectic range of music styles and periods and to the music of other cultures. Variety will provide contrast, sustain interest and stimulate comparisons between scales, rhythms, harmonies, the timbre of instruments and playing styles. (p. 144)

Adults can integrate music into children's daily experiences in many ways. For example, they can provide background music, as is often done in child care centers to promote a calm atmosphere. Besides orchestral and some of the many styles of folk music, "New Age" music of the nineties is well suited for this purpose. It sometimes includes natural sounds, such as bird calls and waves breaking, that children recognize and make part of their play. For parents and children, many moments in the day can be enriched with listening experiences. This can be as simple turning on the radio or a cassette while traveling by car. In moments like these, children's exposure can be broadened by introducing music from other times and places.

To avoid children's initial rejection of music, adults should consider its features carefully. For instance, tempo needs to be a prime consideration, since children are likely to respond more positively to faster than slower music (Kratus, 1993; Montgomery, 1996). While broadening children's musical experience, adults often find they are discovering music *with* children. That is, they open up new worlds of interest for themselves. A word of caution, however: Continual background music can promote musical **desensitization,** in the same way that a con-

stant traffic sound gradually fades into the background and goes unnoticed. Carefully considered, sparing use of music is a more productive approach.

## Considering Children's Perceptual Skills

From an early age, children have impressive perceptual skills. During early childhood, they can learn to use appropriate language to describe music (Sims, 1991). Consequently, adults should model the use of simple terminology, such as high/low and fast/slow. However, young children's perceptual skills do have limitations. For instance, preschool and young school-age children can be encouraged to discriminate multiple features of music, but they will probably be able to focus on only one feature at a time (Sims, 1995). Therefore, when adults encourage children to listen to a particular musical aspect, they should choose music in which that characteristic is clearly apparent and not dominated by other elements.

## Encouraging Active Listening

Children's musical understanding develops during active listening. Movement is a salient way in which young children respond to music (Metz, 1989; Suthers, 1995). Early childhood programs can capitalize on this natural tendency by providing many opportunities for active engagement with music. Appropriate resources must be available, including sufficient space and equipment. Active listening can be a teacher-directed experience, but it should also be part of the play program. As Suthers (1995) states, "Music play can help children develop a disposition to participate in music activities and to create with music" (p. 149).

## Encouraging Children to Talk About Music

Children are able to talk about music (Richardson, 1996; Richardson & Whitaker, 1996) and sometimes describe their emotional response in words (McDowall, 1991). Beginning in early childhood, adults can help children develop evaluative skills. *The Arts—A Curriculum Profile for Australian Schools* (Australian Education Council, 1994) states that students engage in arts criticism as they describe, analyze, interpret, judge, value, and challenge arts works and arts ideas (p. 4). Although these are sophisticated processes, they originate in early childhood as young children talking about their responses to new or familiar music-their preferences, their perceptions of musical characteristics, and how the music makes them feel.

## CONCLUSION

Musical performance, particularly singing, is a common feature of early childhood programs, and few would argue against its importance. However, performance is only one aspect of children's musicality. As this article demonstrates, children are also receivers of music. Adults who aim to foster children's aesthetic sensitivity should pay special attention to this aspect of children's musical experience.

## EVALUATING YOUR MASTERY

1. Research on musical perception reveals
   a.  Children have remarkable perception of melodies by the end of the first year.
   b.  Formal training is necessary for development of sensitivity to musical structure.
   c.  Maturation, but not training, affects musical perception.
   d.  Preschoolers have impressive ability to focus on two perceptual aspects of music simultaneously.

2. At what grade level does it become fairly easy for schoolchildren to make musical discriminations when elements are presented simultaneously?
   a.  Kindergarten and first grade
   b.  First and second grade
   c.  Second and third grade
   d.  Fourth and fifth grade

3. When teachers model ways of moving to music, describing and suggesting particular movement responses has which of the following effects?
   a.  Increases 2- to 4-year-olds' responsiveness.
   b.  Decreases 2- to 4-year-olds' responsiveness.
   c.  Has no effect on 2- to 4-year-olds' responsiveness.
   d.  Increases 2-year-olds' but decreases 3- to 4-year-olds' responsiveness.

4. Research reveals that
   a.  Preschool children are far less sensitive to the emotional qualities of music than are school-age children.
   b.  Individuals of all ages have difficulty expressing their affective responses to music in words.
   c.  Girls are more sensitive to emotional qualities of music than are boys.
   d.  Elementary school children must be taught to associate happy, sad, excited, and calm emotions with music.

5. Which of the following is especially salient in children's affective response to and preference for music?
   a.  Tempo
   b.  Melodic contour
   c.  Pitch
   d.  Intervals between tones

6. True or False: Spanish-speaking children are more likely to misunderstand the musical terms "high" and "low," which refer to pitch, than are English-speaking children.

7. True or False: Maturation places limits on the extent to which training can enhance children's musical perception.

8. Using _____, information can be collected about children's cognitions while they listen to music.

## Critical Thinking

Why is it important to expose children to a wide range of musical styles in the early years? Use research findings to support your answer.

## Applying Your Knowledge

1. What benefits does musical play have for young children? What can parents and teachers learn about children's musical development from observing their musical play? How would you recommend parents and teachers stimulate musical play?

2. List as many ways as you can that parents and teachers can enhance young children's music listening skills.

# 17

*ऌ*

# Perspectives on Cooperative Learning

## SUSAN HILL

### University of South Australia

■

Cooperative learning, or learning with others in a group, is hailed as one of the innovative approaches to education of the future.

■

Group members discuss what was learned and what helped or hindered effective cooperation, and they set goals for what they might do differently next time.

■

Joint goals that engage the interest of all participants plus a task that yields clear feedback about success or failure appears to be central to effective collaboration.

■

Many schools working as "communities of learners" or as "learning organizations" stress the importance of teacher learning to improve classroom practice and collegial processes.

■

Positive interdependence occurs when each person in the group has a part to play.

■

Finally, perhaps the most important aspect of cooperative learning is how the group worked and learned together.

■

Multidisciplinary approaches—social psychology, sociology, sociocultural theory, and critical theory—can be used to provide new insights for the future development of cooperative education.

■

## EDITOR'S INTRODUCTION

This article explores different perspectives on cooperative learning, an innovative approach to instruction that, when effectively implemented, has the potential for improving children' academic achievement, social relationships, and self-esteem. Susan Hill describes the diverse theoretical perspectives that have contributed to cooperative learning, clarifying the major goals and outcomes linked to each. Her review of research challenges the widespread assumption that preschoolers are too egocentric to engage in peer collaboration. She shows that children as young as age 3 consider others' points of view, respond to justice claims, and resolve conflict through negotiation and compromise, as long as teachers coach them in effective strategies while respecting their autonomy. Hill highlights cooperative play and games as vital contexts for development of collaboration, especially for children with limited social skills. She also addresses the vital role of cooperative learning in successful mainstreaming of children with special needs into regular classrooms. Hill concludes with a wealth of research-based recommendations for implementing cooperative learning in preschool and primary school programs.

In this essay, I examine different perspectives on cooperative learning. From these perspectives, key ideas and principles for improving learning in preschool and school will be explored.

Cooperative learning, or learning with others in a group, is hailed as one of the innovative approaches to education of the future. Although educators agree that there is overwhelming evidence about the value of cooperative learning, it is by no means a common practice. For example, recent research into cooperative group work in England suggests that seating children in groups in the early years of school is generally no more than an organizational device. Even when children were seated with a partner, they worked collaboratively only 4 percent of the time (Galton & Patrick, 1990; Galton, Simon, & Croll, 1980).

Furthermore, there has long been a notion that children younger than age 7 are selfish and self-centered, cannot share, think exclusively about their own needs and desires, and fail to understand how other people think and feel. However, this, in most cases, has been shown to be incorrect. Yet on the basis of this erroneous assumption, a number of early childhood educators have concluded that teaching young children through cooperation is developmentally inappropriate (Goffin, 1987; Rubin & Everett, 1982).

In the discussion that follows, I refer to **cooperative learning** as a set of principles, structures, and strategies for schools working to improve academic achievement, social relationships and students' feelings of self-worth. **Collaboration** is a more general term covering the many ways people can work together for a range of purposes.

## MAJOR PERSPECTIVES ON COOPERATIVE LEARNING

Cooperative learning developed out of a variety of theoretical perspectives and associated issues having to do with teaching and learning (see Table 17.1). Historically, it can be traced to the 1940s, when Morton Deutsch, a student of Kurt Lewin, proposed a theory emphasizing different goal structures as the distinguishing features of cooperative, competitive, and individualistic learning environments (Johnson, Johnson, & Holubec, 1989a; Schmuck, 1985). In competitive situations students perceive they can only achieve their goal if other students fail to obtain their goals. In individualistic learning situations, students perceive that their learning goal is unrelated to what other students do. In cooperative learning, the students seek learning outcomes that are beneficial to themselves and beneficial to other group members (Johnson, Johnson, & Holubec, 1993).

Much of the current work in cooperative learning has a base in social psychology, with strong influences from the areas of experimental psychology and behavior analysis (Sapon-Shevin & Schniedewind, 1992).

### Mastery Learning Perspective

The major focus of the **mastery learning perspective** is improved academic learning with a limited focus on positive interpersonal behaviors. Motivation is assumed to depend on extrinsic rewards, such as team scores, stickers, and extra credit for group achievement (Kagan, 1988; Slavin, 1987, 1988). Cooperative learning tasks are structured so students have to work together to master information. Team scores on quizzes are posted on charts to encourage competition between groups (Kagan, 1988). Within the mastery learning approach, it is argued that cooperative structures can be used to teach any content (Kagan, 1989/1990). In fact, one limitation of this approach is that the structures are so powerful they can involve students in learning trivial details and facts—that is, unimportant as opposed to important content (Sapon-Shevin & Schniedewind, 1992).

### Social Psychology Perspective

The **social psychology perspective** focuses on improved cognitive and social learning. According

**Table 17.1 Major Perspectives on Cooperative Learning and
Collaboration**

|  | Mastery learning perspectives | Social psychology perspectives | Sociological perspectives | Sociocultural perspectives | Critical perspectives | Schools as learning communities |
|---|---|---|---|---|---|---|
| **Driving theories** | Behaviorism | Social psychology | Sociology | Sociology, anthropology, psychology | Feminist and critical theories | Organizational theory, teacher as researcher |
| **Researchers and theorists** | Kagan (1988); Slavin (1987) | Johnson & Johnson, (1989, 1990, 1995); Deutsch (1949) | Cohen (1990) | Vygotsky (1978); Moll (1992); Rogoff, (1990) | Sapon-Shevin & Schniede-wind (1992) | Fullan (1993); Senge (1990) |
| **Major goals and outcomes** | Improving academic achievement | Improving cognitive and social learning | Improving group participation; Equalizing status in groups | Improving learning by linking community and everyday knowledge with school knowledge | Identifying and changing the sociopolitical power relationships | Restructuring, reculturing of schools with cooperative learning and collaborative teams of teachers |

to David and Roger Johnson, brothers who have spent two decades cooperating to investigate and refine cooperative learning, the key principles of cooperative learning are (1) positive interdependence, when students need each other to perform the task; (2) structured interactions, when students sit face to face to talk through problems or teach each other; (3) individual accountability, when group members discuss what they contributed, (4) teaching of cooperative skills, such as group membership roles, mediation and negotiation, and problem-solving strategies (for example, brainstorming); and (5) group processing, when group members focus on how well they have worked together. The social psychology approach regards the last of these principles, group processing, as essential for individuals to learn to step outside the group and its functioning to consider feedback and goals for ways to improve. Group members discuss what was learned and what helped or hindered effective cooperation, and they set goals for what they might do differently next time. This form of reflection, especially, is believed to contribute to

academic achievement (Johnson & Johnson, 1987; Johnson, Johnson, Dudley, & Magnuson, 1995; Yager, Johnson, Johnson, & Snider, 1986). Indeed, in a review of 126 studies exploring cooperative, competitive and individualistic classroom structures, cooperative learning consistently led to higher achievement (Johnson & Johnson, 1989a).

It is important to emphasize, however, that cooperation does not imply harmony. In fact, as Kohn (1992) describes, when people are playing with ideas or struggling to make decisions, conflict should and will happen. In preschools and schools, conflict does not need to be soothed or smoothed with artificial consensus or exaggerated through adversarial debate based on winning and losing. A third, preferred alternative is inviting disagreement but nesting it in a framework of positive interdependence. Johnson and Johnson (1987) have referred to this optimal balance as "constructive controversy," "creative conflict," or (put more poetically) "friendly excursions into disequilibrium" (Kohn, 1992). Their research suggests that this approach is preferable to concurrence-seeking or debate. It promotes both more effective learning and better liking of group members for one another (Johnson, Johnson, & Smith, 1986).

## Sociological Perspective

The **sociological perspective** focuses on participation and resolution of status differences among diverse group members. Cooperative learning is "recommended for inner-city classrooms, bilingual and multicultural classrooms, and academically heterogeneous settings" (Cohen, 1990, p. 134). Although the potential for cooperative learning is enormous, Elizabeth Cohen, the major proponent of this view, suggests that there are three requirements for its success:

1. *The development of new curricular materials.* If materials are of the "one-right-answer variety," children will quickly see that one person can do the task quicker than a group. Curriculum materials must be designed so that multiple abilities, such as verbal and spatial reasoning, role playing, and precision, are used.

2. *The ability to treat problems of status that inevitably develop within small groups.* Status problems can affect group participation. High-status students are very likely to take over the group; other students defer to these "stars" because they see them as more competent. Even in groups where members have been selected randomly, students perceive status differences, which affect their participation. As Cohen and Lotan (1995) note,

> [S]mall groups will also develop status orders based on perceived differences in academic status: high-status students will interact more frequently than low-status students. Moreover, those differences in interaction can lead to differences in learning outcomes—that is, those who talk more, learn more. (p. 100)

Without the teacher paying attention to status in cooperative groups, the classroom continues to be a place where "the rich get richer."

Cohen (1990) suggests two ways to change status inequalities: (1) the "**multiple abilities strategy**" and (2) giving positive feedback to low-status students. In the multiple abilities strategy, when a group is faced with a complex task, the teacher states explicitly that "no one will be good at all of these abilities; everyone will be good at at least one" (p. 136). Giving positive feedback is not the same as giving unconditional teacher praise. The feedback must be linked to good performance so that others will find it believable and appreciate each student's strengths.

3. *The availability of collegial relationships and strong organizational support for teachers who use cooperative learning.* When teachers change their traditional roles by delegating more authority to the group, strong collegial relationships and organizational support is required. Cooperative learning strategies cannot be plugged into old organizational arrangements. Teachers need time for planning, for problem solving and for curriculum development and collegial feedback. For collegial feedback to be effective, it must be specific and not general professional talk about implementation. Teachers must be released from their classrooms to observe one another (Cohen, 1990). These collegial observations should focus on the frequency of precise behaviors and provide information about desired strategies and problematic teacher behavior, such as "hovering" over a group. Staff development might be required in learning procedures for conducting formal team meetings for planning and for receiving collegial feedback. The effective implementation of cooperative learning has implications for curriculum, for staff development, and for the organizational support of teaching.

## Sociocultural Perspective

The **sociocultural perspective** focuses on the social and cultural contexts of learning and is concerned with the social construction of meaning (Rogoff, 1990, 1994). To clarify this approach, Rogoff (1990) contrasts the **cognitive-developmental theory** of Piaget with the **sociocultural theory** of Vygotsky. The two approaches differ in the extent to which cognitive development is seen as occurring through social interaction:

> Cognitive development from a Piagetian view is a product of the individual, perhaps sparked by having to account for differences in perspective in others, whereas cognitive development from a Vygotskian point of view involves the individual's appropriation or internalization of the social process as it is carried out externally in joint problem solving. (Rogoff, 1990, p. 150)

In a series of fascinating studies, Tudge (1992) explored peer collaboration from a Vygotskian perspective. First, pairs of same-age, same-sex 6- and 7-year-old classmates were teamed to solve a complex problem. In some pairs, both members were equivalent in their understanding of the problem; in other pairs, one member was advanced over the other. It was expected that cognitive conflict during problem solving would improve learning and that children working in Vygotsky's **zone of proximal development** (a range of tasks that children are ready to master with cooperative assistance) would show special benefits—namely, those children paired with more knowledgeable peers would gain the most. Yet these predictions were not confirmed. Instead, a surprising number of children regressed in their understanding of the problem (did worse on the posttest than on the pretest), and those who worked with more expert peers did not always gain.

Tudge's research shows that merely pairing children and expecting that they will collaborate is not sufficient. Joint goals that engage the interest of all participants plus a task that yields clear feedback about success or failure appears to be central to effective collaboration. Tudge (1992) concludes,

> The implications for teachers are that they must do more than merely ask children to collaborate to solve a problem, or even to pair a child who is more advanced in his thinking with one who is less advanced. It goes without saying that the children should

be interested in the task and share the goal of solving it: In addition, however, the results of their attempted solutions should be both immediate and visible. (p. 167)

Tudge and Caruso (1988) make the following recommendations to teachers for cooperative learning to be successful: (1) plan activities in which children have a shared goal; (2) select tasks that are intrinsically interesting to each child; (3) make sure children can achieve the goal through their own actions; and (4) make sure the results of children's actions are both visible and immediate. As these ingredients reveal, although development is embedded in the larger social and cultural conditions of society, it also depends on particular interactions children have with others. From the sociocultural perspective, the immediate social context has a powerful and lasting effect on children's learning.

According to the sociocultural approach, the sharing of different points of view while attempting to achieve a common goal is the key to cognitive advances. The outcome of collaboration is a transformation of understanding resulting from collective thinking and resolution of arguments, which leads to what Miller termed a "collective valid." The collective valid is a local construction made up of shared meanings and working definitions for describing and classifying reality. From this perspective, learning is a sociocultural activity within a community of learners—*people participating in shared endeavors*. A community of learners contrasts sharply with an *adult-directed* transmission of knowledge approach and with a *child-directed* approach, in which children discover knowledge independently. Instead, children participate in a small society and, as result, are enculturated into its practices, signs, and tools (Cole, 1992; Gallimore & Tharp, 1992; Moll, 1992; Rogoff, 1990; Wertsch, 1992).

## Critical Perspective

This view is similar to the sociocultural perspective, except that critical theorists acknowledge that the power bases within different sociopolitical contexts are not equal ones. The critical perspective is concerned with social action and social change. It contends that social practices are set up to maintain the privileged positions of those within the dominant culture. In other words, the interests of the dominant culture are accepted more readily and have more influence than the interests of any marginalized people who might seek to disrupt existing hierarchical relationships.

According to critical theorists, the implementation of cooperative learning has the potential to be a "wolf in sheep's clothing," promising good things but in fact stifling the power of students to engage in proactive social action. Holloway (1992) tells the story of a six-year-old child Ellie who was playing outside. At one point, she left the group to inform her father, "I'm cooperating, Daddy, and I cooperate at school too." Observing what was happening in the group, Holloway found that one child was insulting her and attempting to exclude her. Ellie had gone along with this. She seemed to be seeking praise from adults by not protesting about other children's behavior. She was being "good."

Cooperative learning viewed as avoidance of conflict amounts to compliance. "When cooperation is interpreted as compliance, power is defined as coercive rather than enabling" (Hollaway, 1992, p. 93). In coercive approaches to cooperation, students often resist enforced compliance by subverting tasks to regain power.

Within the critical perspective, cooperative learning is not something to be tacked on to a competitive classroom structure. Instead, it must permeate the educational environment through implementation at three levels: (1) learning activities that are cooperatively structured, (2) classroom practices that foster sharing, caring, and an overall supportive atmosphere, and (3) the extension of cooperative principles into broader areas of social relations and societal structures (Sapon-Shevin & Schniedewind, 1992).

## SCHOOLS AS LEARNING COMMUNITIES

Cooperative learning and teacher collaboration are found in much of the innovative change involved in school restructuring and reculturing. Schools as learning communities combine sociocultural and critical perspectives. The following projects use teacher collaboration and cooperative learning: The Coalition for Essential Schools (Sizer, 1992); The Comer Process for Reforming Education (Comer, Haynes, Joyner, & Ben-Avie, 1996); School Restructuring (Lieberman, 1995); and the Accelerated Schools Project (Levin & McCarthy, 1995; McCarthy & Mayfield, 1996).

Many schools working as "communities of learners" or as "learning organizations" stress the importance of teacher learning to improve classroom practice and collegial processes. As Senge (1990) states, "Organizations learn through individuals who learn. Individual learning does not guarantee organizational learning. But without it no organizational learning occurs" (p. 139).

In a study of five schools set up as communities of learners Nias, Southworth, and Campbell (1992) found that teachers continually reinforced the expectation and conditions conducive to teacher and student learning. Teacher learning as a collective activity was regarded as a means of increasing one's ability, not as a sign of inadequacy. In these schools, teachers challenge one another's thinking and practice. Fullan (1993), a proponent of collaborative teacher learning, suggests, "[T]he secret of growth and development is learning how to contend with the forces of change, turning positive forces to our advantage, while blunting negative ones. The future of the world is a learning future." (p.vii)

Hargreaves (1994), in his book *Changing Teachers Changing Times,* warns that cooperative learning can be inserted into schools as a set of contrived and controlling structures, practices, and behaviors. Some forms of team work imposed on schools can be superficial, prescribed, and manipulative and, consequently, fail to consider teachers' discretionary judgments about their own classrooms. Fullan (1993) suggests that to really improve learning in schools requires teacher collaborative action, but this must be balanced by the actions and initiatives of individuals.

## COOPERATIVE LEARNING AND THE EARLY YEARS

Research over the last several decades has shown that young children are not self-centered and egocentric but sensitive to the needs of others and able to take their viewpoints into consideration. In one study, children's preferences for conflict management strategies were assessed through interviews about vignettes in which puppets acted out common peer conflicts (Iskandar, Laursen, Finkelstein, & Frederickson, 1995). Two-and-one-half to 6-year-olds showed an overwhelming preference for negotiation rather than power assertion or disengagement. They suggested conflict resolution strategies, such as turn taking and sharing that considered others' rights and desires. No age or sex differences emerged, indicating that young children's preference for resolving conflict through negotiation and cooperation resembles that of older children and adolescents.

Although children as young as 3 years of age prefer constructive conflict resolutions, converting this knowledge into behavior requires instructing young children in *how to use* these sophisticated strategies, in addition to teaching them *which ones to use* (Iskandar, Laursen, Finkelstein, & Frederickson, 1995). Research shows that positive forms of conflict resolution are used by children who are well liked by peers (Asher & Renshaw, 1981) whereas socially rejected (or disliked) children, in contrast, are likely to escalate conflict (Dodge, Coie, Pettit, & Price, 1990). Hill's (1989) work reveals that if teacher intervention does not occur, rejection of children with behavior problems and physical disabilities is exacerbated. Besides coaching in social skills,

helping such children form rewarding friendships can offer preparation for effective collaboration in learning situations. In fact, children are more likely to consider another's point of view when sustaining a relationship is important. In a study that compared conflicts with siblings and friends, young children were more likely to use reasoning that considered another's perspective with friends than with siblings (Dunn, Slomkowski, Donelan, & Herrera, 1995).

Many early childhood educators value spontaneous play for social learning. However, spontaneous play is unlikely to provide collaborative opportunities for children whose social competence is limited (Hill, 1989). Research suggests that during spontaneous play, children's social status—well liked, rejected, or neglected (seldom chosen)—is constantly reinforced by peers (Hill, Parker, & McKenna, 1986). As Katz (1987) points out, "The young child's capacity to understand the cause of his or her social difficulties and to make the necessary adjustments is virtually nil. Adults must intervene to break faulty cycles" (p. 13).

Investigations conducted in Australia reveal that if teachers do not promote cooperative play, young children with limited social skills continue to play alone while those with well-developed social skills play in groups (Hill, 1989). Cooperative games where children have to collaborate to play provide less socially skilled children with ways to join a group and take turns and, therefore, with a greater sense of belonging (Hill, 1992; Orlick, 1981).

In Russia, Zuckerman (1994) claims that children cannot participate effectively in the academic curriculum if they have not mastered cooperative learning before formal school entry. She explored the effects of a ten-day program designed to teach preschoolers explicitly how to cooperate to solve problems—a course aimed at preparing them for greater self-discipline and responsibility in school. Program goals were (1) to expose children to teachers' expectations and give them a chance to try out the student role in a safe situation, without risk of losing the teacher's favor or falling behind in learning; (2) to help children comprehend that the student's role involves expressing personal opinions, even if they differ from the majority; (3) to create a system of cooperation and assistance among students that permits them to take the risks involved in working out and standing up for their own positions; and (4) to dispel anxiety about school by creating groups of support and trust among children.

In the cooperative learning program, children learned to work together in pairs or in circles (larger groups), where they were encouraged to confer before answering a question. The teacher provided feedback about what was positive in the group answer and how well the group worked together. Findings showed that positive self-appraisal changed from "What or why am I doing poorly today?" to a more constructive form of "What help do I need today?" and "Who or what will help me?" The principal effects of the course were the following:

1. Decentration as the ability (a) to act with due account for the actions of one's partner; (b) to realize the relativity of opinions, their dependence on the other side's view; and (c) to discover the difference in the emotional states of participants in a common action.

2. Initiative as (a) the ability to procure missing information with the help of questions and (b) a readiness to suggest a plan of common action to a partner.

3. The ability to intellectualize conflict and to settle it rationally.

The long-term effects of the program on students' ability to **decenter** (take account of the partner's position) were apparent well into the first year of school.

## IMPLEMENTING COOPERATIVE LEARNING IN EARLY CHILDHOOD

Building on the work of Johnson and Johnson (1989a, 1990), there are seven ways in which co-

### Table 17.2 Difference Between Cooperative Groups and Traditional Groups

| Cooperative Groups | Traditional Groups |
|---|---|
| Positive interdependence | No positive interdependence |
| Common goals | No common goals |
| Heterogeneous groups | Homogeneous groups |
| Shared leadership | One leader |
| Changing membership | Static membership |
| Group and individual responsibility | No group or individual responsibility |
| Cooperative skills are taught | No cooperative skills are taught |

operative learning in classrooms for young children differs from traditional grouping (see Table 17.2).

### Positive Interdependence

Positive interdependence occurs when each person in the group has a part to play. Group performances are excellent illustrations of how positive interdependence can work. For example, children can create puppets, assign them roles, and act out a puppet play. Teachers can assist with plots, scripts, and music suggestions. Class projects involve everyone and, consequently, often foster cooperation and a sense of group spirit among children while allowing them to express themselves fully as individuals (Katz & Chard, 1989).

### Common Goals

For a cooperative project to work, the group must have common goals. Kotloff (1993) notes that under these circumstances, both collective and individual work can be promoted. She describes a project in which a small group of children began making an airplane during free-play time. Over a few weeks, the airplane construction evolved into a whole-class endeavor. The children planned the project during a teacher-led discussion. Then, working individually or in small groups, they implemented their plans and

These preschoolers are about to work together in a cooking activity. When adults arrange supportive conditions, young children take others' viewpoints into consideration, negotiate differences of opinion, and cooperate. (Photo: Frederick Ebbeck)

met again as a class to discuss their progress and plan what steps to take next.

## Heterogeneous Groups

At times, it is important to structure groups so children are not always with their friends. When children choose friendship groups, girls go together, boys go together, socially less proficient children go together, and children rejected or neglected are usually not included at all. Children who have limited social skills require demonstrations or examples of behavior from those more competent. Grouping children randomly and changing group membership provide children with the opportunity to work with everyone.

## Changing Group Membership

It is important for groups to change frequently so everyone has a chance to work and play with new people. Rotating group membership often increases heterogeneity by ability, gender, social status, ethnic or economic background, learning styles, and activity preferences (Baloche & Platt, 1993).

## Shared Leadership

The idea of "born" leaders and "born" followers permeates many cultures. Sharing leadership rather than having one person in charge provides opportunities to learn and practice leadership skills. Katz and Chard (1989) describe an excursion in which children visited a market. When they returned, a large piece of paper was placed on the floor with one set of paints. Children discussed what they saw and then took turns painting their ideas. After each child had a turn, he or she called on another child to come and paint. The result was a detailed class mural with each contribution in proportion to the others. Some teachers rotate leadership roles, whereas others apportion leadership responsibilities—for example, into materials organizer, time keeper, negotiator, and clarifier.

## Group and Individual Responsibility

Taking responsibility for both the group and oneself contributes to self-esteem. To build self-esteem through peer support, many teachers have feedback circles or class meetings. After free play children gather in a circle, and the teacher begins by indicating who is absent and welcoming new children as well as those who have just returned from an absence. This shows children that their well-being is important and that they

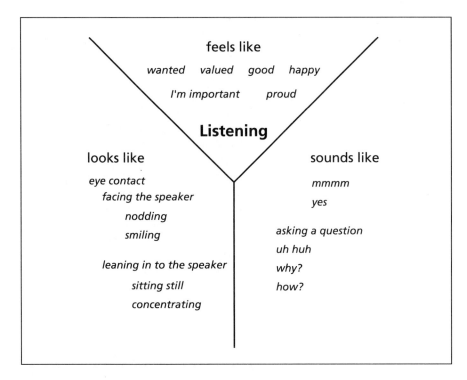

**FIGURE 17.1** Y chart for the cooperative behavior of *listening*. A group of children brainstormed a list of words to make the cooperative behavior explicit.

are members of the group. Children's products made during free play are shared, and the teacher points out features so the whole class can learn from a child's work. As a result, children realize that they can rely on and learn from each other (Greenberg, 1992).

## Cooperative Skills Made Explicit

Cooperative skills range from turn taking to more complex negotiation skills like perspective taking and social problem solving (Hill & Hill, 1994). Children can, with guidance, move from the teacher settling all their disputes to the teacher providing strategies for children to manage differences (Oken-Wright, 1992).

Teachers can record cooperative behaviors on *T charts,* which illustrate what a cooperative skill looks like (Johnson, Johnson, & Holubec, 1993). Building on this idea, **Y charts** can be used,

which describe the look, sound, and feel of particular cooperative behaviors, such as negotiating, clarifying, or listening (see Figure 17-1).

## Group Reflection and Feedback

Finally, perhaps the most important aspect of cooperative learning is how the group worked and learned together. As teachers, we are familiar with providing feedback on the content of learning, but the process of learning requires continuous feedback to remind children to use cooperative skills. Goals for future learning can be set after feedback and reflection. Although much of the implementation of cooperative learning in the early years draws on principles from social psychology there also important links to the sociocultural perspective stressing shared goals, meaningful activities and feedback from tasks.

## COOPERATIVE LEARNING AND INDIVIDUAL DIFFERENCES

Cooperative learning has major benefits for children with special needs, and it also raises several important issues for mixed-age classrooms and gender differences.

### Special Needs and Mainstreaming

A literature review by Miller (1989) provided persuasive evidence that cooperative learning can have positive effects on students with disabilities. Yet when such children are **mainstreamed,** they might be extremely anxious about how they will be treated and, consequently, might withdraw. Children with disabilities need special coaching in social skills. In addition, children without disabilities might have to be taught how to support their disabled classmates' efforts to achieve and behave appropriately. Successful mainstreaming programs have been found to depend on (1) integration of students with disabilities into heterogeneous learning teams in classrooms; (2) cooperative learning programs' use of group goals and individual accountability for working toward those goals; and (3) special education teachers' provision of additional instruction and support to the learning disabled child in the regular classroom (Stevens & Slavin, 1995).

### Mixed Age and Mixed Ability Groups

Research suggests that both more and less advanced students can progress in the same cooperative groups (Cannella, 1993; Zuckerman, 1994). In an investigation involving pairs of 5- and 6-year-olds, Cannella (1993) found that what happens within the pair is of greater importance than is the ability of the partners. When interactions involve constructing joint purposes and knowledge—for example, by looking closely at a partner's idea or asking "What do you think?"—they create new, shared meanings. Consequently, cooperative learning can take place successfully in mixed age and mixed ability groups.

### Gender Differences

Different cultural expectations for cooperative behavior exist for boys and girls (Putallaz, Hellstern, Shepperd, Grimes, & Glodis, 1995). During interactions with other children, boys appear to be more concerned with power and status, girls with relationships and sustaining harmonious interaction (Maccoby, 1990).

In a recent study, however, the effects of gender on 10- and 11-year-old students' behaviors and interactions during cooperative group work was found to be minimal (Gillies & Ashman, 1995). In this study, the more time the group spent working together the more responsive they became to the needs of each other and the more they gave explanations to assist each other's learning. McCaslin, Tuck, Ward, Brown, LaPage, & Pyle (1995) found that cross-gender groups emerged as important dimensions in student's self-reported helping behavior and affective experiences. Shy students, especially, tended to be energized by cross-gender groups. Maccoby (1990) suggests that children's **gender segregation** is situationally specific. The two sexes interact comfortably under certain conditions—for example, in an absorbing joint task when structures and roles are set up by adults. Chambers and Doyon (1994) reported that no sex differences in behavior were evident among preschoolers engaged in a range of cooperative learning tasks. This suggests that 3- to 5-year-olds may not yet have been strongly socialized into the gender roles just described. Indeed, the early introduction of cooperative learning might combat traditional gender roles.

## CONCLUSION

School practices can teach children to compete, work as individuals, or cooperate. Choosing the best paintings to display on the wall or writing the names of children who have not yet finished their work on the board teaches children to exclude others. Classroom academic contests (such as spelling bees) that sort individual children into winners and losers and force them into edging each other out for awards teaches children that "[o]ther people are potential obstacles to my success" (Kohn, 1992, p. 45). This message not only sabotages relationships and undermines self-confidence but impedes achievement and long-term interest in learning (Johnson & Johnson, 1989a; Kohn, 1992).

Where teachers are serious about children learning together, they teach cooperative skills explicitly—not just because these skills contribute to academic gains but because they are valuable in their own right (Graves & Graves, 1990; Kohn, 1992; Johnson & Johnson, 1991a). Besides helping children become good learners, schools should play a role in helping children become good people (Kohn, 1990, 1992). In actuality, these two goals go together. Classrooms most conducive to learning are environments in which children feel socially and intellectually comfortable about expressing their ideas and opinions, resolve these differences in interpersonally respectful ways, and offer support and help to one another (Cannella, 1993).

In classrooms with many children who are troubled, aggressive, and come from stressful homes, three lessons about cooperative group work can be drawn from the research: (1) implementing cooperative activities will not be easy; (2) teachers will need considerable training and assistance to promote cooperative learning; and (3) schools can achieve something, but children's out-of-school environments cannot be ignored (Cowie, Smith, Boulton, & Laver, 1994).

Even when teachers are well trained in cooperative learning strategies, they need additional time to work with individuals and groups. Without being granted this extra time through smaller class sizes or additional classroom staff, when challenges and problems arise, teachers are limited to "fire fighting;" they cannot work these difficulties through in depth. Consequently, sufficient school resources and the support of administrative personnel are vital for cooperative learning to take place at its best.

In conclusion, there are exciting possibilities ahead for cooperative learning, especially if different perspectives can inform one another. Multidisciplinary approaches—from social psychology, sociology, sociocultural theory and critical theory—can be used to provide new insights for the future development of cooperative education. Our capacity to learn, is after all, embedded in our capacity to learn collaboratively *with the help of others*.

# EVALUATING YOUR MASTERY

1. Which of the following is the focus of the mastery learning perspective on cooperative learning?
   a. Intrinsic motivation
   b. Improved academic learning
   c. Resolution of status differences among group members
   d. Social construction of meaning

2. Which of the following is the focus of the sociocultural perspective on cooperative learning?
   a. Intrinsic motivation
   b. Improved academic learning
   c. Resolution of status differences among group members
   d. Social construction of meaning

3. According to Jonathan Tudge's research,
   a. Pair children with one another, and they will automatically cooperate.
   b. Children who work with more expert peers always gain in task performance.
   c. When pairs of children work together, performance is at least maintained; it never gets worse.
   d. Cooperation occurs when the task is interesting to all participants.

4. Mrs. Bloom is concerned about Tammy, a student in her third-grade class, who always tries to avoid conflict while working on tasks with her peers. To understand Tammy's difficulties, Mrs. Bloom should consult the
   a. Mastery learning perspective
   b. Sociological perspective
   c. Sociocultural perspective
   d. Critical perspective

5. True or False: According to the sociocultural perspective, sharing different points of view is the key to cognitive advances in cooperative learning.

6. Young children [are/are not] egocentric and therefore [can/cannot] negotiate in groups and come up with effective conflict resolution strategies.

7. True or False: Group reflection and feedback is the [most/least] important aspect of cooperative learning.

8. Students with disabilities [can/cannot] benefit from cooperative learning. Such children need special coaching in _____.

## Critical Thinking

1. A teacher discovers strong status differences among small work groups in her classroom; some children are much more capable than others. Which perspective on cooperative learning should she turn to for help with this problem? Suggest three steps the teacher should take to resolve status differences.

2. List seven ways in which cooperative learning in classrooms for young children differs from traditional grouping, and explain why each of these ingredients is essential.

## Applying Your Knowledge

1. Visit a child care center, preschool, or elementary school classroom and observe small groups of children working together. Do groups of boys, groups of girls, and mixed-gender groups show different patterns of interaction? Describe these, and indicate whether they are consistent with the findings of research.

2. Try cooperating with a friend in an activity, such as cooking, playing a game, or deciding what to do for pleasure on a weekend afternoon. What strategies did each of you use to sustain cooperation? What could you have done to cooperate more effectively? On the basis of your experiences, explain why children depend on adult assistance to learn how to collaborate.

# 18

## Gender Segregation Among Children

### Understanding the "Cootie Phenomenon"

KIMBERLY K. POWLISHTA

Northern Illinois University

■

This separation of the sexes may have important developmental consequences. In a sense, the two sexes are raised in distinctive "cultures."

■

[One] theory of gender segregation holds that children choose playmates with general styles of play that are similar to their own. For example, children who like to roughhouse will find other children who like to play in this manner; children who prefer more easy-going styles will avoid the roughhousers and instead seek out more compatible playmates.

■

Assuming that children have a relatively positive view of themselves (or are motivated to achieve one), the other people seen as "like me" also will be evaluated positively and thus will be seen as desirable play partners. The result is gender segregation.

■

When boys and girls play separately, they miss out on opportunities to learn from and cooperate with each other. The maintenance of separate groups encourages an acceptance of gender stereotypes, suggesting that boys and girls are more different from each other than they really are.

■

Research evidence supports the notion that teachers often interact with boys and girls differently, in ways that might encourage sex differences in play or interaction style. Specifically, the treatment of girls encourages compliance and dependence, whereas the treatment of boys encourages assertiveness.

■

Although we have seen that gender is typically very salient for children, there are times when they seem able to ignore it, at least temporarily, and allow barriers between the sexes to fall.

■

Emphasizing attributes that boys and girls have in common can also reduce perceived differences between the sexes.

■

## EDITOR'S INTRODUCTION

Why do children prefer playmates of their own sex? In this article, Kimberly Powlishta considers possible answers to this question and discusses the implications of gender segregation for development. She reviews evidence on the extent to which pressures from adults, toy preferences, play styles, and gender categories influence children's choice of same-sex play partners. As Powlishta points out, gender segregation means that the two sexes are essentially raised in different cultures. This separation can inhibit girls' independence and assertiveness, promote the inaccurate belief that men and women are completely different, and inadequately prepare children for the adult world, which is far less gender segregated than are children's peer interactions. Powlishta concludes with ways to encourage more positive interactions between boys and girls. Although sex differences in play styles are unlikely to be eliminated, research suggests that they can be reduced. And teachers can minimize the salience of gender categories to children by arranging activities in which boys and girls collaborate and by emphasizing the attributes both sexes have in common.

One of the most striking findings during the past 20 years of research on gender-role development is that boys and girls are not nearly as different from each other as most people believe them to be. Often, commonly held stereotypes turn out to be false when investigated empirically. Even when sex differences are found, they usually represent highly overlapping distributions. Take visual-spatial skills, for example: Although some studies find that boys do better in this domain than girls, the overall difference is small; furthermore, many girls do better than the average boy, and many boys do worse than the average girl. The variability within each sex is quite large relative to the difference between the sexes.

In the context of these small differences, one gender-related phenomenon stands out: Virtually *all* children show preferences for playmates of their own sex. Anyone who has spent time with groups of children will recognize the following scene:

> In the lunchroom, when the two second grade tables were filling, a high-status boy walked by the inside table, which had a scattering of both boys and girls, and said loudly, "Oooo, too many girls," as he headed for a seat at the far table. The boys at the inside table picked up their trays and moved, and no other boys sat at the inside table, which the pronouncement had effectively made taboo. (Thorne, 1986, p. 171)

Girls display a similar dislike of members of the other sex; for example, an 11-year-old told Maccoby and Jacklin (1987) that sitting next to a boy was like "being in a lower rank or peeing in your pants" (p. 245).

Although the above examples involved elementary-school children, this preference for same-sex playmates, also known as **gender segregation,** actually begins much earlier. For example, in one study of preschoolers (average age = 34 months) observed during free play, 62 per-cent of the girls and 21 percent of the boys displayed significant gender segregation (Powlishta, Serbin, & Moller, 1993). Although girls may get a head start in preference for same-sex playmates, boys soon catch up, and by the end of preschool they sometimes even show stronger same-sex preferences than do girls (LaFreniere, Strayer, & Gauthier, 1984).

For children of both sexes, gender segregation increases dramatically by the elementary school years and remains strong throughout middle childhood. Maccoby and Jacklin (1987), for instance, observed 6½-year-olds with same-sex playmates 11 times as often as with cross-sex playmates. Older children report having almost exclusively same-sex friends (for example, Gottman & Parker, 1987). Gender segregation is found in a wide variety of cultures (Edwards & Whiting, 1988) and in virtually every study that has attempted to measure it, whether the children were observed in natural settings (as described above) or in more structured, experimental contexts (Powlishta, 1995).

## THE CONSEQUENCES OF GENDER SEGREGATION

This separation of the sexes may have important developmental consequences. In a sense, the two sexes are raised in distinctive "cultures." Maccoby (1985) has discussed some of the ways in which the worlds of boys and girls are different: Boys tend to play in larger, hierarchically organized groups; to play more in public places; and to engage in more rough play and aggression than do girls. Girls remain closer to adults than do boys, thereby receiving more exposure to an environment that promotes compliance and dependence while inhibiting independence and assertiveness (Carpenter, Huston, & Holt, 1986). In this manner, gender segregation may amplify or create sex differences— differences that are not based on the individual

Powlishta, K. (1995, May). Gender segregation among children: Understanding the "cootie phenomenon." *Young Children, 50*(4), 61–69. © National Association for the Education of Young Children. Reprinted by permission.

child's interests and abilities but instead are based solely on membership in a particular social category, "male" or "female." Furthermore, the relatively little experience that boys and girls have with each other may inadequately prepare them for the adult world, which, in our society, is not nearly as segregated as are children's groups. The early lack of contact with each other may contribute to communication problems between men and women and, more generally, to promote the perception that males and females are completely different creatures: Men are creatures who refuse to ask for directions when they're lost and always leave the toilet seat up; women are creatures who sob during Hallmark Card commercials and go to public restrooms in groups. These silly examples suggest a more serious problem that gender segregation may promote: reliance on stereotypes and disregard for individual differences.

## WHY DO CHILDREN CHOOSE SAME-SEX PLAYMATES?

Despite the extensive evidence of gender segregation and the importance of its potential consequences, the reasons behind it are not well understood. Several theories have been proposed (see, for example, Maccoby, 1988).

### Direct Socialization

The most straightforward theory holds that children segregate by sex because of pressure from adults. For example, parents may provide their children with more opportunities to play with same-sex than with cross-sex peers, while actively rewarding same-sex contact and discouraging cross-sex contact. Although such pressures may exist, they probably do not fully account for gender segregation; in fact, we see more gender segregation among children when adults are not present than when children are participating in adult-structured activities (Luria & Herzog, 1985; Thorne, 1986). Lockheed and Klein (1985) found greater segregation in the lunchroom than

in the classroom, for example. Because children themselves are crucial for maintaining these behaviors, to understand gender segregation we need to examine the characteristics of boys and of girls.

### Toy Preferences

A second theory of gender segregation focuses on sex differences in toy or activity preferences. This theory states that because of socialization practices or biological differences, boys and girls prefer different kinds of toys and activities from a very early age. When they are placed in a group setting, such as a child-care center or preschool, they gravitate toward their preferred toys. As a result, boys will end up near the traditionally "masculine" toys and girls near the traditionally "feminine" toys. Gender segregation would therefore occur essentially as a by-product of this toy or activity preference. In other words, this theory holds that rather than seeking out same-sex playmates, children look for playmates with similar interests, and these playmates often turn out to be of their own sex.

Is there evidence for this theory? It is clear that sex-differentiated toy preferences emerge early in life—as early as 2 years of age (for example, Fagot, 1974; Fein, Johnson, Kosson, Stork, & Wasserman, 1975). Young children avoid toys associated with the other sex, especially when cross-sex peers are watching (Serbin, Connor, Burchardt, & Citron, 1979). Such preferences become stronger during the preschool years and are evident when children are observed in naturalistic settings or when they are presented with standard sets of toys or activities and asked to make choices from among them (for example, Blakemore, LaRue, & Olejnik, 1979; Connor & Serbin, 1977; Serbin & Sprafkin, 1982).

Because boys and girls prefer different toys at least as early as they begin to segregate by sex, the "toy preference" theory of gender segregation seems plausible. If the theory is accurate, then girls with the greatest preference for "feminine" toys and boys with the greatest preference for "masculine" toys should show the most gender segregation. Although there have been exceptions (Eisenberg, Tryon, & Cameron, 1984), for the most part this pattern has not been upheld. For example, Powlishta, Serbin, and Moller (1993) found both gender segregation and sex-differentiated toy preferences among a group of 2½- to 3-year olds, but the two variables were unrelated. In fact, girls with the most *masculine* toy preferences had a tendency to be the most segregated (that is, to prefer *female* playmates). Similarly, Maccoby and Jacklin (1987) noted that their 4½-year-old research participants spent the majority of time in gender-neutral activities (for example, on swings, in the sandbox, working on puzzles) but continued to segregate by sex. All-girl groups were seen playing on one jungle gym or swing set at the same time that all-boy groups were playing on another. It is clear, then, that gender segregation is not dependent upon sex differences in toy or activity preferences.

## Sex Differences in Play Style

A third theory of gender segregation holds that children choose playmates with general *styles* of play that are similar to their own. For example, children who like to roughhouse will find other children who like to play in this manner; children who prefer more easy-going styles will avoid the roughhousers and instead seek out more compatible playmates. To the extent that boys and girls, on the average, prefer different styles of play, this desire for play-style compatibility will lead to gender segregation. In other words, as with the sex-typed toy hypothesis, this theory states that children do not seek out same-sex playmates directly; instead, gender segregation arises as a consequence of children's choosing playmates with compatible play styles—playmates who happen to be predominantly of the same sex.

There are, in fact, several ways in which typical styles of playing or interacting with others differentiates girls from boys. As noted by Maccoby (1985), boys' play tends to be rougher, with more body contact and aggression and a greater concern for leadership and dominance hierarchies. Girls tend to be more concerned with joint decision making and turn taking. Their friendships tend to be more intensive, more focused on shared personal characteristics, and less focused on shared activities than are friendships between boys. Boys and girls also differ in their styles of influencing others. For example, Serbin and colleagues (1984) found that between the ages of 3 and 5, girls increase the number of polite suggestions they make when attempting to influence a play partner's behavior, whereas boys increase their frequency of direct demands and become less responsive to polite suggestions. At least partly as a function of these different styles, boys often are able to dominate mixed-sex interactions and to obtain more than their share of scarce resources (Charlesworth & LaFreniere, 1983; LaFreniere & Charlesworth, 1987; Powlishta & Maccoby, 1990).

Do these sex differences in play or interaction style contribute to children's tendency to segregate by sex? Unfortunately, research on this topic is relatively sparse. In one recent study (Alexander & Hines, 1994) using somewhat artificial stimuli, children preferred hypothetical playmates whose play styles or activities were consistent with their own sex. A study by Moller and colleagues (Moller, Powlishta, & Serbin, 1990; Moller, 1991) has provided some preliminary support for the play-style hypothesis, using a more naturalistic research paradigm. The researchers videotaped 2½-year-olds during free play at their nursery schools to measure their level of gender segregation and to identify each child's "best friend." Teachers also were asked to rate each child on a series of characteristics, from which four general play or interaction styles were identified: socially sensitive (for example, doesn't give up, is verbally skilled, is not shy, doesn't accept bossiness), popular (for example, meets new situations well, is happy, is accepted by same-sex and other-sex peers), disruptive (for example, is restless, grabs toys, disrupts, is excitable), and adult dependent (for example, seeks attention, maintains high proximity to teacher). Best friends were then compared on their play styles and found to be quite similar. Because at this early age best friends were equally likely to be of the same or of the other sex, this play-style matching appears to develop earlier than full-scale gender segregation. However, when all of the children's interactions were examined (not just their interactions with best friends), early signs of gender segregation emerged. Approximately 42 percent of the children were observed with same-sex playmates more often than would be expected by chance. Whether a child was one of this 42 percent was predictable from his or her play style: Among children who were not yet segregating, there were no sex differences in play style, but among segregating children, girls were rated higher in social sensitivity than were boys. These findings could be interpreted in two ways: Either an emerging sex difference in play style promotes gender segregation, or the emergence of segregation causes the play styles of boys and girls to diverge. In light of the findings regarding best friends, the first explanation seems most plausible—that is, children selected best friends who had similar play styles even before they showed any preference for same-sex best friends. This pattern suggests that play-style compatibility precedes gender segregation: Children seek out peers with play styles that are similar to their own; as these styles become sex-typed, play partners are increasingly likely to be of the same sex as the child.

Although more research must be done on this topic, play-style compatibility seems to be at least one factor that contributes to gender segregation. However, behavioral sex differences still cannot *fully* explain why children prefer their own sex. Children often react more positively to someone of their own sex even when they have had little or no exposure to that person's play style. For example, when provided with verbal descriptions or photographs of people they have never met, children predict that they will like same-sex individuals, select them as preferred playmates, and attribute more positive and fewer negative characteristics to them, relative to ver-

bal descriptions or photos of the other sex (Martin, 1989; Powlishta, 1995; Serbin & Sprafkin, 1986). Children also show preferences for same-sex adults (for example, Serbin & Sprafkin, 1986), for whom the types of play styles measured by Moller and colleagues have little, if any, relevance. These findings suggest that the classification of a person as male or female may have implications for how a child will react to that person. This leads to a fourth theory of gender segregation: cognitive categorization.

## Dividing the World into Male and Female Categories

According to the **cognitive categorization theory,** children's tendency to categorize others on the basis of gender plays a crucial role in gender segregation. Once the child has classified the self and others in this manner, people are viewed as either "like me" or "not like me." Assuming that children have a relatively positive view of themselves (or are motivated to achieve one), the other people seen as "like me" also will be evaluated positively and thus will be seen as desirable play partners. The result is gender segregation.

Is there empirical support for this theory? Children certainly are sensitive to distinctions between males and females at a very early age. Infants as young as 5 months old can tell the difference between men and women depicted in photographs (Fagan & Shepherd, 1981). By 9 to 12 months of age, infants are able to match voices to these pictures (Poulin-Dubois, Serbin, Kenyon, & Derbyshire, 1994; Fagan & Singer, 1979). In other words, even at this early age, children have begun to form gender concepts. As children grow older, their knowledge expands and becomes more explicit. By the age of 3, most children are able to sort photographs on the basis of gender and to use gender labels for themselves and others accurately (Leinbach & Fagot, 1986; Thompson, 1975; Weinraub, Clemens, Sockloff, Ethridge, Gracely, & Meyers, 1984).

Do such abilities contribute to gender segregation? The evidence on this point is mixed.

One group of researchers has found a relation between labeling ability and same-sex peer preferences (Fagot, 1985; Fagot, Leinbach, & Hagan, 1986), while others have not (Moller, Powlishta, & Serbin, 1990). Maccoby (1988) has argued that even though children may be able to label the gender of self and others by the time they start to segregate, it is unlikely that they are efficient yet at matching the two concepts—in other words, reasoning such as "I am a girl; you are a girl; we are therefore the same" is probably too complex for a child in the beginning stages of gender segregation. Perhaps factors such as play-style compatibility more readily account for a child's initial selection of same-sex playmates. With maturity, the division of the social world into in-groups (that is, same-sex) and out-groups (that is, other sex) may play an increasingly important role. As a result, older children gravitate toward same-sex peers even in the absence of play-style information. Whereas young children's behavior may be governed largely by what they see other boys and girls doing, older children's behavior may be governed more by their beliefs about males and females.

## US VERSUS THEM: THE IMPACT OF SOCIAL GROUPS

Research evidence has shown that dividing people into in-groups and out-groups can have important consequences (see Messick & Mackie, 1989 for a recent review). When random groups of adults are created, supposedly on the basis of some trivial distinction (for example, having either over- or underestimated the number of dots in an array), participants show favoritism toward members of their own groups when allocating rewards, making ratings on traits, or evaluating group products. They also exaggerate differences between and similarities within the groups and believe that other groups are more homogeneous than their own ("those people are all just alike") (Messick & Mackie, 1989). These processes may encourage the formation and use of social stereotypes, because stereotypes are based on the notion that all members of a particular social category are alike in some way—a way that makes them distinct from other categories of people. Could these generic group processes help to explain children's attitudes toward males and females?

One study has investigated this possibility (Powlishta, 1995). Third- and fourth-graders watched videotaped scenes and rated each featured unfamiliar child on several characteristics. Both boys and girls perceived children of their own sex as more positive (for example, intelligent), less negative (for example, boring), and more likable, similar to themselves, and varied than children of the other sex. In addition, all children in the video were viewed in a stereotype-consistent manner (that is, boys were seen as more daring and messy than girls; girls were seen as more gentle and prone to crying than boys). In other words, the full range of intergroup phenomena previously demonstrated in laboratory studies of adults was seen in children's attitudes toward unfamiliar boys and girls.

Does this general tendency to favor members of our own groups and to see members of other groups as very different from ourselves help explain gender segregation? It seems logical that children would want to play with peers who they expect to have positive characteristics that are similar to their own. In the study described (Powlishta, 1995), a measure of gender segregation also was collected. Groups of classmates (two boys and two girls) were asked to complete two puzzles. Although extensive gender segregation was found, the amount of time a child spent interacting with a same-sex classmate (that is, gender segregation) was *not* related to his or her attitudes toward the unfamiliar videotaped children.

At first, this finding seems to suggest that general attitudes toward in-groups and out-groups do not contribute to gender segregation. However, almost all groups split into same-sex pairs for the entire duration of the puzzle task. Because everyone was so highly segregated, it is not surprising that a child's degree of segregation was unrelated to his or her attitudes. There was not enough individual variability. Consistent with previous research (for example, Maccoby & Jacklin, 1987; Powlishta, Serbin, & Moller, 1993), nearly all children show equally strong preferences for same-sex playmates, at least under some circumstances.

Why is gender such a salient characteristic for children? First of all, a person's gender usually is immediately apparent from visual cues; it is something we notice right away. As Allport put it, "All our experience teaches us that when things look different they usually are different. A black cloud in the sky has very different significance from a white cloud. A skunk is not a cat. Our comfort and sometimes our lives depend on learning to act differently in the face of unlike objects" (1954, p. 131). In addition to being perceptually salient, gender also is emphasized by our society. Furthermore, because often real differences exist between the sexes within the child's world, using these categories and their corresponding stereotypes (for example, men mow the lawn; women vacuum) often is useful in making predictions about the behavior of males and females (Martin & Halverson, 1981; Serbin, Powlishta, & Gulko, 1993). All of these factors help to explain why children pay so much attention to gender.

## IMPLICATIONS FOR REDUCING GENDER SEGREGATION

One advantage of knowing something about the causes of gender segregation is that such knowledge may suggest possible ways to encourage more positive interactions between boys and girls.

### Should We Try to Reduce It?

Given that gender segregation among children is such a pervasive phenomenon, one that seems to occur naturally, without direct pressure from adults, should we attempt to reduce it? As previously noted, there are a number of reasons why lack of interaction with peers of the other sex

could have negative consequences for children. Gender segregation exposes boys and girls to differing social influences—not on the basis of the individual child's interests and aptitudes but on the basis of gender alone. When boys and girls play separately, they miss out on opportunities to learn from and cooperate with each other. The maintenance of separate groups encourages an acceptance of gender stereotypes, suggesting that boys and girls are more different from each other than they really are.

Research evidence also supports the notion that boys and girls may benefit from interacting with each other. For example, Feiring and Lewis (1991) found that girls who had frequent contact with male peers at ages 3, 6, and 9 were rated as high in social competence by teachers. Although we cannot be certain that the cross-sex contact *caused* social competence to increase, the authors suggest that interacting with male friends may help girls develop social skills such as independence and assertiveness. Howes (1988) has found similar beneficial effects of cross-sex contact for boys as well as girls. In her observational study of 1- to 6-year olds, Howes found that children with at least one cross-sex friend were more socially skilled than children who had only same-sex friends.

### Breaking Down the Gender Barriers

These findings indicate that gender segregation may deprive children of important social opportunities. Is there anything that can be done to encourage positive interactions between boys and girls in school settings? Bianchi and Bakeman (1978) found that segregation was higher in a "traditional" than in an "open" preschool. The open preschool had deliberately set out to minimize sex typing. Its philosophy was described as follows:

> The emphasis is on the individual development of each child; the goal is to respond to children on the basis of their individual behaviors, needs, and characteristics: thus, sex-stereotyped expectations about children's

interests, abilities, or personalities are consciously avoided. Several aspects of school practice reflect this. For example, as often as possible, there are both male and female teachers in the classroom, and both teachers consciously engage in a wide range of activities and roles. (1978, p. 911)

Unfortunately, there is no way of knowing whether these characteristics led to lower levels of gender segregation. Families choosing to place their children in the "open" preschool may have differed from "traditional" school families; their children may have been less prone to segregation for any one of a variety of reasons (for example, maternal employment, parental modeling or encouragement, etc.) regardless of their preschool experience. Nevertheless, these findings do support the notion that gender segregation is not "fixed in stone" but instead is subject to change.

## Rewarding Mixed-Sex Play

Other, more direct attempts to manipulate gender segregation have met with only moderate success. For example, Serbin, Tonick, and Sternglanz (1977) had preschool teachers reward cross-sex play by giving positive attention (for example, praise) any time they saw a boy and girl or a mixed-sex group of children playing together. The teachers' comments were to be made so that the whole class could hear (for example, "I like the tower John and Kathy are building with the blocks"). Rates of cooperative mixed-sex play doubled when this treatment was implemented. However, gender segregation quickly reappeared when teachers returned to their normal classroom procedures. Given that children spend quite a bit of time away from adult surveillance, a teacher reinforcement approach to reducing gender segregation has limited practicality. As the results of this study demonstrated, it is difficult to have lasting effects on gender segregation through short-term efforts to influence the phenomenon directly.

## Encouraging Similar Play Styles

Because gender segregation is not caused by direct pressure from adults but instead is instigated primarily by the children, it should not be surprising that direct teacher pressure has limited effectiveness in reducing segregation. Even though encouragement from adults can push children toward mixed-sex play, other forces pull in the opposite direction. A desire for playmates with similar play styles is one such force. If sex differences in play style drive segregation, then reducing these play-style differences may be more effective in lowering rates of gender segregation than attempting to reduce segregated play directly. Although some aspects of play style seem to be biologically determined (for example, Hines & Kaufman, 1994), socialization practices may enhance these biologically based sex differences and create additional differences, as well.

Research evidence supports the notion that teachers often interact with boys and girls differently, in ways that might encourage sex differences in play or interaction style. Specifically, the treatment of girls encourages compliance and dependence, whereas the treatment of boys encourages assertiveness. Beal (1994) summarized these differences: Girls receive more teacher attention when they are indoors playing quietly. When a misdeed is noted, girls typically receive only quiet reprimands from the teacher. Boys, on the other hand, are likely to receive teacher attention even when they are playing at a distance. Teachers tend to monitor boys for signs of misbehavior and to scold them publicly when it happens. Many boys seems to enjoy this public attention and thus are more likely to misbehave in the future.

It seems logical that if boys and girls were treated more similarly, sex differences in play style would decline, thus reducing gender segregation; however, such attempts are likely to meet with limited success. Although teachers often react to the same behavior differently depending on whether it was enacted by a boy or girl, they also react to actual differences between the sexes.

These boys congregate with other boys as they create a fast-action, imaginary play scene in the sandbox. Their genetically influenced, rambunctious play styles combine with adult socialization to promote gender-segregated play. As children categorize the social world as "like me" and "not like me," preference for same-sex associates strengthens. Although reducing the salience of gender is challenging, it can be done in preschool and elementary school classrooms. (Photo: Laura Berk)

Boys and girls behave differently long before entering school; thus, teachers reinforce lessons that have already been learned at home (Beal, 1994).

Beal (1994) has summarized some of the ways in which adults in general, and parents in particular, treat boys and girls differently. When adults believe that they are playing with a boy baby, they are likely to bounce, toss, and roughhouse with the baby; when they think that the baby is a girl, they talk with her more frequently. Although there are probably more similarities than differences in the way parents treat their sons and daughters, some differences do exist. Mothers tend to hold infant daughters closer and to touch and cuddle them more than they do sons; infant sons are allowed more independence. Fathers are more likely to use a rough-and-tumble style of play with sons than with daughters, a style that is active, unpredictable, and physically stimulating. Differential parental treatment that encourages compliance on the part of girls and independence on the part of boys continues during the toddler and school-age years. Parents react positively

when female toddlers follow them around the house but negatively when boys do the same thing. They worry about a boy who is too compliant. During the elementary school years, girls are granted much less independence than boys, for example, by being picked up after school and by being required to play at home rather than in public places (Beal, 1994).

Such differential treatment, when coupled with potentially innate differences between the sexes, is likely to result in gender-typed play or interaction styles. It is unlikely that teachers could wipe out such differences simply by treating boys and girls similarly. However, play style is only one factor contributing to gender segregation. As noted earlier, children typically choose same-sex playmates even in the absence of information about play style. The mere fact that a person has been cognitively categorized as "like me" (same sex) or "not like me" (other sex) sets group processes in motion, whereby same-sex individuals are preferred. If we could interrupt this categorization process, gender segregation should decline.

## Reducing the Salience of Gender

The salience of gender varies considerably from one situation to another. Deaux and Major (1987), for instance, point out that some events (for example, watching the Miss America Pageant) may prime us to focus on the gender of other people. Although we have seen that gender is typically very salient for children, there are times when they seem able to ignore it, at least temporarily, and allow barriers between the sexes to fall. Thorne (1987) provides the following anecdotal evidence. A group of fourth-graders, who were usually quite gender segregated on the playground, came together in a mixed-sex group to defend and discuss the plight of a classmate who had been unjustly punished by a teacher. The children united on the basis of classroom membership, which temporarily became more salient than gender.

Unfortunately, situations are often created in the classroom that emphasize gender distinctions: In a combined fourth-fifth grade classroom the teacher introduced a math game organized as girls against boys; she would write addition and subtraction problems on the board, and a member of each team would race to be the first to write the correct answer. As the teacher wrote two score-keeping columns headed 'Beastly Boys' and 'Gossipy Girls' several boys yelled out, 'Noisy girls! Gruesome girls!' while some of the girls laughed (Thorne, 1987, p. 10).

Teachers sometimes try to manage the behavior of boys by comparing them to girls or threatening to make them work with girls. "One teacher told the girls to line up first for recess and said, 'Oh, Billy thinks he's a girl' when a boy stood up and tried to head out the door; he promptly sat down again" (Beal, 1994, pp. 141–42). In schools where children wear uniforms, all girls often wear one outfit and all boys wear another outfit. By emphasizing differences between boys and girls and similarities within each sex in these ways, the likelihood of cooperative, mixed-sex interactions is minimized.

Besides avoiding these kinds of artificial distinctions, is there anything that teachers can do to de-emphasize gender? Thorne (1986) has identified some characteristics of settings in which boys and girls are likely to interact with each other:

1. Children are engaged in an absorbing task (for example, a group art project) that encourages cooperation and takes attention away from gender.

2. Children are not responsible for group formation, such as when the teacher has organized mixed-sex encounters.

3. Principles of grouping other than gender are invoked explicitly (for example, by forming "hot lunch" and "cold lunch" lines, or by organizing workgroups on the basis of interests or abilities).

Research evidence has supported the contention that boys and girls interact more frequently, have more positive attitudes about each other, and acknowledge similarities between the sexes under these kinds of circumstances. For example, Lockheed (1986) asked teachers to make use of small, mixed-sex workgroups. Relative to control classrooms, children in these experimental classes engaged in more cross-sex interactions. The experimental treatment also improved boys' preference for working in mixed-age groups. However, the treatment did not influence children's perceptions of each other; children from all classes continued to rate same-sex classmates more positively than cross-sex classmates.

Another similar study was more successful at influencing children's attitudes toward individual boys and girls (Deschamps & Doise, 1978). Groups of 12 children (6 boys, 6 girls) were taken into a room and seated according to gender. For half of these groups, two subgroups were created: Three boys and three girls were given blue pens and labeled "the blue group"; the remaining children were given red pens and labeled "the red group." Each child then individually completed a series of paper-and-pencil games and was asked to estimate how well each of the other children did at these games. When the children had been divided into mixed-sex groups (blue versus red), they predicted that boys and girls would do equally well. When these mixed groups were not created, boys and girls believed that their own sex had done better than the other sex. So the creation of groups that cross gender boundaries and accentuate commonalities between boys and girls, especially when such groupings are made explicit (for example, with distinct names), can be successful at reducing children's biases against the other sex.

Emphasizing attributes that boys and girls have in common can also reduce perceived differences between the sexes. In one study (Powlishta, 1989), children reviewed photographs of unfamiliar boys and girls and judged the similarity of several boy-girl pairs. Pairs were seen as more similar when they were surrounded by photographs of adults and explicitly labeled as "children" than when the same pairs were surrounded by photographs of other children. In the former, more diverse context, focusing attention on a characteristic shared by boys and girls, one that distinguished them from other people (that is, "childhood"), reduced children's tendency to view males and females as different types of creatures.

## CONCLUSION

The previous studies suggest that gender barriers may be less rigid in diverse social contexts in which children share similarities and differences with members of both sexes. By emphasizing variability within each sex and by creating or highlighting commonalities between boys and girls, gender should become a less salient basis for social categorization. This approach argues against the formation of single-sex classes in public schools, an arrangement for which some people have recently been advocating. These advocates have argued that boys and girls have different learning styles (for example, competitive versus cooperative), that girls receive less attention than boys and are discouraged from being assertive in mixed-sex classes, and that teachers of coeducational classes expect boys and girls to adhere to sex-typed norms (deGroot, 1994). This argument overlooks the tremendous individual variability that exists within each sex, and it avoids rather than attempts to correct the problem of differential treatment of boys and girls. More importantly, creating separate classes or workgroups for each sex enhances the salience of gender and legitimizes children's gender stereotypes. It sends the message to children that gender is the most important distinction among people—more important than interests, aptitudes, achievements, values, cultural heritage, and personality. Given the considerable evidence that social categorization leads to stereotyping and biases against those who are viewed as different, enforcing gender segregation through single-sex classes can only aggravate the strained relations that already sometimes exist between boys and girls. Any short-term gains (for example, easier classroom management) will be compensated for by long-term problems (for example, encouraging males and females to be seen as more different than they really are).

Instead of encouraging or accepting gender segregation, we should provide opportunities for positive interactions between boys and girls. It does not seem likely that we can block the basic human tendency to form social categories that help us make sense of the world. However, by creating situations that require cooperation between boys and girls, and by forming groups or pointing out characteristics that unify both sexes, we may be able to discourage children from always reacting to others on the basis of their gender.

## EVALUATING YOUR MASTERY

1. Gender segregation _____ over the preschool years and _____ throughout middle childhood.
   a.   Increases; decreases
   b.   Increases; remains strong
   c.   Decreases; increases
   d.   Remains strong; decreases

2. While playing, girls are more likely than boys to
   a.   Remain closer to adults
   b.   Play in larger, more hierarchical groups
   c.   Play more in public places
   d.   Engage in more rough play

3. Which theory posits that children's tendency to categorize others on the basis of gender plays a crucial role in gender segregation?
   a.   Direct socialization
   b.   Toy preference
   c.   Play-style compatibility
   d.   Cognitive categorization

4. According to Powlishta's findings,
   a.   Both boys and girls perceive members of their own sex more positively.
   b.   Both boys and girls perceive boys more positively.
   c.   Both boys and girls perceive girls more positively.
   d.   Neither boys nor girls perceive one sex more positively than the other.

5. Gender segregation [is/is not] strongly related to sex-differentiated toy preferences.

6. True or False: Research shows that play-style compatibility does not contribute to gender segregation.

7. True or False: According to Powlishta, play-style compatibility might account for gender segregation at younger ages, whereas cognitive categorization might account for it at older ages.

8. True or False: Cross-sex contact has not been found to be beneficial for young children.

## Critical Thinking

1. When teachers emphasize differences between boys and girls and make public comparisons of their behavior, they promote gender segregation. Which theory accounts for these influences? Explain.

2. How can mixed-sex classes and workgroups reduce gender segregation?

## Applying Your Knowledge

Observe children between 3 and 10 years of age playing in a school yard or a city park. To what extent is their play gender segregated? Note any comments and behaviors by children and nearby adults that might either promote or reduce gender segregation. Relate your observations to the diverse social influences on gender segregation discussed by Powlishta.

# 19

## Discipline in Early Childhood

### LOUISE PORTER
### Flinders University of South Australia

■

External reinforcement can cause children to repeat only the behaviors
for which they will receive reinforcement,
limiting their motivation to be more creative and adventurous.

■

Cognitive training involves teaching children to manage themselves through
monitoring their own behavior, giving themselves constructive instructions,
and evaluating (reinforcing) their own efforts.

■

Neo-Adlerians believe that all children are striving to belong and that when they
cannot do so through prosocial behaviors, they resort to antisocial behavior by
seeking attention, power, revenge, or withdrawing from adult demands.

■

The humanists argue that their theory's strength is that it prevents most disruptive
behavior and does not provoke the child to rebel because her autonomy
has been denied by an authoritarian adult.

■

The various theories of behavior management have different goals—
one managerial and four educational goals.

■

When assessing which theory best fits within an early childhood program,
the issue of justice or ethics is fundamental.

■

The democratic or authoritative adult accepts and acknowledges considerate
behavior, using encouragement rather than praise.

■

In the preschool years, the goal of discipline, then, is to give children
the confidence to take increasing responsibility for their own actions
and for their effect on other people.

■

## EDITOR'S INTRODUCTION

Louise Porter argues that a clear theory is vital for an effective approach to discipline in early childhood. She discusses four key approaches to early childhood discipline—applied behavior analysis, cognitive-behaviorism, neo-Adlerian theory, and democratic theories—placing them on a continuum from authoritarian to laissez-faire and clarifying the strengths and weaknesses of each. Because different theories have contradictory underlying philosophies, Porter concludes that an eclectic blend is not a viable way to construct an effective theory of discipline. Instead, she recommends that adults choose a theory that shares their discipline goals, that realizes those goals on the basis of research evidence, and that is ethical and just.

Porter evaluates each theory on the basis of these criteria. An authoritarian approach emphasizes the goals of management and order; in contrast, a democratic approach stresses educational goals of self-discipline, appropriate emotional expression, cooperation, and responsible citizenship—that is, the development of considerate behavior. Democratic procedures have also amassed substantial empirical support for their effectiveness in producing self-controlled, self-confident, and socially mature children. In addition, they fulfill professional ethical standards.

Porter concludes with recommendations for teaching young children the skills for behaving considerately. She clarifies the adult's disciplinary role, advocates a developmental view of children's behavior, and discusses how to respond to both considerate and inconsiderate child conduct.

Advice contained in the well-known adage, "If you want to get ahead, get a theory" is particularly apt for disciplining young children. When we understand the theoretical basis of our practices, we are able to generate a set of coherent ideas to guide consistent practice.

## THEORIES OF BEHAVIOR MANAGEMENT

There are many theories of discipline; however, only some of these translate comfortably into the early childhood age range. Four key approaches are in common use with young children. These are arranged along a continuum, shown in Figure 19.1. On the left are the authoritarian theories in which the adult has control over children. Applied behavior analysis is the main authoritarian theory used in the early childhood years. At the other end of the continuum is the **permissive or laissez-faire** approach that grants children a free rein, with very few adult-imposed restrictions. This approach has no modern adherents. The middle ground is occupied by the democratic theories—humanism and control theory—that promote children's self-control.

### Applied Behavior Analysis (ABA)

**Applied behavior analysis (ABA)** is the new term for behavior modification. According to this theory, individuals acquire new behaviors through imitation and through a process called **shaping,** in which a complex skill is learned by mastering a series of small steps that together make up the total task. Once learned, a behavior is repeated if it works or, in the language of ABA, is **reinforced**—that is, it earns the individual something she values, making it likely that she will repeat the behavior.

Therefore, if adults want a child to stop engaging in a particular behavior, they have to prevent it from working—from receiving a positive response. To do this, ABA rewards alternative behaviors that are more desirable than the disruptive

behavior. The kinds of rewards used in early childhood include social reinforcers such as praise, hugs, or a smile; the opportunity to do a favorite activity; a sticker or some other tangible reward that the child values for itself; and food rewards (although these are not recommended—see Birch, Johnson, & Fisher, Chapter 12 in this volume).

If rewarding an alternative behavior does not work, then punishments can be used as a last resort. **Punishments** are of two types: taking away something that the child wants, or administering something the child does not like. The first class of punishments includes withdrawing a child's privileges, and **time out**—probably the most widely used punishment in child care centers. Time out is based on the assumption that something in the environment is maintaining (reinforcing) the child's undesirable behavior, so if the child is removed from that environment and placed where he cannot receive any reinforcement, the behavior will stop. The second class of punishments—delivering something aversive or unpleasant—includes verbal aversives such as reprimands and physical aversives such as spanking. (Experts agree that physical aversives should never be used. Besides being ineffective in controlling behavior, they prompt anger and resistance in children and can spiral into serious abuse.)

When using ABA, it is absolutely crucial to observe and record the circumstances that precede the behavior (antecedents) and that follow it (consequences). This allows the adult to choose an appropriate intervention. Careful recording of the behavior rate before and during the selected intervention also permits evaluation of whether the behavior management program is working.

The great strength of ABA is its emphasis on unbiased observation of the child's behavior and careful monitoring of the success of a management program. On the other hand, the detailed recording that ABA requires is difficult to do in addition to one's other tasks. A secondary strength, claimed by proponents of this approach (for example, Alberto & Troutman, 1995) is that it has been shown to be highly effective. However, other writers rebut this by saying that most

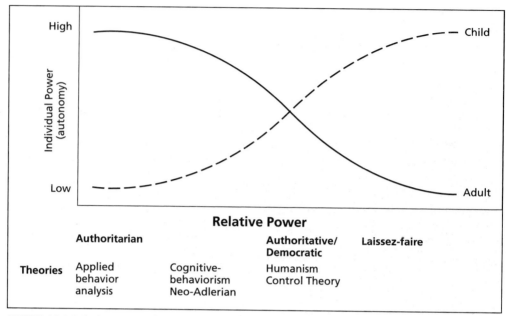

**FIGURE 19.1** Relative power of adults and children upheld by each theory of behavior management.

ABA studies occur in tightly controlled conditions that cannot be duplicated in less structured settings (Kaplan & Drainville, 1991).

Because ABA is highly technical—more technical than this brief summary suggests—it takes a great deal of skill and training to use ABA effectively (Alberto & Troutman, 1995; Wolery, Bailey, & Sugai, 1988). The first challenge is that although the use of rewards and punishments seems like common sense, it is fraught with pitfalls. For instance, the adult cannot observe all the events that led to a behavior, so it is difficult to judge what would be a fair intervention. Second, because adults are in charge, they fail to capitalize on children's inner resources for managing their own behavior. Third, external reinforcement can cause children to repeat only the behaviors for which they will receive reinforcement, limiting their motivation to be more creative and adventurous (Levine & Fasnacht, in Thompson & Rudolph, 1992). Fourth, punishment produces what Gordon (1970) calls the three Rs—resistance, rebellion, and retaliation—

plus escape or submission. Punishment also lowers a child's standing with her peers, who then treat her as "naughty."

Finally, the theory gives little guidance to the practitioner about how to prevent inappropriate behavior and thus avoid the need for a restrictive management program. And there is debate—especially among opponents of ABA—about whether the gains made justify violating the child's autonomy.

## Cognitive-Behaviorism

A recent variation of ABA is **cognitive-behaviorism**, which aims to address these criticisms of ABA (Bandura, 1986; Fontana, 1985). Cognitive-behaviorists believe that, besides the consequences of behavior, individuals' **meta-cognitive** planning, emotional state, developmental stage, and the environment all affect their behavioral choices (Kendall, 1991). **Cognitive training** involves teaching children to manage themselves through monitoring their own behavior, giving themselves constructive instructions, and evaluating (reinforcing) their own efforts. It focuses on the child's thinking and planning processes, such as enhancing problem-solving, improving children's self-esteem, and teaching children that they can regulate their own behavior.

An advantage of cognitive-behavioral methods is that when children are in control of their own behavior, they become more motivated to behave appropriately and more persistent at using the self-regulatory skills that lead to success at an activity (Fontana, 1985). Some, however, criticize cognitive-behaviorism for being imprecise (Benson & Presbury, 1989; Lee, 1993), a criticism that is answered by the assertion that the imprecision of cognitive-behaviorism means that its interventions can be more flexibly tailored to specific individuals (Dobson & Pusch, 1993; Dyck, 1993). A second debate is whether the cognitive and linguistic demands of the cognitive-behavioral methods make them unsuitable for use with very young children. But with suitable adjustments in language, even very young children can be taught to regulate their own behavior. For instance, **inductive discipline**—which explains to children the direct consequences of their behavior on others—will teach children as young as age two to consider the effect of their behavior (Berk, 1997).

### Neo-Adlerian theory

**Neo-Adlerian theory** is so called because it represents modern writers' refinements of Alfred Adler's work early in this century. It was originally popularized in the United States by Don Dinkmeyer and his colleagues in the *Systematic training for effective parenting/teaching* packages (Dinkmeyer & McKay, 1989; Dinkmeyer, McKay, & Dinkmeyer, 1980) and is advocated in Australia by Maurice Balson (1992, 1994) and Jeannette Harrison (1996).

Neo-Adlerian theory has two distinct parts. Its preventive aspect focuses on creating warm relationships with children, listening to them, fostering cooperation and reducing competition between children, and encouraging rather than praising them. Of this list, most features have been borrowed from the democratic theories to be discussed in the next section, although the use of encouragement instead of praise is a unique contribution of this theory. Encouragement differs from praise in the following ways (Dinkmeyer & McKay, 1989; Dinkmeyer, McKay, & Dinkmeyer, 1980):

1. Encouragement teaches children to *evaluate their own efforts*: "What do you think of *that*?" "Was that fun?" "Are you pleased with yourself?" "You seem pleased that you did that so well." In comparison, praise approves of work that meets *adult* standards.

2. Unlike praise, encouragement *does not judge* children or their work, although we still might choose to tell children what we think or feel about what they have achieved. For example, "I like the colors you used," replaces the praising statement that a painting is "beautiful."

3. Encouragement focuses on the *process* rather than the outcome. The adult comments on the child's effort, rather than on the end product: "It looks like you're having fun over there" or, when the child has written her name: "I see you're enjoying writing."

4. Encouragement is a *private* event that does not embarrass children in public or compare them with each other. Unlike praise, it does not try to manipulate other children into copying a child who has been praised. Encouragement simply describes—in private—what the adult appreciated: "Thanks for being quiet while I found a book to read you," or, "I appreciate that you put your equipment away."

Encouragement aims to overcome the disadvantages of praise that arise when children resist being manipulated into repeating behavior of which the adult approves or when, conversely, they become compliant and submissive.

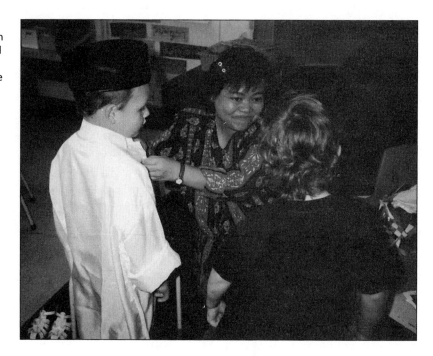

This child waits patiently while a teacher dresses him in a native costume for a special school event. An Adlerian theorist would encourage the boy for favorable behavior rather than praise him. Encouragement teaches children to evaluate their own efforts and minimizes comparisons with agemates. (Photo: Laura Berk)

In contrast with its preventive component, the neo-Adlerian approach to intervention with difficult behavior is largely under adult control. That is, the adult diagnoses children's motivation for their behavior and subsequently chooses an intervention. Neo-Adlerians believe that all children are striving to belong and that when they cannot do so through prosocial behaviors, they resort to antisocial behavior by seeking attention, power, revenge, or withdrawing from adult demands. Adults can diagnose which of these goals is motivating the child by noting their own feelings about the child's behavior, how they normally discipline the child, and how the child responds to that discipline. Table 19.1 summarizes these clues.

Having diagnosed the child's antisocial goal, the adult can then plan an intervention, which will differ for the various goals. For example, the adult can ignore attention-seeking behavior, or apply logical consequences (defined later) when ignoring is not possible. At the same time, the adult can give the child extra attention for

appropriate behavior. In contrast, if the adult believes the child is attempting to withdraw from adult demands, she can refuse to believe that the child is incapable and can endeavor—through acceptance and encouragement—to show the child that he can be successful.

Instead of using punishment to reduce undesirable behavior, neo-Adlerian theory employs **natural** or **logical consequences**. Natural consequences are those—as their title implies—that occur naturally, without adult manipulation. Logical consequences are arranged by the adult but, unlike punishment that can be arbitrary, logical consequences are related to the act. For instance, a natural consequence for a child who throws sand in the sandpit might be that she is asked to play somewhere else so that everyone can be safe; a logical consequence might be that she is banned from the sandpit for a specified time period; a punishment might be sending her to time-out to consider her actions.

Neo-Adlerian theory's strengths lie in its preventive aspects and its use of encouragement

**Table 19.1 Neo-Adlerian Clues to the Goals of Inappropriate Behavior**

| If the adult feels | If the adult responds by | If the child's response to correction is | Then the child's goal is |
| --- | --- | --- | --- |
| Annoyed | Reminding, coaxing | Stops but then repeats the behavior | Attention |
| Angry | Fighting or giving in | Confronts or ignores authority | Power |
| Hurt | Wanting to retaliate or get even | Becomes devious, violent, or hostile | Revenge |
| Despairing or hopeless | Agreeing with the child that nothing can be done | Refuses to participate or cooperate, is uninterested | Withdrawal |

instead of praise. Its interventions, however, attract two criticisms. The first criticism is that the interventions are based on illogical assumptions that the child's behavior *makes* the adult feel a certain way, and that how the adult feels is a reliable indicator of the child's motivation, when an adult can feel disturbed by a child's behavior for reasons other than the actions themselves. The adult might be tired, or the particular behavior might be the last of a series of disruptions, causing the adult to feel more irritated than if the behavior were an isolated incident. A second criticism is that because neo-Adlerian interventions are determined by the adult, they contradict the democratic flavor of this theory's preventive component.

## The Democratic Theories: Humanism and Control (Choice) Theory

The democratic writers include humanists Carl Rogers (1951, 1978; Rogers & Freiberg, 1994); Thomas Gordon (1970, 1974, 1991); Haim Ginott (1972); Dan Gartrell (1994); and control theory's author, Bill Glasser (1986; 1992). (Glasser recently announced that his theory is now to be called *choice theory*, so both terms will be used here.)

Each of these writers accepts the view that although adults and children have different responsibilities, they have the same rights to having their needs met. Under a democratic system, the adult facilitates children's learning by acting as a leader rather than a boss (Glasser, 1992). That is, the adult gains respect by being expert—

by being **authoritative**—rather than by exercising power over children.

The democrats believe that most of children's difficult behavior can be avoided by creating a child-centered program that meets children's educational needs and their emotional needs for self-esteem, belonging, autonomy, and fun (Glasser, 1986; Rogers & Freiberg, 1994). (Note that this list of emotional needs is more comprehensive than the neo-Adlerians' single need to belong.) As can be seen from this description, the prevailing philosophy of early childhood care and education shares many humanist principles.

To satisfy children's need for self-esteem, the democrats avoid praising children and instead teach them to evaluate their own actions. They also ensure that children are successful at learning skills that are relevant to them in the present or will be useful to them in the future (Rogers & Freiberg, 1994). To satisfy children's need to belong, the adults create a warm relationship with each child; they ensure that the children can spend most of their time learning from each other; and they engage the children in cooperative activities and games. Children's need for autonomy is safeguarded by facilitating their self-control rather than imposing discipline on them. Fun is the intangible joy that we experience when our learning and emotional needs are met (Glasser, 1986) and so is a natural by-product of the other measures designed to meet children's needs.

When deciding whether to intervene in a behavior, Gordon (1970, 1974) discriminates between behavior that, even if it is irritating, does not violate anyone's rights—and so is acceptable—versus behavior that interferes with meeting an individual's needs—and so is unacceptable because it is disruptive. The person affected by disruptive behavior might be the child himself, in which case the adult *listens* to the child and helps him find a way to meet his own needs without hurting himself or anyone else. At other times, a child's behavior negatively affects other people. In this case, the adult must speak up, must state honestly and *assertively*—but not aggressively—what effect the behavior has on others.

A third communication skill—**collaborative problem solving**—is used when both the child and the adult are being affected by the child's behavior—except if someone is in danger, in which case the adult takes charge unilaterally. Collaborative problem solving involves both of the other skills—listening and assertiveness—to find out what the child needs, and for the adult to state his or her own needs. Next, the adult and child together suggest some possible solutions that would meet their needs; choose one of these; enact it; and, later, check whether it worked. This process might result in a contract, or "deal," with a child, but with the unique feature that the contract is reciprocal. A reciprocal contract not only specifies what standards the child must achieve, but also states how the adult will help the child to meet those expectations. The process might also result in the adult's adjusting his demands, instead of simply requiring the child to comply with what is being expected of her.

The democratic writers do not use praise, rewards, logical consequences, or punishments. However, if a child breaks a reasonable agreement or cannot behave appropriately, then Glasser (1977) advises the adult to isolate the child until the adult and child can "work it out" again. Unlike time out, this "time away" would be in pleasant surroundings, and the child could occupy herself enjoyably, but she would not regain her freedom until she could find a way to behave prosocially.

The humanists argue that their theory's strength is that it prevents most disruptive behavior and does not provoke the child to rebel because her autonomy has been denied by an authoritarian adult. The strengths of this theory, however, are also its weaknesses. By rejecting all forms of punishment, the democrats have few interventions to use for disruptive behavior. They do believe in natural consequences, but at very young ages, it can be unfair to let children suffer a natural consequence for their inadequate planning when poor planning is developmentally normal in the early years. For example, when a child does not play in a friendly way, other children will dislike him. But instead of allowing him to become isolated as a natural result of his antisocial behavior, it would be better to teach him how to behave prosocially.

## CRITERIA FOR EVALUATING THE THEORIES

Individuals who work with young children will need to evaluate which of these theories can best inform their practice. Their options include blending attractive elements of each theory, choosing a theory with goals that match their own, examining the research evidence for the various approaches, or judging the approaches according to ethical and other guidelines provided by early childhood authorities.

### Eclecticism

When choosing a theory to guide one's practice, it might be tempting to select elements of all the theories to arrive at an eclectic blend. To be **eclectic** means to select the best practices from various theories (Corey, 1991). When the theories have contradictory underlying philosophies, however, their practices cannot be blended into a coherent whole (Porter, 1996). The theories of discipline introduced here differ in their goals and in the resulting status of adults versus children, making many of their practices incompatible with one another.

## Goals of the Theories

Rather than being eclectic, then, the practitioner might choose a theory that shares his or her discipline goals. The various theories of behavior management have different goals—one managerial and four educational goals. These goals are as follows:

1. To create order so that the group can function effectively: This allows adults to teach and children to learn and is the managerial goal of discipline (Doyle, 1986).

2. To teach children *self-discipline*: With support, children learn to take responsibility for their actions with the result that they can be trusted to make wise decisions about their behavior, whether they are being supervised or not (Glasser, 1986; Rogers, 1991).

3. To teach children to express their feelings appropriately, without getting themselves distressed and without upsetting the other people around them (Gartrell, 1994).

4. To teach children to cooperate with other people (Hill & Hill, 1990; Hill, Chapter 17 in this volume; Johnson & Johnson, 1991; Johnson, Johnson & Holubec, 1990).

5. To teach children to be responsible citizens. This requires children to have the confidence and integrity to make ethical choices and to exercise their social responsibilities as well as their rights (Gartrell, 1994; Ginott, 1972; Glasser, 1986, 1992; Gordon, 1970, 1974, 1991; Greenberg 1992a, 1992b; Knight, 1991; Porter, 1996, 1997; C. Rogers, 1951, 1978; Rogers & Freiberg, 1994). Although this is a long-term aim, it begins in early childhood when adults teach the moral principles behind children's decisions, and encourage children to empathize with other people.

The last four educational goals form the essence of *considerate behavior* (Porter, 1997). There are two parts to considerateness: First, that children learn to think in advance about the effect of their behavior on others, and, second, when children are told that their behavior is harming someone else, they can consider this information and adopt a more respectful course of action.

Table 19.2 summarizes the goals of each of the theories of behavior management. The democratic theories have a more comprehensive range of goals than do the authoritarian theories. This is clearly an advantage: Discipline must do more than foster order alone because order is necessary but not sufficient for learning to occur (Doyle, 1986). Instead, discipline has to be educational as well (Rodd & Holland, 1990). And it must reinforce the goals of the wider curriculum because, as McCaslin and Good (1992, p. 13) state, "We cannot expect that [children] will profit from the incongruous messages we send when we manage for obedience and teach for exploration and risk taking." As well as being educational in themselves, the democratic discipline methods are superior to authoritarian approaches because they foster the same skills during intervention with disruptive behavior—such as self-management, considerateness, problem solving, and communication skills—as are promoted by the wider curriculum.

A judgment about an approach must also consider whether, in addition to positive outcomes, the method produces any unwanted side-effects. On this criterion, the democratic approaches are preferable because they avoid the negative emotional side-effects of the rewards and punishments used by the authoritarian approaches. Under a democratic approach, the rights of the miscreant, victim, onlooking children, and adults are all protected by a response that does not blame or shame anyone (Ginott, 1972).

## Research Evidence

Another criterion that might inform the choice of a discipline theory is research evidence about the approaches. Berk (1997) reports that recent research confirms earlier findings by Baumrind and colleagues (for example, Baumrind, 1967)

**Table 19.2 Aims of Each Theory of Discipline**

| | |
|---|---|
| Applied behavior analysis | Compliance/order |
| Cognitive-behaviorism | Compliance/order |
| | Self-discipline |
| | Cooperation |
| Neo-Adlerian theory | Self-discipline |
| | Cooperation |
| Humanism | Self-discipline |
| Control (choice) theory | Emotional expression |
| | Cooperation |
| | Responsible citizenship |
| | Order |

that authoritative discipline produces children who are more self-controlled, self-confident, independent, and social, both in preschool and in later years. It is more likely that children will accept demands that are fair and reasonable, rather than arbitrary, and so they will voluntarily observe fair standards that are expected of them. In contrast, authoritarian discipline that demands compliance produces withdrawn, anxious, unhappy children who become hostile when frustrated and are unwilling to persist at tasks.

## Ethics

When assessing which theory best fits within an early childhood program, the issue of justice or ethics is fundamental. The National Association for the Education of Young Children's (1984) guidelines for quality child care offer some direction on ethics. These guidelines state that high quality staff-child interactions (both verbal and nonverbal) must be warm, convey respect, accept children's individuality, support their social learning, foster their autonomy, be responsive to their needs, and involve positive discipline methods that are based on realistic expectations of children. Although the guidelines do not specify what the term "positive discipline methods" means, the National Child Care Accreditation Council's code of ethical conduct (1989, p. 26) states what they do *not* mean, when it says that

caregivers, "will not participate in practices that are disrespectful, degrading . . . intimidating, psychologically damaging, or physically harmful to children."

## Conclusion: Criteria for Evaluating the Theories

The democratic approach meets the criteria of having comprehensive goals that are both educational in themselves and are congruent with the educational goals of the wider early childhood curriculum. At the same time, the democratic approach is nurturing, which is especially important with very young children (National Child Care Accreditation Council, 1993). Research verifies that the democratic or authoritative approach achieves its educational goals for children. The approach satisfies the quality and ethical guidelines for early childhood programs. Nevertheless, specific democratic disciplinary practices need to be enunciated for very young children and so, to that end, the next section describes how the democratic approach can be enacted for teaching considerate behavior during early childhood.

## TEACHING CHILDREN CONSIDERATE BEHAVIOR

Teaching considerate behavior begins with guiding children to manage their own behavior. Their occasional inconsiderate behavior is regarded as a developmental issue rather than a challenge to the adult's authority. From this perspective come methods to teach children the skills for behaving considerately, rather than punishing them when they cannot.

### Adult Status

Under the authoritarian discipline approach, the adult acts as the boss who has power over children and so imposes rules on them. In contrast, the democratic adult acts as an authoritative leader who guides children to behave considerately. At the same time, the leader takes responsibility for him-self and will speak up when his rights—or the rights of a child in his care—are being infringed.

## A Developmental View of Behavior

The democratic or authoritative adult realizes that learning to behave considerately is a developmental task like any other—although it is far more complex than any other skill that children will learn. Just as children need to learn how to walk, so too they need to learn how to be considerate. When a behavior is disruptive, instead of viewing it as "naughty" or "misbehavior," the democratic adult regards it as developmentally normal for children to lack mature skills and sets about teaching them the required skill.

## Response to Considerate Behavior

The democratic or authoritative adult accepts and acknowledges considerate behavior, using encouragement rather than praise. Instead of praising or rewarding a child for using his manners, the democratic adult might employ a natural positive consequence—such as saying, "You're welcome" when a child has thanked her for something.

## Response to Inconsiderate Behavior

*Prevention.* The democratic adult aims to prevent most instances of disruptive behavior by providing a program that meets children's learning, emotional, and social needs.

*Change the Demands.* The democratic adult will listen to what a child's disruptive behavior is telling her about the child's needs. She might be willing to change what she expects of the child, instead of forcing him to comply with expectations with which he clearly cannot cope.

*Assertiveness.* The authoritative adult is honest when a child's behavior is having a negative effect. She is not aggressive nor blaming of the miscreant, but neither does she force herself to be patient with inconsiderate behavior because tolerating it would teach the child that he can

behave inconsiderately with impunity and would allow the behavior to continue to harm its victims. She asserts her own needs and the needs of other children in her care.

*Collaborative Problem Solving.* The democratic adult offers the child choices about his behavior and might negotiate—using a collaborative problem solving approach—to find ways that the child can meet his needs without violating the needs of other people.

*Flexibility.* Adults who believe in controlling children are inflexible about their discipline so that they are not seen to have "lost" a power battle with a child. Instead of changing a discipline approach that is not working, they attempt to apply it more rigidly or "consistently." In comparison, the adult using an authoritative or democratic approach is concerned not with winning or losing but with meeting everyone's needs. Therefore, she is willing to change her mind about her response to a child's inappropriate behavior—as long as doing so does not violate her own rights.

*Teach Prosocial Skills.* Disruptive behavior usually results from young children's natural skill deficits. The authoritarian approach to such behavior is to punish a child, which amounts to punishing him for *being* a child. Instead, the democratic adult responds by teaching the child the appropriate skill to use and explaining how that skill will benefit him or other people.

*Teach Emotional Self-Control.* Around the age of two years, children begin to display more mature social behavior. But—and this is the reason for the "terrible twos" label—their behavior fluctuates considerably (Stonehouse, 1988). They can show very capable behavior one minute and very disorganized behavior the next. They tire easily and can cope less well than older children with being hungry, overstimulated, or unwell. The result is that, even when they know what to do, they cannot do it. Their feelings get out of control and their behavior becomes "disorganized." For example, they might not use words to ask a playmate for a toy, but will snatch it because they want it *now.* This is perfectly normal given that, as babies, they needed to act on every feeling so that they

**Table 19.3  Summary of Controlling versus Democratic Discipline Skills**

| Discipline style | Control | Democracy/Guidance |
|---|---|---|
| **Goals** | Order<br>Compliance | Consideration<br>• Self-discipline<br>• Handling feelings<br>• Cooperation with others<br>• Responsible citizenship |
| **Adult's status** | Boss | Leader |
| **View of behavior** | Naughty | Developmental |
| **Response to considerate behavior** | Praise<br>Rewards | Encouragement<br>Natural consequences |
| **Response to inconsiderate behavior** | Intervention<br>Change the child<br>Aggression<br>Patient<br>Impose a solution<br>Inflexible<br>Punishment | Prevention<br>Change the demands<br>Assertiveness<br>Honest<br>Find a solution collaboratively<br>Responsive to circumstances<br>Natural consequences<br>Teach mature skills<br>Teach emotional self-control |

could receive the care they needed to survive and given that they have so recently learned how to talk: No one can use new skills when under stress.

When a child is overwhelmed, again the democratic adult would not punish the child for a natural childhood state but instead would help her to calm down—perhaps by giving her some time away to regain control by herself if she enjoys solitude, by cuddling her until she is calm again if she responds to adult comfort, or by showing her how to breathe deeply and relax before returning to a demanding situation (Porter, 1997). These nurturing methods are not used in the authoritarian approach because they appear to give the child attention for inappropriate behavior; under the democratic approach, the aim is to teach the child how to manage her feelings, so that she can return to considerate behavior.

## CONCLUSION

Discipline will only ever safeguard individual children from abuse and protect society from the behavioral excesses of its members when individuals can accept responsibility for themselves and can satisfy their own needs without violating the needs of other people (Gordon, 1991). In the preschool years, the goal of discipline, then, is to give children the confidence to take increasing responsibility for their own actions and for their effect on other people. To achieve this, adults guide rather than control children.

The two approaches to discipline are compared in Table 19.3. As already described here, the fundamental difference between them is their goals, which in turn dictate the amount of power granted to adults and children. The two approaches might appear to use very similar methods: A natural positive consequence can involve virtually the same action as a reward. Nevertheless, the difference is one of flavor or style, of how the adult conveys respect for children. And children *can* detect the difference between the guidance and controlling approaches. They can read adults' nonverbal behavior and will respond very differently to the two approaches.

# EVALUATING YOUR MASTERY

1. Discipline that relies heavily on external reinforcement
   a. Promotes generally good behavior—even responses that have not been reinforced
   b. Has been criticized for being imprecise
   c. Promotes creativity
   d. Risks violating the child's autonomy

2. Which theory of discipline emphasizes cognitive training?
   a. Applied behavior analysis (ABA)
   b. Cognitive-behaviorism
   c. Neo-Adlerian theory
   d. Humanism

3. Which of the following is a strength of *encouragement,* a unique contribution of neo-Adlerian theory?
   a. It provides a judgment of the child and his or her work.
   b. It approves of work that meets adult standards.
   c. It comments on the child's effort rather than end product.
   d. It is a public event that compares children to others.

4. _____ theories advocate collaborative problem solving, which makes use of _____ and _____ skills.
   a. Neo-Adlerian; encouragement; reinforcement
   b. Behaviorist; time out; logical consequences
   c. Democratic; listening; assertiveness
   d. Cognitive-behaviorist; metacognitive planning; inductive

5. True or False: A weakness of neo-Adlerian theory is its assumption that how an adult feels about the child's behavior is a reliable indicator of the child's motivation.

6. True or False: A weakness of democratic theory is that it rejects all forms of punishment.

7. True or False: Democratic theories have a more comprehensive range of goals than do authoritarian theories.

## Critical Thinking

1. What does Porter mean by a disciplinary approach that fosters *considerate behavior?* Which theory of discipline stresses considerateness? Explain.

2. List four criteria for evaluating theories of discipline. Which ones do you prefer, and why?

## Applying Your Knowledge

Using Porter's criteria for evaluating theories of discipline, describe and justify your own theory of discipline.

# 20

# Becoming Bicultural

## An Australian Perspective*

### ANNE GLOVER

### University of the South Pacific

■

In any culturally diverse society, children who do not belong to the dominant
cultural group have a special task to undertake—they must learn to function
effectively in two distinct cultural environments.

■

More recent writing ... emphasizes the way individuals interrelate with two distinct
cultures—the premise being that people do not step in and out of cultures, shedding
one as they enter the other; rather, they continually negotiate the two.

■

Often in early childhood education we try to avoid the very tensions that will help
us learn more about the lives of families and that can prevent us from putting
children in situations of conflict.

■

The factors that influence the process of biculturalism are not easily isolated because
it is a dynamic and complex process with many variables.

---

* The examples in this discussion are drawn mostly from Australian Aboriginal communities. Becoming
bicultural, however, is not a process exclusive to Aboriginal communities—all bicultural communities in
Australia and other multicultural nations face the daily struggle of living in two or more distinct cultural
worlds where values are very often in direct conflict.

■

Searching out and providing translators—individuals from the child's primary
culture who have undergone the process of dual socialization with success ... is
another important strategy.

■

We must seek to establish genuine relationships with all families. As relationships are
built, teachers and parents will learn from each other.

■

### EDITOR'S INTRODUCTION

In this essay, Anne Glover describes the challenges that indigenous minorities—
in particular, Aboriginal peoples—face in rearing young children in Australia.
Discontinuities between the culture of the home and the practices of the school
often create distance rather than build bridges between the minority group and
the majority culture. Glover illustrates by describing Aboriginal parenting values
and behaviors, indicating how their cultural roots and adaptive functions are
often misunderstood by mainstream Australians. Her analysis reveals that misunderstandings of Aboriginal culture often create barriers to effective communication and impede the development of biculturalism—minority children's hope of
sustaining their cultural ties and adapting successfully to mainstream society.
Glover concludes with a variety of suggestions for building bridges between minority homes and early childhood programs. Her message is relevant to individuals everywhere who seek to understand and work with ethnic minority
children and families.

Early childhood educators have long recognized the importance of addressing issues of culture, ethnicity, and race in programs for young children. In our increasingly diverse nations, educators implement various programs to address the linguistic and cultural diversity found in their communities. Some programs focus on the particular needs of ethnic-minority children; others provide a multicultural perspective for all children. In some programs culture is defined broadly and includes many aspects of human difference—culture, ethnicity, gender, class, age, physical and mental ability, and sexual orientation. In others, culture is simply defined as ethnicity and language. Some programs address cultural diversity by actively teaching children to recognize and challenge cultural and racial stereotypes, whereas still others seek to teach children about cultural groups that are outside their daily experience (Glover, 1994).

Each program represents a different response to cultural diversity. The type of program we construct depends on many factors, including how we view early childhood education (what we believe its purpose to be), our understanding of culture and of the link between culture and education, and our beliefs about, and visions for, a fair and just society.

In communities where two or more cultural groups coexist, most programs include some focus on the needs of children who do not belong to the dominant cultural group. Programs usually aim to help children fit into existing social structures by building on their skills, knowledge, and cultural heritage (Sleeter & Grant, 1988). The degree of emphasis given to biculturalism in any program depends on the number of bicultural children represented—the more children, the more emphasis, whereas the selection of teaching and care-giving strategies depends significantly on our understanding of biculturalism (what we understand about the process of becoming bicultural), and on the resources available.

Early childhood is a critical time for the development of group-referenced identities, beliefs about human difference, and interpersonal skills (Beale Spencer & Markstrom-Adams, 1990; Ramsey, 1987). If we are to respond effectively to linguistic and cultural diversity, as we are now being challenged to do (for example, Neuman & Roskos, 1994; NAEYC, 1996), it is timely to consider what becoming bicultural means to the young children in our care.

## LIVING IN TWO WORLDS

In any culturally diverse society, children who do not belong to the dominant cultural group have a special task to undertake—they must learn to function effectively in two distinct cultural environments. That is, they must become **bicultural** (Glover, 1994). In Australia, where the population comprises people representing more than 140 ethnic groups and speaking approximately 150 different languages (including more than 40 Aboriginal languages), becoming bicultural would obviously be advantageous for all children, though not essential for children who are members of the dominant culture. For indigenous Australian children and children of cultural minorities however, there is very little choice. Unless they are to become (or remain) marginalized citizens in their own country, they must learn to function within their primary (home) culture, while learning to function in the institutions of the dominant culture.

For young children, becoming bicultural is the process of learning to live in two worlds. It is a process that usually involves learning two (or more) sets of communication symbols and styles, cognitive orientations, values, behavioral repertoires, and rituals.

All cultures share some activities, including communication, role differentiation and assignment, regulation and socialization (Berry, Poortinga, Segall, & Dasen, 1992). Each activity can be found in every culture, but how each is manifested varies greatly. If young children are to function effectively in two cultures, they must learn, to some degree, the manifestations of each activity in both cultures. This includes learning two distinct ways of behaving—one for time spent in their home culture, the other for time spent outside. Children need to learn, for example, how boys and girls are expected to behave, how adults are addressed and how conflict is handled in each setting. In becoming bicultural, children are therefore engaged in a dual process of enculturation/socialization within their home culture, and acculturation/resocialization as they come into contact with the dominant culture (Berry, et al., 1992).

Although relatively little has been written in early childhood texts about this dual process, the concept of duality for culture, race, and ethnicity has been gaining increasing attention throughout the twentieth century. First documented in 1903 by the African-American W. E. B. du Bois, who described it as "double consciousness" (du Bois, 1903), it has since been described as double vision (Wright, 1953), multidimensional (Cross, 1978), bicultural (Banks, 1988; de Anda, 1984; Ramirez and Castaneda, 1974; Rashid, 1981) and two-way (Harris, 1990).

Ninety years after du Bois presented his idea of a double consciousness, Aboriginal mothers and grandmothers in rural South Australian communities spoke of the same phenomenon. They referred to it as "living in two worlds" (Glover, 1993). The ability to function effectively in both Aboriginal and non-Aboriginal environments is one of, if not the most important developmental task Aboriginal mothers want their children to accomplish (Glover, 1993). Parents' desire for their children to become bicultural is so great that it allows them to send their children, some as young as three and a half, into early childhood centers created, structured, and staffed by non-Aboriginal teachers. Asked why they would place children in centers where Aboriginality is often ignored, trivialized, or stereotyped, mothers spoke of children needing to "learn the ways of the whitefella." Many mothers expressed concern, but saw no alternative—children would learn Aboriginal ways at home, but where else would they learn the ways of the dominant cul-

ture, learning so necessary for future school/life achievement and success? Parents recognized that despite Australia's diversity, schools and other social institutions have remained largely monocultural and Anglo-centric.

Referring to the similar situation of African-American children, Rashid (1981) argued that biculturalism is an essential developmental process. According to Rashid, unless children have the ability to function effectively and productively within the context of America's core institutions while maintaining ethnic identity they will not be able to cope with the challenges of living in contemporary American society.

Rashid (1981) concluded that all children should become bicultural, that is, all children should develop at least two behavioral repertoires. In doing so, children would learn to survive and thrive in at least one other culture, which Rashid believed would provide a foundation for a truly multicultural society. Banks (1988, 1993) also posited the notion of biculturalism for all children. He sees, as ideal, individuals having a balance of ethnic, national, and global identifications, commitments, literacy, and behaviors. Banks (1993) suggests that an individual becomes bicultural when he or she moves from a position of ethnocentrism and separatism to having the attitudes, skills, and commitment to participate both within his or her ethnic or cultural group and within another ethnic or cultural group.

## BECOMING BICULTURAL

Increasing numbers of very young children are being required to make the transition from home to social institutions. For children who do not belong to the dominant cultural group, the adaptation to a new set of "rules, values, expectations and behaviors" (NAEYC, 1996) is beginning earlier than ever before. The theory of biculturalism offers early childhood educators a way of thinking about how children adapt to and match their two environments.

Most writing about biculturalism suggests that it involves individuals stepping in and out of two very different settings. More recent writing, however, emphasizes the way individuals interrelate with two distinct cultures—the premise being that people do not step in and out of cultures, shedding one as they enter the other; rather, they continually negotiate the two. Some of the most radical writing about this interrelationship and its implication for educators is that of Antonia Darder (1991). Darder suggests that biculturalism—the process of becoming bicultural, is essentially a process of mediation. According to Darder, bicultural individuals are constantly negotiating two distinct sociocultural environments, one of which is the dominant mainstream culture. Darder's work has much to offer Australian early childhood educators, particularly as she addresses the issue of unequal power relationships between cultures and describes how this affects the process of biculturalism.

Darder does not see bicultural development as a linear process with a defined endpoint. Individuals do not reach a point of having become bicultural. Rather, Darder (1991) writes of the "biculturalism process" (p. 54) as the process by which children (and adults) mediate between the dominant discourse and the realities of living in a subordinate culture. She likens it to movement backward and forward along a cultural continuum. At one end of the continuum is the individual's primary culture; at the other end sits the dominant culture. Individuals respond to the two cultures in varying ways at various times. Responses depend on many factors, but are always significantly influenced by the unequal distribution of power within culturally diverse societies.

## CULTURE AND POWER

Central to Darder's theory of biculturalism is the issue of power, in particular the unequal power relationship between the dominant and the nondominant cultures. Reviewing traditional definitions of culture, Darder (1991) concludes that

there is an "obvious absence of specific reference to the issue of power and its relationship to the nature in which cultural relationships are structured and perpetuated within and between groups" (p.26). Darder draws heavily on Giroux's (1981, 1983, 1985, 1988) critical connection between power and culture and his notion that the range of relationships developed among social groups is generally determined by the nature of social structures and material conditions that arise from unequal power relationships. Darder (1991) extends Giroux's notion suggesting that biculturalism is a struggle to function in institutions that have been created by, and primarily serve members of the dominant culture. She emphasizes the invasiveness of the dominant culture, whose members dictate to others what is right and proper; who decide the norms by which all will be judged; and whose lifestyles, values, and expectations are seen as the legitimate ones.

In Australia, this invasiveness should not be underestimated by educators. For Aboriginal groups in particular, it has had, and continues to have devastating effects. Dispossessed of their land and relocated on reserves and missions where, legally, all were wards of the State and permission was necessary to come and go, Aboriginal groups became powerless and alienated in their own land. State intrusions into Aboriginal family life systematically undermined the roles of Aboriginal parents (Hunter, 1996) and, under the policy of assimilation that existed in some states until the late 1960s, possibly as many as 30,000 children were taken from their families—sent to government institutions or fostered out to Anglo-Australian families. Two well-known and widely respected Aboriginal educators describe the effects:

Colonisation took away the land and changed the roles of Aboriginal men and women. New laws, values and beliefs were introduced and enforced. Self-reliance and self-esteem were destroyed as Aboriginal society disintegrated and traditional family life was no longer viable. The introduced diseases, alcohol, the abuse of women and the debasement of men left family life in tatters.....The imposition of Christian values and the deliberate removal of children from their parents ensured that Aboriginal families would never again be what they were. (Bourke and Bourke, 1995, p. 59)

Although most discriminatory laws have now been abolished, the legacies of the original invasion, of colonization and dispossession, remain. Thousands of Aboriginal Australians are not housed adequately; have no access to appropriate health services—services that take into account Aboriginal cultural beliefs and practices; and suffer racism as part of their daily lives (HREOC, 1991; Royal Commission into Aboriginal Deaths in Custody, 1991). Aboriginal youths are over-represented at every level of the juvenile justice system (Gale, Bailey-Harris & Wundersitz, 1990), and communities face "the problematic use of alcohol, self-destructive behavior and interpersonal violence" (Royal Commission into Aboriginal Deaths in Custody, 1991, p. 2). The echoes of invasion "reverberate through succeeding generations" (Hunter, 1996, p. 17).

Today, invasions are more subtle and usually less deliberate. Whereas, for example, Aboriginal children are no longer forcibly removed from their homes, and schools have policies stating that cultural diversity will be accepted and appreciated, most teachers are from the dominant group, are trained in institutions that promote Anglo-Australian values, beliefs, and practices, and thus (unintentionally) create classrooms in which children must leave their Aboriginality at the door. As a result, the majority of Aboriginal school children and their families feel alienated by, and marginalized from, the Anglo-Australian dominated school system that, in the main, fails to recognize how its cultural assumptions contribute significantly to the situation. Many immigrant families express similar feelings of marginalization as they struggle to create new lives in Australia.

In early childhood education, invasions occur when educators suggest that there is only one right way to behave—when directly and indirectly we give children messages that there is a right and proper way to hold a baby, eat a snack or interact with others. They occur when we silence or diminish the languages that children bring to our centers, when we make Aboriginal English a source of shame rather than raising it to a place of dignity, and when we stop (or don't encourage) children conversing together in their primary language as part of the classroom experience (Darder, 1991). Invasions occur too, when we assume that certain beliefs and practices, particularly those associated with child rearing, are common and shared. Child rearing varies markedly across cultures; when we don't recognize and accommodate this in our interactions with children and parents, we override the practices of many families. In Aboriginal families, for instance, parents usually encourage children from a very early age to be self-regulating and self-reliant (Malin, Campbell, & Agius, 1996). Thus they encourage children to rely on their own observations to learn new things, to seek help from siblings and peers rather than adults, and to resolve their own disputes. This is in contrast with the majority of Anglo-Australian families where parents invest considerable time in monitoring children's behavior, and children are encouraged to ask questions of parents and seek parental attention and assistance.

When we forget to seek and listen to parents' views and when our teaching practices, including how and why we discipline children, are not open to debate and challenge, our practice is culturally invasive. Among the many differences between Aboriginal and Anglo-Australian child-rearing is how children are disciplined. In some Aboriginal families, for instance, teasing and scaring are used to control children in situations that parents feel are dangerous or inappropriate. Fearful creatures such as mamu (a harmful spirit being) are summoned to frighten children into behaving appropriately. Alternatively, it is common practice in early childhood centers to use time-out (removal from the group) or various forms of deprivation (for example, not being allowed to join in an activity) to coerce children into approved behavior. Rather than viewing each other's strategies negatively, parents and teachers need to discuss and debate them and learn how each is consistent with the encouragement of carefully selected goals for young children.

Often in early childhood education we try to avoid the very tensions that will help us learn more about the lives of families and that can prevent us from putting children in situations of conflict. If parents disagree with our practice we get defensive; if they request something out-of-the-ordinary we resist; if they don't conform to our expectations, we get frustrated. When parents ask for their male children to be served first at snack-time; request that their children not play with the water; dress their young daughters in long, feminine dresses we think inappropriate for outdoor play; or tell their children that they must use titles to address us, we can either take the time to find out what each means to families, or we can dismiss and override parent's requests and actions, thus maintaining the unequal power relationships with which they are constantly struggling. That many Aboriginal parents, as part of their nurturance of independence, are hesitant to intervene in conflicts between children; are reluctant to respond to children's whining, complaining, or seeking of attention; and are accepting of children's reprimanding, contradiction and attempts to rationalize to adults (Malin et al, 1996), can easily be dismissed by early childhood educators as poor parenting. If we take the time to talk with parents and learn of their goal of early independence for their children, we might find ways to work together to ensure that this goal is met and that the children thrive in our joint care.

Recognition of the impact of past and current invasions; acknowledgment of contemporary race relations; and acceptance of culture as embracing power relationships, tensions, and struggles, are essential if early childhood programs are to honor the bicultural realities of Australian children and families and help affirm children's biculturalism.

## INDIVIDUAL RESPONSES

Groups and individuals vary in their participation and response to living in plural societies. Responses can be categorized according to how individuals relate to and interrelate with the dominant group. Given the nature of cultural domination and resistance, Darder (1991), proposes four major response patterns within the bicultural process, which she categorizes as alienation, dualism, separatism, and negotiation. According to Darder, these reflect varying degrees of acceptance and rejection of both the primary and dominant cultures, and are shaped by the individual's accommodation of cultural conflicts, contradictions and tensions. Cultural alienation is an internalized identification with the dominant culture and a rejection of the primary culture; cultural dualism is the perception of having two separate identities; cultural separatism is the rejection of the dominant culture and an attempt to remain within the boundaries of the primary culture; and cultural negotiation is the attempt to mediate the primary and dominant culture.

In indigenous and culturally diverse communities each response pattern exists. Some people reject their primary culture, others embrace it wholeheartedly. Faced with possible discrimination, hostility, and even violence, some adults of Anglo-Aboriginal ancestry have taken the extreme step of denying their Aboriginal heritage, an example of the strongest rejection of one's primary culture. Conversely, others, some of whom were taken from their families as children and encouraged to conceal their Aboriginality, now deny their Anglo-Australian heritage, return to live in homelands, reject Anglo-Australian values and definitions, and take on traditional names.

Recognizing individual and group responses to biculturalism and the factors that shape responses can assist us in understanding behaviors we find baffling—behaviors such as parents wanting their children to speak only English; children wanting to be called by the Anglicized version of their names and refusing to sing songs in their home language; and grandparents wanting

These Australian Aboriginal preschoolers sample native foods at their child-care center. Affirming minority children's family backgrounds tells them that their culture is just as valid as the dominant culture. As a result, they are more likely to respond positively to biculturalism. (Photo: Laura Berk)

ethno-specific programs for their grandchildren. Using Darder's categories, we can see that each behavior reflects a person's response to the bicultural process, at a particular time in his or her life.

Response patterns are not fixed. Children and adults will display many different variations of responses depending on their primary cultural socialization; geographic location; the number of, and their association with, other bicultural children and adults; families' socioeconomic levels; and teachers' responses (Darder, 1991). Different situations evoke different responses. When, for instance, the tensions and contradictions that result from cultural negotiation become too great, individuals often move to cultural alienation. In doing so, they outwardly reject their home culture and identify only with the dominant culture. Terry Ngarritjan-Kessaris, an Aboriginal writer recollecting her school experiences, describes it thus:

> Not once during my twelve years of
> formal schooling did any of my teachers or

anyone else in the school system, affirm my Aboriginality. Instead I grew up feeling ashamed of my Aboriginal heritage and I felt pressured to stress that I was only "part Aboriginal." (Ngarritjan-Kessaris, 1995, p. 1)

Early childhood educators who affirm each child's primary culture through support and promotion of language—by, for example, having parents introduce home languages in stories and songs; using culturally diverse teaching materials; providing opportunities for children to use the knowledge and skills they bring when they enter programs; and the encouragement of families in all aspects of the program (including decision-making)—will help children respond positively to biculturalism. Children will not see their home culture as inferior or irrelevant and will not be forced, albeit subtly, to make cultural choices about which way of being in the world is right and proper.

Teaching materials that present children with diverse cultural images, for example, suggest to children that all cultures, not just the dominant one, are important and valued. Children see that there are many ways to be in the world—many ways to look, foods to eat, clothes to wear, languages to speak, and so forth. They will see manifestations of their home culture, affirming its legitimacy in the center and the world outside of home. Teaching materials, including books, posters, dolls, and dramatic play adjuncts, which reflect only the dominant culture, give children very strong messages about the importance or superiority of the dominant group; similarly, when home cultures are not represented, or are represented tokenistically, stereotypically, or in ways that suggest low status, children gradually become aware that they are less valued. Lack of representation of Aboriginal families in the teaching materials used during her school days caused Ngarritjan-Kessaris to see her family as "abnormal":

> . . . I considered that I came from a crazy, mixed up family that did things upside down and back to front. For instance, for almost the first seven years of our lives my sister Robyn and I lived with my grandmother. Mum and Nana shared our upbringing and Nana was considered to be "Boss" for us. This was a mutual arrangement. It was difficult to explain to White people that I had two sets of parents and that my grandmother had more authority for me than my mother. The books at school only showed nuclear families who visited the grandparents for short periods . . . (we) did not seem to fit a "normal" Australian situation. Somehow we were a little abnormal ... I learnt early from school that we were doing many things "wrong." (Ngarritjan-Kessaris, 1995, p. 2–3)

Children will not respond positively toward biculturalism in environments that require or support cultural homogeneity. Rather, they will be thrust into "state(s) of confusion and anxiety" (Ngarritjan-Kessaris, 1995, p. 5), and will find cultural negotiation an almost impossible task.

## FACTORS AFFECTING BICULTURALISM

The factors that influence the process of biculturalism are not easily isolated because it is a dynamic and complex process with many variables. However, there is general agreement among writers (for example, de Anda, 1984; Ramirez & Castenada, 1974; Rashid, 1981) that the degree of similarity between the two cultures is significant. de Anda (1984) argues that the more similarity or overlap there is between two cultures, the more effective the bicultural process.

She cites the following six factors as influencing the level of biculturalism achieved by an individual:

- The degree of overlap or commonality between the two cultures with regard to norms, values, beliefs, perceptions, and the like
- The availability of cultural translators, mediators, and models
- The amount and type (positive or negative) of corrective feedback provided by each culture
- The conceptual style and problem-solving approach of the minority individual and its mesh with the prevalent or valued styles of the majority culture
- The individual's degree of bilingualism
- The degree of dissimilarity in physical appearance from the majority culture, such as skin color, facial features, and so forth

de Anda's work provides a useful framework for early childhood educators to determine strategies for working with culturally diverse families. That the degree of commonality is a significant factor suggests that exploring areas of both similarity and difference is an important part of our work. Hence, two effective strategies for assisting biculturalism to thrive in early childhood programs are (1) determining those areas of interface between the two cultures that can serve as "doorways," and (2) identifying major points of conflict between cultures. In early childhood programs, a doorway for parents and teachers is the child, specifically a shared concern for children's growth and development, their safety, and their happiness. The degree to which children are expected to obey adults, to take on responsibility and nurturing roles, and to become self-reliant and independent can vary considerably, but an overriding and shared commitment to children provides a meeting place for talking together and for acknowledging common goals and interests.

When points of conflict are identified, they can form the basis of reciprocal learning, rather than being the things that divide teachers and families. In child care some of these points of conflict have been identified as differing attitudes to authority, to possession, to children's separation from parents (when and how this should be done), to routines, including eating and sleeping, and to discipline. Many Aboriginal parents, for example, have significantly different views from non-Aboriginal teachers about obedience, responsibility, nurturance, and independence. The degree to which young Aboriginal children are trained to obey adults is one source of potential conflict for teachers and children, particularly because most teachers require a much higher degree of obedience than do the children's parents (Malin, 1990). Another potential source of conflict arises when Aboriginal children, who are trained to care for their younger siblings, are separated from siblings in programs that group children by age; the older children are thus unable to fulfill their nurturing responsibilities.

Unless we take the time to discover potential points of conflict, we risk putting children in positions of great discomfort and tension, as happens to many Aboriginal children when they begin school.

> The pressure applied to the individual in school by the two often opposing cultures can be immense and requires constant negotiation between the two sets of demands. This can be very tiring and the rewards are not always attainable or satisfying. As a child

I saw the problem as mine, as some inadequacy in my family.... (Ngarritjan-Kessaris, 1995 p. 5.)

Searching out and providing translators (individuals from the child's primary culture who have undergone the process of dual socialization with success), mediators (individuals from the majority culture who serve as guides and providers of information), and models is another important strategy. Colbung and Glover (1996) highlight the importance of exposing Aboriginal children to positive role-models who "show children that they do not have to sacrifice their Aboriginality in order to succeed in mainstream institutions like schools" (p. 38). Ngarritjan-Kessaris (1995) talks of the need for translators, people like herself, who can " say to these kids something that I wished someone had said to me while I was at school; that it was okay to be Aboriginal" (p. 1).

## THE ROLE OF THE EARLY CHILDHOOD EDUCATOR

For more than a decade, there have been calls for culturally responsive approaches to early childhood education. We are urged to provide programs that "affirm children's cultural identity and help develop their understanding and appreciation of other cultures" (Rodd, 1996, p. 327). Yet very little is written about biculturalism and even less is written about what it means for teachers of young children. Perhaps the best starting point for us as teachers is to examine our own skills, knowledge, and attitudes. We can begin by asking this: What do we know about biculturalism, and what must we be able to do to help children become effectively bicultural?

The work of Darder (1991), de Anda (1984) and others suggests the importance of teachers being able to conceptualize the process of becoming bicultural, of acknowledging individual responses to biculturalism, and of recognizing the factors that affect people's responses to the process. Without any personal experience of bi-culturalism, understanding such a complex and dynamic process is difficult, but not impossible. We begin by listening to the stories of others and, in doing so, show our preparedness to be both teachers and learners.

As we hear the stories of bicultural families, our understanding of the process grows. Recently, Lorraine Peeters, an Aboriginal grandmother who was taken away from her family as a child, wrote, "people think the suffering stops with me. But I have passed these feelings on to my children not realising what I was doing" (Peeters, 1995, p. 16). We can learn much from grandmothers like Lorraine, who are willing to share their stories with us, if we are willing to listen.

We need also to try and understand the role of culture in the formation of our own values, beliefs, problem-solving orientation, and patterns of behavior and accept that there are other cultural orientations as legitimate as our own.

Different ways of doing things then become the starting point for talking with parents and other family members, rather than being dismissed or negated. As we talk with parents, we begin to understand how life is for children at home and find ways to help children negotiate life at home and life in the center.

If we belong to the dominant cultural group, we must be willing to acknowledge the unequal power relationships that exist between cultures, and find ways, at least in our centers, of redistributing and sharing the power. We can actively encourage bicultural families to join the center's decision-making groups and create opportunities for discussing our goals and aspirations. We can argue for staff teams to reflect racial and cultural diversity and, if we are in employing positions, actively seek bicultural employees.

We must be able to handle resistance, defensiveness, and frustration (both our own and others), and be open to other possibilities, other ways of being and doing. In doing so, we acknowledge that many trails lead up the mountain.

We must seek to establish genuine relationships with all families. As relationships are built, teachers and parents will learn from each other. Our readiness to talk with parents and other family members, will demonstrate our respect for, and genuine desire to understand children's home socialization, and the goals and expectations families have for their children. When, for example, Aboriginal parents ask that their children not be separated by age but be allowed to remain in family groupings, we are much more likely to consider the request if we know that nurturant acts between siblings are given a high priority in most Aboriginal families who value affiliation more than they value individualism. At the same time, if we are unable to meet parents' requests, we can share our reasons with parents and children. How different too, might be our reaction to teasing, if we have listened to parents and understand that gentle teasing is a traditional method of social control in many Aboriginal communities.

Above all, we must support the parent-child relationship. Many parents, though acknowledging the importance of education, harbor fears that they might lose their children forever through formal education (Darder, 1991). Aboriginal parents have expressed fears that early childhood programs might be just another form of taking the children away (Glover, 1993). They are concerned that long periods of time spent in Anglo-dominated centers can encourage children to feel ashamed of their primary culture and encourage an alienation response to biculturalism. Can we confidently reassure parents that this will not happen in our centers? Can we say with confidence that our practice will support children's cultural negotiation of their two very different worlds?

Australian early childhood educators have a strong tradition of fostering respect for diversity and of addressing prejudice, discrimination, and issues of equity. With increasing numbers of our children coming from linguistically and culturally diverse backgrounds, the challenge for us now is to ensure that children are well anchored in all their worlds. Understanding the process of biculturalism, and making a commitment to assist young children in becoming effectively bicultural will help us to meet this challenge.

## EVALUATING YOUR MASTERY

1. W. E. B. du Bois, who first documented biculturalism in 1903, described it as
   a.   Open-mindedness
   b.   Assimilation
   c.   Double consciousness
   d.   Integration

2. Aboriginal mothers
   a.   Have resisted biculturalism for their children
   b.   Believe biculturalism is one of the most important developmental tasks
   c.   Want the ways of the dominant culture to dominate those of Aboriginal culture
   d.   Have been relatively unconcerned about matters of cultural transmission

3. Recent writing emphasizes that biculturalism involves
   a.   Stepping in and out of two different cultures
   b.   Giving up one culture in favor of another
   c.   Interrelating two distinct cultures
   d.   Learning about both cultures and consciously choosing one

4. In Aboriginal families, parents usually encourage children from an early age to be
   a.   Self-regulating and self-reliant
   b.   Quiet and reserved
   c.   Exploratory and persistent
   d.   Passive and dependent

5. Alice, an early childhood teacher, was amazed when an Aboriginal parent requested that she serve her son before her daughter at snack and lunch time. Alice should
   a.   Tell the parent that the practice is sexist and inappropriate
   b.   Ignore the parent and serve both children at the same time
   c.   Ask the parent to explain the meaning and importance of the practice
   d.   Go along with the parent's wishes, but teach the children the correct practice of serving females before males

6. An ethnic minority parent wants her 4-year-old daughter to speak only English. Which of the following of Darder's four response patterns does this desire reflect?
   a.   Cultural alienation
   b.   Cultural dualism
   c.   Cultural separatism
   d.   Cultural negotiation

7. True or False: A major obstacle to biculturalism is unequal power relationships between the dominant and nondominant cultures.

8. When tensions and contradictions between cultures become very great, ethnic minority people often resort to
   a.  Cultural alienation
   b.  Cultural dualism
   c.  Cultural separatism
   d.  Cultural negotiation

## Critical Thinking

How can parent involvement be used as a powerful instrument of biculturalism in early childhood programs and schools? Cite several examples.

## Applying Your Knowledge

1. It is often possible to tell whether an early childhood program fosters biculturalism by looking at its physical setting. What would you expect to see on the walls and among play materials and equipment in such an environment?

2. Design an experience for young children that exposes them to positive role models as a way of promoting biculturalism. Why are such experiences important?

# 21

## The Importance of Parent Participation in Child Protection Curricula

FREDA BRIGGS with RUSSELL M. F. HAWKINS

University of South Australia

■

Although child protection curricula have been available for almost two decades, designers have virtually ignored the importance of parent participation.

■

Program designers had little professional knowledge of the norms of child development, children's thought processes, their beliefs relating to safety issues, their language, or their capacity to understand the complex adult concepts incorporated in the new curriculum.

■

One weakness of the empowerment model is that it takes little account of the reality that children are only empowered when adults permit it.

■

In sum, the *Touch Continuum* gave children permission to reject unwanted touching, but there was a dangerous, unstated assumption that "if it feels good, it must be okay."

■

Important differences were found between parents who had involved themselves in the protection programs versus others who had relied on the schools and had not been directly involved.

■

Children will not take risks associated with reporting unless they already know with certainty, from past experience, that they will be supported and not blamed.

■

Parents promote family secrecy without understanding the dangers involved.

■

Parents also said that even at 12 years of age, children were "too young to understand," and parents were afraid that they might cause their children to be "unnecessarily" fearful or distrusting.

■

Children gain most when parents become involved in child protection programs when their children are young.

■

To gain maximum benefit from their child protection initiatives, schools and communities should use every available resource to convince parents of their importance in program reinforcement.

■

## EDITOR'S INTRODUCTION

Freda Briggs and Russell Hawkins address the need for parent involvement in preschool- and school-based child-protection programs aimed at preventing child sexual abuse. They note that the pressing need for child protection curricula in the 1970s and 1980s meant that programs proliferated without sound knowledge of child development or evidence to document their effectiveness. Briggs and Hawkins critically review program models and examine new evidence, mobilizing a powerful argument for parent participation. Capitalizing on the emergence of different approaches to child protection in Australia and New Zealand, Briggs and Hawkins compare these programs. They demonstrate that children gain more when curricula are developmentally appropriate and forthright in their presentation of sexual information and parents communicate with teachers and support their child's learning. When parents participate, school-based child protection programs can open up lines of communication about sexual matters between parents and children. Supportive interaction not only prevents sexual abuse, but promotes healthy sexual attitudes and safe sex practices when young people become sexually mature. As Briggs and Hawkins note, a major challenge for child protection programs is to find ways to make parents see the importance of and feel comfortable about joining in with their children.

Even the most widely used child-protection programs have weaknesses that limit their effectiveness. This chapter will illustrate some of the problems with existing models. We will show that child-protection efforts are most effective when teachers find ways of eliciting the interest and involvement of parents.

## CURRICULUM DEVELOPMENT: EARLY INITIATIVES

Efforts to prevent child sexual abuse through school and preschool-based programs began in the United States in the late 1970s. For many years children throughout the English-speaking world were warned only to avoid male strangers. Reasons for the warning were seldom given, and no one seems to have investigated whether young children understood the complex concept of "stranger." In the 1970s, data showed that the stereotyped dangerous stranger was more a myth than a reality and that most child sexual offenders were known and trusted by their victims. This led to a demand for "dangerous stranger" information to be replaced by a more realistic approach to child protection. The urgency of the demand was such that the production and adoption of child-protection programs preceded independent studies to evaluate their various claims to effectiveness.

## WHY PARENTS WERE EXCLUDED FROM CHILD-PROTECTION CURRICULUM

Although child-protection curricula have been available for almost two decades, designers have virtually ignored the importance of parent participation. There are several reasons for this neglect.

### Teachers Lack the Confidence to Involve Parents

Teachers who are new to protective education rarely feel sufficiently confident or knowledgeable to involve parents. Given the sensitivity of the subject matter, they are afraid of making mistakes and of being criticized. Paradoxically, teachers are most likely to be misunderstood and criticisms are most likely to occur when parents are not involved in programs. In New Zealand, for example, a four-year-old involved in a preschool program reprimanded her father for tickling the baby's bottom while he was dressing her. The four-year-old regarded the tickling as a "bad touch." Another preschool child told her father that she no longer wanted to shower with him; she claimed body ownership and the right to wash herself. If these parents had understood the objectives and had been asked to reinforce the concepts at home, they would have been delighted that their children felt sufficiently confident to assert themselves. Instead, they complained to the sensationalist media that teachers were "making children paranoid," "spoiling children's innocence," and exaggerating the risks of abuse. They demanded the abolition of all personal safety curricula in schools.

### Program Designers Believed That Parents Are the Main Abusers

In the 1970s and 1980s, information about the problem of child sexual abuse came from adult female rape and incest survivors. Convinced that fathers were the main offenders and some mothers were accomplices, designers deliberately precluded parents in the belief that some would sabotage protective efforts if they knew what was being taught.

It is now recognized that, although some parents do abuse their children, they constitute a small minority. Furthermore, there is no evidence that abusive parents sabotage school programs; to the contrary, a survey of convicted child molesters showed that some incest offenders were already worried about their behavior and instructed their victims to "do the right thing" and report them when they learned that they were involved in a school program (Briggs and Hawkins, 1996a, Briggs and Hawkins, 1996b).

## WEAKNESSES OF THE EARLY MODELS

Introduced by well-intentioned adult rape-crisis workers, the early programs followed from the adult female's conceptualizations of rape, a manifestation of what David Elkind (1976) referred to as **externalism,** that is, a process of conceptualizing problems and events in children's lives based on adult thinking and the assumption that a simple reductionist translation to children is possible. There was, for example, an assumption that all offenders were male, that all victims were female, and that all sexual touching was unpleasant and unwanted. Boys were assumed (wrongly) to be either less vulnerable to abuse or less likely to be damaged by the effects (Goldman & Goldman, 1988). Program designers had little professional knowledge of the norms of child development, children's thought processes, their beliefs relating to safety issues, their language, or their capacity to understand the complex adult concepts incorporated in the new curriculum. Simultaneously, few child development experts had knowledge of the dynamics of child sexual abuse and the forces involved in the seduction ("grooming") process.

In the early 1980s three distinct program models emerged: the empowerment model, the *Touch Continuum,* and lessons about sexual assault.

### The Empowerment Model

The **empowerment model** was based on the feminist theoretical view of sexual abuse as the abuse of male power (that is, not sex related) (Butler, 1986). It was thought that children could be "empowered" by encouraging assertiveness skills and teaching them about their rights. Some programs claimed to protect children from sexual abuse without referring to human sexuality. This omission was considered to be necessary for teacher acceptance.

One weakness of the empowerment model is that it takes little account of the reality that children are only empowered when adults permit it.

We can teach children that they have the right to say "No" to unwanted touching, but it becomes a cynical exercise if children try to practice their new skills and find parents unsupportive.

When we examine the power differential, the authority of the adult, and the tricks used to seduce children, the expectation that targeted victims can be empowered by information about their rights is clearly too simplistic. Curriculum designers assumed somewhat naively that this knowledge would enable children to overcome compelling needs of affiliation, love, and physical as well as emotional dependence and report sexual abuse involving important people in their lives without feeling guilty or responsible. Program designers also promoted the view that children can be taught not to blame themselves if they have already been abused or if, at some future date, they fail to stop abuse from happening.

When they excluded parent involvement from programs, curriculum designers overlooked the fact that, for children to stay safe from sexual offenders, they have to ignore societal mores and parental teaching relating to obedience to adults and authority figures in particular. They have to ignore what they have been taught about keeping adults' secrets. They have to ignore the taboo on the subject of genitals. Teaching assertiveness skills without parental support places children at risk for psychological and physical abuse when they make their first tentative, sometimes inappropriate attempts to assert themselves at home.

Most programs in the "empowerment" category instruct children to report sexually related anxieties to trusted adults. A survey of New Zealand children (Briggs & Hawkins, 1996b) showed that this is irresponsible when the trusted adults have not been involved in the program and they have not been taught how to handle such disclosures in psychologically helpful ways. Most victims trust their mothers and, despite being told to "tell and keep on telling . . . ," when their trusted persons disbelieve them, few have the confidence to seek help elsewhere.

## The *Touch Continuum*

The *Touch Continuum* (Anderson, 1979) aimed to teach children to identify good, bad, and confusing touches. This approach was too simplistic in its failure to take account of either the complexity of abusive relationships, the adult-child power differential, or the attractive inducements abusers use to get children's cooperation. It failed to take account of children's sexual curiosity, assuming that all sexual touching feels bad or confusing and that children would identify oral sex as "touch."

A recent Australian study by Briggs and Hawkins (1996a) confirmed Cook and Howells' (1981) earlier findings that boys have a high level of sexual curiosity at an early age. They often socialize in highly sexualized male peer groups, are easily stimulated, and sometimes respond positively to genital fondling and oral sex. When unwilling boys experience a physiological response, they accept responsibility for what happens, and guilt then prevents them from making reports. In the recent Australian study (N = 200), 43 percent of male victims reported liking the sexual contact while 78.5 percent had believed that sexual misconduct by youths and adults was "normal" behavior. Liking sexual activity was a significant factor in determining which victims perpetuated the abuse cycle and became offenders (Briggs & Hawkins, 1996a; Hawkins & Briggs, 1995).

In sum, the *Touch Continuum* gave children permission to reject unwanted touching, but there was a dangerous, unstated assumption that "if it feels good, it must be okay." In the meantime, many authors changed the emphasis from identifying "touch" to identifying feelings (for example, the Wisconsin program *Protective Behaviors,* to be discussed shortly).

Krivacska (1990a) criticized both this and the empowerment approach. He expressed concern that children are expected to exercise the good judgment necessary to accurately discriminate when sexual abuse has occurred and respond appropriately, despite having been taught such discrimination using vague and ambiguous concepts such as "rights" and "confusing touching."

## Lessons About Sexual Assault

A more recent approach, probably arising from criticisms of the two models already described, has been to teach young children about sexual assault. Although some program writers claim that their curricula can be used with preschoolers, the approach is seldom appropriate for very young children. Krivacska (1990a) argues that it is "sex negative" and that all child-protection education should be preceded or accompanied by positive information about children's sexuality, body parts, and body functions.

## CONTEMPORARY PROGRAMS

Recently, curriculum designers have incorporated aspects of all three models into their programs. Unfortunately, the tendency is still to refer to an abuser as "he" and the victim as "she," failing to take account of the risks to boys.

In deference to the sensitivity of adults, many (including those involved in the explicit "lessons about sexual assault" approach) have maintained the taboo on genitals, referring to them with such phrases as "private parts" or "parts covered by your . . . swim-suit/bathing suit/underwear (and so on)." In other words, children are receiving conflicting messages. On the one hand, children are assured that they must talk to trusted adults if they encounter sexual misbehavior; on the other hand, teachers and parents are confirming by their very avoidance of correct vocabulary that adults cannot cope with information about sexual parts of the body.

Literally hundreds of child protection programs are now available. In 1996, Tutty reported to the International Congress on Child Abuse and Neglect that, although several American personal safety programs have been evaluated and found effective, school communities are, with little or no expertise, creating their own programs based on what adults want to teach rather than what children can understand. The problem for children is that their parents are deluded into

*Keeping Ourselves Safe,* New Zealand's national child protection program, involves parents through information sessions that tell them about their children's classroom experiences. In addition, parents assist in the development of children's skills through joint child–parent homework. Parent involvement increases the likelihood that children will use the safety strategies they are taught. (Photo: Owen Sanders)

thinking that children are receiving the most reliable protective education when, all too often, they are not.

## THE INTRODUCTION OF CHILD-PROTECTION CURRICULA TO SCHOOLS IN AUSTRALIA AND NEW ZEALAND

### Australia

In the mid 1970s, the United States experienced a substantial increase in the incidence of rape. Experts predicted that this trend would reach other English speaking countries five years later. It did. Australian women followed the American lead by setting up support services for female rape victims.

In 1984, police in the Australian state of Victoria first revealed statistics relating to reports of

sexual offenses. These showed that only 6 percent of reported cases of child sexual abuse involved strangers. The majority of perpetrators were known and trusted by their victims. The women's movement demanded that, as a matter of urgency, "Dangerous Stranger" information should be replaced with a more realistic school-based program.

Police convened a multiprofessional committee to examine a range of options. The committee selected the little-known Wisconsin program, *Protective Behaviors.* The author, Peg West, claimed that the program was appropriate for all ages and the eight sessions had the capacity to stop child sexual abuse in one generation. *Protective Behaviors* assumes that sexual abuse causes children to feel "unsafe" and that children can identify these feelings. Children are taught that "we all have the right to feel safe all of the time" and that "nothing is so awful that we can't talk about it to someone." Sessions are used to teach children to identify "early warning signs"—the physical sensations of fear, tension, and worry, such as "knees shakey," "stomach funny," and "legs want to run"—and to persist in telling until their concerns are responded to (West, 1984).

A major shortcoming of this approach is that "it takes no account of the context of child sexual abuse, which can occur in an affectionate relationship. Nor does it acknowledge the fact that sexual touching may feel exciting and pleasurable rather than unsafe" (Briggs & Hawkins, 1994a, p. 274). One attraction of this program was its claim to protect children from sexual assault without mentioning sex. It was thought that such an omission was necessary to gain the acceptance of teachers and parents.

## New Zealand

In 1985, New Zealand police faced similar community pressures to introduce a new and more relevant national child protection program to schools. Police education officers, teachers and curriculum writers with the Ministry of Education created their own developmentally and culturally appropriate program for children from 5 to 17 years of age. *Keeping Ourselves Safe* was designed by groups of child development specialists and curriculum experts. From the outset, the designers recognized the value of parent cooperation, and parents were consulted throughout the planning process. Some of the key design features of *each module* were:

- Parent information sessions that included the videos and stories to be used with children

- Parent evaluation and provision for feedback to teachers

- Joint child-parent homework that is signed by parents and returned to teachers

- Written information on what is to be taught and how parents can help

- Parent encouragement to assist in the development of children's problem-solving and assertiveness skills

## EVALUATION OF AUSTRALIAN AND NEW ZEALAND PROGRAMS WITH 5- TO 8-YEAR-OLD CHILDREN

Comparisons of the Australian and New Zealand programs (Briggs, 1991; Briggs & Hawkins, 1994b; Briggs & Hawkins, 1996b) showed the New Zealand curriculum to be superior. However, in both countries parent participation was a key mediating variable in determining children's gains from participation in a child protection program.

Important differences were found between parents who had involved themselves in the protection programs versus others who had relied on the schools and had not been directly involved. The uninvolved parents remained relatively uninformed about child-protection issues.

### Uninformed Parents Encourage the Fear of Strangers

Although parents know that most reports of child sexual abuse involve known adults, without access to a school-based program, they concentrate their protection efforts on avoidance of the stereotyped stranger. Unfortunately, these efforts are somewhat futile (and, at worst, negative) because of young children's difficulties in understanding the concept of "stranger."

Before participation in a child-protection program, Australian and New Zealand children were fearful of strangers. They believed that

- Strangers are always male and easily identifiable by their evil appearance, leering eyes, black clothes, masks or knit caps, and black cars

- Strangers steal children from their beds and kill them

- They had never seen a stranger in their lives but would recognize one instantly if they saw one

- People are trustworthy if they look and seem kind, know your name, or claim to know your parents

- Strangers would never be allowed to enter school premises

Children declared almost unanimously that the researcher (who had recently arrived on an international flight) was not a stranger because she was a woman and she looked "quite nice." Because she carried a briefcase, they also assumed that she had a "job" (and strangers "don't work, they only rob people").

## Uninformed Adults Deny Children's Sexuality

Although age-appropriate sexuality education for children (that is, a gradual unfolding of basic information about their own bodies) is known to be a significant factor in child protection (Hard, 1986; Krivacska, 1990b; Hawkins & Briggs, 1995), few parents discuss or teach children the biologically correct vocabulary for their genitals. In a class of South Australian six-year-olds, boys produced twenty different "pet" or ethnic names for "penis." Girls were less familiar with their physiology, and many had been taught to say "down there," "between my legs" or "bottom" to describe all of their organs designed for reproduction and excretion. There are several reasons for the taboo.

First, many parents believe that ignorance keeps children asexual or, at the opposite extreme, that information will encourage early sexual exploration. Goldman and Goldman (1988) found the reverse to be true. In their international study of children's sexuality, the areas with the highest rate of illegitimate births to school-age mothers were those that banned sex education from the school curriculum.

Second, without professional guidance, few parents know how to talk to children about their bodies. Some adults are uncomfortable about their own sexuality. Moreover, adults have traditionally concentrated on protecting themselves from having to answer questions that might cause them embarrassment, and secretive "pet" names are used with that objective in mind.

In pretesting, all of the Australian and New Zealand children of 5 to 8 years knew that matters relating to genitals, nudity, and toileting were taboo subjects when they were in adult company. Without involvement in a child protection program, none of the children felt that they could report sexual misbehavior to an adult. They explained that sexual misbehavior is naughty, and naughty means that

- You are bad and no-one will love you.

- You'll be punished.

- You must have done something to deserve it and it's all your fault

It became clear that a hazard to children's safety was their inability at the 5 to 8 year level to ascribe blame or responsibility accurately when confronted by the possibility of adult disapproval. The study showed that children would tolerate sexual misbehavior rather than risk a parent's wrath. Children will not take risks associated with reporting unless they already know with certainty, from past experience, that they will be supported and not blamed. There was ample evidence of Krivacska's (1990b) concern that children misattribute blame to themselves for other people's misbehavior. Children of 5 to 8 years were disadvantaged by immature notions of guilt and shame, including guilt by association; if the behavior is "naughty," they hold themselves responsible and punishable. If adults misbehaved, children believed that they would be blamed entirely because parents neither believe nor support children in conflict with other adults.

Some parents have resisted the introduction of child-protection programs because they might "damage children's innocence." Such parents tend to assume that children are deaf and blind to the sexual references they hear and the simulated sex they see on TV screens. At the same time, parents often "delude themselves" about the extent of their own contribution to children's sex education. This was confirmed in a study of Australian parents, many of whom told researchers that they had discussed sexual matters, including STDs, homosexuality and safe sex, with their 16-year-old children. The children were interviewed, and few confirmed their parents' claims. When challenged, the parents admitted that they had not engaged in any discussion, but they defended their responses by saying that they were always "open to discussion" (Weekes & Westwood, 1993). Similarly, interviews with the parents of 565 South Australian of 3- to 12 year-olds indicated that they were waiting for their children to make the first approach (Briggs, 1988).

Our Australian and New Zealand studies have consistently shown that children will not approach an adult about sexual matters unless they know, from past experience, that the adult will respond supportively. School-based child-protection programs can help parents open up channels of communication. These programs encourage parents to teach and use the correct biological names for genitals and to teach children to take special care of these body parts. The traditional parental practice of presenting sex education booklets to children when they reach puberty is clearly too little, too late.

## Uninformed Parents Promote Secrecy

It is widely accepted that child sex offenders are protected by the secrecy that surrounds sexual matters. Australian and New Zealand 5-to-8-year-olds who had not been involved in a child protection program with their parents believed that they must keep all adults' secrets and family secrets in particular. They believed that they would always have to keep secrets about sexual misbehavior because disclosure would be punished several times:

■ First, because the misbehavior occurred.

■ Second, because the child told an adult secret.

■ Third, because telling the secret would involve "dirty" or "rude" talk.

■ Finally, because their mothers would tell the offender that the child had told the secret, and the child would be punished yet again.

When children were taught at school that they should tell "bad secrets" and keep "good secrets about birthdays and Christmas surprises," many uninformed parents amended the instruction, adding "mummy's and daddy's and even grandparents'" secrets to the list of those to be kept. Children became confused and resorted to the logical but dangerous conclusion that, "You can tell good secrets because they make people happy but you can't tell bad secrets because they make grown-ups mad/angry/sad."

It became very clear that parents promote family secrecy without understanding the dangers involved. It also became clear that adults must be given explanations for why a "no secrets" policy is necessary to keep children safe.

## Uninformed Parents Give Priority to Adults' Needs and Feelings

Some cultures give priority to adults' needs at the expense of children's rights. When their parents were not involved in the school program, Maori, Asian, and Pacific Island children explained that awareness of their rights was of little value because their parents were powerless to intervene if they reported inappropriate behavior by a senior member of the family hierarchy. Their mothers could not report male family members and their fathers could not ask older brothers or paternal grandfathers to desist.

Before access to a protection program, Australian and New Zealand 5-to-8-year-olds thought that they had to tolerate unpleasant or unwanted touching from adults because to complain would distress both their parents and the offenders. Most children had already sought and failed to gain parents' intervention to stop uncomfortable touching by adult relatives and older siblings. An alarming 26 percent of children believed that they could not trust their parents to support and protect them from other adults.

Parents often criticized their children for seeking support to stop excessive tickling and "sloppy" kissing by adult relatives and friends. The children were accused of misunderstanding adult motives or being inconsiderate of adults' feelings. "Granddad will be upset if you don't let him kiss you. He only does it because he loves you."

In other words, uninformed parents unwittingly give children powerful and dangerous messages to the effect that they have to suffer unwanted and uncomfortable touching to please adults and that their own feelings are unimportant.

### Without Parent Participation in Child Protection, Young Children Only Give Vague Hints That They Have a Sexually Related Problem

In a problem solving situation relating to a babysitter who wanted to play an undressing game, all the children knew that such a game was wrong. Sixteen percent of respondents reported that they had already played sex games with adolescent babysitters. Those who had not undertaken a child-protection program believed that they would have to obey a babysitter because "Mummy always says I have to do what the babysitter tells me to do." Furthermore, children view adolescent and adult babysitters as powerful people who become angry when children disobey their instructions.

Without a child-protection program, children said that they would not report adult misbehavior. With a program but no parent participation (and, therefore, no expectation of support), children would only hint that they did not like the babysitter or that the babysitter was "mean." Such vague hints were unlikely to be understood by their parents.

By contrast, when parents participated in programs, children used whole sentences to make clear reports. They were confident that they would be praised and protected: "I would say, "Mummy! The babysitter told me to take my clothes off and play a bad game and I said 'No'

and got away and mummy would say, 'Good boy' and pat me on the head.'"

### Uninvolved Parents Do Not Know How to Handle Disclosures of Sexual Misbehavior

Eight percent of the New Zealand parents reported that they were aware of acts of sexual abuse involving their children as victims but only 50 percent of these incidents had been reported to police. Interestingly, 21 percent of children told us that they had been raped or sexually abused (Briggs & Hawkins, 1996b).

When juveniles and youths were the offenders, parents of victimized children reported offenses only to the perpetrating boys' parents or their school principals. No formal investigation took place to establish whether youths were habitual offenders or whether they were also victims. Without professional intervention, there was no counseling or therapy for either perpetrators or the victims.

When family members were the offenders, most mothers protected their children by avoiding further contact with the abusing relative. They knew that other children were at risk but were reluctant to report relatives to the authorities because of the risk of public disgrace. Some mothers were aware of ongoing offenses but claimed that they did not report them because they were unaware of child-protection services. These mothers revealed a lack of knowledge about the long-term damage to victims and used "children forget" as an excuse for noninvolvement.

## THE CHALLENGE OF INVOLVING PARENTS IN CHILD-PROTECTION PROGRAMS

### Uninformed Parents Deny That the Risk Exists

Although it is easy to see why parent cooperation in child-protection programs enhances children's safety, parents are highly resistant to involvement. They are also alarmingly complacent about their own family's immunity to the child-abuse problem. When parents of 565 South Australian children were asked how they were protecting their children from the risk of sexual abuse, 75 percent had done nothing and 25 percent had told children not to talk to strangers (Briggs, 1988). When asked to account for their negligence, 68 percent said that personal safety education was irrelevant to their children because they knew no one, in or outside the family, who was mentally ill and sexually deviant. Parents also said that, even at 12 years of age, children were "too young to understand," and parents were afraid that they might cause their children to be "unnecessarily" fearful or distrusting.

With only the dangerous stranger in mind, all the parents thought that, because they transported children to and from school and social functions, their children were safe. Many parents were under the impression that boys were not at risk and that the safety of girls related to the level of parental strictness.

None of the fathers thought that they had a role to play in safety education; they thought that it was the responsibility of their partner. They had not checked whether their partners had undertaken that responsibility.

## Parents Avoid School Meetings About Protection Programs

Mayes, Currie, Macleod, Gillies, & Warden (1992) noted that only 25 to 30 percent of American and British parents attend school meetings about child protection.

The first Australian evaluation of *Protective Behaviors* in primary schools (Briggs, 1990; 1991) showed that only 22 percent of Australian parents attended information sessions and that some were unaware of their children's involvement in the program. Parents who failed to attend meetings excused their absence by saying that they trusted school staff to provide all the necessary information. Unfortunately, their trust was misplaced. Two evaluations revealed that most teachers used the program selectively, omitting the most important information needed by children to identify and reject inappropriate adult behavior (Briggs, 1991; Johnson, 1995).

The New Zealand studies by Briggs and Hawkins (1994b, 1996b) also showed that, at best, only 30 percent of children had any parent representative at any school information session. Most said that they did not attend a meeting because they don't read school newsletters (which announced the meetings), they did not think that attendance was important (that is, schools often adopt a "low-key" approach to avoid controversy; this rebounds when parents interpret it as "my attendance is not important"), work commitments prevented attendance, or attendance was unnecessary because their families are safe.

The vast majority of New Zealand parents wanted more information about how to teach sensitive issues, more child-parent joint homework, leaflets that could be read "between the mail-box and the kitchen," week by week information about how to reinforce safety concepts at home, videos, parent workshops, and small discussion groups about handling sensitive issues. These same parents were nonetheless reticent about attending school meetings, especially because they expected to be "talked at" by professionals. Interestingly, in Australia, Hunt, Hawkins, and Goodlet (1992) found that although parents listed child sexual abuse as their fourth most serious parenting concern, they too said they would not attend child-protection sessions run by professionals.

Even when parents do attend a child protection session, special skills are required to run the meetings in an effective manner. In the United States, Berrick (1988) questioned the value of such sessions because she found that attendance did little or nothing to change parents' views on their own family's immunity and the dangers from strangers. Wurtele, Kvaternick, and Franklin (1992) found that parents of preschoolers favored the use of sexual abuse prevention programs and discussion of the topic of sexual abuse with their preschoolers but the majority focused narrowly on the avoidance of dangerous strangers.

Quite clearly, teachers wishing to involve parents in programs have to find alternatives to school meetings. Some New Zealand parents indicated that they "failed school" and have negative feelings whenever they enter the premises. They suggested that small parent workshops should be held in community centers (Briggs & Hawkins, 1996b).

In Australian and New Zealand surveys, parents were well satisfied with the design and delivery of child-protection curricula in schools. They just wanted schools to deliver the program without involving them. Parents are clearly unaware of their own importance in child protection or of the risks to their own children. The question is, how can schools convince parents of their importance if the parents are not prepared to read newsletters or attend meetings?

## CHILD PROTECTION AT THE PRESCHOOL LEVEL

From Wurtele's work and our own observations, it seems likely that child protection workshops attract the best attendance when children are enrolled in early childhood centers. These meetings usually have a social element, often with the provision of child care for young children.

Men can usually be persuaded to attend a "Dad's night" when they might resist attending a mixed session. Men's needs are often different from women's because of myths and attitudes specific to the male culture and their own fears of being blamed or wrongfully accused.

Wurtele, Kast, and Melzer (1992) compared the knowledge and skills of preschool children who had participated in a personal safety program or a control program taught by a teacher, parent or both. Those in the safety program demonstrated greater knowledge and safety skills than those in the control group, but those taught by parents and teachers together made the greatest gains.

## THE IMPORTANCE OF PARENT PARTICIPATION: FINDINGS FROM STUDIES INVOLVING OLDER CHILDREN

The most important study in recent times has been the survey of 2,000 children for Boy Scouts of America by Finkelhor, Asdigian, and Dziuba-Leatherman (1993). Interviewing children in 440 school districts, the researchers found that 67 percent had participated in school-based child-protection programs of various kinds and duration.

Measuring safety knowledge and how safety strategies had been used over a 12-month period, the researchers showed that any child protection program is better than none. However, those involved in the longest, most comprehensive programs had the highest scores on safety knowledge relevant to protection from sexual abuse. Furthermore the high scorers were the ones most likely to have used their knowledge, reporting abusive incidents and feeling very positive about their own responses. School programs did not necessarily prevent abuse from happening, but they helped reduce its seriousness and increased the number of reports. Comprehensive parental instruction and participation made a substantial difference in children's coping skills and knowledge. Parent participation also resulted in children limiting the seriousness of assaults, escaping, and reporting. Well-informed parents were the most approachable and the most likely to handle reports positively.

Parents and children from the Briggs and Hawkins' (1996b) study of the New Zealand *Keeping Ourselves Safe* program said that they shared information and discussed television reports relating to abuse and a wide range of sensitive topics. When parents were involved in the program from the primary school level, both they and their children viewed the school and home as reinforcing each other. Children and parents gave examples of how the children had used the safety strategies they were taught to stop or prevent an assault of some kind. It is important to note, however, when they were introduced to the program at the 10–12 year age level (that is, the children had not attended a primary school where the modules were taught), parents and children uniformly felt that it was too late to break down the taboos surrounding sensitive issues. Boys were "too embarrassed" to discuss the program, and their parents shared their embarrassment. In other words, children gain most when parents become involved in child-protection programs when their children are young. At 10 to 12 years of age, it seems to be too late for children and parents to begin communicating about previously banned topics.

## CONCLUSIONS

We have seen that developmental issues are central to the success of child-protection programs. Some important concepts are not understood by very young children. Even the widely used concept of "stranger" is much more complex than is generally realized. Some programs ask children to make quite sophisticated judgments about what constitutes good and bad "touching" or good and bad "feelings," and some expect children to ignore parental teaching about secrecy. It is also asking too much of children to make explicit reports about sexual misbehavior when their experiences of adults' reactions to sexually related information demonstrate how unprepared many adults are to receive such reports.

Some critics have argued that child-protection programs place an unreasonable burden on children to stop abuse from happening. The sad reality is that they are necessary because adult caregivers have not provided and cannot provide guarantees of safety. It should also be remembered that child abusers typically repeat their offenses (for example, studies by Bentovim (1991) and Abel, Becker, Mittelman, Cunningham-Rathner, Rouleau, and Murphy (1987) showed that perpetrators had committed, on average, more than 500 offenses each before they were interviewed). Although a prevention program might not prevent

an offense from occurring, if it results in disclosure, the risk of repetition will be reduced.

In addition, teachers and parents should assist children in understanding that they are not responsible for other people's sexual misbehavior. This will give some children the courage to make reports and help others recover from abuse. Child-protection curricula are comparatively new, imperfect, and underresearched, but well-designed programs offer an important contribution to children's safety and well-being. Schools and preschools should exercise care in selecting a well-designed program and in evaluating it regularly through child, parent, and teacher reports to eliminate weaknesses.

The responsibility for teaching personal safety skills was given to schools and preschools because parents have a poor history of providing protection for children. Most programs were written with the assumption that children could be taught to protect themselves without parent involvement. When we examine the adult-child power differential, the highly sophisticated seduction techniques used by offenders, parenting practices and priorities, and the complexity of emotional relationships, this expectation is clearly unreasonable.

Studies have shown that parent support is crucial for ensuring children's personal safety knowledge and safety skills. Telling children about their rights is not sufficient to change their behavior. To become part of children's responses, the desired behavior has to be modeled, repeated, and rewarded. Although parents are more likely than teachers to have the opportunity to encourage appropriate assertiveness, those who are uninvolved and uninformed might react with hostility to school teachings that *appear* to conflict with family values, to promote disobedience, to diminish adult authority, and to place parents at higher risk of being reported for inappropriate touching. Parents are much less likely to be concerned about risks to traditional family values when they have the opportunity to clarify safe strategies to their children and are given ideas about what to say.

Unfortunately, some schools do not perceive parent education and involvement as their responsibility. Potentially supportive parents are not always welcomed by teachers who lack confidence in teaching the program. And when they offer meetings that are not well attended, teachers often become negative and withdraw rather than seek alternative ways of enlisting parental interest.

Parent education can be a major resource in prevention efforts. With training, parents are likely to be more careful in their choice of babysitters and more careful about entrusting others with their children for outings. With education, they should be better able to answer children's questions and evaluate their relationships with older people.

To gain maximum benefit from child protection initiatives, schools and communities should use every available resource to convince parents of their importance in program reinforcement. Adults promise children that if they are victimized, it is in their best interests to report the abuse. We assure children that if they have been abused, they will be believed, supported, and protected if they "tell" someone they trust. To ensure that those promises are meaningful, it is vital that we find ways of developing effective teaching partnerships with parents.

## EVALUATING YOUR MASTERY

1. Which of the following is a reason that the importance of parent participation in child-protection curricula has been ignored?
   a. Teachers do not feel comfortable or knowledgeable about involving parents.
   b. No one saw a need, given that parents rarely abuse their children.
   c. So few children are abused that it did not seem worthwhile to involve parents.
   d. Research indicated it was not necessary to involve parents.

2. Early models of child protection programs, which did not involve parents, were based on the *incorrect* assumption that
   a. Children's thinking is different from that of adults.
   b. Girls are less vulnerable and less likely to be damaged by abuse.
   c. Children have difficulty accurately understanding the concept of stranger.
   d. Abusers are mostly parents.

3. Which of the following is a compelling reason for involving parents in child-protection curricula?
   a. Parents have too little time to teach their children safety skills.
   b. Few parents know how to discuss sexuality with their children.
   c. Parents are reluctant to tell their children to avoid strangers.
   d. Parents need advice on how to keep information about sexual matters secret from children.

4. Which of the following is a major challenge to involving parents in child protection programs?
   a. Parents are so overly concerned that their children will be abused that it is difficult to get them to listen to experts.
   b. Parents do not want more information about how to teach their children about sensitive issues.

    c.   Parents do not think it is important to attend school meetings on child protection.

    d.   Teachers teach parents relevant information in the wrong order.

5. True or False: A main weakness of the empowerment model of child protection is that children cannot be empowered simply by being given information about their rights.

6. Parent participation in child-protection programs [prevents abuse from happening/reduces the serious consequences of abuse].

7. In a study of the New Zealand *Keeping Ourselves Safe* program, Briggs and Hawkins found that intervention is best begun at [the primary school level/the middle school level].

## Critical Thinking

1. Why is teaching children about good, bad, and confusing touches not an effective way to protect them from sexual abuse?

2. What ingredients of the New Zealand *Keeping Ourselves Safe* program are central to its success?

## Applying Your Knowledge

Contact an elementary school principal or teacher and find out what kind of child protection programming exists in his or her school. To what extent does the program involve parents? Are the techniques used likely to work? Explain why or why not, based on research discussed by Briggs and Hawkins.

# PART V

# Pathways to Maturity: Middle Childhood to Adolescence

# 22

## Childhood and the Culture of Consumption

### BERYL LANGER
### LaTrobe University

■

Photographs of the possessions accumulated by each generation of children in a family over the course of this century would provide graphic illustration of how the material culture of western childhood has changed from one of scarcity, in which most children had few if any toys, to one of abundance and "hyper-consumption."

■

A child longs for another "Barbie" or a new set of action figures not just because she or he is "greedy" or "spoiled," but because she or he is targeted by a multibillion-dollar industry in a culture whose dominant messages equate happiness with consumption and novelty.

■

If Manus children were "accustomed to water" from the first years of life, our own are accustomed to shopping, and as the boat was central to the production of material life in Manus culture, the shopping trolley is central to our own.

■

Put simply, there are more things to buy, more abstract ways to buy them, more elaborate and impersonal environments in which to shop, and more time devoted to shopping as a preferred leisure activity rather than as a domestic chore.

■

■

The commoditoy subjects children's culture to the logic of fashion and planned obsolescence used to stimulate turnover in other areas of the economy.

■

The essential feature of the commoditoy, whether durable or transient, is the capacity to stimulate rather than satisfy desire.

■

The commoditoy cycle draws children into generationally specific subcultures, diminishing the possibility of communication with adults based on shared experience.

■

Television situates children as consumers, potential owners or enjoyers of toys, treats, and activities—a process that can only be understood in terms of the broader cultural logic to which it is tied.

■

The question is not whether our children will be consumers, but what kind of consumers they will be.

■

## EDITOR'S INTRODUCTION

Drawing a link between social structure and individual character, Beryl Langer analyzes the changing social and historical conditions of the consumer world, considering its profound impact on children and families. She discusses post–World War II economic, technological, and ideological factors that have changed children and parents as social beings, making them into insatiable consumers, shaped by a culture that offers endless purchasable choices. According to Langer, childhood consumer capitalism reaches its peak in the "commoditoy"—a toy heavily dependent on fashion and designed to stimulate purchase of another toy. Commoditoys, Langer argues, permit children's culture to be governed by constant turnover and planned obsolescence, like other aspects of the economy. The result: Frequent family disputes sparked by pleas to purchase, bedrooms heaped with material goods, and children steeped in materialism.

Langer challenges us to think carefully about our cultural values as a healthy and appropriate context for children's development. Although she views children's consumer desires as the product of contemporary Western capitalism, she underscores that childhood consumerism is not inevitable. Although children cannot be completely shielded from market influences, Langer believes parents and other influential adults can influence what kind of consumers children will be.

The notion of "consumer culture" implies that, in the modern world, core social practices and cultural values, ideas, aspirations and identities are defined and oriented in relation to consumption rather than to other social dimensions such as work or citizenship, religious cosmology or military role. To describe a society in terms of its consumption and to assume that its core values derive from it is unprecedented: A militaristic culture, agrarian culture, maritime culture … but a consumer culture?

Don Slater, *Consumer Culture and Modernity*

It is a middle-class delusion—though one often propagated by child experts—that children can be shielded from consumption, that proper parenting will nip children's interest in toys and television in the bud. Rather, I believe that we need to accept that contemporary parenthood is always already embedded in consumerism, although the scale, the size of the market, and the prestige associated with the goods vary greatly from class to class.

Ellen Seiter, *Sold Separately*

This chapter considers children's relation to the consumer culture in which everyday life in modern developed societies is embedded. A consumer culture makes children's entry to society inseparable from their entry to the market, first through parental consumption of goods and services, then as apprentice consumers. Children's engagement with the world around them is therefore a "frontier" of economic opportunity, and their consumer preferences are a major focus of market research. Little scholarly attention has been directed at children's consumption, however. There is extensive research on children's television, and on gender stereotyping and violence in toys and video games, but the general implications of consumer culture for contemporary childhood have rarely been explored.

My research in this area was prompted by the experience of becoming a parent. Similar accounts of entering the field are offered by Kline (1989, 1993) and Seiter (1995), which says much for the way in which this life stage is now mediated by the market. Parenthood redefines your "consumer profile." You become aware of advertisements that you had never noticed before and of your intense vulnerability to their messages. A new life is an awesome responsibility, and products that offer to keep your baby healthy, happy, and safe have powerful emotional appeal. As Seiter (1995, p. 1) observes,

I had never listened to advertisers' messages so attentively before, because I had never felt spoken to so directly. When I had my first baby, I felt that advertising and advice literature buttonholed me in a way I never dreamed possible.

As your children move through infancy and toddlerhood, you realize that they too have a "consumer profile." To shop with a two-year old is to encounter a new world of "small pleasures" for the fledgling consumer—Golden Books strategically placed near the check-out, model cars hung at trolley-seat eye level, dinosaur-shaped biscuits—which cost so little and bring such delight that their inclusion in the shopping ritual is easy and rewarding. Only when the object of desire costs more than you can afford, or offends your sense of what is appropriate, are children's consumer aspirations experienced as a problem. You are then assailed by a multibillion-dollar global industry that speaks to you in the insistent voice of your own child. Resistance is definitely an option. You say "No" to Nintendo, ban G. I. Joe, insist that Barbie does not need another new outfit, and generally feel that *your* children, at least, are learning to exercise restraint. Then you look at the accumulated clutter in their rooms—closets, shelves and boxes overflowing with "stuff"—and feel that you have let them down by failing to establish appropriate limits.

Once the market speaks directly to your child—on television, at the supermarket, or through friends—you might control what is purchased, but not what is desired. Where once you were a partner in the shared pleasure of unexpected treats, you are now cast in the role of obstacle—a resistant force to be overcome. Engaged in disputes about cultural value with children who have barely mastered the art of riding a bicycle, you wonder how their imaginations have been captured by forces beyond your control so early in their lives.

As a sociologist, I was intrigued by children's consumer behavior, which seemed different from my own at the same age, and even further removed from the childhood experiences of parents and grandparents. The dynamics of contemporary children's relation to toys seemed similar to that of teenagers to popular music—a continuous cycle of "hits" that enjoyed a brief period of popularity before being replaced by new releases. Placed in historical context, this suggested that just as "teenagers" had been constructed as a marketing category through identification with "teen culture" in the 1950s and 1960s, children's culture was being used to develop new market cohorts in the 1980s and 1990s.

The sheer volume of objects in children's rooms suggested that their construction as a niche market was proceeding nicely, but I wondered whether the consequences might be more than material. The sociological imagination (Mills, 1973) moves between history, biography, and social structure, trying to tease out the connections between social and historical conditions and the people who live through them. From this perspective, the toy-filled rooms of my children and their contemporaries posed two kinds of questions. How had they come into being as a routine feature of childhood in the affluent sectors of the developed world? What were their implications for the social practices and cultural values of the children who lived in them, and the adults that they would become?

## THE MATERIAL CULTURE OF CHILDHOOD: FROM SCARCITY TO ABUNDANCE

Photographs of the possessions accumulated by each generation of children in a family over the course of this century would provide graphic illustration of how the material culture of western childhood has changed from one of scarcity, in which most children had few if any toys, to one of abundance and "hyper-consumption." This change was in part a consequence of the shift from craft to factory production, which not only transformed the way basic needs were met but offered an ever-expanding universe of gadgets and appliances for mass consumption (Ewen, 1976; Kline, 1994). At the same time, popularization of educational and psychological theories emphasizing the developmental importance of play redefined toys and games as "needs," legitimizing expenditure once seen as frivolous (Kline, 1993).

The combined effects of new techniques of mass production and marketing and new ideologies of childhood made toys an increasingly important feature of the landscape of childhood. Our photographs would therefore document steady growth in the number of things acquired by each generation, except during the 1930s Depression or Second World War. Until the end of the 1940s, the kinds of toys and play equipment in each photograph would be relatively constant—blocks, dolls, model trains, tricycles—generic items that could be passed down from older to younger siblings, and between generations. Photographs taken from the beginning of the 1950s, however, would document changes in both the toys available and the number of toys owned by each child, which increased at an accelerating rate over the next four decades.

Children's material culture was changed by a complex set of economic, technological, and ideological developments that might seem very remote from the subject of childhood. New technology developed for military purposes during the Second World War, for example, revolutionized postwar manufacturing of consumer durables—including toys. Postwar reconstruction generated employment, producing the sustained growth in capitalist economies that gave "ordinary people" in the 1950s and 1960s more money to spend and more things to spend it on. Affluence would not make willing consumers of parents and grandparents raised in a culture of scarcity that warned against spoiling children without a shift in consumer psychology. This was facilitated by the Cold War, which made consumer abundance an ideological weapon in the fight against communism, elevating the moral status of consumption through association with "freedom" and "democracy" rather than waste. At the same time, anxiety about Russian space research placed the question of whether "Ivan was smarter than Johnny" on the political agenda,[1] situating children's development as an important public issue.

Then there was television—of the new appliances available for mass consumption after the Second World War, the one with most profound social and cultural impact. Television changed the way in which people received information, perceived the world (McLuhan, 1964), spent their leisure time, and related to each other. Its effects on children became an enduring focus of concern and research on the relationship between their viewing habits and their cognitive, social, and moral development. For the purposes of this discussion, television's most important effect was that it allowed advertisers to target children directly rather than through their parents—a niche market of apprentice consumers who could be sold to advertisers via programs like "The Mickey Mouse Club." As Steven Kline (1993:166–167) argues, television was central to the formation of an "exclusively children's subculture."

## THE SOCIAL CONSTRUCTION OF ACQUISITIVE CHILDREN

The fact that the toy-filled rooms that prompted my research on children and consumption can be explained in sociocultural terms does not mean that children are incapable of resisting seduction by advertising, or that parents are powerless to establish limits, but it does place children's consumerism in context. Children long for another "Barbie" or a new set of action figures not just because they are greedy or

spoiled, but because they are targeted by a multibillion-dollar industry in a culture whose dominant messages equate happiness with consumption and novelty. As Slater points out,

> The study of consumer culture is not simply the study … of individual choice and consciousness, of wants and desires, but rather the study of such things in the context of social relations, structures, institutions, systems. It is the study of the social conditions under which personal and social wants and the organization of social resources define each other. (1997, p. 2)

How children and parents respond to these cultural messages varies, not least in relation to social class. Seiter (1995, p. 3) notes that children "whose circumstances do not resemble that of the media world" have limited access to either "the consumer economy of childhood" or the "stimulating" environments prescribed by "child-centered pedagogy." She argues,

> When good parenting is defined as the provision of an appropriate environment for child development, class oppression expresses itself in children's everyday lives through deprivation, through the absence of material goods. (1995, p. 2)

When parents are consumer enthusiasts themselves, children's initiation into the culture sits easily with established family patterns. Only if parents want to place limits on children's consumption does the question of "whether"—as opposed to "what" and "when"—become the subject of negotiation. Within this category, parents occupy positions on a continuum that runs from absolute refusal on religious, political, or environmental grounds[2] through selective resistance to ambivalent complicity. Misgivings about the intensity and continuously shifting focus of children's consumer passions are weighed against the emotional reward of giving a child her or his heart's desire, the relief that comes from putting an end to persistent pleading, and the recognition that at least some participation in consumer

Children in Western industrialized nations learn from an early age to be conspicuous consumers. A never-ending variety of products, made more alluring through new technologies and seductive TV advertising, have increased children's passion to buy the latest toy fads. (Photo: Robert Brenner/ PhotoEdit)

culture is a prerequisite for inclusion in children's social networks.

One way to go beyond feelings of unease about children's relation to the market and think constructively about how to respond is to place it in social and historical context. As C. Wright Mills (1973, p. 14) points out, understanding "the intersections of biography and history within society" enables us to distinguish between "personal troubles" for which we are ourselves responsible, and "social issues" that demand institutional and collective solutions. The child who longs for Pirate Lego when she or he already has enough Space Lego to stock a small day-care center, for example, might be seen as the spoiled offspring of incompetent parents. Viewed as a pattern that repeats itself in families throughout the western world, however, this cycle of perpetual longing reveals itself as a social issue—to be explained in terms of structural and cultural changes rather than individual weakness or greed.

The idea that large-scale socioeconomic and cultural transformation changes not just what

people *do,* but what people *are*—how they *feel* as well as how they think—is unsettling to those who see human nature as a constant. The work of historians of the family, however, provides strong support for the thesis that emotions and interpersonal relations are shaped by social and cultural conditions. Even something as seemingly "natural" as how parents feel about children, or how childhood is defined and experienced, is not constant across either cultures or historical periods (Aries, 1962; de Mause, 1976; Shorter, 1976; Stone, 1977; Walvin, 1982; Zelizer, 1994).

The link between social structure and individual character can be understood through the **symbolic interactionist** account of the emergence of self through social interaction. George Herbert Mead (1934) argues that we develop a sense of ourselves as individual *subjects* by viewing ourselves as *objects,* first from the standpoint of *significant others* in the family, then from the standpoint of the social group as a whole. He conceptualizes the self as a *social process,* an ongoing conversation in which the socially constructed and regulating "me" reflects on the spontaneous and impulsive "I" from the standpoint of *the generalized other*—the understandings and expectations of the social group as learned through a process of interactive role-taking over time. Mead's idea of the self is implicitly historical—emerging not through interaction with an abstract universal "other," but with a *particular family* situated in a *particular society* shaped by a *particular culture* at a *particular time* in its history. The consumer capitalist self emerges through interaction with significant others whose sense of the world is global and electronically mediated and whose generalized other is shaped by a culture that offers endless consumer choice and easy access to credit in the context of perpetual stimulation of desire—not a situation conducive to the development of a sense of sufficiency in the young.

## CHILDHOOD AND MATERIAL LIFE

Contemporary childhood can only be understood in the context of consumer capitalism, but given a division of academic labor that allocates children to psychology or education, and consumer capitalism to social theory or economic history, the connection between the two tends to be overlooked. The familiarity of everyday life in our own society is also an obstacle to understanding. Why bother to study what we already know "from the inside?" Because our own social and material practices are experienced as "natural," requiring no explanation, the everyday life of "normal" children becomes a routine object of study only in relation to "other" cultures where social and material arrangements and cultural assumptions cannot be taken for granted. Ethnographies of child-rearing practices in tribal cultures might be therefore be used as a guide to the questions that need to be asked about "normal" childhood within our own. To take a classic example, when Margaret Mead set

out in 1928 to study child-rearing practices among Manus villagers in the Admiralty Islands north of New Guinea, she defined her task as one of documenting the way in which the Manus prepared their children for life. She began with the question of what must be learned—relatively easy to answer in a monocultural fishing village built in a lagoon. How useful would such a question be in relation to countries like Australia, Canada, or the United States at the end of the twentieth century?

The cultural diversity of populations drawn from all parts of the globe and occupational diversity of consumer capitalist economies makes Mead's simple question seem impossibly naive. If we compare her account of how Manus children learned to negotiate their watery world with the routines of early childhood in our own society, however, we can see how children's initiation into social life is in each case structured by the way in which material needs are met (Mead, 1975). If Manus children were accustomed to water from the first years of life, our own are accustomed to shopping, and as the boat was central to the production of material life in Manus culture, the shopping trolley is central to our own. Manus children had to learn not to fall out of canoes; our own learn to sit in shopping trolleys and car seats. The parallel ends here, for the world that our children enter is constituted not by water/nature but by commerce/culture—a world in which preparation for life is less a matter of learning basic survival skills determined by environmental limits and physical needs, than of defining "need" itself. The survival skills demanded by subsistence settings involve complex technical mastery and detailed knowledge of environments in which needs are imposed and met by nature. Survival in consumer capitalist economies in which needs are continuously redefined to generate profit depends on the capacity to set personal limits in cultural environments saturated with messages that actively target consumer resistance and stimulate desire.

A trip to the local supermarket lacks the exotic appeal of field work in the Admiralty Islands, but the question of how basic needs are defined and met is nonetheless central to understanding contemporary childhood. Supermarkets and malls are the consumer capitalist equivalent of the bush gardens and lagoons in which the ethnographers of the 1920s and 1930s documented the social relations through which material life was produced in tribal societies. If the tribal child's first venture into the world was on mother's back while she dug for yams, our own children's back pack eye-view is of aisles stacked with cans and packets. If tribal children watched their parents working alongside other adults to ensure a meal at the end of the day, our children enter a world in which basic needs are met through consumption—mysterious transactions involving plastic cards and smiling strangers who say "Have a nice day."

The impact of consumer capitalism on childhood is not just a matter of changing the ways in which parents provide for their children, but changing the cultural conditions for the formation of parents and children as social beings. We tend to think that while times change, human nature remains the same—a universal subject with the same cognitive and emotional structures responding to different historical conditions. Nowhere are these assumptions about the fundamental unity of human experience across space and time more deeply embedded than in relation to children, for they are reinforced by developmental and biological universals. It is easy to move from the fact that physical maturation and cognitive development proceed in the same way wherever they take place to the assumption that the outcome of these processes is also basically the same, particularly within our own language and cultural tradition. When we visit simulated social environments such as theme parks and pioneer villages, for example, we imagine ourselves living in the past or the future as the same person—"me"—wearing different clothes and using different technology. What this fantasy overlooks

is that the "me" produced under different social and technological conditions would almost certainly have different cognitive and emotional responses. Social change is not just about modes of production, but about modes of being human.

We cannot document the economic, technological and social changes involved in the transition from *industrial capitalism* to *consumer capitalism* here, but we can broadly indicate some features of consumer capitalism that make contemporary childhood historically distinctive. Put simply, there are more things to buy, more abstract ways to buy them, more elaborate and impersonal environments in which to shop, and more time devoted to shopping as a preferred leisure activity rather than as a domestic chore. The cultural importance of shopping, and the ambivalence that it evokes, is reflected in car stickers and T-shirts whose ironic slogans—"Born to Shop," "I Shop Therefore I Am," "I'd Rather Be Shopping"—can be read as at once affirmative and critical of the place of consumption in our lives. Joking reference to "retail therapy," or to particular individuals (usually women) as "shopaholics" is a further indicator of the cultural importance of consumption, as is recent identification of compulsive shopping as a "psychiatric disorder"(Lejoyeux, Ades, Tassain, & Solomon, 1996).

Domestic environments—children's first point of entry into the social world—have been radically transformed by new technologies of information and communication. VCRs, personal computers, CD ROMs, Nintendos, and Game Boys offer round-the-clock entertainment, intensifying the penetration of everyday life by commercial culture. Given television's place at the center of the family circle since the 1950s, not to mention radio, records and even sheet music long before that, commercial culture is hardly a new presence in the domestic sphere. What is new is the pervasiveness of this presence. It is not just a matter of technological innovation producing new gadgets, but the combination of new technology and the global division of labor lowering the cost of production, making video and sound equipment cheaper and more accessible. Households often have several television sets, older children and adolescents their own CD players and computers,[3] at least in the middle class. Add a modem and the home becomes a multipurpose site of work, play, shopping, and communication, blurring the division between public and private.

The boundaries of the nation state have also become more permeable. Both production and culture are global. Fewer things that we buy are made in the country we live in, or even in any one country at all. Look, for example, at the packaging on toys marketed throughout the world by companies like Mattel or Hasbro and you will probably find that the toy is made in one country, the package in another—neither necessarily the one in which the company has its headquarters. Information transmission from one part of the world to another is instant, and the same television programs, films, music, and books circulate throughout the globe—as do toys, computer games, and designer-label sneakers and clothing. Children in one part of the developed world look much the same as children in another and watch the same television programs promoting consumption of the same range of toys. They also eat the same fast food at global franchises like McDonald's, KFC, and Pizza Hut, whose marketing strategies include promotional link-ups with children's television or film characters. At the height of the Teenage Mutant Ninja Turtles craze, for example, Pizza Hut offered Turtles figures with family orders; McDonald's routinely offers cheap available-only-at-McDonald's collectables for purchase with Mac Meals. The "fun" of eating at McDonald's or Pizza Hut is thus tied to the "fun" associated with the program or movie and its associated toys—all part of children's shared culture, and all dependent on parents' willingness and capacity to pay. As most parents would not willingly consign their child to feeling left out, this is an extraordinarily effective marketing strategy.

## COMMODITOYS

One of the more obvious ways in which children are incorporated into the hyper-consumption of consumer capitalism is through the commoditoy—the toy designed not to satisfy but stimulate the desire and felt need for the purchase of another toy (Langer, 1989; 1994). The commoditoy subjects children's culture to the logic of fashion and planned obsolescence used to stimulate "turnover" in other areas of the economy.

Commoditoys come in two forms. One is the generic product that allows for an infinite number of variations on a theme, like Lego or Barbie. Lego's legitimacy as an "educational toy" that develops fine motor skills and creativity, and Barbie's association with the twin "evils" of gender stereotyping and consumerism,[4] make their location in the same category unlikely. But if you examine the way in which they are marketed, there are many parallels. Lego might have begun its career in bags of gender-neutral blocks, and can still be found in this form under the Lego Basic label, but it is the brightly colored boxed sets associated with different Lego "stories" that capture children's imaginations and parents' money. Each box of Lego, whatever its size, includes instructions on how to construct the model, pictures and serial numbers of other models in the same series, and illustrated examples of each of the other Lego "stories"—Fabuland, Town, Railway, Castle, Pirate, Technic, and Paradiso. As with Barbie, satisfaction of the desire for one serves to stimulate desire for another.

The other variation on the commoditoy is the transient item that enjoys a finite period of popularity before being replaced by something else that children "must have." This comes in two forms. First is the unpredictable generator of consumer panic of the kind surrounding the Christmas supply of Cabbage Patch Dolls in 1983 or Tickle Me Elmo in 1996. Second are the franchised character toys produced in association with films and television cartoons—a process that effectively turns children's "entertainment" into extended advertisements for toys. Englehart (1987) and Kline (1989, 1993) have documented the way in which the success of movies like Star Wars and E.T. in generating markets for franchised products, and the popularity of soft toys based on cartoon characters, attracted toy companies to what Kline (1989, 1994) describes as "the profitable attractions of character marketing."

Instead of simply finding a suitable and popular television program to sponsor, or waiting for a popular series to survive a season and then creating spin-off characters in the time-honored fashion, toy marketers and licensing agents got together early on to develop their own "property"—their own television characters and program concept. Characters marketed to children in this way over the past two decades include *He-Man and the Masters of the Universe, Transformers, Voltron, DinoRiders, Teenage Mutant Ninja Turtles, Power Rangers,* and *Barney.* Add the product spin-offs of television programs like *The Simpsons,* movies like *Jurassic Park, The Lion King, Aladdin, 101 Dalmatians,* and *Star Wars,* and you have the basis for major accumulations of objects, even before the inclusion of Disney and Muppet characters, Thomas the Tank Engine, Snoopy, Garfield, the eternally youthful Barbie, and Lego—in many respects the ultimate commoditoy because you can never have "too much."

Like the "hit music" associated with teen culture, the toys and assorted paraphernalia (backpacks, lunch boxes, stickers, T-shirts, pajamas, underwear, and so on) produced as part of the promotional universe of block-buster movies and children's television enjoy a limited period of popularity. Association with a movie usually means that the toy has a life-span coinciding with the season of its first release. In January 1997, for example, millions of children across the United States and Canada returned to school with *101 Dalmatians* "gear" acquired over Christmas; their peers in Australia and New Zealand started school in February with the same logos on their lunch boxes. By March, the twentieth anniversary re-release of Star Wars "for the big screen" would diminish the satisfaction of owning *Dalmatians*

spin-offs and create a sense of insufficiency in children whose shelves and closets were already full to overflowing with things. What happens, one wonders, to the toys and clothing that, once longed for with an intensity that has to be observed to be believed,[5] have been rendered irrelevant by the release of a new program or film promoting a whole new product universe?

The essential feature of the commoditoy, whether durable or transient, is the capacity to stimulate rather than satisfy desire. The act of consumption is a beginning rather than an end, the first step in an endless series for which each particular toy is an advertisement, first because its package is also a catalog and second because it is part of a tantalizing universe without which the one just purchased is somehow incomplete. Each purchase inserts the next as an object of fantasy, and perpetual desire becomes one of the defining features of children's experience. This cycle of desire and partial satisfaction is central to the process of socializing children into consumer capitalist adulthood, for it is not so much their capacity to produce as their willingness to consume that will define them as economically useful adults.

Increase in the number of things acquired and discarded by children is evidence of a cultural shift that has material consequences. The "children's culture" industry's contribution to environmental degradation—the destruction of forests, the production of nonbiodegradable waste—is one of the crueler ironies of consumer capitalist childhood, which combines high levels of anxiety about the environment with unwitting complicity in its destruction. Just imagine a toy equivalent of car wreck dumps on the outskirts of every city in the developed world, piled high with discarded Machine Men, Transformers, Masters of the Universe, DinoRiders, Ninja Turtles, My Little Ponies, Jurassic Park dinosaurs, Cabbage Patch babies, Darth Vader masks—once objects of intense desire, but no longer of interest to either the children who wanted them in the first place or their younger siblings and cousins. The culture moves on, bringing new fantasies and desires that cannot be fulfilled by last year's toys.

Children's play has long been subject to cycles of change. Nor is the phenomenon of the "toy fad" a new thing—at least since the advent of mass production and mass media of communication. What *is* distinctive about the commoditoy cycle to which children's play is currently linked is the extent to which its changes are initiated by corporations whose first priority is profit.[6] What is involved is not the recurring cycle of games that pass in and out of favor on an annual basis, or games played by each generation of children at particular ages, but the passing in and out of fashion of games that depend on the purchase of toys whose obsolescence is guaranteed by the release of successors whose promotional cartoon series is already in production.

The point at issue is not the desirability of capitalism as a system of economic and social relations, but the implications for children of growing up within a systemic logic that actively subverts enduring attachment and stimulates desire for continuous novelty. Babies and toddlers still manage to attach themselves to much-loved "transitional objects" singled out from the overwhelming array of stuffed toys that typically greets their entry to the world. But full entry into commoditoy culture produces shortening cycles of attachment and accumulations of objects from which fond memories of "favorite toys" would seem an unlikely outcome.

A sense of the extent to which children's relation to the commodity culture of consumer capitalism involves changes in childhood that go deeper than the transformation of its material surfaces was brought home to me some years ago, as I watched an elderly woman choosing a birthday present for her grandson in the toy section of a big department store. It was 1987, and children's desires were fixed on Transformers—robots that could be turned into vehicles by folding their arms and legs—which starred in a television cartoon series ("Transformers, robots in the sky; Transformers, more than meets the eye") depicting a futuristic struggle for control over planet earth between two robot armies—the good Autobots and the evil Decepticons. Autobots and Decepticons came in all shapes and sizes, each one part of a set of five that could be joined together—"transformed"—into a larger robot. I will leave the cost implications of this aspect of their design to your imagination, and concentrate instead on their incomprehensible features when viewed for the first time through adult eyes.

The woman stood gazing at shelves stacked with boxes of Autobots, Decepticons, Stunticons, and Insecticons. In her hands she held a box of toy soldiers—the expensive metal ones associated with English middle-class boyhood for more than one hundred years. She looked from soldiers to Transformers, shaking her head. Finally, she turned to me, gesturing toward the box in her hand. "I was going to get these for my grandson's birthday," she said, " but I don't suppose he'd want them, would he? I suppose he'd rather have one of those." She pointed to a Stunticon called Breakdown. She looked bewildered. How could such a thing be of lasting value? The soldiers, she told me, were like the ones that her son had played with as a child, and her brother before him. Such things could be passed on from one generation to the next, but who would want to play with this Transformer thing once the fad had passed? "I suppose there's no point in getting him something he doesn't want, " she said, "but which one of these things would I get him? He already has so many." "I don't know," she said, shaking her head as she walked along the aisle looking at the alien objects. "I just don't know." The commoditoy cycle draws children into generationally specific subcultures, diminishing the possibility of communication with adults based on shared experience.

Harnessing play to the promotional strategies of toy companies can also have emotional implications for children whose involvement in a fantasy world is disrupted by the commoditoy program-product cycle. Consider the example of a boy called Daniel, who, at the age of four, was not only playing games based on the television series *Inspector Gadget*, but immersed in the fantasy that he *was Inspector Gadget*. As long as "Gadget" occupied the 5:30 P.M. slot watched by Daniel and his friends each afternoon, their days at kindergarten were organized around "playing Gadget" with Daniel in the title role. One day when his mother collected him he seemed subdued. When asked what was wrong, he burst into tears: "They say I can't be Gadget any more because it's not on television. We have to play Voltron." A new series had started on television, a new range of commoditoys had appeared in the stores, and the fantasy identification of one small boy was rendered obsolete.

In accounting for Daniel's predicament, we have to go beyond television to its social and economic context. Daniel had neither been rendered passive (Winn, 1984) nor robbed of innocence (Postman, 1982) by watching Inspector Gadget on television. The basis of his "problem" was the fact that children's television viewing and the desire for toys that flows from it are salable commodities. The fact that what television produces is not entertainment for audiences, but audiences for sponsors, is crucial to its role in the transformation of children's culture. Television situates children as consumers, potential owners or enjoyers of toys, treats, and activities—a process that can only be understood in terms of the broader cultural logic to which it is tied. It is not just television, but its intersection with the entry of children into the "universal market"(Braverman, 1974; Ewen, 1976), which gives contemporary childhood its distinctive character. For English social critic Jeremy Seabrook (1985, p.13) this simply represents a new phase in children's exploitation by capital, which now needs not their labor, but their desires.

Just as the pauper apprentices once provided an inexhaustible supply of hands to the mills, our children become, in this new phase of capitalist expansion, indentured to their own appetites. And the wants which they learn to express in this way are no more their own than the labour they formerly performed was for their own satisfaction....

## KEEPING THINGS IN PERSPECTIVE

Seabrook's analogy is persuasive. The connection he makes between dark satanic mills and shopping malls is a useful corrective to sentimental rhetoric about childhood as a period of freedom from economic exploitation. Children play a crucial role in the generation of profit for capital, and are no less subject to the dominant economic logic of the society they live in than at any other time or place. At the same time, however, it is important to recognize that the equation of imaginations "stunted and crippled" by consumer culture with bodies "stunted and crippled" by malnutrition and long working days trivializes the suffering of child laborers—suffering that continues in the developing world. Given a choice between having our children work fourteen-hour days in a factory, or spend fourteen hours playing with Lego, Barbie, and Nintendo with time out for meal breaks at McDonald's or Pizza Hut, most of us would have little hesitation in choosing consumer capitalist childhood.

Complete rejection of children's involvement in consumer culture assumes an opposition between "real pleasures" untainted by commerce, and "false pleasures" offered by the market—an opposition that is simply not sustainable. A child's joy is no less "real" because the thing that inspired it cost money. The fact that children's desire for fun is manipulated to *sell* the toys does not mean that fun is absent when the children *play* with them. Nor does the fact that parental anxiety about children's development and success is manipulated to sell "educational" or "creative" toys and activities to parents mean that the toys and activities have no educational or creative value.

Uncritical enthusiasm for the pleasures of consumption is no less problematic. Children undoubtedly get pleasure from fashionable toys and paraphernalia, not least from bonding with friends who have the same things, but this does not mean that there is no need for critical engagement with the recurring cycles of desire and the partial satisfaction through which they are hooked in to consumerism. Children's involvement in consumer culture does have positive, even utopian, elements, but given that it also subverts enduring attachments by stimulating desire for continuous novelty, its implications for individual and collective well-being are at least worth debating. To dismiss all criticism as "Puritanism" or middle class moral panic, is, by implication, to leave decision-making about "what's best for children" in the hands of multinational corporations. Even if the only negative consequences of promoting unrestrained consumerism in children were material—domestic clutter and nonbiodegradable waste—this would be a dubious strategy.

To locate children's consumer desires in the context of history, socioeconomic structure, and culture is not to present them as socially and culturally determined and therefore inevitable. Fatalistic resignation is not the only possible response, though it is important to understand that a culture cannot just be turned off. It must be negotiated on a daily basis. As Seiter (1995, p. 3) argues, "we need to accept that contemporary parenthood is always already embedded in consumption." We cannot shield our children from consumer culture, because it surrounds them, as water surrounded the Manus children studied by Mead. The question is not whether our children will be consumers, but what kind of consumers they will be. To leave the answer to this question entirely to marketing executives is to abdicate responsibility—the consumer capitalist equivalent of allowing our children to fall out of the boat.

## NOTES

1. Arthur S. Trace's *What Ivan Knows that Johnny Doesn't*, published in 1961, provides a classic statement of this anxiety. Although the "communist threat" is no longer an issue, national anxiety about children's academic performance continues in relation to economic competition.

2. For example, one father refused permission for his children to participate in my study on the grounds that focus group discussion about toys and leisure activities would serve to "normalize" children's involvement in consumer culture.

3. The idea that a personal computer is essential for learning is widely shared. In the United States, President Clinton has declared a computer on every desk a key educational goal. In Australia, the Victorian Minister for Education recently justified funding cuts with the argument that the Internet would soon make schools irrelevant anyway, as children could learn from home, and many private schools require children to have their own laptop computer.

4. I recently watched an American talk show featuring "victims" who had been "damaged" by their obsession with Barbie. A program on "Lego victims" is hard to imagine.

5. It is not part of my argument that children are passive dupes of capital. They are very active participants in the passionate pursuit of whatever happens to be the current object of their desire, as any parent of young children can testify. What is at issue is the question of whose interests are served by stimulating ever-shortening cycles of desire, satiation, and dissatisfaction.

6. Stern and Schoenhaus (1990) give an anecdotal account of the corporate environment in *Toyland: The High-Stakes Game of the Toy Industry;* Kline's (1993) *Out of the Garden: Toys and Children's Culture in the Age of TV* provides systematic analysis of the history and implications of toy marketing.

## EVALUATING YOUR MASTERY

1. Childhood consumerism today
   a. Is very similar to the culture of a generation or two ago.
   b. Has been heavily influenced by newspaper advertising.
   c. Has roots in new techniques of mass production and marketing.
   d. Is due to a greater number of spoiled, selfish children.

2. Which of the following is television's most important effect on childhood consumerism?
   a. It reduces parents' control over children.
   b. It allows advertisers to target children directly.
   c. It exposes children to violence and a desire for aggressive toys.
   d. It provides children with adult models who "shop until they drop."

3. According to Langer, the consumer capitalist self emerges through
   a. Interaction with significant others
   b. Early make-believe play
   c. Children's basic needs
   d. Too much time spent in day care

4. The commoditoy's essential feature is its capacity to stimulate the following:
   a. Gender stereotyping
   b. Aggressive behavior
   c. A desire to purchase more
   d. Excessive television viewing

5. True or False: Childhood consumerism fosters enduring attachments to favorite toys.

6. True or False: The commoditoy diminishes children's opportunities to communicate with adults based on shared experiences.

### Critical Thinking

1. Langer emphasizes that even though the consumer world inevitably affects children's outlook and desires, parents can influence what kinds of consumers children will be. List several parenting strategies likely to help children become wise and critical consumers. For each technique, explain why it is likely to be effective.

2. Watch children's television programs in the late afternoon and on Saturday morning, focusing on commercials and television series based on commoditoys. Do child-directed commercials, especially those aimed at young children, constitute fair and ethical practice by the broadcasting industry? Should the federal government limit or ban such commercials? Why or why not?

### Applying Your Knowledge

Visit a mall or grocery store and observe several parents interacting with their children while shopping. To what extent did childhood consumerism influence parent-child interaction during the shopping trip? Did parents' responses to their children promote or deter consumerism?

# 23

## School Matters in the Mexican-American Home

### Socializing Children to Education

CONCHA DELGADO-GAITAN

University of California–Davis

■

Socialization of Mexican-American children must be explained within the historical, sociocultural, and socioeconomic conditions that impact Mexican-American families.

■

Mexican-American parents have viewed the educational system as a means of economic mobility for their children. Thus, education is highly valued.

■

Child-rearing practices at home are sociocultural skills that are learned though mediating structures that interlink; these structures include the family, the church, the school, the neighborhood, and the parents' workplace. These undergirding principles of socialization allow us to understand how families develop strengths and how these strengths need to be recognized by educators.

■

Parents created a safe, comfortable, and stable environment that was conducive to children's thinking positively about their schooling.

■

Common to all families was the factor of participation in social networks outside the family, including church and work groups as well as relatives—the extended family.

In Spanish, children are said to be "buen educado" (well educated) when they are well mannered, speak to others kindly and respectfully, and are helpful to those who need help.

■

Parent-child interactions regarding school-related activities illustrated ways in which parents socialized their children to value schooling in a concrete manner.

■

Low socioeconomic conditions limited the parents' material resources, but did not detract from parental discipline, scheduling time for schoolwork and bedtime, and organizing their lives around a familiar routine.

■

In the home, relative to school matters, culture represents a human adaptation to a dynamic environmental situation. It is not a process of parents transmitting educational values to their children. Rather, children are also active agents in facilitating the transmission of knowledge and the creation of a learning environment in the home.

■

## EDITOR'S INTRODUCTION

For many years, the poor school achievement of low-income minority children was attributed to "cultural deficits"—home environments that place little value on education. Concha Delgado-Gaitan's research challenges this assumption. She spent many months getting to know the residents of a Mexican-American community in a small California city. There she collected extensive field notes on six families that had second-grade children and that had recently immigrated to the United States.

Although the parents had little schooling themselves, they regarded education as a great privilege and supported their children's learning in many ways. Yet their success in helping children with assignments and fostering behaviors valued in school depended on social networks outside the home through which they could obtain information about educational matters. Discontinuities between Mexican cultural values (such as respect for elders) and the requirements of the classroom (formulating contrary verbal arguments) were often at the heart of children's academic difficulties.

Delgado-Gaitan's findings reveal that even when ethnic minority parents provide children with appropriate emotional support and place a high value on education, they need ways to become familiar with their children's classroom experiences and priorities. Contact between parents and teachers also helps educators understand and accurately interpret the child's home life.

The role of families as educators has been one of particular interest in educational research. Research on families in their home environments provides intense exposure to the complex layers of communication and cultural systems that organize the everyday life of the family. The home environment provides a wealth of information about the family's interactions, **acculturation,** and values. Mexican-American families have received specific attention because of the large number of students from this group who underachieve in school.[1]

Numerous reasons for this **underachievement** of Mexican-American children have been advanced. When comparing Mexican-American families with Anglo-American families, researchers have found Mexican-American families are inferior with respect to cultural ideals, values, and family organization and generally are unconcerned about education.[2]

Learning differences of Mexican-American children have been attributed to biological and cultural values that render them cognitively deficient and inferior in comparison to their Anglo-American mainstream counterparts.[3] Pejorative characterizations of Mexican-American families have impacted social practices and policies.[4] Failures in the classroom are attributed to inadequate family environments, unlike those of Anglo-American mainstream children whose families provide them with the values, language, and cognitive skills valued by the schools.

Numerous researchers have disputed this deficit thesis by concluding that Mexican-American families indeed value education for their children.[5] These studies have noted that families face **socioeconomic** barriers that need to be overcome in their pursuit of higher education. Context-bound rules for sociocultural adjustment in a social setting seem to play a role in understanding how Mexican-American families participate in the mainstream system.

Socialization of Mexican-American children must be explained within the historical, sociocultural, and socioeconomic conditions that impact Mexican-American families. Although poverty and limited education do affect child rearing, the problem is more generally one of missing out on the resources and access to advantages otherwise available to middle-class families. This problem is attributed, incorrectly, to Mexican ignorance and/or lack of motivation. The study reported in this paper attempts to understand what education means to Mexican-American families within the household setting and to learn about the family's role in children's education.

## HOME LEARNING ENVIRONMENTS

The home learning environment is created through complex interactions between parents and children and is influenced by the adults' background as well as the sociocultural and sociopolitical forces outside the home. Environment is not necessarily a geographic setting, aside from the fact that it refers, in this instance, to a home. The term, in this paper, connotes the social interaction occurring between family members in the home. Children are socialized to education through interpersonal experience with their parents and family members.

I argue that parents train their children to adapt to the social order which they understand and with which they identify. Children learn about the nature of the world in which they live through parental **socialization.**[6] An important aspect of socialization is the transmission of

Delgado-Gaitan, C. (1992). School matters in the Mexican-American home: Socializing children to education. *American Educational Research Journal, 29,* 495–513. © American Educational Research Association. Reprinted by permission.

values, which vary from culture to culture and from family to family. Research has shed light on the strengths of the family through the study of cultural continuity and discontinuity as well as the cultural ecology of the family.[7] Cultural differences such as religion, moral values, recreation, and education are reflected in the ways in which people raise their children. Parents transmit their culture to the young by teaching them how to think, act, and feel. Part of this process is the act of socializing children to value education. In Mexican-American families, the transmission of educational values is shaped by the family's low socioeconomic condition and the parents' low levels of formal education in the United States. Mexican-American parents have viewed the educational system as a means of economic mobility for their children. Thus, education is highly valued.

While it is true that parents and children experience largely similar social environments, it is also true that their environments diverge in significant ways. Parents and children spend much of their time doing different things in different institutions. Theorists have noted that the same social-structural conditions may affect adults and children in decidedly different ways, especially when we account for the difference in the educational experience of parents in their country of origin and that of their children in the United States.[8]

The complex nature of socialization forces us to consider how Mexican-American children learn the value of education. In a model proposed by LeVine for examining the issues of early learning experience in the family, socialization is shaped by the organization of the social systems in the family.[9] The process of socialization influences children in two major ways: (1) through family structure, which determines the nature of the child's earliest interpersonal experiences but which in turn is affected by the wider social system with which it is integrated; and (2) through parental mediation, which allows parents to deliberately train their children for successful adaptation to a changing social order.[10] These areas

establish the strengths in the families. Spanish-speaking families, and families from other culturally different groups, have demonstrated strengths as evidenced by the cultural knowledge they possess to socialize their children to succeed in their culture.[11] This is contrary to the belief that they are culturally deficient.

The process of the transmission of beliefs, values, and experiences from parent to child is imbedded within broader cultural systems that include societal institutions that impact the family.[12] Child-rearing practices at home are sociocultural skills that are learned through mediating structures that interlink; these structures include the family, the church, the school, the neighborhood, and the parents' workplace. These undergirding principles of socialization allow us to understand how families develop strengths and how these strengths need to be recognized by educators.

## METHOD

How parents convey the value of education can be studied within the process of parent-child value transmission. To that effect, I examined the day-to-day parent-child interactions and the household circumstances and conditions. Presumably, children infer parental values not only from parents' verbalizations, but also from their practices. To study this concept, I selected six Mexican-American families from one community located in Carpinteria, California. These six families lived in the Latino neighborhood in Carpinteria.

### Setting and Participants

Carpinteria is a small city of approximately 12,000 residents adjacent to the larger city of Santa Barbara. Whites represent 67 percent of the population, Mexican Americans 31 percent, Asians 1 percent, Blacks .5 percent, and others including American Indians, .55 percent.[13] Agriculture and other low-paying jobs in the tourist industry drew population to settle in the area.

**Table 23.1 Six Children and Their Parents**

| Characteristics | Norma Serna | Jorge Macias | Jose Martinez | Maria Soto | Jaime Sierra | Marta Osuña |
|---|---|---|---|---|---|---|
| Children in the home | 3 | 2 | 3 | 3 | 7 | 2 |
| Number of parents in the home | 2 | 2 | 2 | 2 | 2 | 2 |
| Family yearly income | $13,200 | $11,900 | $13,500 | $14,800 | $12,500 | $11,500 |
| Family's resident time in Carpinteria as of 1990 | 9 years | 15 years | 11 years | 6 years | 10 years | 10 years |
| Parent education in Mexico: | | | | | | |
|   Mother | 6 years | 4 years | 5 years | 6 years | 6 years | 3 years |
|   Father | 3 years | 5 years | 6 years | 2 years | 5 years | 9 years |
| Mother's occupation | Nursery laborer | Factory assembler | Nursery laborer | Ranch tender | Nursery laborer | Nursery laborer |
| Father's occupation | Nursery laborer | Nursery laborer | Private gardener | Ranch tender | Nursery laborer | Factory assembler |
| Primary home language | Spanish | Spanish | Spanish | Spanish | Spanish | Spanish |

Prior to the early 1960s, Anglo Americans and Mexican Americans were segregated geographically by neighborhood and by school. Gradual upward mobility of Mexican-American families and the advent of equal opportunity programs to compensate for segregating have improved the social and educational conditions of Mexican Americans. Although many in Carpinteria have risen to high professional status as physicians, attorneys, teachers, and small business owners and have moved into more comfortable upscale homes, the fact remains that most Mexican Americans are still relegated to unskilled work.

Demographic data and interviews revealed that the families in the study shared these characteristics: (1) membership in the Mexican working-class community; (2) Mexican immigrant status; (3) a common language (Spanish); and (4) a strong desire to have their children succeed in school. Although their children were born in the United States, the parents had all emigrated from Mexico. Five of the families lived as nuclear units in small one-bedroom apartments, occasionally having another family member reside with them on a temporary basis. The sixth family lived in a larger rented home, which it shared with another family. Although commonalities existed (see Table 23.1), family organization and activities differed daily in form, function, and meaning, as described later in this paper.

The six families that participated in the study lived within a 2-mile radius of Aliso Elementary School. Aliso had one of the largest enrollments of Mexican-American children of any school in the district. Of the approximate enrollment of 360 students in the second to sixth grades, 41 percent were Mexican Americans, and 25 percent of those were limited English-speakers.

The families of the six second-graders who participated in the study were selected because the children were placed in both novice and advanced reading groups in the classroom. These families agreed to be studied in their homes; it appeared that they fairly represented the issues under discussion. The teacher placed the students in their respective novice and advanced reading groups (see Table 23.2). Rather than using the label "low" to identify children who achieved below grade level, the researcher referred to the children as "novice" readers.[14] The fact that they were not yet experienced readers may have been due to the fact that they had not

**Table 23.2  Children's Reading Placement in the Classroom**

| Student | Novice | Advanced |
|---|---|---|
| Norma Serna | X | |
| Jorge Macias | X | |
| Jose Martinez | X | |
| Maria Soto | | X |
| Jaime Sierra | | X |
| Marta Osuña | | X |

yet been taught how to read, or more precisely, taught in a manner understandable to them. The term "novice" eliminates the stigma of being a "slow" learner, and better defines the reader's experience and the reality of the reading problem. That is, in actuality students are not necessarily low or incompetent readers, but they are readers who are beginning to learn to read. The students' reading level was a criterion in selecting families for the study because I wanted to observe the home environment to ascertain what it might reveal about the ways in which parents support their children and how children learn to value schooling.

## The Study

Data were collected through **ethnographic observations and interviews**. Spontaneous parent-child interactions in the home were observed. During a 9-month period, all families were observed six times, in visits that lasted on the average of 2 hours each. Data were collected in the form of field notes, audiotapes, and videotapes. Observational strategies were premised on the theory that the categories through which educational encounters are understood are culturally variable. Observation helped achieve an understanding of the particular symbols, categories, and concepts that organized a particular family's everyday life.[15]

In ethnographic interviews of parents, questions were asked about their residence in Carpin-teria, their employment, the meaning of literacy in the home, the network system outside the home (including employment, church, relatives), and their participation in the schools. The core questions focused on the skills required for their jobs, how much their children knew about their employment, what they expected of their children's future employment/careers, and which, and for what purpose, local social resources were utilized. Interviews about specific tasks were aimed at clarifying the observations made in the home.

The school's permission was obtained since selection of the children was through the classroom. This quasi-official affiliation gave me a status that facilitated the families' acceptance of the study and agreement to participate. Trust between the researcher and the families was established within the first or second visit. I visited all the families to determine their routine and the time of day when I would be able to best capture the necessary parent-child interaction.

## Analysis Procedures

Parent-child interactions that concerned education, including selection of literacy activities, were the primary units of analysis. Conceptions about the ways in which family environments condition children's experience were clustered in a variety of ways.

Three major categories surfaced in the analysis, characterizing the patterns of interaction as physical environment, emotional and motivational climate, and interpersonal interactions.[16] These categories were adjusted to depict the data collected in this study and helped to organize the family's conditions and activities in the home. The categories are the following:

1. *Physical Environment:* The level of economic and educational resources, the types of visual stimulation, and the physical arrangements of the family that set the stage for the child's experience.

2. *Emotional and Motivational Climates:* The emotional relationships within the home,

parental recollections of their experiences with literacy, and the aspirations of family members that conditioned the child's experience with school.

3. *Interpersonal Interactions:* The child's literacy opportunities, conditioned by moment-by-moment interpersonal interactions with parents, siblings, and others in the household regarding informal correction, explanation, or other feedback for the child's experiments with schooling.

These categories provide a heuristic framework within which the home environment can be analyzed and discussed and extend the perspective on home socialization and family strengths. Audiotaped and videotaped data (observations and interviews) were transcribed. A summary description was made of each family. Family profiles were analyzed qualitatively for interaction patterns that revealed the cultural contexts created by parent-child emotion, motivation, skill, knowledge of resources, and beliefs about schooling. The thematic categories are used as a basis for discussion of the findings in the following section.

## PHYSICAL ENVIRONMENT

Part of children's home learning environment is shaped by their parents' economic resources. The extent to which parents provide safe and comfortable housing, adequate learning materials, and informed practices regarding school matters is related to the parents' socioeconomic conditions and their knowledge about academic requirements.

### Economic Resources

The parents' educational background plays an important role in their thinking about education for their children. All of the parents had received a few years of education in Mexico, completing some elementary education. One parent completed the sixth grade and another the equivalent of high school. In spite of the fact that the parents did not have extensive formal education, they regarded schooling as a great privilege for their children. Their day-to-day support for their children's schooling efforts was demonstrated in numerous ways.

Parents created a safe, comfortable, and stable environment that was conducive to children's thinking positively about their schooling. Parents supported students' motivation and educational efforts by providing material rewards for good grades, setting a regular bedtime, and, when possible, designating a particular place in the home for school materials. In most cases, physical space was extremely limited, which made it difficult for children to have a private space. Often they used their backpacks to store their school supplies. Specific areas of the house served a dual function and were typically used for school-related activities on a shared basis with other activities. For example, the kitchen table often served as a desk for homework either before or after dinner. The living room couch was sometimes used by parents as a place to read with their children. If children shared a bedroom with their siblings, they sometimes made arrangements to use the room for part of the evening in order to complete their homework. It was not unusual for parents to send the younger children to bed so that they could watch the evening news in Spanish or a favorite Spanish soap opera on television in the living room.

### Social Resources

The study gathered data about the arrangement of furniture and the number of rooms in the house, the family's neighborhood, and its employment. Yet interaction with others also impacted the family and created another component of its physical environment. In turn, the physical environment set the stage for the quality of resources available for children's education and general quality of life. Family social resources were crucial to the ability to access the educational system.[17]

This Mexican-American mother tries to support her daughter's academic development by helping with homework. How well she will succeed depends on access to information and resources from the school. (Photo: Myrleen Ferguson/PhotoEdit)

Familiarity with the educational system had a great deal to do with the parents' ability to shepherd their children through the school system. Thus, parents who had more experience with schools were better informed and could better guide their children. Parents obtained this information about schools and resources in a variety of ways.

Common to all families was the factor of participation in social networks outside the family, including church and work groups as well as relatives—the extended family. Often, the extent to which parents participated in those networks and the nature of their relationships within them

greatly influenced their children's socialization. Social networks help to shape the educational socialization of children.

Families in the study had relatives who lived nearby, and their social life revolved around the extended family. During celebrations or other events, parents divulged to the interviewer that they insulated any evaluation of academic performance from each other; they usually did not discuss their children's grades. Conversations revolved around family, both in Carpinteria and in Mexico, discipline problems with children in the home, and the crucial passages of life, birth, death, and illness.

When school problems persisted, the parents sometimes sought advice from other adults in their workplace or church groups. Problems caused by their child's frustration or their own inability to deal with the system led to a search by mothers for another family member as adviser. Cousins, uncles, and aunts were sometimes able to help the younger children with homework or with other school matters because they might be better versed in English than the parents. Some of the family members had attended high school in Carpinteria and were able to function as a resource to younger children.

Within the context of church groups, parents who were naive about the school's operation found someone to help them resolve their problem. The setting appeared to be nonthreatening for people. Informally, church organizations served as a resource for parents and supported them in their effort to establish a learning environment. Information about scheduling, location of classes, and matters of punctuality, lunch and dress was provided.

Two of the parents, Mrs. Osuña and Mrs. Macias, were active in the Catholic church organization, Los Guadalupeños. They often saw each other in church meetings. Although they usually did not talk about their children's schooling, Mrs. Osuña, Marta's mother, told of her interaction with a father who was baffled by the process of beginning first grade.

El señor me preguntó, "¿Oiga señora, cómo sabe uno cuando comienza la escuela?" El no sabía que hacer con su hijo porque su esposa estaba en México y su hijo ya estaba para entrar al primer grado. No tenía ninguna idea en cual fecha iba a comenzar el niño. Me preguntó si alguien iba a venir a su casa a recojer al niño porque el no tenía carro. Le dije cuál diá comenzaban las clases y cómo llegar a la escuela y cómo podía saber cuál maestra le tocaba. Se quedó pensando de toda la información que le di y yo digo que hay muchas personas así que no saben cómo leer ni saben inglès. No saben de que se tratan las escuelas; así es que los niños se pierden de mucho. Siquiera este señor supo preguntar y pedirme información. Yo creo que sabiá que yo tengo niños en la escuela también.

(The man asked me, "Ma'am, how does one know when school begins?" He did not know what to do with his son because his wife was in Mexico and the boy was ready to enter first grade. He did not have the slightest idea what date his son began school. He asked me if someone was going to pick him up because he did not have a car. I told him the date that school began and how to get to school and how to figure out who his teacher was. He stood there thinking about all of the information I had given him. I think there are many people like this man who do not know how to read in English and they do not know what the school is about. So the children lose out a lot. At least this man knew enough to ask me for information. I think he knew that I had children in school, too.)

The parents' workplace was another setting in which a resource person was found with whom to consult about school problems. Adults who worked outside of the home on ranches, in nurseries, or in factories were likely to be familiar with the same in-town schools. Mrs. Macias,

Jorge's mother, for example, recounted a time when she felt lost as to the directions to take with Jorge's discipline problems in school.

She had received numerous reports from Jorge's teacher, each indicating an increasing problem with his behavior. The last one threatened to suspend Jorge if he did not improve. His mother had talked to him and punished him at home by not letting him watch television or play outside. Obviously, these measures were not successful. Mrs. Macias asked one of her coworkers, who had children in Jorge's school, what she should do. Her coworker told her that she should ask for permission to leave during the lunch hour and go to the school to talk to the teacher. Mrs. Macias accepted her advice and received her supervisor's permission to go to the school to talk with the teacher. The problem was resolved when Jorge, his mother, and his teacher were able to talk and figure out that Jorge needed to stay away from certain boys who were provoking him.

Parents' economic and social resources are important factors in shaping their children's learning environment in the home. Constrained physical space made it necessary for children and their parents to work within the space they had very carefully and to organize the children's school-related tasks. Setting day-to-day standards for complying with school requirements was accomplished within the limits of a family's space, time, and money. Additionally, parents required the knowledge with which to deal with school problems, and this varied among the parents. Parental experience with the schools dictated the type of support that they were able to access for their children. Parents who were less knowledgeable sometimes found that their social connections served as an important supportive component that compensated, in part, for cultural naiveté. Their social networks provided a level of involvement, maintaining the families' connectedness, through the trust and safety of families' ethnic ties.

# EMOTIONAL AND MOTIVATIONAL CLIMATES

All the parents verbally expressed a strong desire to have their children succeed in school. Obviously, education had a very special meaning for these families that went beyond their desire to have them improve their socioeconomic conditions. Parents believed that education meant being considerate of others, kindness, respect for elders and authority, and cooperation. In Spanish, children are said to be "buen educado" (well educated) when they are well mannered, speak to others kindly and respectfully, and are helpful to those who need help. A person who is "buen educado" may not have been formally schooled. The contrary may also be the case; a person may have a great deal of formal education but be considered "mal educado" (poorly educated) if he or she mistreats others and does not respect others' rights. These parents were strongly influenced by their traditional culture and encouraged their children to be "buen educado" as well as to respect the values of the public school.

## Parental Aspirations

As noted earlier, education was important and highly valued in these families. They expected their children to get good educations to expand their opportunities in employment and possibly to become professionals. Emotional support was abundant in these families. Parents shared with their children their own educational limitations as well as their desire that the children remain in school, complete their education, and go beyond the parents' accomplishments. For example, Mrs. Sierra, Jaime's mother, stated that she and her husband frequently reminded their children to take advantage of their opportunity to study:

> Les decimos a nuestros niños que nosotros no tuvimos la oportunidad de estudiar en México donde viviámos porque habiá mucho trabajo que hacer en el rancho pero ellos aquí pueden estudiar para una carrera

buena. Necesitan prepararse para poder conseguir un empleo más de lo que tenemos nosotros ahorita. A veces los niños prefieren jugar en vez de estudiar, y les tenemos que recordar de cómo es vivir cuando no tiene uno educación. También, los animamos a que pongan atención a sus estudios, que hagan su tarea cada noche y que se acuesten temprano porque aveces quieren ver televisión hasta muy noche.

(We tell them that we as children did not have the opportunity to study in Mexico because we had too much work to do on the ranch. But, they have the opportunity to study here for a good career. They [the children] need to prepare themselves to obtain a good job, better than we have right now. Sometimes, the children prefer to play outside rather than to study, and we have to remind them how it is to live without education. We also encourage them to pay attention to their studies and to do their homework nightly and to go to bed early because they often want to watch television until very late.)

Family stories about their life in Mexico, like those told by the Sierra parents to their children, guided the children's moral and emotional learning. Parents provided emotional support in the talks with their children about their schoolwork when teachers' reports arrived on Fridays. Generally, mothers initiated these discussions about reports, but in some families, the fathers took equal interest.

In families where children were in the novice reading group, the parents often accepted the reports about their children without questioning the teachers' evaluation. If the report about their child was negative, they punished the child and did not inquire further. Other parents acted differently. When a child came home with a negative report that suggested additional assistance in the home was required, parents communicated with the teacher through notes or phone calls asking how to help. But there was no contact when children received positive reports. Parents verbally commended the children and then rewarded them with a book or took them to their favorite restaurant.

Parents made strong efforts to provide children with a supportive learning environment. Nevertheless, in spite of many similar demographic characteristics, parents' daily interactions with children varied according to their knowledge about children's school tasks.

## INTERPERSONAL INTERACTIONS

Interpersonal interactions were abundant in the families observed; many of these interactions had little to do with educational values or school performance. However, observations in the family revealed that, during the week, most of the verbal exchanges revolved around the children's homework. Parent-child interactions regarding school-related activities illustrated ways in which parents socialized their children to value schooling in a concrete manner. Homework constituted most of the children's literacy activities in the home, particularly during weekdays when children were expected to return the assigned homework the following day.

Parents' assistance to their children varied due to their different experiences with the schools. Some parents attended school/child development workshops occasionally. Others did not attend workshops but communicated frequently with their children's teachers. Some parents, not as familiar with their child's academic world, helped, nevertheless, in any manner that they could. In families with older siblings, the older ones helped with homework when parents were unable to assist.

### Advanced Readers' Homework Tasks

Strong emotional support for achievement characterized the relationship between parents and children in the advanced reading group. The Soto, Sierra, and Osuña families wanted to help their children to succeed in school work; and they were available "on demand." Reading, workbook, and ditto pages constituted the homework assignments. Most assignments were in Spanish, but a few were in English for students who were in transition to an English curriculum. The homework worksheets were usually assignments that students did not complete during classtime. Advanced students worked more quickly in class than others and therefore seldom had much homework, and what there was they usually easily understood. Children in this group usually did not spend more than a total of 30–40 minutes on their homework assignments, whether they did their homework alone or under parental supervision.

Parents in this group accepted children's scheduling of their homework because they believed that the students best understood their own academic responsibilities. Ritually, the children came home from school and engaged in play with siblings or watched television. They had no fixed time to do their homework. Many of the children in this group did their homework just before dinner and others accomplished this task after dinner.

Parents reported that their children were rather autonomous in completing their homework tasks and requested less assistance from them. Nevertheless, parents provided supervision. For example, Jaime Sierra's parents stated that they did not have to help him because he usually wanted to do his homework by himself. His mother explained:

El casi siempre hace su trabajo correcto. Por eso lo dejamos que haga su trabajo solo. Hay veces que su papá se pone a discutir la tarea [de Jaime] mientras que Jaime hace su tarea. A veces su papá lo espera hasta que termina su trabajo y discuten el trabajo. Mi esposo también trata de asegurar que Jaime termine su tarea como debe ... Jaime es el mayor de los siete niños y tratamos de darles alguna atención a todos los que estan en la escuela también.

(He usually does his homework correctly. That's why we let him do it by himself. There are times, however, when his father discusses the homework while Jaime is doing

it. Most of the time, however, his father waits until he completes his work and then he discusses it and asks him what he has done …
He also makes sure that Jaime has completed the work he was assigned. Jaime is the oldest of 7 children and we also try to help all of our other children who are also in school.)

Mr. Sierra's involvement with Jaime's homework kept him informed of his son's progress in school. His father discussed the homework with Jaime. Parents did not always help children solve homework problems, but they held the children responsible for completing homework. They often requested to see the completed work, or requested that the child report to them after finishing the assignment.

The example below illustrates how Marta, who completed her homework before dinner, showed it to her father. A ditto sheet had vocabulary words listed at the bottom and the student had to fill in the blanks with a synonym.

Marta: [Approached her father sitting on the couch.] Ya. (OK.)

Father: A ver. Dime que hiziste. (Let's see. Tell me what you did.)

[She showed her father the ditto sheet where she had written in the words to the synonyms in English.]

Marta: Aquí me pregunta. Cuál palabra es igual que "grande," mayor. En la segunda pide la palabra que es igual que "mejor," es superior. En la tercera aquí pide la palabra que es "bonita," bella. (Here they ask me which word is the same as "big," and it's "large." In the second one they ask what is the same as "best," and it's "superior." In the third one they ask what is "pretty," and it's "beautiful.")

Father: Oh si, "bella." (Oh yes, "beautiful.")

Marta: En esta pide la palabra que es "encontrar" y le puse que es "rescatar." (In this one it asks for the word that means the same as "find," and I put, "rescue.")

Father: Espera, yo creo que es otra palabra, mi hija. Puede ser "rescatar" pero a ver

cuales otras palabras te dan para escojer. (Wait, dear, I think that it may be another word. It might be "rescatar" but let's see which ones there are to choose from.)

[There were eight fill-ins on the sheet and the father suggested that Marta finish reviewing all of the other fill-ins. They completed the rest of the fill-ins and she had used the word "rescatar" "rescue" twice; they looked at the word "localizar" ("locate") which she had not used. The father suggested that she substitute the word "localizar" for "encontrar" and Marta did.]

Her father helped her organize her thinking according to the instructions on the sheet in order to check her work. He helped Marta match the synonyms by considering her choices at the bottom of the page. Although this case exemplifies a successful exercise, parents often were filled with consternation when helping their children with homework when the tasks required extensive reading and searching for meaning.

These feelings of frustration and confusion often were the reason for parents to communicate with the teacher in order to clarify expectations about their child's progress. Some parents wrote notes or came to the school to talk personally with the teacher when possible. They spoke about not being able to help with the homework and asked for ideas on ways in which they could be of more assistance.

## Novice Readers' Homework Tasks

Reams of workbook pages and ditto sheets made up the homework activities for children in the novice reading group. Parents in this group enforced highly structured rules for doing homework. Norma, Jorge, and Jose had a set specific time to do homework. They were expected to do their homework either before or after dinner. When the parents were employed full-time, the homework was usually done after dinner so that parents could be present to assist them. When parents assisted their children directly, they gave the children their answers.

Norma, Jorge, and Jose spent between one-half to two hours working on their assignments. In spite of this, the students sometimes did not complete their homework because the instructions were unclear.

The following incident demonstrates how Norma's mother helped her with her homework. Although Norma completed the assignment, both she and her mother did not really understand the task:

[Just before dinner, Norma sat at the dinner table: Her mother interrupted dinner preparation long enough to show her how to fill-in the reading worksheet for her assignment.]

Mother: Sí, mi hija ahorita te ayudo. (Yes, dear I'll help you right now.) [Mother sat down with Norma at the kitchen table and began to work with her.] A ver que tienes que hacer. (Let's see what you have to do.)

Norma: ¿Qué es un personaje? (What's a character?)

Mother: A ver, el personaje es … [The mother looked at the book cover.] (Let's see what the character is …) [The mother continued to look at the book cover and pointed to the illustrator's name and commented to Norma.] Yo creo que esta es la persona que necesitas. (I think this is the person you need.) Espera, no es. (Wait, that isn't it.) [Norma watched as her mother continued to search for the author of the book. Her mother looked at the book cover and found the book title with the name *Zorro* written in small letters at the bottom. She told Norma that this was the person who wrote the book.] "Aquí está. Este es el que escribio el libro. (This is it. Here is the one who wrote the book.) [She pointed to the book title. Norma proceeded to write the book title in the space that called for the name of the author.]

Norma's mother's explanations, corrections, and feedback, although sincere and well-intended, misled her. Norma's mother, like other parents whose children were in the novice reading group, tried her best with the homework questions, as she felt it was her responsibility to assist her child with the answers. Norma's mother, however, expressed a sentiment that was common among the parents whose children were placed in novice groups. The parents felt frustrated because they did not understand how to help their children with homework tasks.

These parents often underestimated the degree to which their children were underachieving. Jose, for example, was experiencing many problems in reading that were made explicit in the negative reports sent home. His parents accepted the teacher's report, and he was criticized for not doing well in school. When his academic work improved, however, the teacher's reports also reflected this and his parents were pleased that Jose was performing at his grade level and that his underachievement had been overcome. Jose's parents expressed ignorance about the nature of Jose's reading problems and were frustrated in not knowing what more to do than to help him as the teacher requested.

The fact that the homework grades and the student's overall performance did not correspond caused confusion. There was a general sense of helplessness on the part of this group's parents. Often they were not aware of alternatives available to them, such as contacting the teacher or someone else with whom they could consult to solve their children's problems.

Part of the problem that undermined parents' feelings of competence was related to the nature of the homework literacy activity. **Decontextualized** drill and practice tasks constituted most of the homework activities, making parental assistance uncertain. Such tasks were dependent on subject-matter knowledge covered in the classroom. Assignments reflected literacy as separate, isolated skills to be individually mastered by rote drill and practice. Assignments seldom encouraged higher level cognitive and language exchanges between parents and children.

Although interpersonal interactions among family members were numerous, those related specifically to issues of homework revealed an area of knowledge about school matters unfamiliar to many parents in this group. Some parents seemed to deal with the homework task much better than others, but their understanding was really no better. This, too, was an important characteristic differentiating the groups. Of significance was the fact that advanced readers were better able to complete the assignment than novice readers.

A possible explanation of the difficulty that novice readers had in doing their homework might be found in the type and amount of work that they were assigned. With the novice readers, lower expectations seemed to be signaled by the assignment of more drill work and stricter rules. The parents tried to comply with the teacher's request for home help for the student; such a request indicated that the child was in academic crisis. This crisis message was reinforced by parents. They generally did not understand enough about the school environment to make necessary and appropriate contacts with the teachers as often as was required to support their child. However, some parents in this group did contact teachers regarding their children's academic progress, and thus were able to affect their children's learning at home.

## CONCLUSION

Parents share a great deal with their children in the areas of aspirations, motivations, physical resources, and face-to-face interactions, which organize the total learning environment. With the exception of parental contact with the school, minor differences existed in the home learning environments of children in different reading groups.

Parents in all groups provided, or tried to provide, their children with the necessary material comforts to support the home learning environment. Low socioeconomic conditions limited the parents' material resources, but did not detract from parental discipline, scheduling time for schoolwork and bedtime, and organizing their lives around a familiar routine. Family social networks outside of the home occasionally mediated parents' concerns about their children. By exchanging information about their children, parents learned how others dealt with similar childhood-learning problems. Not all resources related to schooling were known to all parents, and not all were available. Thus, the role of social networks outside of the home was key for some parents, enabling them to become more knowledgeable about resources and school requirements, both formal and informal.

Parents provided children with the appropriate emotional support and placed a high cultural value on education. The parents also used their personal experiences, their own lack of educational opportunity, to motivate their children. Notwithstanding the high value placed on academics, the concept of an educated person was much broader than merely being able to complete a school program. A child that was "buen educado" (well educated) not only attended school, but was also respectful and cooperative with those around him or her. It was this behavior that was the measure of a person's educational achievement. Parents tried to socialize their children to this concept of education but often met resistance from children's peers as well as school personnel.

Variation in the home learning environments among the families was most apparent in the way that they approached homework tasks. Parents felt confident that they knew how to establish an emotionally supportive environment for their children, yet it was homework assignments that caused more frustration and confusion than any other interactional area. Some parents relied on their children for leadership and explanation in confronting the assignment. Others tried to apply their own commonsense interpretations to the task, but parents in this group met with repeated failure. Major differences appeared in the parents' handling of their children's homework and in their contacts with the school regarding their children's academic progress.

There was no contradiction in the fact that parents felt secure in the physical and emotional support they provided their children but were perplexed when it involved actual academic tasks. They had not received much formal schooling in this country and were unfamiliar with its expectations. However, those parents who contacted the respective teachers demonstrated knowledge about how to access resources that would otherwise have been untapped. Clearly, the school contacts made by parents mattered in that teachers believed that the parents cared about the child's learning, and teachers, therefore, provided parents with valuable information. An important lesson derived from the issue of parent-teacher contacts is that the components of the home-learning environment involve and depend upon interpersonal relationships outside of the home.

In the home, relative to school matters, culture represents a human adaptation to a dynamic environmental situation. It is not just a process of parents transmitting educational values to their children. Rather, children are also active agents in facilitating the transmission of knowledge and the creation of a learning environment in the home. There is a continuous interchange between the family and the school that influences the daily familial interactions about educational issues.

It is necessary to continue examining the family learning environments of children from ethnically different groups to help educators better understand and interpret the discrete circumstances of children's home life. Through descriptive research, educators can make recommendations regarding the necessity for schools to open lines of communication with families' access to necessary academic and social resources. The error of relying on overly simplistic explanations about the learning environment in Mexican-American families, such as the **cultural deficit explanation**, is that they deflect atten-

tion away from the schools' responsibility to develop effective programs for students from underrepresented groups. The influences that contribute to the quality of life of a family and its participation in its children's education are many. These include the cultural group identity, parents' educational background, their socioeconomic conditions, and the parents' knowledge about the school. Mexican-American parents and their children create a learning environment in the home that needs to be recognized by the school in order to build effective community communication linkages that enhance schooling opportunities for students and their families.

## NOTES

1. A number of studies discuss how Mexican-American students have been overrepresented as failures in school. See the review of literature by Russel Rumberger, "High School Dropouts: A Review of Issues and Evidence," *Review of Educational Research, 57,* no. 2 (1987): 101–127. Another book also presents a good discussion of the issue: Gary G. Wehlage, Robert A. Rutter, Gregory A. Smith, Nancy Lesko, & Ricardo Fernandez, *Reducing the Risk: Schools as Communities of Support.* London: Falmer, 1989.

2. This work presents Latino students in a cultural deficit model: Lloyd Dunn, *Bilingual Hispanic Children on the U.S. Mainland: A Review of Research on Their Cognitive, Linguistic and Scholastic Development,* Research Monograph (American Guidance Service: Circle Pines, MN: 1987).

3. See Luis Laosa (1983). "Parent Education, Cultural Pluralism and Public Policy: The Uncertain Connection," in R. Haskin, & D. Adams (Eds.), *Parent Education and Policy* (pp. 331–345). Norwood, NJ: Aldine.

4. Ibid.

5. Researchers who have examined the conditions contributing to cultural adjustment issues of Mexican-American families include Shirley Achor & Aida Morales (1989), Chicanas holding doctoral degrees: Social reproduction and cultural ecological approaches. *Anthropology and Education Quarterly, 21,* 269–287; Richard Cromwell & Richard Ruiz (1982), The myth of macho dominance in decision making within Mexican and Chicano families. *Hispanic Journal of Behavioral Sciences, 1,* 355–373; Concha Delgado-Gaitan & Denise Segura (1989), The social context of Chicana women's role in children's school. *Educational Foundations, 3,* 71–92; Patricia Gandara (1982), Passing through the eye of the needle: High-achieving Chicanas. *Hispanic Journal of Behavioral Sciences, 1,* 167–179; Luis Laosa (1978), Maternal teaching strategies in Chicano families of varied educational and socioeconomic levels. *Child Development, 49,* 1129–1135.

6. Issues of early socialization in ethnically different families are discussed in Uri Bronfenbrenner (1979). *The Ecology of Human Development* Cambridge, MA: Harvard University Press; George DeVos (1992) Adaptive strategies in U.S. minorities. In S. J. Korchin (Ed.), *Minority mental health* (pp. 74–117). New York: Praeger; James Gabarino (1982), *Children and families in the social environment*. New York: Aldine; John Ogbu (1981), Origins of human competence: A cultural-ecological perspective. *Child Development, 52,* 413–429; John Ogbu (1982), Cultural discontinuity and schooling. *Anthropology and Education Quarterly, 13,* 290–307; George Spindler (1974), The transmission of culture. In George Spindler (Ed.), *Education and cultural process: Toward an anthropology of education* (pp.237–310). New York: Holt, Rinehart and Winston; Henry Trueba & Concha Delgado-Gaitan (1985), Socialization of Mexican children for cooperation and competition. *Journal of Educational Equity and Leadership, 5,* No. 2, 189–204.

7. Earlier writings of cultural change have provided some of the conceptual development for understanding the role of family, for example, Julian Steward (1955), *Theory of culture change.* Urbana: University of Illinois Press. Strengths of the family have since been documented in research by Shirly Achor (1978), *Mexican Americans in a Dallas barrio.* Tucson: University of Arizona Press; Moncrieff Cochran (1987), The parental empowerment process: Building on family strengths. *Equity and Choice, 4,* 9–23; Concha Delgado-Gaitan (1987). Traditions and transitions in the learning process of Mexican Children: An ethnographic view. In George & Louise Spindler (Eds.), *Interpretive ethnography of education at home and abroad* (pp. 333–362). Hillsdale, NY: Lawrence Erlbaum; Frederick Erickson & Gerald Mohatt (1982), Cultural organizaiton of participation structures in two classrooms of Indian students. In George Spindler (Ed.), *Doing the ethnography of schooling: Educational anthropology in action* (pp. 132–172). Prospect Heights, IL: Waveland; Hope Leichter (1974), *The family as educator.* New York: Teachers College Press; Alan P. Pence (Ed.) (1988), *Ecological research with children and families: From concepts to methodology.* New York: Teachers College Press; Susan Philips (1983), *The invisible culture: Communication in classroom and community on the Warm Springs Indiana Reservation.* New York: Longman; Peter Sindell (1987), Some discontinuities in the enculturation of Mistassini Cree children. In George Spindler (Ed.), *Education and cultural process* (pp. 333–341). New York: Holt, Rinehart and Winston; Kay Sutherland (1983), Parents' beliefs about child socialization: A study of parenting models. In Irving E. Siegel, & Luis M. Laosa (Eds.), *Changing families*

(pp. 337–366). New York: Plenum; Marcelo Suarez-Orosco (1989), *Central American refugees and U.S. high schools.* Stanford, CA: Stanford University Press.

8. See James Garbarino (1982), *Children and families in the social environment.* New York: Aldine; and Melvin Kohn (1983), *Sociology of education and socialization* (pp. 3–12). Greenwich, CT: JAI.

9. Ibid.

10. See Alex Inkeles (1955), Social change and social character: The role of parental mediation. *Journal of Social Issues, 11,* 3–12; Robert A. LeVine (1982), *Culture, behavior, and personality* (p. 66). New York: Aldine.

11. Based on work on emplowerment by the Cornell Empowerment Group and Delgado-Gaitan. See Cochran & Woolever. Beyond the Deficit Model: The Empowerment of Parents with Information and Informal Supports. In Irving E. Siegel, & Luis M. Laosa (Eds.), *Changing families* (pp. 225–245). New York: Plenum; Delgado-Gaitan (1990), *Literacy for empowerment: The role of parents in children's education.* London: Falmer.

12. See Garbarino, *Children and Families in the Social Environment* [cited in note 8]; George Spindler (1987). *Education and cultural process: Anthropological approaches,* 2nd ed. Prospect Heights, IL: Waveland; Sheldon Stryker & Richard Serpe (1983), Toward a theory of family influence in the socialization of children. In A. C. Kerchoff (Ed.), *Research in sociology of education and socialization* Vol. 4 (pp. 47–74). Greenwich, CT: JAI.

13. U. S. Bureau of Census, U. S. Census of Population and Housing: 1990. *Census Track Final Report.* Washington, D. C: Government Printing Office.

14. The children's reading status is identified as "novice" or "advanced," terms used by Cole and Griffin. See Michael Cole & Peggy Griffin (1983), A socio-historical approach to remediation. *The Quarterly Newsletter of the Laboratory of Comparative Human Cognition, 5,* 69–74.

15. Hope Leichter (1984). Families as environments for literacy. In Hillel Goelman & Antoinette Oberg (Eds.), *Awakening to Literacy* (pp. 38–50). Portsmouth, NH: Heinemann Educational Books.

16. The actual labels of these categories and components that make up the labels are adapted from Leichter's conceptions on home literacy environments. See Leichter. Families as environments for literacy [cited in note 15].

17. Delgado-Gaitan. *Literacy for Empowerment. The Role of Parents in Children's Education* [cited in note 11].

## EVALUATING YOUR MASTERY

1. The deficit model sees school failure of children from Mexican-American homes as primarily caused by which of the following?
   a. Poverty
   b. The home not valuing education
   c. Lack of access to educational resources
   d. Cultural differences between home and school

2. Compared with the families of "novice" readers, families of "advanced" readers displayed which of the following characteristics?
   a. Had higher incomes per family member
   b. Had parents who cared more about their children's education
   c. Had parents who were better versed in the educational system
   d. Let their children watch less television

3. Parents of "novice" readers were less powerful in helping their children with homework because
   a. They had difficulty understanding "novice" readers' homework instructions.
   b. They were not capable of engaging in high-level cognitive and language exchanges with their children.
   c. They were unaware of school resources that could assist them.
   d. a and c.

4. Delgado-Gaitan's study is a qualitative investigation because of which of the following?
   a. It is well done.
   b. It looks at what and how things happen rather than at how much or how many things happen.
   c. We cannot be sure of its findings.
   d. It views the Mexican-American home environment from a superior perspective.

5. True or False: Delgado-Gaitan's study identifies problems in Mexican-American "novice" readers' home–school interactions.

6. True or False: Compared with parents of "novice" readers, parents of "advanced" readers more often contacted the school for advice when their children's reading reports were negative.

7. Delgado-Gaitan used [extensive audio and videotaped observations/questionnaires administered to parents] to find out about home–school ties in the Mexican-American community.

## Critical Thinking

1. What is meant by ethnocentrism? How is ethnocentrism relevant to the difficulties Mexican-American parents encountered in trying to support their children's academic performance in school?

2. What does Delgado–Gaitan mean by "home learning environments?" What features of Mexican–American children's homes foster effective learning environments?

## Applying Your Knowledge

1. Arrange to observe a school-age child at home, during a time when the child has homework to complete. Describe the physical environment, the emotional and motivational climate, and interpersonal interactions relating to the child's school activities and performance. Ask the child's parent(s) how often they visit the school and communicate with the child's teachers? Evaluate the quality of (a) the home learning environment and (b) family-school ties.

2. List as many ways as you can think of that schools can assist ethnic minority parents in their efforts to help their children do well in school.

# 24

## Children with Attention Deficits and Disinhibited Behavior

### STEVEN LANDAU
### Illinois State University

■

ADHD reduces the likelihood the child can function successfully in the classroom and peer group, and increases the risk for management problems at home. As such, children with ADHD experience pervasive difficulties in getting along in the everyday world.

■

It is not the case that children with ADHD behave in unusual ways and are unlike other children. Instead, they behave like children much younger than themselves.

■

ADHD boys who were extremely inattentive in the classroom were able to attend to educational television programming to an extremely high degree.... Apparently, the nature of the task is crucial when determining whether the child has significant difficulty paying attention.

■

Studies of ADHD children indicate that those who show conduct disorder not only are more difficult to manage as children, but also will have more serious adolescent and adult adjustment problems.

■

■

Biological relatives—parents, aunts and uncles, and siblings of diagnosed ADHD children—are more likely to be symptomatic themselves, and twin studies indicate that identical twins are much more likely than fraternal twins to be concordant for the disorder.

■

Designing classrooms appropriately for the child's development is an important step toward managing the behavior of a child with ADHD.

■

One unfortunate consequence of pharmacological treatment is that many parents and teachers rely on medication exclusively and do not invest in other, more lasting interventions.

■

Parent daily reports should be used throughout the course of all school-based interventions, not only to assess treatment efficacy, but also to enhance teacher-parent communication and collaboration.

■

## EDITOR'S INTRODUCTION

Steven Landau reviews recent theory and research on the 3 to 5 percent of school-age children diagnosed with attention-deficit hyperactivity disorder. Without treatment, these children's symptoms—severe inattention, overactivity, and impulsive responding—can lead to academic failure and peer rejection.

Landau describes a new theory of ADHD that attributes its diverse symptoms to a single underlying problem: the child's inability to suppress or delay a response. He notes that although many more boys than girls are diagnosed with the disorder, strong evidence indicates that girls are less likely to be referred for services. Yet early diagnosis is crucial because ADHD can lead to serious adjustment difficulties in adolescence and adulthood. Landau dispels claims that ADHD is caused by poor parenting or dietary problems; instead, research indicates that it has genetic origins and, in some cases, might be the result of pregnancy and obstetric complications.

Stimulant medication is the most common treatment for ADHD. Although the majority of children respond positively, its effects are only short term. For lasting improvements in academic performance and social behavior, drug treatment must be combined with behavioral interventions, including rewards for appropriate behavior and training in social problem solving. In addition, flexible classroom environments help make these children's symptoms less distinctive and disturbing. Treatment requires collaboration among parents, teachers, and the school or clinical psychologist for optimal success.

While the other second graders were working quietly at their desks, Bruno squirmed in his seat, dropped his pencil, looked out the window, fiddled with his shoelaces, and talked out. "Hey Joey," he yelled over the top of several desks, "…wanna play ball after school?" Joey didn't answer. He and his classmates knew that conversation during academic seatwork was not permitted. Bruno was always getting in trouble, and Joey and his classmates knew this because of frequent teacher criticism. More important, though, none of these second graders wanted to play with Bruno. On the playground, Bruno became easily frustrated if things didn't go his way. He engaged in numerous behaviors destined to alienate other children, was provoked easily, and would not follow rules of the game. On occasion, he even fought with other youngsters. Bruno was always chosen last for baseball: When up at bat, he would look the wrong way; in the outfield, he tossed his mitt in the air and did not notice when the ball was hit to him. Bruno's desk at school and his room at home were a chaotic mess. He often lost pencils, books, and other materials necessary for completing assignments (Berk, 1997). Each day, Bruno hears disapproval and reprimands from parents, teachers, and peers.

Bruno is representative of many children referred for **attention–deficit hyperactivity disorder (ADHD)**. What is ADHD, and how does it differ from hyperactivity? Many parents and teachers are rightfully confused when encountering these terms, as even a cursory examination of the clinical literature reveals a bewildering change in perspective regarding the origins of this disorder. Adding to the confusion, one discovers concomitant changes in explanation regarding how ADHD symptoms actually contribute to the dysfunctional state of the child.

Throughout the 1960s and 1970s, motor excess or overactivity was considered the hallmark characteristic; these children were known as hyperactive, and the formal psychiatric system of classification used the term *hyperkinetic reaction to childhood*. It was certainly true that excessive movement found in these children was the most salient of symptoms, and probably the most annoying. By the late 1970s, however, overactivity per se was not considered the most problematic for the affected child. With the publication of DSM-III (American Psychiatric Association, 1980), psychiatry endorsed the belief that a deficit in sustained attention—the lack of vigilance—functions as the preeminent explanation of ADHD, thereby accounting for a change in the formal diagnostic label applied to these youngsters. As such, these children were no longer called "hyperactive", instead, they became known as children with attention-deficit disorder and eventually attention-deficit/hyperactivity disorder.

Regardless of its nominal characterization, researchers and clinicians agree the psychiatric term ADHD describes a constellation of behaviors reflecting excessive inattention, overactivity, and impulsive responding. If present, this symptom set reduces the likelihood the child can function successfully in the classroom and peer group, and increases the risk for management problems at home. As such, children with ADHD experience pervasive difficulties getting along in the everyday world.

There is an evolving theoretical debate, however, regarding the veritable nature of this disorder. Most recently, Barkley (1994, 1997) articulated an explanation for ADHD in which all symptoms are attributed to a single phenomenon—**behavioral disinhibition**—in which the child's ability to suppress or delay a response is impaired. Although a comprehensive discussion of Barkley's "unifying theory" is well beyond the scope of this chapter, a few points are worth mentioning. Barkley argues that children with ADHD experience difficulties in executive functioning that interferes with their working memory, internalization of speech, self-regulation of affect and arousal, and **reconstitution** (that is, the ability to rapidly analyze and reconstruct parts of language to constitute meaningful communicative speech). The combination of these deficits best explains the symptom picture of children with ADHD.

In this theoretical model, a deficient working memory accounts for the numerous anecdotal and empirical reports about children with ADHD who fail to efficiently or accurately execute lengthy sequences of goal-directed behavior. This might account for frequent complaints of noncompliance and forgetfulness. In addition, a disrupted sense of time is explained by deficient working memory. Indeed, Barkley (1997) cites numerous studies indicating that children with ADHD experience significant problems negotiating tasks involving temporal relationships.

Second, Barkley (1997) focuses on the **self-regulatory** and **metacognitive** applications of language. In this context, language serves the child as a way to communicate reflectively with self when plans of action are considered, acted out, and tested (Barkley, 1994). This portion of his theoretical model borrows heavily from the work on children's private speech by the Soviet psychologist Lev Vygotsky (1934/1986) and its recent application by Berk and her colleagues (for example, Berk & Landau, 1993; Berk & Potts, 1991). According to Vygotsky, children use private speech (that is, thought spoken out loud) to overcome cognitive challenges and as a means to regulate and control behavior. Research indicates this speech-to-self follows a developmental course proceeding from audible, externalized speech to more internalized, less audible forms. In addition, private speech is evoked in the presence of increasing academic and behavioral challenge (see Berk, 1994, for a review), and its use predicts enhanced attention, reduced motoric behavior, and improved task performance (Berk & Landau, 1993). According to Barkley (1997), children with ADHD are delayed in the ability to internalize language—to make effective use of private speech—for the purpose of inhibiting or controlling a response. Thus, Vygotskian theory, plus data from Berk's lab, are used to link deficient private speech and behavioral disinhibition (that is, Barkley's explanation for ADHD).

The third component of Barkley's model involves an inability to self-regulate emotion, motivation, and arousal. Accordingly, children who are able to control their motor behavior, who appear to cope with negative emotional states (for example, frustration or anger) without becoming explosive, and who accurately anticipate and prepare themselves for emotionally provocative circumstances show a developmentally appropriate ability to self-regulate affect and its attending arousal. Children with ADHD, in contrast, seem to present significant delay in this ability. This hypothesis may explain why youngsters with ADHD become so excited about impending rewards in behavior modification programs that performance is disrupted. In addition, children with ADHD are known to become more frustrated than normal age-mates when rates of reinforcement are systematically diminished over time as part of a school-based intervention (Barkley, in press). As a consequence, they give the appearance of having problems with drive and motivation. In addition, the failure to regulate one's emotional display accounts for some of the disturbed peer relations experienced by children with ADHD (see Landau, Milich, & Diener, 1998). Thus, a deficient ability to regulate affect seems to characterize the ADHD child's functioning in both classroom and free-play situations.

The final executive function described by Barkley (in press) involves the process of reconstitution, the language-based ability to decompose a stimulus event and then reconstruct or generate an adaptive response to the immediate episode. Verbal discourse, peer communications, story-telling and writing narratives, and the creation of alternative messages and solutions exemplify activities that require reconstituted information (Barkley, 1994). Thus, children who show delays in reconstitution (for example, those with ADHD) will have difficulty developing solutions to problems and will seem more rigid and less creative in their adaptation to changing situational demands. Emblematic of a delay in reconstitution is the frequently articulated complaint that children with ADHD have problems with transitions. For example, Landau and

Milich (1988) found that boys with ADHD experienced great difficulty modulating their communication behavior when required to shift between "interviewer" and "guest" in a TV-Talk Show role-playing game. Boys with ADHD behaved in less role-appropriate ways, seemed more disagreeable or argumentative, and showed reduced ability to adjust dyadic communication behavior commensurate with varying role expectations. Their conversational performance reflected the inability to modulate or adapt according to shifting demands—potential evidence for a delay in the ability to reconstitute information.

Although Barkley's (1997) theory of ADHD is both interesting and comprehensive, several qualifying points need to be asserted. First, Barkley's theory has explanatory relevance only for those children who meet diagnostic criteria for Predominantly Hyperactive-Impulsive or Combined Types of the disorder (a distinction to be discussed later). Indeed, he feels the Predominantly Inattentive type of ADHD does not involve difficulties with behavioral disinhibition. Second, one should not infer from this theoretical discussion that children with ADHD are deficient in adaptive skills or knowledge of appropriate behavior. Thus, it would be unfair to argue that these children could behave properly "if only they tried harder." In fact, it is widely accepted that children with ADHD experience a **performance deficit** (that is, the failure to make consistent use of their resources and skills when dealing with everyday situations), not a **skill deficit** (that is, diminished capacity and knowledge of how to behave). As suggested by Barkley (in press), "(t)he problem, then, for those with ADHD is not one of knowing what to do, but one of doing what you know when it would be most adaptive to do so" (p. 44). Finally, it is necessary to remind the reader that Barkley's (1994, in press) model is yet to be verified. It is an excellent guide for future research, but few investigations have actually been designed to verify the theory and only limited validating data are available at this time.

## CLASSIFICATION OF ADHD

With current diagnostic practices (that is, DSM-IV; American Psychiatric Association, 1994), ADHD can appear as three variants of the same disorder (that is, there are three subtypes of ADHD). According to the diagnostic criteria that appear in Table 24.1, the child who meets the criterion for inattention symptoms (that is, at least six of the listed inattention characteristics), but not "six or more" of the hyperactivity-impulsivity symptoms, would receive a diagnosis of ADHD Predominantly Inattentive Type (the subgroup excluded in Barkley's [1997] theoretical model). If, on the other hand, the child who is symptomatic of six or more characteristics in the hyperactivity-impulsivity symptom list, but not of those in the inattention list, would receive a diagnosis of ADHD Predominantly Hyperactive-Impulsive Type. Finally, children who are symptomatic of six or more inattention symptoms and six or more hyperactive-impulsive symptoms would be diagnosed with ADHD Combined Type (see Table 24.1).

Several other inclusion and exclusion criteria must also be considered. Based on a clinical history taken during the evaluation, there should be evidence that the hyperactive-impulsive or inattentive symptoms had an onset before the age of 7. Thus, if a parent or teacher reports that these problems first emerged during third grade, for example, this information would be incompatible with this DSM-IV age-related criterion. Second, for an ADHD diagnosis to be applied, it is necessary to demonstrate that symptoms are present in two or more settings (for example, at school [or work] and at home). In addition, demonstrable evidence must exist indicating significant impairment in social, academic, or occupational functioning. Finally, even though several ambiguous terms are used in this psychiatric system (for example, "significant impairment" or "maladaptive"), each clinician is expected to apply a developmental perspective when confronted with a child referred for ADHD. Thus, it is necessary to establish the degree to which the child with ADHD displays behaviors inconsistent with his or her developmental level; that

## Table 24.1  DSM-IV Diagnostic Criteria for Attention-Deficit/
##              Hyperactivity Disorder

**A. Either (1) or (2):**

(1) six or more of the following symptoms of *Inatten-tion* have persisted for at least 6 months to a degree that is maladaptive and inconsistent with develop-mental level:

**Inattention**

  (a) often fails to give close attention to details or makes careless mistakes in schoolwork, work, or other activities

  (b) often has difficulty sustaining attention in tasks or play activities

  (c) often does not seem to listen when spoken to directly

  (d) often does not follow through on instructions and fails to finish schoolwork, chores, or duties in the workplace (not due to oppositional behavior or failure to understand instructions)

  (e) often has difficulty organizing tasks and activities

  (f) often avoids, dislikes, or is reluctant to engage in tasks that require sustained mental effort (such as schoolwork or homework)

  (g) often loses things necessary for tasks or activi-ties (for example, toys, school assignments, pencils, books, or tools)

  (h) is often easily distracted by extraneous stimuli

  (i)  is often forgetful in daily activities

(2) six or more of the following symptoms of *Hyperac-tivity-Impulsivity* have persisted for at least 6 months to a degree that is maladaptive and inconsistent with developmental level:

**Hyperactivity**

  (a) often fidgets with hands or feet or squirms in seat

  (b) often leaves seat in classroom or in other situa-tions in which remaining seated is expected

  (c) often runs about or climbs excessively in situa-tions in which it is inappropriate (in adolescents or adults, this may be limited to subjective feelings of restlessness)

  (d) often has difficulty playing or engaging in leisure activities quietly

  (e) is often "on the go" or often acts as if "driven by a motor"

  (f) often talks excessively

**Impulsivity**

  (g) often blurts out answers before questions have been completed

  (h) often has difficulty awaiting turn

  (i)  often interrupts or intrudes on others (for example, butts into conversations or games)

From American Psychological Association. (1994). *Diagnostic and statistical manual of mental disorders* (4th. ed.). Washington, D.C.

is, the degree to which behavior is age-inappro-priate. This is necessary because it is not the case that children with ADHD behave in unusual ways and are unlike other children. Instead, they behave like children much younger than them-selves. This fact has important implications for the design of school- and clinic-based assessment protocols: Data should be assembled to establish each child's topography of difficulties and degree of deviance from age-mates.

## EPIDEMIOLOGY OF ADHD

ADHD might be the most prevalent psychiatric disorder of childhood and is found in at least 3-

to 5-percent of the childhood population (APA, 1994). Given this estimate of occurrence, one should anticipate, on the average, approximately one ADHD student per class in the school set-ting. In addition, all **epidemiological** data indi-cate that ADHD is a male-dominated disorder. Even though the specific cause of this disorder continues to elude researchers, there are several explanations for the consistent finding of male dominance. These include gender differences in heritability, greater vulnerability of male versus female fetuses to pre-, peri-, and postnatal insult and complications, and greater parent and teacher intolerance for male deviance (thereby increasing the chance that boys will be referred sooner to clinics even though girls may emit the same unacceptable behavior). However, very little systematic study has been designed to explore the nature of gender differences (if any) in the symptom picture of ADHD. Indeed, this has been a difficult research program to pursue due to the very small number of referred girls who appear with this disorder.

Fortunately, a recent **meta-analysis** described by Gaub and Carlson (1997) offers interesting insight into possible gender differences among children with ADHD. Based on their review of 18 studies in which boys and girls with ADHD were compared, Gaub and Carlson discovered that an important moderating variable—referral status—qualifies all findings regarding gender effects that have been reported in this area. In other words, there is good reason to believe that clinic-referred children with ADHD are not representative of the disordered population in general. For example, one finds a male-to-female prevalence ratio of 3:1 for ADHD within community samples, but at least 6:1 to 9:1 within clinic samples. This provides strong evidence that girls with ADHD are not referred for services as readily as boys. Support for this contention is based on data indicating that girls referred for ADHD are actually more symptomatic of the disorder than are their male counterparts in the clinic, particularly in the area of cognitive or intellectual impairment. Among community samples, however, Gaub and Carlson report few gender-related differences except that boys with ADHD are much more likely to have serious difficulties with externalizing and disruptive behaviors. Thus, it is possible that teachers feel less competent to manage the disturbed conduct of boys with ADHD. However, these same teachers might consider the typical girl with ADHD "more manageable" because her associated problems (for example, learning difficulties) lead to a better fit between teacher-perceived competence and school-based needs of the child (see Greene, 1995). This phenomenon might have more to say about our referral practices than about the epidemiology of ADHD.

# PRIMARY SYMPTOMS OF THE DISORDER

There has been a conceptual shift in emphasis regarding what is considered most central to the disorder. During the preceding two decades, most researchers agreed that a deficit in sustained attention, the inability to remain vigilant, represented the area of greatest difficulty for the ADHD child (Douglas, 1983). Thus, ADHD children were considered significantly less persistent than their classmates. Even though many teachers use the term "distractible" to characterize the ADHD child's school performance, distractibility implies that these youngsters are unable to select relevant from irrelevant stimuli that compete for their attention (that is, a selective attention deficit). The bulk of current research suggests, however, that their greatest difficulties stem from an inability to sustain a response long enough to accomplish assigned tasks; that is, they lack perseverance in their efforts. As a consequence, parents and teachers attribute to them characterizations such as " doesn't seem to listen," "fails to finish assigned tasks," "can't concentrate," "can't work independently of supervision," "requires more redirection," and "confused or seems to be in a fog"—all apparently the result of this inability to sustain attention (Barkley, 1990).

According to the current psychiatric taxonomy (that is, DSM-IV), and numerous **factor analytic** investigations representing the empirical approach to classification (for example, Frick, et al., 1994), the symptoms representing inattention are considered unrelated to symptoms indicative of hyperactivity and impulsivity (the latter two symptom dimensions tend to cluster together). Thus, ADHD children described as Predominantly Inattentive according to DSM-IV criteria do not, by definition, present symptoms indicative of disinhibited behavior (Barkley, 1997).

Efforts to reliably establish the presence of problems representative of inattention can be compromised by setting effects on child functioning. Thus, inattention might not be a source of difficulty in a less structured, free-play setting, but of great consequence for the child in a highly structured academic setting (Milich, Loney, & Landau, 1982). As a consequence, specific expectations and the degree of structure within any given setting play an important role in determining the presence of these difficulties. This might explain, in part, why parents and teachers do not tend to agree when rating many of the symptoms of these children (Achenbach, McConaughy, & Howell, 1987). Expectations in the home environment are simply quite different than those at school.

This point was reinforced in a study by Landau, Lorch, and Milich (1992). These investigators were intrigued by the surprising but frequent parent report that their ADHD child is able to attend to television (for example, "What do you mean he can't pay attention in school? He sits glued to the TV for hours!"). In fact, a recent advice column in *Parents* magazine suggested that parents could rule out thoughts of ADHD if their youngster was able to pay attention to television. Results of the Landau, Lorch, and Milich study indicated that diagnosed ADHD boys who were extremely inattentive in the classroom were able to attend to educational television programming to an extremely high degree, and their attention was indistinguishable from normal agemates under some circumstances. It seems evident that television might hold greater intrinsic appeal than school work for the ADHD child, plus it does not represent the historical source of frustration and failure associated with classroom performance. Apparently, the nature of the task is crucial when determining whether the child has significant difficulty paying attention.

The second primary symptom involves motor excess or overactivity. This, in combination with impulsivity (discussed later) yield a cluster of symptoms that regularly co-occur and represent the essence of Barkley's (in press) notion of behavioral disinhibition. Historically, overactivity was considered the hallmark characteristic of the disorder and served as the source for the enduring "hyperactivity" label applied to these children. In fact, parents of ADHD children retrospectively report overactivity to be an early marker of the disorder (Campbell, 1988), even though it is also a very common complaint from parents of normal children (Lapouse & Monk, 1958; Richman, Stevenson, & Graham, 1982). As with the other symptoms, overactivity can take many forms but is especially apparent as excessive body movements (both major and minor motor) and vocalizations. Thus, for example, these children are described as "always on the go," "squirmy and fidgety," "can't sit still," "hums and makes other odd noises," "talks incessantly," and "climbs excessively" (Barkley, 1990).

When ADHD children engage in table activities or academic seatwork, they constantly get up and down from the desk (or do all seatwork while standing). Many show minor motor fidgeting, such as pencil tapping or leg shaking, and they seem unable to keep their hands off objects unrelated to the task at hand. During individual psychological testing, ADHD children can be extremely challenging subjects, as they attempt to manipulate the examiner's test materials throughout the evaluation. Finally, they are often overactive and incessantly talkative in the context of social play—behaviors that seem to have a negative effect on peer relations (Landau, Milich, & Diener, 1998). Again, it is important to remember that setting demands—in particular, the degree of structure in the environment—affect the extent to which these children are considered problematic by their teachers. For example, the ADHD child might be quite troublesome in a highly structured academic setting, with desks placed in rows and all work to be accomplished in one's seat. In contrast, in the open classroom setting where cooperative learning is encouraged and students are expected to move about and collaborate with others, the ADHD child may be less distinctive and disturbing to others (Jacob, O'Leary, & Rosenblad, 1978).

The third core symptom, and one Barkley (in press) considers central to the disorder, involves problems with impulsive responding. Children with ADHD experience significant difficulty inhibiting their response—they are disinhibited (Barkley, 1994). As with inattention, impulsivity is a multidimensional construct; it can be defined in several ways (Olson, 1989). For example, ADHD children are impulsive when confronted with academic tasks. They are extremely quick to respond without considering all alternatives. Thus, they are known as fast but careless and inaccurate problem solvers. This type of response style can have profound influence on the ADHD child's ability to perform in the academic setting. Besides affecting cognitive performance, impulsivity can also manifest itself as an inability to suppress inappropriate behavior. As such, ADHD children are also known to be high risk takers, as evidenced by running out in traffic. In addition, they seem unable to delay gratification (see Milich, Hartung, Martin, & Haigler, 1994), and do not respond in the same way as agemates to reinforcement and response cost paradigms (Iaboni, Douglas, & Baker, 1995). In school, they experience difficulty waiting their turn in line, blurt out answers in class, constantly touch other children, and tend to be undesirable playmates because of their difficulty with turn-taking, sharing, cooperation, and a low tolerance for frustration while playing games (Landau, Milich, & Diener, 1998).

## SECONDARY PROBLEMS OR ASSOCIATED CHARACTERISTICS

The research literature is replete with demonstrations that clinic-referred children have multiple problems; that is, they are **comorbid** for two or more disorders (Caron & Rutter, 1991). This is especially the case with ADHD children, as they typically experience numerous difficulties that go beyond the primary symptoms of inattention, overactivity, and impulsive responding. These additional problems are secondary to the disorder, not relevant to the diagnosis of ADHD, but are nonetheless found in many cases. This fact accounts for the extreme heterogeneity in samples of ADHD children.

For example, ADHD children are at elevated risk for problems related to **oppositional-defiant (ODD)** and **conduct (CD) disorders**. Although the rates of overlap vary with each study, most investigators agree that at least one-half of all ADHD children also meet diagnostic criteria for ODD or CD. Thus, with ADHD children comorbid for these problems, one finds extreme stubbornness, noncompliance, and hostility, plus rule violations, stealing, lying, and aggressive acts (Erhardt & Hinshaw, 1994). Children with ADHD who present the most serious management challenge for parents and teachers are more likely comorbid for ODD or CD. Studies of ADHD children indicate that those who show conduct disorder not only are more difficult to manage as children, but will also have more serious adolescent and adult adjustment problems (Weiss & Hechtman, 1993).

In addition, many ADHD children experience disturbed peer relations, tend to be rejected by classmates, and have few, if any, friends (Landau, Milich, & Diener, in press). These problems occur with such frequency that some (for example, Whalen & Henker, 1991) have suggested that difficulties in the social domain should serve as a diagnostic indicator of the disorder. In fact, Erhardt and Hinshaw (1994) argue the social problems experienced by children with ADHD might be central to an understanding of their overall psychopathology.

Take, for example, Bruno, who was described at the beginning of this chapter. Although not characteristic of all children with ADHD, Bruno is emblematic of many who, by virtue of their behavioral excesses in the peer group, are considered objectionable playmates and tend to be actively disliked and avoided. Indeed, data indicate that negative reputation among peers can be established after only brief contact (that is, 8 minutes in some cases) with unfamiliar children (Pelham & Bender, 1982). This is an especially troubling domain in which to experience problems: To date, research has consistently identified two risk factors that predict adverse outcomes later in life for children with ADHD. When tracking children diagnosed with ADHD into adolescence and adulthood, those who ultimately experience the most serious clinical problems (for example, substance abuse, criminal arrests and incarceration, psychiatric hospitalization) were previously identified as having difficulties with aggression (Hinshaw, 1987) or social relations (Parker & Asher, 1987). Thus, ADHD children with early peer problems are more likely to experience adolescent and adult disturbance.

Even though it is not possible to advance causal explanations for these disturbed peer relations, most researchers agree that a deficit in social skills per se does not sufficiently explain the peer problems of ADHD children (Cousins & Weiss, 1993). For example, Whalen, Henker, and Granger (1990) found their ADHD subjects as competent as normal children in the ability to detect appropriate and inappropriate social behavior. Unfortunately, children with ADHD might not be able to consistently and efficiently implement their social skills (that is, they know how to make friends, but fail to apply this knowledge in their attempts). As a consequence, one would say these children have a performance deficit in the social domain. There is evidence to support this hypothesis. Despite their best intentions, children with ADHD are notorious for emitting a high rate of aversive behavior in the presence of peers. Like Bruno, they can be noisy, boisterous, intrusive, explosive, critical, and argumentative—behaviors that classmates find highly objectionable. It is no wonder that children with ADHD tend to play with others much younger than themselves. Any of these noxious behaviors could cause the child with ADHD to be rejected. However, aggression—especially physical aggression—seems to account for the largest share of these peer difficulties (Erhardt & Hinshaw, 1994).

In addition to aggressive conduct and peer problems, children with ADHD are at risk for significant achievement difficulties and learning disabilities (McGee & Share, 1988). These academic problems should come as no surprise, as many ADHD youngsters are extremely inefficient and disorganized in the academic setting, and their performance tends to reflect great fluctuation (Barkley, in press). According to both anecdotal reports and systematic observations (Atkins, Pelham, & Licht, 1985), the classroom desk of an ADHD student is easy identified, being the messiest in the room. Grade-appropriate performance in class is also a challenge: Children with ADHD spend significantly less time on task, more often violate classroom rules because of an inability to inhibit behavior (for example, "…you must raise your hand and wait to be called upon!"), have difficulty adjusting to transitions, such as going from recess back to class (Landau & Milich, 1988), and complete fewer assignments. As a consequence, the learning potential of many of these children is compromised by academic performance problems and a grave discrepancy between ability and accomplishment. Because of these difficulties, children with ADHD receive copious amounts of negative teacher attention (Flicek & Landau, 1985); this feedback is an important predictor of peer rejection (Landau & Milich, 1990). Even more unsettling is the finding that teachers tend to be more negative and reprimanding with nonsymptomatic students if a student with ADHD is enrolled in that classroom (Campbell, Endman, & Bernfeld, 1977). Thus, children with ADHD are disruptive forces to the "social ecology" of the school setting (Whalen & Henker, 1985). It is little wonder, therefore, that ADHD children are also at risk for self-esteem deficits and depression because of the cumulative history of negative feedback from parents, teachers, and peers.

## ETIOLOGICAL HYPOTHESES

Many causal explanations for ADHD have been proposed over the years. First, research indicates that genetic transmission of the disorder should be given serious consideration. Biological relatives—parents, aunts and uncles, and siblings of diagnosed ADHD children—are more likely to be symptomatic themselves, and twin studies indicate that identical twins are much more likely than fraternal twins to be **concordant** for the disorder. In addition, siblings of children with ADHD might be at greater risk for learning disabilities, thereby suggesting the possibility of common causal mechanisms for both disorders. Second, researchers are pursuing neurobiological causes, such as a deficiency in neurotransmitters that control attention (Hynd, Hern, Voeller, & Marshall, 1991), or inadequate development in one or more portions of brain structure. For example, Barkley's (1997) theoretical explanation of behavioral disinhibition as the primary deficit of ADHD presumes the prefrontal brain area as locus of the impairment. Unfortunately, much of the supportive data regarding neurobiology are inferential and, in most cases, lack complete explanatory power. Third, intriguing data implicate pregnancy and obstetric complications. For example, correlational studies indicate that maternal smoking or alcohol use during pregnancy are linked to increased risk for ADHD. The fact that children with ADHD have a higher rate of minor physical anomalies (MPAs; for example, asymmetrical ears, third toe longer than second) suggests insult to the fetus during the first trimester of pregnancy. However, the higher count of MPAs among ADHD children can also be explained by genetic aberration. Fourth, despite a widespread belief among lay persons, and the popularity of various dietary treatments, no data suggest that sugar consumption (Wolraich, Milich, Stumbo, & Schultz, 1985) or other food additives (for example, artificial food coloring and salicylates) are related to the onset of ADHD. Finally, even though it has been argued that parents are somehow causally responsible for ADHD symptoms in their children (for example, Winsler, 1994), no evidence suggests aberrant parenting or child rearing is culpable for the disorder. In fact, Barkley (1997) argues persuasively that ADHD can be distinguished from CD

by virtue of etiological hypotheses: The former is indicative of cognitive impairment, whereas the latter more likely results from deleterious child-rearing plus socioeconomic disadvantage.

## ASSESSMENT OF ADHD

Given that the topography of impulsivity, inattention, and activity symptoms differ among ADHD children and across situations, it is necessary to establish precise individual information of each event and a thorough description of every situation in which the problems occur. For this reason, a multidimensional and multisetting approach to assessment is necessary. Parent, teacher, and even peer reports, plus observations in the naturalistic setting, must be employed in the evaluation of ADHD. Certainly the assessment protocol should be designed to go well beyond the objective of generating a psychiatric diagnosis. Because psychiatric classification of ADHD presumes homogeneity of symptoms for all members of the diagnosed group (see Landau, Milich, & Widiger, 1991, for a discussion of this issue), an ADHD diagnosis on its own does not lead to an individualized treatment plan. Instead, a comprehensive school-based evaluation should be launched to provide data that can be linked directly to the design of an intervention for each child (see Landau & Burcham, 1995) for a discussion of a problem-solving approach to this assessment).

### Parents

Parents are, of course, an important source of information about children's behavior, as they observe them daily and in a variety of settings. However, parent reports are not sufficient in the evaluation of ADHD for two reasons. First, parents do not have exposure to the full range of child behavior. They might be unaware of developmental norms and what constitutes age-appropriate behavior. Second, as stated earlier, the symptoms of ADHD might not be as troublesome in the home, a setting that typically is less structured than school. Although parent reports are necessary, information from other informants must be considered as well.

## Teachers

Teachers serve as an essential source in the assessment of ADHD, and they can use several rating scales to communicate their knowledge and concerns regarding the child (see Barkley, 1990, for a review of these scales). Rating scales provide a normative comparison, as teachers are asked to rate the degree to which the child's behavior differs from other children in the class. Like parents, teachers have almost daily contact with these children. Unlike parents, teachers are also exposed to many other children of the same age and can use their normative perspective to determine if the referred child is behaving in age-inappropriate ways (an important question to address during assessment). In addition, teachers observe these children in both unstructured play settings as well as in highly structured academic settings, where symptoms of ADHD are more likely to emerge. Finally, teachers are in a position to notice behavior fluctuations in response to different situations.

In fact, the notion of behavioral variability itself has become an important target for assessment: Because children with ADHD are believed to be deficient in regulation-of-self (see Barkley, 1997), they should not be expected to deviate from agemates if performance is under the control of immediate and frequent contingencies. On the other hand, children with ADHD should become increasingly more distinctive as tasks and settings require longer chains of behavior strung together in the absence of frequent rewards. For the child with ADHD, the consequence of this latter situation is inconsistent effort toward a task because both internal and other external events influence and disrupt behavior. Thus, the child "flits" from one incomplete activity to another (Barkley, 1997), thereby evincing great fluctuations in performance. For treatment purposes,

these fluctuations, and their accompanying situations, must be noted during data collection.

## Naturalistic Observation Data

An important source of information about the ADHD child, and one that has direct implications for treatment planning, involves systematic observation of the child in classroom and play settings. By using previously defined code categories that quantify the amount of time the ADHD child spends engaged in on-task behavior and various inappropriate off-task behaviors, it is possible to get direct information about how the child is functioning. In addition, it is helpful to collect these data on the same-sex classmates of the child. In this way, it is possible to determine that Billy, who presents symptoms suggestive of ADHD, attends to math or story time 22 percent of the time, while the other boys in his class attend an average of 84 percent during that same observation session. Because parent and teacher reports are based on previous contact with the child (that is, numerous retrospective observations), and might be biased by the disruptive nature of the child's behavior, direct observation of the ADHD child is the only way to provide data regarding current behavior, and these data will facilitate interpretation of the reports from parents and teachers. In addition, it is just as crucial to use direct observation for the purpose of evaluating the contingencies and controls operating in the classroom or playground. As previously stated, the fluctuating performance observed in children with ADHD indicates that disinhibited behavior may be attributable to insufficient reinforcers.

## Peers

One final area to be considered in the assessment process involves the child's peer interactions. This is an especially important domain to address during data collection because of the overwhelming evidence that children with ADHD experience disturbed peer relations (Landau, Milich, &

Diener, 1998). For social skills training to have a therapeutic effect, it will be necessary to establish if the child with ADHD has a deficit in social skills or social performance. Teacher and peer ratings of interpersonal behavior, classroom **sociometric assessment** (which can provide information about peer popularity and rejection), self-report measures of social loneliness and social anxiety, all offer valuable information about the child's functioning in the social domain (see Landau & Milich, 1990, for a discussion of these procedures). In addition, direct observation of the child in the presence of peers, especially during free-play and unstructured activities (for example, on the playground, in the cafeteria, before and after school) will provide rich data to be used to establish if and what type of intervention might be needed.

## TREATMENT OF ADHD

Once assessment data indicate the referred child is, indeed, experiencing significant problems with inattention or behavioral disinhibition or both, what should be done? It is important to remember that children with ADHD benefit from the same classroom environments available to all children (that is, there is nothing unique to ADHD indicating the need for special class placement). Thus, designing classrooms appropriately for the child's development is an important step toward managing the behavior of a child with ADHD. For young children, this means a loosely structured environment in which active involvement is an integral part of the learning process. As these children mature, however, the role of curricular interventions takes on greater importance. Finally, all intervention activity should reflect extensive and ongoing collaboration among parents, teachers, the psychologist (school or child clinical), and a medical professional in the community. The two primary methods of intervention are psychopharmacological, involving the use of stimulant medication, and behavioral management. However,

treatment outcome data strongly encourage a combination of the two—that is, multimodal treatment (Pelham, 1993).

## Medication Therapy

The most common treatment for ADHD involves medications that stimulate the central nervous system (Barkley, 1990), with 80 to 90 percent of all children with ADHD experiencing a trial of psychostimulants (DuPaul & Stoner, 1994). Methylphenidate (MPH; Ritalin®) is the most frequently prescribed psychostimulant. Approximately 70 to 75 percent of children show a positive response to this medication, leaving at least one-fourth unaffected (Pelham, 1993). Thus, these medications will help many, but not all children with ADHD. MPH is generally administered twice daily, with dosages ranging from 0.25 to 0.75 mg/kg of body weight per dose. In most clinical trials and research settings, this translates to 7.5 mg to 12.5 mg per dose for a second or third grader of typical size (Pelham, 1993).

## Effects of Medication

For those children who do respond positively, the effects are immediate and typically quite strong. For the average child, conspicuous effects are apparent within 30 minutes following ingestion, peak within two hours, and are gone within four. Attention, impulse control, and short-term memory can all be improved (see Pelham, 1993, for an excellent review of these effects). Children talk less, are less disturbing, follow rules better, and emit fewer hostile exchanges with peers. Thus, children who respond to medication are noticeably less disruptive and more cooperative, leading to improved relations with parents, teachers, and peers. As these children become more cooperative, the need for close adult supervision should diminish. In fact, these desirable short-term effects are considered the most impressive and replicable in the entire pediatric psychopharmacology literature (Brown, Dingle, & Landau, 1994). However, despite a substantial reduction in disruptive behavior, the vast majority of ADHD children continue to show problem behaviors. Thus, medication is often helpful, but not sufficient, in the management of the disorder.

In addition to reducing disruptive behavior, stimulant medication helps children attend better when involved in organized athletic play with other children (Pelham et al., 1990). These activities, such as soccer or T-ball, involve peer interactions, so medication might indirectly improve the peer relations and self-esteem of children with ADHD. Even while on medication, however, most ADHD children have difficulty experiencing any improvement in the negative social status that accrued before drug treatment. There are at least two explanations for this disappointing outcome. First, social status research with children in general is replete with demonstrations of the durability of rejected peer status (Landau & Milich, 1990). Once an unsavory reputation has been created, subsequent appropriate behavior might not be salient enough to disconfirm earlier negative impressions. Thus, even though medication improves the social behavior of ADHD children, this alone might not impress classmates sufficiently to affect a change in how they feel about the medicated child. Second, as suggested by Erhardt and Hinshaw (1994), the curvilinear effect cycle experienced by medicated ADHD children (that is, quick onset that peaks at 2 hours and washes out by lunchtime, followed by a noon-time dose with effects gone by end of school day) will leave most ADHD children in an unmedicated state during the two times of day when they are most likely in unstructured free time with peers: lunchtime and after school. As such, members of the peer group might not have sufficient opportunity to observe the medication-induced improvements in social behavior. Whatever the explanation, the data indicate that medication can exert a desirable effect on the social behaviors of children with ADHD, but without concomitant improvement in their actual status among peers.

Medicated ADHD children are also better able to concentrate on schoolwork. They complete more assignments and are more careful and accurate. In terms of daily observation in the classroom and examination of permanent academic products, MPH clearly exerts a powerful effect on short-term academic performance (see Carlson & Bunner, 1993, for a review). However, pharmacological studies carried over months or years fail to demonstrate a concomitant medication effect on learning, as defined by achievement tests or other measures of academic accomplishment. In other words, medication does not seem to help ADHD children master more difficult tasks and might not relate directly to enhanced learning. Thus, even though the child's academic performance seems improved, academic achievement itself is only minimally, if at all, affected by psychostimulants.

Recently, there has been growing interest in the effects of medication on attitudes and motivation of ADHD children. For example, some experts have suggested that medication might cause children to believe they are responsible for their own misbehavior—that they must rely on some external agent (the drug) for control of their difficulties (see Whalen & Henker, 1976). Thus, when children behave inappropriately or do not succeed at school work, they might conclude their medication must not be working that day—in other words, these problems are not their fault. In contrast, other researchers suggest that because medication leads to improved performance, ADHD children can personalize this newly discovered success. Thus, they feel greater responsibility for their own behavior than if not medicated—they have greater control than ever before. Although more study is necessary, current results support the second hypothesis: Medicated ADHD children seem to credit themselves for good performances (that is, they internalize and personalize their successes) (Milich, 1993). The fact that these children attribute successes to their personal effort, and not to the medication, might contribute to their self-esteem. Indeed, many ADHD children informally report they "can try harder" and feel more effortful during times they are medicated. In summary, medication seems to improve behavior in a variety of ways and can also help children feel better about themselves.

Despite the important effects of medication, several cautions should be kept in mind. First, not all children with ADHD benefit from stimulant medication. Second, preschool-age children do not experience improvement to the same extent as older children (Barkley, 1989). In a review of medication studies with preschoolers, Campbell (1985) noted that few benefits were obtained and that side effects, such as increased solitary play and clinging, appeared serious enough to potentially disrupt social development. Third, all the medication-induced benefits represent short-term effects only. That is, improvements are noticeable only while the child is taking the medication. In the evenings, weekends, and summers when children are typically not medicated, the child's symptoms generally return to pretreatment levels. Thus, there are no lasting benefits from the use of medication.

## Side Effects

Many parents express concern about negative side effects resulting from MPH treatment. For example, there is evidence of mild insomnia and reduced appetite (Pelham, 1993). This latter effect has been thought to lead to suppressed height and weight gains. However, research indicates that effects on growth can be corrected by altering the dosage and by medicating the child only during the hours of school. Therefore, standard pediatric practice involves "drug holidays," in which the child is given an opportunity for extended wash-out during evenings, weekends, and school vacations. This regimen seems to sufficiently address the growth suppressing effects of MPH.

Mild headaches and stomach aches can also occur, but they tend to disappear within a few weeks (Barkley, 1990). These problems, along with mood changes, such as irritability and idiosyncratic responses (for example, lip-licking, rashes), can be alleviated by a simple dosage adjustment. Research indicates there are no known long-term side effects. For example, positive medication status during childhood does not appear to increase the risk for drug abuse later in life (Pelham, 1993). Thus, any side effects tend to be mild, short-term, and easily relieved.

One unfortunate consequence of medication treatment is that many parents and teachers rely on it exclusively and do not invest in other, more lasting interventions. Within the past few years, the lay press has expressed alarm about overmedication of children, and with good reason: The period 1990–1995 witnessed an increase of 250 percent in the prescribed use of MPH ("Mother's Little Helper," 1996). If parents seek medication only for the purpose of managing their child's home-based behavior problems, one could say that medication is being overprescribed, but if medication is used to help the child adjust better to school, the concern is exaggerated. It is important to remember, however, that medicated ADHD children, although improved, are not made symptom-free. For these reasons, medication is not adequate by itself as a treatment for children with ADHD. Thus, the acknowledged best-practice is to combine drug and behavioral treatments in the management of ADHD. This is done not only because medication, although necessary, is not sufficient in the treatment of most cases, but also because it permits the use of a lower dose. The data indicate that a low dose of Ritalin®, in combination with behavioral intervention, results in at least the same behavioral improvement as a high dose alone (Pelham, 1993). In addition, when the low dose is used, most undesirable side effects can be avoided.

## Behavior Modification

Because many children with ADHD demonstrate an inability to follow rules and govern their own behavior (Barkley, 1997), behavioral treatment is a necessary adjunct to medication for these self-regulatory difficulties. Aspects of successful behavioral intervention include rewarding appropriate behavior, giving effective directions and requests, and using consistent methods of discipline. If teachers can receive assistance from consultants (such as school psychologists) with the implementation of these procedures, most ADHD children can have their educational and social needs met in the mainstream or regular class setting. In addition, collaboration with parents is essential, as home-based support will enhance the success of psychosocial interventions at school (see DuPaul & Stoner, 1994, for an excellent discussion of school-based programs).

Regarding the use of rewards, many parents and teachers do not believe that children should be reinforced simply for doing what is appropriate and expected. It is certainly the case that most children do not need a rich schedule of rewards to promote acceptable behavior. However, if a child with ADHD seldom engages in a desirable behavior (such as raising a hand in class), then rewards might be necessary to shape this expected behavior. Eventually, the schedule of rewards can be diminished as the behavior is learned. Research clearly shows the use of rewards is particularly helpful when dealing with ADHD children (Pelham, 1992). Their inappropriate behavior tends to be extremely compelling—adults and peers can not ignore it. As a consequence, much of the feedback they receive from others is expressed as a complaint or reprimand, having implications for self-concept difficulties. Thus, rewarding positive behavior not only shapes the child to continue behaving appropriately, but can also contribute to the child's more favorable sense-of-self.

Verbal praise is crucial and can be especially powerful when the positive behavior is also clarified (for example, "I like the way you waited to be called on before answering"). However, praise alone may not be sufficient because of the ADHD child's greater sensitivity to irrelevant internal and external stimuli (Barkley, 1997). Thus, praise might not engage the child's attention during implementation of the **operant procedure.** At first, parents and teachers might need to give material rewards along with praise to teach appropriate behavior and subsequently use praise

alone to maintain the behavior. For example, smiley faces or gold stars could be given every half hour for engaging in desirable classroom behavior. A star chart in which different classroom activities (for example, math desk work) are separated as intervals, can make implementation easier. Even though some teachers may find these procedures intrusive and distracting, the fact remains that the use of a behavioral intervention disrupts classroom routine much less than an untreated ADHD child. It is important to remember that children with ADHD require more frequent and powerful rewards to assist them with response inhibition (Iaboni, Douglas, & Baker, 1995), and any operant procedure will most likely be strengthened if the child is concurrently receiving pharmacological treatment (Pelham, 1993).

Unfortunately, the disinhibited behavior of ADHD children requires that teachers and parents issue numerous directives and commands to these youngsters throughout the day. To increase the likelihood the child will cooperate with adult requests, directions should be specific and brief (Pelham, 1992). Commands that are vague (for example, "Will you cut that out!"), issued in question format (for example, "Let's get back to work, shall we?"), or involve several directives strung together, are not likely to be obeyed. Instead, adults should obtain the child's attention, issue the direction (for example, "Joey, finish picking up those blocks now"), and wait a few seconds. The child should then be praised for cooperating. These techniques can be very effective, as they prevent adult interactions from escalating into anger and reduce the tendency of ADHD children to ignore or resist.

In circumstances where an ADHD child does not respond to adult direction, teachers can consult with psychologists to implement a variety of other behavioral interventions. Ignoring mildly aversive behaviors can prove effective, but increased adult monitoring and immediate consequences to reduce disruptive acts (for example, asking the child to sit out of an activity) might be indicated. If the child engages in aggressive outbursts or is extremely uncooperative, a time-out procedure should be implemented (DuPaul & Stoner, 1994). Consistency is essential for any of these methods to work well.

## Cognitive-Behavioral Interventions

Interventions with a cognitive or problem-solving focus, designed to improve the peer relations of children with ADHD, have received recent attention (Landau, Milich, & Diener, 1998). The essence of these **social problem-solving interventions** involves a model in which children are taught, through coaching, role-playing, and rehearsal, to identify and define their interpersonal problems, generate various problem-solving strategies for each of the identified problems (brainstorming), assess the potential consequences for each strategy (causal thinking), consider how to implement each potential solution (means-end thinking), and implement a strategy and assess its efficacy (Guevremont & Dumas, 1994). One promising program, known as Anger Coping (see Lochman, White, & Wayland, 1991), addresses both cognitive and affective responses to provocation in the peer group. Although not initially designed for the disturbed peer relations of children with ADHD, this program does focus on the largest single contributor (that is, aggression) to their social difficulties (Erhardt & Hinshaw, 1994). Anger Coping trains children to (1) develop awareness of physiological, affective, and cognitive phenomena related to aroused anger; (2) use self-management and monitoring skills; (3) apply means-end thinking so that alternative responses to provocation are considered, and (4) increase the behavioral repertoire in the face of social conflict. Preliminary data are encouraging (see Landau, Milich, & Diener, in press, for a review).

Finally, there is good reason to believe that parents can serve as an effective back-up to the school-based interventions described earlier, including social skills training programs in school (for example, Sheridan, Dee, Morgan, McCormick, & Walker, 1996). One effective method to enlist the aid of parents involves sending home each day a brief daily report card reflecting the child's performance in school (Barkley, 1990). This card, to be completed by the teacher and shared with the child daily, should reflect the prioritized treatment targets previously agreed on in a parent-teacher-psychologist conference. This procedure has several appealing benefits. First, it ensures that parents remain involved in the child's school-based treatment regimen, and, by rewarding the child for success in school, can support teachers' efforts. Second, this procedure serves as an important medium for communication between school and home. The daily report generates a sense of shared responsibility and problem-solving. Finally, this daily report card should also be considered a critical component in every school-based drug evaluation protocol (Landau & Burcham, 1995; Pelham, 1993). Thus, parents will receive daily feedback to share with the prescribing physician, who must establish the proper dose of MPH. In this context, a daily report card is more appealing than norm-referenced rating scales because its items are unique to each case, having been determined as the most important targets of treatment. Parent daily reports should be used throughout the course of all school-based interventions, not only to assess treatment efficacy, but also to enhance teacher-parent communication and collaboration.

To conclude this discussion of treatment alternatives for children with ADHD, guidelines prescribed by Pelham (1993) and the National Association of School Psychologists (NASP, 1992) deserve utmost consideration: Psychostimulant medication, such as Ritalin®, should be prescribed for children with ADHD only after appropriate psychosocial (for example, behavior modification) and curricular interventions have been implemented and found insufficient. In addition, psychostimulants should only be used in conjunction with other interventions (Pelham,

1993). In this way, maximal benefit for the child can be realized while reducing the likelihood of undesirable consequences that emerge from the treatment experience.

As this review indicates, children with ADHD experience problems in academic and social functioning and are at risk for emotional disorders as well. Their problems tend to be pervasive, influenced by many factors, and resistant to change. Because of the complexity of the dis-order, successful treatment requires the collaboration of many professionals engaged in multiple interventions. No single treatment has been identified that can eliminate all difficulties. A number of treatments, however, do exist that can ameliorate many ADHD symptoms and alter the course of the disorder. If parents and teachers receive assistance through multidisciplinary consultation and collaboration, the quality-of-life for children with ADHD can be improved.

# EVALUATING YOUR MASTERY

1. According to Barkley, all symptoms of ADHD are caused by which of the following?
   a. Deficient working memory
   b. Reconstitution
   c. Behavioral disinhibition
   d. A disrupted time sense

2. According to DSM-IV, a child with _____ of the hyperactivity-impulsivity symptoms but not _____ of the inattention symptoms would receive a diagnosis of ADHD Predominantly Hyperactive-Impulsive Type.
   a. Six or more; three or more
   b. Three or more; six or more
   c. Three or more; three or more
   d. Six or more; six or more

3. Which symptoms of ADHD tend to cluster together?
   a. Inattention and impulsivity
   b. Inattention and hyperactivity
   c. Impulsivity and hyperactivity
   d. Inattention, impulsivity, and hyperactivity

4. Children with ADHD are likely to be comorbid for which of the following?
   a. Oppositional-defiant disorder
   b. Severe depression
   c. Schizophrenia
   d. Anxiety disorder

5. Children with ADHD who are at greatest risk for adolescent and adult disturbance show which of the following difficulties?
   a. Aggression and peer difficulties
   b. Learning problems and anxiety
   c. Aggression and depression
   d. Distractability and dependency

6. True or False: Barkley's theory applies only to children with the predominantly inattentive type of ADHD.

7. For a child to be diagnosed with ADHD, symptoms must have appeared before age ___ and must be present in _____ settings.

8. True or False: Children with ADHD are at risk for disturbed peer relations.

9. True or False: In assessing ADHD, parents provide more valid information than do teachers.

10. True or False: In treating ADHD, medication therapy is not sufficient; it must be combined with behavioral treatments.

## Critical Thinking

1. ADHD is a "male-dominated disorder." Why are girls with ADHD less likely to be referred for services than are boys? What are the long-term implications of overlooking ADHD in girls?

2. Summarize evidence on the causes of ADHD. What are the implications of assuming, erroneously, that ADHD is a parent-caused disorder?

## Applying Your Knowledge

Seven-year-old Gerry has been diagnosed with ADHD. His parents are convinced that all Gerry needs is stimulant medication for his academic performance and peer relations to improve. Explain why Gerry's parents are incorrect. What additional interventions do you recommend for Gerry?

# 25

## Control versus Autonomy During Early Adolescence[1]

JACQUELYNNE S. ECCLES
Universities of Colorado and Michigan

CHRISTY MILLER BUCHANAN, CONSTANCE
FLANAGAN, ANDREW FULIGNI,
CAROL MIDGLEY, & DORIS YEE
University of Michigan

■

Putting this person-environment fit perspective into a developmental framework suggests that parents and teachers need to adjust their exercise of control based on the particular child's developmental stage. Optimal developmental outcomes ought to result from an environment that gradually reduces adult control as children's desire for autonomy increases.

■

As predicted, these early adolescents expressed an increasing desire for input into classroom decision making as they got older....

■

In contrast to these changes in desires, reports of both the adolescents themselves and their teachers indicate that the classroom environment is not positively responsive to the longitudinal increase in the adolescents' desire for autonomy.

■

These findings suggest that the increasing mismatch between early adolescents' desire to have input into classroom decision making and their perceptions of the actual availability of such opportunities that is typically associated with the transition to junior high school could contribute to the decline in motivation to study math in the junior high school that has been reported in several studies.

■

Parent-child relationships offer the inexperienced adolescent essential guidance from a more knowledgeable member of society. They also provide an often-unsure child with a secure base from which to explore his/her identity and the complexities of the adult world. Peer relationships, on the other hand, provide developing adolescents with the opportunity to explore their potential as autonomous, independently thinking and acting individuals.

■

Youths reporting only limited opportunity to participate in family decision making also relied more on their friends than their parents for help with personal problems and future planning and were more willing to disobey their parents and forgo achievement-related activities in order to keep and be popular with friends.

■

Clearly, these results point out the importance of designing educational and family environments for early adolescents that provide a better match to their growing desires for greater control over their own lives.

■

## EDITOR'S INTRODUCTION

Jacqueline Eccles and her collaborators discuss the controversial issue of how much adult control is appropriate for young people in transition from childhood to adolescence. Drawing on person-environment fit theory, the authors hypothesize that optimal motivation and life satisfaction results from a gradual reduction of adult control as the adolescent's desire for autonomy increases. This prediction was tested in a large-scale longitudinal study of the impact of changes in school and family life on early adolescents' achievement-related beliefs, motives, values, and behaviors.

Findings indicate that classroom environments are not responsive to maturational increases in adolescents' autonomy needs. In fact, external control seems to tighten with age rather than relax, leading to declines in young people's intrinsic motivation and interest in school.

Within the family, the more adolescents participate in decision making, the greater their motivation for school work, their liking of school, their self-esteem, and their adjustment to the junior high school transition. In contrast, when parents are not responsive to adolescents' bids for greater autonomy, young people invest too heavily in peers—turning to friends rather than parents for help with personal problems and future planning and engaging in self-defeating behaviors to be popular with agemates. At the same time, too much freedom also has costs; it leads to excessive peer orientation.

The authors conclude that adolescents require changing levels of autonomy that fit their changing developmental needs. Their research is of great practical relevance for parents and, especially, secondary school teachers who aim to provide developmentally appropriate rearing and learning environments during the adolescent years.

Because they are dependent on adults, children experience varying degrees of adult control throughout their development. Theories about the potential impact of adult control on children's social and intellectual development often make what appear to be conflicting recommendations and predictions. On one hand, researchers concerned with **intrinsic motivation** have argued for minimal use of controlling strategies with children (for example, Boggiano & Katz, 1991; Boggiano, Main, & Katz, 1988; Deci & Ryan, 1985, 1987). On the other hand, researchers like Baumrind (1971) and Brophy and Evertson (1976) have argued that relatively high levels of adult control, when exercised in an emotionally supportive relationship, have more positive consequences for child development than do lower levels of adult control exercised in the same type of supportive environment.

The issue becomes even more complex when one takes developmental considerations into account in theorizing about the potential impact of adult control on children's development. Optimal levels of adult control undoubtedly change as children grow older. **Person–environment fit theory** (Hunt, 1975; Lee, Statuto, & Kedar-Voivodas, 1983; Lewin, 1935) suggests that the match between the child's need for **autonomy** and the amount of adult control exercised is critically important. People will have optimal motivation and satisfaction in settings that afford them as much autonomy as they desire. Less than optimal motivation is likely in settings that provide either less control or more control than desired.

Putting this person-environment fit perspective into a developmental framework suggests that parents and teachers need to adjust their exercise of control based on the particular child's developmental stage. Optimal developmental outcomes ought to result from an environment that gradually reduces adult control as children's desire for autonomy increases.

This article draws on the data from an ongoing, large-scale **longitudinal study** of adolescent development (the Michigan Study of Adolescent Life Transitions, MSALT) to examine these issues. More specifically, it presents findings regarding a mismatch between adolescents' increasing desire for autonomy and their perceptions of the autonomy they are allowed, and the consequences of this mismatch for their school motivation and attachment to their teachers and parents. But first the theory of stage-environment fit is described.

## STAGE-ENVIRONMENT FIT

Numerous studies have examined the impact of environmental characteristics on the behavior and motivation of people of all ages. Work in the area of intrinsic motivation, in particular, has documented the impact of controlling environments on children's and adults' behavior and motivation (for example, Boggiano, Main, & Katz 1988; deCharms, 1980; Deci & Ryan, 1985, 1987). These studies demonstrate the negative impact of controlling environments on students' intrinsic motivation, learning, and subsequent interest in the activity. But socialization environments are, by their very nature, controlling to some extent. Therefore, it may be better to think about the relation between controlling environments and motivation in terms of optimal levels of control-levels that further positive growth without undermining intrinsic motivation or attachment to the adult socializers. What might these optimal levels be, how does this optimal level of environmental control change as children get older, and what happens when environmental change does not keep pace with the children's increasing desire for more autonomy as they mature? We know, for example, that children become more extrinsically motivated and less intrinsically motivated to do their schoolwork as they move into

Eccles, J. S., Buchanan, C. M., Flanagan, C., Fuligni, A., Midgley, C., & Yee, D. (1991). Control versus autonomy during early adolescence. *Journal of Social Issues, 47,* 53–68. Reprinted by permission.

junior high schools (Eccles & Midgley, 1988). Many also "turn off" to school and to learning at about this same age. Is this decreased motivation a result of excessive control in the junior high school environment? During the same period, many parents complain about the increasing rebelliousness of their children at home. Is this rebelliousness due, in part, to a lack of parental recognition of, and adaptation to, their young adolescent's growing desire for autonomy?

Person-environment fit theory provides a useful framework in which to think about these issues. According to this theory, there are negative motivational and behavioral consequences of being in an environment that does not match one's subjective needs (Hunt, 1975; Lewin, 1935; Murray, 1938). In contrast, positive motivational consequences should result when there is a good match between individuals' needs and the characteristics of their environments. At the most basic level, this perspective suggests the importance of considering the fit between the needs of early adolescents and the opportunities afforded them in the traditional junior high school and in their homes. A poor fit could explain the declines in motivation associated with the transition to junior high school.

An even more interesting way to use the person-environment fit perspective is to put it into a developmental framework. Hunt (1975) argued for the importance of adopting a developmental perspective on person-environment fit in the classroom. He suggested that the optimal level of classroom structure and control would satisfy two conditions: (a) it would mesh well with the student's current level of maturity and need for both control and autonomy, and (b) it would pull the students along a developmental path toward higher levels of maturity and independence. Furthermore, this suggestion implies that optimal levels of adult control over children's behavior should respond to, and foster, increasing independence and autonomy as children mature. Combining this idea of optimal levels of control with a developmental perspective on likely age-related increases in children's desire for autonomy suggests that children will continue to be positively motivated only if their environments change at least as rapidly as they do. We say "at least" because Hunt's perspective implies that the optimal rate of change in the actual autonomy afforded by the environment may be slightly faster than the rate of change in the children's own desire for autonomy.

These suggestions have intriguing implications for understanding the motivational declines that occur at early adolescence. First, if one accepts the notion that different types of environments are needed for different age groups in order to meet their developmental needs and to foster growth, then it is also likely that similar environments will have different effects on children of different ages. For example, if children develop a greater need for autonomy as they move through adolescence, then living in environments characterized by a constant level of adult control should produce an increasing mismatch over time between the need these adolescents have to be autonomous and the opportunities for autonomy they believe are available to them. In turn, experiencing this increasing mismatch between one's needs and one's environments should have negative consequences for both the adolescent's intrinsic motivation and their attachment to the adults in these environments.

Second, it seems likely that some types of changes in the social environments children confront as they move into adolescence may be especially inappropriate for the early adolescent period. For example, some evidence suggests that junior high school teachers are more controlling than are upper level elementary school teachers (Eccles & Midgley, 1988). This type of environmental change is at odds with the normal course of development and, as such, it could be characterized as "developmentally regressive." Exposure to increased control at this age is likely to lead to a particularly poor person-environment fit, which in turn could account for declines in motivation and in attachment to adults at this developmental period.

This analysis raises an interesting set of questions. First, how do the subjective developmental needs for autonomy from adult control change during the early adolescent period? Second, what kind of socialization environments are developmentally appropriate for this age in terms of both meeting the adolescents' needs and stimulating further development? Finally, and most importantly, is there evidence that moving into regressive (developmentally inappropriate) environments contributes to emergence of the negative motivational outcomes often associated with young adolescents? Such an explanation is in marked contrast to popular views that these negative motivational outcomes reflect the impact of the biological changes associated with **puberty** on psychological states (Blos, 1965; Freud, 1969).

## METHODOLOGICAL OVERVIEW

To answer these questions, we are conducting a large-scale longitudinal study of the impact of changes in school and family environment on adolescents' achievement-related beliefs, motives, values, and behaviors (MSALT). The initial sample of sixth graders was drawn from 12 school districts located in middle-income communities in southeastern Michigan; it included approximately 80 percent of the adolescents asked to participate During the first two years of this study, approximately 2,300 early adolescents (80 percent of the initial Wave I sample) filled out an extensive questionnaire in their math classroom two times in the sixth grade and again two times in the seventh grade (fall and spring of both the 1983/84 and 1984/85 academic years). Each of these questionnaires took two class periods to complete.

Since we were primarily interested in the impact of various types of changing school environments on early adolescents' motivation and self-concepts, we selected school districts in

which the adolescents would experience the traditional junior high school transition as they moved from the sixth to the seventh grade. The following measurement strategies were used in order to get an accurate and detailed description of the changes over this two-year period in these adolescents' home and school environments: (a) at least one classroom for each of the participating teachers was observed by trained field staff members for five consecutive days during late October or November each year, (b) all teachers completed an extensive classroom climate questionnaire at each wave, (c) all adolescents completed a similar classroom climate questionnaire at each wave, and (d) both the parents and the adolescents answered an extensive set of questions assessing the family environment at each wave. Although all parents were asked to participate, only about half agreed to do so at each of the four waves of data collection. The vast majority of the remaining parents indicated that they did not have time to fill out the questionnaires. Only a few attitudinal and demographic differences emerged when the adolescents of participating families were compared with the adolescents of nonparticipating families-most importantly, the adolescents of participating families did slightly better in school and were slightly more likely to come from White middle-class families.

The questionnaire completed by all participants (adolescents, teachers, parents, and observers) contained indicators of a wide range of environmental characteristics and achievement-related motivational constructs. To investigate the impact of physical maturation on early adolescent development, the parents were also asked a series of questions about their children's pubertal development. Most of the items were answered on **Likert scales**. Composite scales were derived from these items using both **factor analysis** and theoretically based clustering, and most of these scales had adequate **internal consistency reliability** (s > .60). Single-item indicators of certain key constructs were also used.

The specific scales and items used in the analyses reported herein are described where appropriate.

## PERCEIVED CONTROL IN THE SCHOOL SETTING

Several analyses tested the developmental hypotheses regarding person-environment fit in the classroom setting (for a full description of these analyses, see Mac Iver & Reuman, 1988; Midgley & Feldlaufer, 1987). In a sample of 2,210 students and their teachers in 117 pretransition and 137 posttransition classrooms, Midgley and Feldlaufer (1987) assessed student and teacher perceptions of actual and preferred decision-making opportunities in the classroom. Yoked pairs of items (Lee, Statuto, & Kedar-Voivodas, 1983) assessed these opportunities in five areas (that is, where to sit, class work, homework, class rules, and what to do next) in which students might be allowed to help make the classroom policy on issues directly affecting them. For example:

> For students: Do you help decide what math you work on during class? *Should* you have a say about this?
>
> For teachers: Do your students have a say about what math they work on during class? Do you think students *should* have a say in this?

Three scores can be derived from this measure: (a) perceived opportunity to participate in decisions regarding each area; (b) desired opportunity to participate in decisions regarding each area; and (c) the congruence or incongruence (mismatch) between the respondents' desired opportunity to participate and their assessment of the actual opportunity to participate. These measures were used to assess (a) longitudinal changes in both the desire for and the perceived opportunity to have this type of autonomous control over the learning environment, (b) developmental differences (as assessed by pubertal maturation rate) in these indicators, and (c) the impact of stage-environmental match or mis-

match on the adolescents' academic motivation and classroom behavior.

## Perceived Control: Developmental Changes in Fit

**Changes in the desire for autonomy.** One way to look at developmental' change is to look for longitudinal changes in the same children across time. Midgley and Feldlaufer (1987) reported the results of such an analysis using the first four waves of data. As predicted, these early adolescents expressed an increasing desire for input into classroom decision making as they got older; that is, they were more likely to indicate that they should have a say in classroom decisions at Waves 3 and 4 (fall and spring of their seventh-grade year) than at Waves 1 and 2 (in their sixth-grade year).

**Maturational differences in the desire for autonomy.** Another way to look at developmental change is to look for interindividual differences between same-aged children of different maturational levels. At this age, the extent of pubertal development of the females provides a good indicator of individual differences in physical maturation; the parents of the female students rated their daughter's pubertal development in terms of changes in (a) breast development, (b) oily hair, (c) skin blemishes, (d) pubic hair, (e) growth spurt, and (f) the onset of menstruation. A 3-point scale ranging from 1 = no development to 3 = substantial development was used to rate breast growth; a yes-no scale was used to rate the presence of (b), (c), (d), and (f); reports of the actual number of inches grown in the last year were used to create a three-level indicator of growth spurt, by dividing the distribution into thirds. These-various indicators were combined and standardized within age groups. This indicator of maturational level was examined in relation to the female adolescents' desire for input into classroom decisions on the Lee, Statuto, & Kedar-Voivodas (1983) items. Consistent with the intra-individual longitudinal pattern of age-related change reported in the previous paragraph, the more developmentally mature female adolescents expressed a greater desire for input into classroom decision making than their less developmentally mature female classmates (Miller, 1986).

**Grade-related changes in the opportunity for autonomy.** In contrast to these changes in desires, reports of both the adolescents themselves and their teachers indicate that the classroom environment is not positively responsive to the longitudinal increase in the adolescents' desire for autonomy. Both the adolescents and their teachers reported that the adolescents actually had fewer decision-making opportunities after the transition to junior high school than before-the classroom environment became more controlling as these adolescent went from sixth to seventh grade. As a result, the mismatch between the adolescents' increasing desire for autonomy and the actual opportunities for participation in decisions regarding their classroom experience increased as the adolescents moved from sixth grade into seventh grade (Midgley & Feldlaufer, 1987).

**Maturation-related differences in the perceived opportunity for autonomy.** A similar pattern of results emerged when we divided the girls into two groups based on their physical maturity in the sixth grade and then compared their sixth grade responses to the same set of decision-making items. Although these girls with varying degrees of pubertal development were in the same classrooms, the more physically mature females (that is, the early developers) reported fewer opportunities for participation in classroom decision making than did their less mature female peers (that is, the on-time and late developers).

This maturational difference was shown even more strikingly in the within-year changes in these female adolescents' perceptions of the opportunities they had to participate in classroom decision making. The mean change in their perceptions of opportunities from the fall to the spring testing was examined as a function of their pubertal status. The early-maturing sixth-grade females showed a negative change (a decline) over the course of the school year in the extent to which they could participate in classroom decision-making. In contrast, the late-maturing females in these same classrooms showed a positive change (an increase) over the course of the school year (Miller, 1986). How can this be, given that these adolescents were in the same classrooms? Did the teachers actually treat these adolescent females differently (that is, did the teachers respond to earlier physical maturity with more controlling behavior)? Or did the adolescents perceive a similar environment differently (that is, did the early-maturing adolescents perceive the same level of adult control as providing less opportunity for self-control than did the later-maturing adolescents)? Evidence from educational psychology, developmental psychology, and general psychology suggests that either or both of these explanations could be accurate: Teachers do respond differently to various children in the same classroom depending on a variety of characteristics (Brophy & Evertson, 1976), and people do perceive similar environments differently depending on their cognitive and/or motivational orientation (see Baron & Graziano, 1991). More detailed classroom observations are needed to determine the exact nature of the relationship between teachers' behavior and adolescents' perceptions.

But more important for the issues central to this article, the pubertal maturity of the female adolescents was related to the degree of mismatch between their desires for input and their perceptions of these opportunities in their classroom environment. By the end of the school year, almost twice as many early maturing females reported experiencing the "can't have a say but should" type of mismatch as did their less physically mature classmates.

This last set of results is especially interesting in light of the findings of Simmons and her colleagues (for example, Simmons & Blyth, 1987; Simmons, Blyth, Van Cleave, & Bush, 1979) on factors related to adolescents' successful adjustment to the junior high school transition. They have found that the pubertal status of female adolescents at the time of the junior high school transition is related to changes in their self-esteem, and to their self-reports of truancy and school misconduct. In particular, the more physically mature females reported the highest amount of truancy and school misconduct after they made the junior high school transition. The researchers suggested that experiencing both school and pubertal transitions simultaneously put these girls at risk for negative outcomes. Alternatively, it is possible that the mismatch between their desire for a less controlling adult environment and their perceptions of the actual opportunities for participation puts these females at risk for negative motivational outcomes.

## Motivational Consequences of Poor Fit in Perceived Control

As outlined earlier, person-environment fit theory suggests that the mismatch between young adolescents' desires for autonomy and control and their perception of such opportunities in their environments should result in a decline in the adolescents' intrinsic motivation and interest in school. Mac Iver, Klingel, and Reuman (1986) tested this prediction using the sixth-grade data of 2,239 of the students. They compared changes in the extent of match (that is, congruence) in students' responses to the "can decide" and "should decide" questions with changes in these early adolescents' motivation and interest in school. Students who showed an increase in this match also showed an increase over this time period in the following single-item indicators of motivation and interest (each measured on a 7-point Likert scale): their rating of math as useful and interesting, their rating of how much they liked both their math teacher and school in general, and their rating of how hard they worked in math. They also reported engaging in less misbehavior than did the students who experienced an increase in mismatch. These findings suggest

that the increasing mismatch between early adolescents' desire to have input into classroom decision making and their perceptions of the actual availability of such opportunities that is typically associated with the transition to junior high school could contribute to the decline in motivation to study math in the junior high school that has been reported in several studies (see Eccles & Midgley, 1988).

**Consequences of less-than-desired autonomy.** More directly related to the stage-environment fit perspective is the hypothesis that adolescents who experience a particular type of increasing mismatch, or incongruence, should be most likely to experience a decline in intrinsic motivation and interest. The Mac Iver, Klingel, and Reuman (1986) study looked only at the extent of the mismatch and did not distinguish between the two possible types of mismatches that can occur: the "can't have a say but should be able to" mismatch and the "can have a say but shouldn't be able to" mismatch. Given the general developmental progression toward increased desire for independence and autonomy during the early adolescent period, Eccles and Midgley (1988) predicted that adolescents who experience too little opportunity for participation in classroom decision making (that is, the "can't but should" mismatch) should be most at risk for negative motivational outcomes. In a longitudinal analysis of the Lee, Statuto, & Kedar-Voivodas (1983) items, Mac Iver and Reuman (1988) provided some support for this prediction, as shown in changes in intrinsic interest in math for adolescents across the four waves of data. Consistent with the prediction, the adolescents who perceived their seventh-grade math classrooms as putting greater constraints on their preferred level of participation in classroom decision making than their sixth-grade math classrooms showed the largest and most consistent declines in their intrinsic interest in math as they moved from the sixth grade into the seventh grade. These were the students who were experiencing the "can't have a say but should" type of developmental mismatch.

## Summary

Thus there is evidence from our longitudinal study of adolescent development that there is an increase in early adolescents' desire for control over their own educational experiences as they move from the sixth through the seventh grade. Unfortunately, there appears a decline, rather than an increase, in the opportunities provided to them for this type of control over this same developmental period. Consequently, the adolescents experience an increasingly poor stage-environment fit between their autonomy needs and their perception of their school environment's responsiveness to these needs. Finally, as would be predicted by stage-environment fit theory, students who experience the greatest mismatch are the ones whose intrinsic interest in school declines over these academic years.

## PERCEIVED CONTROL IN THE FAMILY

We are in the process of examining similar issues in the family context of the adolescents in the MSALT study. Family decision making was assessed in two ways: Both the adolescents and their parents responded to two items derived from the Epstein and McPartland (1977) scale of family decision making. For example, "In general, how do you and your child arrive at decisions?" (1 = *I tell my child just what to do; 3 = We discuss it and then we decide; 5 = I usually let my child decide)*; "How often does your child take part in family decisions that concern her/himself?" (1 = *never; 4 = always)*. The adolescents were also asked to rate how they thought decisions ought to be made in their family, and the extent to which they thought "their parents treated them more like a kid than like an adult."

Adolescent motivational orientation was assessed in a variety of ways. To assess intrinsic interest and motivation in school, the adolescents rated on 7-point Likert scales the extent to which they enjoyed coming to school, liked doing math,

and felt it was important to them to do well in match. They also answered the Harter (1981) Scale of Intrinsic vs. Extrinsic Orientation and the Harter (1982) General Self-Esteem Scale.

Consistent with the analyses reported earlier, the results showed both a longitudinal increase from the sixth to the seventh grade in adolescents' desire for greater participation in family decision making, and positive associations between the extent of the adolescents' participation in family decision making and indicators of both intrinsic school motivation and positive self-esteem (Flanagan, 1986, 1989; Yee, 1986, 1987; Yee & Flanagan, 1985). Specifically, adolescents who reported having greater opportunity to participate in decision making at home also reported having higher intrinsic interest in studying math and a greater liking of school than adolescents who reported less opportunity to participate in decision making at home (Yee, 1986). They also reported higher levels of self-esteem (Yee, 1986) and more intrinsic motivation, particularly with regard to a desire for independent mastery of academic work and a preference for challenging school work (Flanagan, 1985, 1989).

Even more interestingly from the stage-environment fit perspective, the parents generally reported that they included their children more in family decision making than the children perceived to be true (Flanagan, 1986; Yee, 1987). Furthermore, for girls in particular, the discrepancy between the adolescents' and the parents' perception of the opportunities for the adolescents to participate in family decision making increased over the four waves of the study (Yee, 1987). Finally, and most importantly, the pattern of changes in early adolescents' self-esteem and intrinsic versus extrinsic motivation for school work were systematically, and predictably, related to changes in their perceptions of the opportunity to participate in family decision making at home. As the developmental stage environment fit perspective on adult control implies, the adolescents who reported decreasing opportunities to participate in family decision making showed a decrease in their self-esteem and intrinsic motivation over the period of this study;

the opposite pattern of change occurred for the adolescents who reported increasing opportunities to participate (Flanagan, 1989; Yee, 1987). In addition, the opportunity to participate in family decision making also predicted betterment to the junior high school transition (Eccles, McCarthy, Lord, Harold, Wigfield, & Aberbach, 1990).

## Control Fit in the Family and Early Adolescents' Orientation to Peers versus Parents

It seems likely that the provision of developmentally appropriate amounts of autonomy within the family will affect other aspects of adolescent social development in addition to its impact on intrinsic school motivation. One area that is especially important to consider is the relative attachment of adolescents to their parents versus their peers. Adolescence is a time when this relative attachment should gradually shift from the parents to specific members of the peer group. But optimal social development during this period is facilitated by a continuing healthy attachment to one's parents as well as by increasing healthy attachments to specific peers (Ryan & Lynch, 1989). Parent-child relationships offer the inexperienced adolescent essential guidance from a more knowledgeable member of society. They also provide an often-unsure child with a secure base from which to explore his/her identity and the complexities of the adult world. Peer relationships, on the other hand, provide developing adolescents with the opportunity to explore their potential as autonomous, independently thinking and acting individuals. These relationships, by virtue of the similarity in age and expertise, are more likely to have an equal power distribution than are parent-child relationships. Consequently, they are likely to provide the adolescent with more opportunities for autonomous control than are parent-child relationships. Early adolescents need both types of relationships. An excessive amount of one type of relationship not only denies the child the positive aspects of the other, but also increases the negative effects of the dominant relationship. However, if

parents do not provide their early adolescent children with increasing opportunities to control their own lives, the adolescents may turn, prematurely, to peers for their primary social relations.

Social changes in the world of the adolescent substantially increase the opportunity for this premature shift to occur. The transition to junior high school, and cultural beliefs regarding "appropriate" amounts of adult supervision for children of different ages, lead to a dramatic increase in amount of unsupervised age-mate contact during this developmental period (Higgins & Parsons, 1983). This increase creates the opportunity for adolescents to spend a lot of unsupervised time in symmetrical peer relationships. At the same time, adolescents are attempting to introduce more power symmetry into their relationships with their parents so that they may exercise their potential as independent individuals at home as well as with their friends (see studies cited earlier). What happens when parents are not responsive to these bids for greater autonomy from adult control? How do changing power and control relationships in the family affect peer-group attachment? Does the way the family reorganizes its power and authority relationships at this developmental juncture have consequences for the amount of influence both parents and peers have on the child during adolescence?

Most developing adolescents want a balance of independence from, and connectedness with, their parents (Grotevant & Cooper, 1986; Hill & Holmbeck, 1986; Ryan & Lynch, 1989). Consequently, they typically attempt to take a more active role in family and personal decision making, seeking a greater degree of control over their own lives (Steinberg, 1988), but not at the expense of maintaining strong, positive relationships with their parents. It seems likely, then, that an excessive orientation toward peers, coupled with premature detachment from one's parents, arises more from a perceived lack of fit in the family than from the attractiveness of the peer group (Ryan & Lynch, 1989). If early adolescents believe their parents are not going to give them the amount of autonomy they think they deserve, or

The psychological well-being of these young people may be partly the result of effective person-environment fit in their homes and schools. Adolescents need environments that gradually relinquish control as they become ready for greater autonomy. (Photo: Tony Freeman/PhotoEdit)

have provided them with too little guidance and emotional support, they may abandon their efforts to maintain a healthy connection with their parents, and turn instead to the peer group. It is the fit between the adolescent's desire for both increased autonomy and adequate emotional support, and the adolescent's perception of the availability of these opportunities in his/her family environment, that is critical.

We have begun to test these hypotheses using the parent and child reports of decision-making opportunities in the home and the following three indicators of peer attachment (Fuligni & Eccles, 1990): (a) the general value attached to having friends, (b) the extent to which the youths talked to their peers rather than parents about personal problems and future plans, and (c) the extent to which the youths expressed a willingness to engage in behaviors that were self-defeating in order to be popular with friends. The students rated, on 5-point or 7-point Likert scales, the extent to which a series of statements tapping each of these three constructs were true of them. Three composite scales, representing the latent constructs listed above, were created based on factor analysis. Cronbach's alphas [a measure of internal consistency] were .60 or higher.

**Consequences of too much control.** The results supported our hypothesis. The adolescents who perceived that they had relatively little opportunity to participate meaningfully in family decisions had more conflicts with their parents over issues related to autonomy and control than did the adolescents who perceived that they had sufficient opportunity to participate in family decision making. In addition, as predicted, the youths reporting only limited opportunity to participate in family decision making also relied more on their friends than their parents for help with personal problems and future planning and were more willing to disobey their parents and forgo achievement-related activities in order to keep and be popular with friends.

**Consequences of too much freedom.** But what about families in which there is too much opportunity for autonomy and too much freedom from adult control? As noted earlier, if the important factor is the fit between the desires for and perceived opportunities for autonomy, then too much autonomy could have just as negative an effect as too little autonomy. If this is true, then some early and middle adolescents may orient more to peers than to parents because of parental neglect rather than parental overcontrol. Condry and Simon (1974) found support for this argument in a study of peer- and adult-oriented sixth graders. Peer-oriented youth—those who complied with peer norms rather than parental values—reported receiving less parental support than adult-oriented youth. Similarly, Simmons and Blyth (1987) found that the youths who were most at risk for declining school motivation and achievement, and for increasing involvement in deviant subcultures, were the ones whose parents had relinquished control over their children's behavior prematurely. Although on the surface these results and the results we have reported here may seem contradictory, they are consistent if one adopts the stage-environment perspective outlined in this paper. These results and the results from our work suggest that there is likely to be a curvilinear relationship between amount of parental control and peer orientation. Both the lack of opportunities for the desired amount of autonomy, and an excessive amount of autonomy unaccompanied by a sufficient amount of emotional support and guidance, can result in a greater attachment to peers relative to parents. Thus it is overly simplistic to recommend that healthy adolescent development requires more autonomy from adult control. Instead, healthy adolescent development requires changing levels of autonomy that fit the changing needs of the early adolescent.

## CONCLUSION

These findings indicate that adolescents desire a gradual increase in the opportunity to participate in decisions that affect their lives and they seem to develop best when these increasing opportunities occur in environments that are emotionally supportive (Baumrind, 1971; Ryan & Lynch, 1989). Unfortunately, our data suggest that many early adolescents do not experience this increase in autonomy in either the school or family settings. When they move into junior high school, many early adolescents experience a decrease in the opportunity to participate in classroom decision making, and this decrease is accompanied

by a decrease in intrinsic motivation and an increase in school misbehavior. Similarly in the family, excessive parental control is linked to lower intrinsic school motivation, to more negative changes in self-esteem following the junior high school transition, to more school misbehavior, and to relatively greater investment in peer social attachments. Since these results are correlational, it is possible that excessive parental control is the consequence rather than the cause of these negative adolescent outcomes. However, the preliminary longitudinal analyses suggest that the causal links are at least bidirectional.

Clearly, these results point out the importance of designing educational and family environments for early adolescents that provide a better match to their growing desire for greater control over their own lives. The current situation in traditional junior high schools seems especially problematic. Junior high school teachers generally appear overly controlling. Field studies of the more successful junior high schools provide numerous examples of classrooms and schools that are less controlling—ones that provide the students with increasing opportunities for meaningful participation in both school and classroom decision making (see Eccles & Midgley, 1988). Students in these schools do not display the same declines in intrinsic motivation and school attachment stereotypically associated with junior high schools; they also do not engage in the same amount of school misbehavior as students in more traditional junior high schools. Unfortunately, many junior high schools do not provide such a developmentally appropriate environment (Eccles & Midgley, 1988).

## NOTE

1. Work on this article was supported by grants to the first author from the National Institute of Child Health and Human Development and the National Science Foundation. We would like to thank the school districts involved in this study and the following people for their assistance: Allan Wigfield, David Reuman, Douglas MacIver, Harriet Feldlaufer, Dave Klingel, Rena Harold, Mary Lou Tucker, and Bonnie Barber.

# EVALUATING YOUR MASTERY

1. According to findings of the Michigan Study of Adolescent Life Transitions, which of the following environments consistently shows poor stage-environment fit for early adolescents?
   a.   Family
   b.   Workplace
   c.   Community
   d.   School

2. In sixth-grade classrooms, early maturing girls, compared with their on-time and late-maturing female peers, reported _____ opportunity for participation in classroom decision making.
   a.   Greater
   b.   Less
   c.   About the same

3. When early adolescents perceive that they have more opportunities to participate in family decision making, they tend to show which of the following?
   a.   Greater intrinsic interest and motivation in school and greater peer orientation.
   b.   Less intrinsic interest and motivation in school and greater peer orientation.
   c.   Greater intrinsic interest in school and less peer orientation.
   d.   Less intrinsic interest in school and less peer orientation.

4. In families where there is almost complete freedom from adult control, early adolescents are likely to
   a.   Achieve better in school
   b.   Hold part-time jobs
   c.   Become involved in deviant peer subcultures
   d.   Feel more positively about their parents

5. Research suggests that junior high school teachers are [more/less] controlling than upper elementary school teachers, a factor that [supports/undermines] stage-environment fit.

6. True or False: Most adolescents want a balance of independence from and connectedness with parents.

## Critical Thinking

1. According to person-environment fit theory, what accounts for the motivational declines that often occur at early adolescence?

2. Explain the consequences of a perceived lack of person-environment fit in the family for early adolescents' relationships with peers.

## Applying Your Knowledge

Obtain two or three recent issues of a junior high or high school newspaper. What proportion of letters to the editor discuss topics related to adolescents' sense of person–environment fit? List those topics, and for each, briefly describe the writer's perspective. How satisfied do students seem to be with the degree of autonomy granted by their school?

# 26

*⁂*

# Adolescent Suicide Prevention

## Current Research and
## Social Policy Implications

A N N   F .   G A R L A N D   &   E D W A R D   Z I G L E R

Yale University

■

Suicide is the third leading cause of death among [15- to 19-year-olds].

■

Females attempt suicide far more often than do males but with less lethal methods, primarily ingestion of substances, that allow time for treatment. Males are more likely to choose violent and immediately lethal methods, such as gunshots and hanging. These gender differences in method choice are probably related to a complex interaction of biological, intrapsychic, social, and cultural factors.

■

The best single predictor of death by suicide is probably a previous suicide attempt.

■

In one study, adolescent suicide attempters experienced more family turmoil (including parental separation, change in caretaker, and change in living situation) as well as increased social instability in the year before the suicide attempt, compared with depressed but nonsuicidal adolescents and a normal sample of adolescents.

■

Suggested explanations for the increase in the adolescent suicide rate include increased substance abuse, increased use of firearms, increased psychosocial stress among adolescents, and a social imitation effect that may function by modeling the behavior or lowering taboos against it.

■

More efficient and effective strategies to attack the problem of adolescent suicide than curriculum-based programs … include implementation of integrated primary prevention programs, suicide prevention education for professionals, education and policy formation on firearm management, education of media professionals about the social imitation factor in adolescent suicide, more efficient identification and treatment of at-risk youth, and crisis intervention and postvention programs.

■

Although the passage of strict gun control laws may be a valuable long-range goal in suicide prevention, as well homicide and accident prevention, more immediate, less controversial measures could be taken in gun management and education.

■

Hotline services can be encouraged only if there is adequate backup support from mental health services. Anonymity should not be guaranteed because emergencies may require intervention. Calls should be screened for severity by trained paraprofessionals, and mental health workers must be available to respond to calls from adolescents in immediate crisis. Each caller referred for psychological treatment should be followed up.

■

### EDITOR'S INTRODUCTION

The rate of adolescent suicide has increased three-fold in the past few decades. Today, it is the third leading cause of death among 15- to 19-year-olds in the United States. Ann Garland and Edward Zigler consider the complex interaction of biological, psychological, social, and cultural factors that contribute to suicide and take a critical look at prevention efforts. Curriculum-based programs in schools have proliferated, but most are not based on current research findings, misrepresent the facts of suicide to adolescents, and have difficulty reaching the target population (since suicidal adolescents are often absent from school before the suicidal act). Consequently, they have not been effective in preventing suicide and, in some instances, can be harmful. Garland and Zigler recommend a change in focus—toward primary prevention that reduces risk factors, such as substance abuse, depression, lack of social support, and poor problem-solving skills. They also advocate family intervention aimed at improving parents' and children's ability to cope with stress. Rather than directing educational efforts at adolescents (who may imitate another's suicidal behavior), the authors underscore the need to educate teachers and school counselors about identification and referral of children at risk.

In recent years, growing public concern over the increased rate of adolescent suicide has prompted suicide prevention activities at the local level, as well as state and federal policy initiatives to address the problem. A problem as compelling as adolescent suicide can force program planners and policymakers to act hastily, in the absence of empirically derived knowledge on which to base social action. Unfortunately, the communication between policymakers, program developers, and researchers has been inadequate, and some ill-informed curriculum-based prevention programs have proliferated. These ill-informed efforts, no matter how well intentioned, are sometimes ineffective, inefficient, and even potentially deleterious.

In this article we summarize current research on the epidemiology and etiology of adolescent suicide to provide an empirical context in which to evaluate the potential effectiveness of current prevention strategies and policy initiatives. We end with recommendations for integrating current empirical knowledge into policy formulation and intervention efforts. A more comprehensive review of the diverse theoretical perspectives on suicidal behavior, including a more extensive analysis of biological, intrapsychic, cognitive, familial, and social-cultural factors, is beyond the scope of this article, but we refer the readers to Berman and Jobes (1991) for a more comprehensive review of etiological theories and clinical issues regarding adolescent suicide.

## DEMOGRAPHICS OF ADOLESCENT SUICIDE

Public concern over adolescent suicide is justified. In 1988, a total of 2,059 adolescents ages 15–19 and 243 children under age 15 committed suicide (National Center for Health Statistics, 1991).[1] Suicide accounts for 11.3 deaths per 100,000 people in the 15–19 year age group; it is the third leading cause of death in this age group, accounting for 14 percent of all the deaths. Suicide is close behind homicide, which has a rate of 11.7, as the second cause of death. The well-publicized increase in youth suicide rates is disturbing. Between 1960 and 1988, the rate increased from 3.6 to 11.3 per 100,000 population. As Figure 26.1 illustrates, the suicide rate among adolescents has increased much more dramatically than it has in the general population; adolescent suicide rose by more than 200 percent, compared with a general population increase of 17 percent.

Statistics on suicide are generally considered to be low estimates of the true incidence. There has always been a tendency to underreport suicide because of religious implications, concern for the family, and financial considerations regarding insurance payment restrictions. Many sudden deaths are probably suicides, but without any direct evidence, such as a suicide note, the death may be ruled accidental or undetermined. This suspected underreporting of suicide adds emphasis to the severity of the problem but should not be exaggerated. After a careful analysis of mortality data, Kleck (1988) claimed that "little hard evidence supporting claims that suicides are seriously underreported in the United States" could be found (p. 219). However, Jobes, Berman, and Josselson (1987) analyzed the reliability and validity of suicide reporting and concluded that systematic misreporting does exist, and in fact the increase in adolescent suicides (ages 15–24) is even greater than that reported. Clearly more work should be done to illuminate the true incidence issue.

It could be argued that the increase in the suicide rate may simply reflect a change in reporting practices—that is, the increased attention to adolescent suicide may have encouraged medical examiners to use the suicide classification more

Garland, A. F., & Zigler, E. (1993). Adolescent suicide prevention: Current research and social policy implications. *American Psychologist, 48,* 169–182. © American Psychological Association. Reprinted by permission.

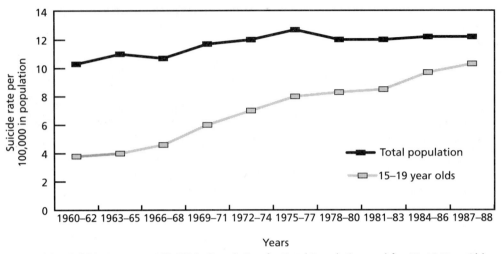

**FIGURE 26.1** Suicide Rates per 100,000 in Population for Total Population and for 15–19-Year-Olds

Note: Data for the years 1966–1988 are from *Vital Statistics of the United States: Volume II. Mortality—Part A.* National Center for Health Statistics, 1968–1991, Washington, D.C.: U.S. Government Printing Office. In the public domain.

often in questionable cases. By analyzing the patterns of the rates of undetermined, accidental, and suicidal deaths across years, some investigators have concluded that suicide is somewhat underreported but that reporting practices have not changed significantly in the past few decades and therefore that the rate increase is not an artifact of changed reporting practices (Brent, Perper, & Allman, 1987; Kleck, 1988; Shaffer & Fisher, 1987).

## Suicide Attempts

Because there is no centralized registry of suicide attempts, the actual rate is unknown, although some estimate it may be as high as 50 to 200 times that of completed suicides (Hawton, 1986; Pfeffer, 1986; Weissman, 1974). Although males *complete* suicide approximately four times as often as females (rate of 18.0 vs. 4.4), females *attempt* suicide at least three times as often as do males (Berman & Jobes, 1991). This difference has been explained primarily in terms of method choice, as described later, but it may also be due partially to case-finding methods. Most studies survey suicide attempt records from health or mental health facilities, which are used more often by females. Weissman (1974) pointed out

that suicide attempts are common among incarcerated males and that if case-finding methods were expanded to include detention facilities, gender differences would diminish.

Between 6 percent and 13 percent of adolescents have reported that they attempted suicide at least once in their lives (Dubow, Kausch, Blum, & Reed, 1989; Gallup Organization, 1991; Meehan, Lamb, Saltzman, & O'Carroll, 1992; Shaffer, Garland, Vieland, Underwood, & Busner, 1991). Rubenstein, Heeren, Housman, Rubin, and Stechler (1989) found a particularly high rate of 20 percent and attributed this to the anonymous design of their survey and the somewhat ambiguous wording of the item, "I tried to hurt myself." Many of these prevalence figures are difficult to interpret because of unclear definitions of suicidal behavior. Meehan et al. (1992) found that 10.4 percent of a college sample reported having made a suicide attempt; however, only 4.6 percent indicated that they had suffered injury or illness as a result of the attempt, only 2.6 percent had sought medical care, and only 1 percent had been hospitalized as a result of an attempt. The vast majority of suicide attempters do not seek or receive medical or mental health care (Smith & Crawford, 1986).

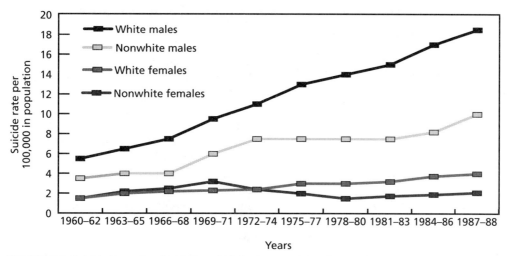

**FIGURE 26.2** Suicide Rates for 15–19-Year-Olds by Race and Gender Group

Note: Data for the years 1966–1988 are from *Vital Statistics of the United States: Volume II. Mortality—Part A.* National Center for Health Statistics, 1968–1991, Washington, D.C.: U.S. Government Printing Office. In the public domain.

## Suicide Ideation

**Suicide ideation** appears to be a common phenomenon. Smith and Crawford (1986) reported 62.6 percent of a Midwestern high school sample reported some suicidal ideation or behavior. Another study reported a lifetime prevalence of suicidal ideation of 54 percent among college students; incidence in the past 12 months was 25.6 percent, and these figures dropped by approximately 10 percent for ideation with a specific method of suicide (Meehan et al., 1992).

## Ethnic and Gender Differences

Figure 26.2 illustrates that the suicide rate is higher among males than among females, and higher for Whites than for other ethnic groups. The increase in the past 28 years is most striking among White males, but the rate for non–White males has also more than doubled.

Several explanations for the differences in rates between the genders and races have been proposed, but there is no clear answer. Early explanations were based on a reciprocal model of suicide and homicide (for example, Henry & Short, 1954), whereby some demographic groups were seen as more likely to express frustration and aggression inwardly and others were more likely to express it outwardly. However, the empirical data do not support this reciprocal relationship. Antisocial, aggressive behavior is highly correlated with suicidal behavior. Cohen-Sandler, Berman, and King (1982) found that internalized and outwardly expressed rage characterized adolescent suicide attempters. Many adolescent suicide attempters and completers have been in trouble with the police, and incarcerated youths are at extreme risk for suicide. Their rates have been reported to be as high as 2,041 per 100,000 juveniles incarcerated in adult jails (Memory, 1989).

Other models to explain the racial differences in suicide have emphasized ideological factors among some cultural or **socioeconomic** groups that may protect or deter them from suicide. Shaffer (1988) suggested that negative cultural values about suicide may inhibit the behavior. Some have also suggested that the extreme stress and discrimination that African Americans confront helps to create protective factors, such as extended social support networks, that lower their risk (Bush, 1976; Gibbs, 1988). Although the reported suicide rate is lower among African

Americans, Gibbs argued that high rates of other self-destructive behaviors, such as substance abuse and victim-precipitated homicides, provide indirect evidence of suicidality in the African-American population.

Native Americans have the highest suicide rates of any ethnic group in the United States, although there is great variability across tribes, with the Navajos having rates close to the national average (12 per 100,000) and some Apache groups having rates as high as 43 per 100,000 (Berlin, 1987). High suicide rates in this population have been associated with high rates of alcoholism, substance abuse, unemployment, availability of firearms, and child abuse and neglect (Berlin, 1987; Berman & Jobes, 1991). In general, less traditional tribes have higher rates of suicide than do more traditional tribes, which may offer a greater sense of belongingness and support to adolescents (Wyche, Obolensky, & Glood, 1990).

Gender differences in suicidal behavior are best examined in the context of an analysis of methods of suicide, as discussed in the following section.

## Methods of Suicide

Firearms are the most frequent method of completed suicide for both genders; the second most common method is hanging, and the third most common is gassing. Males use firearms and hanging more often than do females, but females use gassing and ingestion of substances more often than do males for completed suicide (Berman & Jobes, 1991). The most common method for suicide *attempt* is ingestion or overdose. Spirito, et al. (1992) found that 83 percent of adolescent suicide attempters used this method, and approximately one half of the attempts were rated as mild or moderate in lethality (if they had gone untreated).

The gender differences in the ratios for suicide attempts and completions reflect differences in method choice. Females attempt suicide far more often than do males but with less lethal methods, primarily ingestion of substances, that allow time for treatment. Males are more likely to choose violent and immediately lethal methods, such as gunshots and hanging. The question of whether method choice reflects the sincerity or ambivalence about the wish to die is difficult to answer, especially because adolescents' knowledge about the lethality of various methods is often quite inaccurate (Rotheram, 1987). Berman and Jobes (1991) reviewed many factors in the choice of suicide method, including accessibility, familiarity, meaning and cultural significance, and the individual's state of mind.

These gender differences in method choice are probably related to a complex interaction of biological, intrapsychic, social, and cultural factors. Adolescent males are characteristically more aggressive, impulsive, and violent than are females, and this bias is reflected in the means they choose to attempt. For example, in a study of 229 suicide victims under age 20, Hoberman and Garfinkel (1988) found that "most suicides appeared to be the result of marked impulsivity" (p. 693). Thus, these personality factors put males at a higher risk for suicide. Females may benefit from such protective factors as a greater reliance on interpersonal relationships for support and more positive help-seeking attitudes and behaviors (Garland & Zigler, 1994).

## RISK FACTORS OF SUICIDE

The search for the etiology of suicide spans many fields of study, from the molecular level of biochemistry to the celestial level of astronomy. A sampling of proposed risk factors includes **neurotransmitter** imbalances and genetic predictors (Roy, 1986); psychiatric disorders (Brent et al., 1988; Shaffer, Garland, Gould, Fisher, & Trautman, 1988); poor self-efficacy and problem-solving skills (Cole, 1989); sexual or physical abuse (Deykin, Alpert, & McNamara, 1985); concerns over sexual identity or orientation (Harry, 1989); availability of firearms (Boyd,

1983; Brent et al., 1988); substance abuse (Brent, et al., 1988; McKenry, Tishler, & Kelley, 1983); violent rock music (Wass, Miller, & Stevenson, 1989); divorce in families (Dorpat, Jackson, & Ripley, 1965); unemployment and labor strikes (Platt, 1984; Stack, 1982); and phases of the moon (Jones & Jones, 1977).

Using a method called the **psychological autopsy,** in which psychological profiles of adolescents who committed suicide are reconstructed on the basis of extensive interviews with family members and peers, researchers have identified several **primary risk factors**. These include drug and alcohol abuse, prior suicide attempt, affective illness such as depression or manic depression, antisocial or aggressive behavior, family history of suicidal behavior, and the availability of a firearm (Brent, et al., 1988; Gould, Shaffer, & Davies, 1988; Shaffer, 1974, 1988; Shaffi, Carrigan, Whittinghill, & Derrick, 1985).

It is important to note that the identified risk factors, although very useful from an epidemiological perspective, are not very accurate in predicting suicidal behavior at the individual level. Prediction is an inherently frustrating process because suicide is so rare and knowledge about risk factors, although improving, is still not specific enough to avoid the identification of too many false positives. Many young people will experience some, or many, of these risk factors and will never go on to commit suicide. However, Murphy (1972) argued that adolescents identified because of the false positive problem may require some kind of intervention anyway, even though they are not at imminent risk of suicide.

There is one more important cautionary note to consider when reviewing risk factors associated with suicidal behavior. Much of the research on suicidal behavior is conducted with suicide attempters, for the obvious reason that suicide completers are not available. Risk factors for attempted and completed suicide may be different; therefore we have specified studies that have used attempters as the subjects.

## Psychiatric Disorders

Almost all adolescent suicide victims have suffered from psychiatric illness. Brent, et al. (1988) diagnosed at least one psychiatric disorder in 92.6 percent of their sample of 27 adolescent suicides. Shaffer (1988) concluded that only a very small minority of adolescent suicides are free of discernible psychiatric symptoms. The most prevalent psychiatric disorders among completed adolescent suicides appear to be affective disorders, conduct disorder or antisocial personality disorder, and substance abuse (Brent, et al., 1988; Shaffer, 1988). Among affective disorders, bipolar illness and depressive disorders with comorbidity, specifically attention deficit disorder, conduct disorder, or substance abuse, are also associated with increased risk for suicidal behavior (Brent, et al., 1988; Rohde, Lewinsohn, & Seeley, 1991).

In a study of nearly 200 adolescent suicides in the New York metropolitan area, Shaffer and Gould (1987) found that approximately one-half of the victims had been identified for, or had sought, some kind of mental health intervention. Brent, et al. (1988) found that one-third of their sample of adolescent suicides had had some mental health treatment, but only 7 percent were under active treatment at the time of their deaths. Psychological difficulties are also implicated by the fact that the majority of adolescents who commit suicide experienced long-standing problems in school, with their families, and possibly with the law.

However, adolescent suicide victims are a diverse population. Shaffer (1988) has also identified a very different minority of suicide victims who have not exhibited any behavior or school problems. These young people experience pathological anxiety and are often seen as perfectionistic and rigid; they appear to be particularly vulnerable at times of change or dislocation. Adolescents with eating disorders constitute another risk group because these behaviors are self-destructive. Favazza and Conterio (1989) found that 62 percent of self-mutilating adolescent women reported eating disorders.

## Previous Suicidal Behavior

The best single predictor of death by suicide is probably a previous suicide attempt (Shaffer, Garland, Gould, et al., 1988). Some studies indicate that up to 40 percent of attempters will make more suicide attempts, and as many as 10 percent–14 percent may go on to die by suicide (Diekstra, 1989; Spirito, Brown, Overholser, & Fritz, 1989). In a recent follow-up study of adolescent suicide attempters, 10 percent had made another attempt within three months of the original attempt; 30 percent of the reattempters never received any medical or mental health care (Spirito, et al., 1992).

These data suggest a continuum of severity of suicidal behavior, from suicidal ideation to suicide threats, to attempts, and finally to completed suicide. A person is unlikely to be at the extreme risk end of the continuum without progressing through the less risky behaviors. However, the continuum model is somewhat controversial. Robins (1989), for example, noted that there are clear demographic differences between suicide completers and attempters (for example, gender) and believed there are also motivational differences in that many suicide attempters have no intention of dying and are using the attempt as a cry for help. Other researchers have found that ideators, attempters, and completers may be part of the same population. Kosky, Silburn, and Zubrick (1990) found that ideators and attempters were indistinguishable in clinical symptomotology and demographics except for more chronic family discord and substance abuse among the attempters. However, their findings are quite biased because both groups consisted of children referred to psychiatric outpatient clinics. A comparison of suicide ideators and attempters in an unselected population might have yielded different results.

## Cognitive and Coping Skill Factors

Many researchers have identified cognitive and coping style factors associated with suicidal behaviors. However, most of this research has been done with suicide attempters rather than completers, and generalizations are uncertain. Hopelessness is often associated with suicidal behavior. Kazdin, French, Unis, Esveldt-Dawson, and Sherick (1983) found that children who had made a suicide attempt reported more depression and hopelessness than did children who were suicide ideators. They also concluded that hopelessness may be better than depression for predicting suicidal behavior. Rotheram-Borus and Trautman (1988), however, found that hopelessness was not a significant predictor of suicidal intent among minority adolescents. Holden, Mendonca, and Serin (1989) have found that "a sense of general capability buffers the link of hopelessness to suicidality" (p. 500). Cole (1989) also identified cognitive factors (belief in self-efficacy and coping abilities) that mediate the relationship between hopelessness and suicidality, especially for boys. Deficits in interpersonal problem-solving skills, such as generating fewer alternative solutions to problems and seeking social support less often, are also associated with suicidal behavior (Rotheram-Borus, Trautman, Dopkins, & Shrout, 1990).

## Additional Psychosocial Risk Factors

Drug and alcohol abuse is a significant risk factor for suicidal behavior, both as it affects affective, cognitive, social, familial, and behavioral functioning, and as an immediate precipitant to suicide due to decreased inhibitions (Shaffer, 1988). Brent, et al. (1988) found that at least one third of adolescents who commit suicide are intoxicated at the time of death and many more may be under the influence of drugs. Preliminary findings from a study of almost 200 suicides indicate that more than one-third of the victims had positive toxicology results (P. W. Fisher, personal communication, June, 1990). In another large study of completed suicide in adolescents, 10 percent of the victims were characterized as alcohol abusers, and 12 percent were drug abusers (Hoberman & Garfinkel, 1988).

Changing patterns of drug and alcohol abuse are probably related to the dramatic rise in suicide rates among teenagers. The percentage of adolescents committing suicide under the influence of alcohol increased by 46 percent in only five years between 1978 and 1983 (Brent, Perper, & Allman, 1987). Examining trends in suicide rates in Europe, Diekstra (1989) found that the percentage change in alcohol consumption had the single highest correlation with changes in suicide rates. The deadly combination of firearms and substance abuse is particularly alarming. Suicides committed by firearms are more likely to be committed while the adolescent is intoxicated than are suicides by other methods (Brent, Perper, & Allman, 1987).

Stressful life events have also been associated with increased risk for suicidal behavior (deWilde, Kienhorst, Diekstra, & Wolters, 1992). In one study, adolescent suicide attempters experienced more family turmoil (including parental separation, change in caretaker, and change in living situation) as well as increased social instability in the year before the suicide attempt, compared with depressed but nonsuicidal adolescents and a normal sample of adolescents. Some have argued that the increase in adolescent suicide rates may be related to an increase in psychosocial stressors experienced by young people in today's world (Hendin, 1987). For example, the family lives of children and adolescents are dramatically different than they were just a few decades ago. At least one-half of all children in the United States will live in a single-parent home at some time in their lives, and 70 percent of mothers of school-age children now work outside the home (Zigler, 1989). Young adolescents who are unsupervised for more than 20 hours per week are at twice the risk for alcohol and substance abuse as those who have adult supervision (Richardson, et al., 1989).

Social change is also reflected in the increased accessibility and use of firearms. Between 1968 and 1979, the number of firearms per 100 Americans increased by 47 percent (Boyd & Moscicki, 1986). This may partially explain why, since 1950, the rate of suicide by firearm has increased three times faster than the rates of all other methods for the 15- to 19-year-olds (Boyd & Moscicki, 1986). Lester (1988) found positive correlations between gun ownership rates and firearm suicide rates according to geographic region. Brent, et al. (1988) reported that there was greater availability of firearms in homes of adolescents who committed suicide than in homes of adolescent inpatients who had made suicide attempts.

Elkind (1981) attributed the dramatic increase in adolescent suicide to increased pressure on children to achieve and to be responsible at an early age. He stated that adolescents are particularly "audience conscious" and when they are expected to perform tasks that are beyond their developmental level, perceived public disapproval due to a failure can lead to suicidality.

The increase in adolescent suicide has also been attributed, in part, to the mass media. Several studies have confirmed that suicide rates increase following television or newspaper coverage of suicide, and that teenagers appear to be particularly susceptible to this effect (Gould & Shaffer, 1986; Phillips & Carstenson, 1986). It has also been demonstrated that the extent of publicity given to a suicide (for example, front-page versus back-page coverage) has a significant effect on local suicide rates, as do cases receiving vivid, sensationalistic coverage (Phillips, 1974).

Fictional stories about suicide have also been found to be associated with increases in suicidal behavior. Gould and Shaffer (1986) found a significant increase in the rate of suicide attempts and completions among adolescents in a large metropolitan area following the broadcast of three television movies about suicide. The findings have since been replicated in some areas but not in others (Berman, 1988), suggesting a possible interaction effect by location (Gould, Shaffer, & Kleinman, 1988). At the individual level, there are several confirmed cases of **copycat suicide,** in which children have committed suicide using the identical method to that portrayed in a book or movie they had just read or seen (Shaffer, 1974). This effect is not a new phenomenon; it was first labeled the "Werther effect" after a rash of suicides associated with Goethe's book in the early nineteenth century (Phillips, 1974).

Related to the social imitation explanation for suicidal behavior is the fact that suicidal adolescents are more likely than other adolescents to know someone who has either attempted or committed suicide (Spirito, et al., 1989). Several studies have indicated that a family history of suicide is a significant risk factor for suicide in adolescence. Garfinkel, Froese, and Hood (1982) found that the rate of suicide in the families of adolescent suicide attempters was seven times greater than the rate in families of medical patients. These findings support a social imitation model of suicide, as well as possibly a genetic inheritance model.

## Precipitants

Completed suicide is often immediately precipitated by a shameful or humiliating experience such as an arrest, a perceived failure at school or work, or a rejection or interpersonal conflict with a romantic partner or parent (Brent, et al., 1988; Shaffer, 1974, 1988; Shaffer, Garland, Gould, et al., 1988). The humiliation and frustration suffered by some adolescents struggling with conflicts over their sexual orientation may precipitate suicidal behavior (Harry, 1989), although there is considerable debate over whether homosexuality is a risk factor for suicide (see Blumenthal, 1991; Snelling, 1991). Hoberman and Garfinkel (1988) found that the most common precipitant of suicide in their sample of 229 youth suicides was an argument with a boyfriend or girlfriend or a parent (19 percent of the cases), followed by school problems (14 percent). Brent, et al. (1988) reported that an interpersonal conflict was a precipitant in more than 70 percent of the suicides they studied. Other humiliating and shameful experiences, such as corporal punishment and child abuse, also serve as precipitants. The experience of sexual or physical assault appears to be a particularly significant risk factor for girls (Hoberman & Garfinkel, 1988).

In summary, epidemiological research has indicated that, although suicide ideation is common and suicide attempts are reported by approximately 10 percent of teenagers, suicide is still relatively rare, with a rate of 11.3 per 100,000 among 15- to 19-year-olds. Risk factors associated with completed adolescent suicide include psychiatric illness, specifically conduct disorder and antisocial personality disorder, affective illnesses, substance abuse, eating disorders, and anxiety disorders; family history of suicide or other exposure to suicidal behavior; previous suicide attempt; and availability of a lethal suicide method. Suggested explanations for the increase in the adolescent suicide rate include increased substance abuse, increased use of firearms, increased psychosocial stress among adolescents, and a social imitation effect that may function by modeling the behavior or by lowering taboos against it.

## SUICIDE PREVENTION EFFORTS

The most prevalent types of suicide prevention programs are crisis intervention services. Of these, telephone hotlines are the most popular. There are currently more than 1,000 suicide hotlines in the United States that offer services to adolescents (Garland, Shaffer, & Whittle, 1989). These telephone counseling services are typically available 24 hours a day and are usually staffed by trained volunteers or paraprofessionals. Schneidman and Farberow (1957) originally outlined the rationale for suicide crisis centers as follows: Suicidal behavior is often associated with a crisis situation, and the victim often experiences ambivalence about living and dying. People have a basic need for interpersonal communication that will often be expressed in a last-minute "cry for help."

Although there has been a fair amount of research evaluating this approach, the findings have been somewhat inconclusive. The consensus seems to be that suicide hotlines are minimally effective in reducing suicidal behavior (Shaffer, Garland, Fisher, Bacon, & Vieland, 1990). Miller, Coombs, and Leeper (1984) conducted a well-controlled study and found that communities with suicide hotlines had slightly, although significantly, lower suicide rates among young White women only. Consistent with this, several studies have indicated that these women are the most frequent users of suicide prevention services (see Shaffer, Garland, Fisher, et al., 1990).

## Curriculum-Based Programs

A relatively new approach to suicide prevention that has received a great deal of attention recently involves curriculum-based prevention or education programs. The number of such programs introduced into schools increased by 200 percent between 1984 and 1989 (Garland, Shaffer, & Whittle, 1989) and continues to grow. These programs have been described in detail elsewhere (Garland & Shaffer, 1990; Ross, 1980; Shaffer, Garland, Gould, et al., 1988). Briefly, the main goals are (a) to raise awareness of the problem of adolescent suicide, (b) to train participants to identify adolescents at risk for suicide, and (c) to educate participants about community mental health resources and referral techniques. The programs are presented by mental health professionals or educators and are most commonly directed to secondary school students, their parents, and educators. The mean duration of the programs is approximately two hours.

The content of a typical suicide prevention program for students includes a review of statistics of adolescent suicide; a list of "warning signs" of suicide, usually emphasizing symptoms of depression; a list of community mental health resources and how to contact them; and a discussion of skills for referring a student or peer to counseling, stressing concerns about confidentiality. Many programs also include a component on problem-solving skills training and stress reduction.

Although specific methods and content vary across programs, the theoretical model guiding them is consistent. Virtually all of the suicide prevention programs in a recent review used a stress model of suicide rather than a mental illness model (Garland, Shaffer, & Whittle, 1989). Suicide is presented as a reaction to extreme psychosocial or interpersonal stress and the link to mental illness is strongly denied, or at least underemphasized. The curricula often explicitly state that people who commit suicide are *not* mentally ill and that everyone is vulnerable to suicidal behavior. The rationale behind this approach is that the destigmatization of suicide will encourage students who are feeling suicidal to identify themselves and to seek help.

In reviewing more than 300 prevention programs of various types, Price, Cowen, Lorion, and Ramos-McKay (1989) concluded that the most effective programs are based on a sound foundation of empirical knowledge. That knowledge should include a clear understanding of the risks and problems confronting the target population. Another essential element is the collection of evaluative data to inform planners how well the program achieves its goals or can be modified to do so. Unfortunately, most suicide prevention programs have fallen short on both these requirements.

First, many curriculum-based programs are not clearly founded on current empirical knowledge of the risk factors of adolescent suicide. By deemphasizing or denying the fact that most adolescents who commit suicide are mentally ill, these programs misrepresent the facts. In their attempt to destigmatize suicide in this way they may be, in fact, normalizing the behavior and reducing potentially protective taboos. Suicide is portrayed as a reaction to common stressors of adolescence, namely problems with parents and teachers, problems with relationships, performance anxiety, and peer pressure. Hoberman and Garfinkel (1988) noted that a deemphasis on the relationship between psychopathology and suicide with a focus on normative stresses is likely to be an ineffective preventive intervention. The link between stressful experiences and suicide may be the one message retained by adolescents who attend a suicide prevention program, regardless of the well-intentioned messages about seeking help.

The incidence of adolescent suicide is sometimes exaggerated in suicide prevention programs because one of the programs' goals is to increase awareness and concern about the problem. This exaggeration seems unnecessary; surveys of teens indicate that they are certainly aware of the problem (Gallup Organization, 1991). The danger of exaggeration is that students may perceive suicide as a more common, and therefore more acceptable, act. They may also become unnecessarily anxious about the possibility of suicide in their immediate peer group.

Magnifying the incidence of the problem is one indication that the developers of curriculum-based programs have not heeded the substantial literature on the imitation or contagion factor in adolescent suicide. Another is the common use of print or visual media to present case histories of adolescents who have attempted or committed suicide. The purpose is to teach students how to identify friends who may be at risk for suicidal behavior. However, the method may have a paradoxical effect in that students may closely identify with the problems portrayed by the case examples and may come to see suicide as the logical solution to their own problems. Indirect empirical support for this concern is provided by Gibson and Range (1991), who had teenagers read vignettes about a distressed adolescent. One half were told that this adolescent knew someone with similar problems who had committed suicide and the others were told that the adolescent knew someone with similar problems who sought mental health treatment. When asked how likely the adolescent would be to commit suicide or to seek help, the subjects responded according to the modeled behavior. There was, however, an interaction effect whereby girls responded more positively to help-seeking behavior and boys responded more positively to suicidal behavior.

Finally, at the most practical level, suicide prevention programs may never reach their target population, adolescents most at risk for suicide. Incarcerated and runaway youths, as well as dropouts, have extremely high rates of suicide (Memory, 1989; Stiffman, 1989) and will not be in the audience. Many reports suggest that suicide victims are likely to have been absent from school before their suicidal act (Hawton, 1986), and therefore students who are regularly attending school are not the highest risk group. Program developers might argue that the programs are not primarily intended to address the suicidal child but rather to encourage peers to identify and seek help for someone who may need it. Nevertheless, a program aimed at a general audience of adolescents who are not at highest risk may be inefficient. Future suicide prevention efforts should be based on the valuable empirical data that can help to identify children who may be at risk for suicide so they can be referred to more therapeutic interventions.

## How Effective Are the Efforts?

Although many curriculum-based suicide prevention programs have been operating since 1981 (Garland, Shaffer, & Whittle, 1989), there are only a few published evaluation studies, and most of these are poorly designed in that there is no control group (Nelson, 1987; Ross, 1980). Spirito, Overholser, Ashworth, Morgan, and Benedict-Drew's (1988) evaluation of a suicide awareness program for ninth graders is an exception. Approximately 300 students who attended the program were compared with about 200 students in a geographically matched control group. All students completed a battery of instruments covering suicide, hopelessness, helping behaviors, and coping skills before and 10 weeks after the implementation of the 6-week curriculum in their health classes.

The results indicated that the program was minimally effective in imparting knowledge, and was ineffective in changing attitudes. Slight increases in knowledge among girls were associated with program attendance. In a similar study by the same research group (Overholser, Hemstreet, Spirito, & Vyse, 1989), boys changed in the undesirable direction—that is, they reported increased hopelessness and maladaptive coping responses upon exposure to the suicide prevention curriculum.

In another large, well-controlled study in New Jersey, Shaffer, Garland, Vieland, et al. (1991) found few positive effects of three suicide prevention curriculum programs and a possible negative effect. The programs lasted approximately three hours and were implemented collaboratively by mental health professionals and educators. The sample included approximately 1,000 teenagers who attended the programs and 1,000 students in a demographically matched control group. Pre- and postprogram assessments were made of knowledge and attitudes about suicide and help-seeking from adults, knowledge about mental health resources, and self-reported suicidal behavior.

Most students rated the programs as helpful, but only 41 percent found them interesting; girls and minority students were most likely to rate the programs favorably. The majority of students who attended the programs were fairly knowledgeable about suicide before program participation, and most held favorable attitudes toward help seeking. Specifically, students listed an average of more than three warning signs of suicide, and approximately 80 percent believed that suicidal threats should be taken seriously and said that they would refer a friend to a counselor if they believed the friend to be at risk for suicide. Program attendance did not affect these knowledge or attitude variables. A minority of students expressed unfavorable attitudes, such as the belief that suicide can be a good solution to problems, or that suicidal confidences from friends should never be disclosed. Program attendance did not effect a significant change in these students' attitudes either. Program attendance was associated with a small, but significant, increase in the number of students who responded that suicide could be a possible solution to problems. Most importantly, however, there was no significant increase or reduction in self-reported suicidal ideation or suicide attempts after program implementation. However, there were data suggesting that the students most at risk for suicide (those who said they had made a previous attempt) found the programs upsetting (Shaffer, Vieland, Garland,

Rojas, Underwood, & Busner, 1990). Although this does not necessarily indicate a negative effect, it is cause for concern.

Program evaluation research is underdeveloped, and final conclusions about the effectiveness of suicide prevention programs cannot be drawn on the basis of these two studies. The programs were of short duration (although longer than the national average; Garland, Shaffer, & Whittle, 1989), and the evaluations included only self-report measures of knowledge, attitudes, and behavior. However, there is little evidence that the programs have the desired effect on knowledge and attitude variables, and there is some suggestive evidence that the programs may have a deleterious effect on some students. Further evaluation is clearly needed, with an emphasis on the assessment of behavioral variables including suicidal behavior and help-seeking behavior.

## RECOMMENDATIONS FOR SOCIAL POLICY

The dramatic rise in adolescent suicide has prompted policymakers at all levels of government to introduce legislation on prevention. The Youth Suicide Prevention Act of 1987 (S 1199, 1987) is a good example because it incorporated many of the components contained in other legislative proposals. The bill called for the establishment of a national resource center clearinghouse that would disseminate information, provide training programs, and conduct a national public awareness campaign about youth suicide. The act also encouraged the implementation of suicide prevention and mental health services for troubled youth and funded demonstration programs. There was also financial support for improved data collection on attempted and completed adolescent suicides and for research into causes and prevention of suicidal behavior among youths.

Although this bill was never passed, it was well intentioned and potentially beneficial in many respects. A central resource center, where information is compiled and disseminated, would be very useful. On the other hand, a major public awareness campaign, if not carefully developed, could have potentially dangerous effects in light of the social imitation research findings. In discussing a variety of prevention strategies, Seidman and Rapkin (1983) stated, "considerable caution needs to be exercised in developing public education programs because they run the risk of becoming iatrogenic, alarming individuals and exacerbating the very problems they are intended to reduce and inhibit" (p. 195).

The Youth Suicide Prevention Act of 1987 wisely placed a stronger emphasis on research than does some other legislation. Many bills proposed for adolescent suicide prevention offer financial support for programs without any recommendation or funding for evaluation research. Such legislation is short-sighted in that program implementation without evaluation does not contribute to the knowledge base. Support for innovative prevention efforts should be encouraged, but only when there is an evaluation requirement to guide further program development.

If evaluation had been required in the funding agreements of many suicide prevention programs, perhaps several state laws mandating such programs would not have been passed. California, Louisiana, and Wisconsin are among the states that have required suicide prevention curricula in schools. Similar initiatives have been proposed in several other states. Such legislation is apparently based on the incorrect assumption that suicide prevention programs have reliably demonstrated their effectiveness. The lack of data to support the effectiveness of these programs, as well as the potential dangers discussed earlier, argue strongly against mandating suicide prevention curriculum programs, as they now are implemented, for students. This certainly does not preclude the need for funding innovative demonstration programs and programs directed to adults who work with children, with adequate funds for evaluation.

Current empirical knowledge suggests that there are several more efficient and effective strategies to attack the problem of adolescent suicide than curriculum-based programs. These include implementation of integrated **primary prevention programs,** suicide prevention education for professionals, education and policy formation on firearm management, education of media professionals about the social imitation factor in adolescent suicide, more efficient identification and treatment of at-risk youth, and crisis intervention and postvention programs. None of these approaches requires a drastic reorganization or creation of new services, but rather a reemphasis and determination to set priorities according to available knowledge and resources. Each of these approaches is described in the following sections, beginning with several primary prevention approaches and ending with secondary and tertiary prevention approaches.

## Primary Prevention Programs

The curriculum-based suicide programs are sometimes called primary prevention programs, but in fact they are not truly primary prevention because their purpose is to encourage the identification of adolescents at risk for suicide, rather than to reduce the prevalence of risk factors in the population. Because the known risks for suicide are also common to risks for other major social ills such as delinquency, substance abuse, dropping out of school, and teen pregnancy, primary prevention programs can have far-reaching effects. Substance abuse, for example, permeates all of these problems and affects a much larger number of youths than does the rare instance of suicide. Thus, successful efforts to reduce the prevalence of substance abuse would in fact be excellent primary preventive interventions for suicide, as well as for other difficulties affecting teenagers. Prevention efforts could be focused on the underlying constructs that are risk factors for these negative behaviors such as depression, lack of social support, poor problem-solving skills, and hopelessness.

Schools provide an appropriate setting for potentially useful primary prevention programs, including social competence building programs, problem-solving skills training, and basic mental health education. After thoroughly investigating the psychopathology of adolescent suicide, Cole (1989) concluded that problem-solving skill training and self-efficacy enhancement for adolescents may be the most effective suicide prevention effort. In addition, programs that include general mental health education, health promotion, and help-seeking encouragement might be very beneficial. The destigmatization and demystification of mental illness and the mental health system could encourage troubled youth to seek help. For example, middle and high school students exposed to a 45-minute "Mental Illness Awareness Program" reported more positive help-seeking attitudes than did a group of control subjects (Battaglia, Coverdale, & Bushong, 1990). These types of programs are truly primary prevention and would address many of the underlying risk factors for many current social problems.

Family support programs also address many of the social problems associated with adolescent suicide. In documenting the increase in adolescent suicidal behavior as early as 1974, Weissman (1974) called for increased primary prevention efforts to include strengthening family and community support networks, improving the stability and continuity of children's relationships, and generally improving the quality of the institutions that serve children and youth. These goals were embodied in the family support movement that has spread throughout the nation since that time.

Although a concise definition of family support intervention is difficult to provide because of the diversity of services, the main principles and examples of effective programs have been outlined in several publications (Kagan, Powell, Weissbourd, & Zigler, 1987; Small, 1990; Weiss, 1989; Zigler & Black, 1989). These programs seek to empower families by improving their ability to cope with the debilitating stresses facing families today, such as poverty, single parenthood, dual careers, geographic mobility, substance abuse, and adolescent pregnancy. Although the evaluation of these programs is still under development, several studies have indicated that social support of families can result in improved adjustment and development among children (for a review, see Price, et al., 1989). A recent report indicated that early childhood interventions have been found to significantly reduce subsequent delinquent behavior and to generally increase social competence (Zigler, Taussig, & Black, 1992). Because delinquent behaviors are strongly associated with suicidal behavior as well as substance abuse, these interventions may be effective primary prevention interventions for suicide.

Family support programs range from independent, grass-roots efforts to federally supported programs. Connecticut's Family Resource Centers are one example of the family support model. These centers are based on the "School of the Twenty-first Century" program of child care and family support (Zigler, 1989). The centers offer a wide variety of services, including preschool and school-age child care, parent education, adult literacy, information and referral services, and teen pregnancy prevention. The administration of the programs is centered in the schools, and all families in the district are eligible for services on a sliding fee schedule.

There is a great deal of empirical support for the effectiveness of family support and early childhood interventions (Price, et al., 1989; Seitz, Rosenbaum, & Apfel, 1985). However, there is a tremendous need for more descriptive and evaluative research in this area and for improved communication and cooperation between researchers and program developers (Small, 1990). Current research cannot yet inform us in making recommendations regarding specific program models for certain groups or problems. As the implementation and study of these programs progresses, such recommendations may be possible. In the meantime, these programs should be supported and further evaluated because they have the potential to be effective primary prevention interventions for suicide, as well as a multitude of other social problems.

The demonstrated value of a general system of support, as opposed to an isolated and narrow approach to a specified problem, holds a message for the delivery of suicide prevention programs. Schools are becoming overwhelmed with all of the psychosocial programs they are asked to implement. Many schools may offer individual units on substance abuse, sex education, suicide, education for parenthood, and other topics. The inclusion of so many autonomous programs reflects an inefficient and fragmented approach to solving social problems. The Secretary of the Health and Human Services Task Force on Youth Suicide recommended that "suicide prevention activities should be integrated into broader health promotion programs and health care delivery services directed at preventing other self-destructive behaviors, such as alcohol and substance abuse, teen pregnancy, and interpersonal violence" (Alcohol, Drug Abuse, and Mental Health Administration, 1989, p. 3). It does seem logical that programs aimed at improving general physical and mental health will have a wider scope of success than those addressing specific behaviors that are multidetermined.

## Professional Education for Educators and Health and Mental Health Care Workers

Suicide prevention programs directed to educators often precede programs for students and usually include a didactic presentation about suicide risk factors, sample case histories, and information about identifying and referring students for mental health treatment. Some programs also include small group discussion sessions to enable educators to share their attitudes and concerns about confronting suicidal students. The development and dissemination of explicit school policies for identifying and referring suicidal students is often a very beneficial component of these programs. In addition, the collaboration between community mental health professionals and educators can improve cooperation in the referral process.

Although few studies have been done, suicide prevention activities directed to educators appear to be effective. One brief, two-hour program produced significant increases in knowledge of both suicide warning signs and community mental health resources (Shaffer, Garland, Whittle, & Underwood, 1988). Another more extensive program involved six weekly education and training sessions for school personnel. This outstanding collaborative mental health and education program had positive effects on counselors' knowledge, attitudes, and referral practices (Reisman & Scharfman, 1991). Educating teachers and school counselors about the identification and referral of children at risk for suicide does not carry the same dangers of social imitation as do programs directed to adolescents. These programs must, however, reflect current empirical knowledge regarding the prevalence of adolescent suicide and the most accurate risk factors.

Health and mental health care workers should also be educated about adolescent suicide. Hodgman and Roberts (1982) surveyed pediatricians and found that only 21 percent routinely inquired about suicidal symptoms among their incoming patients. Major medical journals have recently published exemplary articles informing physicians about the risk factors and interventions for adolescent suicide (Adler & Jellinek, 1990; Blumenthal, 1990). Adler and Jellinek's article offered specific guidance to pediatricians consulting to schools in the aftermath of a suicide. They advised physicians to resist the pressure to implement curriculum-based prevention programs that, "at best, have little or no impact" (p. 985), citing research by Spirito, et al. (1988) and Shaffer, Garland, Gould, et al. (1988) reviewed earlier. Pediatricians and other health care workers, including nurses, are urged to take a more active role in identifying children who may be at risk for suicidal behavior.

Mental health care providers could similarly benefit from professional education about suicide; less than one-half of clinical psychology graduate programs offer formal training in the study of suicide (Bongar & Harmatz, 1991). It is particularly important that professionals who work with at-risk youth in such settings as detention facilities or runaway shelters be well educated about adolescent suicide. Training programs for such settings have been developed and have shown effectiveness (Cox, McCarty, Landsberg, & Paravati, 1990; Rotheram-Borus & Bradley, 1991).

## Firearm Management

Restricting access to means of suicide is a common preventive measure (Berman & Jobes, 1991; Shaffer, Garland, Gould, et al., 1988). Because increased availability of firearms is associated with the increase in adolescent suicide rates (Boyd, 1983; Boyd & Moscicki, 1986), several investigators have called for stricter gun control laws as a suicide prevention measure (Boor, 1981; Lester & Murrell, 1980). Lester and Murrell (1980) compared suicide rates in states with strict and more lenient gun control laws. They found that states with stricter laws in 1968 had lower suicide rates among males from 1969 to 1971 and showed an increase in suicide rates smaller than other states over the next 10-year period. The most frequently cited proof that restricting access to means of suicide is an effective preventive measure is the British domestic gasoline example. Carbon monoxide poisoning had been a popular method of suicide in Britain, but beginning in 1960 there was a great reduction in the carbon monoxide residue from domestic gas, and the suicide rate decreased (Brown, 1979). In the United States, Lester and Frank (1989) found that suicide rates by automobile exhaust poisoning were lower in states where car ownership rates and the toxicity of gas emissions were lower.

Although the passage of strict gun control laws may be a valuable long-range goal in suicide prevention, as well as homicide and accident prevention, more immediate, less controversial measures could be taken in gun management and education. For example, public awareness campaigns about the importance of storing guns and ammunition in separate, locked areas could be conducted. As a further step, states could adopt laws to encourage the safe storage of firearms. A model is Connecticut's Public Act 90–144,

which requires gun dealers to provide buyers with trigger locks and makes the unsafe storage of weapons a felony. Such a law is an intermediate alternative to strict gun control legislation, which is more controversial and therefore more difficult to implement.

## Suicide Education for the Media

Workers in the media should be educated about the social imitation effects of suicide. Data reflecting the increase in suicidal deaths and attempts following publicity about suicides should be presented clearly and objectively to journalists and other media professionals. The information should be presented in a nonthreatening, nonaccusatory manner, because the objective presentation of empirical data is more likely to have a beneficial impact than are any dramatic calls for censorship of suicide coverage.

## Secondary Prevention: Identification and Treatment of At-Risk Youth

Efforts to identify and treat at-risk youth are particularly essential following exposure to suicide. The Centers for Disease Control (1988) have recommended that, following a suicide in a school, persons who may be at high risk for suicide (friends and relatives of the victim, and people with a history of depression and suicidality regardless of relationship to the victim) be screened by a trained counselor and referred for further treatment as needed. Such efforts have proved to be effective. For example, after the suicides of two students in a high school of approximately 1,500 students, Brent and colleagues (1989) sent a team of mental health professionals to screen for students at risk for suicidal behavior. They identified 16 students at the school and referred them for treatment; 14 others presented themselves at mental health facilities in the area. No other follow-up information is available. For a more extensive review of crisis management and postvention interventions to schools, families, and other systems in which a suicide has occurred, see

Berman & Jobes (1991, pp. 239–243) and Dunne, McIntosh, & Dunne-Maxim (1987).

Simple survey methods using self-report forms can also be effective in identifying at-risk youths. With a questionnaire survey of more than 2,000 adolescents, Shaffer, Garland, Gould, et al. (1988) reported that 2 percent–3 percent of the students requested help from a counselor for feelings of depression or suicidality. Schools could use health surveys to identify young people with significant risk factors for suicide, allowing students the opportunity to request help if they wish. Suicidal students often hold negative help-seeking attitudes, and therefore outreach efforts to identify and refer them for therapeutic intervention should be encouraged (Shaffer, Vieland, et al., 1990).

Screening methods must be executed with extreme caution. Referring to attempts to identify parents at risk for abusing their children, Kaufman and Zigler (1989) pointed out the hazards of using screening devices to predict individual behavior. Standardized instruments are unable to measure or detect the complexity of behavior; they cannot take into account the effects of chance events or of compensatory factors as well as risk factors. In addition, as stated previously, any identification of young people with risk factors for suicide will produce a large number of false positives. Such misclassification could be devastating because of the stigma associated with suicide. In light of the imitation and contagion effects of adolescent suicide, such labeling could also be potentially dangerous. Screening efforts should therefore not be focused solely on suicidal behavior but should be integrated into other health related screening programs.

## Tertiary Prevention: Crisis Intervention and Treatment of Suicide Attempters

Support for crisis intervention and hotline services also appears worthwhile. Hotline services have been shown to reach a population not served by any other mental health intervention (King, 1977). Such services are likely to appeal to adolescents because of their anonymous nature and the adolescents' perceived control of the interaction—that they can hang up the telephone anytime. As noted above, hotline services have been associated with reduced suicide rates among the population known to use these services most frequently, young White women (Miller, Coombs, & Leeper, 1984). These services should be advertised more heavily among other groups, particularly teenage males. Research has indicated that adolescents are interested in using hotline services, and there is evidence that their interest and knowledge can be increased through educational awareness programs in schools (Shaffer, Garland, Vieland, et al., 1991).

Hotline services can be encouraged only if there is adequate backup support from mental health services. Anonymity should not be guaranteed because emergencies may require intervention. Calls should be screened for severity by trained paraprofessionals, and mental health workers must be available to respond to calls from adolescents in immediate crisis. Each caller referred for psychological treatment should be followed up. Research has confirmed that compliance with a referral improves when an appointment is made for the client, as opposed to simply giving the caller a name and telephone number (Rogawski & Edmundson, 1971).

Finally, successful therapeutic intervention with suicide attempters is certainly a critically important tertiary prevention strategy. Unfortunately, this group is notoriously noncompliant in treatment (Shaffer, Garland, Gould, et al., 1988). A review of clinical issues in the treatment of adolescent suicide attempters and research regarding such treatment is beyond the scope of this article, but we refer readers to reviews by Berman and Jobes (1991, pp. 163–225) and Trautman and Shaffer (1984).

## Informing Policymakers

The exchange of information between researchers, program developers, and policymakers must improve so that coordinated efforts can enhance the knowledge base and capitalize on the most current research methodologies and findings. Although there are certainly discrepancies and gaps in knowledge about the etiology and prevention of adolescent suicide, we must not ignore the vast amount of information available. Armed with an understanding of what we do and do not know about adolescent suicide, we must reevaluate our current approaches to the problem.

Specifically, major risk factors for adolescent suicide have been outlined (substance abuse, affective illness, family history of suicide, conduct disorder and antisocial behavior, access to firearms, and previous suicide attempts), so we should use this information to target our efforts to adolescents who are most at risk. In addition, some of the most potentially effective preventive interventions may be educational efforts targeted to those adults who work with and care for adolescents.

The primary prevention of suicidal behavior may be accomplished most effectively through primary prevention programs such as family support and competence-building interventions that address a wide range of related social problems. Program developers are encouraged to be innovative in their efforts, but they must also be somewhat cautious and respect the potentially iatrogenic effects, such as the social imitation effect of adolescent suicide. As policymakers are pressured to act quickly on this issue, we hope they will be able to benefit from the available data, because data provide a much firmer foundation for social policy than do good intentions.

## NOTE

1. Unless otherwise indicated, all statistics will be reported for the year 1988, the latest year for which national data are available.

## EVALUATING YOUR MASTERY

1. The suicide rate among adolescents
   a. Has decreased in recent decades more than it has in the general population
   b. Has increased in recent decades more than it has in the general population
   c. Has remained about the same as in the general population for several decades
   d. Is the leading cause of death between ages 15 to 19

2. Which of the following is true?
   a. Antisocial, aggressive behavior is not correlated with suicidal behavior.
   b. Extended social support networks may lower the risk of suicide among African Americans.
   c. Native Americans have the lowest suicide rates of any ethnic group in the United States.
   d. Gassing is the most common method of suicide.

3. Adolescent suicide victims
   a. Rarely suffer from psychiatric illness
   b. Often display a sense of hopelessness
   c. Are virtually always poor students in school
   d. Tend to smoke but rarely abuse alcohol

4. For suicide prevention,
   a. Crisis intervention services, such as telephone hotlines, are highly successful.
   b. Curriculum-based programs place too much emphasis on suicide as a reaction to stress and too little on its relation to psychopathology.
   c. Interventions are successful in reaching adolescents at greatest risk.
   d. The majority of students rate programs as both helpful and interesting.

5. True or False. Since 1950, the rate of suicide by firearm has increased faster than the rates of all other methods.

6. Although males [attempt/complete] suicide more often than do females, females [attempt/complete] suicide more often than do males.

7. True or False: Completed suicide is often precipitated by a shameful or humiliating experience.

## Critical Thinking

1. Describe gender differences in suicide. What might explain these differences?

2. Why is restraint by journalists in reporting adolescent suicide on television or in newspapers important?

## Applying Your Knowledge

On the basis of Garland and Zigler's recommendations, list components of a prevention program that would help reduce the incidence of adolescent suicide.

# PART VI

# Looking Back, Looking Forward: Lifespan Implications

# 27

ᔕ

# Shadows of War

## The Impact of Ethnic
## and Political Violence on Children
## Who Found Refuge in Australia
## During World War Two

GLEN PALMER

Griffith University, Queensland

■

The mass arrests, suicides, deportations and emigration that occurred in Germany and Austria throughout 1938 had a disastrous effect on family life—especially, but not exclusively, Jewish family life. As men disappeared, women were left alone to protect their children. In numerous cases, children were left to fend for themselves. Even families that remained intact often could not protect and nurture their children.

■

Through years of living in these circumstances the [German] children bonded closely to each other; they became like siblings, and remain so today. Although it can be said that they received adequate physical care during their years at *Larino*, institutional life did not provide the nurturing environment needed to heal past wounds....

■

For the 20 boys, being selected amounted to winning "the lottery of life." Even at that time, when the Holocaust could not have been foreseen, a permit to Australia offered a rare opportunity to escape the poverty and oppression of Jewish life in Poland.

■

■

Unlike their Polish and German counterparts, child evacuees from Britain were able to return to their homeland and families at the end of the war. Most did, although a large number later returned to Australia as immigrants.

■

Separation alone did not determine the overall impact on any of the children; what preceded and followed separation was equally important—the nature and quality of the substitute care they received, age and maturity at separation, individual temperament, previous family experiences, and trauma.

■

## EDITOR'S INTRODUCTION

This article, joined by the one that follows, offers a lifespan perspective on the impact of childhood experiences. Glen Palmer's research is retrospective; she asked adults to *look back* on an early, traumatic period of their lives and to assess its effects on their life course. Her research participants, all over 70 years of age when interviewed, had been refugees under 16 years of age who came from Germany, Poland, and Britain to Australia without their families, just before or during World War II. Palmer examines the long-term consequences of disintegration of family life for these young people. In doing so, she addresses a topic of profound significance for millions of modern children and youths: the impact of ethnic and political violence on development.

As Palmer notes, the diversity of participants' childhood experiences makes it difficult to draw precise cause-and-effect conclusions. But consistent trends emerged as they told their stories. Childhood well-being depended on the extent to which new adult relationships granted opportunities to form satisfying attachments and involved age-appropriate guidance and limit-setting. At the end of the war, reunions with parents presented new stresses; after years of separation, reestablishing affectionate bonds was often difficult. For those who lost their immediate families, grieving sometimes lasted a lifetime, becoming more intense during later life.

Nevertheless, protective factors within the individual and social supports shielded many refugees from extreme trauma. Although almost all were emotionally scarred by their childhood experiences, most found the personal resources to cope with adversity and led productive, fulfilling lives. Palmer offers several recommendations for easing the severe stresses experienced by refugee children.

Ten million children—one child in every 200 throughout the world—has been affected by war in the last decade (Benjamin, 1994, p. 3). Maimed, orphaned, violated, millions of these children will bear physical and psychological scars for the rest of their lives. For some, the impact will be disabling—a never-ending search and waiting for lost families; others will learn to live with the past and will lead fulfilling lives. What contributes to this differential response, to the impact of ethnic and political violence on children, and what affects the healing process?

Most studies of children and war have been conducted during or soon after the event. Although these provide valuable information about the immediate effects of political and ethnic violence on children, they offer limited insight into long-term effects, or into factors related to resilience and the healing process. By contrast, the following study took a longitudinal and retrospective approach. The participants were adults who came to Australia as unaccompanied refugee or evacuee children immediately before or during World War II. The study involved interviews in Australia, Israel, and England with about one hundred of these former child refugees and evacuees and with people involved in their care; it also involved extensive archival research. The integration of oral history with other primary and secondary sources allowed participants to tell their own stories, from which conclusions have been drawn.

## THE CHILDREN

Those involved in this research came to Australia as children, mainly from Germany, Poland and England, although a small number also came from Austria. All came without their families, were under sixteen years of age, and arrived generally through group schemes.

### German Children

From 1933, when Adolf Hitler became Chancellor of Germany, life for German Jewish children and youth deteriorated. With quotas of 1.5 percent imposed on Jewish enrollment in the noncompulsory years of schooling and with few prospects for employment, thousands of Jewish youth left Germany in the 1930s. The situation was such that by late 1937, German Jews had coined the poignant expression, "Children turn into letters." "There scarcely exists in Germany any Jewish parents who have not got at least one child abroad."[1] Nevertheless, before 1938 emigration was confined mostly to older children, to those at least fourteen years of age who were beyond the compulsory years of schooling. That situation changed dramatically in 1938 as Nazi Germany expanded and persecution intensified.

The mass arrests, suicides, deportations and emigration that occurred in Germany and Austria throughout 1938 had a disastrous effect on family life—especially, but not exclusively, Jewish family life. As men disappeared, women were left alone to protect their children. In numerous cases children were left to fend for themselves. Even families that remained intact often could not protect and nurture their children. Jewish children were banned from state schools, and violence on the streets meant that many were virtually under house arrest. Emigration thus became a matter of urgency for hundreds of thousands of children of all ages.

Organized appeals to help children came rapidly in the wake of the November **pogrom,** *Kristallnacht.* The response from governments was less inspired. Nevertheless, the British government set an example that it hoped other countries would emulate. It approved the temporary admission to Britain of as many children as British refugee organizations could guarantee. Between December 1938 and September 1939, a period of 10 months, the Refugee Children's Movement, a nondenominational organization, moved 9,354 German and Austrian children to Britain. Although the majority were Jewish, about twenty percent of the children were from families of political dissidents, or were at risk for other reasons. Other organizations and individuals also helped remove small numbers of children

Fourteen of the seventeen German Jewish children on board the *Orama,* which left for Australia in June 1939, just before the outbreak of World War II. (Photo: Glen Palmer)

from Czechoslovakia and German children who had been deported to Poland. It was surely a sterling effort. Yet those numbers represent only a fraction of the children by then needing refuge, and whose parents were anxious to send them away.

From 1933, Australia was among those countries receiving requests for the reception of older Jewish children and youth; by the end of 1938 requests were for children of all ages. But, although both the Australian government and the Australian Jewish Welfare Society received many expressions of interest in refugee children, the Australian public, including Jewish families who were not part of the establishment, were given little opportunity to help. Decisions regarding refugee children were in the hands of

the Australian Jewish Welfare Society and the Australian government. Neither seemed in a hurry to take action.

Only in March 1939 did the Australian government agree to admit "up to 250 Jewish refugee orphan children per annum" for three years. At the same time it insisted that the children be included in the 15,000 quota already announced for refugees.[2] Given this, the offer was scarcely a gesture of generosity or humanitarianism. Furthermore it came with severe and unrealistic restrictions; the children were to be "double orphans"—that is, neither parent living—and were to be between the ages of seven and twelve years.

Despite the government restrictions, the Australian Jewish Welfare Society of the time must share the responsibility for the admission of so few children. The first year's quota of 250 children was divided among the Melbourne, Sydney, and Perth branches of the Welfare Society. Although it was now March 1939, there was no sense of urgency in filling the quota. Sydney embarked on a building program and delayed the selection of children until a children's home was ready—in November 1939, by which time it was too late. Perth reneged on its earlier offer, insisting it wanted to select the children, and then only at the rate of four a month. Only Melbourne took immediate action and prepared to receive a small group of children to partially fill its quota.

This group of seventeen children escaped the orphan restriction. The London and German committees responsible for their selection interpreted "orphan" as a child separated from his or her parents, as was the case for children entering England on the kindertransports. When personnel from the Australian Department of the Interior discovered this, they insisted that future children be complete orphans. Only later, following repeated requests from the Australian Jewish Welfare Society, did the government grudgingly relax this position: "Failing complete orphans being available the balance selected should have only one living parent. The admission of any of these children to Australia cannot be used, at any time, to facilitate the entry of their relatives to the Commonwealth."[3] Fear of children beginning a chain of unwanted foreign migration was thus the rationale for Australia's dismal response to refugee children. It was a response shared by most of the world. As Norbert Wollheim, who was involved in the movement of Jewish children overseas, wrote to me,

> There is no doubt in my mind that parents tried desperately to give their children a chance to escape persecution by the Nazis, but the gates of most countries were closed and only England was the shining exception.

These seventeen children became the only young non-British children admitted to Australia either before or during the war. They were aged between seven and twelve and came from various backgrounds. Some had relatives in Australia, but for others the destination was immaterial. "I don't think they cared where they sent me," commented one of the seventeen. "Just to get out—England, Australia . . . I don't think they cared where . . . and I'm sure they would have sent my sister and my brother." There were three couples of brothers and sisters in the group, but brothers and sisters outside the seven to twelve age range were excluded, a restriction that caused unnecessary stress and suffering.

Their experiences of persecution in Germany varied—from the general oppression of being Jewish in pre-war Nazi Germany, to witnessing the death, violent abuse, and humiliation of parents. Hermann Levy spoke of the impact of his father's violent arrest and the destruction of their flat by the Gestapo:

> Up to this point my father was for me the symbol of strength, maturity and responsibility ... now denigrated before my eyes, and I am full of fear ... my mother was broken in the absence of my father. The men who took my father advised her no longer to send me to the local school ... I dared no longer play with or even speak to other children and never ventured on to the street unaccompanied. So mother and I lived alone for seven months until I emigrated.

Family life had thus begun to disintegrate for many of the children, fathers having died, been deported, incarcerated, or forced to flee.

The children left Germany from Bremen in June 1939. They traveled by ship to England, thence to Australia. Having arrived at their destination, they were taken to a rather grand old home in Balwyn, then an outer suburb of Melbourne. This house, called *Larino,* became the children's home for the duration of the war, and beyond. It was run by the Australian Jewish Welfare Society and in a manner that Hedi Fixel, the first matron, described as "Anglo-Jewish Australian." This entailed quite strict adherence to Jewish practices, and a formal religious education.

Nevertheless, great emphasis was also put on the children becoming "100 percent Australian." To this end, names were changed on arrival and the children were expected to shed their German identities and language.

Despite their Jewish upbringing, the children's only regular contact with the Jewish community was through a fortnightly visit to the St. Kilda synagogue, a considerable distance from the home. They also mixed very little with the local community even though they attended state schools. "We were an island. We went to school and we went home. We were taken places occasionally, but always as a group." There was thus no opportunity for family life, while correspondence with natural families was reduced to irregular twenty-five word Red Cross messages. By early 1942 even these had ceased as any remaining Jews in Germany were herded toward the concentration camps.

Through years of living in these circumstances, the children bonded closely to each other; they became like siblings, and remain so today. Although it can be said that they received adequate physical care during their years at *Larino*, institutional life did not provide the nurturing environment needed to heal past wounds; nor did it offer the support they needed as young children and adolescents growing up without their families.

## Polish Children

The experiences of Polish children who came to Australia were somewhat different …

In the bid to remove Jews from Germany, in October 1938 the Reich deported more than 16,000 Polish nationals from Germany. Many were people who had emigrated from Poland to Germany after the First World War. On 28 October, they and their German-born families were rounded up from across Germany, taken to the Polish border in sealed railway carriages, and dumped. Norman Schindler, then a fourteen year old adolescent, described what happened next:

With the German police and their dogs we were marched across No Man's Land, which was a few kilometres. People couldn't carry their belongings any more; they became heavier and heavier as they walked along. They had to drop them because the Germans were pushing them to walk as fast as they could. As far as the eye could see the place was strewn with cases, bed linen, and all sorts of boxes and personal belongings.

"When we got there it was chaos," recalled Werner Teitel, another fourteen year old, picked up separately from his parents. "I finished up in a stable with another boy. He had three sisters, a mother and a grandfather . . . The first night I slept in the stable on the cobble stones. It was bitterly cold, and the grandfather of my friend died during the night."

The deportation coincided with the Australian government's granting permits to a Polish Jewish committee in Melbourne to bring to Australia twenty poor Polish boys aged between fourteen and sixteen. Acknowledging the plight of the Polish refugees, the committee agreed that ten of the twenty boys should come from the Polish refugee camp, the other ten from poor Jewish families within Poland.

For the 20 boys, being selected amounted to winning "the lottery of life." Even at that time, when the Holocaust could not have been foreseen, a permit to Australia offered a rare opportunity to escape the poverty and oppression of Jewish life in Poland. Although partings were emotional, especially for parents, families buoyed themselves with optimistic talk of the future, of a time when they would be together in Australia. "My mother wanted to keep the family together," commented Aleck Katz, "but my father's argument prevailed: We have no way of getting out of here; at this point of time there doesn't seem to be any solution to this problem, so if we get him to go perhaps eventually he can organize something so that we can come too."

The 20 boys traveled to Australia via London, arriving in Melbourne on 29 May 1939.

In Melbourne they were taken to North Carlton, then the hub of eastern Jewish life in Australia, where, in groups of four to six, they stayed in boarding houses within walking distance of each other. It was a business arrangement, but the families with whom they boarded, also recent arrivals, provided the boys with a familiar environment, as well as some guidance and support in their new lives. This was complimented by guardian support, each boy having been allocated a guardian who would "keep an eye on him," and whose family would provide some family life. Although not all the guardian networks were successful, the arrangements seem to have been sound for parentless children of this age and background. The boys had each other, they had access to family experiences and support, and they were relatively independent.

The boys started work immediately; most also began classes at night school. The opportunity to earn money, and so help their families migrate, lured some to farming. However, the outbreak of war halted plans for family reunions so that they, like the younger German children, were obliged to get on with their lives without their families and with little news of their families' fates or whereabouts. Anxious to be part of the war effort, most joined up at the earliest opportunity, serving in the army, airforce, and labor companies.

## British Children

The Australian government's response to British children was a stark contrast to that given non-British children. In June 1940, when a German invasion of Britain seemed inevitable, the British government endorsed a scheme to evacuate children from Britain to the dominions. The Australian government was ecstatic at the opportunity to receive British children, and offered to pay the transport and maintenance expenses of as many children as Britain could send.

Interest in the children as potential immigrants lay behind the Australian government's enthusiasm. The response from the Australian public was more genuine. Offers of hospitality poured in from Australian families offering their homes to children. Many of the offers were inclusive of allied and alien children who had taken refuge in Britain. Despite this, Prime Minister Menzies ensured that the scheme was restricted to British children. Furthermore, restrictions were placed on the number of British Jewish children who could be included; Indian children and children with disabilities were completely excluded. The scheme thus excluded those who would have been most in need had there been a German invasion of Britain.

The movement of children overseas got underway in July 1940, but ended tragically in September when the *City of Benares* was torpedoed on its way to Canada. Seventy-seven evacuees and six escorts died as a result. By that time 577 British children, aged between five and fifteen years, were on their way to Australia; they arrived in three ships in October and November 1940.

On arrival the children were placed with families across Australia. About sixty percent went to relatives and friends nominated by the children's parents, the remainder went to some of the thousands of families who had offered their homes to evacuee children. More than half the children stayed in their first placements for the duration of the war; others moved on, some many times.

Unlike their Polish and German counterparts, child evacuees from Britain were able to return to their homeland and families at the end of the war. Most did, although a large number later returned to Australia as immigrants. In this respect, the government's belief that unaccompanied children would be the vanguard of further migration was realized. Nevertheless it is a blot on Australia's history that the Australian government was so discriminatory in pursuing that belief, in closing the doors on foreign children as it ushered in those who were British.

## FINDINGS

What impact did their experiences have on these former child refugees and evacuees, and what factors contributed to this?

Making cause-effect relationships is fraught with difficulty given the diversity of the children and their situations. Nevertheless, the collective experiences of these children offer insights into a number of issues that continue to confront those working with child victims of political and ethnic violence. I will focus on those findings.

## Separation

Being separated from their families was an experience common to all these children. For some British evacuees the effect was overwhelmingly positive; they found in foster families loving relationships that they had never experienced in their natural families or that allowed them to enjoy the overseas experience despite the absence of their natural families. These former child evacuees declare their overseas evacuation was "the best thing that ever happened to them."

Other children paid various prices for their removal to safety. However, separation alone did not determine the overall impact on any of the children; what preceded and followed separation was equally important—the nature and quality of the substitute care they received, age and maturity at separation, individual temperament, previous family experiences, and trauma. Separation from family was complicated by other separations—from homeland, from familiar cultural and social worlds, and sometimes from attachments formed after leaving home.

For the Jewish children in the study, separation meant survival. Without it, they would probably have joined the 1.5 million Jewish children who were murdered during the Holocaust. At the very least, they were spared horrendous suffering and trauma. From them comes unanimous support for separation, especially in genocidal war, where children are targets. It is not just a matter of personal survival, but survival also of a people.

Also worth noting is that the parents of these children chose separation, and that many thousands of others would have done likewise had they been given the opportunity. In desperate times, parents around the world have always made, and continue to make, this sacrifice—giving up a child to protect the child. Surviving letters tell of the anguish that accompanied the decision, and suggest that in many cases parents suffer more than children from separation.

Past research has tended to condemn separation as a strategy for protecting children (Ressler, Boothby, & Steinbock, 1988). Findings from this research show that although many children exhibited somatic behaviors in the short term—for example, bed wetting, stammering, blushing—these disappeared when good aftercare was provided. The contention of this research is therefore that the debate needs to shift from separation to aftercare—that is, to the care provided children after separation from natural families.

## Aftercare

The children in this study went into a variety of care situations in Australia—foster care, group homes, independent living, and boarding schools. Each had its strengths and weaknesses, with varying outcomes.

Experiences with foster families varied enormously. Placing children where they were wanted and were absorbed into the family was the key to success. Whether or not these families were relatives was immaterial. In fact, where relatives took on children under duress, the results for the children were often disastrous. Joan Sullivan, who was eight when she and her older sister arrived, presents one such case: "We were constantly made to feel unwanted. My aunt and uncle passed this attitude onto others in town. Consequently, other people were always putting us down and saying such things as, 'Do you know how lucky you are?'" Joan was also given a hard time at school: "I was often bashed up by the other children and had to be let out school ten minutes before them."

Where children were wanted and were absorbed into the family, they generally reciprocated by forming new attachments to both family and country. These were often at the expense of former bonds, but that is the price parents paid for their children's safety. As one interviewee commented, "If you send a child away in the formative years you take the risk of losing the affection of that child." At the end of the war, such children faced a dilemma of divided loyalty and, although they might have returned temporarily to their natural families in Britain, many ultimately opted to return to their new family and country.

This process was aided by the fact that young children's memory of their parents generally became vague during the years apart, a phenomenon also reported by Anna Freud in her study of evacuees in Britain (Freud & Burlington, 1943). Young children who were not able to form new attachments were thus left in an emotional limbo, clinging to fading memories of family and sometimes recreating idealized images of families to whom they longed to return.

Older children were more able to divide their loyalties, to develop new relationships while retaining the old. At the same time, many of the adolescents in this study had no wish for new family attachments. "I knew in my mind that I had plenty of family support, though they were not around," commented Max Nagel, one of the Polish adolescents. "I couldn't see when I had parents and brothers, even though they weren't close by, that I wanted somebody else to become a substitute parent." The guardian scheme provided for the Polish adolescents proved to be a very successful model of care. These fourteen and fifteen year olds arrived with few expectations but with a strong resolve to be self-supporting and to help their families. The support they received matched their needs and aspirations. It gave them security while allowing them to be independent. Through connections with people of similar backgrounds, they also had continuity with the past, an important ingredient of successful substitute care for adolescents.

British adolescents, on the other hand, were placed in foster homes where both they and their foster parents often experienced considerable interpersonal difficulty. Successful relationships developed where foster parents set limits and offered guidance, but allowed adolescents to make decisions affecting their lives. Mutual trust and friendship often followed, as was the case for Peter Barnard who went through a series of placements before settling with a family where he was accepted for the reserved, intelligent English boy that he was. "We had a couple of cows," commented his foster father, "and we would talk as we milked the cows—about everything." Peter added, "Phil and I would do things like plastering a ceiling while talking Latin." It was a relationship many adolescents might have envied. Unfortunately, many foster parents took their duty of care so seriously and exerted such strict control over their adolescent charges that relationships were fractious. The situation generally improved as the adolescent evacuees joined the work force or the armed services.

Group homes or boarding schools might be preferable alternatives for adolescents who cannot settle with foster families. This is supported by studies of adolescent evacuees and refugees in both Britain (Isaacs, 1941) and America (Close, 1953). All cases confirm the continued need for guidance and protection throughout adolescence, but the importance of making the support relevant to the needs and maturity of young people.

About sixty percent of British evacuees stayed in their original placements. Pressures of war and changing circumstances of families caused many moves. Children's behavior caused others. Mismatches were inevitable, but most children settled down when moved to another family. Some evacuees went through many moves, but a move was unquestionably better than leaving a child in an unhappy environment. Children who eventually found a happy placement seem not to have experienced any long-term harmful effects from their moves whereas those who stayed in unhappy placements are filled with sad, sometimes bitter, memories. Their cases illustrate the importance of careful and continuous monitoring of foster homes, and the involvement of children in that process.

In the absence of any family life, group care did not fulfill the needs of the young German children who came to Australia. Although they received good physical care, their memories are a painful reminder of what was missing: "There was a desolation because there was no love . . . You need to be able to say to a child, 'You're my special one.'" In the absence of love, their behavior often disguised a deep pain that revealed itself only in the quiet of night. "We used to cry sometimes at night. We wanted someone to hug us and kiss us."

Nevertheless, group care is inevitable in many emergency situations. To this end, the memories and reflections of these former child refugees offer valuable insight into the requirements of group care for young children. Foremost is the need to offer children family experiences and, within the institution, to replicate home life as closely as possible—to have small child-staff ratios, qualified and caring male and female staff, opportunities for children to have regular social contact with children and adults outside the group home, including links with families who can provide each child with satisfying family experiences. Keeping siblings together seemed to be important for younger children, but was less so for older children. A positive outcome of group living for the German children was the development of strong bonds with each other. These bonds have withstood the test of time, providing friendship and support not available to children who went into foster care. In this respect, children in uncaring foster homes were considerably worse off than children in the *Larino* home.

Outcomes for children who went into boarding schools support these conclusions. This includes British children evacuated to Australia from the Pacific Islands and South-East Asia, many of whom were placed in boarding schools. Where care was of a high quality, and children had the support of adults and the friendship of peers, they tended to thrive. Andrea Bannantyne from the Solomon Islands spoke enthusiastically of her years at Frensham, near Sydney:

> Everyone was marvelous to me. The headmistress was really inspired ... I didn't find the separation horrific. I thought it was rather fun really because I had lots of children to play with and that to me was a picnic.

## Family Reunion and Loss

The end of the war brought new stresses to many children, most of whom were by then young adults. This was true even for those who were reunited, as were most British evacuees, and some of the young German children. Reunions rarely fulfilled expectations or had "happy ever after" endings. In the years apart, parents and children had both changed. An escort who returned to Britain with some evacuees, visited them at home some weeks after their return: He found parents reluctant to talk. "They felt their children had been away . . . and when they came back they appeared not to be their children. They'd changed so . . . the parents were pleased to have their kids back again, but were resentful." Many children echoed these sentiments: "I couldn't say my family were my family anymore." Another interviewee articulated the feelings of many returning children when she commented, "It was easier to go than to come back."

The complexity of reunion needs greater recognition. Where separation is prolonged, counseling is essential for both children and parents before and after reunion. Even then, these case studies suggest it is unrealistic to expect children to resettle easily with natural families after prolonged separation, especially when they have formed new bonds. Nevertheless, the reunion is critical, for without it there can be a lifetime of unresolved grief, as has been demonstrated through other cases of separation in Australia—for example, British child migrants and Aboriginal children forcibly separated from their families.

For most of the Polish and German refugee children, there was no reunion; the loss of immediate family was total. For some the grieving, the searching, the sorrowing goes on. "The Holocaust pursues us daily," commented Hermann Levy, a former child refugee. "It is like having a flea in your head." Others have learnt to live with "the cup that is half full instead of the half empty one." Yet, more than 50 years later, the wounds still bleed when touched. Inge

Sadan, who has been involved with hundreds of former child refugees who went to England, spoke of "the dividing line between those whose parents did survive and those who didn't. There's a big pain in them … I don't think I could have survived mentally not knowing what had happened to my parents . . . It's coming home to roost now . . . they've got more time to think and reflect."

Rather than healing with the passing of time, this suggests that the pain of childhood loss and trauma can become more intense in later life. In this respect, reunions and recollections serve an important function—offering opportunities to talk and share with those who have had similar experiences, and to record those experiences for family and for posterity.

For Jewish children, this has been particularly significant as, in the aftermath of the Holocaust, little attention was paid to the experiences of children who escaped overseas before the war. Because they were neither in concentration camps nor in hiding, their experiences were generally overlooked. As one interviewee commented, when she is with concentration camp survivors she sums up her history in a few words: "Germany, Australia, America, and then I came here (Israel)." These children too shared the Jewish fate, and it is important to acknowledge their experiences, suffering, and survival strategies.

## Coping

Political and ethnic violence set in motion a chain of events for all these children and their families. Separation was a shared experience but, apart from it, there were numerous variables that affected how each child responded to the situation, and the long-term outcomes for each person. In an attempt to determine possible causes and relationships, some of the most salient of those variables have been identified, both those that caused stress and those that offered protection against the impact of stressful or traumatic experiences.

### Stressors

#### In childhood

- Trauma before separation (for example, racial harassment, witnessing violence or humiliation of parents, loss of a parent through death, divorce or other means)
- Inadequate and inappropriate aftercare (feeling unwanted, lack of support; for young children included lack of family experiences)
- Maltreatment or abuse
- Being thwarted in pursuing goals and ideals, including religious practices
- Resettlement
- Unsatisfactory family reunion
- Loss of parents and extended family; not knowing what happened to them

#### In later life

- Continuing grief over family loss
- Loss of social support (for example, a partner who has helped the person cope with earlier stress)
- Other personal stresses (for example, illness, the death of children, financial worries, divorce)

### Protective Factors

#### In childhood

- Family practices, before separation, that made children feel secure but that encouraged independence
- High self-esteem and a positive sense of self
- Earlier life experiences or hardship that made children resourceful
- Having adults, other than parents, who gave children support and care that matched their needs
- Being able to form friendships and make new relationships
- Having goals, and the potential and determination to work toward those goals; having dreams
- Having interests (for example, school, sport, hobbies)
- An easy temperament

#### In later life

- A continuing sense of purpose in one's life
- Good social support throughout adult life, including fulfilling family experiences
- Being in control of the past—able to talk about the past, but not dwell on painful memories
- A sense of humor; being able to laugh

Other variables, for example age and maturity at the time of the experience, overlapped these. Young children might have had less opportunity to develop buffers such as independence or a strong sense of self before being separated; adolescents who had lived pampered lives might not have had opportunities to become resourceful. Hans Eisler, for example, who arrived from Austria at age fourteen, confirmed that nothing in his pampered early life prepared him for the hardships and loneliness of life in Australia. Stressful experiences also varied in their intensity; for example, a parent disappearing because of divorce as opposed to witnessing a parent being violently apprehended by the S.S.

It is not difficult to see how British evacuees who went from secure family environments to caring foster families might now feel positively about the overall experience. Many of these children experienced minimal stress and had numerous personal resources to fall back on. Other children, including some British evacuees, experienced multiple stressors, some of which were certainly traumatic. An accumulation of stress factors surely increases the chances of damaging outcomes. However, case studies of these former child refugees and evacuees challenge research that claims that the accumulation of stress or risk factors "tells the story" or explains the variance in child outcomes (for example, Garbarino & Kostelny, 1996). Over the lifespan, protective factors may tell a more remarkable story, a finding also emerging from other longitudinal studies (Werner & Smith, 1982). Many of the participants in this research are like archetypal heroes—they have had everything thrown at them and have survived. How do we account for this ability to cope in the face of such adversity? Habituation might explain some of it. As a Holocaust survivor commented when I phoned to offer my condolences on the death of her husband: "My dear, when you've been through what I've been through you can survive anything." Habituation probably helped some children through the early years without family support—they got used to being on their own.

However, they needed other buffers both then and in later life to maintain their resilience.

Those buffers were often clustered. Easygoing, socially competent children were more likely to have the skills required to form friendships and interests beyond the care situation. They found outlets in sport, school and other people. Secure, independent children were also much better equipped to handle life without their families; this included children who were accustomed to being away from their families or to having other people care for them. On the contrary, withdrawn, insecure children, who lacked interpersonal skills, were more vulnerable to the effects of inadequate care and other stressful experiences. Success in childhood social relationships was also closely linked with the ability to develop effective adult relationships and to create a network of social support in later life.

Although much of the data for these conclusions came from adults' memories of their childhoods, insights into many childhoods were also gleaned from documents and letters. Overall, strong evidence emerged for the constancy of interviewees' temperaments over their lifespan. Invariably the withdrawn, the extroverted, the happy, the worried child who emerged from the documents was present in the adult I interviewed. Although basic temperaments seem not to have changed, insensitive treatment had a profound effect on the lives of more vulnerable children, a finding that supports other contemporary research on stress and resilience in children (see, for example, Haggerty, 1994).

## CONCLUSION

There is a tendency in research on children and war to stress the negative, to focus on the pathology (this point is stressed in a recent literature review by Cairns & Dawes, 1996). Perhaps this reflects the psychological focus of the research and that most studies have not been conducted over the lifespan. Reflecting on the lives of these former child refugees and evacuees, several conclusions can be drawn. First, although many people involved in this study remain deeply affected by their childhood experiences, only a minority might be considered pathologically disturbed. Most found turning points through family, careers, or other interests and have lived fulfilling and productive lives. Second, it is important to acknowledge that even the most resilient of children suffered when their basic needs were not met. Much research on childhood resilience suggests that resilient children emerge unscarred from distressing lives and situations. Testimonies of children in this study dispute this and caution against misinterpreting childhood resilience.

Finally, it is questionable that victims of genocide can ever make a complete recovery. Nor is it realistic to expect resettlement in a country where genocide has been endorsed and perpetrated by the government. Although none of these interviewees has returned to live in Europe, some have visited Austria and Germany, mostly in recent years. It has rarely been a comfortable sojourn. This is a poignant reminder of the pervasive effects of ethnic violence throughout the lifespan.

Past and present conflicts provide ample evidence of the effects of political and ethnic violence on all children, be they victims or perpetrators. In each conflict, the seeds of the next war are sown as children are inculcated into a culture of hate—bearing arms, name calling, or merely imbuing the prevailing propaganda. Intervention with children in war zones, and wherever racism prevails, is critical if the cycle is to be broken.

Counterbalancing the grim statistics of children and war is the extraordinary capacity of many to cope with adversity, and the potential of other people to make a difference. The testimonies in this research are filled with examples of individual courage and commitment. Most chronicles of war are similar—stories of human kindness and courage emerging from the darkness. Nevertheless, when the guns are silenced and the treaties signed, the war is rarely over for children. The shadows remain—even for those who are most resilient.

## NOTES

1. "The position of Jews in Germany," October 1937, file 63, reel 12, Archives of the Central British Fund.

2. Letter from J. A. Carrodus, Department of the Interior, to H. Lesnie, Australian Jewish Welfare Society, 16 March 1939, AA433/1: 43/2/46. On 1 December 1938, the Department for the Interior announced that Australia would admit 15,000 refugees over a period of three years. This was in fact a slight reduction from an unannounced quota that had existed for Jewish refugees since June 1938—3,600 unguaranteed persons and 1,500 guaranteed.

3. Extract from a letter from the AJWS to the Overseas Settlement Department, London, 22 December 1939, AA434/1: 49/3/3.

## EVALUATING YOUR MASTERY

1. The impact of separation from family on refugee and evacuee children depended on which of the following?
   a. Quality of aftercare
   b. Mood of family members when separating
   c. Experiences en route to Australia
   c. Whether the child was cared for by relatives in Australia

2. Which refugee and evacuee children were most likely to maintain ties to their parents?
   a. Younger children
   b. Older children
   c. Children placed in caring foster homes
   d. Children placed in group homes

3. Which living arrangement worked best for adolescent refugees and evacuees?
   a. Boarding houses and schools
   b. Adoption
   c. Foster homes
   d. None of the above; adolescents, regardless of living arrangements, adjusted poorly

4. Which of the following was related to long-term positive outcomes for refugees and evacuees?
   a. Trauma before separation, which eased after arrival in Australia
   b. Family practices before separation, which combined security with independence training
   c. An introverted temperament
   d. An unsatisfactory reunion with family members, which helped the child forget the pain of separation

5. True or False: Keeping siblings together was more important in the adjustment of older than younger children.

6. For children whose emotional ties to parents were disrupted by prolonged separation, reunion with parents was [unimportant/still important] for long-term adjustment.

7. True or False: The pain of childhood loss can become more intense in later life.

### Critical Thinking

Explain how long-term well-being after separation from parents in childhood is a product of both personal and situational factors. Why do the various buffers from stress often cluster together?

## Applying Your Knowledge

Interview an older adult who experienced severe adversity of one kind or another in childhood or adolescence (for example, family separation, death of parents, or a move to a new country because of ethnic or political violence). What factors helped the individual cope? What factors made adjustment more difficult? Is the report of your interviewee consistent with Palmer's generalizations about refugee and evacuee children who came to Australia during World War II?

# 28

## Risk, Resilience, and Recovery

## Perspectives from the Kauai Longitudinal Study

EMMY E. WERNER

University of California, Davis

■

As toddlers, the resilient boys and girls tended to meet the world already on their own terms. The pediatricians and psychologists, who examined them independently at 20 months, noted their alertness and autonomy, their tendency to seek out novel experiences, and their positive social orientation.

■

The resilient boys and girls also sought and found emotional support outside of their own family. They tended to have at least one, and usually several, close friends, especially the girls. They relied on an informal network of kin and neighbors, peers and elders, for counsel and support in times of crises.

■

Personal competence and determination, support from a spouse or mate, and reliance on faith and prayer were the shared qualities that characterized the resilient children in their mid-30s.

■

The presence of an intact family unit in childhood, and especially in adolescence, was a major protective factor in the lives of delinquent youths in this birth cohort who did not commit any offenses in early adulthood.

■

■

When we examined the links between protective factors within the individual and outside sources of support or of stress, we noted a certain continuity that appeared in the life course of the high-risk men and women who successfully overcame a variety of childhood adversities. Their individual dispositions led them to select or construct environments that, in turn, reinforced and sustained their active, outgoing dispositions and rewarded their competencies.

■

One of the most important lessons we learned from our adult follow-up was that *the opening up of opportunities* led to major turning points in the lives of high-risk individuals as they entered their 20s and early 30s.

■

Our findings alert us to the need for setting priorities, to choices we must make in our investment of resources and time. Intervention programs need to focus on children and youths who appear *most* vulnerable because they lack some of the essential personal resources and/or social bonds that buffer chronic adversity or stress.

■

The rediscovery of the healing powers of hope in the stories of individual lives may be the most precious harvest of those who venture forth into research on risk, resilience, and human development.

■

## EDITOR'S INTRODUCTION

Emmy Werner examines the long-term consequences of early risk—in the form of birth complications, chronic poverty, and troubled family environments in childhood—through longitudinal research, by *looking forward*. Her participants are members of the Kauai Longitudinal Study, which followed all children born on the Hawaiian island of Kauai from birth into early adulthood.

The generalizations that emerge from Werner's study complement Palmer's conclusions on children of war. Inner resources (a good-natured temperament), the opportunity to establish a close bond with at least one adult, and emotional support through friendships as children grew older led to resilience in the face of stress. The most recent follow-up, at age 32, reveals that with few exceptions, resilient children had become competent adults who had satisfying marriages and did well educationally and vocationally. Young people whose life stresses piled up early in life tended to display long-term adjustment difficulties. But over time, some youths and young adults became more active in protecting themselves, leaving stressful homes for other environments that helped redirect their life course. Werner suggests a variety of ways adults can offer experiences that bring about changes in the life trajectories of vulnerable children and youths.

In 1955, a team of pediatricians, psychologists, psychiatrists, and public health and social workers began a prospective study of the development of all 698 babies born that year on the Hawaiian island of Kauai, the westernmost county of the United States. The principal goals of our study were (a) to document, in natural history fashion, the course of all pregnancies and their outcomes in the entire island community until the surviving offspring had reached adulthood, and (b) to assess the long-term consequences of perinatal complications and adverse rearing conditions on the individuals' development and adaptation to life. A detailed description of the methodology, data base, and results of this study can be found in *Overcoming the Odds: High Risk Children from Birth to Adulthood* (Werner & Smith, 1992).

The men and women whose lives we followed from birth to their mid-30s are a mixture of ethnic groups—most are of Japanese, Filipino, and Hawaiian descent. About half of the cohort (54 percent) grew up in poverty. They were reared by fathers who were semi- or unskilled laborers on the local sugar and pineapple plantations and by mothers who had not graduated from high school.

We began our study by examining the children's **vulnerability,** that is, their susceptibility to negative developmental outcomes after exposure to serious *risk* factors, such as perinatal stress, poverty, parental psychopathology, and disruptions of their family unit (Werner & Smith, 1977). As our longitudinal investigation progressed, we also looked at the roots of resiliency in those children who successfully coped with such biological and psychosocial risk factors and at protective factors that aided in the *recovery* of troubled children and youths as they made the transition into adulthood (Werner & Smith, 1989, 1992).

We need to keep in perspective that the majority of the members of this birth cohort were born without complications, after uneventful pregnancies, and grew up in supportive home environments. They led lives that were not unusually stressful, and they coped successfully with the developmental tasks of childhood, adolescence, and young adulthood.

We designated about one-third of the surviving boys and girls in this cohort as high-risk children (n = 201) because they were born into poverty, they had experienced moderate to severe degrees of perinatal stress, and they lived in a family environment troubled by chronic discord, parental alcoholism, or mental illness. Two out of three of these vulnerable children (who encountered four or more such risk factors by age 2) did indeed develop serious learning or behavior problems by age 10 and had mental health problems, delinquency records, and/or teenage pregnancies by the time they were 18 years old.

One out of three of these high-risk children (n = 72), however, grew into competent, confident, and caring young adults. None developed serious learning or behavior problems in childhood or adolescence. As far as we could tell from interviews with them in their senior year in high school and from their records in the community, they succeeded in school, managed home and social life well, and expressed a strong desire to take advantage of whatever opportunity came their way.

In our book *Vulnerable but Invincible* (Werner & Smith, 1989), we contrasted the behavior and caregiving environments of these resilient youngsters to those of their high-risk peers of the same age and gender who had developed serious coping problems in the first two decades of life.

Even as infants, the resilient children had elicited positive attention from family members as well as strangers. At age 1, they were frequently described by their caregivers as "very active," with the girls more often as "affectionate" and "cuddly" and the boys more often as "good

Werner, E. E. (1993). Risk, resilience, and recovery: Perspectives from the Kauai Longitudinal Study. *Development and Psychopathology, 5,* 503–515. Reprinted by permission of Cambridge University Press.

natured" and "easy to deal with." The resilient infants also had fewer eating and sleeping habits that were distressing to their parents than did the infants who later developed serious learning or behavior problems.

As toddlers, the resilient boys and girls tended to meet the world already on their own terms. The pediatricians and psychologists, who examined them independently at 20 months, noted their alertness and autonomy, their tendency to seek out novel experiences, and their positive social orientation. They were more advanced in communication, locomotion, and self-help skills than the other high-risk children, who later developed serious coping problems.

In elementary school, teachers reported that the resilient children got along well with their classmates. They had better reasoning and reading skills than the children who later developed problems, especially the girls. Though not unusually gifted, the resilient children used whatever skills they had effectively. Both parents and teachers noted that they had many interests and engaged in activities and hobbies that were not narrowly sex typed. Such activities provided them with solace in adversity and a reason to feel proud.

By the time they graduated from high school, the resilient youths had developed a positive **self-concept** and an **internal locus of control**. On the California Psychological Inventory (Gough, 1969), they displayed a more nurturant, responsible, and achievement-oriented attitude toward life than their high-risk peers, who had developed problems in their teens. The resilient girls, especially, were more assertive and independent than the other females in this cohort.

Most resilient boys and girls had grown up in families with four or fewer children, with a space of 2 years or more between themselves and their next sibling. Few had experienced prolonged separations from their primary caretaker during the first year of life. All had the opportunity to establish a close bond with at least one caregiver from whom they received plenty of positive attention when they were infants.

Some of this nurturing came from substitute parents, such as grandparents or older siblings, or from the ranks of regular babysitters. Such substitute parents also played an important role as positive models of identification. Maternal employment and the need to take care of younger siblings contributed to the pronounced autonomy and sense of responsibility noted among the resilient girls, especially in households where the father was absent. Resilient boys were often first-born sons who did not have to share their parents' attention with many additional children. There were some males in the family who could serve as a role model—if not the father, then a grandfather, older cousin, or uncle. Structure and rules, and assigned chores, were part of their daily routine in adolescence.

The resilient boys and girls also sought and found emotional support outside of their own families. They tended to have at least one, and usually several, close friends, especially the girls. They relied on an informal network of kin and neighbors, peers and elders, for counsel and support in times of crises. Many had a favorite teacher who became a role model, friend, and confidant for them.

Participation in extracurricular activities played an important part in the lives of the resilient youths, especially activities that were cooperative enterprises, such as 4-H and/or the YMCA and YWCA. For others, emotional support came from a youth leader or from a minister or church group. With their help, the resilient children acquired a faith that their lives had meaning and they had control over their fate.

When we interviewed these young men and women at age 18, they were in a transitional phase of their life cycle. They were about to graduate from high school, to leave their parental homes, and to enter their first full-time jobs. Their relationships with members of the opposite sex were still tentative and did not involve any serious long-term commitments. With the exception of the teenage mothers, they had not yet been confronted with the demands of childbearing and child-rearing. The period of maximum risk for mental breakdown was still ahead of them.

## THE ADULT FOLLOW-UP

Our most recent follow-up at age 32 finds these same men and women at a stage in life that provides them an opportunity to reappraise and modify the initial mode of adult living they established in the previous decade. The *age-30 transition period* is biologically the peak of adulthood, a time of great energy, but also among the most stressful of the adult life cycle. The central components of the adult life structure being reappraised are work life, marriage, and parenthood.

The main objectives of our most recent inquiry were, first, to trace the long-term effects of childhood adversity on the adult lives of the men and women who had been exposed to perinatal stress, poverty, parental discord, and psychopathology and, second, to examine the long-term effects of protective factors and processes that led most to a successful adaptation in adulthood (Werner & Smith, 1992).

### Perspectives and Procedures

We used two perspectives to assess the quality of adult adaptation of the men and women in our study. One was the perspective gained from a semistructured interview (questionnaire) that focused on the developmental tasks of early adulthood. The responses to the interview questions permitted us to make some judgment on how well a given individual had negotiated Erikson's stages of identity, intimacy, and generativity.

A second complementary perspective on the quality of adult adaptation of the men and women in this cohort was gleaned from their record(s) in the community. From the District and Circuit courts on Kauai, in Honolulu, and on the other islands (Maui and Hawaii), we obtained information on every member of the 1955 birth cohort residing in the State of Hawaii who was convicted of a crime, involved as a defendant in a civil suit, or whose marriage ended in divorce since our last follow-up. From the State Department of Mental Health, we ascertained information on every member of the 1955 birth cohort who received in- or outpatient treatment for mental health problems. The U.S. Veterans Administration provided us with information on cohort members who had served in the Armed Forces and who had received disability payments or educational benefits.

Our criteria for rating the quality of adult adaptation were based on these two perspectives: the individual's own account of success and satisfaction with work, family and social life, and state of psychological well-being, and on their records in the community. Areas included in the evaluation were achievements in school and/or work; relationships with spouse or mate; relationships with offspring; relationships with parents, in-laws, and siblings; relationships with peers; and the degree of overall satisfaction an individual expressed with his or her present state in life. A criminal record, a record of spouse or child abuse or delinquent child support, and a record of chronic substance abuse and/or psychosomatic or psychiatric disorders were considered signs of unsuccessful adaptation to adult life (see Appendix II in Werner & Smith, 1992).

## THE HIGH-RISK CHILDREN AS ADULTS

We were fortunate to reach a relatively high proportion of the original high-risk sample in our cohort. We have data in adulthood on 88 percent of the resilient high-risk individuals, 90 percent of the teenage mothers, and 80 percent of the high-risk youths who had records of serious mental health problems and/or delinquencies.

### The Resilient Children in Their Mid-30s

With only two exceptions (both offspring of depressed mothers), the resilient children had grown into adults whose educational and vocational accomplishments exceeded those of their high-risk peers and were equal to those of the low-risk children in the cohort who had grown up in more affluent, secure, and stable environments.

Personal competence and determination, support from a spouse or mate, and reliance on faith and prayer were the shared qualities that characterized the resilient children in their mid-30s.

As a group, they worked and loved in contexts far different than the traumatic domestic scenes that had characterized their childhoods. Those who were married (76 percent of the women, 60 percent of the men) had strong commitments to intimacy and sharing with their partners. Those who had children (65 percent of the women, 56 percent of the men) had a strong sense of generativity that enabled them to be caring parents who respected the individuality and encouraged the autonomy of their offspring.

There was a persistent need, however, for detachment from parents and siblings whose domestic and emotional problems still threatened to engulf them. The balancing act between forming new attachments to loved ones of their choice and loosening of old family ties that evoked painful memories had exacted a toll in their adult lives. Among some men in this group, there was a reluctance to make definite long-term commitments to a mate; some of the women exhausted themselves in the balancing act among the demands of marriage, motherhood, and striving for success in a career. The price they paid varied from stress-related health problems such as migraines and backaches (reported by 55 percent of the men and 41 percent of the women) to a certain aloofness that characterized their interpersonal relationships.

## The Teenage Mothers in Their Mid-30s

On the whole, the situation of the 28 teenage mothers in our cohort had improved significantly over time. In almost all respects, except for marital stability, they were better off than at age 18. By age 32, 60 percent of the adolescent mothers on Kauai had obtained additional schooling beyond a high school diploma.

Their employment picture was much more positive as well. Only two of the women, both mothers of young preschool children, were temporarily unemployed. The employment experience of the adolescent mothers on Kauai refutes the popular stereotype of teenage mothers as chronic welfare recipients. Their rate of employment rose steadily during the course of our study, and their levels of employment increased with educational opportunities sought out by them once their own children were in school.

The paths that had led to improvement for the majority of our teenage mothers were similar to those reported by Furstenberg, Brooks-Gunn, and Morgan (1987) for a much larger sample of black adolescent mothers who grew up in metropolitan Baltimore. The development of the women's personal resources, their competence and motivation, the support of kith and kin, and a stable marriage all contributed to positive changes in their life trajectories.

## Delinquents With and Without a Record of Adult Crime

Most of the 103 delinquent youths in this birth cohort did not go on to an adult criminal career. Three-fourths of the males and 90 percent of the females with a record of juvenile offenses avoided arrest upon reaching adulthood. This was especially true for those with only one or two offenses before age 18.

The majority of the adult crimes in this cohort were committed by a small group of juvenile offenders with an average of four or more arrests whose delinquent career had begun in their early teens and who had been considered "troublesome" by both their parents and their teachers at age 10.

The presence of an intact family unit in childhood, and especially in adolescence, was a major protective factor in the lives of delinquent youths in this birth cohort who did not commit any offenses in early adulthood. Only one out of four of this group grew up in a home where either the mother or the father were absent for prolonged periods of times because of separations, desertion, or divorce. In contrast, five out of six among the delinquents who went on to commit adult crimes came from families where one parent was absent for prolonged periods of time during their teens.

Police and court records also revealed that among the delinquent youths who did not go on to a criminal career there was more active involvement by the parents or other elders (grandparents, aunts) in their rehabilitation process. Foster home placement and the Hawaii Youth Correctional Facility did not prove to be adequate parent substitutes for the persistent offenders in this group. For some, however, a promising alternative appeared to be enlistment in the military or a marriage to a stable spouse.

Our findings on Kauai, with a Pacific Asian sample, are very similar to those reported by Wolfgang, Thornberry, and Figlio (1987) from two cohorts of Black and White males born in Philadelphia in 1945 and 1958. Both studies found that, on the average, the earlier an offender started, the more juvenile *and* criminal offenses he accumulated.

## Troubled Youth in Their Early 30s

Only a minority of the 70 individuals with serious mental health problems in their teens were still in need of mental health services by the time they reached their early 30s; however, a higher proportion of males than females with mental health problems in their teens had grown into adults who had difficulties finding and keeping a job, who had marriages that ended in divorce, who were delinquent in spouse and child support, and who had criminal records. Only about one-third of the men and women who had been identified as having serious mental health problems in this cohort received some form of mental health care in adolescence or young adulthood.

A significant minority among the individuals with mental health problems in this cohort (one out of five men, one out of three women) had converted to fundamentalist religions that assured them salvation, security, and a sense of mission. Prominent among them were the Jehovah's Witnesses and, to a lesser extent, the Latter Day Saints. By far the most frequently mentioned source of support in times of difficulties was a supportive spouse or close friend. Nearly half of the men and two-thirds of the women with mental health problems in their youth reported that their spouses had helped them most in dealing with difficulties and stresses in their adult lives. Two-thirds of the men and half of the women also relied on the emotional support of close friends.

Overall, the prognosis for youths who were shy and lacked confidence was considerably better than for youths who displayed antisocial behavior or for youths who had parents with schizophrenia or chronic depression *and* who had been exposed to serious perinatal trauma.

Approximately one out of six (18 percent) in this cohort, however, became troubled adults who had serious coping problems that included at least two of the following conditions: a broken marriage, a criminal record, chronic mental health problems, and a poor self-concept. Two-thirds of these individuals had been high-risk youth who had been exposed to poverty and family disorganization since early childhood and who subsequently developed a record of school failure, repeated delinquencies, and/or mental health problems. Our study of Asian Americans on Kauai and Magnusson's (1988) study of urban Swedish males are consistent in their findings that individuals who are characterized by *several* problem areas at an early age are more stable in their patterns of maladjustment up into adulthood than are persons who have problems in a *single* area.

# LINKS BETWEEN PROTECTIVE FACTORS AND SUCCESSFUL ADULT ADAPTATION IN HIGH-RISK CHILDREN AND YOUTHS

A major objective of our follow-up into adulthood was to document how a chain of protective factors, linked across time, afforded vulnerable children and teenagers an escape from adversity and contributed to positive outcomes in their adult lives.

We used latent-variables **path analyses** (Lohmöller, 1984) to examine the links between protective factors in the individual and outside sources of support in childhood and adolescence that led to successful adult adaptation (see Werner & Smith, 1992, Appendix I, pp. 240–245, for a detailed account of our analysis and the path diagrams).

Several clusters of protective factors appeared in the records and interviews of the high-risk children who made a successful adaptation in adult life. Cluster 1 included **temperamental characteristics** of the individual that helped him or her to elicit positive responses from a variety of caring persons. Cluster 2 included skills and values that led to an efficient use of whatever abilities they had: realistic educational and vocational plans, and regular household chores and domestic responsibilities. Cluster 3 included characteristics and caregiving styles of the parents that reflected competence and fostered self-esteem in the child. Cluster 4 consisted of supportive adults who fostered trust and acted as gatekeepers for the future. Among these "surrogate" parents were grandparents, elder mentors, youth leaders, and members of church groups. Finally, there was the opening of opportunities at major life transitions, from high school to the work place, from civilian to military life, from single state to marriage and parenthood, that turned the trajectory of a significant proportion of the high-risk children on the path to normal adulthood. Among the most potent forces providing a second chance for such youths were adult education programs in community colleges, voluntary national service, and/or an intrinsic religious orientation.

When we examined the links between protective factors within the individual and outside sources of support or of stress, we noted a certain continuity that appeared in the life course of the high-risk men and women who successfully overcame a variety of childhood adversities. Their individual dispositions led them to select or construct environments that, in turn, reinforced and sustained their active, outgoing dispositions and rewarded their competencies. In spite of occasional deviations during transitional periods such as adolescence, their life trajectories revealed cumulative interactional continuity. These continuities have also been demonstrated in other cohorts of high-risk individuals followed into adulthood—for instance, in the life course of shy and ill-tempered white children in the Berkeley Guidance Study (Caspi, Elder, & Bem, 1988) and in the life trajectories of the Black teenage mothers followed by Furstenberg, Brooks-Gunn, & Morgan (1987).

There was, for example, a significant positive link between an easy infant temperament and the sources of support available to the individual in early and middle childhood. Active and sociable babies, without distressing sleeping and feeding habits, tended to elicit more positive responses from their mothers at age 1 and from alternate caregivers by age 2 than did shy and "difficult" babies. In middle childhood, such children tended to rely on a wider network of caring adults both *within* and *outside* the family circle.

Positive parental interactions with the infant and toddler were, in turn, associated with greater autonomy and social maturity at age 2 and with greater scholastic competence at age 10. **Difficult temperament** traits in infancy, in contrast, were moderately linked with behavior problems in the classroom and at home at age 10 and, in turn, generated fewer sources of emotional support during adolescence.

Scholastic competence at age 10, however, was positively linked with the number of sources of help that the teenager attracted, including support from teachers and peers as well as from family members. Scholastic competence at age 10 was also positively linked with a sense of self-efficacy (self-esteem, internal locus of control) at age 18. A greater sense of self-efficacy at age 18 was, in turn, linked to less distress and emotionality for the high-risk men at age 32 and generated a greater number of sources of emotional support for the high-risk women in early adulthood, including support from a spouse or mate.

Parental competence, as manifested in the educational level of the opposite sex parent (fathers for women, mothers for men) also proved to be a significant protective factor in the lives of the men and women on Kauai who grew up in childhood poverty. The majority of the immigrant parents in this birth cohort had only 8 years or less of formal education, but each additional grade completed strengthened the link between parental and child competence—especially graduation from high school. Better educated parents had more positive interactions with their children in the first and second years of life and provided more emotional support for their offspring during early and middle childhood—even when the family lived in poverty. Parental education was also positively linked to the infant's health and physical status by age 2.

There were also significant positive links between parental educational level and the child's scholastic competence at age 10: One path was direct, the other was mediated through the child's health and physical status. Better educated parents had children with better problem-solving and reading skills, but they also had healthier children with few handicaps and absences from school due to repeated serious illnesses.

While parental competence and the sources of support available in the childhood home were modestly linked to the quality of adult adaptation, they made less of a direct impact in adulthood than the individual's competencies, degree of self-esteem and self-efficacy, and temperamental dispositions. Many resilient high-risk youths left the adverse conditions of their childhood homes (and their island community) after high school and sought environments they found more compatible. In short, they picked their own niches (Scarr & McCartney, 1983).

## Individual Dispositions versus Outside Sources of Support

We noted, however, that protective factors *within* the individual (such as temperament, cognitive skills, self-esteem, and locus of control) tended to consistently make a greater impact on the quality of adult coping for the high-risk females than

the high-risk males. *Outside* sources of support tended to make a greater difference in the lives of the high-risk men than the high-risk women.

In infancy, the educational level of the mother, the proportion of positive maternal interactions observed during the developmental examination at age 2, and a rating of family stability (from birth to age 2) predicted successful adult adaptation better for high-risk males than for high-risk females. Behavior characteristics of the 1-year-old infant and the 2-year-old toddler (that is, an engaging, sociable temperament) predicted successful adult adaptation better for high-risk females than for high-risk males.

In middle childhood, the emotional support provided by the family (between ages 2 and 10), the number of children in the family, and the number of adults outside of the household with whom the youngster liked to associate were more potent predictors of successful adult adaptation for the high-risk boys than the high-risk girls. For the high-risk girls, the best predictors of a successful adaptation in early adulthood were a (nonverbal) measure of problem-solving skills at age 10 and the role model of a mother who had graduated from high school and who was steadily employed.

In late adolescence, the availability of a teacher as a mentor or role model and the assignment of regular household chores and responsibilities were better predictors of successful adult adaptation for high-risk men than for high-risk women. A high self-esteem rating, an internal locus of control, and realistic educational and vocational plans were better discriminators for high-risk women than for high-risk men who coped successfully with the demands of adult life.

## IMPLICATIONS FOR DEVELOPMENTAL THEORY

Our findings fit into the framework of a number of complementary developmental models. The perspectives we found most useful in interpreting our data are the structural-behavioral model of development by Horowitz (1987) and the theory of genotype → environment effects by Scarr and McCartney (1983).

Horowitz's structural-behavioral model of development assumes that the adequacy of development of an individual in a particular behavioral domain is the result of individual organismic factors acting in relation to aspects of the environment that facilitate or impede development at any given period of the life cycle. As her model would suggest, we noted a range of relative resiliency or vulnerability in the face of adverse environmental conditions that changed at different points of the life cycle—for example, at the onset of adolescence or in the transition to adulthood. Some children drew consistently on constitutional resources that allowed them to overcome adverse experiences relatively unscathed. Others went through a period of reorganization after a troubled adolescence that changed their place on the continuum from vulnerability to resiliency. The *transaction across time* between constitutional characteristics of the individual and aspects of the caregiving environment that were supportive or stressful determined the quality of adult adaptation in different domains—at work, in interpersonal relationships, and in the person's overall satisfaction with life.

Our findings also lend some empirical support to Scarr and McCartney's (1983) theory about how people *make* their own environment. They proposed three types of **genotype → environment effects** on human development: a *passive* kind, through environments provided by biologically related parents; an *evocative* kind, through responses elicited by the individual from others; and an *active* kind, through the selection of different environments by different people. In line with their propositions, we noted that over time there was a shift from passive to active genotype → environment effects, as the youths and young adults in our study left stressful home environments and sought extrafamilial environments (at school, at work, in the military) that they found more compatible and stimulating. Genotype → environment effects of the evocative sort tended to persist throughout the differ-

ent life stages we studied, as individuals elicited differential responses from other people (parents, teachers, peers) based on their physical characteristics, temperament, and intelligence.

Above all, our findings fit well into the framework of the emerging field of **developmental psychopathology,** an approach that stresses the reciprocal interplay between normal developmental theory and findings derived from studies of high-risk populations (Cicchetti & Toth, 1992). We agree with Cicchetti (1993) that the study of resiliency holds considerable promise for the development of intervention programs. By examining the processes that contribute to positive adaptation in situations that more typically result in maladaptations, we should be better able to devise ways of promoting positive outcomes in high-risk children and youths.

## IMPLICATIONS FOR SOCIAL ACTION

Rutter (1987) reminded us that if we want to help vulnerable youngsters, we need to focus especially on the *protective processes* that bring about changes in life trajectories from risk to adaptation. He included among them (a) those that reduce the risk impact, (b) those that reduce the likelihood of negative chain reactions, (c) those that promote self-esteem and self-efficacy, and (d) those that open up opportunities. We have seen these processes at work among the resilient children in our study and among those youths who recovered from serious coping problems in young adulthood. They represent the essence of any effective intervention program, whether by professional or volunteers.

We noted, for example, that structure and rules in the household reduced the likelihood that youths committed juvenile offenses, even when they lived in a delinquency-prone environment, and that children of parents with chronic psychopathology could detach themselves from the discord in their household by spending time with caring adults outside the family circle. Both processes altered their exposure to the potent risk conditions in their homes. In other cases, the negative chain reactions following the intermittent hospitalizations of psychotic or alcoholic parents, or of divorce, were buffered by the presence of grandparents or older siblings who acted as substitute parents and provided continuity in care.

The promotion of competence and self-esteem in a young person is probably one of the key ingredients in any effective intervention process. We saw, for example, how effective reading skills by Grade 4 were one of the most potent predictors of successful adult adaptation among the high-risk children in our study. More than half of the school failures detected at age 10 were due to deficiencies in that skill. Such children profited substantially from short-term remedial work in the first three grades by teachers' aides and peer tutors at a critical period when achievement motivation is stabilized.

Self-esteem and **self-efficacy** were derived not only from academic competence. Most of the resilient children in our high-risk sample were not unusually talented, but they took great pleasure in interests and hobbies that brought them solace when things fell apart in their home lives. They also engaged in activities that allowed them to be part of a cooperative enterprise, whether being cheerleader for the home team or raising an animal for the 4-H Club.

Self-esteem and self-efficacy also grew when youngsters took on a responsible position commensurate with their ability, whether it was part-time paid work, managing the household when a parent was incapacitated, or, most often, caring for younger siblings. At some point in their young lives, usually in middle childhood and adolescence, the youngsters who grew into resilient adults were required to carry out some socially desirable task to prevent others in their family, neighborhood, or community from experiencing distress or discomfort. Such acts of *required helpfulness* (Rachman, 1979) can also become a crucial element of intervention programs that involve high-risk youth in community service.

Most of all, self-esteem and self-efficacy were promoted through supportive relationships. The resilient youngsters in our study *all* had at least one person in their lives who accepted them unconditionally, regardless of temperamental idiosyncrasies, physical attractiveness, or intelligence. Most established such a close bond early in their lives, if not with a parent, then with another family member—a grandparent or favorite aunt or uncle. Some of the high-risk youths who had problems in their teens, but staged a recovery in young adulthood, gained a more positive self-concept in the context of an intimate relationship with a spouse or mate. The experience from intergenerational mentoring programs also suggest that a close one-to-one relationship with an unrelated elder can foster self-esteem in a troubled child or youth (Freedman, 1993). An essential aspect of the encounter is that the youth feels that he or she is special to the other person.

One of the most important lessons we learned from our adult follow-up was that *the opening up of opportunities* led to major turning points in the lives of high-risk individuals as they entered their 20s and early 30s. Our findings at age 32 indicate that earlier events in the lives of high-risk children and youths are not the only ones to affect their later adjustment to the world of work, marriage, and parenthood. Several routes out of poverty and despair in later life were identified in our study of the Asian American youths on Kauai.

Among the most potent forces for positive change for high-risk youths on Kauai in adulthood were education at community colleges, educational and vocational skills acquired during service in the Armed Forces, and active involvement in a church or religious community.

Attendance at community colleges and enlistment in the Armed Forces were also associated with geographical moves for many of the high-risk youths. Both settings provided them with an opportunity to obtain educational and vocational skills that were instrumental in moving them out of a context of poverty into skilled trades and middle-class status.

Community colleges and courses on Army, Navy, and Air Force bases as well as on board ship for some of the young sailors also offered remedial work that allowed high school dropouts to take the General Education Development Test. Military service turned out to be a constructive option for many delinquent youths in our cohort. The majority utilized the educational benefits they earned both during and after the enlistment period. Military service also provided them with opportunities for personal growth in a structured setting and a chance to take on responsibilities that enhanced their self-esteem.

Involvement in church activities and a strong faith provided meaning to the adult lives of many high-risk youths. Such a faith was tied to identification with fundamentalist religious groups for a significant minority who had been troubled by mental health problems in their teens. Participation in their communal activities provided structure for their lives and assured them salvation, security, and a sense of mission in an "alien world."

However, for the majority of the men and women in this cohort, faith was not tied to a specific formal religious affiliation but, rather, to confidence in some center of value. Their faith enabled them to perceive the traumatic experiences of their childhood or youth constructively, even if they caused pain and suffering.

The central component in the lives of the resilient individuals in this study that contributed to their effective coping in adulthood appeared to be a feeling of confidence that the odds can be surmounted. Some of the luckier ones developed such hopefulness early in their lives, in contact with caring adults. Many of their troubled peers had a second chance at developing a sense of self-efficacy and self-esteem in adulthood, sometimes even by virtue of apparent chance encounters with a person who opened up opportunities and gave meaning to their lives.

We need to keep in mind that our research on individual resilience and protective factors has focused on children and youths "who pulled themselves up by their own bootstraps," with informal support from kith and kin, not children who were recipients of intervention services. Yet, there are some lessons these young people can teach us about the need for setting priorities, about critical time periods for intervention, and about the need for a continuum of care and caring. Cicchetti (1993) argued persuasively that empirical findings from the evaluation of such preventive interventions can challenge or affirm the tenets of our theories of normal development.

Our examination of the long-term effects of childhood adversity and of protective factors and processes in the lives of high-risk youths has shown that some of the most critical determinants of adult outcome are present in the first decade of life. It is also apparent that there are large individual differences among high-risk children in their responses to both negative and positive circumstances in their caregiving environment.

Our findings alert us to the need for setting priorities, to choices we must make in our investment of resources and time. Intervention programs need to focus on children and youths who appear *most* vulnerable because they lack some of the essential personal resources and/or social bonds that buffer chronic adversity or stress. Among them are the increasing numbers of preterm survivors of neonatal intensive care, the offspring of parents with severe psychopathology (chronic substance abuse, affective disorders, and schizophrenia), maltreated children reared by isolated single parents with no roots in a community, and preadolescents with conduct disorders who have poor reading skills. From a longitudinal perspective, these youngsters appear most at risk of developing serious coping problems in adulthood—especially if they are boys.

Assessment and diagnosis—the initial part of any intervention program, whether preventive or ameliorative—need to focus not only on the risk factors in the lives of these children, but also on the protective factors. These include competencies and sources of informal support that already exist in the extended family, the neighborhood, and the community at large and that can be utilized to enlarge a child's repertoire of problem-solving skills and his or her self-esteem.

Our own research and that of our American and European colleagues (Garmezy & Rutter, 1983; Werner, 1990) who have followed resilient children into adulthood has repeatedly shown that, if a parent is incapacitated or unavailable, other persons in a youngster's life can play such an enabling role, whether they are grandparents, older siblings, caring neighbors, family day-care providers, teachers, ministers, youth workers in 4-H or the YMCA/YWCA, Big Brothers or Big Sisters, or elder mentors.

Such informal and personal ties to kith, kin, and community are preferred by most children and families to impersonal contacts with formal bureaucracies. These ties need to be encouraged and strengthened, not weakened or displaced, by legislative action and social programs.

## A CLOSING CAVEAT IS IN ORDER!

Most studies of risk and resiliency undertaken during the past decade have focused on the development of children who live in urban, industrialized societies where parents have options to pursue different child-rearing philosophies and techniques, where children are expected to spend some 10 to 12 years in compulsory schooling, and where much of their socialization is undertaken by a succession of strangers who prepare them for entry into a competitive economy that prizes acquisitiveness, assertiveness, and mobility and values a person's control over his or her social and physical environment. Future research on risk and resilience in children and youth needs to look more systematically at other "developmental niches" that characterize the interface of child and culture (Super & Harkness, 1986). The physical and social settings in which children live, the customs of child care and sex role socialization, and caregivers' beliefs concerning the nature and needs of children vary greatly in those parts of the world where five out of every six children are born today: in Asia, the Middle East, Africa, and Latin America. So do the risk factors that increase the vulnerability and challenge the resilience of children.

Due to the vagaries of contemporary wars and changing immigration laws, the United States sees today a virtual explosion of young people who seek refuge and a chance for better opportunities. In California, *each year* some 1 million young immigrants arrive from Latin America, Southeast Asia, and the Middle East whose resilience has been severely tested by civil wars in El Salvador, Guatemala, and Honduras and by political persecution in Southeast Asia and the Middle East. Among them are the children of the Vietnamese boat people who survived pillage and rape at sea, the Highland Hmong, and Cambodian teenagers who witnessed the holocaust of the Pol Pot regime when they were young children. There is a lot we can learn from these resilient survivors!

Their life stories inform us about individual dispositions, sources of support, and protective mechanisms that transcend cultural boundaries and operative effectively in a variety of high-risk contexts. However, we also need to examine the price exacted from such children and youth—for some protective attributes may promote positive adaptation in one context and have negative effects in another (Masten, 1990). The cost and benefits for men and women will vary with the prevailing values and role expectations of a given culture.

The individuals in our study who overcame the odds and grew into competent and caring adults had a special need for detachment. In some ways, they had learned to keep the memories of their childhood adversities at bay by being in the world but not of it. When they told their life stories, however, it was usually without rancor, but with a sense of compassion and, above all, with optimism and hopefulness. The rediscovery of the healing powers of hope in the stories of individual lives may be the most precious harvest of those who venture forth into research on risk, resilience, and human development. Such hopefulness sustains us as we examine the "mid-life transition" of the men and women in this cohort—on the occasion of their twentieth high school reunion.

## EVALUATING YOUR MASTERY

1. Which of the following characterized resilient children in the Kauai Longitudinal Study?
   a.   Slower communication, locomotion, and self-help skills
   b.   The ability to elicit positive attention from adults
   c.   Gifted performance after entering elementary school
   d.   Strong sex typing

2. In adulthood, the achievements of resilient children resembled those of their low-risk peers in which of the following ways?
   a.   In educational and vocational accomplishment and family life
   b.   In educational and vocational accomplishment but not family life
   c.   In family life but not educational and vocational accomplishment
   d.   None of the above; resilient children did not achieve as well as their low-risk peers

3. Which of the following characterized delinquent youths who did not go on to an adult criminal career?
   a.   Foster home placement
   b.   Earlier beginning as a juvenile offender
   c.   Favorable school achievement
   d.   Active involvement by parents or other family members

4. Which of the following was among the most potent forces in providing a second chance to high-risk youths during the transition to adulthood?
   a.   Education programs in community colleges
   b.   Early marriage
   c.   Employment immediately after high school graduation
   d.   The opportunity to travel

5. True or False: All the resilient children established a close bond with at least one person in their lives.

6. True or False: Most individuals with serious mental health problems in their teens were still in need of mental health services by the time they reached their early 30s.

7. True or False: Protective factors within the individual made a greater difference in the quality of adult coping for (men/women), whereas outside sources of support made a greater difference in the lives of (men/women).

8. _____ led to major turning points in the lives of high-risk individuals as they entered their 20s and 30s.

### Critical Thinking

In Werner's study, higher parental education was related to at-risk children's competence in childhood and adolescence. What explains this association? Why was parental education less predictive of adult adaptation?

## Applying Your Knowledge

What common factors exist in the experiences of resilient individuals in the Kauai Longitudinal Study and in Palmer's study of refugee and evacuee children? Apply these factors to the life story of someone whom you know well who has recovered from adversity. Do they appear to have played an important role?

# 29

# Psychosocial and Behavioral Predictors of Longevity[1]

## The Aging and Death of the "Termites"

HOWARD S. FRIEDMAN
University of California, Riverside

JOAN S. TUCKER
Brandeis University

JOSEPH E. SCHWARTZ
State University of New York, Stony Brook

CAROL TOMLINSON-KEASEY
University of California, Davis

LESLIE R. MARTIN
University of California, Riverside

DEBORAH L. WINGARD
University of California, San Diego

MICHAEL H. CRIQUI
University of California, San Diego

■

Family stress (particularly parental divorce) has been found to predict unhealthy behaviors such as smoking and drug use in adolescence as well as poor psychological adjustment, but the further consequential links to physical health have rarely been studied from long-term longitudinal data.

■

Death of a parent had very little effect, consistent with other research indicating that parental strife and divorce is a greater influence on subsequent psychopathology than is parental death.

■

Advice to get married to promote health seems unjustified. Advice to stay in a satisfactory marriage seems somewhat better, as there are hints of negative health consequences of divorce.

■

The fact that childhood psychosocial information about personality and family stress does as well as gender in predicting longevity is dramatic evidence of the importance of psychosocial factors for understanding premature mortality.

■

## EDITOR'S INTRODUCTION

In this study, a research team capitalized on the rich data base of Lewis Terman's longitudinal investigation of bright California boys and girls, initiated in 1921 and continued throughout the participants' lifespan. Like Palmer and Werner in the previous two articles, the investigators focused on characteristics of resilient individuals, but their interest was in a different outcome: longevity.

To study how personal resources and life stress interact to affect length of life, the researchers examined childhood personality characteristics in conjunction with two sources of stress: parental divorce in childhood and marital instability in adulthood. Their findings revealed that individuals experiencing stress in childhood tended to have stressful adult lives, and each source of stress contributed independently to a shorter lifespan. At the same time, childhood personality traits moderated this stress-longevity relationship. Conscientious, dependable children were resilient in the face of stress, whereas cheerful, "happy-go-lucky" children grew into adults more likely to smoke, drink, and take risks—behaviors known to shorten length of life.

These findings are a fascinating complement to Palmer's study of World War II refugee and evacuee children and Werner's research on early risk. In line with Palmer's and Werner's findings, good-natured, sociable children might be advantaged in surmounting certain childhood stressors, such as birth complications, poverty, a troubled home life, and extended parental separation. But congeniality and gregariousness can be harmful in the long run if they lead a person to be impulsive and irresponsible throughout life.

In 1921, Lewis Terman began one of the most comprehensive and best-known studies in psychology. To investigate his genetic theories of intelligence, Terman recruited 1,528 bright California boys and girls, intensively studied their psychosocial and intellectual development, and followed them into adulthood. These clever participants nicknamed themselves the "Termites." About half of the Termites are now dead, and we have gathered most of their death certificates and coded their dates and causes of death. These life span data provide a unique opportunity to address intriguing questions about the role of psychosocial variables in physical health and through a life span prospective design.

Although there is little doubt that psychosocial factors such as stress and coping play some role in the development or progression of many chronic diseases and in premature death, there is quite a bit of uncertainty about the nature of the causal pathways. Are aspects of personality and social stress related to longevity in general and to heart disease or cancer in particular across the life span? If so, what is the nature of the links? To address these matters, we studied Terman's archives and our new follow-up data to focus on psychosocial disturbance and mortality. We considered three types of variables. First, we examined two major sources of social stress: the patterns of personality evident in childhood and general psychological stability in adulthood. Finally, we considered the possible role of certain unhealthy habits in mediating the influence of stress and personality on longevity. This article integrates the key findings uncovered thus far, in a search for synthesis. A common thread does indeed emerge—a psychosocial risk pattern for premature mortality. Our more technical articles should be consulted for details that cannot be included here.

## THE "TERMITES"

The Terman Life-Cycle Study (formerly called the Genetic Studies of Genius or Gifted Children Study) began in 1921 to 1922, when most of the children were preadolescents (Terman & Oden, 1947). Terman's aim was to secure a reasonably random sample of bright California children, and so most public schools in the San Francisco and Los Angeles areas were searched for bright kids, nominated by their teachers and tested by Terman to have an IQ of at least 135. There were 856 boys and 672 girls in the study; they have been followed at 5- to 10-year intervals ever since. In addition to Terman, many other researchers, including Melita Oden and Robert Sears (himself a Termite), contributed heavily to the archives, and we are certainly in their debt. Our own contribution has been to gather and code death certificates, to gather and refine certain data about smoking, and to develop the many new indexes necessary for studying longevity and cause of death effects.

In this remarkable study, only small percentages (fewer then 10 percent) of participants are unaccounted for. (Size varies somewhat with the subsample of each analysis.) We generally restricted our analyses to those who were of school age in 1922 ($M = 11$ years old), who lived at least until 1930, and for whom there were no substantial missing data. Our childhood personality measures were derived from information obtained by Terman in 1922, and our adult health behaviors, adult marriage information, and adult adjustment measures derived from mid-life follow-ups (usually 1950, but ranging from 1940–1960). This typically resulted in a sample size of between 1,100 and 1,300. Analyses by Terman's researchers as well as our own comparisons indicated that those lost from study did not differ systematically.

Friedman, H. S., Tucker, J. S., Schwartz, J. E., Tomlinson-Keasey, C., Martin, L. R., Wingard, D. L., & Criqui, M. H. (1995). Psychosocial and behavioral predictors of longevity: The aging and death of the "Termites." *American Psychologist, 50,* 69–78. © 1995 by the American Psychological Association. Reprinted with permission.

In our sample, women significantly outlived men. As of 1991, 50 percent of the men but only 35 percent of the women were known to have died. Statistical survival analyses produce a ratio called a relative hazard, which is the relative probability that a person will die at any given time. The hazard rate for women was more than one-third lower than that for men, confirming what is of course generally true in the population. Because women in this sample live about six years longer than men, all our analyses examined or controlled for gender differences.

The Termites were a bright, well-educated group, integrated into American society (but none grew up to win a Nobel prize or to be identified as an obvious genius). They had regular contact with Stanford University. Certain confounds common to other psychosocial health studies are therefore not likely in this sample. The Termites could understand medical advice and prescription, had adequate nutrition, and had access to medical care. Explanations of poor health involving poverty, ignorance. or discrimination are generally not applicable to this sample, and so the sample is valuable for focusing on certain personality and social stress variables.[2] The Termites were successful in public school, at least to the extent that they made it through teachers' nominations and Terman's tough screening for intellectual talent; this is important to keep in mind because it helps rule out certain competing explanations for longevity. The sample is certainly not, however, representative of the U.S. population as a whole (for example, it contains less than 1 percent Asian, African, or Native Americans); results are not necessarily generalizable to subpopulations that are different on health-relevant dimensions.

During the past several years, we have hunted down and gathered up hundreds of death certificates for the dead Termites, often from resistant state bureaucracies (Friedman, Tucker, & Martin, 1994). Following established **epidemiologic** procedures, we coded underlying cause of death according to the *International Classification of Diseases* (9th rev., U.S. Department of Health and Human Services, 1980), with the assistance of a certified nosologist supervised by our team's physician-epidemiologist. As in the general population, the leading cause of death was cardiovascular disease, followed by cancer.

## DIVORCE

### Divorce of Parents

It has been well established that the divorce of one's parents during childhood can have ill effects on one's future mental health. Although some questions remain about the causal processes, there is good **longitudinal** evidence that children of divorce, especially boys, are at greater risk for observable behavior and adjustment problems (Amato & Keith, 1991; J. Block, Block, & Gjerde, 1988; J. H. Block, Block, & Gjerde, 1986; Hetherington, 1991; Jellinek & Slovik, 1981; Shaw, Emery, & Tuer, 1993; Zill, Morrison, & Coiro, 1993). Most of the conceptual analyses concern a lack of social dependability or ego control (that is, impulsivity and nonconformity), although neuroticism or low emotional stability have also often been implicated.

There has never before been a lifelong prospective study of family stress predictors of mortality and cause of death. Even physical health effects of family stress have been the object of little research attention, although some physiological differences among children have been documented (for example, Gerra, et al., 1993; Weidner, Hutt, Connor, & Mendell, 1992). Family stress (particularly parental divorce) has been found to predict unhealthy behaviors such as smoking and drug use in adolescence as well as poor psychological adjustment (Amato & Keith, 1991; Chassin, Presson, Sherman, Corty, & Olshavsky, 1984; Conrad, Flay, & Hill, 1992; Hawkins, Catalano, & Miller, 1992), but the further consequential links to physical health have rarely been studied from long-term longitudinal data. Can these detrimental effects of parental divorce reach across the life span and affect longevity? Do they differentially affect cause of death?

We looked at the children (N = 1,285) whose parents either did or did not divorce before the child reached age 21, who were of school age in 1922, and who lived at least until 1930 (Schwartz, et al., 1995).[3] We used hazard regression analyses (survival analyses) to predict longevity, controlling for gender.

Children of divorced parents faced a one-third greater mortality risk than people whose parents remained married at least until they reached age 21 (p < .01). Among men whose parents divorced while they were children, the predicted median age of death was 76 years old; for men whose parents remained married, the predicted age of death was 80 years old. For women, the corresponding predicted ages of death were 82 and 86 years (Schwartz, et al., 1995).

This striking finding raises many important questions about causal mechanisms. Only 13 percent of the people in the Terman sample had faced the divorce of their parents during childhood, a situation different from that faced by children today. The estimates of the size of the effects on mortality may not be directly comparable for today's children. Still, in light of the overwhelming evidence from other studies indicating damaging psychological effects of parental divorce, this finding does provoke serious concern. Death of a parent had very little effect, consistent with other research indicating that parental strife and divorce is a greater influence on subsequent psychopathology than is parental death (Tennant, 1988). In the Terman sample, our analyses suggested that parental divorce was the key early social predictor of premature mortality, throughout the life span.

We used the information we gathered and coded from the death certificates to examine whether divorce of one's parents related differentially to cause of death. We found that parental divorce was not associated with whether one is more likely to die of cancer or heart disease or other disease. Also, the overall higher mortality risk cannot be explained away by a higher injury rate, although the possibility of an especially increased risk of injury death cannot be ruled out because of the small sample.

## Instability of One's Own Marriage

There is substantial epidemiological evidence that marriage is correlated with longer life (for example, House, Robbins, & Metzner, 1982; Hu & Goldman, 1990; Kotler & Wingard, 1989). This is often viewed as a protective effect of the social support of marriage. "Get married" appears on pop lists of health recommendations. However, embedded in this relation are several distinct issues too rarely discussed. Should we assume that it is the marriage itself that is protective? Marriage brings the risk of marital dissolution. Death of spouse, divorce, and marital separation are the top three most stressful events on the classic Social Readjustment Rating Scale (Holmes & Rahe, 1967), and there seems little doubt that marital dissolution is the most significant common social stressor in American society (with the possible exception of abject poverty). Furthermore, is it possible that an unstable marital history is the result of other psychological and behavioral problems rather than itself being a primary cause of premature mortality?

As of 1950 (when they were about 40 years old), the vast majority of the Termites were alive, mature, and had married if they were ever going to marry. We classified them as currently and steadily married (N = 829), married but not in their first marriage (inconsistently married; N = 142), never married (N = 102), or currently separated, widowed, or divorced (N = 70). Very few Termites had been widowed by this point. Controlling for gender and self-reported health, we found (in survival analyses) that the inconsistently married people were at higher risk for premature mortality than the steadily married people and that the currently separated, widowed, or divorced people were at even higher risk. Inconsistently married men had a relative hazard of mortality of almost 1.4 (40 percent greater risk), and separated or divorced men had a relative hazard of 2.2. For women, the relative hazards were 1.4 and 1.8, respectively. Those who had never married had less of an increased risk and resembled the steadily married when their other social ties were taken into account (men's relative hazard = 1.05 and women's relative hazard = 1.00 when controlling for social ties; Tucker, 1993; Tucker, Friedman, Wingard, & Schwartz, 1996). This last finding concerning the long life of the never marrieds may be particular to the bright, career-oriented nature of the sample. Note that we have purposely considered marital history at a relatively stable, healthy, and mature time of life; the effects might be different in the very young or in much older people.

The steadily married people and the inconsistently married people were all married in 1950, yet they had significantly different life expectancies. This dramatic finding suggests that it may not be marriage's effect as a buffer against stress that is always important. Rather, there seems to be a detrimental effect of previous divorce that is not eliminated when the individuals remarry. Furthermore, additional analyses revealed that part of the association between marital status and mortality risk seems to be due to a selection into steady marriages—Termites who were impulsive children grew up both more likely to be inconsistently married and more likely to die younger (p < .05; Tucker, 1993).

### Parental Divorce and One's Own Divorce

Is the increased mortality risk of children of divorce due in part to these people's own subsequent divorce? People whose parents divorced were indeed more likely to face divorce themselves (p < .05). Furthermore, individuals who were divorced or remarried reported that their childhoods were significantly more stressful than did those who stayed married (p < .05). In other words, Terman study participants who experienced a marital breakup were more likely to have seen the divorce of their own parents, and they were more likely to report having experienced a

stressful home environment as children, such as marked friction among family members.

Given that parental divorce is associated with one's own future divorce, and given that one's divorce is predictive of increased mortality risk, it is indeed the case that one's unstable adult relations "explain" some of the detrimental effects of parental divorce. However, after controlling for one's (adult) divorce, parental divorce during childhood remained a significant predictor of premature mortality (p < .05), suggesting that it has additional adverse consequences in adulthood.

In summary, in this sample, marriage itself was not fully health protective. On the other hand, a stable marriage history was indeed predictive of increased longevity. Advice to get married to promote health seems unjustified. Advice to stay in a satisfactory marriage seems somewhat better, as there are hints of negative health consequences of divorce. Most surprising in light of previous research is the appearance of a psychosocial selection factor: Some people make poor marriage partners and are also prone to die prematurely (Tucker, 1993; Tucker, Friedman, Wingard, & Schwartz, 1994). All in all, family instabilities—parental and one's own divorce—are clearly predictive of premature mortality.

## PERSONALITY AND ADJUSTMENT

### Childhood Personality

There is a long history of research and theory arguing that certain patterns of psychological responding are damaging to physical health—that is, that certain personalities are disease-prone or self-healing (see overviews by Friedman, 1990, 1991, 1992; Pennebaker, 1990). The theorists and researchers have generally argued that resilient personalities—high in stability, sociability, and optimism—are prone to health, whereas aggressive, excitable, impulsive, and neurotic people are prone to disease and mortality.

Among the Termites, socially dependable individuals with stable families lived longer. We cannot be sure that these findings apply to couples like this one, who are toasting their engagement. Yet gains in eradication of disease could mean that psychosocial factors are even more relevant to contemporary longevity. (Photo: Laura Berk)

In 1922, Terman collected trait ratings about the participants from their parents and teachers. The scales he used were remarkably modern in their appearance and provide a better assessment than the primitive personality tests that were available at the time. It is reasonable to expect that parents and teachers have a good idea of whether an 11-year-old child is sociable, popular, conscientious, self-confident, and so on. We constructed six personality dimensions and used them to predict longevity and cause of death through 1986, using survival analyses (see Friedman, Tucker, Schwartz, et al., 1995; Friedman, Tucker, Tomlinson-Keasey, et al., 1993). We used both Cox proportional hazards and Gompertz regressions; they yielded the same results.

Did childhood personality predict premature mortality decades later? The most striking finding in these and follow-up analyses was that childhood social dependability or conscientiousness predicted longevity. Children, especially boys, who were rated as prudent conscientious, truthful, and free from vanity (four separate ratings, which we averaged, $\alpha = .76$) lived significantly longer. They were about 30 percent less likely to die in any given year.[4]

The finding that certain aspects of personality predicted survival across the life span raises many fascinating questions concerning causal mechanisms. Why are conscientious, dependable children who live to adulthood more likely to reach old age than their less conscientious peers? Our survival analyses (N = 1,215) suggested that the protective effect of conscientiousness was not primarily due to a reduction in the risk of injury: Although there is some tendency for the unconscientious to be more likely to die a violent death, conscientiousness is also protective against early death from cardiovascular disease and cancer. A focus on unhealthy behaviors showed them to be somewhat relevant as explanatory mechanisms (see later), but a significant effect of conscientiousness remained after controlling for drinking ($p < .01$) and for smoking and other aspects of personality ($p < .05$; Friedman, Tucker, Schwartz, et al., 1995).

We have found no evidence so far that the personality trait of sociability or other elements of extroversion were strongly related to health and longevity in this sample. This is somewhat surprising, given that biological and social theories of psychosocial factors and health generally predict such effects. Rather, the locus of health-relevant effects seems to be centered in such traits as impulsive, egocentrism, toughmindedness, and undependability. For example, childhood ratings on such variables as popularity and preference for playing with other people did not predict longevity. To further explore the lifelong effects of sociability, we followed up on Terman's (1954) study of scientists. Terman had found that the Termites who grew up to be scientists (broadly construed) were much less sociable early in life than the nonscientists. (Terman studied only male scientists.) In fact, Terman considered the differences in sociability to be quite remarkable. Using the Stanford archives, we recreated Terman's groups (lss = 288 and 326) and compared their longevity through 1991. However, our survival analyses found that the scientists did not die at a younger age. In fact, the scientists tended to live longer (relative hazard = 1.26, $p <$ .09; Friedman, Tucker, Martin, et al., 1994).

What about neuroticism? Although the traits of neuroticism—emotional instability, depression, and hostility—are thought to be correlated with poor health, we have found mixed results in this sample. On the childhood measures, there is some hint that neuroticism may be unhealthy. For example, for men, permanency of mood (as rated in childhood) tended to be associated with increased longevity. Effects of maladjustment appeared in adulthood (see the following section). In general, it has proved challenging to create valid measures of neuroticism because it is desirable to take various elements of the Termites' reaction patterns into account. This is a focus of our ongoing efforts.

Finally, we have been examining childhood cheerfulness-rated optimism and a sense of humor. Contrary to our expectations, we have found that childhood cheerfulness is inversely related to longevity. Survival analyses showed that the cheerful kids grew up to be adults who died younger (about 22 percent increased risk, $p <$ .01; Friedman, Tucker, Tomlinson-Keasey, et al., 1993). Puzzled, we followed up on those Termites rated as cheerful in childhood. We found that they grew up to be more likely to smoke, drink, and take risks (all ps $<$ .05, comparing upper and lower quartiles), although these habits do not fully explain their increased risk of premature mortality (Martin, et al., 1994). It might be the case that cheerfulness is helpful when facing a stress such as surgery, but harmful if it leads one to be careless or carefree throughout one's life (Tennen & Affleck, 1987; Weinstein, 1984). In other words, the health relevance of such traits as optimism may need to be more carefully conceptualized (cf. Wortman, Sheedy, Gluhoski, & Kessler, 1992).

## Personality, Parents' Divorce, Longevity

Children of divorced parents were somewhat less likely to have been seen as conscientious children, r(1283) = -.14, but controlling for parental divorce did not change the relations between childhood personality and longevity. Other correlations of parental divorce with personality characteristics were even smaller. In our sample, personality and parental divorce are independent predictors of longevity (Schwartz, et al., 1995).

Survival functions for a 20-year-old Termite are shown in Figure 29-1. It shows the probability of death as a function of age. The top four curves are for males in the sample. The topmost curve is for men who were rated as unconscientious in childhood and whose parents divorced during childhood; their probability of dying by age 70 was 40 percent. In contrast, for conscientious males whose parents did not divorce, the probability of dying by age 70 was less than 30 percent.

The bottom curve shows the longest-living women—those rated as conscientious and whose parents did not divorce. The difference between

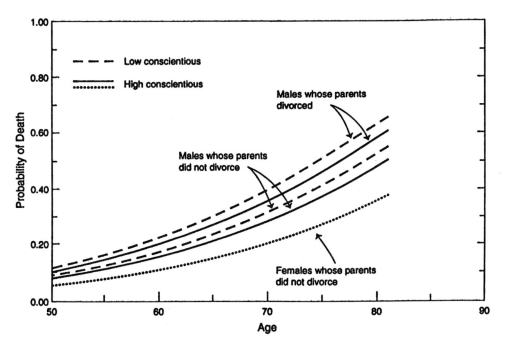

**FIGURE 29.1** Survival Functions for a 20-year-old, by Conscientiousness and Parental Divorce
Note: High and low conscientiousness represent the 75th versus the 25th percentiles. Fitted curves were based on Gompertz hazard function estimates. Copyright 1994, Joseph E. Schwartz and Howard S. Friedman.

this curve and the bottom curve for men represents the gender effect—the longer lives of women. Note that the difference between these two curves at age 70 is smaller than the difference between the highest and lowest male curves. This means that the combined effect of the two psychosocial variables is greater than the well-known major effect of gender on longevity. Although we have purposely selected these two strong psychosocial predictors for this figure, there is (as noted above) excellent theoretical and empirical reason to believe that these childhood factors are highly relevant to subsequent unhealthy psychological functioning and behavior. The fact that childhood psychosocial information about personality and family stress does as well as gender in predicting longevity is dramatic evidence of the importance of psychosocial factors for understanding premature mortality.

## Adult Psychosocial Adjustment

The relation between psychological adjustment and premature mortality has not been much studied in long-term prospective population research. Although special groups such as the clinically depressed or criminals are more likely to face early death (for example, from suicide or homicide), the more general question has received surprisingly little study. It could be argued that psychosocial maladjustment is implicit in the Type A disease-prone pattern, but only the psychosomatic theorists have focused intensively on psychotherapy as a means of promoting general physical health (Dunbar, 1943; see also Berry & Pennebaker, 1993).

In 1950, the Termites were asked about tendencies toward nervousness, anxiety, or nervous breakdown; there had also been personal conferences with participants and with family members. On the basis of this and previous related information in the files dating back a decade, Terman's team then categorized each on a 3-point scale of mental difficulty: *satisfactory adjustment, some maladjustment, or serious maladjustment.* (Almost one-third experienced at least some mental difficulty by this stage.) Survival analyses show that for men, mental difficulty as of 1950 significantly predicted mortality risk through 1991, in the expected direction (relative hazard = 1.30, p < .01, for men and 1.12, ns, for women). Similar results were found on a measure we constructed of poor psychological adjustment as self-reported in 1950 on six 11-point scales that included items like moodiness (significant risk for men, p < .05, but not for women).

Further analyses revealed that the consistently married Termites had the fewest mental difficulties; alternatively, this could be stated as a finding that those with the fewest mental difficulties were most likely to remain married. It is interesting that controlling for mental difficulty weakened but did not eliminate the relation between marital history and longevity. In other words, although mental distress seemed to play the expected role in poor health, a significant detrimental effect of divorce remained, even after taking psychological health in 1950 into account.

In analyses thus far on cause of death, there have been no dramatic differences as a function of psychological adjustment. A general survival analysis model testing for differences among cause of death (cardiovascular disease, cancer, injury, and other diseases) has shown no significant difference. That is, poorly adjusted men are more likely to die from all causes. There is some indication that poorly adjusted participants are especially more likely to die from injury (including suicide), as would be expected. However, because so few people died from injury in this sample, such differences cannot (and do not) account for the main effect of adjustment on longevity There is also a hint that poorly adjusted men may have an extra risk of dying from cardiovascular disease.

## HEALTH BEHAVIORS

Cigarette smoking and heavy use of alcohol (which often occur together) are well established as behavioral causes of significant morbidity and premature mortality. Thus, it is of significant interest to ascertain the extent to which such behaviors can be predicted from childhood and the extent to which they might account for differences in longevity. It is important, however, to keep in mind the time periods in which the various predictors were measured as well as the nature of the Terman sample. We deem it inadvisable to attempt precise effect size comparisons: Rather, these data are best suited for uncovering stable, robust patterns.

Terman collected very good contemporaneous data on alcohol consumption. We used information collected in 1950 and 1960 to classify the Termites as heavy drinkers (N − 226 men and 87 women), as moderate drinkers (seldom or never intoxicated; N = 339 men and 302 women), or as rarely (or never) taking a drink (N = 99 men and 128 women). Alcohol use was quite stable across decades. Because moderate drinking may be protective of heart disease, we also looked for U-shaped effects on mortality, but none were found. Information about smoking was poorly documented in the files, so we collected as much smoking information as possible during 1991 to 1992. We contacted those Termites who could be found, and we attempted to contact relatives of the rest. We gathered smoking data on over 900 Termites, but some of them were missing data on other key variables. Unlike the other measures, there was some evidence of bias in this subsample. Those who died young seemed more likely to have had very unhealthy behaviors and also were less likely to have locatable families. Thus, the mediating effect of smoking may be underestimated.

As expected, smoking and drinking each predicted premature mortality. Did they mediate the relations reported above? Conscientious children grew up to drink and smoke less, but cheerful kids grew up to drink and smoke more (all *ps* < .05;

Tucker, Friedman, Tomlinson-Keasey, Schwartz, Wingard, & Criqui, 1994; cf. J. Block, Block, & Keyes, 1988). However, conscientiousness remained a strong predictor of longevity in various survival analyses, controlling for smoking and drinking (decreased hazard of 20 percent–30 percent). Cheerfulness remained predictive when alcohol use was controlled, but the effects of cheerfulness changed when smoking was controlled; because the sample size dropped by one third, what this means is problematic. Termites (especially girls) who faced parental divorce grew up to smoke a little more (p < .05), but not drink more (possibly due to Prohibition during adolescence).

Analyses of obesity (body mass index in young- to mid-adulthood) showed little systematic relationship to either psychosocial variables or mortality in this intelligent sample, perhaps because obesity was measured in 1940, when few participants were heavily overweight, or because obesity was unusual in bright people of this cohort. What about exercise, hobbies, and other such potentially important mediators? Although there is of course no simple exercise variable per se among the thousands of variables in the data set, information on activity levels and hobbies at various ages is scattered throughout and can eventually be pieced into the puzzle.

It might be the case that psychosocial factors affect a whole host of health behaviors in addition to drinking and smoking-exercise patterns, diet, use of prophylactics, adherence to medication regimens, avoidance of environmental toxins, and more—which, when put together, may explain most of the associations between psychology and longevity. Surprisingly, there has been little prospective study of psychosocial predictors of unhealthy lifestyle patterns across long time periods and how they subsequently and consequently affect health, longevity, and cause of death.

In summary, the data concerning unhealthy behaviors are tantalizing but not definitive. Personal and social factors evident in childhood were predictive of smoking and excessive drinking in adulthood, and these unhealthy behaviors predicted premature mortality in this sample. Yet these behaviors did not come close to fully accounting for the effects of childhood predictors on longevity. It may be the case that more reliable and more extensive measurement of health behaviors could have a major impact in explaining the psychosocial predictors of longevity, without resorting to psychosomatic explanations involving stress. Given the documented associations of stress with both cardiovascular disease mechanisms and suppression of the immune system, however, it is likely that there are multiple pathways linking psychosocial factors to longevity. Our guess is that personality and stress variables have both direct (psychosomatic) and behaviorally mediated effects on health, but ascertaining their relative importance is a difficult empirical question.

## DISCUSSION

A number of intriguing new findings have emerged from efforts thus far in studying longevity and cause of death in the Terman cohort. These enduring patterns could emerge only from a lifelong comprehensive study such as the one that Terman and his colleagues worked so hard to establish.

First, and most basically, the results leave little doubt that aspects of individual psychology are significantly linked to longevity, across the life span. In particular, we found confirmation in the physical health arena of the importance of what psychologists have typically seen as ego strength—dependability, trust, and lack of impulsivity. This pattern of results unites and extends the various related sorts of findings by other researchers.

Second, we found evidence that both personality and social stress factors are independent predictors of longevity. Past findings of psychopathological sequelae of divorce and family conflict can now be extended to the arena of long-term health effects. In both childhood and adulthood, the trauma of divorce clearly predicted premature mortality—but so did personality. Yet the effect of each was substantially independent of the other. Further examination of Figure 29-1 reveals that unconscientious males whose parents divorced crossed the 50th percentile of survival at (that is, lived on average to) 74 years. For conscientious males from stable families, the average survival was to 81 years. (The figures were analogous for females.) Although these numbers probably represent the maximum size of effect that is likely to be found in such a sample, their dramatic nature nevertheless should promote substantial future research focused on this area.

Third, we have not, as yet, found striking associations with specific disease causes of death. Our careful, physician-supervised collection and coding of underlying cause of death from death certificates makes us confident of the reliability of this variable. The fact that personality and social factors predicted all causes of death suggests either that a general homeostasis is critical to good health (Selye, 1976) or that a group of unhealthy behaviors mediates a wide variety of health problems. This is not to say that a specific psychosocial influence cannot further raise the risk of a particular disease. However, to the extent that specific disease-prone patterns do exist (such as a coronary-prone personality), they probably depend on the co-occurence of more than one factor; in other words, interaction effects are likely involved. This could explain why such phenomena have proved so hard to capture.

How large are these effects? Because genetic hardiness, exposure to microbes and toxins, and many random factors affect longevity, researchers should not normally expect an overwhelming effect of psychosocial influences. Yet, where life and death are concerned, an influence that leaves 55 percent of the people alive compared with only 45 percent alive in an uninfluenced comparison group is of great interest. The effects discussed would generally translate into a relative hazard of between 1.2 and 1.5, a correlation of between 0.1 and 0.2, or a decreased life expectancy of two to four years (comparing upper and lower quartiles; cf. Friedman & Booth-Kewley, 1987; Lipsey & Wilson, 1993; Rosenthal, 1991; Schwartz, et al., 1995). These effects are smaller than the influences of gender or smoking on longevity, but comparable to common biological risk factors such as systolic blood pressure and serum cholesterol and to common behavioral risks such as exercise and diet, as they affect all-cause mortality. Nevertheless, caution should be used in making inferences about the magnitude of the effects in other socioeconomic groups and in other historical times; the Terman data are best suited for uncovering robust psychosocial variables that predict longevity rather than for ruling out complex pathways or explicating a full causal model.

Women significantly outlive men in this sample. Consistent with previous research, most of the psychosocial effects were more pronounced for the men (for example, greater effects for childhood conscientiousness, adult mental difficulties, and self-reported early family stress). Like other researchers (Wingard, 1984), we have not yet been able to account for the gender differences in longevity, nor for the greater psychological effects in males, but this is a focus of ongoing efforts.

As in the general population, the significant mortality in this sample occurs after age 55. The important questions that remain unanswered revolve around the mechanisms that lead from seemingly physically healthy but psychosocially impaired middle-aged adulthood to premature mortality. We have seen that smoking and excessive drinking likely play some causal role, but perhaps not a dominant role. Our analyses of cause of death have thus far not provided any dramatic insights into this question. We of course are studying this matter in the Terman sample, but insights will also be gleaned from **cross-sectional** and other shorter-term studies that now can be focused on these issues.

Especially interesting is the importance of stable individual patterns of responding. In light of the current findings, a model that focused on socioenvironmental stress would be clearly inadequate. It is not the case that most people are equally likely to die prematurely until some of them happen to encounter divorce, job loss, or other unexpected stress. Although such factors do play a significant role, it is also the case that personality—a stable individual pattern of responding—is highly relevant. Furthermore, this effect of personality was maintained when we controlled for childhood **socioeconomic status** and for childhood health (that is, parents' reports of health and illnesses in infancy and childhood).

Could it be the case that biological factors are a primary cause of both personality and health, as Eysenck (1985, 1991) has argued? At this point, the evidence is not totally inconsistent with such an explanation. Surprisingly, however, it is what Eysenck termed psychoticism, not neuroticism or introversion, that seems most relevant. (People high on psychoticism are impulsive, cruel, hostile, foolhardy, impersonal, and troublesome.) That is, the unhealthy patterns that have emerged thus far in our study predominantly involved being impulsive, imprudent, and arrogant rather than anxious, shy, pessimistic, and unsociable. This may change somewhat as more complex approaches are taken to these data; there is of course good evidence from other studies that the latter traits are indeed also relevant. More complex models of causality are also plausible. In addition to underlying biology predisposing an individual to both certain styles of behaving and excessive sympathetic reactivity, individuals undoubtedly play some role in selecting their own healthy or unhealthy environments (Magnus, Diener, Fujita, & Payot, 1993; Scarr & McCartney, 1983; also see work on testosterone, Dabbs & Morris, 1990).

Previous notions of a disease-prone personality (Friedman & Booth-Kewley, 1987) and a self-healing personality (Friedman, 1991) seem viable in light of the current findings. Indeed, the long-term predictive value of psychosocial factors, across decades, confirms the utility of thinking in terms of stable individual differences. The past emphasis on emotional reaction patterns, however, must be supplemented by significantly in-

creased attention to behavioral correlates and mediators. For those researchers with a psychodynamic bent, the healthy pattern might be termed mature ego defenses (Vaillant, 1993). For those more focused on behavior, key issues may involve dependability and addictions. In either case, the same sorts of variables emerge—the destructiveness of impulsiveness and substance abuses, and the healthiness of maturity and social stability.

The longitudinal design of the present study points out the importance of not focusing too heavily on short-term coping with stress to the exclusion of lifelong habits and patterns. Although other research gives reason to believe that aspects of personality such as sociability and optimism are related not only to feelings of psychological well-being but also to good health, such influences may be heavily context dependent. For example, it may be helpful to be optimistic when one is facing trauma and it may be helpful to have friends when one is bereaved, but these things may not necessarily be generally health protective by themselves across the life span. Impaired social support can sometimes occur as a result of (as well as be a cause of) psychological maladjustment.

This line of thinking points to the fascinating speculation that problems in psychosocial adjustment that revolve around an egocentric impulsivity are a key general risk factor for all-cause mortality. In terms of healthy aspects of the so-called "Big Five" dimensions of personality, this would probably involve elements of Agreeableness such as trust and straightforwardness, and elements of Conscientiousness such as achievement striving, competence, and deliberation (see McCrae & Costa, 1991; Ones, Viswesvaran, & Schmidt, 1993; Watson & Clark, 1992); closely related are stable interpersonal ties. It has been pointed out that such a pattern might be seen to define "character" (Costa, McCrae, & Dembroski, 1989). Although common wisdom might argue that a selfish, self-indulgent boor may prosper by stepping on others, this does not seem to be the case. Nor do we find a triumph of the lazy, pampered dropout. In terms of the rush toward death, the encouraging news may be that good guys finish last.

The size of the effects we have uncovered, their fit with previous theory, and their support by ancillary lines of research point to the possibility of major public health implications for these psychosocial variables. Although bright children growing up in California in the 1920s obviously faced some unique challenges and one should not carelessly generalize the results to other groups of people in other historical contexts, it is also the case that the findings fit quite well with what is already known about the correlates of better or worse mental health. Indeed, if such patterns of findings were found concerning toxic associations with insecticides, electromagnetic fields, or diets (even in a nonrandom sample), it is likely that a public health emergency would be perceived.

Although improvements in longevity are often assumed to be a function of medical technology, a good case can be made that most of the increase has come from changes in public health—sewage handling, food supply, inoculation, lessened crowding, and so on (McKeown, 1979, makes a cogent case; of course, there are many particular exceptions where medical cures have been discovered). The psychosocial and behavioral variables we have been discussing fit well into such a public health framework—major, lifelong, psychosocial patterns seem highly relevant to longevity. On the other hand, the effects of successful social intervention are not necessarily so clear, as the causal pathways have not been proved. For example, the effects of early psychological and social interventions on subsequent longevity have not been studied, much less documented. Still, given the other known benefits of a society with socially dependable individuals and stable families, the findings of significant relations with longevity should lend a new sense of urgency to addressing these complex issues.

Terman died in 1956. He was almost 80. His wife had died earlier that same year, after more than 50 years of marriage. Terman had set out in 1921 to study the simple bases of intelligence and success, but he came to recognize that it was much more complicated than he had imagined. The same might now be said about our understanding of the psychosocial bases of longevity.

## NOTES

1. This research was supported by National Institute on Aging Grant AG08825. Part of the data was made available by the Terman Life-Cycle Study of Children, begun by Lewis Terman. Assistance was provided by Eleanor Walker and comments by Miriam Schustack and Dan Ozer. We bear responsibility for the death certificate collection and coding, data corrections and refinements, analyses, and interpretations presented in this article. Because of ongoing data refinements and slightly differing subsamples, there are sometimes minor changes in sample and effect sizes as new papers emerge from this project. This article integrates certain key findings from the larger ongoing project.

2. Neither father's education, mother's education, nor father's occupational status predicted longevity of the Termites. Although the bottoms of the distributions of childhood socioeconomic variables were truncated by Terman's selection of bright White schoolchildren, there is considerable socioeconomic variation. The childhood sample is not characterizable as elite on any dimension except intelligence.

3. In about 15 percent of cases that we classed as parental divorce, the parents were actually separated because divorce was not feasible. Analyses without them show a very slight increase in the effect.

4. We used small sets of theoretically chosen predictors (indexes). For example, we created six scales of childhood personality, two measures of family stress, one index of adulthood heavy alcohol use, and two indexes of adult adjustment. Model testing proceeded on the basis of previous theory and research, in a search for patterns; reported $p$ values were not adjusted. Type I errors are possible, but we feel it is more important to avoid Type II errors (that is, missing a key set of predictors) in a study of this type; that is, we used past research to guide our models and then looked for patterns of findings relevant to longevity. Effect size estimates should not be directly generalized to other populations without further confirmatory research.

## EVALUATING YOUR MASTERY

1  Which of the following factors reduced longevity among the Termites?
   a.  Parental death
   b.  Parental divorce
   c.  An unstable marriage in adulthood
   d.  b and c
   e.  a, b, and c

2. Which of the following describes the life trajectories of Termites who were sociable, impulsive children?
   a.  They grew up more likely to be inconsistently married.
   b.  They were more likely to have a parent who died while they were children.
   c.  They were more likely to have parents with stable marriages.
   d.  They tended to be unusually long lived.

3. The researchers believe that the protective effect of being a conscientious, dependable child is largely explained by which of the following?
   a.  A reduction in the risk of injury
   b.  High school achievement
   c.  Good parent–child relations
   d.  Avoidance of unhealthy behaviors, such as drinking and smoking

4. The combined effects of parental divorce and low conscientiousness on length of life is _____ the impact of gender on longevity.
   a.  Greater than
   b.  Less than
   c.  About equal to

5. Which of the following Termites had the fewest mental difficulties?
   a.  Those who were consistently married
   b.  Those high in conscientiousness
   c.  Those who left an unhappy marriage
   d.  Those whose parents divorced

6. True or False: Among the Termites, personality and social factors each contributed independently to longevity.

7. True or False: The psychosocial influences on longevity found in the study of the Termites are comparable to common biological risks, such as high blood pressure and cholesterol, and common behavioral risks, such as exercise and diet.

## Critical Thinking

The Termites were children in the 1920s, more than three-quarters of a century ago. What aspects of the findings of this study do you think would apply to children growing up today? What aspects might not apply? Explain your answer.

## Applying Your Knowledge

The investigators indicate that their findings lend a new sense of urgency to the design of social interventions to increase longevity. Suggest several interventions that might be especially effective in promoting length of life, and justify their value on the basis of outcomes of the Termite research.

# Glossary

**acculturation** The modification of the culture of a group or an individual as a result of contact with a different culture.

**Adult Attachment Interview** An interview that asks adults for childhood memories of attachment experiences along with an evaluation of those memories. Assesses adults' mental representations regarding their early childhood attachment relationships.

**amniocentesis** The most widely used prenatal diagnostic technique, in which a needle is inserted through the abdominal wall and into the uterus to obtain a sample of amniotic fluid, which is examined for genetic defects. Can be performed by 11 to 14 weeks after conception.

**animism** In Piaget's theory, young children's tendency to "psychologize" inanimate objects—to assume that they have lifelike qualities, such as thoughts, wishes, feelings, and intentions.

**applied behavior analysis (ABA)** A set of practical procedures that combines imitation, shaping, reinforcement, and punishment as a last resort to change behavior. Previously termed *behavior modification*.

**assortative mating** The tendency of individuals with certain hereditary characteristics to mate with partners having similar hereditary characteristics.

**atelier** In Reggio Emilia schools, an art studio consisting of a room or set of rooms where art materials and children's art works are stored and can be reviewed by adults and children alike.

**atelierista** In Reggio Emilia schools, a specialized art teacher who works with teachers and children to create, store, and document the activities, projects, and progress of the children and the school.

**Attachment Q-Sort (or Q-Set)** An efficient method for assessing the quality of the attachment bond in which a parent or an expert informant sorts a set of 90 descriptors of attachment related behaviors on the basis of how descriptive they are of the child.

**attachment representations** A set of expectations derived from early caregiving experiences concerning the availability of attachment figures, their likelihood of providing support during times of stress, and the self's interaction with those figures that affect all future close relationships. Also called *internal working model*.

**attachment** The strong affectional tie that humans feel toward special people in their lives.

**attachment theory** Typically refers to a theory a attachment formulated by John Bowlby that views the infant's emotional tie to the familiar caregiver as an adaptive response that promotes survival. The security of infants' attachment to their caregivers is determined by the quality of care they receive.

**attention-deficit hyperactivity disorder (ADHD)** A disorder involving inattention, impulsivity, and excessive motor activity. Often leads to academic failure and social problems.

**authoritarian** A style of child rearing in which conformity and obedience are valued over open communication. Emphasizes adult control. Distinguished from *authoritative* and *permissive,* or *laissez-faire.*

**authoritative** A style of child rearing that is rational and democratic and in which both parents' and children's rights are respected. Promotes self-control. Distinguished from *authoritarian* and *permissive,* or *laissez-faire.*

**autobiographical memory** Long-lasting recollections of personally meaningful events that each of us weaves into a life story.

**autonomy** A sense of oneself as a separate, self-governing individual. An important developmental task of adolescence.

**behavior modification** See *applied behavior analysis (ABA).*

**behavioral disinhibition** An impairment in the ability to suppress or delay a response. Believed to be the central deficiency in attention-deficit hyperactivity disorder.

**bicultural** Able to function effectively in two cultural environments.

**birth cohort** Individuals born at about the same time and who therefore are influenced by the same cultural and historical conditions.

**carrier** An individual who can pass a harmful gene to his or her offspring.

**child-care policy** Laws and government programs specifying and regulating standards of quality for child care.

**childhood, or infantile, amnesia** The inability of older children and adults to recall events that happened to them before about 3 to 4 years of age.

**clinical impressions** Impressions based on the clinical method, in which the researcher attempts to understand a unique individual by combining interview data, observations, and test scores.

**cognitive-behaviorism** A form of applied behavior analysis that assumes that besides the consequences of behavior, individuals' metacognitive planning, emotional state, developmental stage, and environment all affect their behavior.

**cognitive categorization theory** A theory of gender segregation that states that children's tendency to categorize others on the basis of gender plays a crucial role in gender segregation.

**cognitive-developmental theory** An approach introduced by Piaget that views the child as actively building mental structures and cognitive development as taking place in stages.

**cognitive training** In cognitive-behaviorism, teaching children to manage themselves through monitoring their own behavior, giving themselves constructive instructions, and evaluating (reinforcing) their own efforts.

**collaboration** The many ways people can work together for a range of purposes. Distinguished from the more specific term *cooperative learning.*

**collaborative problem solving** A form of problem solving, in response to a child's misbehavior, that uses listening and assertiveness to find out what the child needs and for the adult to state his or her own needs. On the basis of this information, adult and child suggest solutions; choose one; enact it; and, later, check whether it worked.

**comorbidity** The presence of two or more disorders.

**concordance** The percentage of instances in which both members of a twin pair show a trait when it is present in one pair member.

**conditioned aversion** Avoidance of a stimulus associated with an unpleasant outcome. In the case of eating behavior, rejection of a previously consumed food that was associated with nausea and vomiting.

**conduct disorder (CD)** A disorder consisting of a repetitive and persistent behaviors that violate the rights of others and major, age-appropriate societal norms. Symptoms include aggression to people or animals, destruction of property, deceitfulness or theft, and serious violations of rules. *Oppositional-defiant behavior (ODD)* often serves as a precursor (early marker) of CD.

**consanguineous marriage** A marriage in which the partners are genetically related through a common ancestor.

**constructivist approaches to early childhood education** Approaches to early childhood education based on the assumption that the child constructs more adequate and sophisticated understandings through acting directly on the environment as well as being challenged by social experience. Becoming aware of and resolving discrepancies between cognitive structures and external reality is the driving force behind cognitive development.

**cooperative learning** A set of principles, structures, and strategies governing learning with others in a group, used in schools working to improve academic achievement, social relationships, and students' feelings of self-worth. Distinguished from the more general term *collaboration.*

**cooperative play** The most advanced form of social participation during the preschool years, in which children orient toward a common goal by negotiating plans, roles, and divisions of labor.

**copycat suicide** A suicide in which the individual uses a method identical to that portrayed in a book, a news media report, or a movie he or she has just read or seen.

**cosleeping** A sleeping arrangement in which infants and young children go to bed with their mothers at night.

**crib talk** Speech to oneself that toddlers engage in before they go to sleep.

**critical perspective** A perspective on cooperative learning that is similar to the sociocultural perspective and that is also concerned with reducing power differentials among group members.

**cross-sectional study** A study in which groups of participants of different ages are studied at the same point in time. Distinguished from *longitudinal study.*

**cultural deficit explanation** An explanation that attributes the poor school achievement of low-income ethnic minority children to home environments that place little value on education.

**debriefing procedures** Procedures in which research participants are provided a full account and justification of research activities in studies in which deception was used.

**decentration** The ability to focus on several relevant aspects of a situation as opposed to just one aspect.

**declarative memory** Conscious recollection of previous experiences. Also called *explicit memory.*

**decontextualized** Removed from real-life context.

**democratic parenting** See *authoritative child rearing.*

**desensitization** The process of becoming less sensitive to a stimulus, often through repeated or continuous exposure.

**developmental psychopathology** An approach that stresses the reciprocal interplay between normal developmental theory and findings derived from studies of high-risk populations.

**developmentally appropriate practice** A set of standards devised by the National Association for the Education of Young Children that specify program characteristics that meet the developmental and individual needs of young children of varying ages, based on current research and the consensus of experts.

**dialectical model** Model of development, based on Vygotsky's sociocultural theory, in which the child takes over the forms of adult thought through transactions with adults in activity contexts where those forms are employed.

**difficult temperament** The temperament of individuals who are slow to accept new experiences and who tend to react negatively and intensely. Distinguished from *easy temperament.*

**DSM** Abbreviation for Diagnostic and Statistic Manual of Mental Disorders of the American Psychiatric Association. Offers a widely accepted classification system of mental disorders.

**dual representation** Awareness that an object is an interesting object itself as well as a representation of a similar object.

**easy temperament** The temperament of individuals who are generally cheerful and adapt easily to new experiences. Distinguished from *difficult temperament.*

**eclecticism** The process of selecting and blending the bast elements from various theories

**ego** The conscious self, or that part of the personality that most directly controls thought and behavior and is most in touch with the external world.

**egocentrism** The inability to distinguish the viewpoints of others from one's own.

**emotion expectancies** Beliefs about how emotions should be expressed that caregivers convey to children, verbally or nonverbally, in advance of particular events in which children's own emotional reactions are called forth.

**emotion-focused coping style** A coping style that is internal, private, and aimed at controlling distress when a person perceives there is little he or she can do about a situation. Distinguished from *problem-focused coping style.*

**emotion socialization** Caregivers' efforts to redirect or change the way children spontaneously express their emotions to conform more closely with social rules or conventions.

**emotional experience** Interpretation and evaluation of emotions.

**emotional self-regulation** Strategies for adjusting our emotional state to a comfortable level of intensity so we can remain productively engaged in our surroundings.

**empowerment model** A model of child protection based on the feminist theoretical view of sexual abuse as the abuse of male power.

**epidemiology** (adj. epidemiologic or epidemiological) Information on the incidence, distribution, and control of a disorder.

**episodic memory** Memory for personally experienced events that happen once, at a particular time and place. Distinguished from *declarative memory.*

**ethnographic observations and interviews** Observations and interviews aimed at understanding the unique values and social processes of a culture or a distinct social group. Obtained by a researcher who lives with members of the culture or group for an extended period of time.

**eugenics** The hereditary improvement of the human species through controlled selective breeding; deemed by many ethicists and scientists to involve serious questions of morality.

**existential self** Awareness of the self as separate from others and as unique. Forms the foundation for the child's initial self-concept.

**explicit memory** See declarative memory.

**externalism** A process of conceptualizing problems and events in children's lives based on adult thinking and the assumption that a simple reductionist translation to children is possible.

**factor analysis** A complicated statistical procedure that combines scores from many separate test items into a few factors, which substitute for the separate scores.

**false belief** A belief held by a person that does not match reality.

**family systems view** A view of the family as a complex set of interacting relationships in which the quality of interaction between any two members spills over into interactions with other family members.

**field independence** A cognitive style that is analytical as opposed to global (or field-dependent). Typically measured by asking the individual to find a simple hidden figure embedded in a more complex stimulus array or to adjust a rod in a tilted frame, projected on the wall of a dark room, to a vertical position.

**food-acceptance patterns** Which foods people select and how much they consume.

**forgetting curve** The rate at which information is lost, or can no longer be retrieved, from memory.

**gender segregation** Children's tendency to play and interact with children of their own gender.

**generic event memory** Memory for repeated events, such as getting ready in the morning, going to class, or running errands on Saturday morning.

**generic representation** A symbol that stands for a general idea or a class of objects. For example, the Statue of Liberty stands for various abstract principles and ideas; a comercial dollhouse represents a house in general. Distinguished from *specific representation.*

**genetic counseling** A communication process aimed at helping an individual or family accurately comprehend information about a genetic disorder; choose the most appropriate course of action in view of risks and family goals; make the best possible adjustment to occurrence in a family member; and deal with the risk of recurrence.

**genotype → environment effects** Effects in which heredity influences the environments to which individuals are exposed. Three types of genotype → environment effects are possible: *passive,* in which biologically related parents provide the child with an environment influenced by the parents' heredity; *evocative,* in which the individual evokes responses from others influenced by his or her own heredity (for example, an active, friendly child *evokes* positive responses from others); and *active,* in which the individual (at older ages) actively selects environments the fit with his or her genetic tendencies.

**Gestalt psychology** A school of psychology that argues that behavior cannot be studied in parts, but must be viewed as an integrated whole; therefore, Gestalt psychologists focus on the unity of perception and thought.

**Head Start** A U.S. federal program that provides low-income children with a year or two of preschool education before school entry and that encourages parent involvement in children's development.

**Human Genome Project** An ambitious, international research project aimed at mapping human chromosomes, finding the precise location of genes for specific traits, and using this information to identify abnormal conditions with greater accuracy and to devise new, gene-based treatments.

**identity** A well-organized conception of the self made up of values, beliefs, and goals to which the individual is solidly committed. Develops during adolescence.

**inductive discipline** A type of discipline in which the effects of the child's misbehavior on others are communicated to the child.

**insecure attachment** A term that subsumes various uncertain, anxious attachment qualities characterizing infants, including *insecure-resistant* and *insecure-avoidant.*

**insecure-avoidant attachment** The quality of insecure attachment characterizing infants who are usually not distressed by parental separation and who avoid the parent when she returns. Often labeled *attachment pattern A.* Distinguished from *secure attachment* and *insecure-resistant attachment.*

**insecure-resistant attachment** The quality of insecure attachment characterizing infants who remain close to the parent before departure and display angry, resistive behavior when she returns. Often labeled *attachment pattern C.* Distinguished from *secure attachment* and *insecure- avoidant attachment.*

**Institutional Review Boards (IRBs)** Special committees in colleges, universities, and other institutions charged with evaluating the ethical integrity of proposals for conducting research.

**intellectual-domain view of artistic development** Gardner's view, which identifies eight independent intelligences on the basis of distinct mental operations that permit individuals to engage in a wide variety of culturally meaningfully activities. Visual-spatial intelligence is one of the mental abilities identified by Gardner.

**interdependence** A mutually dependent relationship between two or more people in which each relies on the other.

**internal consistency reliability** An approach to reliability in which scores on different halves of a test are compared to see if respondents' answers are internally consistent.

**internal locus of control** Belief in one's own ability to control life events.

**internalization** The process by which communication with symbols between people is transferred to the individual, psychological plane of functioning. As a result, symbols become self-communicative.

**intersubjectivity** A process whereby two individuals who begin with different understandings arrive at a shared understanding.

**intrinsic motivation** Motivation governed by factors within the self, such as pride and pleasure in mastery, rather than external rewards.

**introspection** The activity of turning attention inward toward the processes and contents of the mind.

**joint attention** A form of attention established when two individuals gaze at one another or at the same object or event in the environment.

**kibbutz** (pl. kibbutzim) A cooperative, democratically governed, economically and socially autonomous multigenerational community in Israel with an average population of 400 to 900 people.

**Likert scale** A scale that calls for a graded response to each statement, with response alternatives typically taking the form of strongly disagree (SD), disagree (D), undecided (U), agree (A), strongly agree (SA)—or the reverse order. Its purpose is to get at participants' attitude—favorable or unfavorable—toward the topic under study.

**logical consequences** Consequences for undesirable behavior that are arranged by an adult to be related to that behavior—for example, after throwing sand in the sandpit, being banned from the area for a specified time period.

**longitudinal study** A study in which one group of participants is studied repeatedly at different ages. Distinguished from *cross-sectional study*.

**looking-glass self** C. H. Cooley's view of the self as a blend of what we imagine important people in our lives think of us.

**mainstreaming** The integration of pupils with learning difficulties into regular classrooms for all or part of the school day.

**maltreated children** Children who have experienced child abuse or neglect.

**mastery learning perspective** A perspective on cooperative learning that focuses on improved academic learning, with a limited focus on positive interpersonal behaviors. Motivation is assumed to depend on extrinsic rewards.

**mental rotation paradigm** Use of reaction times (RTs) to determine how long it takes an individual to match a figure with versions of that figure presented in different rotations (for example, sideways or upside down). The more one figure is rotated away from the other, the longer the RT, revealing that mental rotation is being used.

**meta-analysis** A statistical procedure involving reanalysis of the results of many studies on the same topic together, yielding information about whether a difference between groups exists and, if so, an estimate of its size.

**metacognition** Awareness, evaluation, and control of thinking.

**meta-imagination** Awareness and understanding of the mind's ability to imagine; a type of *metacognition*.

**metapelet** (pl. metaplot) In Israeli kibbutzim, a caregiver of infants and young children in the infant house, where children sleep and spend their days communally.

**multifactorial** Influenced by several genetic and environmental factors.

**multiple abilities strategy** A strategy aimed at changing status inequalities during cooperative learning whereby the teacher states explicitly that "no one will be good at all of these abilities; everyone will be good at at least one."

**mutated gene** A sudden, permanent change in a gene, occurring spontaneously, by chance, or due to exposure to a variety of hazardous environmental agents.

**natural consequences** Consequences for undesirable behavior that occur naturally, without adult manipulation—for example, after throwing sand in the sandpit, being asked to play somewhere else.

**neo-Adlerian theory** A modern refinement of Alfred Adler's work early in this century, which emphasizes encouragement to prevent misbehavior and natural or logical consequences to intervene in difficult behavior.

**neophobia** Rejection of the new.

**neurotransmitter** A chemical substance that transmits nerve impulses across a synapse, or gap, between neurons (nerve cells) in the brain, thereby enabling communication among them.

**nonmaleficence** Not of a harmful or evil nature.

**norms** Age-related averages that represent typical development.

**object substitutions** Use of one object to represent another, such as a stick to stand for a horse, in make-believe play.

**Oedipus complex** In psychoanalytic theory, a conflict that occurs between ages 3 and 6 during the phallic stage, a time when sexual impulses transfer to the genital region of the body. The young boy wishes to possess his mother and feels jealous and hostile toward his father. These feelings lead to intense anxiety because the boy fears he will lose his parents' love and be punished for his wishes. To master the anxiety, avoid punishment, and maintain parents' affection, boys renounce these desires, identify with the father, adopt his standards for good conduct, and form a conscience. A similar *Electra complex* is assumed to characterize girls.

**ontogenetic** Relating to the development of an individual, from embryo to adult. Distinguished from *phylogenetic*.

**ontological** Related to the nature of being or existence.

**operant procedure** A procedure that applies operant conditioning, in which a spontaneous behavior is followed by a stimulus that changes the probability that the behavior will occur again. A stimulus that increases the occurrence of the behavior is a reinforcer; a stimulus that decreases the occurrence of the behavior is a punisher.

**oppositional-defiant disorder (ODD)** A disorder consisting of negativistic and noncompliant behaviors that typically involve temper tantrums, argumentativeness with authority figures, defiance, being deliberately annoying and provocative, blaming others for mistakes, and being angry and resentful. Often serves as a precursor (early marker) of *conduct disorder (CD)*.

**panhuman** Relating to all humanity.

**parity** The number of children borne by a woman.

**participant observation techniques** An approach to observing in which the researcher lives with a cultural community for a period of months or years, participating in all aspects of its daily life. Extensive field notes, which consist of a mix of observations, self-reports from members of the culture, and interpretations by the investigator, are gathered. These are put together into a description of the community that tries to capture its unique values and social processes.

**path analysis** A complex statistical procedure that permits researchers to identify probable causal relationships from correlational findings.

**performance deficit** The failure to make consistent use of one's resources and skills when dealing with everyday situations. Distinguished from *skill deficit*.

**permissive or laissez-faire** A style of child rearing in which the child is granted free rein, with very few adult-imposed restrictions. Distinguished from *authoritative* and *authoritarian*.

**person-environment fit theory** Theory that states that there are negative motivational and behavioral consequences of being in an environment that does not match one's subjective needs.

**phylogenetic** Relating to the evolutionary history of a species. Distinguished from *ontogenetic*.

**pogrom** An organized, often officially encouraged persecution or massacre of a minority group, especially one aimed at Jews.

**postpartum depression** Feelings of sadness and withdrawal that appear shortly after childbirth, continue for weeks or months, and are serious enough to interfere with daily functioning.

**primary prevention program** A prevention program directed at reducing the prevalence of risk factors judged to contribute directly to a disorder or problem behavior. *Distinguished from secondary and tertiary prevention programs.*

**primary risk factors** Risk factors judged to contribute directly to a disorder or problem behavior.

**problem-focused coping style** A coping style in which the person appraises the situation as changeable, identifying the difficulty, and decides what to do about it. Distinguished from *emotion-focused coping style.*

**projective psychological tests** Procedures for measuring personality in which individuals are asked to respond to ambiguous stimuli in an unrestricted fashion.

**proxy consent** Consent for a child's participation in research by parents or legal guardians.

**psychoanalytic theory** A theory of personality development originated by Sigmund Freud that assumes children move through a series of stages in which they confront conflicts between biological drives and social expectations of parents. The way these conflicts are resolved determines psychological adjustment.

**psychological autopsy** A method for studying the characteristics of adolescents who committed suicide in which psychological profiles are reconstructed on the basis of extensive interviews with family members and peers.

**puberty** Biological changes during adolescence that lead to an adult-sized body and sexual maturity.

**punishment** Removing a desirable stimulus or presenting an unpleasant one to decrease the occurrence of a response.

**Quality Improvement and Accreditation System (QIAS)** Australia's national system for accrediting child care centers, directed at improving the quality of center-based care by tying government subsidies to accreditation.

**quasi-experimental study** A research design in which the investigator studies already existing treatments in natural settings by carefully selecting groups of participants with similar characteristics. Permits study of naturally occurring variables not subject to experimenter manipulation, but lacks the power of causal inference of a true experimental design.

**realism** In Piaget's theory, young children's tendency to "physicalize" mental states and

processes, to grant them the status of real, material events visible to others.

**reconstitution** The ability to rapidly analyze and reconstruct parts of language to constitute meaningful communicative speech.

**recursive reasoning** A self-embedded form of perspective taking that involves thinking about what another person is thinking.

**rehearsal** The memory strategy of repeating information.

**reinforcement** Following a behavior with a stimulus the individual values, thereby making it more likely that the individual will repeat the behavior.

**reinstatement** The process of restoring information to memory by representing part of the context—for example, through an experience similar to the original event.

**reliability estimates** Numerical estimates of the consistency, or repeatability, of measures of behavior. When percentages are used to estimate the reliability of two or more observers coding the same behaviors, a figure of 80 percent or greater is considered good agreement.

**representational insight** Awareness than an object stands for or represents a similar object.

**resiliency** The ability to successfully cope with risk factors, such as perinatal stress, poverty, parental psychopathology, and disruptions of the family unit.

**risk/benefit calculus** A comparison of the costs of a research study to participants in terms of inconvenience and possible psychological or physical injury against its value for advancing knowledge and improving conditions of life. Used in assessing the ethics of research.

**scaffolding** A changing quality of support over the course of a teaching session in which the adult adjusts the assistance provided to fit the child's current level of performance. As competence increases, the adult permits the child to take over her guiding role and apply it to his own activity.

**script** A type of generic event memory for familiar events, in which we sketch the broad outlines of the experience in terms of main acts, leaving out details. For example, asked to recall what you do when you get ready in the morning, you might report taking a shower, getting dressed, and eating breakfast, without mentioning exactly what you wore or what you ate.

**secondary prevention program** A prevention program—targeted at individuals and families who are already showing problem behaviors—that attempts to reduce current distress and avoid more serious disorders. Distinguished from *primary and tertiary prevention programs.*

**secure attachment** The quality of attachment characterizing infants who are distressed by parental separation and easily comforted by the parent when she returns. Often labeled *attachment pattern B.* Distinguished from *insecure-resistant* and *insecure-avoidant attachment.*

**secure base** The use of the familiar caregiver as a base from which the infant confidently explores the environment and to which the infant returns for emotional support.

**self-concept** The sum total of attributes, abilities, attitudes, and values that an individual believes defines who he or she is.

**self-conscious emotional reactions** Emotional reactions, such as shame, guilt, embarrassment, and pride, that depend on self-understanding.

**self-efficacy** Beliefs about one's own power or capacity to produce a desired effect.

**self-esteem** An aspect of self-concept that involves judgments about one's own worth and the feelings associated with those judgments.

**self-referential** behaviors A set of cognitive skills related to early self-understanding, consisting of (a) an awareness of oneself as separate from others, (b) knowledge that objects independent of oneself have a permanent existence, (c) a sense of oneself as a causal agent, and (d) the ability to visually recognize oneself. These precede and serve as the foundation for self-concept.

**self-regulation** The process of continuously monitoring progress toward a goal, checking outcome, and redirecting unsuccessful efforts.

**sensitive period** A time span that is optimal for certain capacities to emerge and in which the individual is especially responsive to environmental influences.

**separation anxiety** An infant's distressed reaction to the departure of the familiar caregiver.

**shaping** The process whereby a complex skill is learned by mastering a series of small steps that together make up the total task.

**shtetl** A small, Eastern European Jewish community of former times.

**skill deficit** Diminished capacity and knowledge of how to behave when dealing with everyday situations. Distinguished from *performance deficit.*

**social comparison** A judgment of ability, behavior, appearance, or other characteristic in relation to that of others.

**social problem-solving interventions** Interventions in which children are taught, through coaching, role-playing, and rehearsal, to identify and define their interpersonal problems, generate various problem-solving strategies for each of the identified problems, assess the potential consequences for each strategy, consider how to implement each potential solution, and implement a strategy and assess its efficacy.

**social psychology perspective** A perspective on cooperative learning that focuses on improved cognitive and social learning. Group processing, in which group members consider how well they have worked together, is viewed as crucial for reaching these goals.

**social referencing** Relying on another person's emotional reaction to appraise an uncertain situations.

**socialization** The process of training the young to become competent, participating members of society.

**sociocultural perspective** A perspective inspired by Vygotsky's theory that is focuses on the social and cultural contexts of learning and is concerned with the social construction of meaning.

**sociocultural theory or approach** Vygotsky's theory, in which children acquire the ways of thinking and behaving that make up a community's culture through dialogues and participation in joint, meaningful activities with more knowledgeable members of that culture.

**sociodramatic play** The make-believe play with others that is underway by age 2½.

**socioeconomic status (SES)** A measure of a family's social position and economic well-being that combines three interrelated, but not completely overlapping, variables: (1) years of education and (2) the prestige of and skill required by one's job, both of which measure social status; and (3) income, which measures economic status.

**sociological perspective** A perspective on cooperative learning that focuses on participation and resolution of status differences among diverse group members.

**sociometric assessments** Self-report instruments that ask peers to evaluate one another's likability.

**Socratic techniques** Teaching techniques that challenge the individual's current way of thinking through provocative questions and probing dialogue.

**specific representation** Representation that stands for something particular that actually exists—for example, a model of a specific room with certain furniture. Distinguished from *generic representation*.

**strange situation paradigm** A laboratory procedure involving short separations from and reunions with the caregiver that assesses the quality of the attachment bond.

**stranger anxiety** The infant's expression of fear in response to unfamiliar adults. Appears in many babies after 7 months of age.

**suicide ideation** Thoughts about committing suicide.

**symbolic interactionist account** An account, or theory, in which the sense of self develops through social interaction and is viewed, first from the standpoint of significant others in the family, and then from the standpoint of the social group as a whole.

**temperamental characteristics** Stable individual differences in quality and intensity of emotional reaction.

**tertiary prevention program** A prevention program targeted at rehabilitation and further deterioration of individuals and families experiencing serious problems. Distinguished from *primary and secondary prevention programs*.

**theories of mind** Coherent understandings of people as mental beings that children revise as they encounter and make sense of new evidence. Includes children's knowledge of mental activity and their appreciation that people can have different perceptions, thoughts, and feelings about the same event.

**time out** A form of mild punishment in which the child is removed from the immediate environment and placed where he or she cannot receive any reinforcement.

**Touch Continuum** A model of child protection aimed at teaching children to identify good, bad, and confusing touches.

**transitional objects** Objects, such as pacifiers and soft, cuddly toys, that assist infants and young children in coping emotionally with separation from the parent.

**underachievement** Achievement substantially below expectations based on the a child's ability.

**vulnerability** Susceptibility to negative developmental outcomes after exposure to serious risk factors, such as perinatal stress, poverty, parental psychopathology, and disruptions of the family unit.

**Y-charts** In cooperative learning, charts in which students describe the look, sound, and feel of particular cooperative behaviors. Used by teachers to make cooperative skills explicit.

**zone of proximal development** In Vygotsky's sociocultural theory, a range of tasks that the child cannot yet accomplish independently but that the child can do with the assistance of more skilled partners.

# Answers to
# Evaluating Your Mastery

**1. Behavioral Research Involving Children**
1. a; 2. c; 3. c; 4. b; 5. False; 6. True; 7. standards of decent treatment

**2. Genetic Counseling**
1. c; 2. b; 3. b; 4. c; 5. True; 6. True; 7. False; 8. d, b, a, e, c

**3. Interventions to Ease the Transition to Parenthood**
1. d; 2. c; 3. c; 4. d; 5. d; 6. True; 7. False; 8. True; 9. True

**4. Cultural Variation in Infants' Sleeping Arrangements**
1. b; 2. a; 3. c; 4. a; 5. False; 6. False; 7. consistent with

**5. Symbolic Functioning in Preschool Children**
1. c; 2. d; 3. d; 4. a; 5. True; 6. False

**6. The Psychological and Social Origins of Autobiographical Memory**
1. c; 2. c; 3. a; 4. c; 5. elaborative; 6. reinstatement; 7. True

**7. Intersubjectivity in Caregiver–Child Communication**
1. b; 2. a; 3. d; 4. c; 5. building bridges; providing opportunities and support for involvement in meaningful activities; 6. can; 7. need to

**8. Young Children's Understanding of Everyday Emotions**
1. b; 2. c; 3. a; 4. b; 5. d; 6. distance from; 7. False; 8. True

**9. "Children of the Dream" Revisited**
1. b; 2. d; 3. a; 4. b; 5. False; 6. True; 7. False; 8. True; 9. False

**10. Quality of Child Care as an Aspect of Family and Child-Care Policy**
1. b; 2. d; 3. c; 4. c; 5. a; 6. False; 7. 5 to 15; 90; 8. True

**11. Child Care Policy in Australia**
1. a; 2. b; 3. c; 4. c; 5. True; 6. True; 7. False

**12. Children's Eating**
1. a; 2. c; 3. a; 4. a; 5. b; 6. 50; 25; one-third; 7. True; 8. True; 9. Authoritarian

**13. Young Children's Understanding of the Mind**
1. d; 2. a; 3. a; 4. c; 5. True; 6. False; 7. True

**14. Vygotsky's Theory**
1. c; 2. a; 3. c; 4. b; 5. True; 6. False; 7. Inter-subjectivity; 8. True

**15. Art as Development**
1. b; 2. d; 3. b; 4. b; 5. profound; 6. long/process; 7. should/co-artists

**16. Young Children's Responsiveness to Music**
1. a; 2. c; 3. a; 4. b; 5. a; 6. False; 7. True; 8. a "think-aloud" process

**17. Perspectives on Cooperative Learning**
1. b; 2. d; 3. d; 4. d; 5. True; 6. are not/can; 7. most; 8. can/social skills

**18. Gender Segregation Among Children**
1. b; 2. a; 3. d; 4. a; 5. is not; 6. False; 7. True; 8. False

**19. Discipline in Early Childhood**
1. d; 2. b; 3. c; 4. c; 5. True; 6. True; 7. True

**20. Becoming Bicultural**
1. c; 2. b; 3. c; 4. a; 5. c; 6. c; 7. True; 8. a

**21. The Importance of Parent Participation in Child Protection Curricula**
1. a; 2. d; 3. b; 4. c; 5. True; 6. reduces the serious consequences of abuse; 7. the primary school level

**22. Childhood and the Culture of Consumption**
1. c; 2. b; 3. a; 4. c; 5. False; 6. True

**23. School Matters in the Mexican-American Home**
1. b; 2. c; 3. d; 4. b; 5. True; 6. True; 7. extensive audio and videotaped observations

**24. Children with Attention Deficits and Disinhibited Behavior**
1. c; 2. d; 3. c; 4. a; 5. a; 6. False; 7. 7, two or more; 8. True; 9. False; 10. True

**25. Control versus Autonomy During Early Adolescence**
1. d; 2. b; 3. c; 4. c.; 5. more/undermines; 6. True

**26. Adolescent Suicide Prevention**
1. b; 2. b; 3. b; 4. b; 5. True; 6. complete/attempt; 7. True

**27. Shadows of War**
1. a; 2. b; 3. a; 4. b; 5. False; 6. still important; 7. True

**28. Risk, Resilience, and Recovery**
1. b; 2. a; 3. d; 4. a; 5. True; 6. False; 7. women/men; 8. Opening up of opportunities

**29. Psychosocial and Behavioral Predictors of Longevity**
1. d; 2. a; 3. d; 4. a; 5. a; 6. True; 7. True

# References

## 1. Behavioral Research Involving Children

Aber, J. L. & Cicchetti, D. (1984). The socio-emotional development of maltreated children: An empirical and theoretical analysis. In H. E. Fitzgerald, B. M. Lester, & M. W. Yogman (Eds.), *Theory and Research in Behavioral Pediatrics* (Vol. 2). New York: Plenum.

Baumrind, D. (1978). Reciprocal rights and responsibilities in parent-child relations. *Journal of Social Issues, 34,* 179–196.

Campos, J. J., Barrett, K. C., Lamb, M. E., Goldsmith, H. H., & Stenberg, C. (1983). Socioemotional development. In P. H. Mussen (Series Ed.), M. M. Haith & J. J. Compos (Vol. Eds.), *Handbook of child psychology: Vol. 2. Infancy and developmental psychology* (pp. 783–915). New York: Wiley.

Damon, W. & Hart, D. (1982). The development of self-understanding from infancy through adolescence. *Child Development, 53,* 841–864.

Damon, W. (1977). *The social world of the child.* San Francisco: Jossey-Bass.

Dweck, C. S. & Elliot, E. S. (1983). Achievement motivation. In P. H. Mussen (Series Ed.), & E. M. Hetherington (Vol. Ed.), *Handbook of child psychology: Vol. 4. Socialization, personality, and social development* (pp. 643–691). New York: Wiley.

Graham, S., Doubleday, C., & Guarino, P. A. (1984). The development of relations between perceived controllability and the emotions of pity, anger, and guilt. *Child Development, 55,* 561–565.

Harter, S. (1983). Developmental perspectives on the self-system. In P. H. Mussen (Series Ed.) & E. M. Hetherington (Vol. Ed.), *Handbook of child psychology: Vol. 4. Socialization, personality, and social development* (pp. 275–385). New York: Wiley.

Kopp, C. B. (1989). Regulation of distress and negative emotions: A developmental view. *Developmental Psychology, 25,* 343–354.

Maccoby, E. E. (1983). Socio-emotional development and response to stressors. In N. Garmezy & M. Rutter (Eds.), *Stress, coping, and development in children* (pp. 217–234). New York: McGraw-Hill.

Melton, G. B. (1983). Minors and privacy: Are legal and psychological concepts compatible? *Nebraska Law Review, 62,* 455–493.

Melton, G. B. (1987). The clashing of symbols: Prelude to child and family policy. *American Psychologist, 42,* 345–354.

Piaget, J. (1965). *The moral judgment of the child.* (M. Gabain, Trans.). New York: Free Press. (Originally published in 1932.)

Ruble, D. N. (1983). The development of social-comparison processes and their role in achievement-related self-socialization. In E. T. Higgins, D. N. Ruble, & W. W. Hartup (Eds.), *Social cognition and social development* (pp. 143–157). Cambridge: Cambridge University Press.

Shantz, C. U. (1983). Social cognition. In P. H. Mussen (Series Ed.), J. H. Flavell & E. M. Markman (Vol. Eds.), *Handbook of child psychology: Vol. 3. Cognitive development* (pp. 495–555). New York: Wiley.

Thompson, R. A. (1987). Development of children's inferences of the emotions of others. *Developmental Psychology, 23,* 124–131.

Thompson, R. A. (1990). Emotion and self-regulation. In R. A. Thompson (Ed.), *Socioemotional development. Nebraska symposium on motivation:* (Vol. 36, pp. 383–483). Lincoln: University of Nebraska Press.

Williams, P. C. (1984). Why IRBs falter in reviewing risks and benefits. *IRB: A Review of Human Subjects Research, 6,* 1–4.

Wolfe, M. (1978). Childhood and privacy. In I. Altman & J. F. Wohlwill (Eds.), *Children and environment* (pp. 175–222). New York: Plenum.

## 2. Genetic Counseling

Abramovsky, I., Godmilow, L., Hirschhorn, K., & Smith, H., Jr. (1980). Analysis of follow-up study of genetic counseling. *Clinical Genetics, 17,* 1–12.

Affleck, G., McGrade. B. J., Allen, D. A., & McQueeney, M. (1985). Mothers' beliefs about behavioral causes for their developmentally disabled infant's condition: What do they signify? *Journal of Pediatric Psychology, 10,* 293–303.

Antley, R. M., Bringle, R. G., & Kinney, K. L. (1984). Down's syndrome. In A. E. H. Emery & I. Pullen (Eds.), *Psychological aspects of genetic counseling* (pp. 75–94). London: Academic.

Applebaum, E. G., & Firestein, S. K. (1983). *A genetic counseling casebook.* New York: Free Press.

Arnold J. R., & Winsor, E. J. T. (1984). The use of structured scenarios in genetic counseling. *Clinical Genetics, 25,* 485–490.

Beck-Black, R. (1990). Prenatal diagnosis and fetal loss: Psychosocial consequences and professional responsibilities. *American Journal of Medical Genetics, 35,* 586–587.

Beck-Black, R., & Weiss, J. O. (1989). Genetic support groups in the delivery of comprehensive genetic services. *American Journal of Human Genetics, 45,* 647–654.

Beeson, D., & Golbus, M. S. (1985). Decision making: Whether or not to have prenatal diagnosis and abortion for X-linked conditions. *American Journal of Medical Genetics, 20,* 107–114.

Blumberg, B. (1984). The emotional implications of prenatal diagnosis. In A. E. H. Emery & I. Pullen (Eds.), *Psychological aspects of genetic counseling* (pp. 201–217). London: Academic.

Bringle, R. G., & Antley, R. M. (1980). Elaboration of the definition of genetic counseling into a model for counselee decision making. *Social Biology, 27,* 304–318.

Broide, E., Zeigler, M., Eckstein, J., & Bach, G. (1993). Screening for carriers of Tay-Sachs disease in the ultra-orthodox Ashkenazi Jewish community in Israel. *American Journal of Medical Genetics, 47,* 213–215.

Carter, B. D., Urey, J. R., & Eid, N. S. (1992). The chronically ill child and family stress: Family developmental perspectives on cystic fibrosis. *Psychosomatics, 33,* 397–403.

Croyle, R. T. (1992). Appraisal of health threats: Cognition, motivation, and social comparison. *Cognitive Therapy and Research, 16,* 165–182.

Dagg, R. K. B. (1991). The psychological sequelae of therapeutic abortion denied and completed. *American Journal of Psychiatry, 148,* 578–585.

Edwards, W. (1961). Behavioral decision theory. *Annual Review of Psychology, 12,* 473–498.

Ekwo, E. E., Kim, J. O., & Gosselink, C. A. (1987). Parental perceptions of the burden of genetic disease. *American Journal of Medical Genetics, 28,* 955–959.

Ekwo, E. E., Seals, B. E., Kim, J. O., Williamson, R. A., & Hanson, J. W. (1985). Factors influencing maternal estimates of genetic risk. *American Journal of Medical Genetics, 20,* 491–504.

Evers-Kiebooms, G. (1990). Predictive testing for Huntington's disease in Belgium. *Journal of Psychosomatic Obstetrics and Gynecology, 11,* 61–72.

Evers-Kiebooms, G., Denayer, L., & Van den Berghe, H. (1990). A child with cystic fibrosis. 11. Subsequent family planning decisions, reproauction and use of prenatal diagnosis. *Clinical Genetics, 37,* 207–215.

Evers-Kiebooms, G., Fryns, J. R., Cassiman, J. J., & Van den Berghe, H. (1992). Preface. In G. Evers-Kiebooms, J. R Fryns, J. J. Cassiman, & H. Van den Berghe (Eds.), *Psychological aspects of genetic counseling* (pp. xv–xvi). New York: Wiley-Liss.

Evers-Kiebooms, G., Swerts, A., Cassiman, J. J., & Van den Berghe, H. (1989). The motivation of at-risk individuals and their partners in deciding for or against predictive testing for Huntington's disease. *Clinical Genetics, 35,* 29–40.

Evers-Kiebooms. G., Swerts, A., & Van den Berghe, H. (1988). Psychological aspects of amniocentesis: Anxiety feelings in three different risk groups. *Clinical Genetics, 33,* 196–206.

Fishbein, M., & Ajzen, I. (1975). *Relief, attitude, intention and behavior: An introduction to theory and research.* Reading, MA: Addison-Wesley.

Folkman, S. (1984). Personal control and stress and coping processes: A theoretical analysis. *Journal of Personality and Social Psychology, 46,* 839–852.

Folkman, S., & Lazarus, R. S. (1980). An analysis of coping in a middle-aged community sample. *Journal of Health and Social Behavior, 21,* 219–239.

Fost, N. (1989). Guiding principles for prenatal diagnosis. *Prenatal Diagnosis, 9,* 335–337.

Fox, S., Bloch, M., Fahy, M., & Hayden, M. R. (1989). Predictive testing for Huntington disease: 1. Description of a pilot project in British Columbia. *American Journal of Medical Genetics, 32,* 211–216.

Fraser, F. C. (1974). Genetic counseling. *American Journal of Human Genetics, 15,* 1–10.

Frets, R G., Duivenvoorden, H. J., Verhage, E, Ketzer, E., & Niermeijer, M. E (1990). Model identifying the reproductive decision after genetic counseling. *American Journal of Medical Genetics, 35,* 503–509.

Frets, R. G., Duivenvoorden, H. J., Verhage, E., Peters-Romeyn, B. M. T., & Niermeijer, M. F. (1991). Analysis of problems in making the reproductive decision after genetic counseling. *Journal of Medical Genetics, 28,* 194–200.

Gelehrter, T. D., & Collins, E. S. (1990). *Principles of medical genetics.* Baltimore: Williams & Wilkins.

Harper, R. S. (1993). Psychosocial genetics: An emerging scientific discipline. *Journal of Medical Genetics, 30,* 537.

Hietala, M., Hakonen, A., Aro, A. R., Niemela, R., Peltonen, L., & Aula, R. (1995). Attitudes toward genetic testing among the general population and relatives of patients with a severe genetic disease: A survey from Finland. *American Journal of Human Genetics, 56,* 1493–1500.

Hoffman, K. J. (1994). Diffusion of information about Neurofibromatosis Type I DNA testing. *American Journal of Medical Genetics, 49,* 299–301.

Janis, I. L., & Mann, L. (1977). *Decision-making:A psychological analysis of conflict.* New York: Free Press.

Jemmott, J. B.,III, Croyle, R. T., & Ditto, R. H. (1988). Commonsense epidemiology: Self-based judgments from lay persons and physicians. *Health Psychology, 7,* 55–73.

Jorgensen, C., Uddenberg, N., & Ursing, I. (1985). Ultrasound diagnosis of fetal malformations in the second trimester: The psychological reactions of the women. *Journal of Psychosomatic Obstetrics and Gynecology, 4,* 31–40.

Kahneman, D., & Tversky, A. (1982). The simulation heuristic. In D. Kahneman, R. Slovic, & A. Tversky (Eds.), *Judgment under uncertainty: Heuristics and biases* (pp. 201–108). Cambridge: Cambridge University Press.

Kessler, S. (1979). *Genetic counseling: Psychological dimensions.* New York: American.

Kessler, S. (1984). Psychological responses to stresses in genetic diseases. In J. O. Weiss, B. A. Bernhardt, & N. W. Paul (Eds.), *Genetic disorders and birth defects in families and society: Toward interdisciplinary understanding* (pp. 114–117). New York: Alan R. Liss.

Kessler, S. (1989). Psychological aspects of genetic counseling: VI. A critical review of the literature dealing with education and reproduction. *American Journal of Medical Genetics, 34,* 340–353.

Kessler, S., & Bloch, M. (1989). Social system responses to Huntington disease. *Family Process, 28,* 59–68.

Kessler, S., & Levine. E. K. (1987). Psychological aspects of genetic counseling IV: The subjective assessment of probability. *American Journal of Medical Genetics, 28,* 361–370.

Kronenberger, W. G., & Thompson, R. J., Jr. (1992). Psychological adaptation of mothers of children with spina bifida: Association with dimensions of social relationships. *Journal of Pediatric Psychology, 17,* 1–14.

Kunda, Z. (1990). The case for motivated reasoning. *Psychological Bulletin, 108,* 480–498.

Landrine, H., & Klonoff, E. A. (1992). Culture and health-related schemas: A review and proposal for interdisciplinary integration. *Health Psychology, 11,* 267–276.

Lazarus, R. S., & Folkman, S. (1984). *Stress, appraisal, and coping.* New York: Springer.

Leonard, C. Q, & Beck-Black, R. (1984). Decision-making dilemmas in genetic counseling. In J. O. Weiss, B. A. Bernhardt, & N. W. Paul (Eds.), *Genetic disorders and birth defects in families and society: Toward interdisciplinary understanding* (pp. 62–70). New York: Alan R. Liss.

Lerman, C., & Croyle, R. T. (1994). Psychological issues in genetic testing for breast cancer susceptibility. *Archives of Internal Medicine, 154,* 609–616.

Leventhal, H., & Diefenbach, M., & Leventhal, E. A. (1992). Illness cognition: Using common sense to understand treatment adherence and affect cognition interactions. *Cognitive Therapy and Research, 16,* 143–163.

Lippman, A. (1991). Research studies in applied human genetics: A quantitative analysis and critical review of recent literature. *American Journal of Medical Genetics, 41,* 105–111.

Lippman A. (1992). Mother matters: A fresh look at prenatal genetic testing. *Issues in Reproductive and Genetic Engineering, 5,* 141–154.

Lippman, A., & Wilfond, B. S. (1992). Twice-told tales: Stories about genetic disorders. *American Journal of Human Genetics, 51,* 936–937.

Lippman-Hand, A., & Fraser, E C. (1979a). Genetic counseling: Parents' responses to uncertainty. In C. J. Epstein, C. J. R. Curry, S. Packman, S. Sherman, & B. D. Hall (Eds.), *Risk, communication, and decision making in genetic counseling* (pp. 325–339). New York: Alan R. Liss.

Lippman-Hand, A., & Fraser, F. C. (1979b). Genetic counseling: Provision and reception of information. *American Journal of Medical Genetics, 3,* 113–127.

Lippman-Hand, A., & Fraser F. C. (1979c). Genetic counseling—The postcounseling period: 1. Parents' perceptions of uncertainty. *American Journal of Medical Genetics, 4,* 51–71.

Markel, D. S., Young, A. B., & Penney, J. B. (1987). At-risk persons' attitudes toward presymptomatic and prenatal testing of Huntington disease in Michigan. *American Journal of Medical Genetics, 26,* 295–305.

Markova, I., Forbes, C. D., Aledorf, L. M., Inwood, M., Mandalaki, T., Miller, C. M., & Pittadaki, J. (1986). A comparison of the availability and content of genetic counseling as perceived by hemophilic and carriers in the USA, Canada, Scotland and Greece. *American Journal of Medical Genetics, 24,* 7–21.

Marks, J. H. (1989). Forward. In J. H. Marks, A. Heimler, E. Reich, N. S. Wexler, & S. E. Ince (Eds.), *Genetic counseling principles in action: A casebook* (pp. v–vii). New York: National Foundation March of Dimes.

Marks, J. H., Heimler, A., Reich, E., Wexler, N. S., & Ince, S. E. (Eds.). (1989). *Genetic counseling principles in action: A casebook.* New York: National Foundation March of Dimes.

Marteau, T. M. (1989). Framing of information: Its influence upon decisions of doctors and patients. *British Journal of Social Psychology, 28,* 89–94.

Marteau, T. M., Plenicar, M., & Kidd, J. (1993). Obstetricians presenting amniocentesis to pregnant women: Practice observed. *Journal of Reproductive and Infant Psychology, 11,* 5–14.

Marteau, T. M., Van Duijn, M., & Ellis, I. (1992). Effects of genetic screening on perceptions of health: A pilot study. *Journal of Medical Genetics, 29,* 24–26.

McKusick, V., Francomano, C., & Antonarakis, S. (1992). *Mendelian inheritance in man: Catalogs of autosomal dominant, autosomal recessive and X-linked phenotypes.* Baltimore: Johns Hopkins University Press.

McNeil, B. J., Rauker, S. G., Sox, H. C., Jr., & Tversky, A. (1982). On the elicitation of preferences for alternative therapies. *New England Journal of Medicine, 306,* 1259–1262.

Meissen, G. J., Mastromauro, C. A., Kiely, D. K., McNamara, D. S., & Myers, R. H. (1991). Understanding the decision to take the predictive test for Huntington Disease. *American Journal of Medical Genetics, 39,* 404–410.

Murray, T. H. (1984). The ethical use of genetic knowledge. In J. O. Weiss, B. A. Bernhardt, & N. W. Paul (Eds.), *Genetic disorders and birth defects in families and society: Toward interdisciplinary understanding* (pp. 169–174). New York: Alan R. Liss.

Nidorf, J. F., & Ngo, K. Y. (1993). Cultural and psychosocial considerations in screening for Thalassemia in Southeast Asian refugee population. *American Journal of Medical Genetics, 46,* 398–402.

Panter-Brick, C. (1991). Parental responses to consanguinity and genetic disease in Saudi Arabia. *Social Science in Medicine, 33,* 1295–1302.

Partington, M. W (1986). X-linked mental retardation: Caveats in genetic counseling. *American Journal of Medical Genetics, 23,* 101–109.

Pauker S. P., & Pauker, S. G. (1987). The amniocentesis decision: Ten years of decision analytic experience. In G. Evers-Kiebooms, J. J. Cassiman, H. Van den Berghe, & G. d'Ydewalle (Eds.), *Genetic risk, risk perception, and decision making* (pp. 151–169). New York: Alan R. Liss.

Phipps, S., & Zinn, A. B. (1986a). Psychological response to amniocentesis: 1. Mood state and adaptation to pregnancy. *American Journal of Medical Genetics, 25,* 131–142.

Phipps, S., & Zinn, A. B. (1986b). Psychological response to amniocentesis: 11. Effects of coping style. *American Journal of Medical Genetics, 25,* 143–148.

Quill, T. E. (1983). Partnership in patient care: A contractual approach. *Annals of Internal Medicine, 98,* 228–234.

Reading, A. E., Cox, D. N., Sledmere, C. M., & Campbell, S. (1984). Psychological changes over the course of pregnancy: A study of attitudes toward the fetus/neonate. *Health Psychology, 3,* 211–221.

Roberts, L. (1990). To test or not to test? *Science, 247,* 17–19

Rosenstock, I. M. (1974). The health belief model and preventive health behavior. *Health Education Monographs, 2,* 354–386.

Rowley, R. T., Loader, S. L., Sutera, C. J., Walden, M., & Kozyra, A. (1991). Prenatal screening for hemoglobinopathies. III. Applicability of the health belief model. *American Journal of Human Genetics, 48,* 452–459.

Sagi, M., Shiloh, S., & Cohen, T. (1992). Application of the health belief model in a study on parents' intentions to utilize prenatal diagnosis of cleft lip and/or palate. *American Journal of Medical Genetics, 44,* 326–333.

Scott. J. A., Walker, A. P., Eunpu, D. L., & Djurdjinovic, L. (1988). Genetic counselor training: A review and considerations for the future. *American Journal of Human Genetics, 42,* 191–199.

Shiloh, S. (1994). Heuristics and biases in health decision making: Their expression in genetic counseling. In L. Heath, R. S. Tindale, J. Edwards, E. J. Posavac, E. B. Bryant, E. Henderson-King, Y. Suarez-Balcazar, & J. Myers (Eds.), *Applications of heuristics and biases to social issues* (pp. 13–30). New York: Plenum.

Shiloh, S. (1995). Decision-making in the context of genetic risk. In T. Marteau & M. Richards (Eds.), *The troubled helix* (pp. 82–103). Cambridge: Cambridge University Press.

Shiloh, S., Berkenstadt, M., Miran, N., Bat-Miriam-Katznelson, M., & Goldman, B. (1995). *Mediating effects of perceived personal control in coping with a health threat: The case of genetic counseling.* Unpublished manuscript.

Shiloh, S., Reznik, H., Bat-Miriam-Katznelson, M., & Goldman, B. (1995). Pre-marital genetic counseling to consanguineous couples: Attitudes, beliefs and decisions among counseled, non-counseled and unrelated couples in Israel. *Social Science & Medicine, 41,* 1301–1310.

Shiloh, S., & Sagi, M. (1989). Framing effects in the presentation of genetic recurrence risks. *American Journal of Medical Genetics, 33,* 130–135.

Shiloh, S., & Saxe, L. (1989). Perception of recurrence risks by genetic counselees. *Psychology and Health, 3,* 45–61.

Sholomskas, D. E., Steil, J. M., & Plummer, J. K. (1990). The spinal cord injured revised: The relationship between self-blame, other-blame and coping. *Journal of Applied Social Psychology, 20,* 548–574.

Slovic. P. (1987). Perception of risk. *Science, 236,* 280–285.

Somer, M., Mustonen, H., & Norio, R. (1988). Evaluation of genetic counseling: Recall of information, post-counseling reproduction, and attitudes of the counselees. *Clinical Genetics, 34,* 352–365.

Sorenson, J. R., Scotch, N., Swazey, J., Wertz, D. C., & Heeren, T. (1987). Reproductive plans of genetic counseling clients not eligible for prenatal diagnosis. *American Journal of Medical Genetics, 28,* 345–352.

Sorenson, J. R., & Wertz, D. C. (1986). Couple agreement before and after genetic counseling. *American Journal of Medical Genetics, 25,* 549–555.

Speedling, E. J., & Rose, D. N. (1985). Building an effective doctor-patient relationship: From patient satisfaction to patient participation. *Social Science in Medicine, 21,* 115–120.

Strauss, R. R. (1988). Genetic counseling in the cross-cultural context: The case of highly observant Judaism. *Patient Education and Counseling, 11,* 43–52.

Struewing, J. R., Lerman, C., Kase, R. G., Giambarresi, T. R., & Tucker, M. A. (1995). Anticipated uptake and impact of genetic testing in hereditary breast and ovarian cancer families. *Cancer Epidemiology Piomarkers & Prevention, 4,* 169–173.

Sujansky, E., Beeler Kreutzer, S., Johnson, A. M., Lezotte, D. C., Schrier, R. W., & Gabow, P. A. (1990). Attitudes of at-risk and affected individuals regarding presymptomatic testing for autosomal dominant polycystic kidney disease. *American Journal of Medical Genetics, 35,* 510–515.

Tabor, A., & Jonsson, M. H. (1987). Psychological impact of amniocentesis on low-risk women. *Prenatal Diagnosis, 7,* 447–449.

Tadmor, C. S. (1986). A crisis intervention model for a population of mothers who encounter neonatal death. *Journal of Primary Prevention, 7,* 17–26.

Taylor, S. E. (1983). Adjustment to threatening events: A theory of cognitive adaptation. *American Psychologist, 1,* 161–1172.

Taylor, S. E. (1990). Health psychology: The science and the field. *American Psychologist, 45,* 40–50.

Taylor, S. E., & Lobel, M. (1989). Social comparison activity under threat: Downward evaluation and upward contacts. *Psychological Review, 96,* 569–575.

Thompson, E., & Rothenberg, K. (Chairs). (1992). National Institutes of Health workshop statement: Reproductive genetic testing: Impacts on women. *American Journal of Human Genetics, 51,* 1161–1163.

Tibben, A., Vegter-van der Vlis, M., Skraastad, M. I., Frets, R. G., van der Kamp, J. J. R., Niermeijer, M. E., van Ommen, G. J. B., Roos, R. A. C., Rooijmans, H. G. M., Stronks, D., & Verhage, E. (1992). DNA-testing for Huntington's disease in the Netherlands: A retrospective study on psychosocial effects. *American Journal of Medical Genetics, 44,* 94–99.

Tunis, S. L., Golbus, M. S., Copeland, K. L., Fine, B. A., Rosinsky, B. J., & Seely, L. (1990). Patterns of mood states in pregnant women undergoing chorionic villus sampling or amniocentesis. *American Journal of Medical Genetics, 37,* 191–199.

Tversky, A., & Kahneman, D. (1974). Judgment under uncertainty: Heuristics and biases. *Science, 185,* 1124–1131.

Tversky, A., & Kahneman, D. (1981). The framing of decisions and the psychology of choice. *Science, 211,* 453–458.

Watson, J. D. (1990). The human genome project: Past, present, and future. *Science, 24S,* 44–49.

Weatherall, D. J. (1991). *The new genetics and clinical practice* (3rd ed.). Oxford: Oxford University Press.

Weil, J. (1991). Mothers' postcounseling beliefs about the causes of their children's genetic disorders. *American Journal of Human Genetics, 48,* 145–153.

Weinstein, N. D. (1984). Why it won't happen to me. Perceptions of risk factors and susceptibility. *Health Psychology, 3,* 431–457.

Welshimer, K. J., & Earp, J. A. L. (1989). Genetic counseling within the context of existing attitudes and beliefs. *Patient Education and Counseling, 13,* 237–255.

Went, L. (1994). Guidelines for the molecular genetics predictive test in Huntington's disease. *Journal of Medical Genetics, 31,* 555–559.

Wertz, D. C., & Fletcher, J. C. (1988). Attitudes of genetic counselors: A multinational survey. *American Journal of Human Genetics, 42,* 592–600.

Wertz, D. C., & Sorenson, J. R. (1986). Client reactions to genetic counseling: Self reports of influence. *Clinical Genetics, 30,* 494–502.

Wertz, D. C., Sorenson, J. R., & Heeren, T. C. (1984). Genetic counseling and reproductive uncertainty. *American Journal of Medical Genetics, 18,* 79–88.

Wiggins, S., Whyte, R., Huggins, M., Adams, S., Theimann, J., Bloch, M., Sheps, S. B., Schechter, M. T., & Hayden, M. R. (1992). The psychological consequences of predictive testing for Huntington's disease. *New England Journal of Medicine, 327,* 1401–1405.

## 3. Interventions to Ease the Transition to Parenthood

Antonucci, T. C., & Mikus, K. (1988). The power of parenthood: Personality and attitudinal changes during the transition to parenthood. In G. Y. Michaels & W. A. Goldberg (Eds.), *The transition to parenthood: Current theory and research* (pp. 62–84). Cambridge: Cambridge University Press.

Barnard, K. E., Booth, C. L., Mitchell, S. K., & Telzrow, R. W. (1988). Newborn nursing models: A test of early intervention to high-risk infants and families. In E. Hibbs (Ed.), *Children and families: Studies in prevention and intervention* (pp. 63–81). Madison, CT: International Universities Press.

Barnard, K., Morisset, C., & Spieker, S. (1993). Preventive interventions: Enhancing parent-infant relationships. In C. H. Zeanah (Ed.), *Handbook of infant mental health* (pp. 386–401). New York: Guilford.

Belsky, J., & Isabella, R. A. (1985). Marital and parent-child relationships in family of origin and marital change following the birth of a baby: A retrospective analysis. *Child Development, 56,* 342–349.

Belsky, J., & Kelly, J. (1994). *Transition to parenthood.* New York: Delacorte.

Belsky, J., & Pensky, E. (1988). Marital changes across the transition to parenthood. *Marriage and Family Review, 12,* 133–156.

Belsky, J., & Rovine, M. (1990). Patterns of marital change across the transition to parenthood. *Journal of Marriage and the Family, 52,* 109–123.

Belsky, J., Rovine, M., & Fish, J. (1989). The developing family system. In M. Gunnar (Ed.). *Minnesota symposia of child psychology: Vol. 22. Systems and development* (pp. 119–166). Hillsdale, NJ: Erlbaum.

Belsky, J., Spanier, G., & Rovine, M. (1983). Stability and change in marriage across the transition to parenthood. *Journal of Marriage and the Family, 45,* 567–577.

Berman, P. W., & Pedersen, F. A. (1987). *Men's transitions to parenthood.* Hillsdale, NJ: Erlbaum.

Boukydis, C. F. Z. (Ed.). (1987). *Research on support for parents and infants in the postnatal period.* Norwood, NJ: Ablex.

Brazelton, T. B., & Cramer, B. G. (1990). *The earliest relationships: Parents, infants, and the drama of early attachment.* Reading, MA: Addison-Wesley.

Bumpass, L., & Rindfuss, R. R. (1979). Children's experience of marital disruption. *American Journal of Sociology, 85,* 49–65.

Campbell, S. B., Cohn, J. F., Flanagan, C., Popper, S., & Myers, T. (1992). Course and correlates of postpartum depression during the transition to parenthood. *Development and Psychopathology, 4,* 29–48.

Clulow, C. F. (1982). *To have and to hold: Marriage, the first baby and preparing couples for parenthood.* Aberdeen, Scotland: Aberdeen University Press.

Cohn, D. A., Cowan, P. A., Cowan, C. P., & Pearson, J. (1992). Mothers' and fathers' working models of childhood attachment relationships, parenting styles, and child behavior. *Development and Psychopathology, 4,* 417–431.

Coie, J. D., Watt, N. F., West, S. G., Hawkins, D., Asarnow, J. R., Markman, H. J., Ramey, S. L., Shure, M. B., & Long, B. (1993). The science of prevention: A conceptual framework and some directions for a national research program. *American Psychologist, 48,* 1013–1022.

Cowan, C. P., & Cowan, P. A. (1992). *When partners become parents: The big life change for couples.* New York: Basic.

Cowan, C. P., Cowan, P. A., Hemming, G., Garrett, E., Coysh, W. S., Curtis-Boles, H., & Boles, A. J. (1985). Transitions to parenthood: His, hers, and theirs. *Journal of Family Issues, 6,* 451–481.

Cowan, P. A. (1991). Individual and family life transitions: A proposal for a new definition. In P. A. Cowan & E. M. Hetherington (Eds.). *Family transitions: Advances in family research* (Vol. 2, pp. 3–30). Hillsdale, NJ: Erlbaum.

Cowan, P. A., Cohn, D. A., Cowan, C. P. & Pearson, J. (1996). Parents' attachment histories and children's externalizing and internalizing behavior: Exploring family systems models of linkage. *Journal of Clinical and Consulting Psychology, 64,* 53–63.

Cowan, P. A., Cowan, C. P. (1988). Changes in marriage during the transition to parenthood: Must we blame the baby? In G. Y. Michaels & W. A. Goldberg (Eds.). *The transition to parenthood: Current theory and research* (pp. 114–154). Cambridge: Cambridge University Press.

Cowan, P. A., Cowan, C. P., Schulz, M., & Heming, G. (1994). Prebirth to preschool family factors predicting children's adaptation to kindergarten. In R. Parke & S. Kellam (Eds.). *Exploring family relationships with other social contexts: Advances in family research* (Vol. 4, pp. 75–114). Hillsdale, NJ: Erlbaum.

Cox, M. J. (Ed.). (1985). Transition to parenthood [Special issue]. *Journal of Family Issues 6(4).*

Cox, M. J., Owen, M. T., Lewis, J. M., & Henderson, V. K. (1989). Marriage, adult adjustment, and early parenting. *Child Development, 60,* 1015–1024.

Crawford, D. W., & Huston, T. L. (1993). The impact of the transition to parenthood on marital leisure. *Personality and Social Psychology Bulletin, 19,* 39–46.

Crockenberg, S. B. (1981). Infant irritability, mother responsiveness, and social support influences on security of infant-mother attachment. *Child Development, 52,* 857–865.

Cutrona, C. (1982). Nonpsychotic postpartum depression: A review of recent research. *Clinical Psychology Review, 2,* 487–503.

Duncan, S. W., & Markman, H. J. (1988). Intervention programs for the transition to parenthood: Current status from a prevention perspective. In G. Y. Michaels & W. A. Goldberg (Eds.), *The transition to parenthood: Current theory and research* (pp. 270–310). Cambridge: Cambridge University Press.

Egeland, B., & Erickson, M. (1993). Implications of attachment theory for prevention and intervention. In H. Parens and S. Kramer (Eds.). *Prevention in mental health* (pp. 23–50). Northvale, NJ: Jason Aronson.

Eiduson, B. (1981, April). *Parent/child relationships in alternative families and socio-emotional development of the children at three years of age.* Paper presented at the biennial meetings of the Society for Research in Child Development, Boston.

Engfer, A. (1988). The interrelatedness of marriage and the mother-child relationship. In R. A. Hinde & J. Stevenson-Hinde (Eds.). *Relationships within families: Mutual influences* (pp. 104–118). Cambridge: Cambridge University Press.

Entwisle, D. R., & Doering, S. (1981). *The first birth: A family turning point.* Baltimore: Johns Hopkins University Press.

Erickson, M. R., Korfmacher, J., & Egeland, B. (1994). Attachments past and present: Implications for therapeutic intervention with mother-infant dyads. *Development and Psychology, 4,* 495–507.

Feldman, S. S. (1987). Predicting strain in mothers and fathers of 6-month-old infants: A short-term longitudinal study. In P. W. Berman & F. A. Pedersen (Eds.). *Men's transitions to parenthood* (pp. 13–36). Hillsdale, NJ: Erlbaum.

Fidele, N. M., Golding, E. R., Grossman, F. K. & Pollack, W. S. (1988). Psychological issues in adjustment to first parenthood. In G. Y. Michaels & W. A. Goldberg (Eds.). *The transition to parenthood: Current theory and research* (pp. 85–113). Cambridge: Cambridge University Press.

Field, T. M., Healy, B., Goldstein, S. & Guthertz, M. (1990). Behavior-state matching and synchrony in mother-infant interactions of nondepressed versus depressed dyads. *Developmental Psychology, 26,* 7–14.

Fleming, A. S., Ruble, D. N., Flett, G. L., & Shaul, D. L. (1988). Postpartum adjustment in first-time mothers: Relations between mood, maternal attitudes, and mother-infant interaction. *Developmental Psychology, 24,* 71–81.

Gershenson, C. (1993). The child well-being conundrum. *Readings, 8*(2), 8–11.

Gotlib, I. H., Lewinsohn, P. M., & Seeley, J. R. (1995). Symptoms versus a diagnosis of depression: Differences in psychosocial functioning. *Journal of Consulting and Clinical Psychology, 63,* 90–100.

Grossman, R., Eichler, L., & Winickoff, S. (1980). *Pregnancy, birth, and parenthood.* San Francisco: Jossey-Bass.

Gurman, A. S., & Kniskern, D. P. (1978). Deterioration in marital and family therapy: Empirical, clinical and conceptual issues. *Family Process, 17,* 3–20.

Hamilton, J. A. (1962). *Postpartum psychiatric problems.* St. Louis: Mosby.

Heinicke, C. M. (1993). Factors affecting the efficacy of early family intervention. In N. J. Anastasiow & S. Harel (Eds.). *At-risk infants: Interventions, families, and research* (pp. 91–100). Baltimore: Paul H. Brookes.

Heinicke, C. M. (1995, March). *Initial support and maternal personality status and the outcome of home intervention.* Paper presented at the biennial meetings of the Society for Research in Child Development, Indianapolis.

Heinicke, C. M., Beckwith, L., & Thompson, A. (1988). Early intervention in the family system: A framework and review. *Infant Mental Health Journal, 9,* 111–141.

Heinicke, C. M., Diskin, S. D., Ramsay-Klee, D. M., & Oates, D. S. (1986). Pre- and postbirth antecedents of 2-year-old attention, capacity for relationships and verbal expressiveness (1986). *Developmental Psychology, 22,* 777–787.

Heming, G. (1985). *Predicting adaptation in the transition to parenthood.* Unpublished doctoral dissertation, University of California, Berkeley.

Hinde, R. A., & Stevenson-Hinde, J. (1988). *Relationships within families: Mutual influences.* Cambridge: Cambridge University Press.

Hobbs, D. F., Jr. (1965). Parenthood as crisis: A third study. *Journal of Marriage and the Family, 27,* 367–372.

Hobbs, D., & Cole, S. (1977). Transition to parenthood: A decade replication. *Journal of Marriage and the Family, 38,* 723–731.

Junge, M., & Elwood, A. (1986). MELD: Parent information and support groups. *Infant Mental Health Journal, 7,* 146–155.

Kumar, R., & Robson, K. M. (1984). A prospective study of emotional disorders in childbearing women. *British Journal of Psychiatry, 144,* 35–47.

LaRossa, R., & LaRossa, M. M. (1981). *Transition to parenthood: How infants change families.* Beverly Hills: Sage.

Laslett, B., & Rapoport, R. (1975). Collaborative interviewing and interactive research. *Journal of Marriage and the Family, 37,* 968–977.

Leifer, M. (1980). *Psychological effects of motherhood: A study of first pregnancy.* New York: Praeger.

LeMasters, E. E. (1957). Parenthood as crisis. *Marriage and Family Living, 19,* 352–355.

Levant, R. F. (1988). Education for fatherhood. In P. Bronstein & C. P. Cowan (Eds.), *Fatherhood today: Men's changing role in the family* (pp. 253–275). New York: Wiley.

Lieberman, A. F., & Pawl, G. H. (1993). Infant-parent psychotherapy. In C. H. Zeanah (Ed.), *Handbook of Infant Mental Health* (pp. 427–442). New York: Guilford.

Locke, H., & Wallace, K. (1959). Short marital adjustment and prediction tests: Their reliability and validity. *Marriage and Family Living, 21,* 251–255.

Macdermid, S. M., Huston, T. L., & McHale, S. M. (1990). Changes in marriage associated with the transition to parenthood: Individual differences as a function of sex role attitudes and changes in the division of household labor. *Journal of Marriage and the Family, 52,* 475–486.

May, K. A., & Perrin, S. P. (1982). Prelude: Pregnancy and birth. In S. M. H. Hanson & F. W. Bozett (Eds.), *Dimensions of fatherhood* (pp. 64–91). Beverly Hills: Sage.

McHale, S. M. & Huston, T. I. (1985). The effect of the transition to parenthood on the marriage relationship: A longitudinal study. *Journal of Family Issues, 6,* 409–433.

McLoyd, V. C. (1990). The impact of economic hardship on Black families and children: Psychological distress, parenting, and socioemotional development. *Child Development 61,* 311–346.

Meisels, S. J., Dichtelmiller, M., & Liaw, F. R. (1993). A multidimensional analysis of early childhood intervention programs. In C. H. Zeanah (Ed.), *Handbook of Infant Mental Health* (pp. 361–385). New York: Guilford.

Michaels, G. Y., & Goldberg, W. A. (Eds.). (1988). *The transition to parenthood: Current theory and research.* Cambridge: Cambridge University Press.

Olds, D. L. & Kitzman, H. (1993). Review of research on home visiting for pregnant women and parents of young children. *The Future of Children, 3,* 53–93.

Olds, D. L., Kitzman, H., & Cole, R. (1995, March). *Influence of prenatal and infancy home visitation on the outcomes of pregnancy and childbearing in the first year of life.* Paper presented at the biennial meeting of the Society for Research in Child Development, Indianapolis.

Osofsky, J. D., & Osofsky, H. J. (1984). Psychological and developmental perspectives on expectant and new parenthood. In R. D. Parke (Ed.), *Review of child development research: Vol. 7. The family* (pp. 372–397). Chicago: University of Chicago Press.

Palkovitz, R., & Sussman, M. B. (Eds.). (1988). Transitions to parenthood [Special issue]. *Marriage and Family Review, 12*(3–4).

Powell, D. R. (1993). Inside home visiting programs. *The Future of Children, 3,* 23–38.

Radloff, L. (1977). Sex differences in depression: The effects of occupation and marital status. *Sex Roles, 1,* 249–265.

Sameroff, A. J., & Chandler, M. J. (1975). Reproductive risk and the continuum of caretaking casualty. In F. D. Horowitz, E. M. Hetherington, S. Scarr-Salapatek, & G. Siegel (Eds.), *Review of child development research* (Vol. 4, pp. 187–244). Chicago: University of Chicago Press.

Schneewind, K. A. (1983) Konsequenzen der Erstelternschaft [Consequences of the transition to parenthood: An overview]. *Psychologie in Erziehung und Unterricht, 30,* 161–172.

Shereshefsky, P., & Yarrow, L. J. (Eds.) (1973). *Psychological aspects of a first pregnancy and early postnatal adaptation.* New York: Raven.

Spanier, G. B. (1976). Measuring dyadic adjustment. *Journal of Marriage and the Family, 38,* 15–28.

White, L. K., & Booth, A. (1985). The transition to parenthood and marital quality. *Journal of Family Issues, 6,* 435–450.

Worthington, E. L., & Buston, B. G. (1987). The marriage relationship during the transition to parenthood: A review and a model. *Journal of Family Issues, 7,* 443–473.

## 4. Cultural Variation in Infants' Sleeping Arrangements

Abbott, S. (1992). Holding on and pushing away: Comparative perspectives on an Eastern Kentucky child-rearing practice. *Ethos, 20,* 33–65.

Albert, S. (1977). *Rites of passage: Study of children's bedtime rituals.* Paper presented at the 85th Annual Convention of the American Psychological Association. San Francisco.

Anders, T. (1979). Night-waking in infants during the first year of life. *Pediatrics, 63*(6), 860–864.

Barry, H., & Paxson, L. (1971). Infancy and early childhood: Cross-cultural codes 2. *Ethnology, 10,* 466–508.

Benedict, R. (1955). Continuities and discontinuities in cultural conditioning. In M. Mead & M. Wolfenstein (Eds.), *Childhood in contemporary cultures* (pp. 21–30). Chicago: University of Chicago Press.

Brazelton, T. (1978, October). Why your baby won't sleep. *Redbook,* p. 82.

Brazelton, T. (1979, June). What parents told me about handling children's sleep problems. *Redbook,* pp. 54–54.

Brazelton, T. B. (1990). Parent-infant cosleeping revisited. *Ab Initio, 2*(1), 1, 7.

Bundesen, H. (1944). *The baby manual.* New York: Simon & Schuster.

Burton, R., & Whiting, J. (1961). The absent father and cross-sex identity. *Merrill-Palmer Quarterly, 7,* 85–95.

Caudill, W., & Plath, D. (1966). Who sleeps by whom? Parent-child involvement in urban Japanese families. *Psychiatry, 29,* 344–366.

Caudill, W., & Weinstein, H. (1969). Maternal care and infant behavior in Japan and America. *Psychiatry, 32,* 12–43.

Cole, M. (1985). The zone of proximal development. Where culture and cognition create each other. In J. V. Wertsch (Ed.), *Culture, communication, and cognition: Vygotskian perspectives* (pp. 146–161). Cambridge: Cambridge University Press.

Crowell, J., Keener, M., Ginsburg, H., & Anders, T. (1987). Sleep habits in toddlers 18 to 36 months old. *American Journal of Child and Adolescent Psychiatry, 26*(4), 510–515.

Edelman, G. N. (1983, November). When kids won't sleep. *Parents Magazine.* pp. 74–77.

Ferber, R. (1986). *Solve your child's sleep problems.* New York: Simon & Schuster.

Gaddini, R., & Gaddini, E. (1971). Transitional objects and the process of individuation. *Journal of the American Academy of Child Psychiatry, 9,* 347–365.

Gandini, L. (1986, September). *Parent-child interaction at bedtime: Strategies and rituals in families with young children.* Paper presented at the European Conference on Developmental Psychology, Rome, Italy.

Gandini, L. (1990). Children and parents at bedtime in two cultures. *Ab Initio, 2*(1), 5, 7.

Hanks, C., & Rebelsky, F. (1977). Mommy and the midnight visitor: A study of occasional co-sleeping. *Psychiatry, 40,* 277–280.

Holt, E. (1957). *How children fail.* New York: Dell.

Hong, K., & Townes, B. (1976). Infants' attachment to inanimate objects: A cross-cultural study. *Journal of the American Academy of Child Psychiatry, 15,* 49–61.

Hoover, M. B. (1978, November). Does your bed belong to baby? *Parents Magazine,* p. 129.

Kawakami, K. (1987, July). *Comparison of mother-infant relationships in Japanese and American families.* Paper presented at the meeting of the International Society for the Study of Behavioral Development, Tokyo, Japan.

Keener, M. A., Zeanah, C. H., & Anders, T. F. (1988). Infant temperament, sleep organization, and parental interventions. *Pediatrics, 81*(6), 762–771.

Konner, M. J., & Super, C. M. (1987). Sudden Infant Death Syndrome: An anthropological hypothesis. In C. M. Super (Ed.), *The role of culture in developmental disorder* (pp. 95–108). San Diego: Academic.

Kugelmass, N. (1959). *Complete child care.* New York: Holt, Rinehart, & Winston.

LeVine, R. (1980). A cross-cultural perspective on parenting. In M. D. Fantini & R. Cardenas (Eds.), *Parenting in a multicultural society* (pp. 17–26). San Diego: Academic.

LeVine, R. (1990). Infant environments in psychoanalysis. In J. W. Stigler, R. A. Shweder, & G. Herdt (Eds.), *Cultural psychology: Essays on comparative human development* (pp. 454–474). Cambridge: Cambridge University Press.

Lozoff, B., Wolf, A., & Davis, N. (1984). Cosleeping in urban families with young children in the United States. *Pediatrics, 74*(2), 171–182.

Mandansky, D., & Edelbrock, C. (1990). Cosleeping in a community sample of 2- and 3-year-old children. *Pediatrics, 86,* 197–280.

McKenna, J. (1986). An anthropological perspective on the Sudden Infant Death Syndrome (SIDS): The role of parental breathing cues and speech breathing adaptations. *Medical Anthropology, 10* (1), 9–92.

Munroe, R. L., Munroe, R. H., & Whiting, J. W. M. (1981). Male sex-role resolutions. In R. H. Munroe, R. L. Munroe, & B. B. Whiting (Eds.), *Handbook of cross-cultural human development* (pp. 611–632). New York: Garland.

New, R. (1984). *Italian mothers and infants: Patterns of care and social development.* Unpublished doctoral dissertation, School of Education, Harvard University.

Richman, A. L., Miller, P. M., & Solomon, M. J. (1988). The socialization of infants in suburban Boston. In R. A. LeVine, P. M. Miller, & M. M. West (Eds.), *Parental behavior in diverse societies* (pp. 65–74). San Francisco: Jossey Bass.

Rogoff, B. (1977). *A portrait of memory in cultural context.* Unpublished doctoral dissertation, Harvard University.

Rogoff, B. (1990). *Apprenticeship in thinking: Cognitive development in social context.* New York: Oxford University Press.

Rogoff, B., & Morelli, G. (1989). Perspectives on development from cultural psychology. *American Psychologist, 44,* 343–348.

Rogoff, B., Mosier, C., Mistry, J., & Göncü, A. (1993). Toddlers' guided participation with their caregivers in cultural activity. In E. Forman, N. Minick, & A. Stone (Eds.), (pp. 230–253) *Contexts for learning: Sociocultural dynamics in children's development.* New York: Oxford University Press.

Rosenfeld, A., Wenegrat, A., Haavik, D., Wenegrat, B., & Smith, C. (1982). Sleeping patterns in upper-middle-class families when the child awakens ill or frightened. *Archives of General Psychiatry, 39,* 943–947.

Spock, B. J. (1945). *The common sense book of child and baby care.* New York: Duell, Sloan, & Pearce.

Spock, B. J. (1984, December). Mommy, can I sleep in your bed? *Parents Magazine,* p. 129.

Super, C. M., & Harkness, C. (1982). The infant's niche in rural Kenya and metropolitan America. In L. L. Adler (Ed.), *Cross-cultural research at issue* (pp. 47–55). San Diego: Academic.

Takahashi, (1990). Are the key assumptions of the "Strange Situation" procedure universal? A view from Japanese research. *Human Development, 33,* 23–30.

Thevinin, T. (1976). *The family bed: An age old concept in childrearing.* Minneapolis: Author.

Valsiner, J., & Hall, D. (1983). *Parents' strategies for the organization of child-environment relationships in home settings.* Paper presented at the Seventh Biennial Meeting of the International Society for the Study of Behavioral Development, München, Bundesrepub, Germany.

Ward, M. C. (1971). *Them children.* New York: Holt, Rinehart, & Winston.

Whiting, B. B., & Edwards, C. (1988). *Children of different worlds: The formation of social behavior.* Cambridge, MA: Harvard University Press.

Whiting, J. W. M. (1964). The effects of climate on certain cultural practices. In W. H. Goodenough (Ed.), *Explorations in cultural anthropology: Essays in honor of George Peter Murdock* (pp. 511–544). New York: McGraw-Hill.

Wolf, A., & Lozoff, B. (1989). Object attachment, thumbsucking, and the passage to sleep. *Journal of the American Academy of Child and Adolescent Psychiatry, 28,* 287–292.

## 5. Symbolic Functioning in Preschool Children

Burns, N. M. (1990). *Emergence of the understanding of pictures as symbols in very young children.* Unpublished master's thesis, University of Illinois, Urbana-Champaign.

Daehler, M. W., Lonardo, R., & Bukatko, D. (1979). Matching and equivalence judgement in very young children. *Child Development, 50,* 170–179.

DeLoache, J. S. (1986). Memory in very young children: Exploitation of cues to the location of a hidden object. *Cognitive Development, 1,* 123–137.

DeLoache, J. S. (1987). Rapid change in the symbolic functioning of very young children. *Science, 238,* 1556–1557.

DeLoache, J. S. (1989a). The development of representation in young children. In H. W. Reese (Ed.), *Advances in child development and behavior* (Vol. 22, pp. 1–39). New York: Academic.

DeLoache, J. S. (1989b). Young children's understanding of the correspondence between a scale model and a larger space. *Cognitive Development, 4,* 121–139.

DeLoache, J. S. (1990). Young children's understanding of scale models. In R. Fivush & J. Hudson (Eds.), *Knowing and remembering in young children* (pp. 94–126). New York: Cambridge University Press.

DeLoache, J. S. (1991). Symbolic functioning in very young children: Understanding of pictures and models. *Child Development, 62,* 736–752.

DeLoache, J. S., & Burns, N. M. (1994). Early understanding of the representational function of pictures. *Cognition, 52,* 83–110.

DeLoache, J. S., Kolstad, V., & Anderson, K. (1991). Physical similarity and young children's understanding of scale models. *Child Development, 62,* 111–126.

Dow, G. A., & Pick, H. (1990). Young children's use of models and photographs as spatial representations. *Cognitive Development, 7,* 351–363.

Hartley, D. G. (1976). The effects of perceptual salience on reflective-impulsive performance differences. *Developmental Psychology, 12,* 218–225.

Sigel, I. E. (1953). Developmental trends in the abstraction ability of children. *Child Development, 24,* 131–144.

Sigel, I. E. (1978). The development of pictoral comprehension. In B. S. Randhawa & W. E. Coffmann (Eds.), *Visual learning, thinking, and communication* (pp. 93–111). New York: Academic.

Sigel, I. E., Anderson, L. M., & Shapiro, H. (1966). Categorization behavior of lower and middle class Negro preschool children: Differences in dealing with representation of familiar objects. *Journal of Negro Education, 35,* 218–229.

Sigel, I. E., & Cocking. R. R. (1977). *Cognitive development from childhood to adolescence: A constructivist perspective.* New York: Holt, Rinehart & Winston.

Sigel, I. E., & Olmsted. P. (1970). Modification of cognitive skills among lower-class black children. In J. Hellmuth (Ed.), *The disadvantaged child* (Vol. 3, pp. 300–338). New York: Brunner-Mazel.

Sorce, J. (1980). The role of operative knowledge in picture comprehension. *Journal of Genetic Psychology, 136,* 173–183.

Steinberg, B. M. (1974). Information processing in the third year: Coding, memory, transfer. *Child Development, 45,* 503–507.

# 6. The Psychological and Social Origins of Autobiographical Memory

Bartlett, F. C. (1932) *Remembering: A study in experimental and social psychology.* Cambridge: Cambridge University Press.

Dudycha, G. J., & Dudycha, M. M. (1941). Childhood memories: A review of the literature. *Psychological Bulletin, 38,* 668–682.

Eisenberg, A. R. (1985). Learning to describe past experiences in conversation. *Discourse Processes, 8,* 177–204.

Engel, S. (1986). *Learning to reminisce: A developmental study of how young children talk about the past.* Unpublished doctoral dissertation. City University of New York Graduate Center, New York.

Fivush, R. (1988). The functions of event memory: Some comments on Nelson and Barsalou. In U. Neisser & E. Winograd (Eds.), *Remembering reconsidered: Ecological and traditional approaches to the study of memory* (pp. 277–282). New York: Cambridge University Press.

Fivush, R., & Fromhoff, F. A. (1988). Style and structure in mother-child conversations about the past. *Discourse Processes, 11,* 337–355.

Fivush, R., & Hamond, N. R. (1989). Time and again: Effects of repetition and retention interval on two year olds' event recall. *Journal of Experimental Child Psychology, 47,* 259–273.

Fivush, R., & Hudson, J. A. (Eds.) (1990). *Knowing and remembering in young children.* New York: Cambridge University Press.

Fivush, R., & Reese, F. (1991, July). *Parental styles for talking about the past.* Paper presented at the International Conference on Memory, Lancaster, England.

Freud, S. (1963). Three essays on the theory of sexuality. In J. Strachey (Ed.), *The standard edition of the complete works of Freud* (Vol. 7). London: Hogarth.

Gopnik, A., & Graf, P. (1988). Knowing how you know: Young children's ability to identify and remember the sources of their beliefs. *Child Development, 59,* 1366–1371.

Hudson, J. A. (1986). Memories are made of this: General event knowledge and the development of autobiographic memory. In K. Nelson, *Event knowledge: Structure and function in development* (pp. 97–118). Hillsdale, NJ: Erlbaum.

Hudson, J. A. (1990). The emergence of autobiographic memory in mother-child conversation. In R. Fivush & J. A. Hudson (Eds.), *Knowing and remembering in young children* (pp. 166–196). New York: Cambridge University Press.

Hudson, J. A., & Fivush, R. (1991). As time goes by: Sixth graders remember a kindergarten experience. *Applied Cognitive Psychology, 5,* 347–360.

Hudson, J. A., & Nelson, K. (1986). Repeated encounters of a similar kind: Effects of familiarity on children's autobiographical memory. *Cognitive Development, 1,* 253–271.

Miller, G. A. (1990). The place of language in a scientific psychology. *Psychological Science, 1,* 7–14.

Neisser, U. (1962). Cultural and cognitive discontinuity. In T. E. Glodwin & W. Sturtevant (Eds.), *Anthropology and human behavior* (pp. 54–71). Washington, DC: Anthropological Society of Washington.

Nelson, K. (1978). How young children represent knowledge of their world in and out of language. In R. S. Siegler (Ed.), *Children's thinking: What develops?* (pp. 225–273). Hillsdale, NJ: Erlbaum.

Nelson, K. (1986). *Event knowledge: Structure and function in development.* Hillsdale, NJ: Erlbaum.

Nelson, K. (Ed.) (1989). *Narratives from the crib.* Cambridge, MA: Harvard University Press.

Nelson, K. (1990). Event knowledge and the development of language functions. In J. Miller (Ed.) *Research on child language disorders* (pp. 125–141). New York: Little, Brown.

Nelson, K., & Gruendel, J. (1981). Generalized event representations: Basic building blocks of cognitive development. In M. Lamb & A. Brown (Eds.), *Advances in developmental psychology* (Vol. 1, pp. 131–158). Hillsdale, NJ: Erlbaum.

Perner, J. (1991). *Understanding the representational mind.* Cambridge, MA: MIT Press.

Pillemer, D. B., & White, S. H. (1989). Childhood events recalled by children and adults. In H. W. Reese (Ed.), *Advances in child development and behavior* (Vol. 21, pp. 297–340). New York: Academic.

Ratner, H. H. (1980). The role of social context in memory development. In M. Perlmutter (Ed.), *Children's memory: New directions for child development* (Vol. 10, pp. 49–68). San Francisco: Jossey-Bass.

Rogoff, B., & Mistry, J. (1990). The social and functional context of children's remembering. In R. Fivush & J. A. Hudson (Eds.), *Knowing and remembering in young children* (pp. 197–223). New York: Cambridge University Press.

Royce-Collier, C., & Hayne, H. (1987). Reactivation of infant memory: Implications for cognitive development. In H. W. Reese (Ed.), *Advances in child development and behavior* (Vol. 20, pp. 185–283). New York: Academic.

Schachtel, E. (1947). On memory and childhood amnesia. *Psychiatry, 10,* 1–26.

Schacter, D. L. (1992). Understanding implicit memory. *American Psychologist, 47,* 559–569.

Schank, R. C., & Abelson, R. P. (1977). *Scripts, plans, goals, and understanding.* Hillsdale, NJ: Erlbaum.

Sheingold, K., & Tenney, Y. J. (1982). Memory for a salient childhood event. In U. Neisser (Ed.), *Memory observed* (pp. 201–212). San Francisco: W. H. Freeman.

Squire, L. R. (1992). Memory and the hippocampus: A synthesis from finding with rats, monkeys, and humans. *Psychological Review, 99,* 195–231.

Tessler, M. (1986). *Mother-child talk in a museum: The socialization of a memory.* Unpublished manuscript, City University of New York Graduate Center, New York.

Tessler, M. (1991). *Making memories together: The influence of mother-child joint encoding on the development of autobiographical memory style.* Unpublished doctoral dissertation, City University of New York Graduate Center, New York.

Tulving, E. (1983). *Elements of episodic memory.* New York: Oxford University Press.

Tulving, E. (1984). Precis of *Elements of episodic memory* with open peer commentary. *Behavioral and Brain Sciences, 7,* 223–268.

Usher, J. A., & Neisser, U. (1991). *Childhood amnesia in the recall of four target events* (Emory Cognition Project Report No. 20). Atlanta: Emory University, Department of Psychology.

Vygotsky, L. S. (1978). *Mind in society: The development of higher psychological processes.* Cambridge, MA: Harvard University Press.

Wetzler, S. E., & Sweeney, J. A. (1986). Childhood amnesia: An empirical demonstration. In D. C. Rubin (Ed.), *Autobiographical memory* (pp. 191–201). New York: Cambridge University Press.

## 7. Intersubjectivity in Caregiver–Child Communication

Ainslie, R. C. & Anderson, C. W. (1984). Day-care children's relationships to their mothers and caregivers: An enquiry into the conditions for the development of attachment. In R. C. Ainslie (Ed.), *Qualitative variations and development* (pp. 98–132). New York: Praeger.

Australian Bureau of Statistics (1993). *Women in Australia.* Catalogue No. 4402, Canberra.

Berk, L. E. (1985). Relationship of caregiver education to child-oriented attitudes, job satisfaction, and behaviours towards children. *Child Care Quarterly, 14,* 103–129.

Berk, L. E. & Winsler, A. (1995). *Scaffolding children's learning: Vygotsky and early childhood education.* Washington, DC: National Association for the Education of Young Children.

Birdwhistlell, R. L. (1970). *Kinesics and content.* Philadelphia: University of Philadelphia Press.

Dunham, P. J., Dunham, F., & Curwin, A. (1993). Joint-attentional states and lexical acquisition at 18 months. *Developmental Psychology, 29,* 827–831.

File, N. (1995). Applications of Vygotskian theory to early childhood education. *Advances in Early Education and Day Care, 7,* 295–317.

Gallimore, R., Tharp, R. G., & John-Steiner, V. (1992). *The developmental and sociocultural foundations of mentoring.* Institute for Urban and Minority Education, Columbia University, New York (ED354292).

Garton, A. F. (1992). *Social interaction and the development of language and cognition.* Hove, The Netherlands: Erlbaum.

Göncü, A. (1993a). Development of intersubjectivity in the dyadic play of preschoolers. *Early Childhood Research Quarterly, 8,* 99–116.

Goncu, A. (1993b). Development of intersubjectivity in social pretend play. *Human Development, 36,* 185–198.

Halverson, A. M. (1994).The importance of caring and attachment in direct practice with adolescents. *Child and Youth Care Forum, 24,* 169–173.

Hoffman, S. & Lilja, L. D. (1988). *An analysis of language transactions within the storybook reading environment in selected out-of-home childcare centers.* Missouri University, Columbia College of Education (ED 302 816).

Howes, C., & Matheson, C. C. (1992). Contextual constraints on the concordance of mother-child and teacher-child relationships. In R. C. Pianta (Ed.), *Beyond the parent: The role of other adults in children's lives* (pp. 25–40). San Francisco: Jossey-Bass.

Jamieson, J. R. (1994). Teaching as transaction: Vygotskian perspectives on deafness and mother-child interaction. *Exceptional Children, 60,* 434–449.

Leadbeater, B. J. (1989, April). *Between subjects: Shared meanings of intersubjectivity.* Paper presented at the National Biennial Meeting of the Society for Research in Child Development, No. 21, Kansas City, Missouri.

Maxwell, S. (1996). Meaningful interaction. In S. Robson & S. Smedley (Eds.), *Education in early childhood: First things first.* London: David Fulton.

Meadow-Orlans, K. P. (1993). *Interaction of deaf and hearing mothers and their deaf and hearing children at 12 and 18 months.* Paper presented at the biennial meeting of the Society for Research in Child Development, New Orleans.

Murray, L. (1991). Intersubjectivity, object relations theory, and empirical evidence from mother-infant interactions. *Infant Mental Health Journal, 12,* 219–232.

Mundy, P., Kasari, C., & Sigman, M. (1992). Nonverbal communication, affective sharing, and intersubjectivity. *Infant Behavior & Development, 15,* 377–381.

Newson, J. & Newson, E. (1975). Intersubjectivity and the transmission of culture: On the social origins of symbolic functioning. *Bulletin of the British Psychological Society, 28,* 437–446.

Raikes, H. (1993). Relationship duration in infant care: Time with a high-ability teacher and infant-teacher attachment. *Early Childhood Research Quarterly, 8,* 309–325.

Ratner, H. H. & Stettner, L. J. (1991). Thinking and feeling: Putting Humpty Dumpty together again. *Merrill-Palmer Quarterly, 37,* 1–26.

Rogoff, B. (1990). *Apprenticeship in thinking: Cognitive development in social context.* New York: Oxford University Press.

Rogoff, B., Mosier, C., Mistry, J., & Goncü, A. (1993). Toddlers' guided participation with their caregivers in cultural activity. In E. A. Forman, N. Minick, & C. A. Stone (Eds.), *Contexts for learning* (pp. 230–253). New York: Oxford University Press.

Rommetveit, J. (1985). Language acquisition as increasing linguistic structuring of experience and symbolic behaviour control. In J. V. Wertsch (Ed.), *Culture, Communication and Cognition* (pp.183–204). Cambridge: Cambridge University Press.

Schieffelin, B. B. & Ochs, E. (1987). *Language socialization across cultures.* New York: Cambridge University Press.

Smith, A. B. (1993). Early childhood educare: Seeking a theoretical framework in Vygotsky's work. *International Journal of Early Years Education, 1,* 47–61.

Stremmel, A. J. & Fu, V. R. (1993). Teaching in the zone of proximal development: Implications for responsive teaching practice. *Child and Youth Care Forum, 25,* 337–350.

Trevarthen, C. (1977). Descriptive analyses of infant communication behavior. In H. R. Schaffer (Ed.), *Studies in Mother-Infant Interaction: The Loch Lomond Symposium* (pp. 227–270). London: Academic.

Trevarthen, C. (1979). Communication and cooperation in early infancy: A description of primary intersubjectivity. In M. Bullowa (Ed.), *Before speech: The beginning of interpersonal communication* (pp. 321–347). Cambridge: Cambridge University Press.

Trevarthen, C. (1988). Universal cooperative motives: How infants begin to know the language and culture of their parents. In G. Jahoda & I. M. Lewis (Eds.), *Acquiring culture: Cross cultural studies in child development* (pp. 37–90). London: Croom Helm.

Trevarthen, C. & Hubley, P. (1978). Secondary intersubjectivity: Confidence, confiding and acts of meaning in the first year. In A. Lock (Ed.), *Action, Gesture and Symbol* (pp. 183–229). London: Academic.

U.S. Bureau of the Census (1996). *Statistical abstract of the United States* (116th ed.). Washington, DC: U.S. Government Printing Office.

Vygotsky, L. (1984). *Mind in society: The development of higher psychological processes.* Cambridge, MA: Harvard University Press.

Wood, D., Bruner, J. S., & Ross, G. (1976). The role of tutoring in problem solving. *Journal of Child Psychology and Psychiatry, 17,* 80–100.

## 8. Young Children's Understanding of Everyday Emotions

Allen, J. G., & Haccoun, D. M. (1976). Sex differences in emotionality: A multidimensional approach. *Human Relations, 29*(8), 711–722.

Allen, J. G., & Hamsher, J. H. (1974). The development and validation of a test of emotional styles. *Journal of Consulting and Clinical Psychology, 42*(5), 663–668.

Balswick, H., & Avertt, C. P. (1977). Differences in expressiveness: Gender, interpersonal orientation, and perceived parental expressiveness as contributing factors. *Journal of Marriage and the Family, 39*(1), 121–127.

Barden, R. C., Zelko, F., Duncan, S. W., & Masters, J. C. (1980). Children's consensual knowledge about the experiential determinants of emotion. *Journal of Personality and Social Psychology, 39*(5), 968–976.

Bertenthal, B. I., & Fisher, K. W. (1978). Development of self-recognition in the infant. *Developmental Psychology, 14*(1), 44–50.

Borke, H. (1971). Interpersonal perception of young children: Egocentricism or empathy. *Developmental Psychology, 5*(2), 263–269.

Bretherton, I., & Beeghly, M. (1982). Talking about internal states: The acquisition of an explicit theory of mind. *Developmental Psychology, 18*(6), 906–921.

Bretherton, I., Fritz, J., Zahn-Waxler, C., & Ridgeway, D. (1986). Learning to talk about emotions: A functionalist perspective. *Child Development, 57*(3), 529–548.

Brody, L. R. (1984). Sex and age variations in the quality and intensity of children's emotional attributions to hypothetical situations. *Sex Roles, 11*(1/2), 51–59.

Brody, L. R., & Harrison, R. H. (1987). Development changes in children's abilities to match and label emotionally laden situations. *Motivation and Emotion, 11*(4), 347–365.

Campos, J. J., Barrett, K. C., Lamb, M. E., Goldsmith, H. H., & Stenberg, C. (1983). Socioemotional development. In M. Haith & J. J. Campos (Eds.), *Handbook of child psychology: Vol. 2 Infancy and developmental psychobiology* (pp. 783–915). New York: Wiley.

Camras, L. A., & Allison, K. (1989). Children's and adults' beliefs about emotion elicitation. *Motivation and Emotion, 13*(1), 53–70.

Carroll, J. J., & Steward, M. S. (1984). The role of cognitive development in children's understanding of their own feelings. *Child Development, 55*(4), 1486–1492.

Conway, M., Giannopoulos, C., & Stiefenhofer, K. (1990). Response styles to sadness are related to sex and sex-role orientation. *Sex Roles, 22*(9/10), 579–587.

Cooley, C. H. (1902). *Human nature and the social order.* New York: Scribner's.

Davis, T. L. (1992, April). *Sex differences in the masking of children's negative emotions: Ability or motivation?* Paper presented at the Human Development Conferences, Atlanta, GA.

Denham, S. A., & Zoller, D. (1991). "When my hamster died, I cried": Preschoolers' attributions of the causes of emotions. *Journal of Genetic Psychology, 152,* 371–373

Donaldson, S. K., & Westerman, M. A. (1986). Development of children's understanding of ambivalence and causal theories of emotions. *Developmental Psychology, 22*(5), 655–662.

Dunn, J., Bretherton, I., & Munn, P. (1987). Conversations about feeling states between mothers and their young children. *Developmental Psychology, 23*(1), 132–139.

Dunn, J., Brown, J., & Beardsall, L. (1991). Family talk about feeling states and children's later understanding of others' emotions. *Developmental Psychology, 27*(3), 448–455.

Dunn, J., & Kendrick, C. (1982). *Siblings: Love, envy and understanding.* Cambridge, MA: Harvard University Press.

Dunn, J., & Munn, P. (1985). Becoming a family member: Family conflict and the development of social understanding in the second year. *Child Development, 56*(2), 480–492.

Feinman, S., & Lewis, M. (1983). Social referencing at ten-months: A second-order effect on infants' responses to strangers. *Child Development, 54*(4), 878–887.

Fitzpatrick, M. A., & Indvik, J. (1982). The instrumental and expressive domains of marital communication. *Human Communications Research, 8*(3), 195–213.

Fivush, R. (1989). Exploring sex differences in the emotional content of mother-child conversations about the past. *Sex Roles, 20*(11/12), 675–691.

Fivush, R. (1991). Gender and emotion in mother-child conversations about the past. *Journal of Narrative and Life History, 1*(4), 325–341.

Glasberg, R., & Aboud, F. (1982). Keeping one's distance from sadness: Children's self-reports of emotional experience. *Development Psychology, 18*(2), 287–293.

Gordon, S. L. (1989). The socialization of children's emotions: Emotional competence, culture, and exposure. In C. Saarni & P. L. Harris (Eds.), *Children's understanding of emotion* (pp. 319–349). New York: Cambridge University Press.

Gove, F. L., & Keating, D. P. (1979). Empathic role-taking precursors. *Developmental Psychology, 15*(6), 594–600.

Graham, S. (1988). Children's developing understanding of the motivational role of affect: An attributional analysis. *Cognitive Development, 3*(2), 71–88.

Graham, S., Doubleday, C., & Guarino, P. A. (1984). The development of relations between perceived controllability and the emotions of pity, anger, and guilt. *Child Development, 55*(2), 561–565.

Harter, S. (1983). Developmental perspectives on the self-system. In E. M. Hetherington (Ed.), *Socialization, personality and social development, Vol IV, Handbook of Child Psychology* (pp. 275–385). New York: Wiley.

Harter, S., & Buddin, B. J. (1987). Children's understanding of the simultaneity of two emotions: A five-stage development acquisition sequence. *Developmental Psychology, 23*(3), 388–399.

Harter, S., & Whitesell, N. R. (1989). Developmental changes in children's understanding of single, multiple, and blended emotion concepts. In C. Saarni & P. L. Harris (Eds.), *Children's understanding of emotion* (pp. 81–116). Cambridge: Cambridge University Press.

Hochschild, A. R. (1983). *The managed heart: Commercialization of human feelings.* Berkeley: University of California Press.

Izard, C. E., & Malatesta, C. A. (1987). Perspectives on emotional development I: Differential emotions theory of early emotional development. In J. D. Osofsky (Ed.), *Handbook of infant development* (2nd ed.) (pp. 494–554). New York: Wiley.

Kagan, J. (1981). *The second year: The emergence of self-awareness.* Cambridge, MA: Harvard University Press.

Kuebli, J., & Fivush, R. (1992). Gender differences in parent-child conversations about past emotions. *Sex Roles, 27*(11/12), 683–698.

Kuebli, J., & Fivush, R. (1993, March). *Children's developing understanding of emotion and mind.* Paper presented at the biennial meetings of the Society for Research in Child Development, New Orleans, LA.

Leavitt, R. L., & Power, M. B. (1989). Emotional socialization in the postmodern era: Children in day care. *Social Psychology Quarterly, 52*(1), 35–43.

Levy, R. I. (1984). Emotion, knowing, and culture. In R. A. Shweder & R. A. LeVine (Eds.), *Culture theory: Essays on mind, self, and emotion* (pp. 214–237). Cambridge: Cambridge University Press.

Lewis, M. (1992). *Shame: The exposed self.* New York: Free Press.

Lewis, M., & Brooks-Gunn, J. (1979). *Social cognition and acquisition of self.* New York: Plenum.

Lewis, M., & Michalson, L. (1983). *Children's emotions and moods.* New York: Plenum.

Lewis, M., & Saarni, C. (1985). Culture and emotions. In M. Lewis & C. Saarni (Eds.), *The socialization of emotions* (pp. 1–17). New York: Plenum.

Lewis, M., Sullivan, M. W., Stanger, C., & Weiss, M. (1989). Self-development and self-conscious emotions. *Child Development, 60*(1), 146–156.

Lutz, C. (1983). Parental goals, ethnopsychology, and the development of emotional meaning. *Ethos, 11*(4), 246–262.

Lutz, C. (1985). Cultural patterns and individual differences in the child's emotional meaning system. In M. Lewis & C. Saarni (Eds.), *The socialization of emotions* (pp. 37–53). New York: Plenum.

Lutz, C., & White, G. M. (1986). The anthropology of emotions. *Annual Review of Anthropology, 15,* 405–436.

Markus, H. R., & Kitayama, S. (1991). Culture and the self: Implications for cognition, emotion, and motivation. *Psychological Review, 98*(2), 224–253.

Matsumoto, D., Kudoh, T., Scherer, K., & Wallbott, H. (1988). Antecedents of and reactions to emotions in the United States and Japan. *Journal of Cross-Cultural Psychology, 19*(3), 267–286.

Mead, G. H. (1913). The social self. In A. J. Reck (Ed.), *Selected writings: George Herbert Mead* (pp. 142–149). Chicago: University of Chicago Press.

Mead, G. H. (1956). *On social psychology: Selected papers.* Chicago: University of Chicago Press.

Michalson, L., & Lewis, M. (1985). What do children know about emotions and when do they know it? In M. Lewis & C. Saarni (Eds.), *The socialization of emotions* (pp. 117–139). New York: Plenum.

Miller, P., & Sperry, L. L. (1987). The socialization of anger and aggression. *Merrill-Palmer Quarterly, 33*(1), 1–31.

Peng, M., Johnson, C., Pollock, J., Glasspool, R., & Harris, P. (1992). Training young children to acknowledge mixed emotions. *Cognition and Emotion, 6*(5), 387–401.

Reichenbach, L., & Masters, J. C. (1983). Children's use of expressive and contextual cues in judgments of emotion. *Child Development, 54*(4), 992–1004.

Ridgeway, D., Waters, E., & Kuczaj, S. A. (1985). Acquisition of emotion-descriptive language: Receptive and productive vocabulary norms for ages 18 months to 6 years. *Developmental Psychology, 21*(5), 901–908.

Saarni, C. (1984). An observational study of children's attempts to monitor their expressive behavior. *Child Development, 55*(4), 1504–1513.

Saarni, C. (1985). Indirect processes in affect socialization. In M. Lewis & C. Saarni (Eds.), *The socialization of emotions* (pp. 187–209). New York: Plenum.

Saarni, C., & Crowley, M. (1990). The development of emotion regulation: Effects on emotional state and expression. In E. A. Blechman (Ed.), *Emotions and the family: For better or for worse* (pp. 53–73). Hillsdale, NJ: Erlbaum.

Sroufe, L. A. (1979). Socioemotional development. In J. D. Osofsky (Ed.), *Handbook of infant development* (pp. 462–516). New York: Wiley.

Stenberg, C., Campos, J., & Emde, R. (1983). The facial expression of anger in seven-month-old infants. *Child Development, 54*(1), 178–184.

Stern, D. (1985). *The interpersonal world of the infant.* New York: Basic.

Stipek, D., Weiner, B., & Li, K. (1989). Testing some attribution-emotion relations in the People's Republic of China. *Journal of Personality and Social Psychology, 56*(1), 109–116.

Strayer, J. (1986). Children's attributions regarding the situational determinants of emotion in self and others. *Developmental Psychology, 22*(5), 649–654.

Vygotsky, L. S. (1978). *Mind in society: The development of higher psychological processes.* Cambridge, MA: Harvard University Press.

Vygotsky, L. S. (1981). The genesis of higher mental functions. In J. V. Wertsch (Ed.), *The concept of activity in Soviet psychology.* Armonk, NY: M. E. Sharpe.

Wintre, M. G., Polivy, J., & Murray, M. A. (1990). Self-predictions of emotional-response patterns: Age, sex, and situational determinants. *Child Development, 61*(4), 1124–1133.

# 9. "Children of the Dream" Revisited

Ainsworth, M. D. S., Blehar, M., Waters, E., & Wall, S. (1978). *Patterns of attachment.* Hillsdale, NJ: Erlbaum.

Alon, M. (1976). Mishnato hachinuchit shel Shmuel Golan [The educational thought of Shmuel Golan]. In Y. Arnon (Ed.), *Hachinuch hameshutaf* (pp. 11–24). Tel Aviv, Israel: Sifriyat Poalim.

Anthony, E. J., & Bene, E. (1957). A technique from the objective assessment of the child's family relationships. *Journal of Mental Science, 103,* 541–555.

Barry, H., & Paxton, L. M. (1971). Infancy and early childhood: Cross-cultural codes 2. *Ethnology, 10,* 466–508.

Bar-Yosef, R. (1959). The pattern of early socialization in the collective settlements of Israel. *Human Relations, 12,* 345–360.

Beck, S. J. (1950). *Rorschach's test* (Vol. 1). New York: Grune & Stratton.

Beit-Hallahmi, B. (1981). The kibbutz family revival or survival. *Journal of Family Issues, 2,* 259–274.

Beit-Hallahmi, B., & Rabin, A. (1977). The kibbutz as a social experiment and as a child-rearing laboratory. *American Psychologist, 12,* 57–69.

Belsky, J. (1988). The effects of infant day-care reconsidered. *Early Childhood Research Quarterly, 3,* 235–272.

Belsky, J. (1990). Parental and nonparental child care and children's socioemotional development: A decade in review. *Journal of Marriage and the Family, 52,* 885–903.

Ben-Yaakov, Y. (1972). Methods of kibbutz collective education during early childhood. In J. Marcus (Ed.), *Growing up in groups* (pp. 197–295). London: Gordon & Beach.

Berman, E. (1988). Communal upbringing in the kibbutz. *Psychoanalytic Study of the Child, 41,* 319–335.

Bettelheim, B. (1969). *The children of the dream.* London: Collier-Macmillan.

Bowlby, J. (1951). *Maternal care and mental health.* Geneva: World Health Organization.

Bowlby, J. (1982). *Attachment and loss: Vol 1, Attachment.* New York: Basic. (Originally published in 1969.)

Bronson, G. W. (1968). The development of fear in man and other animals. *Child Development, 39,* 409–432.

Clarke-Stewart, K. A. (1988). "The effects of infant day-care reconsidered" reconsidered: Risks for parents, children, and researchers. *Early Childhood Research Quarterly, 3,* 292–318.

Clarke-Stewart, K. A. (1989). Infant day care: Maligned or malignant? *American Psychologist, 44,* 266–273.

Doyle, A., Connolly, J., & Rivest, L. (1980). The effect of playmate familiarity on the social interaction of young children. *Child Development, 51,* 217–223.

Droege, K. L., & Howes, C. (1991, July). *The influence of caregiver behavior on children's affective displays.* Paper presented at the biennial meeting of the International Society for the Study of Behavioral Development, Minneapolis.

Easterbrooks, M. A., & Lamb, M. (1979). The relationship between quality of infant-mother attachment and infant competence in initial encounters with peers. *Child Development, 50,* 380–387.

Eckerman, C. O., & Didow, S. M. (1988). Lessons drawn from observing young peers together. *Acta Padiatrica Scandinavica, 77*(Suppl. 344), 55–70.

Epstein, R. (1992, March). *Sheina bakibbutz—Lina meshutefet mul lina mishpachtit* [Sleep in the kibbutz—collective versus home-base sleeping]. Paper presented at the Technion Workshop on Studies of Sleep in Children, Haifa, Israel.

Faigin, H. (1958). Social behavior of young children in the kibbutz. *Journal of Abnormal and Social Psychology, 56,* 117–129.

Farran, D. C., & Ramey, C. T. (1977). Infant day care and attachment behaviors toward mothers and teachers. *Child Development, 48,* 1112–1116.

Fein, G. G., & Fox, N. (1988). Infant day care: A special issue. *Early Childhood Research Quarterly, 3,* 227–234.

Feldman, S. S., & Yirmiya, N. (1986). Perception of socialization roles: A study of Israeli mothers in town and kibbutz. *International Journal of Psychology, 21,* 153–165.

Fölling-Albers, M. (1988a, July). *Education in the kibbutz as "women's business": Emancipation of women between idea and reality.* Paper presented at Utopian Thought and Communal Experience, New Lanark, Scotland.

Fölling-Albers, M. (1988b). Erziehung und frauenfrage im kibbutz [Child rearing and women's emancipation in the kibbutz]. In W. Melzer & G. Neubauer (Eds.), *Der kibbutz als utopie* (pp. 88–120). Basel, Switzerland: Beltz.

Fox, N. (1977). Attachment of kibbutz infants to mother and metapelet. *Child Development, 48,* 1228–1239.

Fox, N., Kimmerly, N. L., & Schafer, W. D. (1991). Attachment to mother/attachment to father: A meta-analysis. *Child Development, 62,* 210–225.

Freud, A. (1973). *Normality and pathology in childhood.* London: Hogarth.

Gamble, T. J., & Zigler, E. (1986). Effects of infant daycare: Another look at the evidence. *American Journal of Orthopsychiatry, 56,* 26–42.

Gerson, M. (1976). Hitnahaguta hachinuchit shel metapelet bapeuton [The educational behavior of a caregiver in the toddlers' house]. In Y. Arnon (Ed.), *Hachinuch hameshutaf* (pp. 123–144). Tel Aviv, Israel: Sifriyat Hapoalim.

Gerson, M. (1978). *Family, women, and socialization in the kibbutz.* Lexington, MA: Heath.

Gerson, M., & Nathan, M. (1969). Seker hametaplot bagil harach batnua hakibutzit [A survey of care-givers in early education in the kibbutz movement]. *Yediot (3).* Oranim, Israel: Institute for Research on Collective Education.

Gerson, M., & Schnabel-Brandes, A. (1990). The educational approach of the metapelet of young children in the kibbutz. In Z. Lavi (Ed.), *Kibbutz members study kibbutz children* (pp. 40–49). New York: Greenwood.

Gewirtz, J. (1965). The course of infant smiling in four child-rearing environments in Israel. In B. M. Foss (Ed.), *Determinants of infant behavior III* (pp. 205–260). New York: Wiley.

Golan, S. (1958). Collective education in the kibbutz. *American Journal of Orthopsychiatry, 28,* 549–556.

Golan, S. (1959). Collective education in the kibbutz. *Psychiatry, 22,* 167–177.

Golan, S. (1961). *Hachinuch hameshutaf* [Collective education]. Tel Aviv, Israel: Sifriat Poalim.

Goossens, F. A. (1987). Maternal employment and day care: Effects on attachment. In L. W. C. Tavecchio & M. H. Van IJzandoorn (Eds.), *Attachment in social networks* (pp. 135–183). Amsterdam: Elsevier.

Goossens, F. A., & Van IJzendoorn, M. H. (1990). Quality of infants' attachment to professional care-givers: Relations to infant-parent attachment and day-care characteristics. *Child Development, 61,* 832–837.

Greenbaum, C. W., & Landau, R. (1977). Mothers' speech and the early development of vocal behavior: Findings from a cross-cultural observation study in Israel. In P. H. Leiderman, S. R. Tulkin, & A. Rosenfeld (Eds.), *Culture and infancy: Variations in the human experience* (pp. 245–270). San Diego: Academic.

Grossman, K., Grossmann, K. E., Spangler, G., Suess, G., & Unzner, L. (1985). Maternal sensitivity and newborns' orientation responses as related to quality of attachment in northern Germany. *Monographs of the Society for Research in Child Development, 50*(1–2, Serial No. 209).

Haas, M. (1986). *Peutim poalim umitnasim beargaz hagru-taot ubeteivot peilut* [Toddlers acting and experiencing the junk and activity boxes]. Oranim, Israel: Institute for the Teaching of Science and the Improvement of Teaching Methods.

Harel, M. (1986, September). *Dialogues at risk.* Paper presented at the International Conference for Infant Mental Health, Chicago.

Harel, Y. (1979). *Hitnahagut chevratit bikvutsat peutot bakibbutz* [Social behavior in toddlers' groups in the kibbutz]. Unpublished masters' thesis, University of Haifa, Haifa, Israel.

Hazan, B. (1973). Introduction. In A. I. Rabin & B. Hazan (Eds.), *Collective education in the kibbutz* (pp. 1–10). New York: Springer.

Holdstein, I., & Borus, J. F. (1976). Kibbutz and city children: A comparative study of syntactic and articulatory abilities. *Journal of Speech and Hearing Disorders, 4,* 10–15.

Howes, C. (1988a). Peer interaction of young children. *Monographs of the Society for Research in Child Development, 53*(1, Serial No. 217).

Howes, C. (1988b). Relations between early child care and schooling. *Developmental Psychology, 24,* 53–57.

Howes, C. (1990). Can age of entry into child care and the quality of child care predict adjustment in kindergarten? *Developmental Psychology, 26,* 292–303.

Howes, C., Phillips, D. A., & Whitebook, M. (1992). Thresholds of quality: Implications for the social development of children in center-based child care. *Child Development, 63,* 449–460.

Howes, C., Rodning, C., Galluzzo, D. C., & Meyers, L. (1988). Attachment and child care: Relationships with mother and caregiver. *Early Childhood Research Quarterly, 3,* 403–416.

Irvine, E. E. (1952). Observations on the aims and methods of child rearing in communal settlements in Israel. *Human Relations, 5,* 247–275.

Isaacs, S. (1948). *Social development in young children.* London: Kegan Paul, Trench, & Trubner.

Kaffman, M. (1965). A comparison of psychopathology: Israeli children from kibbutz and from urban surroundings. *American Journal of Orthopsychiatry, 35,* 509–520.

Kaffman, M., Elizur, E., & Rabinowitz, M. (1990). Early childhood in the kibbutz: The 1980s. In Z. Lavi (Ed.), *Kibbutz members study kibbutz children* (pp. 17–33). New York: Greenwood.

Keller, S. (1983). The family in the kibbutz: What lessons for us? In M. Palgi, J. R. Blasi, M. Rosner, & M. Safir (Eds.), *Sexual equality: The Israeli kibbutz tests the theories* (pp. 227–251). Norwood, PA: Norwood.

Kohen-Raz, R. (1968). Mental and motor development of kibbutz, institutionalized and home-reared infants in Israel. *Child Development, 39,* 489–504.

Konner, M. (1977). Infancy among the Kalahari desert San. In P. H. Leiderman, S. R. Tulkin, & A. H. Rosenfeld (Eds.), *Culture and infancy* (pp. 287–328). San Diego: Academic.

Laikin, N. G., Laikin, M., & Costanzo, P. R. (1979). Group processes in early childhood: A dimension of human development. *International Journal of Behavioral Development, 2,* 171–183.

Lamb, M. E., Sternberg, K. J., Hwang, C. P., & Broberg, A. G. (Eds.) (1992). *Child care in context: Cross cultural perspectives.* Hillsdale, NJ: Erlbaum.

Lamb, M. E., Thompson, R. A., & Gardner, W. (1985). Measuring individual differences in strange situation behavior. In M. E. Lamb, R. A. Thompson, W. Gardner, & E. L. Charnov (Eds.), *Infant-mother attachment* (pp. 203–222). Hillsdale, NJ: Erlbaum.

Lavi, Z. (1984, April). *Correlates of sleeping arrangements of infants in kibbutzim.* Paper presented at the International Conference for Infant Studies, New York.

Lavi, Z. (1990a). Introduction. In Z. Lavi (Ed.), *Kibbutz members study kibbutz children* (pp. 1–16). New York: Greenwood.

Lavi, Z. (1990b). Transition from communal to family sleeping arrangement of children in kibbutzim: Causes and outcome. In Z. Lavi (Ed.), *Kibbutz members study kibbutz children* (pp. 51–55). New York: Greenwood.

Leshem, N. (1991). *Shirat hadeshe* [The song of the grass: Conversations with women of the kibbutz first generation]. Ramat Efal, Israel: Yad Tabenkin.

Levy-Shiff, R. (1983). Adaptation and competence in early childhood: Communally raised kibbutz children versus family raised children in the city. *Child Development, 54,* 1606–1614.

Levy-Shiff, R., & Hoffman, M. A. (1985). Social behavior of urban and kibbutz preschool children in Israel. *Developmental Psychology, 21,* 1204–1205.

Levy-Shiff, R., & Israelashvili, R. (1988). Antecedents of fathering: Some further exploration. *Developmental Psychology, 24* 434–440.

Lewin, G. (1982). Megamot bachinuch bagil harach [Trends in early education]. *Hachinuch Hameshutaf, 105,* 29–35.

Lewin, G. (1983). Kvutsat hapeutim vehametapelot—Ma kore lema'ase? [The toddlers' group and the caregivers—What happens in practice?]. *Hachinuch Hameshutaf, 108,* 4–24.

Lewin, G. (1985). *Tahalichei shinui bachinuch hameshutaf bagil harach* [Processes of change in early care in collective education]. Oranim, Israel: Institute for the Teaching of Science and the Improvement of Teaching Methods.

Lewin, G. (1986). Hachinuch hameshutaf leor hazichronot [Collective education as reflected in memories]. *Hachinuch Hameshutaf, 122,* 4–83.

Lewin, G. (1990). Motherhood in the kibbutz. In Z. Lavi (Ed.), *Kibbutz members study kibbutz children* (pp. 34–39). New York: Greenwood.

Liegle, L. (1974). *Gezin en gemeenschap in de kibboetz* [Family and community in the kibbutz]. Utrecht, The Netherlands: Spectrum.

Maccoby, E., & Feldman, S. (1972). Mother attachment and stranger reactions in the third year of life. *Monographs of the Society for Research in Child Development, 37*(1, Serial No. 146).

Main, M. (1990). Cross-cultural studies of attachment organization: Recent studies, changing methodologies, and the concept of conditional strategies. *Human Development, 33,* 48–61.

Main, M., & Goldwyn, R. (1991). *Adult attachment rating and classification systems.* Unpublished manuscript, University of California, Berkeley.

Main, M., & Weston, D. R. (1981). The quality of toddler's relationship to mother and to father: Related to conflict behavior and the readiness to establish new relationships. *Child Development, 52,* 932–940.

Meerovitch, A. (1990). *Hitpatchut hamischak bagil harach bair ubakibbutz—Hashpa'at hasviva al hitpatchut hahebetim hakognitivi vehachevrati shel hamischak bagil harach* [Early childhood play development in the kibbutz and in the city—Influence of the environment on development of the cognitive and social aspects of play in early childhood]. Unpublished master's thesis, Bar Ilan University, Ramat Gan, Israel.

Melhuish, E. C., & Moss, P. (1991). *Day care for young children: International perspectives.* London: Tavistock.

Melzer, W. (1988). Die bedeutung von utopien fur die genese der kibbutzim und ihres erziehungsarrangements [The importance of utopias for the creation of kibbutzim and their educational practices]. In W. Melzer & G. Neubauer (Eds.), *Der kibbutz als utopie* (pp. 38–69). Basel, Switzerland: Beltz.

Melzer, W., & Neubauer, G. (1988). Was ist ein kibbutz? Theoretischer anspruch und wirklichkeit-erfahren in kibbutz Ayeleth Hashahar [What is a kibbutz? Theory and practice in kibbutz Ayeleth-Hashahar]. In W. Melzer & G. Neubauer (Eds.), *Der kibbutz als utopie* (pp. 24–37). Basel, Switzerland: Beltz.

Morelli, G. A., & Tronick, E. Z. (1991). Efe multiple caretaking and attachment. In J. L. Gewirtz & W. M. Kurtines (Eds.), *Intersections with attachment* (pp. 41–51). Hillsdale, NJ: Erlbaum.

Nathan, M. (1984). *Lina meshutefet—Lina mishpahtit, takzirei vesikoumei mechkarim* [Communal versus familial children's sleeping arrangement: Abstract and summaries of studies]. *Yediot (15)*. Oranim, Israel: Institute for Research on Collective Education.

Ophir-Cohen, M., Epstein, R., Tzischinsky, O., Tirosh, E., & Lavie, P. (1993). Sleep patterns of children sleeping in residential care, in kibbutz dormitories and at home—A comparative study. *Sleep, 16,* 428–432.

Oppenheim, D., Sagi, A., & Lamb, M. E. (1988). Infant-adult attachments on the kibbutz and their relation to socioemotional development 4 years later. *Developmental Psychology, 24,* 427–433.

Palgi, M., Blasi, J. R., Rosner, M., & Safir, M. (Eds.). (1983). *Sexual equality: The Israeli kibbutz tests the theories.* Norwood, PA: Norwood.

Phillips, D. A., & Howes, C. (1987). Indicators of quality in child care: Review of research. In D. A. Phillips (Ed.), *Quality in child care: What does research tell us?* (pp. 1–20). Washington, DC: National Association for the Education of Young Children.

Piaget, J. (1959). *The language and thought of the child.* London: Routledge & Kegan.

Rabin, A. I. (1958). Infants and children under conditions of "intermittent" mothering in the kibbutz. *American Journal of Orthopsychiatry, 28,* 576–586.

Rabin, A. I. (1965). *Growing up in the kibbutz.* New York: Springer.

Rabin, A. I., & Beit-Hallahmi, B. (1982). *Twenty years later.* New York: Springer.

Rapaport, D. (1958). The study of kibbutz education and its bearing on the theory of development. *American Journal of Orthopsychiatry, 28,* 587–597.

Regev, E., Beit-Hallahmi, B., & Sharabany, R. (1980). Affective expression in kibbutz-communal, kibbutz-familial, and city-raised children in Israel. *Child Development, 51,* 223–237.

Richman, C. L. (1990, May). *Factors related to the prosocial development of kibbutz children.* Paper presented at the meeting of the American Psychological Society, Dallas, TX.

Rosenthal, M. (1991). Daily experiences of toddlers in three child care settings in Israel. *Child and Youth Care Forum, 20,* 37–58.

Ross, H. S., Conant, C., Cheyne, J. A., & Alevizos, E. (1992). Relationships and alliances in the social interaction of kibbutz toddler. *Social Development, 1,* 1–16.

Sacks, J. M., & Levy, S. (1950). The sentence completion test. In L. E. Abt & L. Bellak (Eds.), *Projective psychology* (pp. 357–402). New York: Knopf.

Sadeh, A., Lavie, P., Scher, A., Tirosh, E., & Epstein, R. (1991). Actigraphic home monitoring of sleep-disturbed and control infants and young children: A new method for pediatric assessment of sleep-wake patterns. *Pediatrics, 87,* 494–499.

Sagi, A. (1990). Attachment theory and research from a cross-cultural perspective. *Human Development, 33,* 10–22.

Sagi, A., Aviezer, O., Joels, T., Koren-Karie, N., Mayseless, O., Sharf, M., & Van IJzendoorn, M. H. (1992, July). *The correspondence of mother's adult attachment with infant-mother attachment relationship in traditional and non-traditional kibbutzim.* Paper presented at the XXV International Congress of Psychology, Brussels, Belgium.

Sagi, A., Koren, N., & Weinberg, M. (1987). Fathers in Israel. In M. E. Lamb (Ed.), *The father's role: Cross-cultural perspectives* (pp. 197–226). Hillsdale, NJ: Erlbaum.

Sagi, A., & Koren-Karie, N. (1993). Day-care centers in Israel: An overview. In M. Cochran (Ed.), *International handbook of day-care policies and programs* (pp. 269–290). New York: Greenwood.

Sagi, A., Lamb, M. E., Lewkowicz, K., Shoham, R., Dvir, R., & Estes, D. (1985). Security of infant-mother, -father, and -metapelet attachments among kibbutz-reared Israeli children. *Monographs of the Society for Research in Child Development, 50*(1–2, Serial No. 209).

Sagi, A., Lamb, M. E., Shoham, R., Dvir, R., & Lewkowicz, J. (1985). Parent-infant interaction in families on Israeli kibbutzim. *International Journal of Behavioral Development, 8,* 273–284.

Sagi, A., & Van IJzendoorn, M. H. (in press). Multiple caregiving environments: The kibbutz experience. In S. Harel & J. P. Shonkoff (Eds.), *Early childhood intervention and family support programs: Accomplishments and challenges*. Baltimore: Paul H. Brooks.

Sagi, A., Van IJzendoorn, M. H., Aviezer, O., Donnell, F., & Mayseless, O. (1994). Sleeping out of home in a kibbutz communal arrangement: It makes a difference for infant-mother attachment. *Child Development, 65,* 991–1004.

Sagi, A., Van IJzendoorn, M. H., & Koren-Karie, N. (1991). Primary appraisal of the strange situation: A cross-cultural analysis of the pre-separation episodes. *Developmental Psychology, 27,* 587–596.

Selier, F. J. M. (1977). *Kibboetz, gezin en gelijkheidsideaal* [Kibbutz, family and the ideal of equality]. Assen, The Netherlands: Van Gorcum.

Shamai, S. (1992). *Patterns of paternal involvement in the kibbutz: The role of fathers in intact families in the education of their preadolescent children.* Unpublished master's thesis, Haifa University, Haifa, Israel.

Shepher, J. (1971). Mate selection among second generation kibbutz adolescents and adults: Incest avoidance and negative imprinting. *Archives of Sexual Behavior, 1,* 293–307.

Spiro, M. E. (1958). *Children of the kibbutz.* Cambridge, MA: Harvard University Press.

Spiro, M. E. (1979). *Gender and culture: Kibbutz women revisited.* Durham, NC: Duke University Press.

Spitz, R. A. (1946). Hospitalism: A follow-up report. In *The psychoanalytic study of the child* (Vol. 2, pp. 113–117). Madison, CT: International Universities Press.

Spitz, R. A. (1965). *The first year of life: A psychoanalytic study of deviant object relations.* Madison, CT: International Universities Press.

Sroufe, L. A. (1985). Attachment classification from the perspective of infant-caregiver relationships and infant temperament. *Child Development, 56,* 1–14.

Sroufe, L. A., & Fleeson, J. (1986). Attachment and the construction of relationships. In W. Hartup & Z. Rubin (Eds.), *Relationships and development* (pp. 51–71). Hillsdale, NJ: Erlbaum.

Steele, M., Steele, H., & Fonagy, P. (1993, August). *Associations among attachment classifications of mothers, fathers, and their infants: Evidence for a relationship-specific perspective.* Paper presented at the 4th European Conference on Developmental Psychology, Bonn.

Tavecchio, L. W. C., & Van IJzendoorn, M. H. (Eds.). (1987). *Attachment in social networks.* Amsterdam: Elsevier.

Tiger, L., & Shepher, J. (1975). *Women in the kibbutz.* San Diego: Harcourt Brace Jovanovich.

Tronick, E. Z., Winn, S., & Morelli, G. A. (1985). Multiple caretaking in the context of human evolution: Why don't the Efe know the Western prescription for child care In M. Reite & T. Field (Eds.), *The psychology of attachment and separation* (pp. 293–322). San Diego: Academic.

Van IJzendoorn, M. H. (1990). Developments in cross-cultural research on attachment: Some methodological notes. *Human Development, 33,* 3–9.

Van IJzendoorn, M. H., & Bakermans-Kranenburg, M. J. (1996). Attachment representations in mothers, fathers, and clinical groups: A meta-analytic search for normative data. *Journal of Consulting and Clinical Psychology, 64,* 8–21.

Van IJzendoorn, M. H., Goldberg, S., Kroonenberg, P. M., & Frenkel, O. J. (1992). The relative effects of maternal and child problems on the quality of attachment: A meta-analysis of attachment in clinical samples. *Child Development, 63,* 840–858.

Van IJzendoorn, M. H., & Kroonenberg, P. M. (1988). Cross-cultural patterns of attachment: A meta-analysis of the strange situation. *Child Development, 59,* 147–159.

Van IJzendoorn, M. H., Sagi, A., & Lambermon, M. W. (1992). The multiple caretaker paradox: Some data from Holland and Israel. *New Directions in Child Development, 57,* 5–24.

Weigl, I., & Weber, C. (1991). Day care for young children in the German Democratic Republic. In E. C. Melhuish & P. Moss (Eds.), *Day care for young children: International perspectives* (pp. 46–55). London: Tavistock.

Weinbaum, E. (1990, August). *Family and kibbutz child-rearing effects on emotional moderation.* Paper presented at the 98th Annual Convention of the American Psychological Association, Boston.

Whitebook, M., Howes, C., & Phillips, D. (1989). *Who cares? Child care teachers and the quality of care in America: The national child care staffing study.* Oakland, CA: Child Care Employee Project.

Winograd, M. (1958). The development of the young child in a collective settlement. *American Journal of Orthopsychiatry, 28,* 557–562.

Zaslow, M. (1980). Relationships among peers in kibbutz toddler groups. *Child Psychiatry and Human Development, 10,* 178–189.

Zellermayer, J., & Marcus, J. (1971). Kibbutz adolescents: Relevance to personality development theory. *Journal of Youth and Adolescence, 1,* 143–153.

## 10. Quality of Child Care as an Aspect of Family and Child-Care Policy in the United States

Abbott-Shim, M., & Sibley, A. (1987). *Assessment Profile for Childhood Programs.* Atlanta: Quality Assist Inc.

Bernardo, D. H., Shehan, C. L., & Leslie G. R. (1987). A residue of tradition: Jobs, careers, and spouse time in housework. *Marriage and Family, 49,* 381–390.

Harms, T., & Clifford, R. (1980). *Early Childhood Environmental Rating Scale.* New York: Teachers' College, Columbia University.

Harms, T., Cryer, D., & Clifford, R. (1987). *The Infant and Toddler Environmental Rating Scale.* New York: Teachers' College Press.

Hewlett, S. A. (1986). *A Lesser Life.* New York, NY: Morrow.

Kamerman, S. B. (1989). Child care, women, work, and the family: An international overview of child care services and related policies. In J. Lande & S. Scarr (Eds.), *Caring for Children: Challenge to America.* (Vol. 98). Hillsdale, NJ: Erlbaum.

Maynard, R., & McGinnis, E. (1993). Policies to meet the need for high quality child care. In A. Booth (Ed.), *Child Care for the '90s* (pp. 189–208). Hillsdale, NJ: Erlbaum.

Wessel, D. (1991, June 11). Paved with good intentions, tax writers' road to help the working poor turns into a maze. *Wall Street Journal,* p. A16.

## 11. Child Care Policy in Australia

Australian Bureau of Statistics (1994). *Child Care Australia.* Canberra.

Economic Planning and Advisory Commission (1995). *Interim report of the Child Care Task Force.* Canberra.

Economic Planning and Advisory Commission (1996). *Future childcare provision in Australia* (Report of the Child Care Task Force). Canberra.

National Childcare Accreditation Council (1993). *Putting children first: Quality Improvement and Accreditation System Handbook* (1st ed.). Sydney.

Helburn, S. W. (Ed.) (1995). *Cost, quality and outcomes in child care centers.* Denver: University of Colorado.

Phillips, D. A., Howes, C., & Whitebook, M. (1992). The social policy context of child care: Effects on quality. *American Journal of Community Psychology, 20,* 25–51.

National Association for the Education of Young Children (1991). *Accreditation criteria and procedures of the National Academy of Early Childhood Programs* (rev. ed.). Washington, DC.

## 12. Children's Eating

Baumrind, D. (1973). The development of instrumental competence through socialization. In A. D. Pick (Ed.), *Minnesota symposium on child psychology* (Vol. 7). University of Minnesota Press.

Birch, L. L. (1979). Dimensions of preschool children's food preference. *Journal of Nutritional Education, 11*(2), 77–80.

Birch, L. L. (1980). Effects of peer models' food choices and eating behaviors on preschoolers' food preferences. *Child Development, 51,* 489–496.

Birch, L. L. (1993). Children's eating: Are manners enough? *The Journal of Gastronomy, 7*(1), 18–25.

Birch, L. L., & Deysher, M. (1985). Conditioned and unconditioned caloric compensation: Evidence for self-regulation of food intake by young children. *Learning and Motivation, 16,* 341–355.

Birch, L. L., & Deysher, M. (1986). Caloric compensation and sensory specific satiety: Evidence for self regulation of food intake by young children. *Appetite, 7,* 323–331.

Birch, L. L., & Marlin, D. W. (1982). "I don't like it; I never tried it": Effects of exposure to food on two-year-old children's food preferences. *Appetite, 4,* 353–360.

Birch, L. L., Marlin, D. W., & Rotter, J. (1984). Eating as the "means" activity in a contingency: Effects on young children's food preference. *Child Development, 55,* 432–439.

Birch, L. L., Johnson, S. L., Jones, M. B., & Peters, J. C. (1993). Effects of a non-energy fat substitute on children's energy and macronutrient intake. *American Journal of Clinical Nutrition, 5,* 326–333.

Birch, L. L., Johnson, S. L., Andresen, G., Peters, J. C., & Schulte, M. C. (1991). The variability of young children's energy intake. *New England Journal of Medicine, 324,* 232–235.

Birch, L. L., McPhee, L., Shoba, B. C., Pirok, E. & Steinberg, L. (1987). What kind of exposure reduces children's food neophobia? *Appetite, 9,* 171–178.

Birch, L. L., McPhee, L., Shoba, B. C., Steinberg, L., & Krehbiel, R. (1987). "Clean up your plate": Effects of child feeding practices on the conditioning of meal size. *Learning and Motivation, 18,* 301–317.

Birch, L. L., McPhee, L., Steinberg, L., & Sullivan, S. (1990). Conditional flavor preferences in young children. *Physiology & Behavior, 47,* 501–505.

Birch, L. L., Zimmerman, S., & Hind, H. (1980). The influence of social-affective context on preschool children's food preferences. *Child Development, 51,* 856–861.

Chiva, M. (1983). Gout et communication nonverbale chez le jeune enfant. *Enfance, 1–2,* 53–64.

Costanzo, P. R., & Woody, E. Z. (1985). Domain-specific parenting styles and their impact on the child's development of particular deviance: The example of obesity proneness. *Journal of Social and Clinical Psychology, 4,* 425–445.

Cowart, B. (1981). Development of taste perception in humans: Sensitivity and preferences throughout the life span. *Psychological Bulletin, 90*(1), 43–73.

Cowart, B., & Beauchamp, G. (1986). The importance of sensory context in young children's acceptance of salty tastes. *Child Development, 57,* 1034–1039.

Davis, C. M. (1928). Self-selection of diet by newly weaned infants: An experimental study. *American Journal of Diseases of Children, 36,* 651–679.

Dietz, W. (1991). Factors associated with childhood obesity. *Nutrition, 7,* 290–291.

Fallon, A. E., Rozin, P., & Pliner, P. (1984). The child's conception of food: The development of food rejections with special reference to disgust and contamination sensitivity. *Child Development, 55,* 566–575.

Fomon, S. J. (1974). Voluntary food intake and its regulation. In W. B. Saunders *Infant nutrition* (2nd ed.) Philadelphia.

Johnson, S. L., & Birch, L. L. (1993). Parenting style and the regulation of food intake in children. *Abstracts of the Biennial Meeting for the Society for Research in Children Development* (Vol. 9). Chicago: University of Chicago Press.

Johnson, S. L., McPhee, L., & Birch, L. L. (1991). Conditioned preferences: Young children prefer flavors associated with high dietary fat. *Physiology & Behavior, 50,* 1245–1251.

Kalat, J. W., & Rozin, P. (1973). "Learned safety" as a mechanism in long-delay taste-aversion learning in rats. *Journal of Comparative and Physiological Psychology, 83*(2), 198–207.

Kern, D. L., McPhee, L., Fisher, J., Johnson, S., & Birch, L. L. (1993). The post-ingestive consequences of fat condition preferences for flavors associated with high dietary fat. *Physiology and Behavior, 54,* 71–76.

Pliner, P., Pelchat, M., & Grobinski, M. (1993). Neophobia in humans by exposure to novel foods. *Appetite, 20,* 111–123.

Satter, E. (1986). *Child of mine, feeding with love and good sense* (Exp. ed.) Palo Alto, CA: Bull.

Satter, E. (1987). *How to get your kid to eat—but not too much.* Palo Alto, CA: Bull.

Shea, S., Stein, A. D., Basch, C. E., Contento, I. R., & Zybert, P. (1992). Variability and self-regulation of energy intake in young children in their everyday environment. *Pediatrics, 90*(4), 542–546.

Sullivan, S., & Birch, L. L. (1990). Pass the sugar, pass the salt: Experience dictates preference. *Developmental Psychology, 26,* 546–551.

Sullivan, S., & Birch, L. L. (1994). Infant dietary experience and acceptance of solid foods. *Pediatrics, 93*(2), 271–77.

## 13. Young Children's Understanding of the Mind

Barlow, H., Blakemore, C., & Weston-Smith, M. (Eds). (1990). *Images and understanding.* Cambridge: Cambridge University Press.

Bartsch, K., & Wellman, H. M. (1995). *Children talk about the mind.* Oxford: Oxford University Press.

Boring, E. G. (1952). *A history of psychology in autobiography.* Worcester, MA: Clark University Press.

Bredekamp, S. (1987). *Developmentally appropriate practice.* Washington, DC: National Association for the Education of Young Children.

Bronowski, J. (1978). Development of concepts of self, mind, reality, and knowledge. In W. Damon (Ed.), *New directions for child development* (pp. 77–100). San Francisco: Jossey-Bass.

Brown, A. L., Bransford, J. D., Ferrara, R. A., & Campione, J. C. (1983). Learning, remembering, and understanding. In P. Mussen, J. Flavell, & E. Markman (Eds.), *Handbook of child psychology: Vol. 3. Cognitive development* (pp. 77–166). New York: Wiley.

Bruner, J. S. (1983). Play, thought, and language. *Peabody Journal of Education, 60,* 60–69.

Campione, J. C. (1987). Metacognitive components of instructional research with problem learners. In F. E. Weinert & R. H. Kluwe (Eds.), *Metacognition, motivation, and understanding* (pp. 117–140). Hillsdale, NJ: Erlbaum.

Cavanaugh, J. C., & Perlmutter, M. (1982). Metamemory: A critical examination. *Child Development, 53,* 11–28.

Chandler, M., Fritz, A. S., & Hala, S. (1989). Small scale deceit: Deception as a marker of 2-, 3-, and 4-year-olds' early theories of mind. *Child Development, 60,* 1263–1277.

Churchland, P. M. (1979). *Scientific realism and the plasticity of mind.* Cambridge: Cambridge University Press.

Copple, C., Sigel, I. E., & Saunders, R. (1984). *Educating the young thinker. Classroom strategies for cognitive growth.* Hillsdale, NJ: Erlbaum.

Cox, M. V. (1991). *The child's point of view.* London: Guilford.

Estes, D. E., Wellman, H. W., & Woolley, J. D. (1989). Children's understanding of mental phenomena. In H. W. Reese (Ed.), *Advances in child development and behavior.* New York: Academic.

Fein, G. G. (1982). Pretend play: New perspectives. In J. F. Brown (Ed.), *Curriculum planning for young children* (pp. 61–66). Washington, DC: National Association for the Education of Young Children.

Feynman, R. (1988). *"What do you care what other people think?"* New York: Bantam.

Flavell, J. H. (1963). *The developmental psychology of Jean Piaget.* New York: Van Nostrand.

Flavell, J. H. (1979). Metacognition and cognitive monitoring: A new area of cognitive-developmental inquiry. *American Psychologist, 34,* 906–911.

Flavell, J. H. (1992). Cognitive development: Past, present, and future. *Developmental Psychology, 28,* 998–1005.

Flavell, J. H., Green, F. L., & Flavell, E. R. (1993). Children's understanding of the stream of consciousness. *Child Development, 64,* 387–398.

Flavell, J. H., Miller, P. H., & Miller, S. A. (1993). *Cognitive development* (3rd ed.). Englewood Cliffs, NJ: Prentice-Hall.

Gelman, R., & Baillargeon, R. (1983). A review of some Piagetian concepts. In P. Mussen, J. H. Flavell, & E. Markman (Eds.), *Handbook of child psychology: Vol. 3. Cognitive development* (pp. 167–230). New York: Wiley.

Greeson, L. E., & Zigarmi, D. (1985). Piaget, learning theory, and mental imagery: Toward a curriculum of visual thinking. *Journal of Humanistic Education and Development, 24,* 40–49.

Hadamard, J. (1945). *The psychology of invention in the mathematical field.* Princeton, NJ: Princeton University Press.

Hillerman, T., & Bulow, E. (1991). *Talking mysteries: A conversation with Tony Hillerman.* Albuquerque: University of New Mexico Press.

Jacobs, J. E., & Paris, S. G. (1987). Children's metacognition about reading: Issues in definition, measurement, and instruction. *Educational Psychologist, 22,* 255–278.

Keil, F. C. (1979). *Semantic and conceptual development.* Cambridge, MA: Harvard University Press.

Kuhn, D. (1992). Cognitive development. In M. H. Bornstein & M. E. Lamb (Eds.), *Developmental psychology: An advanced textbook* (3rd ed., pp. 211–272). Hillsdale, NJ: Erlbaum.

Marmor, G. S. (1975). Development of kinetic images: When does the child first represent movement in mental images. *Cognitive Psychology, 7,* 548–559.

Miller, A. I. (1984). *Imagery in scientific thought.* Boston: Birkhauser.

Perner, J. (1991). *Understanding the representational mind.* Cambridge, MA: MIT Press.

Piaget, J. (1928). *Judgment and reasoning in the child.* London: Routledge & Kegan Paul.

Piaget, J. (1929). *The child's conception of the world.* London: Routledge & Kegan Paul.

Piaget, J. & Inhelder, B. (1971). *Mental imagery in the child.* London: Routledge & Kegan Paul.

Platt, J. E., & Cohen, S. (1981). Mental rotation task performance as a function of age and training. *The Journal of Psychology, 108,* 173–178.

Shepard, R. N. (1988). The imagination of the scientist. In K. Egan & D. Nadaner (Eds.), *Imagination and education* (pp. 153–185). New York: Teachers College Press.

Shepard, R. N., & Cooper, L. (1982). *Mental images and their transformations.* Cambridge, MA: MIT Press.

Sigel, I. E. (1990). Journeys in serendipity. In I. E. Sigel & G. H. Brody (Eds.), *Methods of family research: Vol 1, Normal families* (pp. 87–120). Hillsdale, NJ: Erlbaum.

Speidel, G. E., & Troy, M. E. (1985). The ebb and flow of mental imagery in education. In A. A. Sheikh & K. S. Sheikh (Eds.), *Imagery in education* (pp. 11–38). Farmingdale, NY: Baywood.

Stich, S. (1983). *From folk psychology to cognitive science.* Cambridge, MA: MIT Press.

Weinert, F. E., & Kluwe, R. H. (1987). *Metacognition, motivation, and understanding.* Hillsdale, NJ: Erlbaum.

Wellman, H. M. (1985). The origins of metacognition. In D. L. Forrest-Pressley, G. E. MacKinnon, & T. G. Waller (Eds.), *Metacognition, cognition, and human performance: Vol. 1. Theoretical perspectives* (pp. 1–31). New York: Academic.

Wellman, H. M. (1990). *The child's theory of mind.* Cambridge, MA: MIT Press.

Wellman, H. M., & Estes, D. (1986). Early understanding of mental entities: A reexamination of childhood realism. *Child Development, 57,* 910–923.

## 14. Vygotsky's Theory: The Importance of Make-Believe Play

Berk, L. E. (1992). Children's private speech: An overview of theory and the status of research. In R. M. Diaz, & L. E. Berk (Eds.), *Private speech: From social interaction to self-regulation* (pp. 17–53). Hillsdale, NJ: Erlbaum.

Berk, L. E. (1993) *Infants, children, and adolescents.* Boston: Allyn & Bacon.

Bretherton, I., O'Connell, B., Shore, C., & Bates, E. (1984). The effect of contextual variation on symbolic play: Development from 20 to 28 months. In I. Bretherton (Ed.), *Symbolic play and the development of social understanding* (pp. 271–298). New York: Academic.

Burns, S. M., & Brainerd, C. J. (1979). Effects of constructive and dramatic play on perspective taking in very young children. *Developmental Psychology, 15,* 512–521.

Connolly, J. A., & Doyle, A. B. (1984). Relations of social fantasy play to social competence in preschoolers. *Developmental Psychology, 20,* 797–806.

Connolly, J. A., Doyle, A. B., & Reznick, E. (1988). Social pretend play and social interaction in preschoolers. *Journal of Applied Developmental Psychology, 9,* 301–313.

Corrigan, R. (1987). A developmental sequence of actor-object pretend play in young children. *Merrill-Palmer Quarterly, 33,* 87–106.

Dansky, J. L. (1980). Make-believe: A mediator of the relationship between play and associative fluency. *Child Development, 51,* 576–579.

Dias, M. G., & Harris, P. L. (1988). The effect of make-believe play on deductive reasoning. *British Journal of Developmental Psychology, 6,* 207–221.

Dias, M. G., & Harris, P. L. (1990). The influence of the imagination of reasoning by young children. *British Journal of Developmental Psychology, 8,* 305–318.

Dunn, J., & Dale, N. (1984). I a daddy: 2-year-olds' collaboration in joint pretend with sibling and with mother. In I. Bretherton (Ed.), *Symbolic play* (pp. 131–158). New York. Academic.

Dunn, J., & Wooding, C. (1977). Play in the home and its implications for learning. In B. Tizard & D. Harvey (Eds.), *Biology of play* (pp. 45–58). London: Heinemann.

El'konin, D. (1966). Symbolics and its functions in the play of children. *Soviet Education, 8,* 35–41.

Ervin-Tripp, S. (1991). Play in language development. In B. Scales, M. Almy, A. Nicolopoulou, & S. Ervin-Tripp (Eds.), *Play and the social context of development in early care and education* (pp. 84–97). New York: Teachers College Press.

Farver, J. M. (1993). Cultural differences in scaffolding pretend play: A comparison of American and Mexican mother-child and sibling-child pairs. In K. MacDonald (Ed.), *Parent-child play* (pp. 349–66). Albany: State University of New York Press.

Fein, G. (1981). Pretend play: An integrative review. *Child Development, 52,* 1095–1118.

Fiese, B. (1990). Playful relationships: A contextual analysis of mother-toddler interaction and symbolic play. *Child Development, 61,* 1648–1656.

File, N. (1993). The teacher as guide of children's competence with peers. *Child & Youth Care Forum, 22,* 351–360.

Forman, E. A. (1987). Learning through peer interaction: A Vygotskian perspective. *Genetic Epistemologist, 15,* 6–15.

Forman, E. A., Minick, N. & Stone, C. A. (1993). *Contexts for learning*. New York: Oxford University Press.

Garvey, C. (1990). *Play*. Cambridge, MA: Harvard University Press.

Göncü, A. (1993). Development of intersubjectivity in the dyadic play of preschoolers. *Early Childhood Research Quarterly, 8*, 99–116.

Gralinski, J. H., & Kopp, C. B. (1993). Everyday rules for behavior: Mothers' requests to young children. *Developmental Psychology, 29*, 573–584.

Haight, W. L., & Miller, P. J. (1993). *Pretending at home: Early development in a sociocultural context*. Albany: State University of New York Press.

Kavanaugh, R. D., Whittington, S., & Cerbone, M. J. (1983). Mothers' use of fantasy in speech to young children. *Journal of Child Language, 10*, 45–55.

Lucariello, J. (1987). Spinning fantasy: Themes, structure, and the knowledge base. *Child Development, 58*, 434–442.

Miller, P., & Garvey, C. (1984). Mother-baby role play: Its origins in social support. In I. Bretherton (Ed.), *Symbolic play* (pp. 101–130). New York: Academic.

Moll, L. C. (1990). *Vygotsky and education*. New York: Cambridge University Press.

Newman, L. S. (1990). Intentional versus unintentional memory in young children: Remembering versus playing. *Journal of Experimental Child Psychology, 50*, 243–258.

Nicolopoulou, A. (1991). Play, cognitive development, and the social world. In B. Scales, M. Almy, A. Nicolopoulou, & S. Ervin-Tripp (Eds.), *Play and the social context of development in early care and education* (pp. 129–42). New York: Teachers College Press.

O'Connell, B., & Bretherton, I. (1984). Toddler's play alone and with mother: The role of maternal guidance. In I. Bretherton (Ed.), *Symbolic play* (pp. 337–368). New York: Academic.

O'Reilly, A. W., & Bornstein, M. H. (1993). Caregiver-child interaction in play. In M. H. Bornstein, & A. W. O'Reilly (Eds.), *New directions for child development* (pp. 55–66). San Francisco: Jossey Bass.

Parten, M. (1932). Social participation among preschool children. *Journal of Abnormal and Social Psychology, 27*, 243–269.

Pellegrini, A. D., & Galda, L. (1982). The effects of thematic-fantasy play training on the development of children's story comprehension. *American Educational Research Journal, 19*, 443–452.

Pepler, D. J., & Ross, H. S. (1981). The effect of play on convergent and divergent problem solving. *Child Development, 52*, 1202–1210.

Piaget, J. (1951). *Play, dreams, and imitation in childhood*. New York: Norton. (Original work published 1945.)

Rafferty, T. (1988, August 8). The current cinema: All sizes. *New Yorker*, p. 77.

Saltz, E., Dixon, D., & Johnson, J. (1977). Training disadvantaged preschoolers on various fantasy activities: Effects on cognitive functioning and impulse control. *Child Development, 46*, 367–380.

Slade, A. (1987). A longitudinal study of maternal involvement and symbolic play during the toddler period. *Child Development, 58*, 367–375.

Smolucha, F. (1992). Social origins of private speech in pretend play. In R. M. Diaz, & L. E. Berk (Eds.), *Private speech: From social interaction to self-regulation* (pp. 123–141). Hillsdale, NJ: Erlbaum.

Tamis-LeMonda, C. S., & Bornstein, M. H. (1991). Individual variation, correspondence, stability, and change in mother and toddler play. *Infant Behavior and Development, 14*, 143–162.

Tudge, J. R. H. (1992). Processes and consequences of peer collaboration: A Vygotskian analysis. *Child Development, 63*, 1364–1379.

Tudge, J. R. H., & Rogoff, B. (1987). Peer influences on cognitive development: Piagetian and Vygotskian perspectives. In M. H. Bornstein, & J. S. Bruner (Eds.), *Interaction in human development* (pp. 17–40). Hillsdale, NJ: Erlbaum.

Vygotsky, L. S. (1978). The role of play in development. In M. Cole, V. John-Steiner, S. Scribner, & E. Souberman (Eds.), *Mind in society* (pp. 92–104). Cambridge, MA: Harvard University Press. (Original work published 1933.)

Vygotsky, L. S. (1987). Thinking and speech. In R. Rieber & A. S. Carton (Eds.), N. Minick (trans.), *The collected works of L. S. Vygotsky: Vol. 1. Problems of general psychology* (pp. 37–285). New York: Plenum. (Originally published 1in 934.)

Vygotsky, L. S. (1990). Imagination and creativity in childhood. *Soviet Psychology, 28*, 84–96. (Originally published in 1930.)

Wertsch, J. W. (1991). A sociocultural approach to socially shared cognition. In L. B. Resnick, J. M. Levine, & S. D. Teasley (Eds.), *Perspectives on socially shared cognition* (pp. 85–100). Washington, D. C: American Psychological Association.

Wood, D. J. (1989). Social interaction as tutoring. In M. H. Bornstein, & J. S. Bruner (Eds.), *Interaction in human development* (pp. 59–80). Hillsdale, NJ: Erlbaum.

Wood, D. J., & Middleton, D. (1975). A study of assisted problem solving. *British Journal of Psychology, 66,* 181–191.

Zukow, P. G. (1986). The relationship between interaction with the caregiver and the emergence of play activities during the one-word period. *British Journal of Developmental Psychology, 4,* 223–234.

## 15. Art as Development

Allen, P. (1982). *Who sank the boat?* Melbourne, Australia: Nelson.

Arnheim, R. (1974). *Art and visual perception: A psychology of the creative eye.* Berkeley: University of California Press.

Australian Education council (1994). *The arts—A curriculum profile for Australian schools.* Carlton, Victoria: Curriculum Corporation.

Baker, J. (1991). *Window.* London: Julia MacRae.

Bishop, M. (1989). *Young artist: Visual arts activities for young artists at home and at school.* Sydney: Piper.

Blyton, E. (1950). *Five Fall into Adventure.* Illus. Eileen A. Soper. London: Hodder-Stoughton.

Bredekamp, S. (Ed.). (1987). *Developmentally appropriate practice in early childhood programs serving children from birth through to age 8 (expanded edition).* Washington, DC: National Association for the Education of Young Children.

Bresler, L. (1992). Visual art in primary grades: A portrait and analysis. *Early Childhood Research Quarterly, 7,* 397–414.

Burningham, J. (1970). *Mr. Gumpy's Outing.* London: Jonathon Cape.

Davis, J. & Gardner, H. (1992). The cognitive revolution: Consequences for the understanding of the child as artist. In B. Reimer, & R. Smith (Eds.), *The arts education and aesthetic knowing (91st Yearbook of the National Society for the Study of Education)* (pp. 92–123). Chicago: University of Chicago Press.

Davis, J., & Gardner, H. (1993). The arts and early childhood education: A cognitive developmental portrait of the young child as artist. In B. Spodek (Ed.), *Handbook of research on the education of young children* (pp. 191–206). New York: Macmillan.

Dyson, A. H. (1990, January). Symbol makers, symbol weavers: How children play, pictures in print. *Young Children, 45*(2), 50–57.

Edwards, C., Gandini, L., & Forman, G. (Eds.). (1994). *The hundred languages of children: The Reggio Emilia approach to early childhood education.* New Jersey: Ablex.

Eisner, E. W. (1992, November). The misunderstood role of the arts in human development. *Phi Delta Kappan,* pp. 54–58.

Gallas, K. (1995). Arts as epistemology: Enabling children to know what they know. In M. R. Goldberg & A. Phillips (Eds.), *Arts as education* (pp. 19–31). Cambridge, MA: Harvard University Press.

Goldberg, M. R. & Phillips, A. (Eds.). (1995). *Arts as education.* Cambridge, MA: Harvard University Press.

Goodman, N. (1976). *The languages of art.* Indianapolis: Hackett.

Greene, M. (1978). *Landscapes of learning.* New York: Teachers College Press.

Greene, M. (1995). Texts and margins. In M. R. Goldberg & A. Phillips (Eds.), *Arts as education* (pp. 19–31). Cambridge, MA: Harvard University Press.

Hardiman, G. W., & Zernich, T. (1981). *Art activities for children.* Englewood Cliffs, NJ: Prentice Hall.

The Jewish Museum of Prague (1993). *I have not seen a butterfly around here.* (Children's drawings and poems from Terezin) Prague: Jewish Museum.

Keats, E. J. (1964). *Whistle for Willie.* London: Bodley Head.

Kolbe, U. (1996a). Co-player and co-artist: New roles for the adult in children's visual arts experiences. In W. Schiller (Ed.), *Issues in Expressive Arts Curriculum for Early Childhood: An Australian Perspective* (pp. 73–82). Amsterdam: Gordon and Breach.

Kolbe, U. (1996b). *Mia Mia: A new vision for day care (Parts 1 and 2).* North Ryde, Australia: Macquarie University.

Lowenfeld, V. & Brittain, L. (1964). *Creative and mental growth.* New York: Macmillan.

New, R. S. (1990, September). Excellent early education: A city in Italy has it. *Young Children, 45*(1), 4–10.

Piscitelli, B. (1991). Children in Museums. In S. Wright (Ed.), *The arts in early childhood* (pp. 195–216). Sydney: Prentice Hall.

Rabitti, G. (1991). *Preschool at La Viletta: Reggio Emilia.* Unpublished thesis, University of Illinois, Urbana-Champaign.

Readdick, C. A. (1995). Young children's symbol making, tools and factors influencing their availability and use: An international survey. *International Journal of Early Years Education, 3*(1), 93–100.

Schiller, W., & Veale, A. (1996). The arts: The real business of education. In W. Schiller (Ed.), *Issues in expressive arts, curriculum for early childhood: An Australian perspective* (pp. 5–13). Amsterdam: Gordon and Breach.

Silberstein-Storfer, M. & Jones, M. (1981). *Doing art together.* New York: Simon & Schuster.

United Nations General Assembly. (1989, November). *The Convention on the Rights of the Child.* New York.

Vygotsky, L. (1987). *Thought and language.* (A. Kozulin, Trans.). Cambridge, MA: MIT Press.

Wright, S. (Ed.). (1991). *The arts in early childhood.* Sydney: Prentice Hall.

## 16. Young Children's Responsiveness to Music

Campbell, M. (1991). Musical learning and the development of psychological processes in perception and cognition. *Bulletin of the Council for Research in Music Education, 107,* 35–48.

Costa-Giomi, E. (1994) Recognition of chord changes by 4- and 5-year-old American and Argentinian children. *Journal of Research in Music Education, 42* (1), 68–85.

Australian Education Council (1994) *The arts—a curriculum profile for Australian schools.* Carlton, Victoria: Curriculum Corporation.

Finnas, L. (1989) How can musical preferences be modified? A research review. *Bulletin of the Council for Research in Music Education, 102,* 1–58.

Flowers, P. & Costa-Giomi, E. (1991). Verbal and non-verbal identification of pitch change in a familiar song by English and Spanish speaking preschool children. *Bulletin of the Council for Research in Music Education, 107,* 1–12.

Giomo, C. (1993). An experimental study of children's sensitivity to mood in music. *Psychology of Music, 21,* 141–162.

Heller, J. & Campbell, W. (1981) A theoretical model of music perception and talent. *Bulletin of the Council for Research in Music Education, 66–67,* 20–24.

Kratus, J. (1993). A developmental study of children's interpretation of emotion in music. *Psychology of music, 21,* 3–19.

Krumhansl, C. L., & Jsczyk, P. W. (1990). Infants' perception of phrase structure in music. *Psycholotical Science, 1,* 70–73.

Le Blanc, A. (1987). The development of music preferences in children. In J. C. Peery, I. W. Peery, & T. W. Draper (Eds.), *Music and child development* (pp. 137–157). New York: Springer-Verlag.

Le Blanc, A., Sims, W., Siivola, C., & Obert, M. (1996). Music style preferences of different age listeners. *Journal of Research in Music Education, 43*(3), 49–59.

McDowall, J. (1991) *An investigation of eight year old children's musical preferences and related contextual matters.* Unpublished research paper, Geelong: Deakin University.

Meerum Terwogt, M. & van Grinsven, F. (1991). Musical expression of mood states. *Psychology of music, 19,* 99–109.

Metz, E. (1989). Movement as a musical response among preschool children. *Journal of Research in Music Education 37*(1), 48–60.

Montgomery, A. (1996). Effect of tempo on music preferences of children in elementary and middle school. *Journal of Research in Music Education, 44,* 134–146.

Morrongiello, B. (1986). Infants' perception of multiple-group auditory patterns. *Infant Behavior and Development, 9,* 307–319.

Morrongiello, B. (1992). Effects of training on children's perceptions of music A review. *Psychology of music, 20,* 29–41.

Peery, J. C. & Peery, I. W. (1986). Effects of exposure to classical music on the musical preferences of preschool children. *Journal of Research in Music Education, 34*(1), 24–33.

Peery, J. C. & Peery, I. W. (1987) The role of music in child development. In J. C. Peery, I. W. Peery & T. W. Draper (Eds.), *Music and child development* (pp. 3–31). New York, Springer-Verlag.

Richardson, C. (1996). A theoretical model of the connoisseur's musical thought. *Bulletin of the Council for Research in Music Education, 128,* 15–24.

Richardson, C. & Whitaker, N. (1996). Thinking about think alouds in music education research. *Research Studies in Music Education, 6,* 38–49.

Shehan-Campbell, P. & Scott-Kassner, C. (1995*). Music in childhood. From preschool through the elementary grades.* New York: Schirmer.

Sims, W. (1991). Effects of instruction and task format on preschool children's music concept discrimination. *Journal of Research in Music Education, 39*(4), 298–310.

Sims, W. (1995). Children's ability to demonstrate music concept discriminations in listening and singing. *Journal of Research in Music Education, 43*(3), 204–221.

Suthers, L. (1995) Music, play and toddlers. *International play journal, 3,* 142–151.

Trehub, S., Bull, D. & Thorpe, L. (1984). Infants' perception of melodies: The role of melodic contour. *Child Development, 55,* 821–830.

Wright, S. (Ed.) (1991). *The arts in early childhood.* Sydney: Prentice Hall.

Zimmerman, M. (1993). An overview of developmental research in music. *Bulletin of the Council for Research in Music Education, 116,* 1–21.

## 17. Perspectives on Cooperative Learning

Asher, S., & Renshaw, P. (1981). Children without friends: Social knowledge and social skills training. In S. R. Asher & J. M. Gottman (Eds.), *The development of children's friendships* (pp. 273–296). New York: Cambridge University Press.

Baloche, L., & Platt, T. (1993). Sprouting magic beans; Exploring literature through creative questioning and cooperative learning. *Language Arts, 70*(4), 264–271.

Cannella, G. (1993). Learning through social interaction: Shared cognitive experiences, negotiation strategies and joint concept construction for young children. *Early Childhood Research Quarterly, 8,* 427–444.

Chambers, B., & Doyon, P. (1994). The effects of group size on preschoolers' learning. Unpublished paper presented at the *International Conference for Cooperative Education,* Queensland.

Cohen, E. (1990). Continuing to cooperate: Prerequisites for persistence, *Phi Delta Kappan, 72*(1) 134–139.

Cohen, E., & Lotan, R. (1995). Producing equal-status interaction in the heterogeneous classroom. *American Educational Research Journal, 32*(1), 99–120.

Cole, M. (1992). Cognitive development and formal schooling: The evidence from cross cultural research. In L. Moll (Ed.), *Vygotsky and Education* (pp. 89–110). New York: Cambridge University Press.

Comer, J., Haynes, N., Joyner, E., & Ben-Avie, M. (1996). *Rallying the whole village: The Comer process for reforming school.* New York: Teachers College Press.

Cowie, H., Smith, P., Boulton, M., & Laver, R. (1994). *Cooperation in the multi-ethnic classroom: The impact of cooperative group work on social relationships in middle schools.* London: David Fulton.

Dodge, K., Coie, J., Pettit, G., & Price, J. (1990). Peer status and aggression in boys' groups: Developmental and contextual analyses. *Developmental Psychology, 26,* 612–620.

Dunn, J., Slomkowski, C., Donelan, N., & Herrera, C. (1995). Conflict, understanding, and relationships: Development and difference in the preschool years. *Early Education and Development, 6*(4), 302–316.

Fullan, M. (1993). *Change Forces: Probing the depth of educational reform.* London: Falmer.

Gallimore, R., & Tharp, R. (1992). Teaching mind in society: Teaching, schooling, and literate discourse. In L. Moll (Ed.) *Vygotsky and Education* (pp. 175–205). New York: Cambridge University Press.

Galton, M., & Patrick, H. (Eds.). (1990). *Curriculum provisions in small primary schools.* London, Routledge.

Galton, M., Simon, B., & Croll, P. (1980). *Inside the primary classroom.* London: Routledge & Kegan Paul.

Galton, M., & Williamson, J. (1992). *Group work in the classroom.* London, Routledge.

Gillies, R., & Ashman, A. (1995). The effects of gender and ability on students' behaviours and interactions in classroom-based work groups. *British Journal of Educational Psychology, 65,* 211–225.

Goffin, S. (1987). Cooperative behaviours: They need our support. *Young Children, 42*(2), 75–81.

Graves, N., & Graves, T. (1990). *A part to play: Tips, techniques and tools for learning.* Melbourne, Australia: Latitude Media.

Greenberg, P. (1992). How to institute some simple democratic practices pertaining to respect, rights, roots and responsibilities in any classroom (without losing your leadership position). *Young Children, 47*(5), 10–17.

Hargreaves, A. (1994). *Changing teachers changing times; Teachers' work and culture in the post modern age.* London: Cassel.

Hill, S., & Hill, T. (1994). *The Collaborative classroom.* New Hampshire, Heinemann.

Hill, S. (1994). Cooperative communities in early childhood. *Australian Journal of Early Childhood Education, 19*(4), 44–48.

Hill, S., & Hancock, J. (1993). *Reading and writing communities.* Melbourne, Australia: Eleanor Curtain.

Hill, S. (1992). *Games that work: Co-operative games and activities for the primary classroom.* Melbourne, Australia: Eleanor Curtain.

Hill, T. (1989). Neglected and rejected children: Promoting social competence in early childhood settings. *Australian Journal of Early Childhood Education, 14* (1), 11–16.

Hill, T., Parker, K., & McKenna, A. (1986). Social acceptance: How it relates to children's freeplay behaviour in kindergarten settings. *Australian Journal of Early Childhood Education, 11*(2), 28–33.

Holloway S. (1992). A potential wolf in sheep's clothing: The ambiguity of "cooperation." *Journal of Education 174*(2), 80–99.

Iskandar, N., Laursen, B., Finkelstein B., & Frederickson, L. (1995). Conflict resolution among preschool children: The appeal of negotiation in hypothetical disputes. *Early Education and Development, 6*(4), 359–376.

Johnson, D., & Johnson, R. (1987). *Creative conflict.* Edina, MN: Interaction.

Johnson, D., & Johnson, R. (1989a). *Cooperation and competition: Theory and research.* Edina MN: Interaction Book Company.

Johnson, D., & Johnson, R. (1989b). Cooperative learning and mainstreaming. In R. Gaylord-Ross (Ed.), *Integration strategies for students with handicaps* (pp. 233–248), Baltimore: Paul H. Brookes.

Johnson, D., & Johnson, R. (1990). What is cooperative learning? In M. Brubacher, R. Payne & K. Rickett (Eds.), *Perspectives on small group learning: Theory and practice.* Canada: Rubicon.

Johnson, D., & Johnson, R. (1991a). *Learning together and apart: Cooperative, competitive and individualistic learning* (3rd ed.). Englewood Cliffs, NJ: Prentice Hall.

Johnson, D., & Johnson, R. (1991b). *Teaching children to be peacemakers.* Edina, MN: Interaction.

Johnson, D., Johnson, R. & Dudley, B. (1992). Effects of peer mediation training on elementary students. *Mediation Quarterly, 10,* 89–99.

Johnson, D., Johnson, R., Dudley, B., & Magnuson, D. (1995). Training elementary school students to manage conflict. *Journal of Social Psychology, 135*(6), 673–688.

Johnson, D., Johnson, R., Holubec E. (1993). *Cooperation in the classroom* (6th ed.). Edina, MN: Interaction.

Johnson, D. W., Johnson, R. T. , & Smith, K. A. (1986). *Academic conflict among students: Controversy and learning.* New York: Cambridge University Press.

Kagan, S. (1988). *Cooperative learning: Resources for teachers.* San Juan Capistrano CA: Resources for teachers.

Kagan, S. (1989/90). The structural approach to cooperative learning. *Educational Leadership, 46*(4), 12–15.

Kantor, R., Elgas, P., & Fernie, D. (1992). Cultural knowledge and social competence within a preschool peer culture group. *Early Childhood Research Quarterly, 8,* 125–147.

Katz, L. (1987). *Early Education: What should young children be doing?* ERIC Document 279 407.

Katz, L., & Chard, S. (1989). *Engaging children's minds: The project approach.* Norwood, NJ: Ablex.

Killen, M. (1995). Preface to the special issue: Conflict resolution in early social development, *Early Education and Development, 6*(4), 298–302.

Kohn, A. (1986). *No Contest: The case against competition.* Boston: Houghton Mifflin.

Kohn, A. (1992). *Journal of Education, 174*(2),

Kotloff, L. (1993). Fostering cooperative group spirit and individuality: Examples from a Japanese Preschool. *Young Children, 48*(3), 17–23.

Levin, H., & McCarthy, J. (1995). Full inclusion in accelerated schools: Equal access to powerful learning. In C. Finnan, E. St. John, J. McCarthy, & S. Slovacek (Eds.), *Accelerated schools in action: Lessons from the field.* Newbury Park, CA: Corwin.

Lewis, C. C. (1995). *Educating hearts and minds: Reflections on Japanese preschool and elementary education.* Cambridge: Cambridge University Press.

Lieberman, A. (Ed.). (1995). *The work of restructuring schools: Building from the ground up.* New York: Teachers College Press.

Maccoby, E. E. (1990). Gender and relationships: A developmental account. *American Psychologist, 45,* 513–520.

MaCarthy, J., & Mayfield, F. (1996). The influence and impact of inquiry in accelerated schools: Action research and the creation of a professional learning culture. Paper presented at the annual meeting of the *American Educational Research Association.* New York, April, 1996.

McCaslin, M., Tuck, D., Ward, A., Brown, B., LaPage, J., & Pyle, J. (1994). Gender composition and small group learning in fourth-grade mathematics. *Elementary School Journal, 94*(5), 467–482.

Miller, K. (1989). Enhancing early childhood mainstreaming through cooperative learning: A brief literature review. *Child Study Journal, 19* (4), 285–292.

Miller, M. (1987). Argument and cognition. In M. Hickman (Ed.), *Social and Functional approaches to Language and Thought* (pp 225–249). San Diego: Academic.

Moll, L. C., Amanti, C., Neff, D., & Gonzalez, N. (1992). Funds of knowledge for teaching: Using a qualitative approach to connect homes and classrooms, *Theory into Practice, 31*(2) (132–141).

Moll, L. (Ed.). (1992). *Vygotsky and education.* New York: Cambridge University Press.

Nias, J., Southworth, G., & Campbell, P. (1992). *Whole school curriculum development in the primary school.* Lewes, England: Falmer.

Oken-Wright, P. (1992). From tug of war to let's make a deal: The teacher's role. *Young Children, 48*(1), 15–20.

Orlick, T. (1981). *The second co-operative sports and games book.* New York: Pantheon .

Pike, G., & Selby, D. (1988). *Global teacher: Global Learner.* London: Hodder and Stoughton.

Putallaz, M., Hellstern, L., Shepperd, B., Grimes, C., & Glodis, K. (1995). Conflict, social competence, and gender: Maternal and peer contexts. *Early Education and Development, 6*(4), 434–448.

Ramsey, P. (1982). Multicultural education in early childhood. *Young Children, 37*(2), 13–25.

Rogoff, B. (1990). *Apprenticeship in thinking.* New York: Oxford University Press.

Rogoff, B. (1994). *Developing understanding of the idea of communities of learners.* The Scribner Award Address, American Educational Research Association, New Orleans.

Rubin, K., & Everett, B. (1982). Social perspective taking in young children. In S. G. Moore & C. R. Cooper (Eds.), *The young child: Reviews of research* (3), 97–114, Washington DC: NAEYC.

Sapon-Shevin, M. (1994). Cooperative learning and middle schools: What would it take to really do it right? *Theory into Practice, 33*(3), 183–190.

Sapon-Shevin, M., & Schniedewind, N. (1992). If cooperative learning's the answer, what are the questions? *Journal of Education, 174*(2), 11–37.

Schmuck, R. (1985). Learning to cooperate, cooperating to learn; Basic concepts. In R. Slavin, S. Sharan, S. Kagan, R. Hert Lazarowitz, C. Webb & R. Schmuck (Eds.), *Learning to cooperate, cooperating to learn* (pp. 1–4). New York: Plenum.

Senge, P. (1990). *The Fifth Discipline.* New York: Random House.

Sizer, T. (1992). *Horace's School.* Boston: Houghton Mifflin.

Slavin, R. (1987). Cooperative learning in the cooperative school. *Educational Leadership, 45*(3), 7–13.

Slavin, R. (1988). Cooperation and student achievement. *Educational Leadership 46*(2), 31–33.

Stevens, R., & Slavin, R. (1995). The Cooperative elementary school: Effects on students' achievement, attitudes and social relations. *American Educational Research Journal, 32*(2), 321–351.

Tobin, J., Wu, D., & Davidson, D. (1989). *Preschools in three cultures: Japan, China and the United States.* New Haven, CT: Yale University Press.

Tudge, J. (1992). Vygotsky, the zone of proximal development, and peer collaboration: Implications for classroom practice. In L. Moll (Ed.), *Vygotsky and education* (pp. 155–172). New York: Cambridge University Press.

Tudge, J., & Caruso, D. (1988). Cooperative problem solving in the classroom: Enhancing young children's cognitive development. *Young Children, 44,* 46–52.

Wertsch, J. (1992). The voice of rationality in a sociocultural approach to mind. In L. Moll (Ed.), *Vygotsky and education* (pp. 111–126). New York: Cambridge University Press.

Vygotsky, L. S. (1978). *Mind in society: The development of higher psychological processes.* Cambridge, MA: Harvard University Press.

Yager, S., Johnson, R., Johnson, D., & Snider, B. (1986). The impact of group processing on achievement in cooperative learning groups. *Journal of Social Psychology, 126*(30) 389–397.

Zuckerman, G. (1994). A pilot study of a ten-day course in cooperative learning for beginning Russian first graders. *The Elementary School Journal, 94*(4), 405–420.

## 18. Gender Segregation Among Children

Alexander, G. M., & Hines, M. (1994). Gender labels and play styles: Their relative contribution to children's selection of playmates. *Child Development, 65,* 869–879.

Allport, G. (1954). *The nature of prejudice.* Cambridge, MA: Addison-Wesley.

Beal, C. R. (1994). *Boys and girls: The development of gender roles.* New York: McGraw-Hill.

Bianchi, B. D., & Bakeman, R. (1978). Sex-typed affiliation preferences observed in preschoolers: Traditional and open school differences. *Child Development, 49,* 910–912.

Blakemore, J. E. O., LaRue, A. A., & Olejnik, A. B. (1979). Sex appropriate toy preference and the ability to conceptualize toys as sex-role related. *Developmental Psychology, 15,* 339–40.

Carpenter, C. J., Huston, A. C., & Holt, W. (1986). Modification of preschool sex-typed behaviors by participation in adult structured activities. *Sex Roles, 14,* 603–615.

Charlesworth, W. R., & LaFreniere, P. (1983). Dominance, friendship, and resource utilization in preschool children's groups. *Ethology and Sociobiology, 4,* 15–26.

Connor, J. M., & Serbin, L. A. (1977). Behaviorally based masculine- and feminine-activity-preference scales for preschoolers: Correlates with other classroom behaviors and cognitive tests. *Child Development, 48,* 1411–1416.

Deaux, K., & Major, B. (1987). Putting gender into context: An interactive model of gender-related behavior. *Psychological Review, 94,* 369–389.

deGroot, G. (1994, July). Do single-sex classes foster better learning? *The APA Monitor,* pp. 60–61.

Deschamps, J. C., & Doise, W. (1978). Crossed category memberships in intergroup relations. In H. Tajfel (Ed.), *Differentiation between social groups* (pp. 141–58). London: Academic.

Edwards, C. P., & Whiting, B. B. (1988). *Children of different worlds.* Cambridge, MA: Harvard University Press.

Eisenberg, N., Tryon, K., & Cameron, E. (1984). The relation of preschoolers' social interaction to their sex-typed toy choices. *Child Development, 55,* 1044–1050.

Fagan, J. F., III, & Shepherd, P. A. (1981). Theoretical issues in the early development of visual perception. In M. Lewis & L. Taft (Eds.), *Developmental disabilities in preschool children.* New York: Spectrum.

Fagan, J. F., III, & Singer, L. T. (1979). The role of simple feature differences in infants' recognition of faces. *Infant Behavior and Development, 2,* 39–45.

Fagot, B. I. (1974). Sex differences in toddlers' behavior and parental reaction. *Developmental Psychology, 10,* 554–558.

Fagot, B. I. (1985). Changes in thinking about early sex role development. *Developmental Review, 5,* 83–98.

Fagot, B. I., Leinbach, M. D., & Hagan, R. (1986). Gender labeling and the adoption of sex-typed behaviors. *Developmental Psychology, 22,* 440–443.

Fein, G., Johnson, D., Kosson, N., Stork, L., & Wasserman, L. (1975). Sex stereotypes and preferences in the toy choices of 20-month-old boys and girls. *Developmental Psychology, 11,* 527–528.

Feiring, C., & Lewis, M. (1991). The development of social networks from early to middle childhood: Gender differences and the relation to school competence. *Sex Roles, 25,* 237–253.

Gottman, J. M., & Parker, J. G. (Eds.) (1987). *Conversations of friends: Speculations in affective development.* New York: Cambridge University Press.

Hines, M., & Kaufman, F. R. (1994). Androgen and the development of human sex-typical behavior: Rough-and-tumble play and sex of preferred playmates in children with congenital adrenal hyperplasia (CAH). *Child Development, 65,* 1042–1053.

Howes, C. (1988). Same- and cross-sex friends: Implications for interaction and social skills. *Early Childhood Research Quarterly, 3,* 21–37.

LaFreniere, P. J., & Charlesworth, W. R. (1987). Preschool peer status, behavior and resource utilization in a cooperative/competitive situation. *International Journal of Behavioral Development, 10,* 345–358.

LaFreniere, P., Strayer, F. F., & Gauthier, R. (1984). The emergence of same-sex preferences among preschool peers. *Child Development, 55,* 1958–1966.

Leinbach, M. D., & Fagot, B. I. (1986). Acquisition of gender labels: A test for toddlers. *Sex Roles, 15,* 655–67.

Lockheed, M. E. (1986). Reshaping the social order: The case of gender segregation. *Sex Roles, 14,* 617–628.

Lockheed, M. E., & Klein, S. S. (1985). Sex equity in classroom organization and climate. In S. Klein (Ed.), *Handbook for achieving sex equity through education* (pp.189–217). Baltimore: Johns Hopkins University Press.

Luria, Z., & Herzog, E. (1985, April). *Gender segregation across and within settings.* Paper presented at the Biennial Meeting of the Society for Research in Child Development, Toronto, Ontario, Canada.

Maccoby, E. E. (1985). Social groupings in childhood: Their relationship to prosocial and antisocial behavior in boys and girls. In D. Olweus, J. Block, & M. Radke-Yarrow (Eds.), *Development of antisocial and prosocial behavior: Theories, research and issues.* San Diego: Academic.

Maccoby, E. E. (1988). Gender as a social category. *Developmental Psychology, 24,* 755–765.

Maccoby, E. E., & Jacklin, C. N. (1987). Gender segregation in childhood. In H. Reese (Ed.), *Advances in child development and behavior* (Vol. 20, pp. 239–288). New York: Academic.

Martin, C. L. (1989). Children's use of gender-related information in making social judgements. *Developmental Psychology, 25,* 80–88.

Martin, C. L., & Halverson, C. F. (1981). A schematic processing model of sex typing and stereotyping in children. *Child Development, 52,* 1119–1134.

Messick, D. M., & Mackie, D. M. (1989). Intergroup relations. *Annual Review of Psychology, 40,* 45–81.

Moller, L. C. (1991). *Toddler peer preferences: The role of gender awareness, sex-typed toy preferences and compatible play styles.* Ph. D. dissertation, Concordia University, Montreal, Quebec, Canada.

Moller, L. C., Powlishta, K. K., & Serbin, L. A. (1990, November). *Three theories of gender segregation: Cognitive consonance, sex-typed toy play and play style compatibility.* Paper presented at the 13th Annual Conference of the Societe Quebecoise pour la Recherche en Psychologie, Montreal.

Poulin-Dubois, D., Serbin, L. A., Kenyon, B., & Derbyshire, A. (1994). Infants' intermodal knowledge about gender. *Developmental Psychology, 30,* 436–442.

Powlishta, K. K. (1989, April). *Perceived similarity and the salience of gender.* Paper presented at the Biennial Meeting of the Society for Research in Child Development, Kansas City, MO.

Powlishta, K. K. (1995). Intergroup processes in childhood: Social categorization and sex-role development. *Developmental Psychology 31,* 781–788.

Powlishta, K. K., & Maccoby, E. E. (1990). Resource utilization in mixed-sex dyads: The influence of adult presence and task type. *Sex Roles, 23,* 223–240.

Powlishta, K. K., Serbin, L. A., & Moller, L. C. (1993). The stability of individual differences in gender-typing: Implications for understanding gender segregation. *Sex Roles, 29,* 723–737.

Serbin, L. A., & Sprafkin, C. (1982). Measurement of sex-typed play: A comparison between laboratory and naturalistic observation procedures. *Behavioral Assessment, 4,* 225–235.

Serbin, L. A., & Sprafkin, C. (1986). The salience of gender and the process of sex-typing in three- to seven-year-old children. *Child Development, 57,* 1188–1199.

Serbin, L. A., Powlishta, K. K., & Gulko, J. (1993). The development of sex-typing in middle childhood. *Monographs of the Society for Research in Child Development, 52*(2).

Serbin, L. A., Tonick, I. J., & Sternglanz, S. H. (1977). Shaping cooperative cross-sex play. *Child Development, 48,* 924–929.

Serbin, L. A., Connor, J. M., Burchardt, C. J., & Citron, C. C. (1979). Effects of peer presence on sex-typing of children's play behavior. *Journal of Experimental Child Psychology, 27,* 303–309.

Serbin, L. A., Sprafkin, C., Elman, M., & Doyle, A. B. (1984). The early development of sex differentiated patterns and social influence. *Canadian Journal of Social Science, 14,* 350–68.

Thompson, S. K. (1975). Gender labels and early sex role development. *Child Development, 46,* 339–47.

Thorne, B. (1986). Girls and boys together, but mostly apart. In W. W. Hartup, & Z. Rubin (Eds.), *Relationships and development* (pp. 167–184). Hillsdale, NJ: Erlbaum.

Thorne, B. (1987, February). *Children and gender: Constructions of difference.* Paper presented at the conference on Theoretical Perspectives on Sexual Difference, Stanford University, Stanford, CA.

Weinraub, M., Clemens, L. P., Sockloff, A., Ethridge, T., Gracely, E., & Meyers, B. (1984). The development of sex role stereotypes in the third year: Relationship to gender labeling, identity, sex-typed toy preference and family characteristics. *Child Development, 55,* 1493–1503.

## 19. Discipline in Early Childhood

Alberto, P. A. & Troutman, A. C. (1995). *Applied behavior analysis for teachers* (4th ed.). Columbus, OH: Merrill.

Balson, M. (1992). *Understanding classroom behaviour* (3rd ed.). Melbourne: A.C.E.R.

Balson, M. (1994). *Becoming better parents* (4th. ed.). Melbourne: A.C.E.R.

Bandura, A. (1986). *Social foundations of thought and action*. Englewood Cliffs, NJ: Prentice Hall.

Baumrind, D. (1967). Child care practices anteceding three patterns of preschool behavior. *Genetic Psychology Monographs, 75,* 43–88.

Benson, A. J., & Presbury, J. H. (1989). The cognitive tradition in schools. In J. N. Hughes & R. J. Hall (Eds.) *Cognitive-behavioral psychology in the schools*. New York: Guilford.

Berk, L. (1997). *Child development* (4th. ed.). Boston: Allyn & Bacon.

Corey, G. (1991). *Theory and practice of counseling and psychotherapy* (4th ed.). Monterey, CA: Brooks/Cole.

Dinkmeyer, D. & McKay, G. (1989). *Systematic training for effective parenting* (3rd ed.). Minneapolis: American Guidance Service.

Dinkmeyer, D., McKay, G. & Dinkmeyer, D. (1980). *Systematic training for effective teaching*. Minneapolis: American Guidance Service.

Dobson, K. S. & Pusch, D. (1993). Towards a definition of the conceptual and empirical boundaries of cognitive therapy. *Australian Psychologist, 28*(3), 137–144.

Doyle, W. (1986). Classroom organization and management. In M.C. Wittrock (Ed.) *Handbook of research on teaching* (3rd ed.). New York: Macmillan.

Dyck, M. J. (1993). New directions in cognitive-behavior therapy. *Australian Psychologist, 28*(3), 133–136.

Fontana, D. (1985). *Classroom control*. London: British Psychological Society and Methuen.

Gartrell, D. (1994). *A guidance approach to discipline*. New York: Delmar.

Ginott, H. (1972). *Teacher and child*. New York: Macmillan.

Glasser, W. (1977). Ten steps to good discipline. *Today's Education, 66,* 61–63.

Glasser, W. (1986). *Control theory in the classroom*. New York: Harper & Row.

Glasser, W. (1992). *The quality school* (2nd ed.). New York: Harper & Row.

Gordon, T. (1970). *Parent effectiveness training*. New York: Plume.

Gordon, T. (1974). *Teacher effectiveness training*. New York: Peter H. Wyden.

Gordon, T. (1991). *Teaching children self-discipline at home and at school*. Sydney: Random House.

Greenberg, P. (1992a). Why not academic preschool? (Part 2) Autocracy or democracy in the classroom? *Young children, 47*(3), 54–64.

Greenberg, P. (1992b). Ideas that work with young children: How to institute some simple democratic practices pertaining to respect, rights, roots and responsibilities in any classroom (without losing your leadership position). *Young children, 47*(5), 10–17.

Harrison, J. (1996). *Understanding children: Towards responsive relationships* (2nd ed.). Melbourne, Australia: A.C.E.R.

Hill, S. & Hill, T. (1990). *The collaborative classroom: A guide to cooperative learning*. Melbourne, Australia: Eleanor Curtin.

Johnson, D.W. & Johnson, R.T. (1991). *Learning together and alone* (3rd ed.). Boston: Allyn & Bacon.

Johnson, D. W., Johnson, R. T., & Holubec, E. J. (1990). *Circles of learning: Cooperation in the classroom* (3rd ed.). Edina, MN: Interaction.

Kaplan, J.S. & Drainville, B. (1991). *Beyond behavior modification: A cognitive-behavioral approach to behavior management in the school* (2nd ed.). Austin, TX: Pro-Ed.

Kendall, P.C. (Ed.) (1991). *Child and adolescent therapy: Cognitive-behavioral procedures*. New York: Guilford.

Knight, T. (1991). Democratic schooling: Basis for a school code of behaviour. In M. N. Lovegrove & R. Lewis (Eds.), *Classroom discipline*. Melbourne: Longman Cheshire.

Lee, C. (1993). Cognitive theory and therapy: Distinguishing psychology from ideology. *Australian Psychologist, 28*(3), 136–160.

McCaslin, M. & Good, T. L. (1992). Compliant cognition: The misalliance of management and instructional goals in current school reform. *Educational Researcher, 21*(3), 4–17.

National Association for the Education of Young Children (1984). Criteria for high quality early childhood programs. *Position paper from the National Academy of Early Childhood Programs,* 3–13.

National Child Care Accreditation Council (1989). Code of ethical conduct. *Young children, 45*(1), 25–29.

National Child Care Accreditation Council (1993). *Putting children first: Quality improvement and accreditation system handbook*. Sydney.

Porter, L. (1996). *Student behaviour: Theory and practice for teachers*. Sydney: Allen & Unwin.

Porter, L. (1997). *Children are people too* (2nd ed.). Sydney: Allen & Unwin.

Rodd, J. & Holland, A. (1990). Am I doing the right thing? What else could I do? Approaches to child management. *Australian Journal of Early Childhood, 15*(4), 28–34.

Rogers, C. (1951). *Client-centred therapy.* London: Constable.

Rogers, C. (1978). *On personal power.* London: Constable.

Rogers, C.R. & Freiberg, H. (1994). *Freedom to learn* (3rd ed.). Columbus, OH: Merrill.

Rogers, W. (1990). *"You know the fair rule."* Melbourne, Australia: A.C.E.R.

Rogers, W. (1991). Decisive discipline. In M. N. Lovegrove & R. Lewis (Eds.), *Classroom discipline.* Melbourne, Australia: Longman Cheshire.

Stonehouse, A. (Ed.). (1988). *Trusting toddlers: Programming for one to three year olds in child care centres.* Watson, ACT: Australian Early Childhood Association.

Thompson, C. L. & Rudolph, L. B. (1992) *Counselling children* (3rd ed.). Pacific Grove, CA: Brooks/Cole.

Wolery, M., Bailey, D. B., & Sugai, G. M. (1988). *Effective teaching: Principles and procedures of applied behavior analysis with exceptional students.* Boston: Allyn & Bacon.

## 20. Becoming Bicultural: An Australian Perspective

Banks, J. (1988). *Multi-ethnic education: Theory and practice.* Boston: Allyn & Bacon.

Banks, J. (1993). Multicultural education for young children: Racial and ethnic attitudes and their modification. In B. Spodek (Ed.), *Handbook of research on the education of young children* (pp. 236–250). New York: Macmillan.

Beale Spencer, M. & Markstrom-Adams, C. (1990). Identity processes among racial and ethnic minority children in America. *Child Development, 61,* 290–310.

Berry, J., Poortinga, Y., Segall, M., & Dasen, P. (1992). *Cross cultural psychology, research and applications.* Cambridge: Cambridge University Press.

Bourke, E. & Bourke, C. (1995). Aboriginal families in Australia. In R. Hartley (Ed.), *Families and cultural diversity in Australia* (pp. 48–59). Melbourne, Australia: Allen & Unwin.

Colbung, M., & Glover, A. (1996). In partnership with Aboriginal children. In M. Fleer (Ed.), *Conversations about teaching in early childhood settings* (pp. 32–40). Watson, ACT: Australian Early Childhood Association.

Cross, W. (1978). The Thomas and Cross models on psychological nigrescence: A literature review. *Journal of Black Psychology, 4,* 13–31.

Darder, A. (1991). *Culture and power in the classroom.* New York: Bergin & Garvey.

de Anda, D. (1984). Bicultural socialization. Factors affecting the minority experience. *Social Work, 2,* 101–107.

du Bois, W.E.B. (1903). *Souls of black folk.* Chicago: A. C. McClurg.

Gale, F., Bailey-Harris, R. & Wundersitz, J. (1990). *Aboriginal youth and the criminal justice system: The injustice of justice.* Cambridge: Cambridge University Press.

Giroux, H. (1981). *Ideology, culture and the process of schooling.* Philadelphia: Temple University Press.

Giroux, H. (1983). *Theory and resistance in education.* New York: Bergin & Garvey.

Giroux, H. (1985.) Teachers as transformative intellectuals. *Social Education, 2,* 376–379.

Giroux, H. (1988). *Teachers as Intellectuals.* New York: Bergin & Garvey.

Glover, A. (1993). *The early childhood service needs of Aboriginal Communities in the northern country areas of South Australia.* Adelaide: Children's Services Office.

Glover, A. (1994). Issues of culture and race. In E. Mellor & K. Coombe (Eds.), *Issues in early childhood services. An Australian perspective.* (pp. 81–90). Iowa: Brown.

Harris, S. (1990). *Two-Way Schooling.* Canberra: Aboriginal Studies.

HREOC. (1991). *Racist violence: Report of the national inquiry into racist violence in Australia.* Canberra, Australia: Australian Government Publishing Service.

Hunter, E. (1996). Denial, rationalisation and trivialisation of state intrusion into Aboriginal family life. *Family Matters, 44,* 16–19.

Malin, M. (1990). Why is life so hard for Aboriginal students in urban classrooms? *Aboriginal Child at School, 18* (1), 9–29.

Malin, M., Campbell, K., & Agius, L. (1996). Raising children in the nunga Aboriginal way. *Family Matters, 40,* 43–47.

National Association for the Education of Young Children (1996). NAEYC Position Statement: Responding to linguistic and cultural diversity–recommendations for effective early childhood education. *Young Children, 51*(2), 4–12.

Neuman, S. & Roskos, K. (1994). Bridging home and school with a culturally responsive approach. *Childhood Education, 70,* 210–214.

Ngarritjan-Kessaris, T. (1995). Memories of a Millner kid. In S. Harris & M. Malin (Eds.), *Aboriginal kids in urban classrooms* (pp. 1–6). Canberra, Australia: Aboriginal Studies.

Peeters, L. (1995). The years that never were. *Aboriginal and Islander Health Worker Journal, 19*(3), 16–19.

Ramirez, M. & Castenada, A. (1974). *Cultural democracy. Bicognitive development and education.* New York: Academic.

Ramsey, P. (1987). *Teaching and learning in a diverse world. Multicultural education for young children.* New York: Teachers College Press.

Rashid, H. (1981). Early childhood education as cultural transition for African-American children. *Educational Research Quarterly, 6,* 55–63.

Rodd, J. (1996). Children, culture and education. *Childhood Education, 72,* 325–329.

Royal Commission into Aboriginal Deaths in Custody. (1991). *Final report.* Canberra: Australian Government Publishing Service.

Sleeter, C. & Grant, C. (1988). *Making choices for multicultural education. Five approaches to race, class and gender.* Columbus: Merrill.

Wright, R. (1953). *The outsider.* New York: Harper & Row.

## 21. The Importance of Parent Participation in Child Protection Curricula

Abel, G. G., Becker, J. V., Mittelman, M. S., Cunningham-Rathner, J., Rouleau, J. L., Murphy, W. D. (1987). Self-reported sex crimes of non-incarcerated paraphiliacs. *Journal of Interpersonal Violence, 2,* 3–25.

Anderson, C. (1979). *Child sexual abuse prevention project. An educational model for working with children.* Minneapolis: Hennepin County Attorney's Office.

Berrick, J. D. (1988). Parental involvement in child abuse prevention training: What do they learn? *Child Abuse and Neglect, 12,* 543–553.

Bentovim, A. (1991, July). *Evaluation of a comprehensive treatment approach to child sexual abuse within the family.* Third European Conference on Child Abuse and Neglect, Prague.

Briggs, F. (1988). South Australian parents want child protection programs to be offered in schools and pre-schools. *Early Child Development and Care, 34,* 167–178.

Briggs, F. (1990). Evaluation of "Keeping Ourselves Safe": Curriculum used with children 5–8 years in New Zealand schools (Report to the Commissioner of Police, New Zealand). Magill, South Australia: University of South Australia.

Briggs, F. (1991). Child protection programs: Can they protect young children? *Early Child Development and Care, 67,* 61–72.

Briggs, F. & Hawkins, R. M. F. (1994a). Choosing between child protection programmes. *Child Abuse Review, 3,* 272–284.

Briggs, F,. & Hawkins, R. M. F (1994b). *Follow up data on the effectiveness of Keeping Ourselves Safe when used with children of 5–8 years.* Report to New Zealand Police Law Related Education, Wellington.

Briggs, F., & Hawkins, R. M. F. (1996a). A comparison of the childhood experiences of convicted male child molesters and men who were sexually abused in childhood and claimed to be "non offenders." *Child Abuse and Neglect, The International Journal, 20,* 221–234.

Briggs, F., & Hawkins, R.M.F. (1996b). *"Keeping Ourselves Safe": A survey of New Zealand school children aged 10–12 years and their parents.* Final report for the Commissioner of Police and Ministry of Education, New Zealand.

Butler, S. (1986). Thinking about prevention education. In M. Nelson & K. Clark (Eds) *The educator's guide to preventing child sexual abuse,* Santa Cruz, CA: Network.

Cook, M., & Howells, K. (Eds.). (1981) *Adult sexual interest in children.* New York: Academic.

Elkind, D. (1976). *Child development and education: A Piagetian perspective.* New York: Oxford University Press.

Finkelhor, D., Asidigian, N. & Dziuba-Leatherman, J. (1993). *Victimization prevention training in action: A National survey of children's experiences coping with actual threats and assaults.* Durham: Family Research Laboratory, University of New Hampshire.

Goldman, R. & Goldman, J. (1988). *Show me yours: Understanding children's sexuality.* Ringwood, Australia: Penguin.

Hard, S. (1986). Sexual abuse of the developmentally disabled: A case study. Paper presented to the National Conference of Executives of Associations of Retarded Citizens, Omaha, Nebraska, October 22nd. Cited in C.Y. Senn (1988) *Vulnerable: Sexual abuse and people with an intellectual handicap.* Ontario: G. Allen Roehr Institute.

Hawkins, R. M. F., & Briggs, F. (1995). Early childhood experiences of men sexually abused as children. *Children Australia, 20,* 18–23.

Hunt, G., Hawkins, R. & Goodlet, T. (1992). Parenting: A survey of community needs. *Children Australia 17*(3), 9–12.

Johnson, B. (1995). *Teaching and learning about personal safety. Report of the review of Protective Behaviours in South Australia.* Adelaide: Painters Prints.

Krivacska, J. (1990a, August 14). *Sexual abuse prevention programs. Can they cause false allegations?* Paper presented at 98th Annual Convention of the American Psychological Association, Boston.

Krivacska, J. (1990b). *Designing child sexual abuse prevention programs.* Springfield, IL: Charles C. Thomas.

Mayes, G. M., Currie, E. F., Macleod, L., Gillies, J. B., & Warden, D. A. (1992). *Child sexual abuse: A review of literature and educational materials.* Edinburgh: Scottish Academic.

Tutty, L. (1996, August). The efficacy of a child abuse prevention program for elementary school children. *International Congress on Child Abuse and Neglect,* Dublin.

Weekes, P., & Westwood, M. (1993, August 31). Parents deluded on teen sex lives. *Australian,* p. 3.

West, P. F. (1984). Protective behaviors: Anti-victim training for children, adolescents and adults (4th revision). Madison, WI: Protective Behaviors.

West, P. F. (1989). *The basic essentials: Protective behaviors, anti-victimization and empowerment process.* Madison, WI: Protective Behaviors.

Wurtele, S. K., Kvaternick, M. & Franklin, C. F. (1992). Sexual abuse prevention for pre-schoolers: A survey of parents' behaviours, attitudes and beliefs. *Journal of Child Sexual Abuse, 1,* 113–128.

Wurtele, S. K., Kast, L. A & Melzer, A. M. (1992). Sexual abuse prevention education for young children: A comparison of teachers and parents as instructors. *Child Abuse and Neglect, 16,* 865–876.

## 22. Childhood and the Culture of Consumption

Ariès, P. (1962). *Centuries of childhood: A social history of family life.* New York: Vintage.

Braverman, H. (1974). *Labour and Monopoly Capital.* New York: Monthly Review Press.

de Mause, L. (1976). *The history of childhood.* London: Souvenir.

Engelhart, T. (1987). The shortcake strategy. In T. Gitlin (Ed.), *Watching Television* (pp. 68–110). New York: Pantheon.

Ewen, S. (1976). *Captains of consciousness: Advertising and the social roots of consumer culture.* New York: McGraw-Hill.

Kline, S. (1989). Limits to the imagination: Marketing and children's culture. In I. Angus & S. Jhally (Eds.), *Cultural Politics in Contemporary America* (pp. 299–316). New York: Routledge.

Kline, S. (1993). *Out of the garden: Toys and children's culture in the age of TV marketing.* London: Routledge.

Langer, B. (1989). Commoditoys: Marketing childhood. *Arena 87,* 29–37.

Langer, B. (1994). Born to shop: Children and consumer capitalism. In F. Briggs (Ed.), *Children and families: Australian perspectives* (pp. 142–159). Sydney: Allen & Unwin.

Lejoyeux, M., Ades, J. Tassain, V., & Solomon, J. (1996). Phenomenology and psychopathology of uncontrolled buying. *American Journal of Psychiatry, 153,* 12.

McLuhan, H. M. (1964). *Understanding Media.* London: Routledge & Kegan Paul.

Mead, G. H. (1934). *Mind, self, and society.* Chicago: University of Chicago Press.

Mead, M. (1975). *Growing up in New Guinea.* Harmondsworth, Australia: Penguin.

Mead, M. (1972). *Blackberry winter.* New York: Touchstone.

Meyrowitz, J. (1984). The adultlike child and the childlike adult: Socialization in an electronic age. *Daedalus, 13,* 19–48.

Mills, C. Wright (1973). *The sociological imagination.* Harmondsworth, Australia: Penguin.

Postman, N. (1982). *The disappearance of childhood.* New York: Delacourt.

Seabrook, J. (1985). *Landscapes of poverty.* Oxford: Basil Blackwell.

Seiter, E. (1995). *Sold separately:Children and parents in consumer culture.* New Brunswick, NJ: Rutgers University Press.

Shorter, E. (1976). *The making of the modern family.* New York: Basic.

Slater, D. (1997). *Consumer culture and modernity.* London: Polity.

Stern, S., & Schoenhaus, T. (1990). *Toyland: The high-stakes game of the toy industry.* Chicago: Contemporary.

Stone, L. (1977). *The family, sex and marriage in England 1500–1800.* New York: Harper & Row.

Trace, A. S. (1961). *What Ivan knows that Johnny doesn't.* New York: Random House.

Walvin, J. (1982). *A Child's World.* Harmondsworth, Australia: Penguin.

Winn, M. (1984). *Children Without Childhood.* Harmondsworth, Australia: Penguin.

Zelizer, V. A. (1994). *Pricing the priceless child: The changing social value of children.* Princeton, NJ: Princeton University Press.

## 24. Children with Attention Deficits and Disinhibited Behavior

Achenbach, T. M., McConaughy, S. H., & Howell, C. T. (1987). Child/adolescent behavioral and emotional problems: Implications of cross-informant correlations for situational specificity. *Psychological Bulletin, 101,* 213–232.

American Psychiatric Association (1980). *Diagnostic and statistical manual of mental disorders* (3rd ed.). Washington, DC.

American Psychiatric Association (1994). *Diagnostic and statistical manual of mental disorders* (4th ed.). Washington, DC.

Atkins, M. S., Pelham, W. E., & Licht, M. (1985). A comparison of objective classroom measures and teacher ratings of attention deficit disorder. *Journal of Abnormal Child Psychology, 13,* 155–167.

Barkley, R. A. (1989). Attention deficit-hyperactivity disorder. In E. J. Mash & R. A. Barkley (Eds.), *Treatment of childhood disorders* (pp. 39–72). New York: Guilford.

Barkley, R. A. (1990). *Attention-deficit hyperactivity disorder: A handbook for diagnosis and treatment.* New York: Guilford.

Barkley, R. A. (1994). Impaired delayed responding: A unified theory of Attention-Deficit Hyperactivity Disorder. In D. K. Routh (Ed.), *Disruptive behavior disorders: Essays in honor of Herbert Quay* (pp. 11–57). New York: Plenum.

Barkley, R. A. (1997). Behavioral inhibition, sustained attention, and executive functions: Constructing a unified theory of ADHD. *Psychological Bulletin, 121,* 65–94.

Berk, L. E. (1994, November). Why children talk to themselves. *Scientific American, 271*(5) 78–83.

Berk, L. E. (1997). *Child development* (4th ed.). Boston: Allyn & Bacon.

Berk, L. E., & Landau, S. (1993). Private speech of learning disabled and normally achieving children in classroom academic and laboratory contexts. *Child Development, 64,* 556–571.

Berk, L. E., & Potts, M. K. (1991). Development and functional significance of private speech among attention-deficit hyperactivity disordered and normal boys. *Journal of Abnormal Child Psychology, 19,* 357–377.

Brown, R. T., Dingle, A., & Landau, S. (1994). Overview of psychopharmacology in children and adolescents. *School Psychology Quarterly, 9,* 4–25.

Campbell, S. (1988, October). *Longitudinal studies of active and aggressive preschoolers: Individual differences in early behavior and in outcome.* Paper presented at the Second Rochester Symposium on Developmental Psychopathology, Rochester, NY.

Campbell, S. B. (1985). Hyperactivity in preschoolers: Correlates and prognostic implications. *Clinical Psychology Review, 5,* 405–428.

Campbell, S. B., Endman, M. W., & Bernfeld, G. (1977). Three year follow-up of hyperactive preschoolers into elementary school. *Journal of Child Psychology and Psychiatry, 18,* 239–249.

Caron, C. & Rutter, M. (1991). Comorbidity in child psychopathology: Concepts, issues, and research strategies. *Journal of Child Psychology and Psychiatry, 32,* 1063–1080.

Carlson, C. L., & Bunner, M. R. (1993). Effects of methylphenidate on the academic performance of children with attention-deficit hyperactivity disorder and learning disabilities. *School Psychology Review, 22,* 184–198.

Cousins, L. S., & Weiss, G. (1993). Parent training and social skills training for children with attention-deficit hyperactivity disorder: How can they be combined for greater effectiveness? *Canadian Journal of Psychiatry, 38,* 449–457.

Douglas, V. I. (1983). Attention and cognitive problems. In M. Rutter (Ed.), *Developmental neuropsychiatry.* (pp. 280–329). New York: Guilford.

DuPaul, G. J., & Stoner, G. (1994). *ADHD in the schools.* New York: Guilford.

Erhardt, D. & Hinshaw, S. P. (1994). Initial sociometric impressions of attention-deficit hyperactivity disorder and comparison boys: Predictors from social behaviors and nonbehavioral variables. *Journal of Consulting and Clinical Psychology, 62,* 833–842.

Flicek, M., & Landau, S. (1985). Social status problems of learning disabled and hyperactive/learning disabled boys. *Journal of Clinical Child Psychology, 14,* 340–344.

Frick, P. J. et al. (1994). DSM-VI field trials for the disruptive behavior disorders: Symptom utility estimates. *Journal of the American Academy of Child and Adolescent Psychiatry, 33,* 529–539.

Frick, P. J., Lahey, B. B., Loeber, R., Tannenbaum, L. Van Horn, Y., Christ, M. A. G., Hart, E. A., & Hanson, L. (1993). Oppositional defiant disorder and conduct disorder: A meta-analytic review of factor analyses and cross-validation in a clinic sample. *Clinical Psychology Review, 13,* 319–340.

Gaub, M. & Carlson, C. L. (1997). Gender differences in ADHD: A meta-analysis and critical review. *Journal of the American Academy of Child and Adolescent Psychiatry, 36,* 1036–1045.

Greene, R. (1995). Students with ADHD in school classrooms: Teacher factors related to compatibility, assessment, and intervention. *School Psychology Review, 24,* 81–93.

Guevremont, D. C., & Dumas, M. C. (1994). Peer relationship problems and disruptive behavior disorders. *Journal of Emotional & Behavior Disorders, 2,* 164–172.

Hinshaw, S. P. (1987). On the distinction between attentional deficits/hyperactivity and conduct problems/aggression in child psychopathology. *Psychological Bulletin, 101,* 443–463.

Hynd, G. W., Hern, K. L., Voeller, K. K., & Marshall, R. M. (1991). Neurobiological basis of attention-deficit hyperactivity disorder (ADHD). *School Psychology Review, 20,* 174–186.

Iaboni, F., Douglas, V. I., & Baker, A. G. (1995). Effects of reward and response costs on inhibition in ADHD children. *Journal of Abnormal Psychology, 104,* 232–240.

Jacob, R. B., O'Leary, K. D., & Rosenblad C. (1978). Formal and informal classroom settings: Effects on hyperactivity. *Journal of Abnormal Child Psychology, 6,* 47–59.

Landau, S., & Burcham, B. G. (1995). Best practices in the assessment of children with attention disorders. In A. Thomas & J. Grimes (Eds.), *Best practices in school psychology—III* (pp. 817–829). Washington, DC: National Association of School Psychologists.

Landau, S., Lorch, E. P., & Milich, R. (1992). Visual attention to and comprehension of television in attention-deficit hyperactivity disordered and normal boys. *Child Development, 63,* 928–937.

Landau, S., & Milich, R. (1988). Social communication patterns of attention-deficit-disordered boys. *Journal of Abnormal Child Psychology, 16,* 69–81.

Landau, S., & Milich, R. (1990). Assessment of Children's social status and peer relations. In A. M. La Greca (Ed.), *Through the eyes of the child* (pp. 259–291). Boston: Allyn & Bacon.

Landau, S., Milich, R., & Diener, M. B. (1998). Peer relations of children with attention-deficit hyperactivity disorder. *Reading and Writing Quarterly, 14, 83–105.*

Landau, S., Milich, R., & Widiger, T. A. (1991). Conditional probabilities of child interview symptoms in the diagnosis of attention deficit disorder. *Journal of Child Psychology and Psychiatry, 32,* 501–513.

Lapouse, R., & Monk, M. (1958). An epidemiologic Al study of behavior characteristics in children. *American Journal of Public Health, 48,* 1134–1144.

Lochman, J. E., White, K. J., & Wayland, K. J. (1991). Cognitive-behavioral assessment and treatment with aggressive children. In P. C. Kendall (Ed.), *Child and adolescent therapy: Cognitive-behavioral procedures* (pp. 25–65). New York: Guilford.

McGee, R., & Share, D. L. (1988). Attention deficit disorder-hyperactivity and academic failure: Which comes first and what should be treated? *Journal of the American Academy of Child and Adolescent Psychiatry, 27,* 318–325.

Milich, R. (1993). The response of children with ADHD to failure: If at first you don't succeed, do you try, try again? *School Psychology Review, 23,* 11–28.

Milich, R., Hartung, C. M., Martin, C. A., & Haigler, E. D. (1994). Behavioral disinhibition and underlying processes in adolescents with disruptive behavior disorders. In D. K. Routh (Ed.), *Disruptive Behavior Disorders: Essays in honor of Herbert Quay* (pp. 109–138). New York: Plenum.

Milich, R., Loney, J., & Landau, S. (1982). The independent dimensions of hyperactivity and aggression: A validation with playroom observation data. *Journal of Abnormal Psychology, 91,* 183–198.

Mother's little helper (1996, March 18). *Newsweek.* pp. 51–56.

National Association of School Psychologists (1992, May). Position statement on students with attention deficits. *Communique, 20,* 5.

Olson, S. L. (1989). Assessment of impulsivity in preschoolers: Cross-measure convergence, longitudinal stability, and relevance to social competence. *Journal of Clinical Child Psychology, 8,* 176–183.

Parker, J. G., & Asher, S. R. (1987). Peer relations and later personal adjustment: Are low-accepted children at risk: *Psychological Bulletin, 102,* 357–389.

Pelham, W. E. (1992). *Children's summer day treatment program: 1992 program manual.* Unpublished manuscript, University of Pittsburgh School of Medicine, Western Psychiatric Institute and Clinic, Pittsburgh.

Pelham, W. E. (1993). Pharmacotherapy for children with attention-deficit hyperactivity disorder. *School Psychology Review, 22,* 199–227.

Pelham, W. E., & Bender, M. E. (1982). Peer relationships in hyperactive children: Description and treatment. In D. D. Gadow & I. Bialer (Eds.), *Advances in learning and behavioral disabilities: A research annual* (Vol. 1, pp. 365–436). Greenwich, CT: JAI.

Pelham, W. E., Jr., McBurnett, K., Harper, G. W., Milich, R., Murphy, D. A., Clinton, J., & Thiele, C. (1990). Methylphenidate and baseball playing in ADHD children: Who's on first? *Journal of Consulting and Clinical Psychology, 58,* 130–133.

Richman, N., Stevenson, J., & Graham, J. J. (1982). *Preschool to school: A behavioral study.* London: Academic.

Sheridan, S. M., Dee, C. C., Morgan, J. C., McCormick, M. E., & Walker, D. (1996). A multimethod intervention for social skills deficits in children with ADHD and their parents. *School Psychology Review, 25,* 57–76.

Vygotsky, L. S. (1934/1986). *Thought and language* (A. Kozulin, Trans.). Cambridge, MA: MIT Press.

Weiss, B., & Hechtman, L. T. (1993). *Hyperactive children grown up* (2nd ed.). New York: Guilford .

Whalen, C. K., & Henker, B. (1991). The social impact of stimulant treatment for hyperactive children. *Journal of Learning Disabilities, 24,* 231–241.

Whalen, C. K., & Henker, B. (1985). The social worlds of hyperactive children. *Clinical Psychology Review, 5,* 1–32.

Whalen, C. K., & Henker, B. (1976). Psychostimulants and children: A review and analysis. *Psychological Bulletin, 83,* 1113–1130.

Whalen, C. K., Henker, B., & Granger, D. A. (1990). Social judgment process in hyperactive boys: Effects of methylphenidate and comparisons with normal peers. *Journal of Abnormal Child Psychology, 18,* 297–316.

Winsler, A. (1994). *The social origins and self-regulatory quality of private speech in hyperactive and normal children.* Unpublished doctoral dissertation, Stanford University, Stanford, CA.

Wolraich, M., Milich, R., Stumbo, P., & Schultz, F. (1985). The effects of sucrose ingestion on the behavior of hyperactive boys. *Pediatrics, 106,* 675–682.

## 25. Control versus Autonomy During Early Adolescence

Baron, R. M., & Graziano, W. G. (1991). *Social psychology.* Chicago: Holt, Rinehart & Winston.

Baumrind, D. (1971). Current patterns of parental authority. *Developmental Psychology Monograph, 4* (1, Pt. 2).

Blos, P. (1965). The initial stage of male adolescence. *The Psychoanalytic Study of the Child, 20,* 145–164.

Boggiano, A. K. & Katz, P. (1991). Maladaptive achievement patterns in students: The role of teachers' controlling strategies. *Journal of Social Issues, 47,* 35–51.

Boggiano, A. K., Main, D. S., & Katz, P. A. (1988). Children's preference for challenge: The role of perceived competence and control. *Journal of Personality and Social Psychology, 54,* 134–141.

Brophy, J. E., & Evertson, C. M. (1976). *Learning from teaching: A developmental perspective.* Boston: Allyn & Bacon.

Condry, J., & Simon, M. L. (1974). Characteristics of peer- and parent-oriented children. *Journal of Marriage and the Family, 36,* 543–554.

deCharms, R. (1980). The origins of competence and achievement motivation in personal causation. In L. J. Fyans, Jr. (Ed.), *Achievement motivation: Recent trends in theory and research* (pp. 22–23). New York: Plenum.

Deci, E. L., & Ryan, R. M. (1985). *Intrinsic motivation and self determination in human behavior.* New York: Plenum.

Deci, E. L., & Ryan, R. M. (1987). The support of autonomy and the control of behavior. *Journal of Personality and Social Psychology, 53,* 1024–1037.

Eccles, J. S., McCarthy, K. A., Lord, S. E., Harold, R., Wigfield, A., & Aberbach, A. (1990, April). *The relationship of family factors to self-esteem and teacher-rated adjustment following the transition to junior high school environment.* Paper presented at Society for Research on Adolescence meeting, Atlanta.

Eccles, J. S., & Midgley, C. (1988). Stage/environment fit: Developmentally appropriate classrooms for young adolescents. In R. E. Ames & C. Ames (Eds.), *Research on motivation in education* (Vol. 3, pp. 139–186). New York: Academic.

Epstein. J. L., & McPartland, J. M. (1977). The Quality of School Life Scale and administrative and technical manual. Boston: Houghton Mifflin.

Flanagan, C. (1985, April). *The relationship of family environments in early adolescence and intrinsic motivation in the classroom.* Paper presented at American Educational Research Association meeting, Chicago.

Flanagan, C. (1986, April). *Early adolescent needs and family decision-making environments: A study of person-environment fit.* Paper presented at American Educational Research Association meeting, San Francisco.

Flanagan, C. (1989, April). *Adolescents' autonomy at home: Effects on self-consciousness and intrinsic motivation at school.* Paper presented at American Educational Research Association meeting, Montreal.

Freud, A. (1969). Adolescence as a developmental disturbance. In G. Kaplan & S. Lebovici (Eds.), *Adolescence: Psychosocial perspectives* (pp. 5–10). New York: Basic.

Fuligni, A. J., & Eccles, J. S. (1990). *Early adolescent peer orientation and parent-child relationships.* Unpublished manuscript, Institute for Social Research, University of Michigan, Ann Arbor.

Grotevant, H. D., & Cooper, C. R. (1986). Individuation in family relationships: A perspective on individual differences in the development of identity and role-taking skill in adolescence. *Human Development, 29,* 82–100.

Harter, S. (1981). A new self-report scale of intrinsic versus extrinsic motivation in the classroom: Motivational and information components. *Developmental Psychology, 17,* 300–312.

Harter, S. (1982). The Perceived Competence Scale for Children. *Child Development, 53,* 87–97.

Higgins, E. T., & Parsons, J. E. (1983). Social cognition and the social life of the child: Stages as subcultures. In E. T. Higgins, D. W, Ruble, & W. W. Hartup (Eds.), *Social cognition and social behavior: Developmental issues* (pp. 19–62) New York: Cambridge University Press.

Hill, J. P., & Holmbeck, G. (1986). Attachment and autonomy during adolescence. In G. Whitehurst (Ed.), *Annals of Child Development* (Vol. 3, pp. 145–189). Greenwich, CT: JAI.

Hunt, D. E. (1975). Person-environment interaction: A challenge found wanting before it was tried. *Review of Educational Research, 45,* 209–230.

Lee, P., Statuto, C. S., & Kedar-Voivodas, G. (1983). Elementary school children's perceptions of their actual and ideal school experience: A developmental study. *Journal of Educational Psychology, 75,* 839–847.

Lewin, K. (1935). A dynamic theory of personality. New York: McGraw-Hill.

Mac Iver, D., Klingel, D. M., &: Reuman, D. A. (1986, April). *Students' decision-making congruence in mathematics classrooms: A person-environment fit analysis.* Paper presented at American Educational Research Association meeting, San Francisco.

Mac Iver, D., & Reuman, D. A. (1988, April). *Decision-making in the classroom and early adolescents' valuing of mathematics.* Paper presented at American Educational Research Association meeting, New Orleans.

Midgley, C., & Feldlaufer, H. (1987). Students' and teachers' decision-making fit before and after the transition to junior high school. *Journal of Early Adolescence, 7,* 225–241.

Miller, C. L. (1986, April). *Puberty and person-environment fit in the classroom.* Paper presented at American Educational Research Association meeting, San Francisco.

Murray, H. A. (1938). *Explorations in personality.* New York: Oxford University Press.

Ryan, R. M., & Lynch, J. H. (1989). Emotional autonomy versus detachment: Revisiting the vicissitues of adolescence and young adulthood. *Child Development, 60,* 340–356

Simmons, R. G., & Blyth, D. A. (1987). *Moving into adolescence: The impact of pubertal change and school context.* New York: Aldine de Gruyter.

Simmons, R. G., Blyth, D. A., Van Cleave, E. F., & Bush, D. (1979). Entry into early adolescence: The impact of school structure, puberty, and early dating on self-esteem. *American Sociological Review. 44,* 948–967.

Steinberg, L. (1988). Reciprocal relations between parent-child distance and pubertal maturation. *Developmental Psychology, 24,* 122–128.

Yee, D. K. (1986, April). *Family decision-making. classroom decision-making. and student serf-and achievement-related attitudes.* Paper presented at American Educational Research Association meeting, San Francisco.

Yee, D. K. (1987, April). *Participation in family decision-making: Parent and child perspectives.* Paper presented at Society for Research in Child Development meeting, Baltimore.

Yee, D. K., & Flanagan, C. (1985). Family environments and self-consciousness in early adolescence. *Journal of Early Adolescence, 5,* 59–68.

## 26. Adolescent Suicide Prevention

Adler, R. S., & Jellinek, M. S. (1990). After teen suicide: Issues for pediatricians who are asked to consult to schools. *Pediatrics, 86,* 982–987.

Alcohol, Drug Abuse, and Mental Health Administration. (1989). *Report of the Secretary's Task Force on Youth Suicide: Volume 1. Overview and recommendations* (DHHS Publication No. ADM 89–1621). Washington, DC: U.S. Government Printing Office.

Battaglia, J., Coverdale, J. H., & Bushong, C. P. (1990). Evaluation of a mental illness awareness week program in public schools. *American Journal of Psychiatry, 147,* 324–329.

Berlin, I. N. (1987). Suicide among American Indian adolescents: An overview. *Suicide and Life-Threatening Behavior, 17,* 218–232.

Berman, A. L. (1988). Fictional depiction of suicide in television films and imitation effects. *American Journal of Psychiatry, 145,* 982–986.

Berman, A. L., & Jobes, D. A. (1991). *Adolescent suicide: Assessment and intervention.* Washington, DC: American Psychological Association.

Blumenthal, S. J. (1990). Youth suicide: The physician's role in suicide prevention. *JAMA: The Journal of the American Medical Association, 264,* 3194–3196.

Blumenthal, S. J. (1991). Letter to the Editor. *JAMA: The Journal of the American Medical Association, 265,* 2806–2807.

Bongar, B., & Harmatz, M. (1991). Clinical psychology graduate education in the study of suicide: Availability, resources, and importance. *Suicide and Life-Threatening Behavior, 21,* 231–235.

Boor, M. (1981). Methods of suicide and implications for suicide prevention. *Journal of Clinical Psychology, 37,* 70–75.

Boyd, J. H. (1983). The increasing rate of suicide by firearms. *New England Journal of Medicine, 308,* 872–874.

Boyd, J. H., & Moscicki, E. K. (1986). Firearms and youth suicide. *American Journal of Public Health, 76,* 1240–1242.

Brent, D. A., Kerr, M. M., Goldstein, C., Bozigar, J., Wartell, M., & Allan, M. S. (1989). An outbreak of suicide and suicidal behavior in a high school. *Journal of the American Academy of Child and Adolescent Psychiatry, 28,* 918–924.

Brent, D. A., Perper, J. A., & Allman, C. J. (1987). Alcohol, firearms and suicide among youth. *JAMA: The Journal of the American Medical Association, 257,* 3369–3372.

Brent, D. A., Perper, J. A., Goldstein, C. E., Kolko, D. J., Allan, M. J., Allman, C. J., & Zelenak, J. P. (1988). Risk factors for adolescent suicide: A comparison of adolescent suicide victims with suicidal inpatients. *Archives of General Psychiatry, 45,* 581–588.

Brown, J. H. (1979). Suicide in Britain. *Archives of General Psychiatry, 36,* 1119–1124.

Bush, J. A. (1976). Suicide and blacks. *Suicide and Life-Threatening Behavior, 6,* 216–222.

Centers for Disease Control (1988). CDC recommendations for a community plan for the prevention and containment of suicide clusters. *Morbidity and Mortality Weekly Report* (Supplement no. 5–6), *37,* 1–12.

Cohen-Sandler, R., Berman, A. L., & King, R. A. (1982). Life stress and symptomatology: Determinants of suicidal behavior in children. *Journal of the American Academy of Child Psychiatry, 21,* 178–186.

Cole, D. A. (1989). Psychopathology of adolescent suicide: Hopelessness, coping beliefs, and depression. *Journal of Abnormal Psychology, 98,* 248–255.

Cox, J. F., McCarty, D. W., Landsberg, G., & Paravati, M. P. (1990). Local jails and police lockups. In M. J. Rotheram-Borus, J. Bradley, & N. Obolensky (Eds.), *Planning to live: Evaluating and treating suicidal teens in community settings* (pp. 317–332). Tulsa: University of Oklahoma Press.

deWilde, E. J., Kienhorst, I. C. W. M., Diekstra, R. F. W., & Wolters, W. H. G. (1992). The relationship between adolescent suicidal behavior and life events in childhood and adolescence. *American Journal of Psychiatry, 149,* 45–51.

Deykin, E. Y., Alpert, J. J., & McNamara, J. J. (1985). A pilot study of the effect of exposure to child abuse or neglect on adolescent suicidal behavior. *American Journal of Psychiatry, 142,* 1299–1303.

Diekstra, R. F. (1989). Suicidal behavior in adolescents and young adults: The international picture. *Crisis, 10,* 16–35.

Dorpat, T. L., Jackson, J. K., & Ripley, H. S. (1965). Broken homes and attempted and completed suicide. *Archives of General Psychiatry, 12,* 213–216.

Dubow, E. F., Kausch, D. F., Blum, M. C., & Reed, J. (1989). Correlates of suicidal ideation and attempts in a community sample of high school students. *Journal of Clinical Child Psychology, 18,* 158–166.

Dunne, E. J., McIntosh, J. L., Dunne-Maxim, K. (Eds.). (1987). *Suicide and its aftermath.* New York: Norton.

Elkind, D. (1981). *The hurried child: Growing up too fast too soon.* Reading, MA: Addison-Wesley.

Favazza, A., & Conterio, K. (1989). Female habitual self-mutilators. *Acta Psychiatrica Scandinavica, 79,* 283–289.

Gallup Organization (1991). *Teenage suicide study: Executive summary.* (Available from the Gallup Organization, Inc., Princeton, NJ).

Garfinkel, B. D., Froese, A., & Hood, J. (1982). Suicide attempts in children and adolescents. *American Journal of Psychiatry, 139,* 1257–1261.

Garland, A., & Shaffer, D. (1990). School-based adolescent suicide prevention programs. In M. J. Rotheram-Borus, J. Bradley, & N. Obolensky (Eds.), *Planning to live: Evaluating and treating suicidal teens in community settings* (pp. 57–86). Tulsa: University of Oklahoma Press.

Garland, A., Shaffer, D., & Whittle, B. (1989). A national survey of adolescent suicide prevention programs. *Journal of the American Academy of Child and Adolescent Psychiatry, 28,* 931–934.

Garland, A., & Zigler, E. (1991). *Correlates of help-seeking attitudes among children and adolescents.* Manuscript submitted for publication.

Garland, A. F., & Zigler, E. F. (1994). Psychological correlates of help-seeking attitudes among children and adolescents. *American Journal of Orthopsychiatry, 64,* 586–593.

Gibbs, J. T. (1988). Conceptual, methodological, and sociocultural issues in Black youth suicide: Implications for assessment and early intervention. *Suicide and Life Threatening Behavior, 18,* 73–89.

Gibson, J. A. P., & Range, L. M. (1991). Are written reports of suicide and seeking help contagious? High schoolers' perceptions. *Journal of Applied Social Psychology, 21,* 1517–1523.

Gould, M. S., & Shaffer, D. (1986). The impact of suicide in television movies. *New England Journal of Medicine, 315,* 690–694.

Gould, M. S., Shaffer, D., & Davies, M. (1988). Truncated pathways from childhood. In L. Robins & M. Rutter (Eds.), *Straight and devious pathways to adulthood* (pp. 3–9). Cambridge: Cambridge University Press.

Gould, M. S., Shaffer, D., & Kleinman, M. (1988). The impact of suicide in television movies: Replication and commentary. *Suicide and Life-Threatening Behavior, 18,* 90–99.

Harry, J. (1989). Sexual identity issues. *Report of the Secretary's Task Force on Youth Suicide: Vol. 2. Risk factors for youth suicide* (DHHS Publication No. ADM 89–1622). Washington, DC: U.S. Government Printing Office.

Hawton, K. (1986). *Suicide and attempted suicide among children and adolescents.* Newbury Park, CA: Sage.

Hendin, J. (1987). Youth suicide: A psychosocial perspective. *Suicide and Life-Threatening Behavior, 17,* 151–165.

Henry, A. F., & Short, J. F. (1954). *Suicide and homicide.* Glencoe, IL: Free Press.

Hoberman, H. M., & Garfinkel, B. D. (1988). Completed suicide in children and adolescents. *Journal of the American Academy of Child and Adolescent Psychiatry, 27,* 689–695.

Hodgman, C. H., & Roberts, F. N. (1982). Adolescent suicide and the pediatrician. *Adolescent Medicine, 101,* 118–123.

Holden, R. R., Mendonca, J. D., & Serin, R. C. (1989). Suicide, hopelessness, and social desirability: A test of an interactive model. *Journal of Consulting and Clinical Psychology, 57,* 500–504.

Jobes, D. A., Berman, A. L., & Josselson, A. R. (1987). Improving the validity and reliability of medical-legal certifications of suicide. *Suicide and Life-Threatening Behavior, 17,* 310–325.

Jones, D. K., & Jones, S. L. (1977). Lunar association with suicide. *Suicide and Life-Threatening Behavior, 7,* 31.

Kagan, S. L., Powell, D. R., Weissbourd, B., & Zigler, E. F. (1987). *America's family support programs.* New Haven, CT: Yale University Press.

Kaufman, J., & Zigler, E. (1989). The intergenerational transmission of child abuse. In D. Cicchetti, & V. Carlson (Eds.), *Child maltreatment: Theory and research on the causes and consequences of child abuse and neglect* (pp. 129–150). New York: Cambridge University Press.

Kazdin, A. E., French, N. H., Unis, A. S., Esveldt-Dawson, K., & Sherick, R. B. (1983). Hopelessness, depression, and suicidal intent among psychiatrically disturbed inpatient children. *Journal of Consulting and Clinical Psychology, 51,* 504–510.

King, G. D. (1977). An evaluation of the effectiveness of a telephone counselling center. *American Journal of Community Psychology, 5,* 75–83.

Kleck, G. (1988). Miscounting suicides. *Suicide and Life-Threatening Behavior, 18,* 219–236.

Kosky, R., Silburn, S., & Zubrick, S. R. (1990). Are children and adolescents who have suicidal thoughts different from those who attempt suicide? *Journal of Nervous and Mental Disease, 178,* 38–43.

Lester, D. (1988). Gun control, gun ownership, and suicide prevention. *Suicide and Life-Threatening Behavior, 18,* 176–180.

Lester, D., & Frank, M. L. (1989). The use of motor vehicle exhaust for suicide and the availability of cars. *Acta Psychiatrica Scandinavica, 79,* 238–240.

Lester, D., & Murrell, M. E. (1980). The influence of gun control laws on suicidal behavior. *American Journal of Psychiatry, 137,* 121–122.

McKenry, P. C., Tishler, C. L., & Kelley, C. (1983). The role of drugs in adolescent suicide attempts. *Suicide and Life-Threatening Behavior, 13,* 166–175.

Meehan, P. J., Lamb, J. A., Saltzman, L. E., & O'Carroll, P. W. (1992). Attempted suicide among young adults: Progress toward a meaningful estimate of prevalence. *American Journal of Psychiatry, 149,* 41–44.

Memory, J. M. (1989). Juvenile suicides in secure detention facilities: Correction of published rates. *Death Studies, 13,* 455–463.

Miller, H. L., Coombs, D. W., & Leeper, J. D. (1984). An analysis of the effects of suicide prevention facilities on suicide rates in the United States. *American Journal of Public Health, 74,* 340–343.

Murphy, G. E. (1972). Clinical identification of suicidal risk. *Archives of General Psychiatry, 27,* 356–359.

National Center for Health Statistics (1968–1991). *Vital statistics of the United States; Vol. 2. Mortality—Part A* [for the years 1966–1988]. Washington, DC: U.S. Government Printing Office.

Nelson, F. L. (1987). Evaluation of a youth suicide prevention school program. *Adolescence, 38,* 813–825.

Overholser, J., Hemstreet, A. H., Spirito, A., & Vyse, S. (1989). Suicide awareness programs in the schools: Effects of gender and personal experience. *Journal of the American Academy of Child and Adolescent Psychiatry, 28,* 925–930.

Pfeffer, C. R. (1986). *The suicidal child.* New York: Guilford.

Phillips, D. P. (1974). The influence of suggestion on suicide: Substantive and theoretical implication of the Werther effect. *American Sociology Review, 39,* 340–354.

Phillips, D. P., & Carstenson, L. L. (1986). Clustering of teenage suicides after television news stories about suicide. *New England Journal of Medicine, 315,* 685–689.

Platt, S. (1984). Unemployment and suicidal behavior: A review of the literature. *Social Science and Medicine, 19,* 93–115.

Price, R. H., Cowen, E. L., Lorion, R. P., & Ramos-McKay, J. (1989). The search for effective prevention programs: What we learned along the way. *American Journal of Orthopsychiatry, 59,* 49–58.

Reisman, B. A., & Scharfman, M. A. (1991). *Teenage suicide prevention workshops for guidance counselors (trainer's manual & resource materials).* Douglaston, NY: Pride of Judea Mental Health Center.

Richardson, J. L., Dwyer, K., McQuigan, K., Hansen, W. B., Dent, C., Johnson, C. A., Sussman, S. Y., Brannon, B., & Flay, B. (1989). Substance use among eighth-grade students who take care of themselves after school. *Pediatrics, 84,* 556–566.

Robins, L. N. (1989). Suicide attempts in teen-aged medical patients. *Report of the Secretary's Task Force on Youth Suicide: Vol. 4. Strategies for the prevention of youth suicide.* (DHHS Publication No. ADM 89–1624). Washington, DC: U.S. Government Printing Office.

Rogawski, A. B., & Edmundson, B. (1971). Factors affecting the outcome of psychiatric interagency referral. *American Journal of Psychiatry, 127,* 925–934.

Rohde, P., Lewinsohn, P., & Seeley, J. R. (1991). Comorbidity of unipolar depression: Comorbidity with other mental disorders in adolescents and adults. *Journal of Abnormal Psychology, 100,* 214–222.

Ross, C. P. (1980). Mobilizing schools for suicide prevention. *Suicide and Life-Threatening Behavior, 10,* 239–243.

Rotheram, M. J. (1987). Evaluation of imminent danger for suicide among youth. *American Journal of Orthopsychiatry, 57,* 102–110.

Rotheram-Borus, M. J., & Bradley, J. (1991). Triage model for suicidal runaways. *American Journal of Orthopsychiatry, 61,* 122–127.

Rotheram-Borus, M. J., & Trautman, P. (1988). Hopelessness, depression, and suicidal intent among adolescent suicide attempters. *Journal of the American Academy of Child and Adolescent Psychiatry, 27,* 700–704.

Rotheram-Borus, M. J., Trautman, P. D., Dopkins, S. C., & Shrout, P. E. (1990). Cognitive style and pleasant activities among female adolescent suicide attempters. *Journal of Consulting and Clinical Psychology, 58,* 554–561.

Roy, A. (1986). Genetic factors in suicide. *Psychopharmacology Bulletin, 22,* 666–668.

Rubenstein, J. L., Heeren, T., Housman, D., Rubin, D., & Stechler, G. (1989). Suicidal behavior in "normal" adolescents: Risk and protective factors. *American Journal of Orthopsychiatry, 59,* 59–71.

Schneidman, E. S., & Farberow, N. L. (1957). *Clues to suicide.* New York: Blakison.

Seidman, E., & Rapkin, B. (1983). Economics and psychosocial dysfunction: Toward a conceptual framework and prevention strategies. In R. D. Felner, L. A. Jason, J. N. Moritsugu, & S. S. Farber (Eds.), *Preventive psychology* (pp. 175–198). New York: Pergamon Press.

Seitz, V., Rosenbaum, L., & Apfel, N. (1985). Effects of family support intervention: A ten-year follow-up. *Child Development, 54,* 376–391.

Shaffer, D. (1974). Suicide in childhood and early adolescence. *Journal of Child Psychology and Psychiatry, 45,* 406–451.

Shaffer, D. (1988). The epidemiology of teen suicide: An examination of risk factors. *Journal of Clinical Psychiatry, 49,* 36–41.

Shaffer, D., & Fisher, P. (1987). *Commentary and discussion: Research on completed suicides.* (DHHS Publication No. ADM 278–85–0026). Washington, DC: U.S. Government Printing Office.

Shaffer, D., Garland, A., Fisher, P., Bacon, K., & Vieland, V. (1990). Suicide crisis centers. A critical reappraisal with special reference to the prevention of youth suicide. In F. E. Goldston, C. M. Heinicke, R. S. Pynoos, & J. Yager (Eds.), *Prevention of mental health disturbance in childhood* (pp. 135–166). Washington, DC: American Psychiatric Association Press.

Shaffer, D., Garland, A., Gould, M., Fisher, P., & Trautman, P. (1988). Preventing teenage suicide: A critical review. *Journal of the American Academy of Child and Adolescent Psychiatry, 27,* 675–687.

Shaffer, D., Garland, A., Vieland, V., Underwood, M., & Busner, C. (1991). The impact of curriculum-based suicide prevention programs for teenagers. *Journal of the American Academy of Child and Adolescent Psychiatry, 30,* 588–596.

Shaffer, D., Garland, A., Whittle, B., & Underwood, M. (1988). *An evaluation of three adolescent suicide prevention programs* (Contract No. 50013). Trenton: New Jersey Governor's Council on Adolescent Suicide.

Shaffer, D., & Gould, M. S. (1987). Progress report: Study of completed and attempted suicides in adolescents (Contract No. R01-MH-38198). Bethesda, MD: National Institute of Mental Health.

Shaffer, D., Vieland, V., Garland, A., Rojas, M., Underwood, M., & Busner, C. (1990). Adolescent suicide attempters: Response to suicide prevention programs. *JAMA: The Journal of the American Medical Association, 264,* 3151–3155.

Shaffi, M., Carrigan, S., Whittinghill, J. R., & Derrick, A. (1985). Psychological autopsy of completed suicide in children and adolescents. *American Journal of Psychiatry, 142,* 1061–1064.

Small, S. (1990). *Preventive programs that support families with adolescents.* (Available from Carnegie Council on Adolescent Development, 2400 N Street, NW, Washington, DC, 20037).

Smith, K., & Crawford, S. (1986). Suicidal behavior among "normal" high school students. *Suicide and Life-Threatening Behavior, 16,* 313–325.

Snelling, L. K. (1991). Letter to the editor. *JAMA: The Journal of the American Medical Association, 265,* 2806.

Spirito, A., Brown, L., Overholser, J., & Fritz, G. (1989). Attempted suicide in adolescence: A review and critique of the literature. *Clinical Psychology Review, 9,* 335–363.

Spirito, A., Overholser, J., Ashworth, S., Morgan, J., & Benedict-Drew, C. (1988). Evaluation of a suicide awareness curriculum for high-school students. *Journal of the American Academy of Child and Adolescent Psychiatry, 27,* 705–711.

Spirito, A., Plummer, B., Gispert, M., Levy, S., Kurkjian, J., Lewander, W., Hagberg, S., & Devost, L. (1992). Adolescent suicide attempts: Outcomes at follow-up. *American Journal of Orthopsychiatry, 62,* 464–468.

Stack, S. (1982). The effect of strikes on suicide: A cross national analysis. *Sociological Focus, 15,* 135–146.

Stiffman, A. R. (1989). Suicide attempts in runaway youths. *Suicide and Life-Threatening Behavior, 19,* 147–159.

Trautman, P. D., & Shaffer, D. (1984). Treatment of child and adolescent suicide attempters. In H. S. Sudak, A. B. Ford, & N. B. Rushforth (Eds.), *Suicide in the young* (pp. 307–323). Boston: John Wright PSG.

Wass, H., Miller, M. D., & Stevenson, R. G. (1989). Factors affecting adolescents' behavior and attitudes toward destructive rock lyrics. *Death Studies, 13,* 287–303.

Weiss, H. B. (1989). State family support and education programs: Lessons from the pioneers. *American Journal of Orthopsychiatry, 59,* 32–48.

Weissman, M. M. (1974). The epidemiology of suicide attempts. *Archives of General Psychiatry, 30,* 737–746.

Wyche, K., Obolensky, N., & Glood, E. (1990). American Indian, Black American, and Hispanic American Youth. In M. J. Rotheram-Borus, J. Bradley, & N. Obolensky (Eds.), *Planning to live: Evaluating and treating suicidal teens in community settings* (pp. 355–389). Tulsa: University of Oklahoma Press.

Zigler, E. F. (1989). Addressing the nation's child care crisis: The school of the twenty-first century. *American Journal of Orthopsychiatry, 59,* 484–491.

Zigler, E. F., & Black, K. (1989). America's family support movement: Strengths and limitations. *American Journal of Orthopsychiatry, 59,* 6–19.

Zigler, E. F., Taussig, C., & Black, K. (1992). Early childhood intervention: A promising preventative for juvenile delinquency. *American Psychologist, 47,* 997–1006.

## 27. Shadows of War

Benjamin, A. (1994). *Children at war.* London: Save the Children.

Cairns, E. & Dawes, A. (1996). Children: Ethnic and political violence—A commentary. *Child Development, 67,* 1, 129–139.

Close, K. (1953). *Transplanted children: A history.* New York: United States Committee for the Care of European Children.

Freud, A & Burlington, D. (1943). *War and children.* New York: Medical War Books.

Garbarino, G. and Kostelny, K. (1996). The effects of political violence on Palestinian children's behaviour problems: A risk accumulation model. *Child Development, 67,* 1, 33–45.

Haggerty, R. (1994) *Stress, risk, and resilience in children and adolescents.* Cambridge: Cambridge University Press.

Isaacs, S. (1941). *The Cambridge evacuation survey.* London: Methuen.

Palmer, G. (1995). Reluctant refuge: Unaccompanied refugee and evacuee children in Australia 1933–45. Ph.D thesis, University of Adelaide, Adelaide.

Palmer G. (in press). *Reluctant refuge.* Sydney: Kangaroo.

Ressler, E., Boothby, N., & Steinbock, D. (1988). *Unaccompanied children.* Oxford: Oxford University Press.

Werner, E. and Smith, R. (1982). *Vulnerable but invincible: A longitudinal study of resilient children and youth.* New York: McGraw-Hill.

## 28. Risk, Resilience, and Recovery

Caspi, A., Elder, G. H., & Bem, D. J. (1988). Moving away from the world: Life course patterns of shy children. *Developmental Psychology, 24,* 824–831.

Cicchetti, D. (1993). Developmental psychopathology: Reactions, reflections, projections. *Developmental Review, 13,* 471–502.

Cicchetti, D., & Toth, S. L. (1992). The role of developmental theory in prevention and intervention. *Development and Psychopathology, 4,* 489–493.

Freedman, M. (1993). *The kindness of strangers.* San Francisco: Jossey-Bass.

Furstenberg, F. F., Brooks-Gunn, J., & Morgan, S. P. (1987). *Adolescent mothers in later life.* Cambridge: Cambridge University Press.

Garmezy, N., & Rutter, M. (Eds.) (1983). *Stress, coping and development in children.* New York: McGraw-Hill.

Gough, H. (1969). *California psychological inventory manual* (Rev. ed.). Palo Alto, CA: Consulting Psychologists Press.

Horowitz, F. D. (1987). *Exploring developmental theories: Toward a structural/behavioral model of development.* Hillsdale, NJ: Erlbaum.

Lohmöller, J. G. (1984). *LVPLS program manual with partial least-square estimates.* Cologne: Zentralarchiv für Empirische Sozial Forschung.

Magnusson, D. (1988). *Individual development from an interactional perspective.* Hillsdale, NJ: Erlbaum.

Masten, A. (1990). Resilience in development: Implications of the study of successful adaptation for developmental psychopathology. In D. Cicchetti (Ed.), *Rochester Symposium on Developmental Psychopathology: Vol 1. The emergence of a discipline* (pp. 261–294). Hillsdale, NJ: Erlbaum.

Rachman, S. (1979). The concept of required helpfulness. *Behavior Research and Therapy, 17,* 1–6.

Rutter, M. (1987). Psychosocial resilience and protective mechanisms. *American Journal of Orthopsychiatry, 57,* 316–331.

Scarr, S., & McCartney, K. (1983). How people make their own environments: A theory of genotype → environment effects. *Child Development, 54,* 424–435.

Super, C., & Harkness, S. (1986). The developmental niche: A conceptualization of the interface between child and culture. *International Journal of Behavioral Development, 9,* 545–569.

Werner, E. E. (1990). Protective factors and individual resilience. In S. Meisel & J. Shonkoff (Eds.), *Handbook of early intervention* (pp. 97–116). Cambridge: Cambridge University Press.

Werner, E. E., & Smith, R. S. (1977). *Kauai's children come of age.* Honolulu: University of Hawaii Press.

Werner, E. E., & Smith, R. S. (1989). *Vulnerable but invincible: A longitudinal study of resilient children and youth.* New York: Adams-Bannister-Cox. (Original work published 1982).

Werner, E. E., & Smith, R. S. (1992). *Overcoming the odds: High risk children from birth to adulthood.* Ithaca, NY: Cornell University Press.

Wolfgang, M. E., Thornberry, T. P., & Figlio, R. M. (1987). *From boy to man: From delinquency to crime.* Chicago: University of Chicago Press.

## 29. Psychosocial and Behavioral Predictors of Longevity

Amato, P. R., & Keith. B. (1991). Parental divorce and the well-being of children: A meta-analysis. *Psychological Bulletin, 110,* 26–46.

Berry, D. S., & Pennebaker, J. W. (1993). Nonverbal and verbal emotional expression and health. *Psychotherapy and Psychosomalics, 59,* 1119.

Block, J., Block, J. H., & Gjerde, R E. (1988). Parental functioning and the home environment in families of divorce: Prospective and concurrent analyses. *Journal of the American Academy of Child & Adolescen Psychiatry, 27,* 207–213.

Block., J., Block, J. H., & Keyes, S. (1988). Longitudinally foretelling drug usage in adolescence: Early childhood personality and environmental precursors. *Child Development, 59,* 336–355.

Block, J. H., Block, J., & Gjerde, R E. (1986). The personality of children prior to divorce: A prospective study. *Child Development, 57,* 827–840.

Chassin. L., Presson, C. C., Sherman, S. J., Corty, E., & Olshavsky, R. W. (1984). Predicting the onset of cigarene smoking in adolescents: A longitudinal study. *Journal uf Applied Social Psychology, 14,* 224–243.

Conrad, K. M., Flay, B. R., & Hill, D. (1992). Why children start smoking cigarettes: Predictors of onset. *British Journal of Addiction, 87,* 17111724.

Costa, R T., Jr., McCrae, R. R., & Dembroski, T. (1989). Agrceableness versus antagonism: Explication of a potential risk factor for CHD. In A. W. SieBman & T. M. Dembroski (Eds.), *In search of coronary-prone behavior* (pp. 41–64). Hillsdale, NJ: Erlbaum.

Dabbs, J. M., Jr., & Morris, R. (1990). Testosterone, social class, and antisocial behavior in a sample of 4,462 men. *Psychological Science, 1,* 209–211.

Dunbar, H. F. (1943). *Psychosomatic diagnosis.* New York: R B. Hoeber.

Eysenck. H. J. (1985). Personality, cancer, and cardiovascular disease. *Personalily and Individual Differences, 5,* 535–557.

Eysenck. H. J. (1991). Personality, stress, and disease: An interactionist perspective. *Psychological Inquiry, 2,* 221 –232.

Friedman, H. S. (Ed.). (1990). *Personality and disease.* New York: Wiley.

Friedman, H. S. (1991). *The self-healing personality: Why some people achieve health and others succumb to illness.* New York: Henry Holt.

Friedman, H. S. (Ed.). (1992). *Hostility coping, and health.* Washington, DC: American Psychological Association.

Friedman, H. S., & Booth-Kewley, S. (1987). The "disease-prone personality": A meta-analytic view of the construct. *American Psychologist, 42,* 539–555.

Friedman, H. S., Tucker, J. S., & Martin, L. R. (1994). If you want to be studied by health psychology, don't die in New York City. *The Health Psychologist, 16,* 13–20.

Friedman, H. S., Tucker J. S., Martin, L. R., Tomlinson-Keasey, C., Schwartz, J. E., Wingard, D. L., & Criqui, M. H. (1994). Do nonscientists really live longer? *The Lancet, 343,* 296.

Friedman, H. S., Tucker, J. S., Schwartz, J. E, Martin, L. R., Tomlinson Keasey, C., Wingard, D. L., & Criqui, M. H. (1995). Childhood conscientiousness and longevity: Health behaviors and cause of death. *Journal of Personality and Social Psychology, 68,* 696–703.

Friedman, H. S., Tucker. J. S., Tomlinson-Keasey, C., Schwartz, J. E., Wingard, D. L., & Criqui, M. H. (1993). Does childhood personality predict longevity? *Journal of Personalily and Social Psychology, 65,* 176–185.

Gerra, G., Caccavari, R., Delsignore, R., Passeri, M., Fortonani, A. G., Maestri, D., Monica, C., & Brambilla, F. (1993). Parental divorce and neuroendocrine changes in adolescents. *Acta Psychiatrica Scandinavica, 87,* 350–354.

Hawkins, J. D., Catalano, R. E, & Miller, J. Y. (1992). Risk and protective factors for alcohol and otha drug problems in adolescence and early adulthood: Implications for substance abuse prevention. *Psychological Bulletin, 112,* 64–105.

Hetherington, E. M. (1991). Presidential address Families, lies, and videotapes. Presidential Address of the Society for Research in Adolescence. *Journal of Research on Adolescence, 1,* 323–348.

Holmes, T. H., & Rahe, R. H. (1967). The Social Readjustment Rating Scale. *Journal of Psychosomatic Research, 11,* 213–218.

House, J. S., Robbins, C., & Metzner. H. L. (1982). The association of social relationships and activities with mortality: Prospective evidence from the Tecumseh community health study. *American Journal of Epidemiology, 116,* 123–140.

Hu, Y. & Goldman, N. (1990). Mortality differentials by marital status: An international comparison. *Demography, 27,* 233–250.

Jellinek M. S., & Slovik, L. S. (1981). Current concepts in psychiatry: Divorce. Impact on children. *New England Journal of Medicine, 305*(10), 557–560.

Kotler. R. & Wingard, D. L. (1989). The effect of occupational, marital and parental roles on mortality: The Alameda County study. *American Journal of Public Healih, 79,* 607–612.

Lipsey, M. W., & Wilson, D. B. (1993). The efficacy of psychological, educational, and behavioral treatment. *American Psychologist,* 48. 1181–1209.

Magnus, K., Diener, E., Fujita, F., & Payot, W (1993). Extraversion and neuroticism as predictors of objective life events: A longitudinal analysis. *Journal of Personality & Social Psychology, 65,* 1046–1053.

Martin, L. R., Friedman, H. S., Tucker, J. S., Tomlinson-Keasey, C., Criqui. M. H. Wingard, D. L., & Schwartz, J. E. (1994). *Cheerfulness and longevity.* Manuscript submitted for publication.

McCrae, R. R., & Costa, R. T. (1991). Adding Liebe und Arbeit: The full five-factor model and well-being. *Personality & Social Psychology Bulletin, 17,* 227–232.

McKeown, T. (1979). *The role of medicine: Dream, mirage, or nemesis?* Princeton, NJ: Princeton University Press.

Ones, D. S., Viswesvaran, C., & Schmidt, E L. (1993). Comprehensive meta-analysis of integrity test validities: Findings and implications for personnel selection and theories of job performance. *Journal of Applied Psychology, 78,* 679–703.

Pennebaker, J. W. (1990). *Opening up: The healing power of confiding in others.* New York: Morrow.

Rosenthal, R. (1991). Meta-analysis: A review. *Psychosomalic Medicine, 53,* 247–271.

Scarr, S., & McCartney, K. (1983). How people make their own environments: A theory of genotype environment effects. *Child Development,* 54. 424–435.

Schwartz. J. E., Friedman, H. S., Tucker, J. S., Tomlinson-Keasey, C., Wingard. D. L. & Criqui, M. H. (1995). Childhood sociodemographic and psychosocial factors as predictors of longevity across the lifespan. *American Journal of Public Health, 85,* 1237–1245.

Selye, H. (1976). *The stress of life* (Rev. ed.). New York: McGraw-Hill.

Shaw, D. S., Emery, R. E., & Tuer. M. D. (1993). Parental functioning and children's adjustment in families of divorce: A prospective study. *Journal of Abnormal Child Psychology, 21,* 119–134.

Tennant, C. (1988). Parental loss in childhood: Its effect in adult life. *Archives of General Psychiatry, 45,* 1045–1050.

Tennen, H., & Affleck, G. (1987). The costs and benefits of optimistic explanations and dispositional optimism. *Journal of Personality,* 55, 377–393.

Taman, L. M. (1954). Scientists and nonscientists in a group of 800 gifted men. *Psychological Monographs: General and Applied 68,* 144.

Terman, L. M., & Oden, M. H. (1947). *Genetic studies of genius The gifted child grows up* (Vol. 4). Stanford, CA: Stanford University Press.

Tucker, J. S. (1993). *The association of marital status with mortality across the life span for females and males.* Unpublished doctoral dissertation, University of California, Riverside.

Tucker, J. S., Friedman, H. S., Tomlinson-Keasey, C. Schwartz, J. E., Wingard. D. L. & Crioui. M. H. (1994). *Childhood psychosocial predictors of adulthood smoking, alcohol consumption, and obesin:* Manuscript submined for publication.

Tucker, J. S., Friedman, H. S., Wingard, D. L., & Schwartz, J. E. (1996). Marital history at mid-life as a predictor of longevity: *Alternative explanations of the protective effect of marriage. Health Psychology, 15,* 94–101.

U. S. Department of Health and Human Services. (1980). *International clasification of diseases, ninth revision, clinical modification* (2nd ed.). Washington, DC: Public Health Services.

Vaillant, G. E. (1993). *The wisdom of the ego.* Cambridge, MA: Harvard University Press.

Watson, D., & Clark, L. A. (1992). On traits and temperament: General and specific factors of emotional experience and their relation to the five-factor model. *Journal of Personality, 60,* 441–476.

Weidner, G., Hutt, J., Connor, S. L., & Mendell, N. R. (1992). Family stress and coronary risk in children. *Psychosomatic Medicine, 54,* 471–479.

Weinstein, N. (1984). Why it won't happen to me. Perceptions of risk factors and susceptibility. *Health Psychology, 3,* 431–457.

Wingard, D. L. (1984). The sex differential in morbidity, mortality, and life-style. *Annual Review of Public Health, 5,* 433–458.

Wortman, C. B., Sheedy, C., Gluhoski, V., & Kessler, R. C. (1992). Stress, coping, and health: Conceptual issues and directions for future research. In H. S. Friedman (Ed.), *Hostility, coping & health* (pp. 227–256). Washington, DC: American Psychological Association.

Zill. N., Morrison, D. R., & Coiro, M. J. (1993). Longtam effects of parental divorce on parent-child relationships, adjustment. and achievement in young adulthood. *Journal of Family Psychology,* 91–103.